Keywords for American Cultural Studies

Keywords

Collaborative in design and execution, the books in the Keywords series bring together scholars across a wide range of disciplines in the humanities and social sciences. These books speak to today's most dynamic and vexed discussions of political and social life, both inside and outside of the academy.

For additional online resources, visit *keywords.nyupress.org*

Keywords for African American Studies
Edited by Erica R. Edwards, Roderick A. Ferguson, and Jeffrey O. G. Ogbar

Keywords for American Cultural Studies, Third Edition
Edited by Bruce Burgett and Glenn Hendler

Keywords for Asian American Studies
Edited by Cathy J. Schlund-Vials, Linda Trinh Võ, and K. Scott Wong

Keywords for Children's Literature, Second Edition
Edited by Philip Nel, Lissa Paul, and Nina Christensen

Keywords for Disability Studies
Edited by Rachel Adams, Benjamin Reiss, and David Serlin

Keywords for Environmental Studies
Edited by Joni Adamson, William A. Gleason, and David N. Pellow

Keywords for Latina/o Studies
Edited by Deborah R. Vargas, Nancy Raquel Mirabal, and Lawrence La Fountain-Stokes

Keywords for Media Studies
Edited by Laurie Ouellette and Jonathan Gray

Keywords for American Cultural Studies

Third Edition

Edited by
Bruce Burgett and Glenn Hendler

NEW YORK UNIVERSITY PRESS New York

NEW YORK UNIVERSITY PRESS
New York
www.nyupress.org

References to internet websites (URLs) were accurate at the time
of writing. Neither the author nor New York University Press is
responsible for URLs that may have expired or changed since the
manuscript was prepared.

Cataloging-in-Publication data is available from the publisher

New York University Press books are printed on acid-free paper, and
their binding materials are chosen for strength and durability. We
strive to use environmentally responsible suppliers and materials to
the greatest extent possible in publishing our books.

Manufactured in the United States of America

10 9 8 7 6 5 4 3 2 1

Also available as an ebook

Contents

Keywords for American Cultural Studies is a print-digital publication. Essays listed with page numbers are included in the print volume; essays without page numbers can be found online at https://keywords.nyupress.org.

Keywords

An Introduction

Bruce Burgett and Glenn Hendler

What Is a Keyword?

Why are you reading *Keywords for American Cultural Studies*? You may have been assigned some of the print or digital essays in this volume as part of a class. You may be making your way through some challenging works of scholarship and hoping that *Keywords* will help you develop the vocabulary you need to understand them. You may be reading around in the essays to help you enter into one of the many scholarly conversations going on in interdisciplinary American studies, cultural studies, or some related field. Or you may be reading *Keywords* simply because it looks interesting.

These are all good reasons. But for your reading to be useful for any of these purposes, it will be important that you understand what a keyword essay is and what it can and can't do, since *Keywords for American Studies* is not what many readers assume it to be. Though its table of contents is a list of words in alphabetical order, it is not a dictionary. It will not give you simple, stable definitions for the words in that list. Though many of the essays make reference to etymologies or usage histories in dictionaries such as the *Oxford English Dictionary* (*OED*) or the *American Heritage Dictionary of the English Language*, keyword essays tell different stories about how the meanings of words change through time and across space, how they have shaped our thinking, and how they could be deployed in relation to future debates about concerns addressed by the fields of American studies and culture studies. The term "keyword" itself is an example of this dynamic, so let's briefly treat it as a keyword.

In contemporary usage, "keyword" generally refers to a type of information. The *OED*'s primary definition is "a word serving as a key to a cipher or code," one that provides "a solution or explanation" or one that is "of particular importance or significance." Dating from the mid-eighteenth century, these usages represent keywords as data that unlock mysteries. The *OED*'s second definition is a term "chosen to indicate or represent the content of a larger text or record" in an "index, catalogue, or database" (*Oxford English Dictionary Online* 2018). Dating from the early nineteenth century, this usage represents keywords as tools for information retrieval within various archiving systems. This second meaning points toward the most familiar usage of the term today. Keywords are forms of metadata that authors, librarians, book indexers, concordance makers, web designers, and database builders add to a print or digital text to guide users to significant clusters of meaning. The interactive information ecologies of "Web 2.0" extend this usage in interesting ways. They enable consumers of information to produce their own metadata, which can then be visualized as word clouds or tag clouds. Metadata becomes a user-centered and interactive means of organizing, customizing, and sharing data.

When you look up a term in *Keywords for American Cultural Studies*, you will find that these *OED* definitions are both resonant and limited. The essays you will encounter synthesize a great deal of information about the historical and contemporary meanings of terms that structure the fields of American studies and cultural studies. By discussing how the meanings of those terms have developed over time, they may even unlock some mysteries and crack a few codes. In this sense, the essays help readers understand the concepts they encounter and chart relations among them. But *Keywords for American Cultural Studies* is not a reference guide written for novices by academic cryptologists revealing the secrets of American studies and cultural studies. Nor is it an effort to set or fix the meanings of words on the basis of past usage, as a dictionary might. Rather, it is an attempt to explore and explain the social and historical contexts of those usages, trace the genealogy of debates over key terms that have structured the fields of American studies and cultural studies, and speculate about the ongoing significance of those debates. As a whole, *Keywords for American Cultural Studies* aims to map the fissures and fault lines of the past, present, and future, treating the terms within it as sites of unresolved conflict and contestation.

Where Does *Keywords for American Cultural Studies* Come From?

The understanding of keywords central to this publication—both the print book and the digital site—is rooted in the writings of the British cultural studies scholar Raymond Williams. Upon his return from World War II, Williams became interested in how the meanings of certain words, which he only later called "keywords," seemed to have shifted during his absence. Two books that were to hold great importance for the emerging field of cultural studies resulted from this experiential insight. The first, *Culture and Society,*

1780–1950 (1958), traced a genealogy of the complex and contradictory mid-twentieth-century usages of the word "culture" through nearly two centuries of writings by British intellectuals concerned with the antagonistic relations between political democracy and capitalist industrialization. The second, *Keywords: A Vocabulary of Culture and Society* (1976), collected 134 short essays (151 in the 1983 revised edition), all of which gloss shifts over the same two centuries in the meanings of terms ranging from "behavior" and "charity" to "sensibility" and "work." As Williams explained in his introduction to the first edition of *Keywords*, he wrote these short essays in his spare moments and originally conceived of them as an appendix to *Culture and Society*. Only later did he develop them into a separate publication, as their sum grew in scope and complexity and as he began to understand and articulate the methodological stakes of the project he had undertaken. *Keywords* is, Williams insisted, "not a dictionary or glossary of a particular academic subject. It is not a series of footnotes to dictionary histories or definitions of a number of words. It is, rather, the record of an inquiry into a *vocabulary*" (15).

"Vocabulary" is in many ways the unacknowledged keyword of Williams's introduction. His use of that term can help us explain how *Keywords for American Cultural Studies* works and clarify how it differs from more conventional reference books. Williams deployed the term in order to distinguish his project not only from those of dictionary editors and glossary makers but also from the research and writings of academic philologists and linguists, who examine the formal and structural components of language systems and their evolution. In contrast, Williams focused his keyword essays on what he called "historical semantics" ([1976] 1983, 23), emphasizing the ways in which meanings are made and altered over time through contestations among the usages of diverse social groups and movements. "What can be done in dictionaries," Williams wrote, "is necessarily limited by their proper universality and by the long time-scale of revision which that, among other factors, imposes. The present inquiry, being more limited—not a dictionary, but a vocabulary—is more flexible" (26). This underlining of the flexibility of a "vocabulary"—as opposed to the universality of a "dictionary"—points to Williams's general premise that language systems develop and change in relation to local and practical usages. Dictionaries, glossaries, and other reference books rely on experts and reproduce a discourse of expertise by downplaying the creative and unpredictable aspects of interactive and idiosyncratic forms of meaning making. Vocabularies provide a counterpoint to this reliance on experts and expertise. They treat knowledge as a process that is responsive to the diverse constituencies that use and revise the meanings of the keywords that shape our understandings of the present, the future, and the past. To return to our opening conceit, they think about keywords as metadata produced socially and historically in relation to specific communities of users and emerging forms of practice.

Keywords for American Cultural Studies shares a number of these fundamental premises with Williams's volume, as well as its other successors (Bennett, Grossberg, and Morris 2005) and the various *Keywords* volumes published by New York University Press (listed at keywords.nyupress.org). It provides an accessible and readable introduction to some of the central terms and debates that shape the study of culture and society today. It circles around the keyword "culture" in the same way Williams's two volumes did as they explored that central term's interactions with neighboring concepts such as art, industry, class, and democracy. And it insists that our understanding of these terms and the interactions among them can be enhanced—rather than settled or shut down—by a heightened awareness of their

historical genealogies and the conflicts embedded in differing and even contradictory uses of those terms.

At the same time, there are several aspects of *Keywords for American Cultural Studies* that distinguish it from Williams's *Keywords*. Most obviously, it is a collaborative enterprise involving more than one hundred authors working across a range of disciplinary and interdisciplinary fields that overlap with—but seldom map neatly onto—either American studies or cultural studies. It shares this polyvocal structure with the other volumes in the New York University Press's *Keywords* series that followed after the publication of the first edition of this volume. Most importantly, its exploration of culture and society is explicitly linked to a nation (the United States), a concept or ideology (America or Americanness), and, at times, a geography (the Americas).

The keyword "America" is thus essential to our project in two ways. First, the term in all its mutations—"American," "Americas," "Americanization," "Americanist"—has to be defined in relation to what Williams called "particular formations of meaning" ([1976] 1983, 15). "America," in other words, is a category with particularizing effects that are as central to how we think about the possibilities and limitations of the field of American studies as the universalizing term "culture" is to our understanding of the shape of the field of cultural studies. Second, contemporary disagreements over the category's field-defining function point toward a wide range of debates related to what is now commonly called the postnational or transnational turn in American studies. Just as the universalizing referents of Williams's own project have been troubled by subsequent work in cultural studies that has rendered explicit his tendency to assume a narrowly "British" (largely white, working-class) readership and archive for that project (Gilroy 1987), the category "America" has been troubled within American studies in part through the field's interactions with cultural studies, though more pressingly by its engagements with new "formations of meaning" emerging from shifting patterns of migration and immigration, existing and evolving diasporic communities, and the neoliberal cultural and economic phenomena associated with financialization and globalization. The fact that twelve of the words in this last sentence—"culture," "white," "class," "America," "migration," "immigration," "diaspora," "community," "economy," "neoliberal," "finance," and "globalization"—are titles of essays in *Keywords for American Cultural Studies* indicates how rich and complex this research has become.

In our editorial conversations with our contributors, we have attempted to draw out this richness and complexity by insisting—as Kirsten Silva Gruesz does in her essay on "America"—that authors specify when they are talking about "America" and when they are talking about the "United States." It is an editorial decision that has produced some useful results. Nearly all the essays reach across US national borders to track usages of terms such as "America," "South," and "West" and across disciplinary formations such as political philosophy and social theory, where terms ranging from "neoliberalism" and "religion" to "populism" and "fascism" may be inflected in particular ways in the United States but cannot be subsumed under either an "American" or an "Americanist" rubric. Similarly, terms that might from one perspective be viewed as a subset of American studies (or cultural studies focused on the United States) are consistently shown to have transnational histories and future trajectories. Essays on "African," "Asian," "creole," "Latinx," "indigenous," "black," and "whiteness" all map cultural formations and develop lines of inquiry that are neither exclusive to the United States nor exhausted by US-based versions of ethnic studies. Transnational understandings of keywords such as "diaspora,"

"migration," "youth," and "nature" similarly push us to reimagine the political geographies of the United States, as well as the nation-based intellectual geographies of the institutions that study it. And they indicate the involvement of our contributors in a wide variety of critical interdisciplinarities, ranging from queer studies to indigenous studies to community studies.

A final difference between this project and Williams's *Keywords* is evident in the fact nearly all our contributors have followed our editorial lead by referring in their essays to American studies and cultural studies as two distinct fields of inquiry, even as our title seems to name just one: American cultural studies. The point of this analytic separation is to stage an ongoing encounter between the two fields. That encounter is not new, of course, and critical engagement with the usage history of key terms ranging from "pastoralism" (L. Marx [1964] 2000) to "gay" (Chauncey 1994) to "racism" (Fields and Fields 2012) has been as central to American studies as it has been to cultural studies. As Michael Denning (2004) observes, the reasons for this parallel development are complex. Both American studies and cultural studies emerged in the 1940s, '50s, and '60s as critical responses to reductionist versions of literary formalism and Marxist materialism, and both advocated for cultural criticism as a means of reconstructing a usable past oriented toward a more democratic and socially just future. Yet the two fields also evolved differently, with cultural studies taking on the question "What is culture?" while American studies focused on the question "What is American?" Denning suggests that the first question proved more useful than the second, since it opened inquiry onto a wider range of cultural forms and forms of political action. Since Denning drew this conclusion in the mid-1980s, the field of American studies itself has turned toward those modes of inquiry, partly as a result of its encounter with work in cultural studies on questions of region, migration, and diaspora but also due to the engagement of both fields with other forms of intersectional analysis, including work produced in the new interdisciplinary formations that emerged from the social movements of the 1960s and have evolved significantly since then, such as ethnic studies, postcolonial studies, disability studies, working-class studies, and women, gender, and sexuality studies.

What Does *Keywords for American Cultural Studies* Do?

Keywords for American Cultural Studies provides readers with a map of the shifting terrain created by several decades of work located at the intersections of American studies, cultural studies, and other emergent interdisciplinary fields. A rigorous encounter with these relatively new intellectual and institutional formations requires recognition of one of their central lessons: all forms of inquiry and sites of institutionalization, including academic departments, conferences, and journals, police their boundaries by leaving something—and often someone—out of the analytical frame. This boundedness is not simply a result of the limitations of time and space. Exploring its causes is central to the core methodology of those fields, all of which stress the importance of reflexivity with respect to both the social and political commitments of readers, interpreters, and researchers and their temporal and spatial positionalities. For this reason, it is critical to understand *Keywords for American Cultural Studies* not only as a map of contemporary scholarship or a lexicon of critical terms but also as a methodological provocation to think about inquiry in ways that are self-reflexive, open-ended, and future oriented. All the essays frame and pursue research questions that are situated responses to shifts in contemporary political, social, and institutional life. We want

to provoke our readers to do the same by encouraging them to think critically and creatively about how knowledge about "America" and its "cultures" has been, is, and should be made. *Keywords for American Cultural Studies* is, in this sense, both a guide to some of the best existing research in and across the fields it maps and an argument for maintaining and enhancing a commitment to critical and interdisciplinary approaches to the future evolution of those fields.

In *Keywords*, Williams demonstrated his commitment to a self-reflexive and future-oriented approach to inquiry by including several blank pages at the end of his book. These pages were intended, as he put it, "not only for the convenience of making notes, but as a sign that the inquiry remains open, and that the author will welcome all amendments, corrections, and additions" ([1976] 1983, 26). We share this desire to mark the boundedness—and openness—of the inquiry, though readers will find no blank pages at the back of *Keywords for American Cultural Studies*. Instead, we want to underscore the obvious point that many keywords of American studies and cultural studies do not appear here. Take as an example the keyword "individual." A reader who in high school was exposed to the old saw that "American" (read: US) culture is characterized by an ideology of "individualism" might at first be dismayed to find no essay on that term. But that reader might then look for—or be guided to—terms closely related to the concept of individuality: most clearly "subject" and "identity" but also "interiority" and "body." From there, they could move either to keywords that qualify and constitute individuality, such as "race," "ethnicity," "gender," "sex," "normal," "disability," and "intersectionality," or to keywords that name places and concepts within which "individualism" is contested and constructed, such as "family," "rights," "religion," "corporation," "state," "city," and "university." This line of inquiry could then bring the reader to "public" and "community" for broader framings of the missing essay on "individual." And they might even end up reading the essay on "society," recognizing that individualism is always in tension with social norms. At this point, the reader would have a much more nuanced understanding of what other keywords and concepts are necessary to map the relationship between "individual" and "society."

We imagine that this hypothetical example will strike some readers as persuasive, while others will remain skeptical of our editorial choices. In relation to both groups, we want to echo Williams by extending an invitation to our readers to become collaborators in keywords projects that extend beyond the essays in *Keywords for American Cultural Studies*. We ask you to revise, reject, and respond to the essays that do—and do not—appear in this publication, to create new clusters of meaning among them, and to develop deeper and richer discussions of what a given term does and can mean when used in specific local and global contexts. To this end, we offer the following, necessarily incomplete list of words about which we, as co-editors of *Keywords for American Cultural Studies*, would like to hear and read more: activism, age, agency, alien, anarchy, Arab, archive, art, bureaucracy, canon, care, celebrity, character, child, Christian, commodity, consent, country, creativity, depression, derivative, desire, development, disciplinary, education, elite, equality, European, evolution, experience, expert, feminine, fiction, folk, food, friendship, hegemony, heritage, heterosexual, homosexual, human, imagination, individual, intellectual, Jewish, justice, liberty, literacy, local, management, manufacture, masculine, minority, mission, multicultural, Muslim, native, opinion, oratory, patriotism, performativity, place, pleasure, pluralism, police, popular, poverty, pragmatism, print, psychology, radical, reality,

representation, republicanism, reservation, resistance, revolution, romance, security, segregation, settler, socialism, sodomy, sovereignty, subaltern, text, theory, tourism, tradition, trans, translation, trauma, utopia, virtual, virtue, wealth, welfare, work.

This already too-long list could go on for pages, and even then it would be easy to conjure other possibilities. Whether keywords projects take the form of classroom assignments, research and working groups, edited volumes, or public forums, they must remain open to further elaboration and amendment not simply due to dynamics of inclusion and exclusion or limitations of time and space. Rather, their incompletion is methodologically central to any self-reflexive and future-oriented understanding of how research is conducted and how knowledge is made, both inside and outside academic settings. Claiming the ability to map complex fields of knowledge while also maintaining a critical approach to how the questions and problems that constitute those fields are—and should be—framed requires both intellectual modesty and an openness to further collaboration. One useful response to this modesty and openness may be a critique of what is included in and excluded from this publication. We welcome this response, and we also want to encourage readers to take this response a step further by making something new, whether that new thing is as minor as a conversation or as major as a digital archive or public initiative. The true measure of the success of *Keywords for American Cultural Studies* will continue to be its ability to clear conceptual space for these future projects. Since the book's first edition in 2007, readers, scholars, teachers, and students have developed new and challenging research questions in dialogue with others who may not quite share a common vocabulary but who do know something about where conflicts and debates over meaning come from, why they matter, and how they might matter differently in the future. Projects coming out of these new research questions have taken forms ranging from individual classroom assignments to the multiple edited volumes in New York University Press's *Keywords* series. We look forward to reading and hearing about more in the coming years.

Why Is *Keywords for American Cultural Studies* a Print-Digital Hybrid?

When we published the first edition of *Keywords for American Cultural Studies*, we knew that our gestures toward creative response and open-ended inquiry would be empty if we did not follow through on them. This knowledge led us to design, with the generous and generative assistance of Deborah Kimmey, a digital supplement to the print book where readers could work individually or collaboratively to create new keyword essays. The Keywords Collaboratory—which was later administered and developed further by Elizabeth Cornell—was our Web 2.0 version of Williams's blank pages. It was an experiment designed to supplement the first and second editions of the print volume by catalyzing collaboration and publishing responses to the essays the book did and did not contain. As we discuss in "A Note on Classroom Use," the experiment worked, at least in some college classrooms where students collaborated on a variety of assignments that asked them either to supplement existing essays or to create new ones. Like our authors, students developed different approaches to the keywords they had been assigned. Some of the essays in the book and some of the responses to course assignments are explicitly argumentative and polemical, while others are more descriptive and ecumenical. A few are willfully idiosyncratic, and several hint at implicit disagreements among their authors. Yet across all this work, the reader will find scholarly writing that models critical and creative thinking and authors who simultaneously analyze and evince the ways in which keywords are, as Williams put it, both "binding words in certain activities and their interpretation" and "indicative words in certain forms of thought" (1976, 15).

In our planning for the second edition of *Keywords for American Cultural Studies*, we extended this experiment by talking about the publication as a "print-digital hybrid," a term we used with New York University Press even before we knew exactly what it would mean. This commitment is carried further in this third edition, which includes approximately equal numbers of essays on the website as appear in the print volume and e-book. When linked to the print book, the site provides four opportunities that the print book could not: it enables us to publish more essays without expanding the physical volume beyond a manageable and affordable size, it allows for a broader circulation of the essays that appear on the site, it enables an interactive indexing of all the essays in the publication, and it opens the possibility of multimodal composition and postpublication revision. Readers interested in these possibilities—especially instructors of courses—should consult "A Note on Classroom Use" for ideas about how to get started.

A Note on Classroom Use

Please be aware that some of the essays that are part of *Keywords for American Cultural Studies* are available in the print volume and e-book, while others are on the web at http://keywords.nyupress.org. If you are reading this note on the website, please look at the sixty-plus essays in print. If you are reading this in the paper or electronic version of the book, please know that there are as many provocative and useful keyword essays available on the website as there are where you are reading now. There are many brand-new essays, and many of the essays in print and in pixels have been newly revised for this 2020 edition. For this third edition, we felt it important to locate the essays historically by placing one or two dates at the end of each. The first date is the date of original publication of the essay. That date stands alone if the essay has never been substantively revised, or if this 2020 edition is its first appearance. Where there is a second date after an essay, it indicates the essay's most recent revision. In constructing a syllabus or assignment, a list of recommended readings for your students, or a qualifying exam list or in using keyword essays in any other way, please do take into consideration all 120-plus essays that make up *Keywords for American Cultural Studies*.

* * *

One way to teach with *Keywords for American Cultural Studies* is to assign print and online essays either as central readings for your course or as supplementary texts that will help students understand the vocabulary of your course's field of study. If you are teaching, for instance, Sojourner Truth's "Ar'n't I a Woman" speech or the Combahee River Collective Statement, either would pair well with Daniel Martinez HoSang's essay on "Intersectionality," which provides students with a term they can use to interpret those documents and their resonance with both contemporaneous and current issues. The same essay could pair just as well with a recent work of scholarship that uses "intersectionality" in a prominent manner, raising productive questions about that work's deployment of the keyword. "What does this scholar *mean* when they say 'intersectional'?" can be a generative question in a class discussion; the keyword essay can help them respond to such a question.

In any of these contexts and especially in introductory or survey courses, it is important to *teach* the assigned keyword essays by providing some time in class to unpack them rather than simply assigning them and assuming their immediate legibility. The reason for this caution is not that the essays are particularly dense or jargon laden. Rather, we and other instructors have found that students need to learn how to approach a keyword essay, to understand it as a specific genre of writing and mode of inquiry. If this preparatory work is not done, students may misread the individual essays and the publication as a whole as a reference guide whose aim is to define or fix the meanings of terms. If they adopt this approach, they will be frustrated, largely because the essays quite deliberately take a more critical, self-reflexive, and speculative stance in relation to their objects of inquiry. We wrote "Keywords: An Introduction" in part to provide a resource if you want to teach *Keywords for American Cultural Studies* as a methodology, not just a mapping of clusters of important concepts and terms. You may not usually ask students to read a textbook's introduction, but we suggest that you consider assigning this one or reading it yourself and discussing its main points with your students.

For these reasons, we urge you to follow the strategies developed by other successful instructors by using *Keywords for American Cultural Studies* as something other than a traditional textbook that provides a map of the fields it surveys. We emphasize in "Keywords: An Introduction" that one of the primary aims of this project is to provoke readers to engage in self-reflexive, open-ended, and future-oriented forms of inquiry as they conduct research on and make claims about "America" and its various "cultures." Some of the most generative responses to *Keywords for American Cultural Studies*—and some of the most productive class assignments—have come when students and other readers have worked, often on digital platforms, to assemble and publish responses and additions to what we offer in the book and on the web.

In that spirit, many instructors have had great success with assignments that ask students to produce keyword projects of their own. Some assignments require students to revise or supplement published keyword essays; others invite them to create essays about terms not included there. Some are individual assignments; others are collaborative. Many of the most successful have divided the process into two stages:

1. *Archiving usages of a particular keyword.* Many assignments begin by asking students to archive usages of their keyword. Archiving can involve simply copying or typing out every sentence they read that uses their keyword. That archive need not be textual. It can also involve images and sound, conversations overheard on the street, or exchanges on a bus. Depending on the course, the process of archiving can build core skills in close reading, participant observation, and other forms of data collection. These processes usefully focus on the nuances of language and inflection in students' readings and interactions but can also reveal the tensions and contradictions in that language, underscoring the crucial point that keywords are sites of contestation. It can be useful to ask students to keep a usage log in which they record the spatial and temporal location of each specific use of the term.

2. *Composing a keyword essay.* Once students have constructed this archive of usages, you can ask them to draw on that archive to tell a story about their keyword. From reading essays in *Keywords for American Cultural Studies*, students should already know that it is rarely possible to produce a linear narrative about a complex term; the effort to do so themselves underscores this point. Especially in an interdisciplinary context in which students are asked to make sense of an array of materials that use different vocabularies and methodologies, the effort to bring together the varying usages of a single keyword can make the content of the course clearer and more coherent. Ethnographic assignments can serve a similar function by asking students to attend to the contexts of specific usages. Depending on the context and objectives of any given course, these types of assignments can be completed either individually or collaboratively. They may involve written, visual, or multimodal composition strategies.

It is possible to assign the first part of this two-step process without the second. The process of archiving usages of a keyword can increase students' attentiveness to the language of criticism in productive ways even if they do not produce their own essays. Doing the second part without the first has been less successful when it has been tried, because without specific usage examples to draw on, students (and others) tend to write about themes or concepts without paying attention to language and usage. They write about the *thing* the keyword seems to reference, rather than the *word* and its usages.

Assignments that do include the essay-writing stage often start from a version of the prompts we asked our authors to use in constructing their essays:

- What kinds of critical projects does your keyword enable?
- What are the critical genealogies of the term, and how do these genealogies affect its use today?
- Are there ways of thinking that are occluded or obstructed by the use of this term?
- What other keywords constellate around it?

We intended these prompts to spur our contributors to map the contemporary critical terrain as they see it developing through their keyword. They can serve a similar purpose in relation to student work, so long as students understand that their critical terrain is more limited in scope than those surveyed by the essays in *Keywords for American Cultural Studies*. After all, your students are drawing on significantly different (and usually smaller) archives. Our contributors work primarily with historical and contemporary research in American studies, cultural studies, and related fields. For students assigned to compose a keyword essay, the primary archive is often the materials they encounter in a

particular course. Indeed, it can be helpful to tell students that while the essays they have *read* are from *Keywords for American Cultural Studies*, the essays they are *writing* are for an imaginary volume titled *Keywords for This Course*, with the imagined audience being other students in the course. Since the meanings and connotations of keywords are never settled and depend significantly on the local context in which they are used, students can write original essays based on these narrower or more focused materials. They can produce essays on terms that may not be keywords for the broader field but are crucial sites of debate and conflict within the scope of your course's subject matter.

On the website that was built for this book and others in the series (http://keywords.nyupress.org), we include several sample assignments that we and other instructors have developed as we have taught with previous editions of *Keywords*. Many of them follow the two-stage model just described, archiving usages followed by composing an essay. But there are other models represented there as well. Some of these assignments were developed and implemented on the interactive forum built for the first edition of *Keywords*, the Keywords Collaboratory, which housed, between 2007 and 2014, assignments in courses that included first-year writing sections, large undergraduate lectures, small upper-division seminars, and advanced graduate courses. Since that time, interactive and collaborative platforms have proliferated and become widely and easily available to instructors and students. Most course management systems such as Blackboard and Canvas include internal wikis, and Google Docs is easily accessible. As a result, it no longer seemed necessary to build and maintain a wiki specifically dedicated to this project. Thus the Keywords Collaboratory is no longer active. To demonstrate what is possible in these online and sometimes collaborative assignments, we have collected a sampling of student writing from the Collaboratory at http://keywords.nyupress.org.

As you develop your own assignments using whatever platform is at hand, you may opt to encourage or require collaboration among your students. For instance, you can break your class into working groups of three to five, each focused on a different keyword that is central to the course. You can then create two Google Docs for each group: one where they will build an archive of usages of their keyword and one where they will collaborate on an essay based on that archive. You can use a wiki or a blog in a similar way. Alternatively, an entire seminar can work together on a single keyword. Either way, producing a keyword essay, rather than just reading them, helps students grasp and internalize the intellectual and theoretical points implicit in a keywords project.

In these assignments, instructors have found that collaboration itself is a skill or form of knowledge production that has to be taught to students. You cannot always assume that students have experience collaborating on the platform you use—whether it is written, audio, visual, or some combination of the three—let alone that they know how to collaborate in the development of ideas. Here again, the two-step process is a practical approach, since the students learn the mechanics of adding text to the online platform when they are archiving usages and only later need to develop the more complex skill of collective composition.

One value of this approach is that it tends to jolt students out of the idea that writing and composition must be the solitary and individualistic activity typical of college classrooms, especially in the humanities and humanistic social sciences. As such, these assignments illustrate a point made by some of the most ardent advocates for the digital humanities: digital work tends to push scholars in the cultural disciplines toward more collaborative research methodologies and composition practices. It also makes clear one point that college instructors labor to teach: the audience for classroom assignments is not limited to the person who is grading them. Our earlier Collaboratory made this point especially vividly because it was completely open to the public, but even a collaborative Google Doc read by the other students in the class is more "public" than an individualized missive from a student to a professor. This orientation toward a larger audience encourages students to think more carefully and, often, more ambitiously about their writing and composition choices.

We urge you to go to keywords.nyupress.org to look over some of the technological options, sample assignments, and syllabi provided by instructors who have used *Keywords for American Cultural Studies* in the past, along with tips about what has worked and what has not. If you try one of these suggestions—or devise your own—we want to know how it went. You will find on the site a means of communicating with us and of sending us your own sample syllabi and assignments. If your students produce especially strong work, we would like to see that too. We look forward to hearing from you, to learning from your teaching experiences, and to sharing your pedagogical ideas with others.

1

Abolition

Robert Fanuzzi

"Abolition" is a word often used to create a sense of urgency, relevance, or potential for social change. It allows scholars of American studies and cultural studies to maintain a close, productive relationship between their research inquiries and progressive social movements, with at least two results. On the one hand, the use of the word "abolition" offers a way back into US and global history; it deepens our understanding of structural, long-standing inequalities in the United States by inviting comparisons to past social justice struggles, especially the early nineteenth-century movement against slavery that adopted "abolition" as its watchword. On the other hand, "abolition" unsettles the conventional timelines of US cultural history by reminding us that nothing has been adequately or effectively abolished and that abolition's meaning—as well as its objectives—remain open-ended. Abolition provides us with new directions, applications, and methods because it points to social change that has *not yet* occurred.

The author and activist W. E. B. Du Bois showed the potential for this second, forward-thinking usage when he framed *Black Reconstruction*—his far-reaching 1935 account of the thwarted promise of egalitarian Reconstruction policies and the contributions of free and emancipated African Americans to racial justice in the late nineteenth century—around the need for what he

called an "abolition democracy." By adding the modifier "democracy" to the keyword, Du Bois transformed abolition from a word associated with a historical event into a name for a historical process: a call to resist the ongoing oppression of a "colored proletariat, . . . the basic majority of workers who are yellow, black, and brown" and the growing power of white supremacy under modern global capitalism and European and US imperialism ([1935] 1999, 184). Current demands to "abolish ICE" or "prisons" or "the police" extend Du Bois's usage to critiques of US immigration restrictions, border security, and the criminal justice system, challenging us to imagine a democracy that is committed to the continuous "abolition" of social and racial injustice. "Abolition," the legal scholar Michelle Alexander explains in an interview with Rachel Kushner, "is a theory of change" (qtd. in Kushner 2019, 17).

The increasing currency of "abolition" in policy and activism today invites us to think through—and sometimes think against—past usages and historical frames for its meaning. Indeed, abolition is a fruitful term for rethinking and resisting current policies and institutions because of its long association with efforts to reform and redirect capitalist systems responsible for the modern world. This association began in the late eighteenth century, when reformers in Britain, the British American colonies, and France organized an ambitious international movement to end the transatlantic slave trade around the term "abolition." Inspiring a broad coalition of political theorists, political leaders, political economists, and literary and religious thinkers, this usage of abolition represented the slave trade, a pillar of the British and European colonial economy, as a "barbaric traffic" that incentivized the enslavement of Africans in Africa, converted them into articles of commerce, and transported them in unspeakable conditions through the infamous Middle Passage so they could be sold and brutalized on Caribbean and American plantations (Gould 2003).

Though this usage of "abolition" laid the foundation for policies and movements that seek an end to racial oppression, it is important to note what it did not seek to accomplish: the abolition of slavery in the Americas. In its eighteenth-century incarnation, "abolition" gave powerful expression to principles of liberty, autonomy, and humanitarianism that helped white people in Britain, the Americas, and Europe describe themselves—and their transatlantic commerce—as liberal. Abolition contributed to these emerging descriptions in two ways. First, abolition inspired a popular culture, an aesthetics, and a moral philosophy that encouraged Anglo-Americans and Anglo-Europeans to elevate themselves above their governments' narrow economic interests and adopt a "humanitarian sensibility" that engaged them with the suffering of enslaved Africans, re-created through graphic documentation, illustrations, poetry, and fiction (Bender 1992; Drescher 2009). The contribution of wrenching firsthand accounts of family separation, enslavement, and Christian redemption by formerly enslaved writers such as Ottobah Cugoanoa and Olaudah Equiano and African American poet Phyllis Wheatley to the growing body of abolitionist literature helped make abolition synonymous with universal

human principles that circulated among writers and readers across the Atlantic and which transcended both country and race (D. Davis 1975; Nwankwo 2005; Cugoano 1999; Equiano [1785] 2003; Wheatley [1773] 1999).

The counterpart to abolition's liberal and humanitarian vision was an economic plan that called for more not less capitalism: a modern, liberal, self-improving capitalism that could deliver freedom and human dignity to everyone on the globe in incremental fashion once the chains of the transatlantic slave trade were removed. Though firmly associated with the progress of freedom, abolition in this context did not mean the opposite of slavery. As scholars have noted, the capitalist engine of this "Atlantic modernity" was the American and Caribbean plantation system, its financial calculations of human value, and its extraction of profit from Africans' coerced labor (Dillon 2014; Lowe 2015; Baucom 2005). The close connection between abolition and the freedom promised by this capitalist economy helped render all acts of African and Afro-creole self-liberation, especially those that led to the success and spread of the Haitian Revolution throughout the hemisphere, as pointlessly tragic and tragically retrograde, contrary to modern progress and universal principles of humanity (Blackburn 1988; Fischer 2003; Trouillot 1995; James [1938] 1989; Scott 2005; Williams [1944] 1994). Abolition, as first embraced and utilized for liberal and humanitarian goals, thus raises difficult questions about how we define social change and whom we permit to define it.

The more socially egalitarian meanings of "abolition" that emerged in the nineteenth century forecast its potential for redistributing and rebalancing racial positions within and through the struggle for racial justice (Sinha 2017). Until the early 1830s, the word had fallen into disuse as a symbol of antislavery politics in the United States. Its place had been taken by the term "colonization," an initiative supported by political, academic, and Protestant religious elites that sought to reverse the legacy of the transatlantic slave trade and end slavery in the United States by inducing slave owners to free enslaved black Americans and expedite their resettlement on the west coast of Africa, where they would found a new black nation appropriately named Liberia. Free African Americans called out the blatant racism of an antislavery initiative intended to remove black people from the country of their birth and strengthen white peoples' exclusive claim to US nationality, circulating radical critiques of the Protestant religion and liberal reform under the banner of "anticolonization" (Goodman 1998; Jordan 1969; Kazanjian 2003; Hinks 1997). "Abolition" supplanted "colonization" as a signifier of antislavery and incorporated the meanings of "anticolonization" through the efforts of newspaper editor William Lloyd Garrison, who launched the *Liberator* as the voice and forum for a new abolition movement in 1831 with the support of black readers and, even more importantly, texts and commentaries by prominent African American political leaders. Representing a diverse coalition of black anticolonizationists, white temperance reformers, deists, women's rights advocates, and Protestant evangelicals, the resurgent abolition movement modified its earlier usage with its demand for the immediate as opposed to the gradual abolition of slavery and explicit references to Britain's emancipation of enslaved people throughout the Caribbean in 1833. Abolition, as redeployed for the next generation of antislavery resistance, married the prospect of freedom for enslaved African Americans to the establishment of an inclusive democracy that erased sexist and racist limits on political participation and power (Fanuzzi 2003; Schoolman 2014; Stauffer 2004).

Following the example of Du Bois, American studies scholars have used the example of the nineteenth-century abolition movement and the democratic inflection of the keyword "abolition" to signal the potential for progressive social change within US cultural and social history. In the 1960s, historians called African American student leaders "the new abolitionists" in an effort to cast the civil rights and black liberation movements as the overdue, climactic chapters of nineteenth-century antislavery activism (Zinn 1965). Women's studies scholars of the 1980s and '90s sought to cultivate transracial solidarity among white and black feminists through historical scholarship that renamed the nineteenth-century antislavery struggle as "feminist abolitionist" (Sánchez-Eppler 1993; Yellin 1992; S. Samuels 1996). Scholars working from the standpoint of US labor history in the 1990s helped pivot the term from its historical reference toward post-Marxist cultural studies and critiques of contemporary racial formations with their call for the "abolition of whiteness" (Roediger 1994, 2007; Ignatiev and Garvey 1996; Bonilla-Silva 2003; Painter 2010; Frankenberg 1993; Olson 2014).

The wide currency and visibility of "prison abolition" today reflects this forward-looking, political meaning of Du Bois's "abolition democracy" and the influence of the black radical intellectual tradition over its usage. As deployed by many African American and Black studies scholars and activists today, "abolition" represents the disruption of US culture and history, not its culmination or its potential for redemption; it stands for antiracism but takes the historical structures and modern institutions of racism for its point of departure. First proposed by the scholar-activist Angela Davis as an alternative intellectual and policy framework for black liberation, "prison abolition," unlike prison reform, investigates the role of racially discriminatory policies of mass incarceration within larger structures of racial and gender oppression, legacies of economic exploitation, and the physical (mal)distribution of benefits, resources, and populations within a global capitalist system (A. Davis 2003, 2005; R. Gilmore 2007; Knopp, Howard, and Morris 1976; Abolition Collective 2018). "Abolition feminism" is a complimentary usage that seeks to empower women of color and LBTQ+, undocumented, and displaced people—those most vulnerable to cycles of violence, punishment, and retribution that operate through and across the criminal justice system, the legal system, social policies, and educational institutions—to guide and build new social structures for the repair and reduction of harm (Davis 2016; Meiners 2007). Because "prison abolition" and "abolition feminism" refuse to adopt already compromised structures of policy-making as their instruments and arbiters of social change, they have helped make "abolition" a byword for opposition to reasonable moderation and conventional reform.

Emerging usages of abolition, which include "schools of abolition," "abolition universities," and "abolition university studies," explicitly apply the goals of "prison abolition" and "abolition feminism" to higher education. Drawing connections between the exploitative features of global capitalism and national expansion, penal institutions, and the corporate policies of universities, these usages mark the complicity of US educational institutions in racial and gender oppression (Boggs 2019; Marez 2014; Rodriguez 2012). In doing so, they also reference the horizon of change that radical intellectuals have invested in the word "abolition": an end to traditions, or epistemologies, that normalize centuries of racial oppression and gender inequality as inevitable, if regrettable, features of modernity and which center or overrepresent Western European male concepts of humanity as their default. As used in this context, abolition makes the historical experiences and knowledge making of oppressed peoples the critical focus, not an aberration (Harney and Moten 2013; Washington 1998; Wynter 2003). As the term "abolition" becomes more closely associated with creative and future-oriented acts of resistance, it invites us to stop preparing our minds, our policies, and our morality for the world racism has made and to imagine and demand new worlds without it.

2014/2020

2

Affect

Ann Cvetkovich

"Affect" names a conceptual problem as much as a tangible thing. As such, it is best understood as an umbrella term that covers related and more familiar words, such as "feeling" and "emotion," as well as efforts to make distinctions among them. The *Oxford English Dictionary* (*OED*) traces the history of the term to the seventeenth century, aligning it with "desire" or "passion" and opposing it to "reason." Further specifying that "affect" is both a "mental" and a "bodily" disposition, the *OED* sets in place a persistent ambiguity that challenges distinctions between mind and body. More technical uses of the term emerge from mid-twentieth-century scientific psychology, where "affect" designates sensory processes or experiences prior to cognition and distinguishes such sensations from the cognitive processes that produce emotions (Damasio 1994). Because affect, emotions, and feelings stand at the intersection of mind and body, cognition and sensation, and conscious and unconscious or autonomic processes, it is not easy to identify the material basis for their social and historical construction, which includes parts of the body (nerves, brains, or guts) as well as environments and transpersonal relations.

As the declaration of an "affective turn" in American studies and cultural studies suggests (Clough and Halley 2007; Gregg and Seigworth 2010), the current prominence of "affect" as a keyword represents the convergence of many strands of thinking. Foundational for both fields are French theorist Michel Foucault's histories of the social construction of categories such as body, gender, and sex that seem like natural phenomena. These categories form the basis for modern notions of subjectivity and power that conceive of the self as possessing a depth or interiority evident in the supposed natural truth of feelings (Foucault [1976] 1990). Following this line of research, the affective turn takes up debates both about the construction of binary oppositions between reason and emotion and about the reversal of hierarchies that subordinate emotion to reason as part of a mind/body split often associated with the seventeenth-century philosopher René Descartes. In the Cartesian worldview, passions, instincts, and feelings are unruly and uncontrollable, requiring subordination to the rational control of reason and the mind—a hierarchical ordering that has sometimes led to a romantic embrace of their subversive power. In response to such reversals, Foucault's critique of the idea that freedom of expression and resistance to repression constitute political liberation has inspired cautionary accounts of the politics of affect. Efforts to historicize subjectivity and to conceive of the self in non-Cartesian terms have required new conceptions of affect, emotion, and feeling. Indeed, the use of the term "affect" rather than "feeling" or "emotion" arguably stems from the desire to find a more neutral word, given the strong vernacular associations of "feeling" and "emotion" with irrationality.

Within cultural studies, the project of accounting for social life and political economy through everyday and sensory experiences, including feelings, has an extensive history. Affect, emotion, and feeling have been central to long-standing efforts to combine Marxism and psychoanalysis and to theorize the relations between the psychic and the social, the private and the public. Psychoanalysis has used "affect" and related categories as part of a vocabulary for drives, unconscious processes, and the psychic energies created by both internal and external stimuli. The term "affect" is also present in social and cultural theories that seek alternatives to psychoanalytic models, such as Eve Sedgwick's use of Sylvan Tompkins, who describes nine affects that link outward behavior with mental and physical states (Sedgwick and Frank 1995; Sedgwick 2003). Whether drawing on psychoanalysis or its alternatives, accounts of psychic life and felt experience have been important to cultural studies in its efforts to explain the social and political uses of feeling (including the divide between reason and emotion) and to negotiate differences of scale between the local and the global, the intimate and the collective. Raymond Williams's elusively suggestive term "structure of feeling" ([1977] 1997, 128–35) is a good example of the use of the vocabulary of feeling to describe how social conditions are manifest in everyday life and how felt experience can be the foundation for emergent social formations. Rather than being attached to one theoretical school or discipline, "affect" has named multiple projects and agendas, including a broad inquiry into the public life of feelings. Following Williams, the vernacular term "feeling" remains a useful way to signify these projects, which extend beyond the question of specifying what affects are.

Though the affective turn has conceptual roots in Marxism and psychoanalysis, it has also been significantly catalyzed by feminist critiques of the gendering of dichotomies between reason and emotion, which made their way into the academy from popular culture and political movements. The 1970s feminist cultures of consciousness raising reversed the disparaging association of femininity with feeling and, in a version of the discourse of sexual revolution, celebrated emotional expression as a source of feminine power associated with social and political liberation (Sarachild 1978; Lorde 1984b). Subsequent generations of scholarship in feminist cultural studies have been more skeptical about an easy reversal of the reason/emotion binary, the often essentializing assumption that women are more emotional or nurturing than men, and claims for affective expression's liberatory possibilities. Instead, this scholarship has provided rich and nuanced histories of the centrality of feeling to the relations between private and public spheres and especially of how the intimate life of romance, the family, and the domestic sphere serves as the foundation for social relations of power (Davidson and Hatcher 2002). In the field of American studies, scholarship on categories such as sentimentality, sensationalism, sympathy, melodrama, and the gothic has shown how cultural genres, especially fiction, produce social effects through mobilizing feeling (Tompkins 1985; S. Samuels 1992; Cvetkovich 1992; Halberstam 1995). Attention to affect is the culmination of several decades of feminist scholarship on clusters of related terms such as "domesticity," "family," and "marriage" as well as on the historical continuities that link women's popular genres, such as domestic and sentimental novels, theatrical melodrama, and women's film (L. Williams 2002; Berlant 2008).

The far-reaching impact of feminist approaches to feeling and politics, including their relevance to histories of racism and colonialism, is exemplified by scholarship on the sentimental politics of abolition in texts such as Harriet Beecher Stowe's *Uncle Tom's Cabin* ([1852] 1981), nineteenth-century slave narratives, and more recent neo–slave narratives. Stowe uses representations of slave mothers separated from their children and innocent slaves being beaten to generate appeals to universal feeling as the marker of the humanity of slaves and as the inherent result of witnessing the evils of slavery. Scenes of sexual intimacy between master and slave prove more affectively complex, however, in *Incidents in the Life of a Slave Girl* ([1861] 2001), in which Harriet Jacobs grapples with how to represent her sexual relations with white men without losing the reader's sympathy. Toni Morrison's historical novel *Beloved* (1987) further challenges the tradition of the sympathetic slave mother by telling the story of a woman who tries to kill her three children in order to protect them from slavery, aiming for a more complex representation of the affective life of slavery than stark scenes of innocence and guilt. The powerful fusion of secular forms of religious feeling and maternal sentiment in abolitionist discourses provides a model for the representation of social suffering that has had a lasting impact on US cultural politics in both popular entertainment and the news media. What Lauren Berlant (2008) has called the "unfinished business of sentimentality" persists not just in popular genres produced for women but also in realist and documentary forms of representation, including human rights discourses, in which spectacles of suffering are used to mobilize public action. Affectively charged representation is part of everyday life across the political spectrum. The Trump mass rallies leading to and following his election, his anti-immigration politics, and the Black Lives Matter and #MeToo movements all prompt ongoing debate about the politics of sensation, sentiment, and sympathy (Berlant 2004; Staiger, Cvetkovich, and Reynolds 2010).

Another important area of scholarship in which feeling and affect are central are discussions of trauma and cultural memory that have emerged in American studies as it reckons with the legacies of slavery, genocide, and colonialism. Although the urgencies of Holocaust memory have inspired the creation of public memorials and testimony as forums for emotional expression in Europe and elsewhere, slavery and genocide provide a specifically US genealogy for trauma studies and cultural memory. In seeking to address traumatic histories, public cultures of memory raise questions about what emotional responses constitute a reparative relation to the past and whether it is ever possible to complete the work of mourning, particularly while social suffering is ongoing. Drawing on psychoanalytic categories of mourning and melancholy, critical race theory and queer studies (especially work on AIDS) have produced new theories of melancholy or unfinished mourning as productive rather than pathological. These fields depart from psychoanalytic categories of affect and trauma in favor of vernacular vocabularies of affect in indigenous, diasporic, and queer cultures (Crimp 2002; Eng and Kazanjian 2002; Cvetkovich 2003). Queer studies has also made important contributions to embracing ostensibly negative emotions such as shame and melancholy, as well as theorizing queer temporalities that favor affectively meaningful representations of the past rather than accurate or realist documentation (Love 2007; Muñoz 2009; E. Freeman 2010; Berlant and Edelman 2013).

While these critical histories of affect as a cultural and social construct have been extremely generative in American studies, a second important line of research has returned to theories of embodiment and sensation to ask new questions about the material basis for affect, emotions, and feelings. The use of the term "affect" by Gilles Deleuze and Félix Guattari to describe the impersonal intensities, forces, and movements that cause bodies and objects to affect and be affected by one another has been especially influential in recent scholarship (Deleuze and Guattari 1987; Massumi 2002b; Stewart 2007; Puar 2007). Deleuze's work usefully displaces psychoanalysis and decenters the individuated subject of cognition, locating unconscious bodily processes and sensory life at the center of social life. Deleuze has also been a major catalyst for new materialist notions of affect that distinguish more sharply between "affect" and "emotion," preserving "affect" for noncognitive processes and using "emotion" to describe socially constructed behavior.

Clearly, the multidisciplinary question of what it means to be a sensory being cannot be confined to one theoretical school, and American studies and cultural studies have been invigorated by proliferating forms of affect studies. Phenomenology and cultural geography have provided resources for materialist histories of sensory experience as well as new accounts of the relations between bodies, objects, and environments and of terms such as "mood" and "atmosphere" (Ahmed 2006; Thrift 2008). Neurobiology and cognitive science have been embraced by scholars in the humanities interested in the interface between brain and body in constituting sensory experience (E. Wilson 2004, 2015; Pitts-Taylor 2016; Tougaw 2018). Animal studies and ecocriticism contribute to a posthumanist concept of humans as integrated with animals, things, and nature and understandings of affective experience as bodily sensation and vital force (Haraway 2008; Grosz 2011; J. Bennett 2010; Chen 2012; Alaimo 2016; Haraway 2016). Disability studies (Kafer 2013; Clare 2017; Puar 2017) and black feminist discussions of flesh (Musser 2014; Weheliye 2014) also combine affect and sensation to enable new understandings of embodied experience. With the project of overturning old hierarchies between mind and body, cognition and feeling, reason and emotion largely accomplished, these forms of affect studies are promoting interdisciplinary inquiry across science and humanities. In so doing, they offer answers to the long-standing problem in social theory of how to think the relation between the psychic and the social worlds and provide resources for building new cultures of public feeling.

2014/2020

3

African
Kevin K. Gaines

The keyword "African" has been and remains a touchstone for African-descended peoples' struggle for identity and inclusion, encompassing extremes of racial denigration and vindication in a nation founded on the enslavement of Africans. Both the African presence throughout the Americas and its significance for constructions of national culture in the United States have remained fraught with racialized and exclusionary power relations. In a nation that has traditionally imagined its culture and legislated its polity as "white," "African" has often provided for African Americans a default basis for identity in direct proportion to their exclusion from national citizenship.

As scholars ranging from Winthrop Jordan (1969) to Jennifer L. Morgan (2004) have noted, there was nothing natural or inevitable about the development of racial slavery in the Americas. Nor was the emergence of the racialized category of the African as permanent slave foreordained. European travelers who recorded their initial encounters with Africans did not perceive them as slaves. But their ethnocentric self-regard informed their descriptions of Africans as extremely different from themselves in appearance, religious beliefs, and behavior. European constructions of the bodily difference, heathenism, and beastliness of Africans mitigated occasional observations of their morality and humanity. As European nations experimented with systems of forced labor in the Americas, initially enlisting indigenous peoples and European indentured servants as well as Africans, ideologies of African inferiority facilitated the permanent enslavement of Africans as an expedient labor practice. With the legal codification of lifetime African slavery, European settlers completed the racial degradation of African men and women, a process anticipated in Enlightenment conceptions of difference and hierarchy. In keeping with the contingency of its origins, the idea of the African in America was subject to change and contestation. An awareness on the part of travelers and slave owners of ethnic and regional distinctions among peoples from Africa yielded to the homogenizing idea of *the* African. Throughout the eighteenth century, slave owners in the Caribbean and North America attributed rebellions to "wild and savage" Africans, leading, on occasion, to restrictions on the importation of African slaves.

During the nineteenth century, free African Americans held an ambivalent attitude toward all things African. It could hardly have been otherwise, given the existential burdens of chattel slavery and the exclusion of Africa and its peoples from Enlightenment ideas of historical agency, modernity, and civilization. Prominent African Americans such as the shipping merchant Paul Cuffee championed emigration from the United States to West Africa. Despite his personal success, Cuffee despaired at the prospects for African-descended people to achieve equality in the United States. Inspired by the global antislavery movement, as well as the establishment of the British colony of Sierra Leone as an asylum for Africans rescued from the slave trade, Cuffee believed that emigration would allow Africans and African Americans to realize their full potential. But Cuffee led only one voyage of settlers to West Africa, leaving his entrepreneurial and evangelical objectives unfulfilled. African American enthusiasm for emigration was further dampened by the rise in the early nineteenth century of an explicitly racist colonization movement.

The impetus for this movement, which sought the removal of free blacks and emancipated slaves to Africa, came from powerful whites, including slave owners and members of Congress.

Free blacks resented the proslavery motives of colonizationists and increasingly rejected an identification with Africa largely as a matter of self-defense. While the initial wave of schools, churches, mutual-aid societies, and other institutions established by northern free blacks in the late eighteenth century often bore the name "African," this nomenclature was largely abandoned by the mid-nineteenth century. The reasons for this shift were complex, including demands for US citizenship, black abolitionists' opposition to the colonization movement, the dwindling population of African-born blacks, and an acknowledgment, at some level, of a multihued African American community resulting from the systemic rape of enslaved black women by white male slave owners. Above all, the term epitomized the stark conditions of exile faced by African Americans, excluded from US citizenship and society and deprived of an affirming connection to an ancestral homeland. Even for leaders of the African Methodist Episcopal (AME) Church, founded in Philadelphia in 1816 when white Methodists refused to worship alongside blacks, wariness toward Africa and a deep suspicion toward its indigenous cultures informed their efforts to evangelize the continent (J. Campbell 1995).

While emigration and colonization movements resulted in the resettlement of relatively few African Americans, the violent exclusion of African Americans from southern politics after emancipation renewed the appeal of Africa as a foundation of African American identity. As Africa came under the sway of European missions and colonialism, the involvement of AME Church missions in Africa and the scholarship of Edward W. Blyden ([1887] 1967) helped promote among some African Americans a general interest in the welfare of Africans and a greater tolerance for indigenous African cultures. Blyden's work was part of a long-standing African American intellectual tradition seeking to vindicate Africa by documenting its contributions to Western civilization (Moses 1998). Such scholarship, combined with the worldwide impact of Marcus Garvey's post–World War I mass movement, helped sow the seeds of African nationalism and anticolonialism. The Garvey movement, which flourished amid a national wave of urban race riots and antiblack violence, built on popular emigrationism and inspired African-descended peoples all over the world with its secular gospel of economic cooperation toward African redemption, even as some African American intellectuals dismissed it as a quixotic "back to Africa" movement. Such controversy may well have informed subsequent debates among black studies scholars over whether it was valid to speak of African cultural retentions, or "survivals," among the descendants of enslaved Africans in the Americas. The sociologist E. Franklin Frazier and the social anthropologist Melville Herskovits represent the opposing positions in the debate (Raboteau 1978). Frazier believed that the traumas of enslavement and the rigors of urbanization had extinguished all cultural ties to Africa. Herskovits based his support for the idea of African cultural retentions on his research on Caribbean societies and cultural practices. If recent scholarship in history, anthropology, linguistics, religion, literary and cultural studies, historical archaeology, and population genetics is any indication, Herskovits's position that some African cultural practices persisted in the Americas appears to have prevailed.

As African national independence movements capitalized on the decline of European colonialism after World War II, the idea of the African underwent yet another profound revision in the minds of many African Americans, from intellectual and popular stereotypes of African savagery to images of black power and modernity. The emergence of newly independent African nations beginning in the late 1950s became a source of pride for many people of African descent. Even as blacks believed that the new African presence in world affairs signaled the continent's full participation in, if not redefinition of, the modern world, members of the US and European political establishment opposed African demands for freedom and true self-determination, trafficking, more or less discreetly, in racist attitudes. In 1960, widely touted as "the year of Africa," more than thirty African states gained national independence; that year also witnessed the bloody repression of demands for freedom in apartheid South Africa and the Congo. For many northern urban African Americans a generation removed from the violence of the Jim Crow South and facing marginalization in such cities as New York, Chicago, and Detroit, new African states and their leaders, including Ghana's Kwame Nkrumah and the Congo's Patrice Lumumba, rivaled the southern civil rights movement in importance. When Lumumba was assassinated during the civil disorder in the Congo fomented by Belgium, African Americans in Harlem and Chicago angrily demonstrated against the complicity of Western governments and the United Nations in the murder. In doing so, they joined members of the black left and working-class black nationalists in a nascent political formation that envisioned their US citizenship in solidarity with African peoples, uniting their own demands for freedom and democracy in the United States with those of peoples of African descent the world over (Singh 2004; Gaines 2006).

Within this context of decolonization, the term "African" became a battleground. To the architects of US foreign policy, African American solidarity with African peoples and their struggles exceeded the ideological boundaries of US citizenship. African American criticism of US foreign policy and advocacy on behalf of African peoples transgressed the limits imposed by a liberalism whose expressed support for civil rights and decolonization was qualified by Cold War national security concerns (and opposed outright by segregationist elements). As some African governments joined US blacks in denouncing violent white resistance to demands for equality, US officials' assertions of the American Negro's fundamental Americanness became a staple of liberal discourse. Their view was echoed in press accounts asserting that Africans and American Negroes were fundamentally estranged from one another. No doubt many African Americans still looked on Africans with ambivalence. However, this normative liberal, assimilationist notion of African American identity and citizenship provided a context for subsequent debates among African Americans during the Black Power era of the late 1960s and beyond over the terms of an authentic black identity. Contested claims about authentic blackness, particularly when inflected with issues of gender and sexual orientation, can and have had a divisive and self-destructive impact among African Americans (E. Johnson 2003).

As a Janus-faced US nationalism trumpeted its civil rights reforms—seemingly in exchange for consent to its political and military repression of African and, in the 1960s, Vietnamese nationalists—mainstream civil rights leaders endeavored, without success, to formalize an African American position on US foreign policy. It was Malcolm X, among African American spokespersons, who most effectively articulated a growing frustration with the federal government's domestic and foreign policies toward black and African peoples (Gaines 2006). Along with such post–World War II figures as Paul Robeson, St. Clair Drake, and Lorraine Hansberry, Malcolm X reanimated W. E. B. Du Bois's decades-old

assertion that African Americans sought no less than full US citizenship without sacrificing their "Negro" identity and heritage, helping African Americans to embrace rather than shun the designation "African" (Plummer 1996; Von Eschen 1997; Meriwether 2002).

During the 1980s, African American leadership, including many elected officials, waged an effective civil disobedience campaign against the apartheid regime in South Africa and the Reagan administration's support for it. The rapid acceptance of the term "African American," championed by Jesse Jackson and others and used in the context of the antiapartheid struggle, represents a profound reversal of decades of shame and ambivalence. Yet it is unclear what relationship the general (though by no means universal) acceptance of "African" as a marker of US black identity today bears to the black transnational consciousness that developed during the 1960s and that flourished during the Free South Africa movement. A major legacy of these social movements for black equality and African liberation has been the legitimation of scholarly investigations of the African foundations of African American history and culture, including studies of the African diaspora and what Paul Gilroy (1993) has termed the "Black Atlantic."

At the beginning of the twenty-first century, the term "African" remains highly contested in politics and popular culture. On the one hand, crises of poverty, famine, disease (including the AIDS epidemic), and armed conflict reinforce an Afro-pessimism in the Western imagination not far removed from the colonial idea of the "Dark Continent," a place untouched by civility and modernity. While the human toll of such crises is undeniable, the US media generally devote far less attention to democratically elected civilian governments, some of which have supplanted brutal and corrupt military dictatorships supported by the West during the Cold War. These representations continue to view Africans and

African Americans through alternately romanticizing and demeaning prisms of race.

On the other hand, the term "African" has come full circle within a society capable of sustaining wildly contradictory views of race. Apart from the usual Afropessimism, the African has been incorporated in some accounts into the quintessential US immigrant success narrative, as the upward mobility of highly educated African immigrants is portrayed as an implicit reproach to underachieving native-born African American descendants of slaves. The idea of the otherness of African immigrants in relation to the native-born US black community was widely debated during the 2008 presidential campaign of Barack Obama. Some African American pundits asserted that Obama's African parentage made him less authentically black than US-born African Americans descended from slaves and, arguably, less entitled to the black vote than his rival in the Democratic primary in 2008, Hillary Rodham Clinton. This view was discredited as Obama's candidacy gained momentum and as African Americans equated Obama's run for the presidency with African Americans' historical struggles for equality. Obama's election was celebrated internationally, including throughout Africa and in the Kenyan village of his father's family. As the first African American president, Obama faced an unusual level of attacks to his person and the dignity of his office, often of a blatantly racist nature. Right-wing pundits and politicians routinely portrayed Obama's African heritage as a threat to the republic; Newt Gingrich, during his 2012 run for the presidency, claimed that Obama's "Kenyan, anticolonial" worldview was proof of his disloyalty and subversive influence (Costa 2010).

Whatever their origin or occasion, media and political narratives emphasizing tensions between African Americans and African immigrants are the present-day equivalent of Tarzan movies, whose effect is to erase the history and modernity of transnational black subjectivities. While recent scholarship in American studies has called for a rethinking of the black-white color line in US race relations, the tensions expressed by the question of who is an "African" and who is an "African American" are symptomatic of the nation's continued struggle over the significance of the African presence, past and present, real and symbolic. Of course, the contested meaning and legacy of the African presence is not peculiar to the United States, as many Latino immigrants to the United States bring with them histories and identities shaped by the vexed legacy of racial slavery in their countries of origin. The foundations of Latin American societies, with their diverse populations of Africans, indigenous peoples, Europeans, and Asians, suggests that the expansion of the Hispanic population in the United States does not render the black-white color line obsolete but rather makes it all the more salient as a benchmark for social affiliation.

2007/2014

4

America

Kirsten Silva Gruesz

"We hold these truths to be self-evident" begins the main body of the Declaration of Independence, and the definition of "America" may likewise seem utterly self-evident: the short form of the nation's official name. Yet its meaning becomes more elusive the closer we scrutinize it. Since "America" names the entire hemisphere from the Yukon to Patagonia, its common use as a synonym for the United States of America is technically a misnomer, as Latin Americans and Canadians continually (if resignedly) point out. Is their objection just a small question of geographical semantics? The self-evidence of "America" is troubled from the start not only by ambiguities about the geographical extent of the territory it delineates but by the unspoken meanings it bears: deeper connotations that go far beyond the literal referent of the nation-state. In the statement "As Americans, we prize freedom," "American" may at first seem to refer simply to US citizens, but the context of the sentence strongly implies a consensual understanding of shared values, not just shared passports. The literal and figurative meanings tend to collapse into each other. Who gets to define these consensual understandings? Under what historical conditions does one group's definition have more or less power than another's? Without looking critically at these questions, studies of "America" and its cultures cannot claim self-awareness about its premises or its practices.

Because the meaning of "America" and its corollaries— "American," "Americanization," "Americanism," and "Americanness"—seems so self-evident but is in fact so imprecise, using the term in conversation or debate tends to reinforce certain ways of thinking while repressing others. In the slyly comic *Devil's Dictionary* (1911), pundit Ambrose Bierce includes the term only in the form of its opposite: "un-American, adj. Wicked, intolerable, heathenish." Bierce implies that using the adjective "un-American" shuts down an argument by impugning your opponent's values. Thus the power to define what is genuinely American is a considerable one. The political slogan "Make America Great Again," revived from the Reagan era by Donald Trump's 2016 campaign, exemplifies how a seemingly straightforward use of the word can carry a highly divisive and volatile charge.

By the time Bierce penned this undefinition in 1911, the use of "America" as a synonym for "the United States" was a habit already deeply ingrained, thanks in part to nationalistic writers of the nineteenth century such as Walt Whitman. Whitman's original preface to *Leaves of Grass* tries to get at the essence of the nation by using both terms in rapid-fire succession: "The genius of the United States is not best or most in its executives or legislatures, nor in its ambassadors or authors or colleges or churches or parlors, . . . but always most in the common people." "America is the race of races," he continues. "The Americans of all nations at any time upon the earth have probably the fullest poetical nature. The United States themselves are essentially the greatest poem" ([1855] 1999, 4–5). Toggling freely between "America" and "the United States," Whitman celebrates his particular vision of what set the nation apart from all others: "the common people," the heterogeneous mixing of immigrants into a "race of races," and everyday, vernacular speech as the stuff of poetry. Yet Whitman also includes scenes from Mexico, Canada, and the Caribbean in his panoramic vision of America, revealing not only the expansionist beliefs Whitman held at the time but the extraordinary persistence of an older sense of America as the name for the whole of the New World. This too is a misnomer sanctified by the passage of time: tens of millions of indigenous inhabitants neither saw it as new nor imagined it on the large, abstract scale of the Europeans.

Against Columbus's insistence that the landmass he had "discovered" was Asia, the Italian explorer Amerigo Vespucci first dubbed it a "New World." It was not Vespucci himself but a contemporary mapmaker, Martin Waldseemuller, who then christened the region "America," originally referring only to the southern lands. Later cartographers broadened the designation to include the lesser-known continent we now call North America: a historical irony, given the way that US Americans would later strictly exclude those lands from "America." However, alternative theories of the naming of the hemisphere flourish. Solid evidence links a British merchant named Richard Ameryk to John Cabot's voyages along the North Atlantic coast, leading to speculation that Cabot named "America" for his patron a decade or so before Waldseemuller's map. More circumstantial claims have been made on the basis of tenuous etymologies: some argue that the name comes from Vikings who called their Newfoundland settlement "Mark" or "Maruk"—"Land of Darkness"; still others speculate that it derives from a root word in Phoenician, Hebrew, or Hindu, suggesting that one of these groups encountered America before Europeans did. Another provocative theory arises from the fact that one indigenous group in Nicaragua had traditionally referred to one gold-rich district in their territory as "Amerrique," and some Mayan languages use a similar-sounding word (J. Cohen 2004).

Historical linguists advise caution in drawing conclusions from such sonic resonances, but they do suggest the possibility that the name "America" may come from within the New World rather than being imposed on it. The continuing life of this debate about naming suggests that what is really at stake is not some ultimate etymological truth but a claim to origins and therefore to ownership. Each claim grants symbolic primacy to a different group, as Annette Kolodny demonstrates in her examination of the Anglo-American fascination with a Viking "first contact," which emphasized Norse whiteness while erasing the testimony of Wabanaki and other Native peoples about those settlements (Kolodny 2012).

Whatever the ultimate derivation of the name, Waldseemuller's choice to pen it onto his map had profound consequences. Until the beginning of the nineteenth century, "America" and its analogs in Spanish, French, and other European languages designated the whole of the New World. After Columbus, earlier Christian models of a three-continent globe were amended to include America as the fourth. To create two-dimensional representations of a round world, Renaissance mapmakers split the globe visually into distinct hemispheres—Europe, Africa, and Asia as the Eastern, and the Americas isolated into the Western. The Atlantic remained at the map's center, as if America were linked only to Europe (further, the distorted Mercator projection grossly minimized Africa). This geographical convenience has become so naturalized that it remains difficult to envision what Lisa Lowe (2015) calls "the intimacies of four continents": how East and South Asia were closely tied to the transatlantic triangle trade of sugar, rum, and enslaved people. Differently oriented maps can help break these habits of thought: just look at a Pacific-centered or polar-centered map or one that flips the traditional plotting of north and south to locate Australia and Antarctica at the top. Similarly, the idea of "Latin America"—comprising not just the continent of South America but a hefty portion of North

America as well—is a product of fairly recent cultural practices, not geophysical reality. In the nineteenth century, Spanish-speaking elites began using the term to defend and distinguish Franco-Iberian Catholic values from Anglo-Saxon Protestant ones. Walter Mignolo writes, "Once America was named as such in the sixteenth century and Latin America named as such in the nineteenth, it appeared as if they had been there forever" (2005, 2).

Of the many figurative meanings that the American hemisphere acquired for Europeans following first contact, most involve notions of novelty, new beginnings, and utopian promise. The Mexican historian Edmundo O'Gorman (1961) influentially wrote that America was "invented" before it was "discovered," demonstrating that Europeans had long imagined a mythical land of marvels and riches that they then projected onto the unfamiliar terrain. Throughout the hemisphere, most European settlers did not at first refer to themselves as "Americans," reserving that term for indigenous people. Instead, they nostalgically called their home spaces "New-England," "Nieuw-Amsterdam," and "Nueva España," reflecting the fact that, for most, traditional Old World identities took precedence over rootedness in the soil on which they stood: a problem that the architects of nationhood would eventually have to solve. The associations that Europeans projected onto this "new" hemisphere were not always positive, even though the wealth of the American colonies was absolutely vital to the historical shifts we associate with modernity. The common representation of a "virgin land" waiting to be explored, dominated, and domesticated relegates the natural world to the passive, inferior position then associated with the feminine. The French naturalist George-Louis Leclerc de Buffon (1749–89) had even argued that the region was geologically newer, and thus its very flora and fauna were less developed than Europe's—a claim

Thomas Jefferson ([1787] 1984) took pains to refute, using examples from South as well as North America. Nonetheless, the notion of the novelty of the Americas persisted, extending to the supposedly immature culture of its inhabitants as well.

Early debates over literature and fine arts in the English, Spanish, Portuguese, and French Americas all focused on the question of whether the residents of a land without history could cultivate a genuine or original aesthetic. Some Romantic writers tried on Indian themes (Deloria 1998), while others spun this "historylessness" in America's favor. The philosopher G. W. F. Hegel delivered an influential address in 1830 that claimed, "America is therefore the land of the future, where, in all the ages that lie before us, the burden of the World's History shall reveal itself—perhaps in a contest between North and South America. It is a land of desire for all those who are weary of the historical lumber-room of old Europe" ([1837] 1956, 86). Note that Hegel still uses the term to indicate the whole hemisphere, not just the United States. By this point, most residents of the new nation—citizens and noncitizens, free and enslaved—had embraced "American" as their demonym, or proper noun naming the inhabitants of a nation. But there have always been counterarguments made for alternate terms.

As far back as the sixteenth-century Dominican priest Bartolomé de las Casas, some objected to the happenstance of Amerigo Vespucci's name coming to dominate the region. Las Casas proposed rechristening it "Columba," and many place-names in Latin America reflect that suggestion. Two of the most powerful writers of the later Puritan period, Samuel Sewall and Cotton Mather, were convinced by Las Casas's argument and tried to evangelize the rest of the New World so that it would "deserve the significant name of *Columbina*" (Sewall [1697] 1997, 59). (Mather was one of the few settlers to describe himself as an "American" in the introduction to his historical chronicle *Magnalia Christi Americana* in 1702.) The case for honoring Columbus over Vespucci was revived after the Revolution when the iconographic figure of the goddess Columbia became a popular symbol for the United States. In the hands of artists and poets, this idealized feminine figure lent a tinge of classical refinement to the nation-building project; the African American Phillis Wheatley ([1775] 2001) penned one of the very first poems to deploy this image. The figure of Columbia—which had the advantage of distinguishing the national from the hemispheric—prompted patriotic musings on "the Columbian ideal" as well as events such as the 1893 World's Columbian Exposition in Chicago; it continued to appear on coins into the early twentieth century. Other potential alternative names for a resident of the United States have stumbled on the lack of a ready adjectival form in English. A few writers, such as the late Chicano scholar Juan Bruce-Novoa (2004), have recalled into service the neologism that Frank Lloyd Wright coined in the 1930s to describe his nonderivative, middle-class house designs: "Usonian." Others simply substitute "US" or "United Statesian" for "American," arguing that the very awkwardness of such terms has a heuristic value.

Like the adjective "American," the noun "Americanism" had become an everyday term by the beginning of the nineteenth century to designate something particular to the US, referring to evolving linguistic differences from the English spoken in Great Britain. But "Americanization," in the sense of transforming foreign people and their ways into more acceptably familiar ones, did not enter common usage until the turn of the twentieth century and its early decades. This was a period of surging immigration of people whose cultures and religions lay mostly outside the existing Anglo-Celtic-Germanic mainstream, and it brought strong nativist sentiments

to the surface. Americanization became a focus of social and educational programs designed to assimilate perceived outsiders to normative customs and values, in a one-way process. But what are these norms, and who gets to set them? Donald Trump's campaign slogan "America First," for example, was more than a shorthand for an isolationist approach to foreign affairs and a protectionist trade policy. It obscured its own tainted history as a racist rallying cry of the Ku Klux Klan and of a 1940s committee made up of prominent white citizens that opposed intervention in World War II using dubious antisemitic rhetoric. As Bierce's satirical definition implies, the ideas both spoken and unspoken that cluster around "America" in a given utterance will color what the term is intended to include and—in this case—to exclude.

From the nineteenth century forward, then, "America" and its derivations have been used in the US national context to consolidate, homogenize, and unify. Distilling the essence of the nation into a few common character traits or a single idea has been just as tempting to scholars as to politicians and pundits. In the early years of American studies as an academic discipline in the 1950s, the field's foundational texts located the distinctive qualities of Americans variously in the history of westward movement, in philosophical and economic individualism, or in a hopeful orientation toward the future (the "American dream"). As the discipline has evolved, however, it has shied away from advancing theories of what makes the US exceptional. Instead, American studies scholars try to show how such mythic definitions arise in response to specific needs and conditions and then change over time and how the actual history of US actions and policies has often diverged from those expectations.

Since the 1990s, interdisciplinary work in American studies has mainly focused on illustrating the ways in which "American national identity is . . . constructed in and through relations of difference," as one former president of the American Studies Association put it, proposing that the organization rename itself with the plural "Americas" (Radway 2002, 54). Those "relations of difference" are highly visible in the gaps between indigenous people and settlers, between the hemispheric meaning and the national one. A transnational approach to American studies considers US cultural productions and social formations in relation to those of Latin America, the Caribbean, Canada, Africa, the Middle East, and the Asia-Pacific, as well as the more frequently studied contributions of England and Europe. In addition to Alexis de Tocqueville and Michel Crèvecoeur, recent scholarship turns to lesser-known commentators on the meaning of "America" such as the Cuban José Martí—who in an 1891 speech famously distinguished between "Nuestra" (Our) America, with its mestizo or mixed-race origins, and the racist, profit-driven culture he saw dominating the United States. Martí, like the later activist-writers of African origin W. E. B. Du Bois and C. L. R. James, was critical of the growing interventionist tendencies of the United States in the Western Hemisphere and sought to shift the connotations of the term in provocative ways.

Undoing what most Latin Americans see as an imperial arrogation of the name of the hemisphere by the most powerful nation in it has been central to the project of a pluralized, relational Americas studies. Bell Gale Chevigny and Gari Laguardia, in the preface to their landmark essay collection *Reinventing the Americas*, write that "by dismantling the U.S. appropriation of the name 'America,' we will better see what the United States is and what it is not" (1986, viii). Yet simply using the plural form of "Americas" does not always translate into an oppositional stance toward US hegemony in the hemisphere: for example, the US Army School of the Americas was a military training center for Latin Americans whose graduates were implicated in multiple cases of human rights violations in the 1980s and 1990s (it was later renamed the Western Hemisphere Institute for Security Cooperation).

In addition to understanding such patterns of dominance over other nations, comparative Americanist work often locates its inquiry in spaces once relegated to the periphery of scholarly attention, such as the Spanish-speaking borderlands that were formerly part of Mexico. As contact zones between North and South, Anglo and Latino, such areas have long produced hybrid and multilingual cultural formations. At the same time, the massive wave of new migrants from Latin America that began to spike in the 1980s has transformed small towns and large cities in the Midwest, the Deep South, and other areas of the US that fall outside what one might traditionally think of as border spaces. The proportion of foreign-born residents in the US has climbed to nearly the heights it had reached at the turn of the twentieth century, the peak of the previous immigration surge, after declining for decades. This time, however, the question of how to marshal educational and governmental policy to "Americanize" new migrants—and thus contain the threat posed by their cultural differences—is complicated by the fact that they are already American. In response to the perceived threat posed by large-scale migration, many now prefer deportation and expulsion to assimilation. It is the role of a critical American studies to demonstrate—through the recognition of difference, dissonance, and plurality—that other options are possible.

2007/2020

5

Asian

John Kuo Wei Tchen

"Orientals are carpets!" is a common Asian American retort today, one that rejects the linkage between objects of desire—whether hand-woven carpets made in central and western Asia or porcelains made in China—and the people who make them. During the late 1960s phase of the civil rights movement, second- and third-generation, college-age, mainly Chinese and Japanese Americans from the United States and Canada protested the term "Oriental," seeking to replace it with the seemingly less fraught term "Asian." But as in any debate about naming practices, the names rejected and defended reflect differing points of view, as groups troubled certain terms and adopted others in order to shape and reshape meanings for themselves. "Asia," "Asian," and "Asiatic" are still common, though the latter is far less preferred. Variations such as "Asianic," "Asiaticism," "Asiatise," "Asiatall," "Asiatican," and "Asiatically" are now archaic.

Each of these terms comes loaded with particular spatial orientations rooted in temporal relationships. "Asia" has Arabic, Aramaic, Ethiopian, and Greek origins signifying "was or became beautiful," "to rise" (said of the sun), "burst forth" or "went out," and "to go out." Demetrius J. Georgacas (1969, 33) speculates that "Asia" comes from the ancient Greeks, who adopted a cuneiform Hittite word *assuva* when traveling to the western shores of Anatolia (present-day Turkish Asia) around 1235 BCE. *Assuva*, in turn, may have originally been a pre-Persian name referring to a town in Crete with an ancient temple to Zeus or a "land or country with good soil" (73–75). Georgacas adds that Greek mariners first articulated a nautical boundary between the lands of the rising sun and those of the setting sun by traversing the saltwater straits of the Aegean through the Dardanelles, the Sea of Marmara, the Bosphorus, the Black Sea through the Straits of Kerch, and ending in the Sea of Azov, where the landmass to the north did not have such a divide (11–12). Hence "Asia" as "east" began as a local definition.

Asia in these contexts appeared as separated by water from the Greek world, leading to the inaccurate idée fixe of a separable landmass and people. The categorization of continents that emerged from this idea reproduced early notions of racial superiority and inferiority. By the fifth century CE, "Asiatic" was clearly associated with vulgarity, arbitrary authority, and luxurious splendor—qualities deemed antithetical to Greek values (Hay 1957, 3). An early eleventh-century "T-O" map reveals a clear religious cosmos of the world. A "T" within a circle divides three continents: Asia, marked "oriens," is over Europe and Africa (or Libya), which are both marked "occidens." The "T" itself represented both a Christian cross and the Nile River, believed by some people to be the divide between Africa, Asia, and the Mediterranean (plate 1b, 54). Noah's sons, Japheth, Shem, and Ham, were said to have dispersed to Europe, Asia, and Africa, respectively, thereby affixing their characters to geographic spaces. For Western Christians, the Ottoman Empire to the east was formidable. As their city-states became more secular and colonized non-Christian lands westward, northward, and southward, Renaissance intellectuals redefined "civilization" and "progress" as moving westward like the arc of the sun. A double shift took place: the West became synonymous with Christianity, and Western ideologues claimed direct continuity with Greek civilization.

In this centuries-long process, the appropriation of the word "Europe" for this Western Christian political culture also projected the imagined heathenism affixed to peoples onto the continents of "Asia" and "Africa." Intercultural influences that produced overlapping renaissances in the Mediterranean world were appropriated as *the* (one and only) Renaissance, at once Eurocentric and colonizing. Taxonomist Carolus Linnaeus (1735) formulated "four races of mankind," from primitive Africans to civilized Europeans, with Asians or "Mongoloids" said to be the "semi-civilized" peoples of once-great material civilizations now stifled by despotic rulers. The formulation by Karl Marx ([1867] 1976) of "the Asiatic mode of production" as despotic bore the assumptions of this worldview. The rising European and colonial middle classes desired Asian goods, with their cachet of luxury, opulence, and decadence—a practice emulating the European courts' consumption fashions. Yet this fascination was also laced by threat. Startled by Japan's swift defeat of China, Kaiser Wilhelm II first dreamed of an impending "yellow peril" in 1895. The *Fu Manchu* novels of Sax Rohmer (Arthur Sarsfield Ward) soon followed, selling millions of copies throughout the twentieth century and popularizing representations of the "Near East," as ascribed by self-named "Occidentists," as utterly opposite and alien to the European self (Said 1978). This alterity was both derisive and romantic, coding "Asian" difference as gendered and sexualized. French Orientalists, for example, were fascinated by the eroticism of Persian odalisques, such as those represented in Jean-León Gérôme's paintings. This alterity enabled the self-delusional Eurocentric myth of a singular Western modernity: "In adopting the name 'Europe' as a substitute for Western Christendom, the Modern Western World had replaced a misnomer that was merely an anachronism by a misnomer that was seriously misleading" (Georgacas 1969, 29).

This misnaming has a long history. In 1507, German mapmaker Martin Waldseemuller named "America" after the Italian explorer Amerigo Vespucci's charting of South America. At that moment, a fourth continent upset the tripartite "T-O" map, and the Americas became the place where populations—indigenous, Africans, Europeans, and Asians—intermingled. Spanish colonials established the Manila–Acapulco trade from 1565 to 1815, bringing Filipinos/as, Chinese, and other "Asians" to the "New World." By 1635, Chinese barbers were reportedly monopolizing the trade in Mexico City. Chinese silk shawls and other desired goods traveled the Camino Real north to Santa Fe. Filipino sailors resettled in the French colonial lands of Louisiane. As the northeastern ports of the newly established United States began direct trade with China in 1784, people, goods, and influences crisscrossed with ports of the Pacific and Indian Oceans. Yet with Euro-American colonization, transplanted Eurocentric ideas of "Asia," "the Orient," and "the East" were reproduced ever farther westward. The more the people of the Americas shared this Eurocentrism, the more their national identities proved to be a variation of white herrenvolk nationalism.

Despite this long genealogy, "Asian" bodies in the Americas have been viewed as phenotypically foreign—a demarcation of otherness as foundational as the "T-O" map. "Far Eastern" bodies, ideas, and things were mapped onto existent binaries of "Near Eastern" Orientalism. Anglo-American phrases emerged, such as "the yellow peril," "Mongoloid idiot," and "Asiatic hordes," along with names for diseases such as "Asiatic cholera" and the omnipresent "Asian flu." "Asiatics" were portrayed as threatening and inferior to white Euro-American masculinity. The Asian American critique of stereotypes is useful here. Writer-critics Jeffrey Paul Chan and Frank Chin (1972) have delineated "racist hate" as what most US Americans imagine anti-Asian racism to be and "racist love" as the affections formed by the dominant culture toward those Asians who conform to stereotype. The exotic-erotic lotus-blossom geisha, for example, is the object of Orientalist desire—an extension of the odalisque. And detective Charlie Chan always solved the white man's mystery with good, humble humor. At the same time, white, straight, male control has been repulsed (and titillated) by the dominatrix Dragon Lady type or "the devil incarnate" Fu Manchu role.

Contemporary US notions of "terrorism" are undergirded by such stereotypical structures of thought. When media mogul Henry R. Luce (1941) celebrated the "American Century" as a mid-twentieth-century enlightenment project for the world, the primary area of US economic and political expansion was westward into the Pacific. For 170 years, US military actions and wars in the Pacific Rim have been justified by national security and self-interest. The Asia Pacific War, usually understood as a response to Japan's expansionism and efforts to formulate a "Greater East Asia Co-prosperity Sphere," might be better understood in this broader context of competition for Pacific and Asian resources and markets. Historian William Appleman Williams (1992) charted the linkages between US western expansionism and US "foreign" policy annexations into the Pacific. "Manifest Destiny" did not stop at the shores of California. A list of US military, diplomatic, and trade initiatives clearly delineates deep, sustained US involvements in the Asia Pacific region. Witness the US involvement in the British-led opium trade and wars with China (1830s); Commodore Perry's "opening" of Japan (1853); the annexation of Hawaii, Guam, and the Philippines (1898) and Samoa (1900); the countless military actions of the twentieth century establishing strategic military bases; and the early twenty-first-century battle with the "Axis of Evil."

Military actions, missionary work, and trade, along with labor recruitment and immigration policies, linked the fate of Asians and Pacific Islanders in the United States to national foreign policy in Asia and the Pacific. Liberation movements necessarily became critiques of US expansionism and self-interest, while policies toward Asia and the Pacific were articulated to domestic civil rights. Harvard historian and adviser to the US in the war against Japan Edwin O. Reischauer is one example. He urged improved treatment of interned Japanese Americans to counter Imperial Japan's criticism of Western racism and imperialism—the primary argument for developing a pan-Asian and pan-Pacific Japanese-controlled "prosperity" confederation. While pan-Asianism has mainly been identified with the reactionary expansionism of the Japanese empire, it is important to note that there have been many moments when pan-Asian ideas and actions emerged from revolutionary nationalists—often adapting US ideals of freedom and liberty. Tokyo in the 1900s brought together many left-leaning Chinese and Koreans with Japanese socialists; anarchists and various radicals gathered in Paris before World War I, and the Bandung Conference in 1955 articulated an Asian and African "third world" unity. These movements have argued for multiple modernities, not one singular "Western" path. The ongoing post-civil-rights-era "culture wars" have cast Asian American and other identity-based rights movements as a de facto "Balkanizing" of Euro-America (Schlesinger 1998; Huntington 2004b). More progressive scholars argue for the ongoing struggle to expand the meaning of "we, the people" and "the American experiment" at home and democracy and human rights abroad.

Given this long and complex history, the challenges for American studies and cultural studies scholarship and practice are numerous. A thorough critique of Eurocentric knowledge needs to continue and to be extended into curricula. As Naoki Sakai (2000) insists, modernity needs to be pluralized to recognize multiple paths for a people's development. Those who have experienced disempowerment and marginalization help us understand and gain insight into the ways reality is constructed and policies are formulated. This insight, when cultivated with deeper historical, cultural, social, and political analysis, restructures what we understand and how we understand it. In addition, it enables the recognition and translation of diverse and dynamic economic, cultural, and political developments in various parts of "east," "southeast," "south," "central," and "western" Asia (all these directional terms are partial and misleading). This rethinking can begin with the available literature of those Asians, Pacific Islanders, and Asian Americans writing and being translated into English but must be extended to help US Americans understand the local struggles of grain farmers in Kazakhstan or female Nike factory workers in Bangladesh in terms truthful to those people's own worldviews. This requires dialogue and the insistence that disempowered peoples gain the capacity to "name" their own world.

How the United States and various Asian governments respond to the political-economic rivalries of the "New World Order" will frame the spaces in which this scholarship and activism can take place. Calls for pan-Asianism, used in various ways in different places and at different times, can contribute to a process that opens up participation and grassroots mobilizations, or they can serve to close down understanding by offering simplistic solutions to complex political-economic questions. Uneven development and hierarchical knowledges challenge us to better imagine and work for a fair and equitable global vision. "Development" and "modernization" must be reformulated to produce sustainable local practices without romanticizing a prelapsarian past. Here, feminists, labor activists, and students who have access to both local and transnational knowledges—often via digital networks—have led the way, while ambitious corporate power players from "developing nations" and peoples have become the new comprador managers of internationalizing North American, European, and Asian finance capital. The contestation of values and meanings is critical to our future collective well-being. Like other keywords of these globalized struggles, it is the fate of "Asian" to be contested—locally and regionally—in contending, politicized practices of naming.

2007/2014

6

Biopolitics

Kyla Schuller

In 2013, the Black Lives Matter movement took to the streets to protest the police forces and private citizens who kill Black people yet receive no penalty of any kind. The movement directly names and confronts a signature aspect of the US government: that it treats Black people as disposable *bodies* valuable only for the labor that may be extracted from them and who thus can be killed with impunity by its agents. The movement fights back by valuing Black *lives* and holding police forces and private citizens accountable for murder. By emphasizing *lives* over *bodies*, Black Lives Matter's name exposes these assumptions, which have been baked for centuries into the history of the United States.

The wish to expose and contest the state's self-granted right to kill people of color animates like-minded left-leaning projects such as Black Trans Lives Matter and Native Lives Matter. Cops, too, have formed their own campaign by adopting this language. The slogan "Blue Lives Matter" identifies police, rather than the people they kill, as the true victims of violence. But this last parallelism is false. It is true that police are wounded and killed in the line of duty. But in contrast to Black, trans, and Native people, the police are not socially constructed as a disposable population. There exists no state apparatus with the purpose of regulating "police bodies" in the way that there does exist a police force to regulate Black, brown, and trans bodies.

This is the power of "Black Lives Matter" as a phrase and a movement: it identifies deep racial inequality as a structural feature of modern power. American studies or cultural studies scholars might for this reason say that the movement has a theory of "biopolitics," an analysis of how state power treats white, cisnormative people as the cherished heart of the nation and regards people of color and queers as disposable material who threaten the nation's peace and prosperity. Biopolitics names a style of governance that has little interest in guaranteeing equal rights for all. Rather, it approaches the task of governing as administrating the biological life of a population. It aims to maximize the biological quality and productive capacity of a population by dividing people into subcategories that are either valuable to the stability and profitability of the nation-state or not. In the US context, biopolitical regimes deem white, normative members of a population to be assets and attempt to further improve their lives by granting them more and more state resources—for example, cutting-edge health care and education designed to optimize their potential. At the same time, biopolitical regimes dismiss people of color as disposable material who threaten the population's stability and are thus useful only as exhaustible labor.

This use of the term "biopolitics" emerged over the past hundred years. Since the early twentieth century, the term has occasionally been used to refer to the intersection of biology and politics. Its initial usage, proposed by the Swedish political theorist Rudolf Kjellén in 1905, designated theories that saw the state itself to be an organic being. "Biopolitics" then appeared occasionally in Nazi writings to describe their goal of governing through population cleansing (Lemke 2011). But it was French philosopher and theorist Michel Foucault in the 1970s who began using the term to describe how modern governments consider organic existence itself to be their primary target, a mode of power he called "biopower" (2003). Biopolitics, for

Foucault, is one of the two main forms biopower takes (E. Cohen 2009). The first to develop was disciplinary power, which targets the individual body. Discipline takes form in institutions such as hospitals, schools, and prisons that aim to create "docile bodies," or individuals whose own subjectivity is thoroughly entwined with the needs of the state and its drive to capital accumulation (Foucault [1975] 1995). While the nineteenth century was its heyday, disciplinary power continues into the present.

The second mode of biopower to appear was biopolitics, which targets the "population": a key term closely affiliated with biopolitics that takes on a specific meaning in this context. A "population" is not just a group of individuals who live within a territory or nation, akin to the citizenry or the body politic. Rather, the term denotes a specifically biological conception of the people who reside within a nation-state. As elaborated by Foucault, the population is an entity imagined on the biological dimension of a species. It is an organic whole unto itself that exists over the time of generations and perpetually needs stabilizing and securing (2003, 2004). The task of biopolitics is to secure the population through marking some of its members valuable and others superfluous. The thriving of the former becomes a state imperative; the others can be portrayed as contaminants who threaten society's overall health and must be left to die. Biopolitics, Foucault argues, emerged in the late eighteenth century and became dominant in the twentieth, particularly during the Nazis' rule of Germany.

In this framework, modern racism rooted in ideas of biological difference does the work of evaluating the relative quality of the bodies that make up a population, delineating those who must thrive from those who must be disposed of. In contrast, influential Italian philosopher Giorgio Agamben dates biopolitical regimes back to ancient Greece. Agamben argues that such regimes produce two distinct notions of life originally conceptualized by Aristotle as "bare life," or *zoe*, and "qualified life," or *bios* (1998). Bare life / *zoe* connotes a state of raw organic existence as a biological being, while qualified life / *bios* refers to a plane of existence produced within culture and/or politics as a particular mode of living. Agamben proposes that biopolitics strips some members to the status of bare life, subject to a permanent state of exception in which they form the outside of the domain of politics itself.

Many of the debates about "biopolitics" center on the differences between Foucault's and Agamben's approaches. Foucault's use of the concept of biopolitics emphasizes how biological life has been placed at the center of modern politics, creating a shift toward maximizing the "health, excellence, and vitality" of its population (Blencowe 2010, 114). Biopolitics, in his use, animates everything from sewers and public health projects to modern university education. For Agamben, "biopolitics" as a term exposes the authoritarianism hiding in the midst of western legal and political theory. He emphasizes that biopolitics is primarily repressive, revolving around demoting some individuals to nothing but a raw organic existence, a threat that has always been integral to the democratic project. Recent cultural theory, however, puts pressure on Agamben's idea that raw biological life can ever be said to preexist the social, stressing that political effects shape organic existence at every stage of the life cycle (Weheliye 2014). Other critics of Agamben emphasize that the meanings of the biological itself shift dramatically over time; they question the existence of a transhistorical biopolitics that came into being millennia before the modern concepts of species, the field of biology, and the systematic study of natural life that marks the post-enlightenment era (Blencowe 2010; Haines 2019).

Across these historiographical and theoretical differences, "biopolitics" designates technologies of knowledge making as well as governing. The life sciences, demography, political science, and statistics are among the disciplines and methods that have been central to creating the idea that internal difference threatens the population and to calculating the relative risks posed by its members. Biopolitics thus works both to optimize a population and to cleanse it of disposable bodies. For this reason, users of the term "biopolitics" such as Foucault and Agamben generally agree that the Nazi Holocaust that murdered six million Jewish, disabled, and queer people offers the paradigmatic example of biopolitical governance. Others point out the Eurocentric bias of this claim (Mbembe 2003; Dillon 2019). Who exactly counts as members of a population given that Europe and North America's economic success were built on extractive capitalism, settler colonialism, and chattel slavery, all of which made metropolitan sites dependent on flows of people, goods, and capital within and across its borders? Since extractive capitalism and settler colonialism date back centuries, why should we see the twentieth century as representing the full flowering of biopolitics? Was it rather the scene for refining practices initially developed and tested in overseas colonies and domestic settlements and plantations?

Cameroonian theorist Achille Mbembe offers the term "necropolitics" as a modification of and corrective to the conventional use of biopolitics. Necropolitics demarcates the vast technologies of death originating in the plantation and colony and now serving as the guiding force in the war on terror and the Israeli occupation of Palestine (Mbembe 2003). It "account[s] for the various ways in which, in our contemporary world, weapons are deployed in the interest of maximum destruction of persons and the creation of death-worlds, new and unique forms of social existence in which vast populations are subjected to conditions of life conferring upon them the status of *living dead*" (40). For Mbembe, biopolitics on its own is insufficient to comprehend the ubiquity and authority of "contemporary forms of subjugation of life to the power of death," a praxis he names necropower (39). Other decolonial theorists stress that administrative technologies for fostering life (biopolitics) and proliferating mass death (necropolitics) unfurl in an "intimate" interplay (Ahuja 2016, xi). Drawing on and extending these insights, American studies scholars use the term "biopolitics" to reinterpret the genocide of Native peoples from the beginnings of settlement to the end of the Indian Wars in the 1890s, underscoring how the elimination of racialized lives has long been central to the function of US democracy, with settler colonialism serving as a primary manifestation of biopolitics (Morgensen 2011a; Rifkin 2011a). American studies scholars have also emphasized how biopolitical power is wielded by nonstate actors: by individuals and private institutions such as charities, reform movements, religious organizations, or mass-cultural formations like popular novels (Tompkins 2012; Schuller 2018).

On what grounds does US state power differentiate and rank members of populations as worthy or unworthy to the life of the whole? Gender studies theorist Jasbir K. Puar uses the keyword "biopolitics" in her examination of the war on terror that followed 9/11, identifying how white, middle-class, gay men and lesbian women often positioned themselves as good, patriotic citizens of the nation, while brown, queer, and non-Christian people from the Middle East were positioned as threats to national security. Normative biopolitical citizenship, she argues, has expanded to include middle-class white gays among those deemed worthy of life, while it has doubled down on the persecution of brown, queer, and non-Christian people (Puar 2007). Other scholars have used the term "biopolitics" to identify problems with the binary sex logic that sees male and female as the only socially legitimate forms a body can take. This work has revealed that the notion of "gender," used to name the social roles assigned to sexual difference, first emerged out of post–World War II psychology and psychiatry as a treatment strategy for transgender and intersex patients. Individuals were assigned a single gender role in order to eliminate the threat these queer bodies pose to the binary logic of male and female. Thus scholars argue that "the biopolitics of gender" reveals that gender has a stabilizing, securing function meant to make bodies that violate the norms of the sex binary invisible (Preciado 2013; Repo 2016; Gill-Peterson 2018). Scholars also argue that "biopolitics" is a useful keyword for analyzing the treatment of nonhuman lives. Species difference and the technologies of administering animal life—for example, factory farming—are key ways that biopolitics carves up life into bodies that are useful primarily in death and those who will benefit from this unwitting sacrifice (Shukin 2009; Boggs 2013).

Some scholars push on the binary within the theory of biopolitics itself: that power operates primarily through either fostering life or allowing death. American studies and cultural studies research reveals that biopolitical technologies often function in the spaces in between life and death, in the domains of individuals and populations. Puar argues that biopolitics works as a "capacitation machine" that invests in the vital potential of some bodies and deliberately debilitates others. What she calls "the right to maim" considerably nuances the distinction between biopower and necropower quadrants of power that delimit the state's actions as the right to make and let live and make and let die (Puar 2017). Critical disability studies theorist Mel Chen characterizes biopolitics as partitioning out relative qualities of "liveliness" among its members and thus determining the relative worthiness of life (2012, 2). Chen captures this process through the use of another keyword, "animacy," which denotes cognitive hierarchies built into language. Animacy here marks a broad hierarchy of vitality that has governed the logic of race, gender, and species difference. Related work points to a key feature of modern capitalism: vast industries that distribute, market, and enhance biological material down to the microlevel, such as technologies of tissue transfer, molecular optimization, and genetic engineering (M. Cooper 2008; Lee 2014). These "vital politics" represent a shift in biopolitics' central domains from the dimensions of the individual organism and the population to the molecular level in which the continual regeneration of cellular capacity represents one of neoliberalism's most profitable markets (Rose 2006).

At stake in the use of biopolitics as a concept is the notion that state violence and drastic social inequality are fundamental, rather than incidental, to modern democracy. The term does similar work as "society" in that both keywords are used by American studies and cultural studies scholars to illuminate how social and political life are organized by a set of structures and principles that shape individuals' experiences and construct their identities. Biopolitics identifies violence as a structural aspect of state power. It emphasizes the interlocking nature of capitalism, colonialism, and racism at the level of administrative power, formations that in turn produce identity categories as their effects. In other words, "biopolitics" is used to name some of the principles of power through which our identities, experiences, opportunities, and challenges are constructed. Using "biopolitics" as a keyword offers ways of analyzing how exactly power materializes at the site of identity formation. It can help us go beyond the additive logic of enumeration that governs familiar lists of "difference": race, gender, class, sexuality, and ability, among others.

As with other keywords ("neoliberalism," "capitalism," "nationalism"), the structural analysis invited by the term "biopolitics" is a strength. But it can also be a weakness, since many usages of the term risk glossing over nuance and variation. To say that an event or text or movement is "biopolitical" (or "neoliberal" or "capitalist" or "nationalist") is not saying all that much. The use of the keyword in this way can prevent a fine-grained accounting of precisely how power is wielded and by whom in distinct circumstances. Even if we restrict "biopolitics" to the modern world, excluding ancient Greece, our use of the term to describe the overarching practice of power risks riding roughshod over significant geopolitical differences. These include differences between European extractive colonialisms, settler colonialisms that try to replace an existing indigenous population, and economies founded on enslavement, only some of which were initially plantation economies. The proliferation of activist movements today that expose and resist the disposability logic biopolitics embraces—such as Black Lives Matter, Native Lives Matter, and Trans Lives Matter—suggests that while a common strategy of power unites these oppressions, key distinctions nonetheless remain. "Biopolitics" as a keyword does not offer a nuanced account of how, say, anti-Blackness both resonates with and differs from settler-colonial fantasies of erasing indigenous peoples from the United States, much less how racialization is crosscut by gender and sexuality. In other words, "biopolitics" offers a substantive, but far from exhaustive, diagnosis of power's function and effects.

Yet the overarching theory that drastic social inequality functions as a structural feature of modern democracies has been extraordinarily generative, both inside and outside academia. Crossing the worlds of high theory, American studies, cultural studies, and social movements, the term "biopolitics" is most useful when it enables us to interrogate how the state governs not by protecting the abstract notion of individuals' equality under the rule of law but through direct strategies that determine and regulate bodies' relative value. These strategies take shape at the national level of security and wealth accumulation and at the individual level of our own racial, gender, and sexual identities.

2020

7

Black
E. Patrick Johnson

The word "black" has a long and vexed history both inside and outside the United States. Typically used as a neutral reference to the darkest color on the spectrum, the word has also taken on negative cultural and moral meanings. It describes both something that is "soiled," "stained," "evil," or "morally vapid" and people of a darker hue. The *American Heritage Dictionary* provides a typical example of this dual usage. One of the entries under "black" as an adjective is "gloomy, pessimistic, dismal," while another is "of or belonging to a racial group having brown to black skin, especially one of African origin: *the Black population of South Africa.*" The slippage in the latter definition from "brown to black" highlights the ways in which the term's negative cultural and moral connotations are racialized through reference to not-quite-white but also not-always-black bodies. This slippage maintains hierarchies among the races scaled from white to black. While the origin of this mixed usage of the term "black" is hard to pin down, negative associations of cultural and moral blackness with dark-skinned people appear regularly during the Renaissance, as in Shakespeare's play *Othello*, in which the dark-skinned protagonist of the same name is referred to as a "Barbary horse" and a "lascivious Moor." Over time and in opposition to the dominant discourses of their historical moments, people who belonged to these racialized groups have often followed Othello's lead by reappropriating the term "black" to signify something culturally and morally empowering and, in some instances, a quality superior to whiteness.

As this brief overview suggests, the adjective "black" is, in the words of the *Oxford English Dictionary*, "a word of difficult history." Part of that difficulty has to do with the various geographical and historical contexts of its usage. In relation to US slavery, the term was not as prominent a descriptor for enslaved Africans as were the derogatory "nigger" or the seemingly more benign "Negro" and "colored." After emancipation, the term "black" gained increased prominence in the legal and political realms, as the 1865 "black codes" were enacted to restrict the rights of the newly freed by reinforcing white supremacy during Reconstruction (Meier and Rudwick 1976). For the people directly affected by those codes, the term "black" still did not hold as much political weight as "Negro" and "colored" until later in the twentieth century. The result is that "black" was not used in the names of the political organizations that emerged in the late nineteenth and early twentieth centuries, such as the National Association of Colored Women (NACW), founded in 1895, and the National Association for the Advancement of Colored People (NAACP), founded in 1909.

The now common "African American" (or hyphenated "African-American") has a similarly complex history. It did not become a popular term until almost a century later, in the late 1980s. A black army veteran from Alabama by the name of Johnny Duncan claims that he was the first to use the term in his poem "I Can," which he wrote for a 1987 Black History Month calendar. In the last four lines of the poem, Duncan writes, "The last 4 letters of my heritage and my creed spell 'I can,' heritage being Afr-i-can and creed being Amer-i-can." According to Duncan, Coretta Scott King first introduced Jesse Jackson to the poem in 1989 when she showed him the calendar. In 1990, at a speech in New

Orleans, Jackson read the poem and began using the term "African American" (Duncan 2010). Like the term "black," "African American" has a complex and highly politicized history: some people of African descent still prefer "black" because they do not associate themselves with Africa, while others embrace "African American" precisely because of its explicit acknowledgment of an African heritage. Still others deploy "black" as a way of marking global affiliations that exceed "America" (Gilroy 1993; Singh 2004).

In black intellectual circles at the turn of the twentieth century, the term "black" began to emerge as an antiracist response to ideologies of white supremacy disseminated through science. W. E. B. Du Bois, for example, delivered a paper in 1887 at the founding conference of the American Negro Academy in which he critiqued the biological determinism prevalent in nineteenth-century scientific discourse. The form of racism that Du Bois attacked maintained that physical differences between the races account for social and psychological differences—that black (i.e., dark and not-yet- or not-quite-white) skin corresponds to a lower socially developed human form. Du Bois critiqued this racist science by calling attention to the role that history, law, and religion—humanistic rather than scientific theories—have played in the differences among the races. This critique was important because it called attention to the effects of history and sociocultural factors to explain racial differences as opposed to biophysical ones. His argument was the foundation for his most oft-quoted line from *The Souls of Black Folk*—"The problem of the twentieth century is the problem of the color-line"—and for his notion of "double consciousness" ([1903] 1997, 45).

Du Bois's critique of racial essentialism is foundational to approaches in American studies and cultural studies that have become known as racial constructivism. These approaches focus on historical processes of racialization, suggesting that essentialist racial identity categories are stable only due to their repeated references in the context of specific racial projects (J. Butler 1990; Omi and Winant [1986] 1994). Theorists today stress the need to read race as a result of dialogic processes between material bodies and sociocultural influences. An important forerunner of these theories and theorists, Du Bois's critique was aimed at racist scientific discourses promulgated not just by whites but also by leaders in the black community, such as Marcus Garvey and his Universal Negro Improvement Association (UNIA), which promoted the return to Africa as well as racial uplift and a radical black consciousness. Du Bois's critique of race discourse and Garvey's mobilization of that discourse to promote political consciousness around blackness prefigured debates in the 1960s during the emergence of the civil rights movement, as black leaders and artists began to struggle to expand notions of blackness (as Du Bois had) while also solidifying a common definition around which divergent factions could organize as a community against racism (as Garvey had; Blight and Gooding-Williams 1997; Dawson 2001; Ongiri 2010).

These forms of political and cultural activism drew on a rich and often ignored history of cultural production during the Harlem Renaissance. In the 1920s, a consolidation of black pride formed in the African diaspora, especially in the French Caribbean and in Paris, through what became known as the Négritude movement. The Martinique poet Aimé Césaire coined the term "négritude" as a way to recuperate the French *négre*, often translated as "nigger," to signify something closer to the more prideful "black" that was circulating in North America (Nesbitt 1999). "Négritude" was further developed and revised by a number of thinkers and writers, ranging from poet, philosopher, and Senegalese

BLACK   E. PATRICK JOHNSON

president Léopold Sedar Senghor to the influential Martinique psychoanalyst Frantz Fanon (Senghor 1964; Fanon [1963] 2004, 1967b).

Emerging within this global frame and in the context of the civil rights movement, the word "black" became highly politicized. It replaced terms such as "colored" and "Negro" that had become associated with Jim Crow laws and outdated views of people of African descent as benignly subordinate to whites. It also indexed a conscious effort to reappropriate the negative connotations of the term in order to instill race pride among blacks. The term became a part of the name of almost every political organization or movement, including the Black Panther Party and the Black Arts Movement. The heightening of what became known as "black consciousness" and "black nationalism" in the 1960s was critical for the deployment of the term "black" as a cultural mode of being, an analytic, and a site of organized resistance to the global history of white supremacy. Political figures such as Malcolm X and Bobby Seale and organizations such as the Student Nonviolent Coordinating Committee (SNCC) and the Black Panther Party encouraged blacks to disavow white values, beliefs, and ways of knowing and to replace them with black or African worldviews. Signifying oppositionally on the notion that black was somehow inferior to white, Americans of African descent deployed the term "black" to demonstrate their rich cultural heritage through diverse aspects of both expressive and consumer culture—clothing (dashikis), music (rhythm and blues and soul music), hair (the afro and braids), language ("black English"), theater (Black Arts Repertory Theater), foodways (soul food), and literature (the Black Arts Movement). Vernacular expressions that reinforced this race pride also circulated during this time: "Black is beautiful. Brown is it. Yellow is something. White ain't shit." James Brown's 1968 hit "Say It Loud (I'm Black and I'm Proud)" became a signature anthem.

As during the Harlem Renaissance, art and politics were intimately intertwined during this period as the Black Arts Movement emerged as the cultural front of the Black Power Movement. The poetic and theatrical expressions of Amiri Baraka (LeRoi Jones), Haki Madhubuti (Don L. Lee), Sonia Sanchez, Nikki Giovanni, and others reflected the imbrication of aesthetics and politics. These artists and performers spoke of their art both as weapons against oppression and as the vanguard of black creative expression. Kimberly Benston argues that for these black artists of the 1960s, "writing, properly reconceived and directed as utterance and as act, was advanced as a signal instrument of cultural liberation" (2000, 2). Cultural liberation meant an adherence to what was coined "the black aesthetic," a set of principles and standards by which all expressive arts by people of African descent should conform and to which they should aspire. Addison Gayle codified the aesthetic dimensions of this struggle in *The Black Aesthetic* (1971), a collection of essays that elaborated the goals and characteristics of Black Arts. Stephen Henderson's *Understanding the New Black Poetry* (1973) was similar to Gayle's book but with a focus on the tenets of black poetry and its distinguishing features. The artists and intellectuals who were a part of the movement held a range of political views and beliefs about how best to empower the community, but the one through line was a common belief in an authentic or essential blackness.

The effects of this strategic deployment of black essentialism were twofold. On the one hand, the movement enabled a proliferation of artistic expression. The publishing houses, theaters, and intellectual activity it produced made possible the emergence of area and ethnic studies departments devoted to the study of race in academic institutions. Black student riots and takeovers at institutions of higher education across the country demanded that administrators take seriously the intellectual and artistic contributions of people of African descent, which undoubtedly grew out of the fomenting Black Power and Black Arts Movements (Baker, Diawara, and Lindeborg 1996). On the other hand, the movement's reliance on essentialist understandings of blackness created a complex matrix of politics about who could be included under "black" as an umbrella term. While the male leadership of the Black Power Movement believed that black women were a part of the category "black," their views about the role that women should play in the movement mitigated their inclusion. Other identity markers such as sexuality and class status also determined the degree of one's blackness, with homosexuality being viewed as a white disease that had infected the black community and middle-class status viewed as a site of total political capitulation to the white status quo (Cleaver 1968; V. Smith 1998; E. Johnson 2003). This tendency toward selective exclusion and inclusion entered into and structured academic debate as scholars and activists focused on the question of what and who constitutes blackness (Asante 1987; Baker 1987a; Gates 1987; Joyce 1987a, 1987b; Johnson and Henderson 2005). One result of this struggle is that most departments and programs battled over nomenclature, with suggestions for naming ranging from "Black Studies" and "Afro-American Studies" in the 1960s and early 1970s to "African American Studies," "Africana Studies," and "African and African Diasporic Studies" from the late 1970s to the present.

These struggles over naming and the meaning of blackness coincided with the emergence of structuralism and poststructuralism in the academy. These approaches to the study of culture threw into question notions of authenticity and stable meanings of texts. Some black theorists, especially literary critics, drew heavily on poststructuralism to expand what might count as a "black" text and who might count as a "black" author.

These critics often focused on black women writers (M. Henderson 1989), gays and lesbians (B. Smith 1982), or a general engagement with the ways black texts signify beyond a specific referent (Gates 1978; Baker 1986). They gained a platform in a white academy friendly to both poststructuralism and racial antiessentialism but not without pushback from traditional black scholars who saw the adoption of mostly Western theories to analyze black literature as leading to the devaluation of its political and cultural intent (Christian 1987; Joyce 1987a).

Outside the United States, usages of the term "black" followed a similar pattern as they entered into and catalyzed debates about identity and identity politics. In several contexts, the term does not necessarily have as a referent Africa or people of African descent. Aboriginals in Australia are referred to as "black" (Broome 2010), and the subcaste of people in India known as "dalit" or the "untouchables" are referenced as "black," as were many Indians during British colonialism (L. James 2000; Rajshekar 2009). With the advent of mass immigration from the British colonies to the metropole during the 1970s and '80s, the term "black" began to be used to reference any former colonial subject: West Indian, African, South Asian. One result was the intellectual formation known in Britain as black cultural studies (Gilroy 1991, 1993; Mercer 1994; S. Hall 1973, 1992b). These writings were influential on black critical thought in the United States and encouraged scholars to conceive of blackness as a much more capacious signifier, provoking them to rethink racialized knowledge production, identity formation and history, and the circulation of blackness within a global context (Gilroy 1991; Favor 1999; Walcott 2000; E. Johnson 2003; Michelle Wright 2004, 2015; Elam and Jackson, 2005; Hine, Keaton, and Small 2009). In each of these contexts, the designation of blackness had as much to do with politics as phenotype.

Even in the United States, groups we now think of as "white" were earlier described as "black." The Irish, for example, were considered the "blacks of Europe" due to their status as British colonials. They became white only once they had immigrated to the United States and ascended the socioeconomic scale (Ignatiev 1995).

During the 2000s, an interest in postidentity studies fueled a new revision of blackness and its meanings. Mixed-raced scholars writing about their own life experiences (Senna 1999, 2010; R. Walker 2002) and mixed-raced artists who claim multiple identities (e.g., Mariah Carey, Alicia Keys, Halle Berry) began to engage the rhetoric of the US "postracial" moment in the context of the election of Barack Obama (Elam 2011). This interest in postraciality suggested that the importance of "black" as a racial signifier was waning, but the public backlash against the most prominent of the self-identified mixed-raced figures such as Tiger Woods and Barack Obama as well as the election of Donald Trump have dispelled the myth that the US has evolved into a postracial era. More pointedly, the emergence of contemporary social movements, such as Black Lives Matter, which again turn to the term "black" to index race pride against antiblack racism, teach us that the historical weight of blackness haunts the present and shapes the future. If the history of the term "black" has taught us anything, it is that racialized symbols—those that are disparaging and those that are affirming—never quite fade from sight or consciousness but constantly evolve alongside the people who create them.

2014/2020

8

Book
Amaranth Borsuk

As a reader of this volume, you are certainly familiar with the term "book." You are gazing upon one at this very moment—whether in the form of a paperback, its hyperlinked web companion, or an e-book accessed through your phone, tablet, or e-reader. You likely have a dedicated piece of furniture where you store other such volumes, one given the name "bookshelf" to describe its specialized function (though it likely provides space for more than its namesake). The same cannot be said of the other places you put them, which have decidedly unbookish names: coffee table, desktop, pocket, and backpack, for instance. Yet you and I keep our books there as well, placing each where its material form is most at home: the coffee table for oversized volumes of visual heft and aesthetic interest, the metaphorical digital desktop for interactive works of electronic literature and portable document files (or PDFs) to be cross-referenced and searched, the pocket and bag for smaller works we wish to enjoy on-the-go—those designed for commuting or leisure. Our books adopt varied physical forms that influence our interactions with them, yet we have come to take this materiality for granted.

The proliferation of formats to which the designation "book" might be applied causes consternation among bibliophiles for whom digital reading devices presage "the death of the book," a topic that comes up with regularity in news, on blogs, and in public discourse (Birkerts 1994; Carr 2013; Coldewey 2010;

Grossman 2011; Morrison 2011). For such readers, an "e-book" can never properly be considered a "book" because it lacks the tactile experience they associate with the word. Yet when we talk about "the death of the book," as it seems we have for decades (and with special fervor since the release of the Amazon Kindle in 2007), we are anticipating the loss of a highly specific book form—one that has been with us a relatively short time in the grand scheme of recorded knowledge. Known to bibliographers and book historians as the "codex," this structure, a block of pages bound on one side and enclosed between covers, derives its name from the Latin *caudex*, or "tree trunk," a clue to the object's origins. The ancient Romans used that term to describe gatherings of waxed wooden tablets on which they recorded information, and in the early days of the bound book of pages, caudex was used interchangeably to describe both wax-filled hollowed-out wooden boards and gatherings of folded parchment (cleaned and stretched animal hide that has been treated for durability) enclosed between wooden covers. Likewise, "book" stakes its name on a timber source: it derives from the Indo-European root *bhāgo-*, or "beech tree," linking it to the Germanic tradition of carving runes in beechwood. The materiality inherent in our bookish terminology belies the fact that we have come to use "book" to refer to form and content interchangeably. It is a noun, the *Oxford English Dictionary* (*OED*) tells us, that describes "a portable volume consisting of a series of written, printed, or illustrated pages bound together for ease of reading" and "a written composition long enough to fill one or more such volumes." The possibilities of the blank codex, which we also recognize as a book, are acknowledged deeper in the entry, but from the start, the word "book" reflects both object and idea.

The field of book studies reminds us that texts are inseparable from the physical support in which we encounter them and from the moment of that encounter (Cavallo and Chartier 1999; Cohen and Glover 2014; Hall 2014; Levander and Levine 2011; Suarez and Woodhuysen 2010). A book is a technology, and as such, it is not neutral, though it is naturalized. Its material form and history, like that of all media, circumscribe our engagement with it, dictating how we may use and misuse it, what we do with it, and what it does with us (Hayles 2002). A book can thus be seen as a performance undertaken by a reader—one that is different at each instance of access and one that is changed by that reader's embodiment and situation (Drucker 2013; Dworkin 2013). Culturally, we have conflated book and codex so thoroughly that we have built a system of metaphors that posit the codex as the fixed form of the written word: we do things "by the book," we read others "like an open book," we contrast "book learning" with the wisdom of experience, and we preface our judgments with "in my book," conjuring imaginary tomes that confer authority metonymically.

As the presumed official repository of our intellectual and artistic activity, the book thus stands, for many speakers, as the epitome of culture. To study it is to study its form and content but also the systems—intellectual, artistic, and economic—within which it circulates. Designed in proportion to the human body, the codex's own body reflects its place in that system: large manuscripts and early printed books like the antiphonal and missal were designed as objects of devotion—hefty enough to rest on a podium during prayer—while Penguin paperbacks of the 1950s were designed for portability by pocket and purse and marketed to commuters at newsstands and train stations. Books of all shapes and structures are designed to propagate information, and as such, they are vectors for relations among those involved in their production, dissemination, and consumption. They constellate a "communications circuit" or network that at various times has included scribes, rulers, monks, academics, bookbinders, papermakers, printers, artists, authors, publishers, and readers—all of whose skills, interests, needs, and desires have been brought to bear on the book's body (Darnton 2009, 179). If we follow the *OED*'s lead and unbind the book from the codex to think of it as a *portable information storage and retrieval device*, we can move away from the teleological and Eurocentric perspective that privileges the side-bound stack of pages as the epitome of literate society. This allows us to acknowledge the deep history of material forms that precede the codex, all of which were the books of their time and place: a long list that includes tablets, scrolls, and accordions; that encompasses fibers ranging from silk and bamboo to wool and skin; and that comprises a range of record-keeping practices dating as early as 3300 BCE, three millennia before the codex. It also makes space for the book's current and future digital incarnations without setting them up in a false binary as either savior or slayer of print.

Books arise to support the changing information needs of the societies in which they appear, and their material structure reflects the social and cultural context in which they take shape. The clay tablet, for instance, one of our earliest book forms, was developed in the third millennium BCE from a material the Ancient Sumerians had in abundance: the clay provided by the Tigris and Euphrates for which Mesopotamia, the region "between two rivers," is named. They already had refined techniques for working with clay in their architecture and durable goods, and their proficiency coupled with its abundance made clay a natural substrate for their early writing. Scooped from the banks of the river, the clay tablet reflects the hand of the scribe who fashioned it: most are sized to the cupped palm, slightly convex, and no larger than a cell phone (Kallendorf 2010). The book's body is proportional to that of its maker and reader, and its structure is predicated on its materiality. Fired in ovens or baked in the sun, these tablets served as both receipts and repositories of culture. Seventh-century Assyrian king Ashurbanipal of Nineveh amassed over thirty thousand such tablets, including letters, government documents, proverbs, songs, epics, and myths as well as scientific, medical, and mathematical treatises. Arrayed in his great library, they served not as a public good but as an emblem of his stature and intellect (Kilgour 1998).

In every region in which information-recording technology arises, the story is similar: a material ready at hand and established in use serves as the ideal substrate for the book. The affordances or possibilities for use presented by their forms in turn shape how we write and what is written. In Egypt, the Nile provides papyrus, which can be adhered into sheets and scrolls (Bülow-Jacobsen 2011); in China, bamboo is separated into vertical strips that are polished and bound together with cords into *jiance*, whose name means "volume of strips"; in Peru, alpacas, lamas, and other camelids provide wool for knotted *khipu* that are maintained by a select group of *khipukamayuq* who hold the secret to their interpretation; and in India and Sri Lanka, palm leaves are burnished and trimmed into horizontal strips on which Buddhist monks copy down *sutras*, whose Sanskrit name, meaning "thread or string," indicates the way they were bound: with a cord threaded through them like a venetian blind. These materials, far from being neutral, in turn influence the shape of language itself and the kinds of things that get recorded. The affordances of wet clay, for example, make it challenging to inscribe with a pointed stylus but ideal for impression; thus the Sumerians developed the wedge-shaped tool that gives cuneiform its name, drawing again from the riverbanks for an abundant supply of reeds (Schmandt-Besserat and Erard 2008). Likewise, bamboo scrolls were painted with characters from top to bottom and right to left, since each narrow strip was only wide enough for a single character and the strips were inscribed one at a time prior to binding—a technique that became so ingrained in Chinese writing that it carried over into manuscript and print (Tsien 2014).

These different book formats, only a few of those preceding the codex, did not simply give way to one another in a tidy timeline of improvement. The clay tablet and papyrus scroll coexisted for more than two millennia. Likewise, the papyrus scroll and wax tablet were used alongside one another for over a thousand years. And even the codex did not supplant scrolls when it emerged—they continued to be used through much of the first millennium of the Common Era. The codex only began to rise to prominence with the spread of Christianity as a means of differentiating Christian texts from their Jewish counterparts (Stallybrass 2001). Multiple forms coexist in part because they can serve the needs of different writers and readers in divergent cultural contexts: a handwritten manuscript can be composed more clandestinely than a printed one, for instance, if you need to keep your text secret from government censors. And a subversive monotheistic religious tract can be passed from one person to another as a sheaf of folded and sewn pages more readily than a hefty collection of waxed wood tablets or a lengthy scroll can.

In each of its forms, the book is portable, shareable, and durable—a transportability that makes it a handy vehicle for the dissemination of ideas. For this reason, books, in all their forms, are a means for the spread of empire. When the Conquistadors colonized Mesoamerica in the sixteenth century, for example, they encountered book structures they viewed as unsophisticated in comparison with the codex that had reached ascendancy in the Renaissance imagination. They destroyed

Inkan khipu, books composed of knotted wool strings, and Mesoamerican codices of folded barkcloth and animal skin, considering them inferior pagan documents. Disregarding the complex methods of information recording these books represented, they pressed their subjects to rewrite their histories for a Spanish readership in the form of European scrolls and codices, leaving a particularly significant gap in our knowledge of the knotted books and the information they recorded (Bauer 2014; Urton 2003).

A history of the term book that is attentive to its shifting material forms reveals that "books" are socially constructed, their "proper" form agreed upon by the community in which they are used—a community that shapes and is shaped by its medium. Different configurations for books continue to proliferate, from complex pop-up books with movable parts (a form originating in the fifteenth century) to interactive app-based books that incorporate video, audio, and touch-screen interfaces (a form made possible by widely available touchscreen devices; Borsuk and Bouse 2016; Cannizzaro and Gorman 2014; Loyer 2010). If we think of the book in terms not of its form but of its function—the portable storage and distribution of information—then the e-reader is simply another method, adapted from the materials at hand and drawing on the familiar interface of the codex, for collecting our thoughts. The e-reader is clearly an interface, but so are each of the formats mentioned earlier, including the codex itself: each shapes the way we read, write, and think. While we have become accustomed to the paperback and hardbound volume to such a degree that we tend not to notice its physical form, the codex does indeed have a body, and it is full of indicators that frame our experience of it. Chapter numbers, tables of contents, and indexes help us locate the information we seek quickly. Page numbers and running heads

BOOK AMARANTH BORSUK

differentiate between one page of prose and the next. A title and the author's name denote which side of the book is the front cover, and an ISBN indicates the back, helping readers determine which way is up and aiding booksellers in tracking their inventory. These conventions are not inherent in the codex but are adaptations to the needs of readers and of the market.

The book is not only an object of concern for scholars of print history or bibliographers. A term that intersects with media and technology as well as art and literature, "book" is of special interest to American studies and cultural studies precisely because of its protean nature. The keyword "book" does not name a static object; it points toward a history of material change that is shaped by its sociocultural moment and by systems of power that determine which voices are recorded and how. As both an object and idea, the book arises in the moment of the reader's encounter: a performance for two bodies. Understood in this way, the term can help us imagine the book to come, even as it continues to shapeshift along with us.

2020

9

Boycott
Cynthia G. Franklin

The *Oxford English Dictionary* (*OED*) defines "boycott" in its noun form as follows: the "withdrawal from social or commercial interaction or cooperation with a group, nation, person, etc., intended as a protest or punishment" and also "a refusal to buy certain goods or participate in a particular event, as a form of protest or punishment." Also a verb, "boycott" is used to describe a nonviolent tactic directed at inflicting economic loss, expressing principled outrage, and/or changing or ending practices considered harmful or unjust. Boycotts can refer to protests undertaken for a range of often overlapping ethical, social, political, or environmental reasons: to change legislation; to challenge the legitimacy of nation-states (including an occupying power); to counter corporate malfeasance; to protest racial, religious, ideological, or ethnic groups or practices; to contest forms of repression; and to protest individuals with power.

The term originated with the Irish Land League's 1880 protest against Captain Charles C. Boycott, a British land agent. The league's successful campaign to isolate Boycott received international attention (Collins 1993; Marlow 1973), and the word "boycott" came into usage, spreading quickly to other European languages including French (1880), German (1883), Russian (1891), and Dutch (1904; *OED*). As is typical with keywords, the term was later used retroactively, in this case to describe various strategies of resistance or rebellion. For instance, the 1773 Boston Tea Party—enacted as part of colonists' longer-standing refusal to buy Manchester tea in protest of British-imposed tea taxes—is often cited as the first US instance of a boycott. The British responded with the Coercive Acts that shut down Boston's port; this, in turn, prompted colonists to pass a 1774 resolution at the newly formed First Continental Congress to "stop all importations . . . and exportations" of British goods (Ammerman 1974, 23). These organized refusals to buy British goods, undertaken initially under the cry "No taxation without representation!" have become part of US history and of the genealogy of the term.

Tracking this genealogy requires attention to its many particular forms and to how "boycott" defies clear definitional boundaries or neat mappings or historicizing. Today, boycotts are often categorized through adjectives that specify the various spheres in which they operate to pursue their objectives: "consumer," "political," "academic," or "cultural." A boycott is sometimes defined as a form of free expression and other times as an action, in ways that problematize distinctions between the two in the legal sphere and in debates regarding boycotts' power to affect political change. Associations that accrue to the word "boycott" and its definition in relation to words such as "sanctions," "embargo," and "censorship" vary over time and place.

When a government in one nation-state refuses to engage with another, this falls under the definition of "sanctions" or an "embargo," though the word "boycott" is sometimes employed instead, arguably to apply ethical pressure. Sanctions and embargoes, in other words, describe top-down government actions or directives—they comprise policy rather than attempts to influence policy. As Judith Butler (2013) has noted, economic sanctions constitute "a way that states engage in boycotts against one another." At the same time, and as Butler's remark indicates, slippage exists among these terms. In 1980, when Jimmy Carter wanted to pressure the Soviet Union to withdraw from Afghanistan, he called for a boycott of the Moscow Olympics as an instrument to attempt to change state policy. So too the states that make up the Arab League have named their refusal to engage in economic and other relations with Israel a "boycott." As these examples suggest, the meanings of boycott and sanctions are not always distinguishable, even as they are often called for as distinct but complementary tactics, as happened, for example, in South Africa, when sanctions played a powerful role alongside boycott in the movement to end apartheid. In another example, Palestinians have called for both in launching an international "Boycott, Divestment, and Sanctions" (BDS) campaign in 2005 to pressure Israel to comply with international law, even as sanctions thus far figure minimally in the BDS movement, perhaps owing to Israel's close ties to states—including the US—that claim it as a partner and a democracy.

Whereas "sanctions" convey state-exercised forms of authority, "boycott" has more populist appeal. John Berger (2006) notes that it "allows people, as distinct from their elected but often craven governments, to apply a certain pressure on those wielding power in what they, the boycotters, consider to be an unjust or immoral way." To call for a "boycott," then, constitutes a way to mobilize significant numbers of people who can participate in an action voluntarily, simply by withholding support or buying power. The word "boycott" operates as a rallying call, as a form of expression that is not merely symbolic or individual since it involves participants in a collective, nonviolent struggle for justice. For this reason, "boycott" has been associated with taking ethical action that leads to self-improvement and collective change. Dating back to M. K. (Mahatma) Gandhi, this use of the word referred to an act of passive resistance to violence and a conduit for spiritual transformation, for the boycotter and also for the wrongdoer subjected to boycott (Giri 2004). Gandhi's exhortation to hand-spin cloth rather than buy it from the British was couched as a refusal of materialism, imperialism, and exploitation and as a pathway, through the grounded and meditative practice of spinning cloth, to moral betterment, domesticity, and peaceful living. He stated, "Boycott of foreign cloth through picketing may easily be violent; through the use of khadi it is most natural and easily nonviolent" (qtd. in Joshi 2002). Gandhi's boycott in the first part of the twentieth century grew out of the Swadeshi ("of one's own country") movement, which started in the late 1800s and involved promoting Indian industry, burning British goods, and picketing. Although Gandhi continued the Swadeshi movement's commitment to openly challenging British authority in a struggle for Indian independence, he also infused it with spirituality—with the belief that boycott's benefits, if brought about by khadi, would extend to the British and spread love between the oppressed and the oppressor.

The best-known boycotts have reinforced their associations with Gandhian values, imbuing participants with a sense of moral rightness for engaging in a nonviolent struggle for civil and human rights. These include the 1955 Montgomery and Tallahassee bus boycotts protesting the Jim Crow South; the 1965–69 National Farm Workers Association Grape Boycott to support laborers in California; and the 1959 global Boycott Movement, later renamed the Anti-apartheid Movement, which ended the apartheid regime in South Africa in the 1990s. The figures most often perceived as representative of these movements—Martin Luther King Jr., Cesar Chavez and Dolores Huerta, and Desmond Tutu and Nelson Mandela—took direct inspiration from Gandhi by representing the boycott as a nonviolent practice aimed at correcting injustice while being life affirming and raising consciousness. Calls to boycott thus carry a

political weight and moral power that exceed their economic impact. As Cesar Chavez noted, boycotts build workers' self-respect and dignity and serve as forms of political education, observing, "The best educational process in the union is the picket line and the boycott" (Chavez 1970). The term "boycott" may owe its popularity to its open invitation to participate in a political campaign that requires only abstention from action, but it is also closely associated with some of history's most renowned leaders and organizers. In other words, the boycott is at once a grassroots and highly accessible practice and one that carries the imprint of legendary figures.

With the rise of "ethical consumerism" starting in the 1980s (Irving, Harrison, and Rayner 2002), the word "boycott" has come into increasing prominence, along with the variation "buycott." "Buycotts" are campaigns initiated to encourage consumers to buy products or services of a particular company or country—either to counter a boycott or to support a business for its values or practices. By some calculations, buycotts have surpassed boycotts in popularity (McGregor 2018), with the word catching on as a way to popularize consumer activism. "Buycotts" can complement "boycotts"; for example, #BoycottNRA targets companies that support the gun lobby and also has led to buycotting companies that have stopped selling guns. Consumers who wish to send a political message through their purchases are assisted by smartphone apps and websites. Launched in 2013, the "Buycott.com" app reads Universal Product Codes and assists consumers with buying goods that accord with their values as well as with avoiding products subject to particular boycott campaigns. This type of hashtag or social media activism has decreased the effort of mounting boycott campaigns and led to their ubiquity, albeit with mixed results as to their efficacy and/or resilience (Delacotte 2009). Whereas, for example, the frequent calls to boycott Amazon.com have been largely ineffectual, campaigns including #StopFundingHate or the sustained boycotts of Chick-fil-A, Sodastream, and Airbnb have met with more success.

Over the last decade, "boycott" has entered the lexicon of American studies and cultural studies as a keyword in institutional contestations over race, gender, sexuality, immigration, settler colonialism, corporate capitalism, gentrification, what counts as art, the neoliberal university, censorship, and free speech (Davis 2016; Dawson and Mullen 2015; Maira 2018). For example, in 2010, Arizona passed State Bill 1070, a racist attack on immigrants that ignited a boycott of the state supported by over fifty civil rights, labor, and justice organizations. Although it did not formally endorse this boycott, the American Studies Association (ASA) signed onto a joint statement made by a consortium of professional and academic associations condemning SB 1070 and Arizona's House Bill 2281, which issued a prohibition on ethnic studies programs (Consortium 2010). In 2016, the passage of another piece of legislation—House Bill 2, infamous for nullifying a Charlotte city ordinance for gender-neutral bathrooms—led to a boycott of North Carolina supported by American studies scholars. The ASA statement announcing that boycott (2016), which foregrounds issues of sexuality, labor, race, age, disability, gender, and national origin, reflects the commitment in contemporary American studies to intersectional analysis and also suggests how the word "boycott" is evolving to encompass forms of intersectionality and solidarity.

The BDS campaign has been especially influential in shaping "boycott's" contemporary associations. The campaign has put "boycott" in the political limelight, centrally locating it in heated contestations over free speech and aligning it with other social justice movements. Having revived the associations of the word "boycott" with the struggle against apartheid in South Africa, BDS has been endorsed by high-profile public figures and by churches, labor unions, student organizations, political organizations, and academic organizations, including the ASA's headline-making 2013 passage of an academic boycott resolution. Other social justice movements work in solidarity with BDS. The Movement for Black Lives (M4BL) Platform foregrounds their articulated concerns, condemning the United States for diverting funding from "domestic education and social programs" in order to provide military aid to "an apartheid state" that is engaged in a "genocide" against the Palestinian people. The 2016 M4BL "Invest/Divest" policy statement urges support for divestment campaigns and opposition to anti-BDS legislation, noting that such laws not only harm BDS but also are "a threat to the constitutional right to free speech and protest." Through BDS's impact, "boycott" carries with it considerations of the economic and political ties between the United States and Israel and attention to their commonalities as white-supremacist, settler-colonial states that oppress their indigenous populations and operate undemocratically.

As BDS approaches what founding member Omar Barghouti (2011, 233) declares as Palestine's "South Africa moment," its mainstream success in the United States has led to the criminalization of boycotts. Although the Supreme Court affirmed boycotts to be a protected form of free speech in *NAACP v. Claiborne Hardware Co.* (1982), twenty-five states have passed anti-BDS laws with legislation pending in twelve more. Two federal anti-BDS bills have garnered bipartisan support in Congress. Some of this legislation hinges on exploiting legal distinctions between boycotts enacted for political reform and those defined as "secondary boycotts" with purely economic aims. "Secondary boycotts" have been ruled outside the protection of the

First Amendment and prohibited by labor union laws (Purvis 2016). The rationale for the federal bipartisan Israel Anti-Boycott Act that seeks to punish individuals and businesses that support BDS with severe fines and up to twenty years in prison depends on defining this support as a form of secondary boycott—logic that the American Civil Liberties Union repudiates (ACLU 2017). Other anti-BDS legislation, fueled by the US State Department's definition of antisemitism that includes any criticism of Israel, is premised on defining "boycott" as antisemitic hate speech. Lawfare against BDS has also taken the form of lawsuits, including one against the American Studies Association for its academic boycott resolution. Thus far, these bills and lawsuits have been overturned for their First Amendment violations. But the Trump era, which actively promotes the definition of anti-Zionism as antisemitism and has shown a flagrant disregard for First Amendment rights, leaves questions open about if or how boycotts will be (re)defined as hate speech and criminal activity.

In this context, academic and cultural boycotts have come to be cast as forms of censorship. In universities that are increasingly corporatized and influenced by Zionist donors and white supremacist organizing, proponents of boycotts are charged with—and often disciplined for—their alleged incivility, violations of academic freedom, promulgation of hate, hostility to dialogue, and antisemitism. Letters from over 250 university presidents and the US Congress condemning the ASA's academic boycott resolution provide one index of how the boycott is coming to be redefined in Orwellian terms that invert its intent as an ethical tactic to effect political transformation. For a democracy in crisis—under pressure from corporate and state violence and a creeping fascism—struggles over the definition of "boycott" have high stakes. The word carries with it a constellation of the most pressing issues in the United States and in the increasingly internationalized field of American studies. Knowing the word's genealogy—including its history of collective, nonviolent struggles against injustices—can help carry "boycott" into the future.

2020

10

Capitalism

David F. Ruccio

While the capitalist system is generally celebrated by mainstream economists, American studies and cultural studies scholars and students will search in vain through their writings for actual discussions of the term "capitalism." Instead, neoclassical and Keynesian economists refer to the "market economy" (in which individuals and private firms make decisions in decentralized markets) or just "the economy" (defined by scarce means and unlimited desires, the correct balancing of which is said to characterize all societies; Bhagwati 2003; Wolff and Resnick 2012; Krugman and Wells 2017; Mankiw 2017).

In contrast, discussions of the term "capitalism" have long occupied a central position in the vocabulary of Marxian economic theory. References to capitalism in American studies and cultural studies draw, implicitly or explicitly, on the Marxian critique of political economy: a critique of capitalism as an economic and social system and a critique of mainstream economic theory. Karl Marx and latter-day Marxists criticize capitalism because it is based on exploitation, in the sense that capitalists appropriate and decide how to distribute the surplus labor performed by the direct producers, and because it periodically enters into crisis, imposing tremendous economic and social costs on the majority of people. They also criticize the work of mainstream economists for celebrating the existence of capitalism and for treating capitalist institutions and behaviors as corresponding to human nature (Mandel 1976; Resnick and Wolff 1987; Harvey 1989).

Much of this scholarship draws on Marx and Friedrich Engels's critique of political economy in the *Manifesto of the Communist Party* (1848) and the three volumes of *Capital* (1867, 1884, 1894). In the *Manifesto*, Marx and Engels compare capitalism to other forms of economic and social organization such as feudalism and slavery. What they have in common is that all are based on class exploitation, defined as one group (feudal lords, slave owners, and capitalists) appropriating the surplus labor of another (serfs, slaves, and wage laborers). At the same time, capitalism exhibits a distinct dynamic. For the first time in history, it "established the world market," making it possible for the capitalist class to "nestle everywhere, settle everywhere, establish connexions everywhere" and giving "a cosmopolitan character to production and consumption in every country" (Marx and Engels [1848] 1976, 486, 487). It leads to radical and continuous changes throughout the economy and society, since, as Marx and Engels famously put it, "all that is solid melts into air" (487).

If the goal of the *Manifesto* was to challenge the prevailing belief that capitalism had eliminated classes and class struggles, the point of *Capital* was to criticize mainstream economic theory and analyze the specific conditions and consequences of the class dimensions of a society in which the capitalist mode of production prevails. Capitalism presumes that the products of labor have become commodities in the sense that the goods and services that human beings produce have both a use value (they satisfy some social need) and an exchange value (they can be exchanged for other commodities or money). The existence of commodity exchange, in turn, presupposes a culture congruent with the "fetishism of commodities": a culture whereby individuals come to believe and act such that they have the freedom to buy and sell commodities, that the commodities they exchange are equal in value, that the commodity owners meet one another as equals in the marketplace, that individuals have well-defined property rights in the commodities they sell and purchase, and that they are able to calculate the ability of external objects to satisfy their needs and desires. The existence of commodity exchange is not based on the essential and universal human rationality assumed within mainstream economics from Adam Smith to the present. Nor can the cultures and identities of commodity-exchanging individuals be derived solely from economic activities and institutions. Rather, commodity exchange both presumes and constitutes particular subjectivities—forms of rationality and calculation—on the part of economic agents (Amariglio and Callari 1993).

In both the *Manifesto* and *Capital*, capitalism refers to a system in which capitalists are able to produce commodities that will, at least in principle, yield them a profit. The source of the profit is the value created by the laborers who have been forced (historically, through a process Marx referred to as "primitive accumulation" and, socially, through capitalist institutions and cultures [(1867) 1976, 1:871–940]) to exercise the specifically capitalist "freedom" to sell their ability to labor as a commodity. Under the assumption that all commodities (including labor power) are exchanged at their values, a surplus value arises based on the ability of capitalists to appropriate the surplus labor performed by the wage laborers and to realize that extra labor by selling the commodities that are produced. Struggles consequently arise over the "rate of exploitation" (the ratio of surplus value to the value of labor power) and over the subsequent distributions of surplus value (to corporate managers, state officials, banks, and other capitalists, who receive portions of the surplus). The keyword "capitalism" thus designates not just an economic structure but also the conflicts, contradictions, and subjectivities inherent in that structure. Both the initial emergence and the subsequent reproduction of capitalism, if and when they occur, often lead to social dislocations and acute crises; they are also conditioned by the most varied cultures and social identities.

In the case of the United States, the past two centuries have witnessed the widening and deepening of capitalism, both domestically and internationally. Initially a market for foreign (especially British) capitalist commodities, the original thirteen colonies oversaw the establishment and growth of domestic capitalist enterprises, which sought both raw materials and markets for final goods within expanding geographical boundaries and across a heterogeneous class landscape. One result was that noncapitalist (communal, independent, slave, and feudal) producers were eventually undermined or displaced, thereby causing waves of rural peoples (men, women, and children of diverse racial and ethnic origins) to migrate to existing and newly established cities and to sell their labor power to industrial capitalists. The opening up of new domestic markets (through the determined efforts of retail merchants, advertisers, and banks), capitalist competition (which drove down the unit costs of production), and government programs (to establish a national currency and to regulate trusts and working conditions) spurred further capitalist growth. The continued development of capitalist manufacturing provoked vast international migrations of laborers: initially from Africa and western Europe; later and continuing to this day, from Latin America, Asia, eastern Europe, and Africa (Dowd 1977; Duboff 1989; Amott and Matthaei 1996).

The movement of capital that accompanied the expansion of markets and the search for cheaper raw materials transformed regions outside the industrialized Northeast, including the relocation of textile mills to the South, the creation of steel foundries and automobile factories in the Midwest, the development of the oil industry in the Southwest, and the flourishing of capitalist agriculture and the movie industry on the West Coast. Capital was also exported to other countries to take advantage of lower wage levels and other cost advantages, thereby introducing economic and social dislocations similar to those that had occurred inside the United States. In both cases, governments, business groups, and social movements (such as trade unions, civil rights organizations, and political parties) struggled over the economic and social conditions and consequences of the new industrial capitalist investments—the boom-and-bust cycles of domestic economic growth, large-scale movements of populations, the formation of new social identities, and imperial interventions. The uneven development of capitalism at home and abroad has left its mark on the culture of the United States (Kaplan and Pease 1993; Jacobson 2000).

In the first decades of the twenty-first century, as during the Great Depression of the 1930s and many other times throughout US history, capitalism entered into an economic and cultural crisis. The conditions leading up to the most recent crisis have put new issues on the agenda of American studies and cultural studies—the exponential growth of inequality (Collins, di Leonardo, and Williams 2008), the role of economists in creating the crisis (Grossberg 2010b), the increasing importance of the financial sector (R. Martin 2010), the continued racialization of the housing market through subprime lending practices (Lipsitz 2011), and the heightened role of communication technologies and culture in processes of capital accumulation (Fuchs et al. 2010). The severity of the crisis and the subsequent one-sided recovery have cast doubt on the legitimacy of neoliberalism (Duggan 2003) and

of capitalism itself (J. Clarke 2010), leading to a new interest in Marxian theory (Harvey 2017; Davis 2018; Peck 2017), utopia (Reece 2016; Jennings 2016), and socialism (Gallup 2016), especially on the part of young people.

In the analysis of this nexus of capitalism and US culture, we face three major challenges that in turn open up new paths of investigation for American studies and cultural studies. The first concerns globalization. It is often assumed that the internationalization of the US economy and society is a radically new phenomenon, something that burst on the scene in the 1980s. However, when measured in terms of movements of people (migration), goods and services (imports and exports), and money (capital inflows and outflows), the globalization of capitalism achieved in that decade levels that are quite similar to those experienced almost a century earlier (Ruccio 2003). Because of these similarities and others (particularly the rise in the rate of exploitation and, with it, the increasingly unequal distribution of income and wealth), it is a mistake to describe contemporary developments as unprecedented (Phillips 2002). This is not to say that the forms of capitalist development during the two periods are the same. One of the challenges for students of US culture is to register these differences—such as the outsourcing of jobs, the growth of Wal-Mart, the spread of financial markets, the conduct of wars to protect petroleum supplies, and the emergence of new media and communication technologies—without losing sight of the past.

The second challenge is to avoid treating capitalism as a purely economic system, separate from culture. The influence of capitalism on the culture industry, including the rise of a capitalist film industry and the export of US culture (Miller et al. 2001; Wayne 2003), has been widely studied and debated. What is less clear is that the capitalist economy is saturated by cultural meanings and identities. From this perspective, each moment of capitalism, from the existence of commodity exchange to the export of capital, is simultaneously economic and cultural. The point is not to substitute cultural studies for political economy but to recognize and analyze, concretely and historically, the cultural conditions of capitalism as well as the capitalist conditions of culture. Money, commodities, labor power, surplus value, profits: all these economic forms require the performance of historically and socially constructed meanings and identities. It is also important to understand the role of economic thought in influencing the development of US capitalism and US culture generally. These topics remain open, though a fruitful place to begin is by understanding the role that "languages of class" play in creating new class identities (Gibson-Graham, Resnick, and Wolff 2001), the complex interplay of capitalist and noncapitalist economic imaginaries (Watkins 1998), and the need to rethink the economy and economic knowledge (Grossberg 2010a).

The third potential stumbling block is the treatment of capitalism as an all-encompassing, unitary system that has colonized every social arena and region of the globe. While capitalism certainly represents a powerful project for making and remaking the world, deploying the concept of capitalism (or, for that matter, markets) as a complete mapping of the economic and social landscape has the effect of obscuring noncapitalist forms of economic organization and cultural sense making, now as in the past. "Capitalocentrism" (akin to the role played by "phallocentrism" and "logocentrism" with respect to gender and language, respectively) hides from view the historical roots of capitalism in other economic systems, especially racialization practices (Robinson 1984; Johnson and Kelley 2017) and slavery (Baptist 2014; Beckert 2014; Grandin 2014; Rosenthal 2018; Wilder 2013). It also obscures the diverse ways in which people in the United States and elsewhere participate in individual and collective noncapitalist economies—including barter, communal production, gift giving, and solidarity—that today fall outside the practices and presumed logic of capitalism (Gibson-Graham 1996; Ruccio and Gibson-Graham 2001; Roelvink, St. Martin, and Gibson-Graham 2015). In this view, US culture has long been and remains today heterogeneous and contradictory with respect to different class structures and cultures. It contains elements that foster and reproduce capitalism and, at the same time, its noncapitalist others.

2007/2020

11

Citizenship
Lauren Berlant

Although we tend to think of citizenship as something national, originally the citizen was simply a certain kind of someone who lived in a Greek city: a member of an elite class who was said to be capable of self-governance and therefore of the legal and military governance of the city. But the ancient history of the term tells us little about the constellation of rights, laws, obligations, interests, fantasies, and expectations that shape the modern scene of citizenship, which is generally said to have been initiated by the democratic revolutions of the eighteenth century (B. Anderson 1991; B. Turner 1993; Mouffe 1995). Most simply, citizenship refers to a standing within the law (this is often called *formal* citizenship); jus soli citizenship allots citizenship to people born within the geographical territory, and jus sanguinis awards citizenship by way of a parental inheritance.

At the same time, citizenship is a relation among strangers who learn to feel it as a common identity based on shared historical, legal, or familial connection to a geopolitical space. Many institutional and social practices are aimed at inducing a visceral linkage of personal identity with nationality. In the United States, this process has often involved the orchestration of fantasies about the promise of the state and the nation to cultivate and protect a consensually recognized ideal of the "good life"; in return for cultural, legal, and military security, people are asked to love their country and to recognize certain stories, events, experiences, practices, and ways of life as related to the core of who they are, their public status, and their resemblance to other people. This training in politicized intimacy has served as a way of turning political boundaries into visceral, emotional, and seemingly hardwired responses of "insiders" to "outsiders." Thus we can say that citizenship's legal architecture manifests itself and is continually reshaped in the space of transactions between intimates and strangers. The term "civil society" is often applied to these scenes of *substantive* citizenship, though discussions of civil society tend to focus only on the rational aspects of communication and interaction that contribute to the state's reproduction of mainstream society and not to the ordinary affective or interactive aspects of social exchange (Habermas 1999).

The concept of sovereignty is a crucial bridge between the legal and the substantive domains of US citizenship. This term presupposes a relation between the nation's legal control over what happens in its territory and the presumption that citizens should have control over their lives and bodies, a condition of limited personal autonomy that the state has a responsibility to protect. But the promise of US citizenship to deliver sovereignty to all its citizens has always been practiced unevenly, in contradiction with most understandings of democratic ideals (Rancière 1998). The historical conditions of legal and social belonging have been manipulated to serve the concentration of economic, racial, and sexual power in the society's ruling blocs.

This shaping of the political experience of citizens and noncitizens has been a focus of much recent scholarship and political struggle. These discussions contest the term "citizenship" in various ways: "cultural citizenship" describes the histories of subordinated groups within the nation-state that might not be covered by official legal or political narratives (T. Miller 1993, 2001; Ong 1996; R. Rosaldo 1999); "consumer citizenship" designates contemporary practices of social belonging and political pacification in the United States (Shanley 1997; Cronin 2000; L. Cohen 2003); "sexual citizenship" references the ongoing struggle to gain full legal rights for gendered and sexual minorities (Berlant and Warner 2000; Cott 2000; M. Kaplan 1997); and "global citizenship" describes a project of deriving a concept of justice from linkages among people on a transnational or global scale (Falk 1994; Bosniak 1998; Hardt and Negri 2000). This list could be vastly expanded. Patriotic citizenship, economic citizenship, and legal citizenship have all been shaped not just within a political public sphere, not just within the logic of mass culture and consumer capitalism, but also within a discussion among various collective interest groups struggling over the core norms, practices, and mentalities of a putatively general US population.

The histories of racial and sexual standing in the United States provide the clearest examples of the uneven access to the full benefits of citizenship. But historically, citizenship has also shaped less recognized kinds of distinction. Central among these is that US citizenship has always involved tensions between federal and state systems. Indeed, for most of US history, state citizenship had priority, and the history of civil and suffrage rights centrally involved arguments over the relative priority of state versus federal law. For example, the 1967 Supreme Court case *Loving v. Virginia* (388 U.S. 1), which deemed it unconstitutional to forbid marriage among heterosexuals identified as being of different races, nullified "antimiscegenation" laws not only in Virginia but in thirty-seven other states as well. In so doing, the Supreme Court argued that it is a general rule of US citizenship that marriage cannot be governed by racial restrictions. Prior to that, states were more important than the nation in determining the racial component of legal marriage among heterosexuals, as well as

in many other sexual, familial, and commercial matters, including the legal standing of Mormon, lesbian, gay, and women's marital practices, age of consent, marital rape, reproduction (e.g., abortion, surrogacy, and adoption), and child protection.

Given these complex legal and social histories, US citizenship may be best thought of as an intricate scene where competing forces, definitions, and geographies of freedom and liberty are lived concretely. Citizenship is the practical site of a theoretical existence, in that it allows for the reproduction of a variety of kinds of law in everyday life. It is an abstract idea on behalf of which people engage in personal and political acts, from cheating on taxes to pledging allegiance to fomenting revolutions. It is also, importantly, an ordinary space of activity that many people occupy without thinking much about it, as the administration of citizenship is usually delegated to the political sphere and only periodically worried over during exceptional crises or the election season.

Recent scholarship has pursued this insight into the everyday life of citizenship by exploring some of the most contested scenes in which citizenship has been battled over in US history: immigration, voting rights, sexuality, and labor. Immigration and suffrage have been closely linked at least since the US Naturalization Act of 1790 allowed only "free white persons" to be naturalized as full US citizens. Implicitly this act began the shift from a definition of citizenship as the *ownership of property* to citizenship as the *ownership of labor*, since the word "free" in this act defined freedom as not being economically enslaved—that is, free to sell one's labor in a market for wages (Glenn 2004). The history of US immigrant rights (and exclusions) is thus tied up with desires to control the conditions under which certain populations would be "free" to perform labor in the United States without access to many of the privileges of "free white persons," such as the vote and the legal standing to enforce contracts (Haney López 1996; Lipsitz 2006; Roediger 1999).

So, for example, between 1882 and 1952, virtually all Asian immigrants except for a small number of Filipino laborers were excluded from full US citizenship. During this period, the United States was also opening and closing the gates to Latin American peoples, especially Mexicans, hundreds of thousands of whom were forcibly repatriated to Mexico a number of times, following fluctuations in capitalists' needs and white racial anxieties about disease and moral degeneracy, along with the usual and always false fear that "alien" poor people take more from the economy than they contribute to it. The courts adjudicating these shifts veered between using racial science and "common knowledge," especially in the visual register, as justification for discrimination (Honig 1998; Jacobson 1998, 2000; Roberts 1998). Similarly, arguments for *and* against suffrage for women appealed to common sense, racist science, and biblical authority to protect patriarchal privilege. Suffrage was achieved only when President Woodrow Wilson found it politically expedient to use an image of emancipated femininity to establish US modernity and moral superiority on a global scale (Berlant 2002). Federal and state manipulation of voting rights continues to threaten the representation of many citizens, especially the poor and the incarcerated.

The same pseudoscientific rationales that maintained white supremacy in the performance of US citizenship were also crucial in shaping reproductive law. It may not seem a question of citizenship when a court determines, as it did in the early twentieth century, that it is proper to sterilize women deemed mentally ill, intellectually limited, or epileptic. But the presumption was that these women would be incompetent as mothers and would pass their incompetence on to their children and that the nation would be burdened by the social and economic costs of reproduction by the poor. Poor women and women of color, especially African American and Native American women, were isolated by this juridical-medical ideology: in California, until the late nineteenth century, Native American children could be taken from their families without due process; until 1972, the state of Virginia routinely sterilized poor women without their consent if their offspring were deemed vulnerable to taking on a "degenerate" form (Ginsburg 1998; Stern 1999b). These examples demonstrate that certain perquisites of citizenship, such as the material experience of sovereignty and sexual "privacy" (a modern development within sovereignty), have often been unavailable to the poor, thereby privileging the wealthier classes and the sexually "normal."

What connects these cases to the keyword "citizenship" is not that they are denials of state-protected *rights* (there has never been a "right" to medical care in the United States). Rather, the contradiction between the sovereignty of abstract citizens and the everyday lives of embodied subjects has been structured by the administration of class hierarchies alongside formal democracy. So it is no surprise that citizenship norms and laws have been highly contested in the workplace as well. Should places of business be allowed to function by different standards than the public domain? Should the protections of citizenship punch out when the worker punches in? Should there be different rules for free speech and political speech on private property and public property? These and other legal questions of citizen sovereignty are put to the test in labor relations. It was not until the last decades of the nineteenth century that workers won the right to an eight-hour day, and during the post–World War II era, many employers made "concessions" to their workers, such as the family wage, health insurance, pensions, and protecting workers from undue physical harm on the job. None of these concessions would have happened without the organizing energy of the labor movement, as we can see when, in tight economic times, corporations renege on contracts with workers and states cut back on oversight of corporations' economic, environmental, and worker-health practices. Most histories of US citizenship would not place worker rights at the center of a consideration of the practice of equality in the law and social spaces. But insofar as citizens and workers live citizenship as an experience of sovereignty in their everyday lives, the conditions of labor and the formal and informal rules about organizing worker demands for employer accountability have to be at the center of the story.

Many other vectors of normative and legal adjudication that have structured citizenship could be isolated and enumerated, such as human rights, family law, public education, military conscription, real estate zoning, tax structure, religion, and various state entitlement programs. Such seemingly separate domains are actually mutually defining. What, for example, has Christianity had to do with US citizenship, given the constitutionally mandated prohibition of an official state religion? While some theorists have correlated the development of modern public spheres with the secularization of the shared social world, this evolutionary liberal model has recently been shattered by a cluster of different arguments: that the founding fathers were installing political modernity within the strictures of a Protestant morality of conscience; that the history of legislation around marriage, the family, and children has inevitably been influenced by religious movements advocating for and against traditional patriarchal control; that religious organizations have shaped powerfully the historical relation of the public and the private in terms of rights and proprieties; that the development of the welfare state and the civil rights understanding

of the economic basis of rights was crucially shaped by religious thinkers (Harding 2001; Morone 2003; Bruce and Voas 2004). At the same time, local communities often engender notions of proper citizenship through churches, schools, and other institutions that involve face-to-face social participation (Ong 1996). The religious question has also been central to the story of the citizenship of Mormons, Native Americans, and many immigrant groups, involving taxation, reproductive rights, free speech, public education, and diverse discussions of the material relation of morality to political and economic concerns.

Many of the progressive developments in US citizenship would not have been achieved without the internationally based struggles of socialism, feminism, and the labor movement. Today, the United States feels pressure from other international movements dedicated to transforming its practices of citizenship: religious movements (Christian fundamentalism and evangelicalism, Islam, Catholicism), antineoliberalism (antiglobalization movements dedicated to a sustaining rather than exploitative and depleting version of global integration), and international legal and policy institutions (the United Nations and the International Court of Justice; Doctors without Borders). While international institutions tend to be oriented toward a one-world model of justice, resource distribution, and peace, there is no singular direction or vision of the good life projected by these movements. Antineoliberalism is a *motive* rather than a program, coordinating liberal reformist models of ameliorative activity (environmentalism, welfare statism) with more radical anarchist, queer, antiracist models of refusal and demand. Global religious movements link anticapitalist (antipoverty) messages with a variety of assertions of local sovereignty against the abstract imperialism and general liberality of the modernist state.

Innovations in communication and transportation technology, most notably the internet, have revitalized and even enabled new inter- and transnational movements and have often produced new understandings of citizenship (Dahlberg 2001; Graeber 2002; Poster 1997). Local determination is not a major stress point among internet utopians: personal attachments across the globe are made possible by the speed of information transmission. The seemingly infinitely expanding possibilities of niche political developments and micromovements have reanimated citizenship as an aspirational concept in discussions of diverse communities, real and imagined. Thus the nation-state as such has become only one player in struggles over political and social justice, so much so that many states feel threatened by the transnational flow of information and have responded with censorship. Still, the delocalization of citizenship has not made the world simply postnational. Corporations are like empires; both work transnationally to reshape national standards of conduct. So too the activity of ordinary people to force accountability and to imagine new possibilities for democratic collective life and the sovereignty of people—whether or not they are citizens—continues to revitalize the political sphere everywhere.

2007/2020

12

Class
Eric Lott

As an analytical tool and historiographical category, "class" has an important place in American studies and cultural studies, if only because so many people have thought it irrelevant to the study of the United States. Unlike Europe's old countries, with their feudal pasts and monarchical legacies, the United States, it has often been said, is a land of unlimited economic and geographical mobility. Abraham Lincoln was only one of the most notable believers in "American exceptionalism," the idea that the United States, uniquely among the globe's nations, assigned its citizens no fixed class definition and afforded boundless opportunity to those who would only work hard and look beyond the next horizon. The reality is much more complicated, as scholars and critics have to some extent always known and over the past fifty years have demonstrated in studies of US class formation, cultural allegiance, and artistic expression.

Some form of class consciousness has existed in North America at least since white settlers arrived; John Winthrop's ([1630] 1838) well-known sermon aboard the *Arbella*, "A Modell of Christian Charity," in part justifies the existence of class differences by making them crucial to God's plan of binding through charity the socially stratified community of Puritan believers. The descendants of those believers became an ever-rising post-Puritan middle class, as German sociologist Max Weber ([1905] 1958) famously suggested when he linked the "Protestant ethic" with capitalist economic energies. Simultaneously, the development of a specifically working-class or "plebeian" consciousness came out of the early US situation of class stratification, and the scholarly dilemma ever since has been how to account for such stratification historically, socially, and culturally.

Closely related to such categories as "station," "status," "group," "caste," and "kind," "class" resonates with implications of value, quality, respectability, and religious virtue. Goodness is gilded in much US cultural thought, and it has been difficult to pry capital loose from rectitude. A related difficulty is that class can seem a natural and fixed category; certainly one strain of social and historical analysis in American studies has been marked by a static account of class and class belonging, with discrete strata exhibiting characteristic habits and allegiances and existing in hierarchical formation. In one of the best theoretical accounts, Erik Olin Wright (1985) makes useful distinctions among class *structure*, class *formation*, and class *consciousness*. Class structure is that ensemble of social relations into which individuals enter and which shapes their class consciousness; class formations are those organized collectivities that come about as a result of the interests shaped by the class structure or system. As Wright sums it up, classes "have a structural existence which is irreducible to the kinds of collective organizations which develop historically (class formations), the class ideologies held by individuals and organizations (class consciousness) or the forms of conflict engaged in by individuals as class members or by class organizations (class struggle), and . . . such class structures impose basic constraints on these other elements in the concept of class" (28).

These distinctions help keep in view the fact that class and classification are dynamic processes, more the result than the cause of historical events. Class, as British historian and cultural studies scholar E. P. Thompson (1963) insisted, is a *relational* category, always defined against and in tension with its dialectical others. In response to British cultural theorist Raymond Williams's (1958, xvi) claim that culture should be defined as a "whole way of life," Thompson (1961a, 33; 1961b) redefined culture as a "whole way of conflict," structured in dominance and constantly contested by its various social actors. Work on class in American studies has done much to substantiate Thompson's thesis, and the connections between Thompson's historical reconstruction of British working-class formation, Williams's influential model of cultural studies, and American studies scholarship focused on class have been often intimate.

This emphasis has battered time-honored and influential ideas about US culture and society such as Frederick Jackson Turner's "frontier thesis" ([1893] 1920), in which westward-roving US Americans continually reestablish the conditions for social mobility and rising wages, or Louis Hartz's lament that a hegemonic "liberal tradition" rendered US Americans incapable of thinking outside the contours of social consensus (1955). American studies scholars have shown, for example, how self-conscious, articulate, and combative early working-class or "artisan republican" ideologies were in waging rhetorical—and sometimes actual—war on what they termed the "nonproducing classes" or "the upper ten." Sean Wilentz's *Chants Democratic: New York City and the Rise of the American Working Class, 1788–1850* (1984b) is one of the finest studies of the former, while Stuart Blumin's *The Emergence of the Middle Class: Social Experience in the American City, 1760–1900* (1989) is one of the best on the latter. Both capture how extensively the cultural and affective life of social class shaped democracy in the United States.

Each of these studies exemplifies a body of historiography that first emerged in the 1960s to explain the shape and nature of various class formations. Wilentz is the beneficiary of the "new social history," of which Herbert Gutman (1976) was perhaps the chief US representative. Subsequent studies of the labor process, shop-floor cultures, workers' leisure activities, and other matters have decisively demonstrated the tenacious, conflictual character of working-class belonging—even, or most particularly, when that belonging is overdetermined by being African American or female (Peiss 1986; Kelley 1994; Aronowitz 2003). Meanwhile, studies of bourgeois or middle-class cultural formations have long shown how ruling-class desires and cultural investments have influenced everything from modern art to modern therapy, as well as the degree to which such canonical ideas as the "American character," "American progress," and the "American dream" are inflected by class (Susman 1984; Lears 1981). Perhaps most illuminating have been studies that examine the complex interrelations among various (raced and gendered) class fractions and formations (Stansell 1986; Slotkin 1985; Carby 1987; Trachtenberg 1982; Lizabeth Cohen 2003; Green 2007; Baldwin 2007).

One of the common findings of the latter sort of study is how often cross-class interaction works not to dissolve class boundaries but to buttress them. Examples include cross-class philanthropic enterprises that wind up solidifying bourgeois formations and alienating their would-be working-class wards and African American strategies of racial uplift that too often demonize the black working class. For this reason and others, the category of class has been immensely useful in American studies as an analytical tool capable of unpacking the sometimes surprising dynamics of cultural and textual processes and products, from social clubs and theatrical performances to dime novels and Disney films. The class segregation

of mid-nineteenth-century US theaters, for example, has earned a whole tradition of scholarship, with its attention to class-bound characters, plots, settings, and themes; much the same has been done for the history of US fiction, which has, scholars argue, differing trajectories based not only on plot, character, and outcome but also on mode of production and distribution. Cultural forms hardly recognized at all under erstwhile rubrics of US cultural expression—balladry, ribaldry, mob action, table manners, amusement parks—have found a place in scholarly debates precisely as classed forms of cultural life. The saloon is now recognized no less than the literary salon as a space of cultural and social self-organization.

Just as importantly, quintessential public artifacts of US culture such as New York City's Central Park need to be understood as complex mediations of conflicting class, party, and historical factors. Witness too studies of US newspapers, in which various class accents have been seen to vie for control of a given editorial tendency, newsworthy event, or style of audience address. The key emphasis in such studies is that US cultural forms do not so much belong to a given class or class fraction as become sites in which class struggles are fought out. The political rhetoric of class itself has occasionally been one such arena, whether used defensively against partisans of "identity politics" (usually code for women, queers, and people of color) or weaponized by the Right as a racial appeal.

At their best, class-sensitive versions of American studies and cultural studies are animated by the attempt to grasp the complex structuring of US society by the unequal and uneven social relations of labor and the ways in which those relations give rise to a vast array of cultural forms and formations. The social location of the artist, the assembly-line production of films and cheap fiction, the character and function of manufacturing sweatshops (Ross 1997), the emergence of internationalist social movements (Reed 2005), the place of US cultural formations in the world system (Denning 2004): whatever the case, class analysis has immeasurably benefited our understanding of the sociocultural scene. The United States may be an exceptional place—what country is not?—but it has seen its fair share of class conflict in the sphere of culture, conflict that is intense, productive, and ongoing.

2007/2020

13

Climate
Ashley Dawson

Assumptions about environmental stasis are embedded in historical usage of the word "climate." According to the *Oxford English Dictionary* (*OED*), the first recorded use of the term in English is by medieval geographers, who wrote about a series of fixed bands or belts stretching across the Earth's surface like parallels of latitude. These belts were believed to divide the habitable world into seven distinct climatic zones, which astrologers assumed corresponded to the seven known planets. This idea of a static geography undergirds a now archaic use of "climate" to refer to particular regions of the earth as well as the current usage of the term to name prevailing weather conditions in particular regions of the world. Richard Hakluyt's *The Principall Navigations, Voiages, and Discoveries of the English Nation* (1589) contains the first use of "climate" in this sense recorded by the *OED*: "New found land is in a temperate Climate." This use of the word came to be extended figuratively to the attitudes or opinions prevailing among a body of people or nation so that it became common to speak of a "climate of opinion" or an "economic climate." Significantly, this figurative usage emerges in the context of the social and political disruptions of the seventeenth century, when, as also cited in the *OED*, Joseph Glanvill wrote in his 1661 book *The Vanity of Dogmatizing* that "the larger Souls, that have travail'd the divers Climates of Opinions, are more cautious in their resolves." Thus while the term "climate" generally implies a certain fixity in meteorological conditions, it is also inextricably linked to awareness of geographical or temporal variability in weather patterns.

References to climate began to proliferate during the era of European colonial expansion. Mass deaths as a result of European colonization of the Americas after 1492 sparked a new environmental era, one that disrupted the stability that had shaped prior ideas about climate (Lewis and Maslin 2015). The death by disease and warfare of an estimated fifty million Native Americans—as well as the enslavement of millions of Africans to work the newly depopulated land—allowed forests to grow in former farmlands in the Americas and Africa. The growth of all those trees had sucked enough carbon dioxide out of the atmosphere by 1610 to trigger a period of global cooling. Writing in 1614, the Swiss botanist and historian Renward Cysat observed that "a strange and wondrous succession of changes in the weather" had begun around the globe (cited in G. Parker 2014, 1). Later in the century, in China, the Kangxi emperor collected weather reports from all over China and noted that "the climate has changed" (8). These climatic shifts disrupted growing seasons, producing widespread famine and disease that killed up to a third of human populations around the world. This instability sparked social turmoil, including regicides, revolutions, invasions, and wars. Although this global cooling led to the growth of early forms of scientific observation such as the measurement of sunspots using telescopes, the century's disruptions were more often seen as divine punishment for human misbehavior, which led to acts of scapegoating such as the demolition of theaters and the burning of witches (9).

Environmental and cultural dislocation became abiding elements of experience for the Indigenous people and Africans who survived colonial genocide and slavery in the Americas. Prior to the arrival of colonizers, the cultural and political systems of many Native Americans were based on adaptation to what would now be termed "climate change" (Whyte 2016, 89). In the flexible system that was referred to among the Anishinaabe/Neshnabé peoples as the "seasonable round," the size, organization, and purpose of native institutions such as villages, bands, and ceremonies would shift throughout the year as the plants and animals that needed to be harvested, stored, or honored changed. The "seasonal round" insured that institutions contracted or expanded as environmental circumstances dictated so that resiliency to changes in climate were built into native culture. The arrival of settler colonialism disrupted this system of flexible cultural and environmental adaptation by imposing rapid and unprecedented environmental transformation, including ecosystem collapse, species loss, economic crashes, and wholesale geographical relocation on Indigenous populations across the Americas. Much of the havoc that climate change is predicted to wreak in the twenty-first century, Indigenous scholars have observed, has been inflicted on Indigenous people and people of African descent in the Americas for generations (Callison 2014; Wildcat 2009).

For European colonizers, the term "climate" began to serve as an explanation for a broad array of social, racial, economic, and even moral differences. Climate in this sense was both a meteorological phenomenon *and* a cultural construct, a tool that legitimated colonial domination. Key in this regard was the perceived difference between the relatively temperate climates of European colonial powers and the tropical climates where much European settlement took place. From the time of Columbus, colonizers used observations about perceived tropical abundance to argue that inhabitants of colonized regions were rendered indolent and even morally degenerate by the purported ease of life in the tropics. The more trying European climate, it was held, produced hardier "races" more suited to rule. Accompanying this notion of inheritable racial superiority was a determination to tame and transform the climate in occupied lands. In his 1664 poem *Sylva*, Royal Society member John Evelyn argued that high humidity in Ireland and North America was a product of dense forests and that clearing these forests would therefore create a more "salubrious climate" (qtd. in Fleming 2005, 27). Joel Barlow's epic poem *The Columbiad* ([1807] 2006) linked oppressive climatic conditions in the North American colonies to the yoke of British imperial rule and heralded the liberating impact of independence on the colonists, who would be free to "conquer the land and the atmosphere." Following the precepts of John Locke, *improvement* of the climate was seen as a key part of the colonial enterprise, part of the broader European mission to civilize both barbarous peoples and the savage wilderness (Golinski 2007).

One problem with such colonial accounts of climatic and cultural superiority was that European settlers were noticeably more vulnerable to disease and debility linked to tropical climates. Climatic explanations of this differential mortality were based on the notion that inhabitants of tropical climates had developed resistance to tropical pathologies through adaptation. European settlers needed to learn how to adapt similarly to these "alien" climates. "Acclimatization" consequently became a key term and civilizational project for much of the colonial era. Much emphasis was laid initially on the appropriation of indigenous habits and material forms. In India, for example, British colonizers during the period before the nineteenth century adopted Indian architectural solutions to the tropical climate such as the bungalow as well as mechanisms for interior climate control like the verandah and the punkha (Chang 2016). As concerns about European mortality in such environments grew, however, acclimatization was

rejected in favor of creating a cordon sanitaire between colonizers and colonized, who were increasingly perceived not as inherently immune to disease but instead as carriers of biological pathogens to which white settlers were uniquely vulnerable. Seen through this new lens, it was not the tropical climate alone that was a threat in colonies such as the Philippines but rather the supposedly unhygienic behavior and cultural practices of the colonized (Anderson 2006).

As European colonial administrators turned to new technologies of hygiene and sanitation to control mortality in tropical climates, they also developed ideas about what was known at the time as desiccation: the damaging impact of excessive deforestation (Grove 1996). Forest conservation policies were put in place in colonial territories in order to combat the forms of climate change and aridity that were increasingly apparent in the treeless landscapes created by colonial deforestation and plantation agriculture. By the mid-nineteenth century, a discourse of "climate Orientalism," predicated on stereotypical and derogatory depictions of colonized nations in the Middle East, warned colonial states about the civilizational collapse that deforestation could provoke by pointing to ruined cities in the midst of Middle Eastern deserts (Bonneuil and Fressoz 2015). Conservation and scientific management of forests were seen to be the antidote to desiccation, measures that would not only preserve rainfall but also ensure the sustainability of colonial power.

The establishment of increasingly reliable global information about environmental changes as a result of imperial scientific networks led to speculation about—and intervention in—climatic cycles. During the "magnetic crusade" of the 1840s, the British set up magnetic, meteorological, and tidal observatories at key points around the empire, including Toronto, the Cape of Good Hope, Bombay, and Singapore, a far-flung observation apparatus that made it possible to study the atmospheric dynamics of the potential failure of the annual monsoon season—so integral to subsistence in South and Southeast Asia. By the late nineteenth century, the US was deeply embroiled in similar efforts not just to observe but also to control the weather (Harper 2017). These projects reached a fever pitch during the Cold War era, when US military leaders supported the schemes of scientists like John von Neumann and Theodore von Kármán to create weapons capable of altering the climate of enemy nations (Marzec 2015, 17). If climate once seemed to refer to natural conditions wholly beyond human control, whose closest approximation was the celestial spheres, by this time, it had become the subject of globe-girdling engineering schemes with potentially apocalyptic impact.

While one wing of the scientific establishment in the United States was seeking to weaponize the climate, another was beginning to document the forms of climate change that were already taking place. Building on the work of predecessors like Joseph Fourier and John Tyndall, Swedish chemist Svante Arrhenius (Arrhenius 1896) published the first calculation of global warming resulting from human emissions of carbon dioxide in the late nineteenth century, but his predictions were purely theoretical. In the late 1950s, Charles David Keeling began collecting carbon dioxide samples at an observatory on the Mauna Loa volcano in Hawaii that he set up with support from the recently established International Geophysical Year initiative. In 1960, Keeling published his findings documenting annual rises in concentrations of atmospheric carbon dioxide (Keeling 1960). By the end of the decade, scientific studies began to lay bare the implications of this change in the chemistry of the air, including some that predicted a wholesale collapse of the Antarctic ice sheets, an event that would raise global sea levels significantly, thereby drowning many of the world's principal cities. But other climate scientists speculated that the atmosphere might cool as a result of industrial emissions of airborne particles called aerosols. For that reason, most scientific studies continued to refer to the phenomenon as "inadvertent climate modification" or "climate change" until the mid-1970s.

The first use of the term "global warming" was in a paper published in 1975 by the geochemist Wallace Broecker (Broecker 1975). Four years later, the National Academy of Sciences published a definitive study of carbon dioxide's impact on the atmosphere that referred explicitly to changes in Earth's average surface temperature as global warming while also using the term "climate change" to allude to the multiple other impacts of increasing levels of carbon dioxide (National Academy of Science 1979, vii). It was only in 1988, when NASA scientist James Hansen testified before Congress (US Senate 1988), that the general public became aware of the dangers of global warming. By this point, the environmental movements in the United States and Europe had scored many legislative and legal victories. But climate change constituted a bigger challenge for the environmental movement, since it called for a wholesale transformation of capitalist approaches to economics and policy, not the banning of individual toxins that earlier activists such as Rachel Carson (1962) had advocated. The specter of the "Anthropocene," the anthropogenic or human-caused transformation of the atmosphere evident in geologic records, began to come into view, and with it, the even more worrying awareness of planetary ecocide driven by an economic system bent on infinite expansion on a finite resource base that is captured in the allied term the "Capitalocene" (Moore 2016).

Corporations clearly understood the threat that potential action on climate change represented. The same year that James Hansen testified before Congress and that the Intergovernmental Panel on Climate Change was formed, Big Oil and other energy organizations founded the Global Climate Coalition. Taking a leaf from the tobacco industry's prior efforts to cast doubt on the link between smoking and cancer, this industry tool sought to disseminate doubt about climate change in order to influence both politicians and the US public more broadly. The climate, they argued, has always changed, and science cannot be certain that carbon emissions are responsible for the mutations documented in recent decades. Their efforts to halt climate action bore fruit almost immediately, as the United States blocked calls for serious responses to climate change at the 1992 Rio Conference that led to the UN Framework Convention on Climate Change. Climate change denial became a lucrative business for many industry-backed think tanks. There are clear links between the public understandings of climate change that emerged in this period and the discourse and strategies of globalization, since ostensibly neutral descriptions of geographical scale embedded new and strident forms of imperial power.

Frontline communities that stand to lose the most from climate change are chief protagonists in the fight against the climate change denial industry and the obstructionism of polluting nations. In the United States, the movement for climate justice emerged from protests by African American activists against the disproportionate siting of toxic facilities like landfills and coal-fired power plants in or near communities of color (Bullard 2000). Based in both rural areas and cities, the environmental justice movement drew on the protest repertoire of the civil rights movement to challenge the unequal environmental distribution of life and death in the United States. In 1991, at the historic People of Color Environmental Leadership Summit, activists drafted a set of seventeen principles for environmental justice whose core tenets underlined that the movement not only was about environmental issues but also hinged on social justice goals such as economic equity, cultural liberation, and the political participation of people of color at all levels of decision-making (Dawson 2010). Recognizing parallels between their own struggles and those of marginalized communities like the Ogoni in Nigeria and the indigenous peoples of Ecuador, activists in the environmental justice movement argue that those who suffer most from the environmentally and socially brutalizing impacts of fossil capitalism are also those who are being most adversely affected by climate change. Activists insist that reparations are due to such frontline communities and to the many communities displaced by climate change. Through such transnational solidarity, the environmental justice movement in the US has linked arms with an emerging global movement for climate justice.

2020

14

Colonial

David Kazanjian

"Colonial" has very old roots. The Latin word *colonia* was used during the Roman Empire to mean a settlement of Roman citizens in a newly conquered territory. Often these citizens were retired soldiers who received land as a reward for their service and as a display of Roman authority to the conquered inhabitants. For Roman writers, *colonia* translated the Greek word *apoikia*, which meant a settlement away from one's home state, as opposed to the *polis*, meaning one's own city or country as well as a community of citizens, or the *metropolis*, literally one's mother city or mother country.

Despite these etymological ties to the violence and power of conquest, the English word "colony" was until the eighteenth century as likely to mean simply a farm or a country estate as a settlement in conquered land subject to a parent state. The cognate "colonial" was not coined until the late eighteenth century (it is not in Samuel Johnson's 1755 dictionary), when it was used as an adjective to mean "of a colony" and as a noun to mean "a person from a colony," most often referring to Europeans who conquered and settled in North America and the West Indies.

This eighteenth-century usage acquired an important and odd wrinkle in the United States, one that is particularly relevant to US variants of cultural studies: "colonial" and "colonist" have often been used as if they were simple descriptors for early Americans and unrelated to conquest. For instance, while the popular

dictionary *Colonial American English* does not include a definition for the word "colonial," it does define "colony" as "a government in which the governor is elected by the inhabitants under a charter of incorporation by the king, in contrast to one in which the governor is appointed" (Lederer 1985, 54). Here, we can see how far this usage strays from the word's roots in conquest by suggesting that "colonial" signifies a kind of democracy. Indeed, "colonials," "American colonists," "the colonial period," and "colonial literature" in the US context have often invoked images of plucky settlers fleeing persecution in Europe, overthrowing their oppressive European rulers, establishing rich new states and cultures against all odds through hard work, and founding a free, democratic, and unified nation. The word "colonial" thus oddly comes to connote resistance *to* the violence and power of conquest.

In 1847, influential political economist Henry Charles Carey (1967, 345) extended this usage in a way that links it to a history of American exceptionalism: "The colonization of the United States differs from that of the two countries we have considered [Britain and France], in the great fact that they [the United States] desire no subjects. The colonists are equal with the people of the States from which they sprang, and hence the quiet and beautiful action of the system." While Britain and France send their citizens to the far corners of the world to conquer territory and subjugate native inhabitants, Carey tautologically claims, the United States was founded by colonists who colonized themselves. As he goes on to argue, the resulting nation is both exceptional, or unique in the history of the world, and exemplary, or destined to be emulated by the rest of the world.

This US understanding of colonization expresses a deeply nationalist mythology that continues to thrive today: the United States was founded exclusively on the just and noble principles of freedom, equality, and democracy, and it continues to spread those principles around the world. This mythology has been challenged from a number of directions. Scholars and activists in African American and Native American studies have shown how the "quiet and beautiful action" that Carey describes actually involved some of the most brutal systems of dispossession that the modern world has known: the conquest of Native American lands, the enslavement and genocide of native peoples and Africans, and the establishment of a vast transatlantic and transcontinental system of race-based chattel slavery. Much of this scholarship has argued that these practices were not simply aberrations from or exceptions to the history and culture of the United States but rather constitutive of all that it was to become.

Forms of dispossession in which colonists take up permanent residence in the territories they appropriate are called "settler colonialism." As Karl Marx ([1867] 1976) explained in the first volume of *Capital*, such dispossession—along with the enclosure of the agricultural commons throughout Europe, the expropriation of peasants from those expropriated lands, and the transformation of those peasants into wage laborers, global migrants, and settler colonials—was a central means by which capitalists, starting in the sixteenth century, accumulated the wealth they needed to increase the productive efficiency of agricultural and industrial production and to extract ever-increasing rates of surplus value from peasants, the poor, and indigenous and enslaved populations. Mythologized as "primitive accumulation" by classical political economists, accumulation by dispossession was in fact the brutal condition of possibility for modern global capitalism and its attendant political form, the nation-state (Emmanuel 1972). The white settler foundations of the United States—in which European settler colonials violently expropriated lands from Native Americans—can

thus be linked with other histories of settler colonialism across the Caribbean, Latin America, and Canada, as well as in South Africa, Australia, and New Zealand (Wolfe 2006; Black Hawk [1833] 2008; Goldstein and Lubin 2008; Andrea Smith 2010; Byrd 2011; Morgensen 2011b; Goldstein 2012). The concept of settler colonization has also been used to link more recent examples of dispossession, such as the black settler colonization of Liberia and the Zionist project in Israel, to this long history of capitalism's rise to hegemony (Massad 2006; Afzal-Khan and Seshadri 2000; Pedersen and Elkins 2005; Kazanjian 2011, 2012). Indeed, accumulation by dispossession has been extended to contemporary neoliberal policies throughout the globe, policies that have managed waves of economic crisis from the 1970s forward, including the privatization of public assets, seizures of indigenous lands, and the rise of so-called financialization (Harvey 2003).

Attention to histories of settler colonialism unsettles the myth of the North American colonial as a "quiet and beautiful," even heroic actor. Take as an instance of this myth the text that can be said to have founded it: the Declaration of Independence. The Declaration represents North American colonials as innocent victims of British tyranny ("Such has been the patient sufferance of these Colonies") as well as harmless witnesses to violence against Native Americans by blaming both the Crown and Native Americans themselves for resistance to colonization ("the present king of Great Britain . . . has endeavored to bring on the inhabitants of our frontiers the merciless Indian savages"; Jefferson [1776] 1984, 19, 21). Even as white settlers were engaged in these battles, they paradoxically drew on their fantasies about "Indians" to fashion their own identities as American colonials distinct from their British brethren. Sometimes they "played Indian," as Philip J. Deloria (1998) has carefully recounted, in private societies and at protests such as the Boston Tea Party. At other times, they combed through Native American graves to show that America had its own ancient history to rival that of Europe (Jefferson [1787] 1984). And increasingly after the Revolution, white US American writers depicted Native Americans in order to distinguish "American" from "English" literature. Performed alongside violence against Native Americans, this fashioning of a US American identity helped generate the mythology of the innocent North American colonial who became a heroic rebel and eventually an exceptional US citizen.

While the Declaration of Independence does not mention slavery directly, in an early draft, it did include a passage that both criticized slavery and perpetuated the mythology of North American colonials as innocent victims of conquest. The passage personified the entire transatlantic slave trade in the king ("He has waged cruel war against human nature itself") and equated enslaved Africans with free white settlers as fellow victims ("he is now exciting those very people [slaves] to rise in arms among us, and to purchase the liberty of which he has deprived them, by murdering the people on whom he also obtruded them" [Jefferson (1776) 1984, 22]). By suppressing the alliance between Europeans and North American colonials in the system of chattel slavery, this passage transforms the latter from conquerors to conquered. Unabashedly proslavery colonials found even this argument too threatening to their interests and fought successfully for its deletion.

By recovering and reinterpreting early colonial and national texts that were crucial in their day but had long been excluded from disciplinary canons, twentieth-century scholars traced histories and practices of dissent that challenged the mythological conception of the American colonial. New social historians reminded us that the list of men who signed the Declaration of Independence is not simply a list of heroic rebels; it is a list of elites. Their declaration would have had no force behind it had poor people throughout the colonies not been struggling for decades against exploitation at the hands of wealthy and powerful colonials as well as British authorities. The North American colonial looks neither innocent nor uniform from the perspective of an early dissident such as Stephen Hopkins, who helped organize a rebellion and then a furtive utopian community after a Virginia Company vessel shipwrecked on Bermuda in 1609 (Strachey [1610] 1964); or Richard Frethhorn, an indentured servant who was transported to Virginia in 1623 and wrote back to his parents of the brutal conditions he faced (Jehlen and Warner 1997, 123); or Anne Bonny and Mary Read, two cross-dressing women pirates who worked with the predominantly male pirate population of the early eighteenth century to disrupt the social and cultural norms, and the emerging imperial state, of the British Empire (Hogeland et al. 2004, 98–106); or rural colonial rebels who challenged the British colonial elite for control over land and political decision-making before the American Revolution and then took on the early social and political elite in the Shays Rebellion of 1786 (Alfred Young 1976, 1993; Zinn 1980; G. Nash 1986; New Social History Project 1989–92; Raphael 2001).

In the eighteenth and nineteenth centuries, African Americans and Native Americans took the lead in challenging the mythology of the North American colonial. In 1829, a free black tailor and activist from Boston named David Walker published a pamphlet that excoriated whites for their systematic racism and called on blacks to claim the land that slavery had forcibly made their own, effectively recalling the etymological roots of "colonial" in the violence and power of conquest as well as disrupting analogies between white settler colonials and slaves ([1829] 1995, 74–76). William Apess, a Pequot born in 1798, published an 1833 essay in which he charged that US Christians failed to live up to the Revolutionary ideals of freedom and equality as well as the spirit of Christianity: "By what you read, you may learn how deep your principles are. I should say they were skin-deep" ([1833] 1992, 160). Even in the title of his essay ("An Indian's Looking-Glass for the White Man"), Apess reverses the dynamic of "playing Indian"; he claims a European technology, the looking glass, and turns it on white men so that they may see themselves not as innocent colonials but as violent colonizers.

This minority tradition of challenging the mythology of the US American colonial was renewed after the US-Mexico War of 1846–48 by Mexicanos, Tejanos, and, in the twentieth century, Chicanos who insisted that it was US imperialism—not innocent, plucky settlers—that made them as well as the entire geography of the Southwest and California part of the United States. Chicanos in the second half of the twentieth century collaborated with African Americans, Asian Americans, and Native Americans to appropriate the word "colonial" by situating their own histories in the context of third world liberation movements ("Alcatraz Reclaimed" [1970] 1971; Valdez and Steiner [1969] 1972; Ho 2000). Black activists Stokely Carmichael and Charles Hamilton (1967, 5–6) exemplify this mode of analysis in their book *Black Power: The Politics of Liberation in America*: "Black people are legal citizens of the United States with, for the most part, the same *legal* rights as other citizens. Yet they stand as colonial subjects in relation to the white society. Thus institutional racism has another name: colonialism. Obviously, the analogy is not perfect." By acknowledging the imperfections of this "internal colonization" argument at the very moment of formulating it, Carmichael and Hamilton foreground both the difficulty and the importance

of thinking about the keyword "colonial" in an international context.

Such international thinking took place in the early United States as well: Walker's *Appeal*, for instance, is addressed to "the coloured citizens of the world." And it continues today: in an echo of the Declaration of Independence's claim that white North American colonials are victims of imperialism along with slaves and "savages," some contemporary scholars have suggested that the United States should be considered a postcolonial nation (Ashcroft, Griffiths, and Tiffin 1989; Buell 1995). In contrast, others have picked up on the implications of the internal colonization thesis and insisted on the differential relations among variously racialized minorities and whites (Spivak 1993; Sharpe 1995; Saldaña-Portillo 2001). The latter scholarship relies on rich historical understandings of the differences among modes of imperialism, particularly white settler colonialism, comprador capitalism, and neocolonialism.

Contemporary scholars have also shown how a historical understanding of these differences requires a close attention to gender and sexuality. Indeed, we can hear an echo of gender and sexuality in the very word "colonial." As noted earlier, the Latin *colonia* was a translation of the Greek word *apoikia* (literally, "away from the domestic sphere"), which itself was opposed in Greek to the *polis* and the *metropolis*, "the city" and "the mother country." This distinction survives in English in the opposition between "metropole" and "colony." If the home or domestic sphere is figured as maternal, then the colonial sphere is readily figured as public, political, and masculine, which makes the word "colonial" subject to the vast feminist scholarship on the separation—or inseparability—of public and private spheres (Kerber 1980; Isenberg 1998; Davidson and Hatcher 2002). One aspect of this scholarship is exemplified by studies of North American colonial women such as Anne Hutchinson, who challenged the male dominance of mainstream Puritanism in seventeenth-century New England (Kerber and De Hart 2004, 25–120). Other studies suggest that the very concept of the domestic invokes the process of domestication, the incorporation and subjection of that which is not yet fully domesticated (A. Kaplan 2002).

It is thus not surprising to see early champions of women's work in the domestic sphere, such as Catharine Beecher (1841), imagine in imperial terms the ordering and unifying of the home as an ever-expanding process destined to encompass the entire world. In addition, black women who were enslaved in the Americas, as well as contemporary black feminist critics, have shown how the gendering of the colonial had deep racial implications (A. Davis 1983; H. Wilson [1859] 1983; Hartman 1997; Prince [1831] 2000; Spillers 2003). Eighteenth-century laws that based a black person's status as free or enslaved on that of the mother encouraged the sexual exploitation of black women by white men. Consequently, the black domestic sphere became, to white men, a breeding ground for slavery. To further complicate matters, feminist postcolonial scholars have shown how the colony as such is often figured as feminine in order to make it subject to the power and authority of the metropole, while others have complicated this general model by tracking the uneven deployments of gender across the postcolonial world (Mohanty, Russo, and Torres 1991; McClintock 1995; Yuval-Davis 1997; Spivak 1999). Queer studies has also opened up the study of sexuality in the colonial context, examining closely the ways heterosexuality was made culturally and legally normative among early North American colonists, and in turn revealed the challenges that sexually dissident cultures presented to this normativity (Jonathan Goldberg 1992; Burgett 1998).

The complex history of the word "colonial" indexes the equally complex politics that have characterized US imperialism. In the first decades of the twenty-first century, debates about colonialism—and settler colonialism, in particular—remain at the forefront of research in American studies and cultural studies. As struggles over the future of the US empire proliferate, it is all the more urgent for cultural studies to take stock of the history of such a contested keyword.

2007/2014

15

Conservatism
Angela D. Dillard

In common usage, the term "conservatism" names a belief that hierarchies constituting the status quo are worth preserving and protecting, that inequality is not a necessary evil but a positive good, and that the defense of individual liberty is the best bulwark against the so-called totalitarian tendencies of an egalitarian politics. One popular variation of this usage posits conservatism as a transhistorical reaction against revolution from below: the emancipation of the lower orders in France, the rebellions of slaves in the Americas; the struggles of the white working class in nineteenth-century United States; and in successive generations, the demands of women, the poor, nonwhite and racialized minorities, and people with marginalized gender identities. In short, conservatism is synonymous with power and the defense of power in ways that are enlivened by violence and war (Robin 2011).

In the first couple of decades of the new millennium, this usage of the term feels consistent with the performance of conservative politics on Fox News and its articulation in publications such as Breitbart. It also accords well with the "dark money" vision (Mayer 2016) of the political machinations of the Koch brothers and others judged to be responsible for funding and fueling the radical Right. And it reflects a belief that conservatism is embroiled in a "deep history" of "stealth planning" to alter the rules of democratic governance in the United States (MacLean 2017). A key feature of this approach to defining—and exposing—conservatism is the charge that impossibly wealthy interests promote and then cynically use the resentment of the working classes, especially the white working classes, to advance their own agenda. As with the "business conservatism" perspective urged by Kim Phillips-Fein (2009), this definition views conservatism not as a manifestation of the post–World War II "crisis of liberalism" but as a long, historical process of consolidating political, social, and corporate power in the United States while paying lip service to ideas of democracy and individualism.

This dark vision of conservatism, and the politics of the contemporary Republican Party it is said to support, reached a watershed in cultural analysis in Thomas Frank's *What's the Matter with Kansas?* (2004). Frank explored the rise of supposedly grassroots and "anti-elitist" conservatism refracted through his home state of Kansas and the use of cultural wedge issues such as gay marriage, prayer in schools, and misdirected anger toward liberal elites to cement conservative electoral victories. Frank updated the interpretive emphasis on the interconnections among conservatism, power, and resentment with considerable wit. But the general outlines of his argument stretch back at least as far as Richard Hofstadter's *The Paranoid Style in American Politics*. Published in the wake of Barry Goldwater winning the presidential nomination over Nelson D. Rockefeller (and the moderate wing of the Republican Party) in 1964, the book describes the Goldwater brand of conservatism as marked by three tendencies: "heated exaggeration," "suspiciousness," and "conspiratorial fantasy." Hofstadter was struck by what was for him the unfathomable unwillingness of Republicans to sever ties to right-wing extremist organizations such as the John Birch Society. For Hofstadter and others who contributed to the edited volume *The New American Right* (Bell 1955), this was at best a "pseudoconservatism" well outside of the liberal consensus.

Defining conservatism in these ways—through a lens of criticism and suspicion—means that the term cannot be understood without the preservation of racial hierarchies in and through racist and xenophobic ideologies. But what of those who seek to use the term from a position of affiliation and even affection? Conservatives themselves have mostly rejected the assertion that conservatism is indelibly racist and overly beholden to forms of white nationalism. This tendency manifests in multiple ways: in assertions that slavery and Jim Crow segregation were not racist but an outgrowth of the natural inferiority of Black and other nonwhite peoples—a view updated in the twentieth century in assertions of cultural pathology; in claims that appeals to doctrines such as "state's rights" have nothing to do with race or civil rights activism and everything to do with critiques of federal power; and in claims that conservatism is in fact "color-blind."

In one especially provocative series of rhetorical moves, it became common by the 1990s to view conservatism—and not liberalism—as responsible for preserving and extending the values of the civil rights movement. Daniel Patrick Moynihan (often labeled a "neoconservative") describes this turn as "semantic infiltration"—that is, "the appropriation of the language of one's opponent for the purpose of blurring distinctions and molding it to one's own political position" (Moynihan 1979; Steinberg 1995, 166). Hence legislation designed to dismantle affirmative action and other race-conscious strategies gets defined as a "civil rights" initiative, and racism is promoted without a direct articulation of race through a "dog whistle" politics (Haney López 2014)—with the metaphor pointing to the ways in which seemingly neutral turns of phrase can confirm a speaker's support for racist ideologies, though only for those in the audience attuned to those meanings. These ideas reached an apogee with President George Bush's hesitancy over signing the 1990 Civil Rights Act on the grounds that it was a "quota bill."

In a less disingenuous vein, some definitions of conservatism have grappled more forthrightly with the degree to which the preservation of a social, political, and moral order structured by hierarchies will inexorably embrace racism and other forms of exclusion and discrimination. Calls to protect the southern "way of life" are indicative of this definitional tendency. In the preface to *The Southern Tradition*, Eugene Genovese (1994) addresses the race question head-on: "It is one thing to demand—and it must be demanded—that white southerners repudiate white supremacy. . . . It is quite another to demand that they deny the finest and most generous features of southern life" (xiii). What Genovese values most are the communitarian aspects of a southern conservatism rooted in an organic, interdependent vision of the social order. This conservativism regards change as a necessarily slow process and seeks gradual improvement over sudden and therefore dangerous social engineering. It can include a belief that the past is better than the present as well as an emphasis on restoration over revolution. It is often religiously inflected and informed by assumptions about the "right relations" of parts to the whole as ordained by God. These "right relations" are, more often than not, unequal and hierarchical. But this is acceptable precisely because inequality is, in this understanding of conservatism, a positive good and an important wellspring of diversity. And it is this understanding of diversity—that we are born different, not equal—that renders egalitarianism at once perilous and impossible.

A century earlier, George Fitzhugh presented this argument in his two classic proslavery texts, *Sociology for the South* (1854) and *Cannibals All* ([1857] 2006). Fitzhugh held that nature makes some men fit to rule and command and others most suitable to be enslaved and governed. Because of this, it is the duty of the strong to protect and defend the weak. Thus slavery is understood as a form of protection for slaves unable to be fully self-governing, along with women ("the weaker sex") and children. With this argument, Fitzhugh did more than champion slavery in the South. He also denounced the society emerging around industrial capitalism in the North. *Cannibals All* was an especially sharp critique of the "wage slavery" in the North and offered a form of universal (i.e., nonracialized) slavery as a remedy for this "unnatural" form of inequality that unfairly penalizes those who are unfit to compete in a free-market society.

In less extreme forms, these ideas can help us understand usages of the term "conservatism" that are rooted in ideas about "natural" differences that produce "positive" inequalities. Consider, for instance, the ways of defining conservatism that stress fidelity to traditional gender and sexual norms that rest on binary notions that men and women are fundamentally different. Even when the sexes are viewed as complementary, it is typically clear that men rule and women serve. Books and articles that seek to understand the attraction of social and religious conservatism to women—and that reject easy claims of "false consciousness"—are the most representative of this framework. Kathleen Blee's (1992) study of women in the KKK was groundbreaking in this regard. It has been followed by studies of women and the post–World War II Right (Nickerson 2012) and the cultural logics of free Christian enterprise (Moreton 2009). Cumulatively, they offer a very different style of analysis from that of Frank, rejecting false consciousness as the reason some people, especially women, embrace conservatism. In these studies, adherents are not being entirely duped by powerful and often unseen forces. They are not being wholly manipulated. They are being inspired.

Some scholarship on conservatism among racial and ethnic minorities has also adopted this more positive framework (Dillard 2001). In a study of working-class supporters of Thatcherism in Britain, Stuart Hall argued against any "theory about the world which has to assume that vast numbers of ordinary people, mentally equipped in much the same way as you or I, can simply be thoroughly and systematically duped into misrecognizing entirely where their real interests lie" (1988, 44). More often, however, researchers suggest that members of the social and religious Right have manipulated ideas of gender and sexuality, particularly related to reproductive politics and policy-making. Some of the earliest critical analyses of conservatism and the New Right were written by feminist scholars seeking to understand—and undermine—conservative antifeminism in movements against abortion and the Equal Rights Amendment and for the rights of gays and lesbians (Petchesky 1981; Luker 1984; De Hart 1991). They also explored the larger connections between these highly gendered ideologies and the ways that gender shaped thinking about the proper role of the state, nationalism, economic regulation, and moral "contamination" from communists and other subversives. This is arguably the dominant way that American studies and cultural studies have contended with the ascendency of conservative thought in general—and with the rise of Republican and right-wing women, including Anita Bryant, Christina Hoff Sommers, Katie Roiphe, and Phyllis Schlafly. Susan Faludi's *Backlash* (1991) is a key popular text in this genre.

Attempts to define conservatism can also draw our attention to important debates about the meaning of freedom. Put in the starkest terms possible, those who view conservatism in positive ways have tended to define freedom in terms of liberty and individualism—the *negative* liberty not to be harassed or unduly controlled or limited. Conservatives eventually made an uneasy peace with notions of equality, but only as "equality of opportunity" as opposed to "equality of results," which, they maintain, can breed an egalitarian leveling downward. This libertarian streak can be seen most readily in the 1960 Sharon Statement, the founding document of Young Americans for Freedom. It held that individual freedom is a natural and God-given right, that political freedom is impossible without economic freedom, that limited government and a strict interpretation of the Constitution are essential, that the free market system is preferable over all others, and that communism must be defeated at all costs. For this brand of conservativism, anti-communism served as the ideological glue that bound together traditionalists and Christian conservatives, advocates of laissez-faire economics and free-market idealism, and cold warriors dedicated to defeating all vestiges of communism, at home and abroad. In international relations, this bargain led to the support of brutal regimes aligned with the "free world"; domestically, it grafted a fear of subversion at the hands of communists onto an aversion to race mixing, rock 'n' roll, gender-bending, sexual liberation, and other "assaults" on traditional morality. The contemporary notion of "culture wars" between the Left and the Right date from this period (Hartman 2015).

This usage of conservatism has been vigorously contested by what is, once again, a much darker and more skeptical rendering. One of the most useful—and sweeping—cultural studies critiques of conservative ideologies of freedom is Michael Rogin's (1987) work on the "countersubversive tradition" of "political demonology" in US political culture. These terms point to the "creation of monsters as a continuing feature of American politics by inflation, stigmatization, and dehumanization of political foes," Rogin argues, from depictions of "savage Indians" to bomb-throwing anarchists to the "evil empire," and more recently "feminazis" and terrorists who allegedly hate our freedom and our way of life (xiii). At every turn, the world is split into good and evil, and anything is permissible in the fight against evil. In the end, Rogin argued that the process of demonization allows the "countersubversive, in the name of battling the subversive, to imitate his enemy"—that is, to become terrorist-like and abridge freedom in the heroic fight against terrorism, variously defined (xiii). This powerful cluster of ideas has been informed by the rise of the New Right from the post–World War II era to the ascendency of Ronald Reagan and beyond. And American cultural studies, at least since George Nash (1976), has been puzzling over this fusion of seemingly incompatible and inconsistent ideas ever since (Perlstein 2001, 2008, 2014; Kintz 1997; Marable 1999; Kruse 2005).

In the early twenty-first century, debates over the proper usage of the term are complicated by the unexpected 2016 electoral victory of Donald Trump and the degree to which Trumpism has come to define both the Republican Party and the conservative movement. With its stress on tax cuts for the wealthiest of Americans, an overwhelming fidelity to the Second Amendment, and a desire to overturn *Roe v. Wade* by remaking the Supreme Court, Trumpian conservatism is well in line with some past traditions. Yet there are "Never Trump" conservatives and other skeptics within the Republican Party and among Libertarians who judge his strategy to be indecipherable and his message a muddle. Trump's embrace of reactionary white nationalism, anti-immigration policies augmented by closed borders and barrier walls, authoritarian pretensions, and global isolationism appear far from a direct evolution of a tradition once rooted in small government, fiscal responsibility, and a fear of disorder. A vindictive, mercurial, and erratic standard-bearer ought to be anathema to classical conservatism.

It is true that a retroactive interpretation of US political history might find that Trump's "America First" nationalism, with its toxic brew of governance by social media and constant insults, connects to some of the most disreputable episodes of the nation's past. In particular, one can recall the antirationalist "know-nothing" politics of a Huey Long or a Joseph McCarthy or even a Sarah Palin, whose vice presidential candidacy in many ways prefigured Trumpian conservatism. The perilous unpredictability of decisions and situations is why we lack a grand unified theory of conservatism. In the age of Trump, we are presented with protean usages of a term whose future consequences are impossible to predict.

2020

16

Copyright
Kembrew McLeod

Embedded within the word "copyright" is a simple and succinct self-definition. It means, quite literally, the right to copy. Unlike "intellectual property," a term that did not come into common usage until the mid-twentieth century, "copyright" has been used for centuries, dating from 1735. The term accurately describes what this legal doctrine is and how it functions. Often understood as a synonym for "copyright," "intellectual property" is actually a deceptive neologism. That is because copyrighted, patented, and trademarked works are not in fact *property*—they are instead protected by government-granted rights that are limited in how they can be enforced. The term "intellectual property" functions ideologically because it naturalizes an association with physical property that does not exist in law. This encourages many false analogies, such as the common claim that the unauthorized download of a song or a film is like breaking into someone's car and driving it away. The comparison is misleading because stolen physical property is no longer accessible to the owner, something that is not true when a copyrighted work is appropriated. Put in economic terms, physical property is a rivalrous good, and copyrighted works are nonrivalrous because their use by one consumer does not preclude their simultaneous consumption by another (Boyle 2010; Lessig 2002).

Copyright applies to all types of original expression, including art, choreography, literature, music, songs, maps, software, film, and graphic design. A work only needs to rise to the most minimal level of originality to be copyrightable, though it is important to note that one cannot copyright an idea—only the *expression* of an idea. This distinction is known among legal theorists as the "idea-expression dichotomy." It may seem obvious that a copyrighted work cannot be produced without an author—whether corporate or human—but upon closer inspection, "the author" reveals itself to be an unstable and slippery category. During the first half of the eighteenth century, before copyright law as we know it existed, two competing conceptions of authorship prevailed. On the one hand, the author was thought to be much like a "craftsman" who created poems by mining linguistic raw materials and following literary conventions, not unlike a carpenter. On the other hand, the author was viewed as one who transcends workmanlike procedures and channels something higher, such as a muse or God. These two understandings of authorship shared the assumption that authors had no right to own their creations. After all, how could one claim exclusive ownership over a product constructed with commonly shared words or, for that matter, something that originated from a divine source (Vaidhyanathan 2001; Woodmansee and Jaszi 1994)?

Over the course of the eighteenth century, a more individualist notion of authorship emerged as the result of several important economic and cultural changes. The patronage system that had supported artistic production was breaking down during the transition from feudalism to early capitalism, and there was nothing that prevented one's creative labor from being appropriated in a literary marketplace where reproduction had been mechanized. Authors were struggling to make a living from the written word. Without any consensus about what authorship was, literary works could not be legitimated as property in commonsense notions of ownership. Responding to this vacuum, many writers

and thinkers very consciously attempted to redefine texts as commodities. The resulting legal battles that codified copyright as a legal doctrine were informed by emerging Enlightenment notions of what constitutes originality, authorship, and ownership. In eighteenth-century England and nineteenth-century Germany, authorship increasingly became associated with economic discourses about property and Romantic notions about "original genius." Within this context, it became possible for authors (or, more commonly, publishers) to secure the exclusive "right to copy." Put simply, copyright law emerged out of contradictions produced by the rise of capitalism, the invention of the printing press, and the commodification of culture (M. Rose 1995; Woodmansee and Jaszi 1994).

In 1710, Britain passed the Statute of Anne, which is widely recognized as a predecessor to modern copyright. Then in 1790, the US Congress enacted the world's first copyright law. The US Constitution states that copyright is intended to "promote the progress of science and useful arts, by securing for limited times to authors and inventors the exclusive right to their respective writings and discoveries" (art. I, § 8, cl. 8). As many legal scholars have noted, the primary constitutional objective of copyright is to promote the creation and dissemination of knowledge, inventions, and creative expression. Because the United States was a very young country, it had no established culture or literary tradition to call its own. As a project of nation formation, the Constitution treated copyright law as a tool that could solve this problem. It was conceived as a kind of bribe that gave authors a limited right to commercially exploit their work—after a maximum term of twenty-eight years, previously copyrighted works entered the public domain so anyone could make use of them. This is one example of how the US Constitution treated the author as the secondary beneficiary of copyright law; the public interest always came first (Boyle 2010; Coombe 1998; Wirtén 2008).

The framers of the Constitution articulated a theory of copyright that rewarded creativity, but they did not want to give creators complete control over their work in ways that would inhibit the "progress of science and useful arts." As a result, the concept of fair use developed into a robust legal doctrine that was eventually codified into US federal law in 1976. The fair use statute allows people to quote from or repurpose elements of copyrighted works without asking permission, as long as it is for educational, critical, journalistic, or other transformative purposes. Like the word "copyright," fair use is intuitively named: it applies to any usage that a reasonable jurist would consider *fair*. One of the most influential US Supreme Court cases involving fair use was the *Sony Corp. of America v. Universal City Studios, Inc.* (464 U.S. 417, *reh'g denied*, 465 U.S. 1112 (1984))—better known as the 1984 Betamax case—which legalized the videocassette recorder. In this 5–4 decision, Supreme Court Justice John Paul Stevens makes clear copyright law's constitutional mandate. Its purpose, Justice Stevens argued in the majority opinion, is *not* to provide a special private benefit to an individual or corporation: "The limited grant is a means by which an important public purpose may be achieved. It is intended to motivate the creative activity of authors and inventors by the provision of a special reward, and to allow the public access to the products of their genius after the limited period of exclusive control has expired. The copyright law, like the patent statutes, makes reward to the owner a secondary consideration" (*Sony*, 464 U.S. at 429). This assertion is grounded in the "limited" rights language found in the US Constitution, as well as subsequent case law that developed over the course of two centuries (Aufderheidi and Jaszi 2011; Hilderbrand 2009; Litman 2001; McLeod 2007).

Today, fair use functions as a free-speech safety valve within copyright law, one that has become even more important since the US Congress extended the term of copyright in 1998. The Sonny Bono Copyright Term Extension Act lengthened these protections by twenty years: copyright protection now lasts ninety-five years for corporate authors; for individuals, it lasts their entire lifetime, plus seventy years. In contrast, between 1790 and 1978, the average work passed into the public domain after just thirty-two years. This precedent honored the constitutional mandate that stipulated copyright protections should last for "limited times." Some people sarcastically refer to the Bono Act as the Mickey Mouse Protection Act, and with good reason. Without it, *Steamboat Willie*—the first appearance of the transmedia rodent—would have fallen into the public domain in 2003, and several other valuable classics would have followed. The constitutionality of this extension was challenged, but in 2003, the Supreme Court upheld the right of Congress to determine how long was meant by "limited." As a result of this law, nothing would enter the public domain for another twenty years, not until 2019. This means that the right to copy and transform many decades-old works remained in the hands of individual and corporate copyright owners, who had veto power. This environment makes it difficult, legally, to reshape and react to the popular culture that surrounds us because so much of it is locked up and out of reach (Aufderheidi and Jaszi 2011; Boyle 2010; Coombe 1998; Lessig 2002).

Beyond the controversies that greeted the advent of the photocopier, the videocassette recorder, and other disruptive duplication technologies, we can trace the origins of the contemporary copyright wars to the practice of digital sampling that emerged in the mid-1980s. "Sampling" refers to the act of digitally rerecording pieces of preexisting music and placing those bits in a new song. Artists have always borrowed from each other, but hip-hop musicians took these appropriation practices to their furthest logical conclusions. Sampling can be viewed as an extension of earlier African American musical traditions such as the blues, jazz, and gospel. During the 1970s, hip-hop DJs in the South Bronx reimagined the turntable as a device that could *create* music rather than just *replay* songs. In the 1980s, hip-hop artists reinvented newly emerging digital sampling technologies by making them do things their inventors never imagined. As with the sharing of MP3 music files today, many artists and record companies believed that digital sampling was the equivalent of stealing. By 1991, the music industry began rigorously enforcing copyright law, and the industry developed a cumbersome and expensive "sample clearance" system. All samples, even the shortest and most unrecognizable, now had to be approved and paid for. Since this period, the cost of licensing samples has continued to increase, as have the costs associated with negotiating those licenses. This made it impossible for certain kinds of music to be legally made, especially those collage-heavy records that typified hip-hop's "golden age"—a period that lasted roughly from the mid-1980s to the early 1990s (Demers 2006; McLeod 2007; McLeod and DiCola 2011).

Many artists and critics have argued that the contemporary sample licensing system had a negative impact on the creative potential of hip-hop before it had a chance to flower. These critics argue that the growth of twentieth-century jazz would have been similarly stunted if jazz musicians—who regularly "riffed" on others' songs—had been burdened by the requirement of getting permission from music publishers for even the smallest melodic quotations. It is important to note that the licensing log jam produced by the modern-day "clearance culture" has implications that stretch

far beyond the concerns of the hip-hop world. Music, including sample-based music, is regularly integrated into television shows, movies, video games, and user-generated online content. When one is dealing with songs that sample songs that contain other samples, the stack of licenses one must acquire can grow quite tall. The same is increasingly true of remixed video content. As a cultural practice and a legal lightning rod, sampling has implications that stretch far beyond the domain of musical remixing. The crisis it provoked within copyright regimes was the canary in the intellectual property coal mine. Sampling kick-started a conversation about copyright years before the latter became front-page news after the file-sharing service Napster debuted in 1999. Hip-hop artists in the mid-1980s raised many of the same ethical and economic questions that people are still wrestling with now but on a broader scale. Today, new technologies give most people the *ability* to copy, whether or not they legally have the *right* to copy. Given the complexity of this situation, it is unlikely that these contradictions will be resolved anytime soon (Boon 2010; McLeod and DiCola 2011).

2014

17

Corporation

Christopher Newfield

In current usage, the keyword "corporation" is synonymous with "business corporation," generally referring to a for-profit organization that can operate at the discretion of its owners and managers free of social and legislative control. The term is derived from the Latin *corporatus*, the present participle of *corporare*, which means "form into a body," and appeared in English by 1530. A business corporation can own property; buy, sell, and control assets, including other corporations; pay or avoid taxes; write or break contracts; make and market products; and engage in every kind of economic activity. At the same time, the persons involved in a corporation have under most circumstances no liability for its debts. Since 1900, the corporation has been the dominant form for organizing capital, production, and financial transactions. By 2000, the corporation had become a dominant force in the global economy, the only alternative to the state as an organizer of large-scale production, a rival to national governments, and a powerful presence in the world's cultures. Of the world's hundred largest economies in 2000, forty-seven were nation-states and fifty-three were corporations.

Before the mid-nineteenth century, the corporation was a public franchise—a ferry or turnpike company, for example—that received a profit in exchange for reliable service to the common or public good. After the Civil War, corporations increasingly came to reflect private economic interests. In *Santa Clara County v.*

Southern Pacific Railroad Company (118 U.S. 394 (1886)), the Supreme Court asserted, without supporting argumentation, that the corporation was a legal person and could not have its property regulated in a way not in conformity with the due process provisions of the Fourteenth Amendment, thus allowing corporate independence to be consolidated as the essence of the corporate form. Subsequent decisions furthered this tendency by setting forth a doctrine of limited liability, in which the shareholder was personally insulated from claims for damages or the repayment of debts, and by providing corporations with the right to own stock in other companies (Roy 1997). This legal framework gave the firm's executives significant independence from the firm's owners, a framework that was influentially defined as the separation of ownership and control (Berle and Means 1932). The simultaneous development of concentration of control and immunity from interference transformed the corporation from a public trust into a potential monopoly power with most of the capacities of a parallel government.

Support for the corporation came more frequently from courts and legislators than from public opinion. Even legislation such as the landmark Sherman Antitrust Act (1890) was so vague that its powers were in effect created through enforcement or through later legislation: the Hepburn Act (1906), the Mann-Elkins Act (1910), the Glass-Steagall Act (1933), and the Bank Holding Company Act (1956). Over the same period, the labor movement consistently more successfully challenged three of the corporation's most important impacts on working conditions, laying the groundwork for the derogatory use of the term in the mid- and late twentieth century in phrases such as "corporate drone," "soulless corporation," or the "corporatization of the university," not to mention in *Dilbert* cartoons or on any episode of the television show *The Office*. These conditions were the accelerated absorption of skilled, relatively independent workers into the factory system; Taylorization, which micromanaged production workers in a routinized assembly-line process; and managerialism, whose meaning for labor was unilateral control of pay and working conditions by layers of management separated from and generally set against labor. More than a century of major strikes—such as those at Carnegie's steelworks at Homestead, Pennsylvania (1892), and the Loray Mill in Gastonia, North Carolina (1929), and the Flint sit-down strike (1936), the United Parcel Service strike (1997), the Los Angeles janitors strike (2000), and the Chicago teachers strike (2012)—were among the most visible expressions of popular opposition to the corporation's independence of, or sovereignty over, the wider society.

These struggles against corporate power bore fruit in a decades-long movement for "industrial democracy" that sought to put corporate governance on a constitutionalist and democratic footing. Some observers saw collective bargaining, finally legalized by the Wagner Act (1935), as an industrial civil rights movement that transformed management into a government of laws (Lichtenstein 2002, 32–38). But labor never did achieve meaningful joint sovereignty with management in the context of the large corporation. The Taft-Hartley Act (1947) required all trade-union officials to sign an affidavit that they were not Communists, impugning the collective loyalty of labor leaders (managers were not required to sign), and also forbade cross-firm and cross-industry labor coordination (Lichtenstein 2002, 114–18). Union membership and influence declined precipitously from the 1970s onward, and the idea of industrial democracy had by the end of the century virtually disappeared from public view. Even as the corporation continued to rely on the state for contracts and standards enforcement, banking law, educated workers,

and the like, it consolidated its relative autonomy from employees and the public.

Over this period, the corporation became part of the culture of the United States and other countries, and the resulting corporate culture had four dominant features. First, consumption became central. When the corporation collectivized labor and coordinated the production process on a large scale, it enabled the mass production of consumer goods and encouraged an understanding of consumption as a virtually universal activity and primary means of expressing personal identity and desire. Second, democracy was equated with capitalism. Mass production and consumption, freedom, self-expression, and personal satisfaction came to be seen as interchangeable and as enabled by corporate capitalism; consumption came to eclipse, if not exactly replace, political sovereignty. Third, efficient organization became synonymous with hierarchical bureaucracy. As the twentieth century wore on, it became increasingly difficult to imagine truth, power, or innovation arising from personal effort, insight, and inspiration unharnessed by economic roles or effective cooperation without command from above. Fourth, philosophical, spiritual, cultural, and social definitions of progress were eclipsed by technological ones. The rapid commercialization of technical inventions—radio, radiology, transistors—became the measure of the health of a society, and thus society came to require healthy corporations.

The tremendous cultural power of the corporate form has not spared it turbulence and even decline. Annual economic growth in the United States and Europe slowed markedly in the 1970s, as did rates of increase in profitability and productivity. Business efforts to maintain profit margins led to continuous price increases that in turn increased wage demands and overall inflation. The United States lost its unchallenged economic preeminence as countries such as France, Germany, Italy, and Japan fully recovered from the devastation of World War II and as the newly industrializing countries of Asia became important competitors. Oil-price shocks and the end of the Bretton Woods currency system were only the most visible signs of this changing economic order (Rosenberg 2003). Internal pressures added to external ones. Job satisfaction was low enough to prompt an important study from the Nixon administration's Department of Labor, and "human relations" management theory increased its attacks on Taylorist regimentation (Newfield 1998). These trends contributed to a sense among many observers that the large corporation was part of the problem, that it had become too inflexible, hierarchical, and expensive to lead the way in a new era of "post-Fordist" globalization (Harvey 1989).

In the first decades of the twenty-first century, the corporation has been at the center of several major developments. Following the September 11, 2001, attacks on New York and Washington, DC, some corporations became directly involved in military operations as private contractors (Singer 2003; Dickinson 2011). In various sectors, the privatization of public functions and their revenue streams became a large-scale business opportunity. Information and communications technology reached in new ways into private life, ranging from customized marketing and internet-based data collection via Amazon, Facebook, Google, and similar firms (Andrews 2012) to the collection and delivery to the government of unprecedented and still-unknown quantities of personal data for security and surveillance purposes (Greenwald 2013). Legislation and legal decisions allowed corporations to exert new levels of political management. The most famous case, *Citizens United v. Federal Election Commission* (558 U.S. 310 (2010)), sanctioned new corporate bodies, often organized as nonprofits, to channel unlimited private funds into elections (Briffault 2012). One basis for the majority's opinion was the court's recognition in *Santa Clara* and other cases that "First Amendment protection extends to corporations" (*Citizens*, 558 U.S. at 25). The court affirmed the precedent that "the Government cannot restrict political speech based on the speaker's corporate identity" (*Citizens*, 558 U.S. at 30).

The corporation increasingly separated its own fortunes from those of the middle class whose prosperity had been the core political justification for tax, trade, employment, and innovation policies that favored business interests. The gap between executive pay and ordinary corporate wages had grown relentlessly through the 1980s and 1990s: the increasingly common term used to describe the situation in the following decade was "plutocracy" (Krugman 2002). The beginning of the twenty-first century was a "lost decade" for the wages of the vast majority of US workers. The mainstream media routinely offered evidence that whatever else corporations had been doing for the previous decades, they had not given the majority of the US workforce an inflation-adjusted raise (Mishel et al. 2012; Parlapiano 2011; Schwartz 2013). The sense of majoritarian economic failure was confirmed by the financial crisis of 2007–8 and the contrasting fates of Wall Street, which recovered, and Main Street, which did not. The growing sense that corporations produced inequality rather than prosperity triggered another form of resistance, the Occupy movement's call in 2011 for a society run by and for the 99 percent.

Corporations had always been viewed as both financial assets and organizations for production. Their asset value became more important in the 1980s, as financiers specializing in mergers and acquisitions increasingly treated companies and their divisions as commodities to be bought (at discounts) and sold (at large markups). The most popular way to increase a firm's asset value was to fire workers, and the mass layoff, previously rare and regarded as a sign of gross management failure, became common (Uchitelle 2007). Corporate production became less likely to cut against asset bubbles and crashes as corporate valuations came to reflect those cycles. The popping of the housing bubble in 2008 destroyed trillions of dollars of wealth, with effects felt with particular severity among communities of color and the working classes who had counted on housing wealth to compensate for the absence of real wage gains. The post-2008 decade saw most people's wages go down, which allowed more than 100 percent of overall wage growth to accrue to the top 10 percent of wage earners. Policymakers led by the Federal Reserve Bank decided to stabilize the economy with near-zero interest rates, with the explicit goal of inflating asset prices in housing and securities—and with the wholly predictable effect of taking the United States to another level of economic inequality.

The ordinary meaning of the word "corporation" had diverged from corporate practice. The term still suggests a hierarchical organization focused on the production of goods and services that is generally politically conservative—opposed to social and civil rights and environmental movements and to labor or citizen cogovernance of economic decisions. This image of "corporate America" did not become less accurate than it had been before, and yet it eclipsed the extent to which the corporation functions as an asset to be valued and traded in financial markets (Feher 2018). For example, the politically less conservative tech sector has expanded the use of dual-class stock ownership, in which company founders like Mark Zuckerberg at Facebook command ten votes rather than one vote per share, which allows ultraconcentrated managerial power. Meanwhile, between 2000 and 2010, the number of public companies fell by half (Davis 2016), to be in part replaced by privately held corporations. The market in initial public offerings (IPOs) of company shares looked less and less like an open marketplace and more like a mechanism through which contractually defined inequalities of investor placement create stratified financial outcomes for investors. One analyst argued that the goal of IPOs has been decoupled from production: "Their rationale for going public—to pay off employees and early investors, rather than to raise capital to invest in long-lived assets—suggests that such firms are not sustainable as public companies for the long term, although demand for returns by investors may sustain them for some time" (Davis 2016).

This phenomenon would help explain the judgment of the single most visible work of economics of the 2010s, the French economist Thomas Piketty's *Capitalism in the 21st Century*, which showed that the historical norm of capitalism has been for investment returns to grow more quickly than the economy (and wages) and that the post–World War II suspension of this norm ended several decades ago (Piketty 2014). The combination of long-term wage stagnation and racial scapegoating—which ignored the disproportionately negative effect of economic stagnation on people of color (Bayer and Charles 2016)—was widely credited with the Brexit and Trump elections in 2016. Piketty described the US economic zeitgeist of the later 2010s as sinking "into a hyper-nationalist, anti-immigrant and anti-Islam discourse . . . and a limitless glorification of the fortune amassed by rich white people" (2016). None of this suggests the tightly managed production machine marked by the earlier term "corporate capitalism." A new US corporate tax cut in 2017 and other uncoordinated short-term stimulants imply weakness in the corporate sector rather than strength.

Evidence continues to grow that the everyday meaning of the word "corporation" has not caught up with changes in practice. The practice implies acceptance of long-standing claims that the corporate form is less functional, affordable, and durable than most leaders had assumed (D. Gordon 1996; Ross 1997; Bamberger and Davidson 1999; Piketty 2014). A more accurate usage of the term would reference the corporation's partial conversion into an exotic asset class for wealthy investors and funds. The process of inventing postcorporate economic forms will require deeper public knowledge of corporate operations than prevails in the wealthy countries of the early twenty-first century as well as clearer, more imaginative definitions of democratic economics.

2007/2020

18

Creole
Marlene L. Daut

The word "Creole" is perhaps the most mystifying racial and ethnic descriptor used in the Americas. Not only are the origins and precise meanings of the term unclear, but there are many variations in usage, spelling, and grammar. Should the word be capitalized or not? Is "Creole" a noun describing a certain type of person or an adjective, as in creole flavor, creole culture, creole people, and creole music? If "Creole" does refer to certain groups of people rather than certain kinds of things, does it identify those who have common physical characteristics such as skin color or is it a more ephemeral marker, gathering together people who share particular histories, migratory patterns, and geographies or linguistic, cultural, and ethnic identities? At different historical moments, the word could have been (and may still be) used in any or all of these ways. Indeed, my top three Google search results in the United States for the term at the time of the writing of this essay refer to the people of Louisiana and New Orleans in particular; to various languages called Creole in the regions of the Gulf Coast and the Caribbean; and to a plethora of foods and "Creole restaurants." These usages reflect the ambiguous, ambivalent, and vexing origins of the word itself. Examining the genesis of the term "Creole" as well as its many cultural evolutions reveals both how it was used by colonialists to *racialize* the structure of colonial society in the Americas and how it was transformed by later Caribbean artists and intellectuals who developed an entire theoretical field called *créolité* or creolization.

The Royal Spanish Academy of Arts and Letters maintains that "Creole" derives from the Spanish word *criollo*, which was "invented by Spanish explorers and settlers during the initial stages of the conquest of the West Indies" to name "all locally born persons of non-native origin" (Dominguez 1986, 13–14). The *Oxford English Dictionary* (*OED*) traces the origins of the word to Europe more generally and defines a Creole as the "descendant of white European settlers (esp. Spanish or French) who is born in a colonized country." The *OED*'s first English usage of the term is from 1697: "Criole, as we call all born of European Parents in the West Indies." Émile Littré's *Dictionnaire de la langue française* (1863–72) traces the term from the Italian *creolo* and the Spanish *criollo*, adding that the word may also come from an indigenous Caribbean language.

Subsequent researchers have claimed even more alternatives for the origins of the word, tracing it to the Latin verb *creare*, meaning "to create" (Goudie 2006, 8); calling it a "corruption" of the Spanish "*criadillo* (from the diminutive for 'servant' or 'child')" (J. Ward 2017, 8); and proposing that the word could have a "Koongo origin" in the word "*nukuulolo* meaning 'alien person,' or 'outsider'" (Warner-Lewis 1998, 60n1). The first known recorded usage in print of any of the cognates of the word supports the idea that the enslaved Africans of the Americas may have been the ones to introduce the term to European colonizers. In his early seventeenth-century history of the Incas, Garcilaso de la Vega claims that the Spanish derived it from the enslaved "negroes": "The children of the Spanish who were born in the Indies are called *criollo* or *criolla*; the negroes gave this name to their children who were born in the Indies in order to distinguish them from those who were born in Guinea, their country . . . the Spanish borrowed this name" (1704, 460). Hans Sloane's 1707 *A Voyage to the Islands* supports this claim, noting that *Creolian* is what

Africans called those "born in the Islands" (qtd. in Gibson 1982, 104). In partial contrast, the French dictionary *Larousse* stresses that only a "Caucasian" person of French or Spanish descent born in the Americas could be properly designated *as a creole*, while a person of Negro descent born in the Americas could be described *as creole* (Dominguez 1986, 15).

One of the few consistencies across these usages is that "Creole," as a noun or an adjective, marks difference and otherness from a dominant culture, whether racial, cultural, ethnic, or linguistic. An 1842 novel called *Creoleana*, for instance, professes to describe the "customs, manners, and habits of Creolean society" in Barbados in contrast to those of England (Orderson [1842] 2002, 21). Indeed, the way differences between colonial American and metropolitan European societies were manifested by the term is perhaps best understood by turning to its highly variable use in the literary worlds of the eighteenth and nineteenth centuries. Early nineteenth-century French novelists used "Creole" to describe a wide variety of characters. In one, the term referred to a heroine of mixed race from Saint-Domingue (J. T. 1801); in another, it referenced the mother of a mixed-race character but also "a Frenchman . . . from Santo Domingo, whose skin is rather swarthy" (Beaumont [1835] 1958, 5). Yet another French novel applied this identity marker not to the "mulatto" character, but instead to a "beautiful creole" of "Portuguese descent" (Daminois 1824, 1:6). Still another used the term "Creole slaves" to distinguish between those enslaved Africans born in the French colonies and those born on the content of Africa who were called "Congo slaves" (Hugo [1826] 1890, 55, 133).

US authors are equally inconsistent. In Leonora Sansay's *Secret History, or the Horrors of St. Domingo* ([1808] 2007), it is the white women born in the colony who are unfavorably referred to as creoles (95), yet in *Zelica, the*

Creole (1820), which also takes place in French colonial Saint-Domingue and is sometimes attributed to Sansay, the Creole referred to in the title is a virtuous character of mixed race, capable of passing for white. When Walt Whitman's 1842 temperance novel refers to an enslaved woman as a "creole," it not only marks her near-white racial identity but also implies that her racial status is responsible for her homicidal behavior. As these examples make clear, such wildly different applications of the word "Creole" to refer to various kinds of people in the eighteenth and nineteenth centuries were hardly neutral descriptors of identity.

Although colonial Louisianans of all skin colors, as well as many white people from the early modern and nineteenth-century Caribbean, used the term "Creole" to refer to themselves unselfconsciously, the appellation was often directed in a defamatory sense. Marcus Rainsford, who penned one of the first full-length histories of the Haitian Revolution in English, characterizes "Creoles or descendants of Europeans settled in America" as lazy and inept people who lived in the "vilest sloth" (1805, 73). This kind of characterization led some self-defined Creoles in the Americas to attempt to defend themselves against stereotypes associated with the term. The Jamaican woman of color Mary Seacole, who identified herself as a Creole, directly rebutted the kinds of charges made by writers like Rainsford: "I have often heard the term 'lazy Creole' applied to my country people; but I am sure I do not know what it is to be indolent" (2005, 11). The famous naturalist M. L. E. Moreau-de-Saint-Méry, a self-professed white Creole from Martinique, also contested negative narratives about Europeans born in the colonies in his two-volume proslavery defense of French colonialism (Fabella 2010). Despite such defenses, painting "creole attitudes" as dangerous became a mainstay in the United States, sparking not only a "Creole/American opposition" that

lasted into the 1840s (Dominguez 1986, 110–21) but the argument made by the celebrated US novelist George Washington Cable that "Southern Americans," in general, and "white" Louisianans, in particular, needed to undergo a process of "resaxonizing" in order to eliminate the "laxity of morals" associated with French and Spanish influence (Hornung 1998, 244, 231).

These various and seemingly random appearances of "Creole" across historical and literary texts demonstrate that it has nearly infinite flexibility and wide geographical variations. Contrary to Benedict Anderson's influential claim that all nations in the Americas were "creole states . . . formed and led by people who shared a common language and common descent with those against whom they fought" (1983, 49), the term "Creole" is best understood in local and immediate contexts. Enslaved people of African descent who were referred to as creoles in French-claimed Saint-Domingue, for instance, fought during the Haitian Revolution against the white population of European descent, also called creoles. That is to say that the meaning of the term "Creole" does not track consistently with geography, language, colonial legacy, or time period.

The one exception to this sort of variability may be contemporary Haiti, where the term almost universally refers to the primary language of the Haitian people rather than to Haitian people themselves (DeGraff 2016). Some of the earliest recorded usages of the term similarly referred to language. In 1688, M. J. de la Courbe's *Premier voyage . . . fait à la coste d'Afrique en 1685* defined the "langue créole" or "creole language" as that "jargon" "spoken by the negroes and mulattoes" of Senegal "who call themselves Portuguese because they are the descendants of some of the Portuguese who lived there in other times" (192). In the introduction to an 1811 published book of Creole songs published in Philadelphia, signed by a person who claimed to be "an inhabitant of Hayti," "the creole language" is defined as a "corrupted, bastardized French," which was "sort of jargon generally spoken by the Negroes, the Creoles, and the majority of the Colonists in our islands of America" (Habitant d'Hayti 1811, 57). In contrast, René de Chateaubriand claimed in *Memoir d'Outre-Tomb* (1848) that it was "the language of the great writers of England" that had become "creolized, provincialized, barbarized" (1:149). Still others have promoted Creole as a national language of its own (Valdman 2005; Glissant 1989). As early as 1818, the Haitian writer Juste Chanlatte used a version of the word to refer to the language of the newly independent Haitian state when a character in one of his plays chides another for singing a song in French rather than in "criole" (6).

Despite these efforts, one of the factors that prevented Haitian Creole from being recognized as a separate and distinct language from French is that for centuries it was primarily an oral rather than a written language. This meant that although Haitians won their independence from France in 1804, for more than 150 years, French remained the sole official language of the country. In order to combat the devalorization of Creole that caused a linguistic diglossia, whereby one language was considered *high* and the other *low*, a state-sponsored literacy campaign took place in mid-twentieth-century Haiti to create a standard orthography for the Haitian language that would be independent of the French spelling system (Laroche 2001, 85). The system in use today has achieved this *Americanization* (in the broadest sense of the word) by eliminating the letters *c* and *q* and replacing them with the letters *s* and *k* (Valdman 1984). This is why "Créole" in contemporary Haiti is now spelled as "Kreyòl." And in 1961, Haitian Creole/Kreyòl joined French as an official language of the Republic of Haiti, no doubt facilitating the publication of the first novel written in Kreyòl, Franketienne's *Dezafi* (1975), as well as the first history of the Haitian Revolution to be published in Kreyòl, Michel-Rolph Trouillot's *Ti Dife Boule sou istwa Ayiti* (1977). The use of Kreyòl as an emblem of national power was made even more apparent when President Jean Bertrand Aristide insisted upon using it to criticize foreign leaders at the UN General Assembly in 1992 ("Diskou Aristide"). The fifth commandment of Aristide's now-famous ten commandments speech contained the line "What belongs to us is ours. Ours is not yours" (Aristide 2001, 311). Aristide's insistence on using the language of the Haitian people in this particular context underscores the politics of speaking Creole/Kreyòl and its potential role in "unsettling" imperialist and colonial forms of domination instantiated in the Caribbean by colonizing empires (Bonilla 2017, 330).

The social and political dynamics involved in recognizing Creole as the first language of all people in Haiti, as well as in the French departments of the Caribbean, is precisely what led to the development of creolization/creoleness/*créolité* as a prominent site of theorization in cultural studies. Some postcolonial theorists have claimed that creolization (the "the cultural confrontation" of indigenous Americans, Africans, and Europeans in the New World) produced societies and languages unique to the French Caribbean and, as a result, that Caribbean writers should publish solely in Creole languages (Bernabé et al. 1990, 93). The Guadeloupean novelist Maryse Condé has contested this claim in her well-known essay, "Créolité without the creole language?" (1998). Condé prefers to understand Creole languages as relics of the historically violent exigencies of communication that brought them into being on the plantation and less as a way to promote contemporary decolonial movements (2013). The Jamaican writer Edward Kamau Brathwaite, while also recognizing that the violence of colonialization produced the Creole languages and societies of the Anglophone West Indies, has argued that the resulting transculturation has been "creative" for Caribbean intellectuals and artists (1971, 307), making creolization what we might call a "productive paradox" (Garraway 2005, 1). Édouard Glissant, for his part, has made a much more radical claim about the possibilities opened up by the term. He has argued that the cultural heterogeneity that creolization names—whether in language, ethnicity, religion, or race—represents an outright contradiction of the existence of all forms of national homogeneity and a rejection of the notion of purity in origins that constitutes white supremacy (1989).

In the end, it may be that the various usages of the word "Creole" are best understood in the context of unavoidable heterogeneity and endless diversity that Glissant describes. Our continued attempts to use the word "Creole" to create metaphors for decolonization struggles or postcolonial nationalisms reflect the conflicts, clashes, and convergences that shaped the term's emergence out of colonialism to begin with. Because of its messy history as both a concept and a word, "Creole" and all its linguistic and theoretical cognates will likely remain as hard to define as the peoples and languages to which it refers.

2020

19

Culture

George Yúdice

The concept of culture has had widespread use since the late eighteenth century, when it was synonymous with civilization and still indicated a sense of cultivation and growth derived from its Latin root, *colere*, which also included in its original meanings "inhabit" (as in "colonize"), "protect," and "honor with worship" (as in "cult"). According to Raymond Williams ([1976] 1983, 87–93), the noun form took, by extension, three inflections that encompass most of its modern uses: intellectual, spiritual, and aesthetic development; the way of life of a people, group, or humanity in general; and the works and practices of intellectual and artistic activity (music, literature, painting, theater, and film, among many others). Although Williams considers the last to be the most prevalent usage, the extension of anthropology to urban life and the rise of identity politics in the 1980s (two changes that have left a mark on both cultural studies and American studies) have given greater force to the communal definition, particularly since this notion of culture serves as a warrant for legitimizing identity-based group claims and for differentiating among groups, societies, and nations. More recently, the centrality of culture as the spawning ground of creativity, which in turn is the major resource in the so-called new economy, has opened up a relatively unprecedented understanding of culture in which all three usages are harnessed to utility.

The meaning of "culture" varies within and across disciplines, thus making it difficult to narrate a neat linear history. Nevertheless, one can discern a major dichotomy between a universalist notion of development and progress and a pluralistic or relativistic understanding of diverse and incommensurate cultures that resist change from outside and cannot be ranked according to one set of criteria. Beginning in the late eighteenth century, universalist formulations understood culture as a disinterested end in itself (Kant [1790] 1952) and aesthetic judgment as the foundation for all freedom (Schiller [1794] 1982). Anglo-American versions of this universalism later linked it to specific cultural canons: Matthew Arnold ([1869] 1994, 6) referred to culture as "the best which has been thought and said in the world" and posed it as an antidote to "anarchy"; T. S. Eliot (1949, 106) legitimated Europe's claim to be "the highest culture that the world has ever known." Such assertions, which justified US and European imperialism, are newly disputed in postcolonial studies (Said 1993), but they were already rejected early on by defenders of cultural pluralism and relativism, such as Johann Gottfried von Herder ([1766] 2002), who argued that each particular culture has its own value that cannot be measured according to criteria derived from another culture. This critique of the culture-civilization equation had its ideological correlate, first formulated by Karl Marx and Frederick Engels ([1845–46] 1972), in the premise that culture is the superstructure that emanates from the social relations involved in economic production; hence, it is simply a translation of the ruling class's domination into the realm of ideas.

The view of culture—and the civilizing process—as a form of control is consistent with the turn in cultural studies and cultural policy toward a focus on the ways in which institutions discipline populations. In the post-Enlightenment, when sovereignty is posited in the people, the institutions of civil society deploy culture as a means of internalizing control, not in an obviously coercive manner but by constituting citizens as well-tempered, manageable subjects who collaborate in the collective exercise of power (T. Miller 1993; Bennett 1995). The universal address of cultural institutions, ranging from museums to literary canons, tends either to obliterate difference or to stereotype it through racist and imperialist appropriation and scientism, sexist exclusion and mystification, and class-based narratives of progress. Populations that "fail" to meet standards of taste or conduct, or that "reject culture" because it is defined against their own values, are subject to constitutive exclusion within these canons and institutions (Bourdieu 1987). Challenges to these exclusions generate a politics of representational proportionality such that culture becomes the space of incremental incorporation whereby diverse social groups struggle to establish their intellectual, cultural, and moral influence over each other. Rather than privilege the role of the economic in determining social relations, this process of hegemony, first described by Antonio Gramsci (1971, 247), pays attention to the "multiplicity of fronts" on which struggle must take place. The Gramscian turn in cultural studies (American and otherwise) is evident in Raymond Williams's ([1977] 1997, 108–9) incorporation of hegemony into his focus on the "whole way of life": "[Hegemony] is in the strongest sense a 'culture,' but a culture which has also to be seen as the lived dominance and subordination of particular classes."

But hegemony is not synonymous with domination. It also names the realm in which subcultures and subaltern groups wield their politics in the registers of style and culture (Hebdige 1979). Indeed, in societies such as the United States, where needs are often interpreted in relation to identity factors and cultural difference, culture becomes a significant ground for extending a right to groups that have otherwise been excluded on those terms. The very notion of cultural citizenship implies recognition of cultural difference as a basis for making claims. This view has even been incorporated in epistemology to capture the premise that groups with different cultural horizons have different and hence legitimate bases for construing knowledge; they develop different "standpoint epistemologies" (Haraway 1991; Delgado Bernal 1998). The problem is that bureaucracies often establish the terms by which cultural difference is recognized and rewarded. In response, some subcultures (and their spokespersons) reject bureaucratic forms of recognition and identification, not permitting their identities and practices to become functional in the process of "governmentality," the term Michel Foucault (1982, 221) uses to capture "the way in which the conduct of individuals or groups might be directed." On this view, strategies and policies for inclusion are an exercise of power through which, in the US post–civil rights era, institutional administrators recognize women, "people of color," and gays and lesbians as "others" according to a multiculturalist paradigm, a form of recognition that often empowers those administrators to act as "brokers" of otherness (Cruikshank 1994).

These contemporary struggles over cultural citizenship and recognition can be traced to earlier battles over the attributes according to which anthropologists and sociologists in the 1950s and '60s cataloged certain non-European and minority populations as "cultures of poverty." This diagnostic label, first formulated by Oscar Lewis in 1959, references the presumed characterological traits—passivity, apathy, and impulsivity—that in underdeveloped societies impede social and economic mobility. We see at work here the narrative of progress and civilization that had been the frame within which anthropology emerged more than a hundred years earlier. Many anthropologists' methods had been comparative in a nonrelativistic sense, as they assumed that all societies passed through a single evolutionary process

from the most primitive to the most advanced. Culture, which has been variously defined as the structured set or pattern of behaviors, beliefs, traditions, symbols, and practices (Tylor 1871; Boas 1911; Benedict 1934; Mead 1937; Kroeber and Kluckhohn 1952) by means of which humans "communicate, perpetuate and develop their knowledge about and attitudes toward life" (Geertz [1966] 1983, 89), was the ground on which anthropologists, even into the 1920s, sought to track the origins of all societies as well as their progress toward (European and/or Anglo-American) modernity.

In partial contrast, the relativist or pluralist cultural anthropology that arose in the 1920s and is often associated with Franz Boas (1928) began to critique the scientific racism that underwrote many of these accounts, to question the premise that any such accounting could be objective, and to argue that there were neither superior nor inferior cultures. Nevertheless, Boas and his US and Latin American followers (Kroeber 1917; Freyre [1933] 1956; Benedict 1934; Mead 1937; F. Ortiz 1946) believed that culture could be studied objectively, as a science, so long as description and analysis were not hamstrung by the anthropologist's cultural horizon. Many of the US studies were explicitly designed, in Margaret Mead's words, to "giv[e] Americans a sense of their particular strengths as a people and of the part they may play in the world" ([1942] 1965, xlii).

By the end of the 1950s (coincident with the rise of cultural studies in Britain and American studies in the United States), the Boasian legacy and other salient anthropological tendencies such as British structural-functionalism and US evolutionism waned, and other trends rose in influence: symbolic anthropology (culture as social communication and action by means of symbols; Geertz [1966] 1983), cultural ecology (culture as a means of adaptation to environment and maintenance of social systems; M. Harris 1977), and structuralism (culture as a universal grammar arranged in binary oppositions that rendered intelligible the form of a society; Lévi-Strauss 1963). These largely systemic analyses then gave way in the 1980s to a focus on practice, action, and agency as the main categories of anthropological explanation and also to a self-reflexivity that put the very enterprise of cultural analysis in question. Self-reflexive or postmodern anthropology criticized the writing practices of ethnographers for obscuring the power relations that subtend the ethnographic encounter, the status of the knowledge that is derived from that encounter, the relationship of ethnography to other genres (Marcus and Fischer 1986; Clifford and Marcus 1986), and even the analytical and political usefulness of the concept of culture itself (Abu-Lughod 1991; Gupta and Ferguson 1992; R. Fox 1995). Related developments in postcolonial studies focused on transnational hybridity in contradistinction to national cultural homogeneity. With the introduction of television and other electronic media, mass migrations from former colonies to metropolitan centers, and modern transportation and communications technologies, cultures could no longer be imagined as circumscribed by national boundaries. Metaphors such as "montage" and "pastiche" replaced the "melting pot" in accounts of Brazilian culture (Schwarz [1970] 1992; Santiago [1971] 1973), echoing "Néstor García Canclini's description of popular culture as the product of 'complex hybrid processes using as signs of identification elements originating from diverse classes and nations'" (Dunn 2001, 97, quoting García Canclini 1995; Appadurai 1996). More recently, García Canclini (2004) has added access to new information and communication technologies as another dimension to consider when weighing the effects that globalization has on culture-based understandings of difference and equality.

For many US scholars, this troubling of culture as a category of analysis opened up a critique of the ways in which culture expanded in the late twentieth century to serve as an almost knee-jerk descriptor of nearly any identity group. While this expansion responds to the political desire to incorporate "cultures of difference" within (or against) the mainstream, it often ends up weakening culture's critical value. Especially frustrating for critics working in these fields is the co-optation of local culture and difference by a relativism that becomes indifferent to difference and by a cultural capitalism that feeds off and makes a profit from difference (Eagleton 2000). If a key premise of modernity is that tradition is eroded by the constant changes introduced by industrialization, new divisions of labor, and concomitant effects such as migration and consumer capitalism, then recent theories of disorganized capitalism entertain the possibility that the "system" itself gains by the erosion of such traditions, for it can capitalize on the changes through commodity consumption, cultural tourism, and increasing attention to heritage. In this case, both the changes and the attempts to recuperate tradition feed the political-economic and cultural system; nonnormative behavior, rather than threatening the system in a counter- or subcultural mode, actually enhances it.

Critical responses to corporate and bureaucratic modes of multicultural recognition are useful, but they often lack a grounded account of how the expedient use of culture as resource emerged. Culture has increasingly been wielded as a resource for enhancing participation in this era of waning political involvement, conflicts over citizenship (I. Young 2000), and the rise of what Jeremy Rifkin (2000, 251) has called "cultural capitalism." The immaterialization that is characteristic of many new sources of economic growth (intellectual property rights as defined by the General Agreement on

Tariffs and Trade and the World Trade Organization) and the increasing share of world trade captured by symbolic goods (movies, television programs, music, tourism) have given the cultural sphere greater importance than at any other moment in the history of modernity. Culture may have simply become a pretext for sociopolitical amelioration and economic growth. But even if that were the case, the proliferation of such arguments—in forums provided by local culture-and-development projects as well as by the United Nations Educational Scientific and Cultural Organization (UNESCO), the World Bank, and the so-called globalized civil society of international foundations and nongovernmental organizations (NGOs)—has produced a transformation in what we understand by the notion of culture and what we do in its name (Yúdice 2003). Applying the logic that a creative environment begets innovation, urban culture has been touted as the foundation for the so-called new economy based on "content provision," which is supposed to be the engine of accumulation (Castells 2000). This premise is quite widespread, with the US and British hype about the "creative economy" echoing in similar initiatives throughout the world (Caves 2000; Landry 2000; Venturelli 2001; Florida 2002).

As should be clear, current understandings and practices of culture are complex, located at the intersection of economic and social justice agendas. Considered as a keyword, "culture" is undergoing a transformation that "already is challenging many of our most basic assumptions about what constitutes human society" (Rifkin 2000, 10–11). In the first half of the twentieth century, Theodor Adorno ([1970] 1984, 25) could define art as the process through which the individual gains freedom by externalizing himself, in contrast to the philistine, "who craves art for what he can get out of it." Today, it is nearly impossible to find public statements that do not recruit art and culture either to better social conditions through the creation of multicultural tolerance and civic participation or to spur economic growth through urban cultural development projects and the concomitant proliferation of museums for cultural tourism, epitomized by the increasing number of Guggenheim franchises. At the same time, this blurring of distinctions between cultural, economic, and social programs has created a conservative backlash. Political scientists such as Samuel Huntington have argued (once again) that cultural factors account for the prosperity or backwardness, transparency or corruption, entrepreneurship or bureaucratic inertia of "world cultures" such as Asia, Latin America, and Africa (Huntington 1996; Harrison and Huntington 2000), while the Rand Corporation's policy paper *Gifts of the Muse: Reframing the Debate about the Benefits of the Arts* has resurrected the understanding of culture as referring to the "intrinsic benefits" of pleasure and captivation, which are "central in . . . generating all benefits deriving from the arts" (McCarthy et al. 2005, 12).

This complexity is heightened by other considerations deriving from the effects of artificial intelligence (AI) and big data; they have already been part of the transformation of how we produce, receive, and interact with traditional culture industries such as music, film/video, books, and the news. And, of course, the transmission of beliefs, customs, and behaviors constitute a major idea of culture. How we understand culture when we speak to/with "intelligent" virtual assistants like Alexa in the environment of the Internet of Things/Everything or when our music and other tastes are "curated" by algorithms, which also involve and ratchet up the notion of a society of control, especially because biases make their way into these technologies (Angwin et al. 2016), is no longer a matter of science fiction. How do we practice the critical study of culture in this new AI-driven era of "disorganized" capitalism (Yúdice 2018)?

The challenge today for both cultural studies and American studies is to think through this complexity, especially as the notion of cultural citizenship has hit (or built) a wall with the rise of Trumpism in the United States, Brexit in the United Kingdom, and the populist Right in many European countries. This rightward and "anticultural" turn has sparked progressive opposition, but it is not clear whether existing political parties or cultural strategies can take that opposition in an effective direction. In an earlier moment, one could base rights claims on cultural difference; from the perspective of the populist Right, that cultural difference is the basis for restricting rights. And crucial institutions like the Supreme Court are being stacked with justices who will likely strike down more than a half century of precedents consecrating the usefulness of the principle of cultural difference. Yet it may be too soon to make a definitive statement about action and agency oriented toward progressive politics and the role that culture plays in it.

2007/2020

20

Data
Lauren Klein and Miriam Posner

In 1858, a group of ministers associated with the African Methodist Episcopal (AME) Church launched a new journal, the *Repository of Religion and Literature and of Science and Art*. There were already numerous newspapers and magazines aimed at the growing Black reading public, but these ministers—who, Frances Smith Foster tells us, "were also teachers, community activists, and entrepreneurs"—identified an as-yet-unmet need: "To develop the talents of our young people, and to furnish data for future comparison" (2005, 730).

This usage of the term "data," from over 150 years ago, might strike contemporary readers as unusually prescient. And in some ways it was: "data" appears here to mean something like "an empirical observation," which the *Repository*'s editors recognized as a potential tool for achieving justice. This commitment to wielding data on behalf of marginalized people anticipated arguments made by contemporary data justice groups, such as San Francisco's Anti-Eviction Mapping Project or the Boston-based organization Data for Black Lives. The *Repository*'s editorial committee recognized that the act of data collection can do more than document lived experience, capture scientific observations, or represent social relations. When directed by the communities that the data seek to represent, data can provide a powerful means of expressing individual and collective agency as well as shaping future conversations and debates.

Of course, the data of the *Repository* did not take digital form, nor did the *Repository*'s editors describe their work in terms of "data collection" per se. While they seemed to understand that the "data" of the *Repository* could function as a representation of its various constituencies, the popularization of the term "data" itself would not occur until the rise of digital computing in the 1960s and 1970s. Nevertheless, the editorial committee's understanding of the journal's contents as data helps distill the term's multiple layers of meaning in the present. "Data" does not simply denote numerical information, as one might initially assume. Rather, the term "data" indicates any form of information—itself a loaded term—that is intended to be put to use. The *Repository*'s editors were drawing upon this connotation of the term when they described the "future comparison[s]" that their "data" of Black cultural life would enable.

This use of the term further implies that data is information intended to be deployed in a particular way: in support of an argument. This meaning, too, predates digital instantiations of the term. When the word "data" was introduced into English (in 1646, according to the *Oxford English Dictionary*), it was intended to supplement existing terms such as "evidence" and "fact." Unlike those other terms, as Daniel Rosenberg explains, "the semantic function of data" was—and remains— "*specifically* rhetorical" (2013, 18). Then as now, people made recourse to "data" when they sought to establish certain information as the ground truth—the stable basis on which arguments could then be made.

This association of "data" with argument derives from the term's earliest English usages in the domains of theology and math. In those contexts, Rosenberg explains, "'data' was used to refer either to [mathematical] principles accepted as a basis of argument or to facts gleaned from scripture that were unavailable to questioning" (2013, 33). Over the course of the eighteenth century, as more modern ideas about what constituted scientific evidence began to take hold, the term evolved to describe

information or evidence gleaned *from* experiments rather than the facts or principles that provided the rationale for those experiments in the first place. But the residual connections to a priori knowledge soon became a feature of the term. In other words, data might be the result of an experiment or observation, but their factual status was—or, at least, seemed to be—no less open to debate.

Here it is worth making explicit that the word "data" is plural. It derives from the Latin word *datum*, or "given." But *datum* refers only to a single data point. It may, as David Marsh has opined, sound "old-fashioned and pompous" to treat "data" as a plural noun—no one says "agendum," he observes (qtd. in Rogers 2010). But the plural treatment of the term does emphasize a data set's heterogeneity (Loukissas 2019). The term's Latin derivation also underlies its rhetorical force: the term "data" may derive from a word meaning "given," but the concept of data is more accurately understood as *capta*—something not "given" but actively and intentionally "taken" to be true (Drucker 2011). This distinction—between something actively taken to be true and something simply accepted—is presumably among the major reasons that data collection projects, including the *Repository*, seek to compile their own data about a topic. By understanding how data is necessarily constructed by people and yet accepted by those same people (and others) as fact, such projects recognize a powerful mechanism, simultaneously rhetorical and concrete, through which to communicate their truths to the broader public. As data practitioners know, all data is constructed by humans, and yet its veneer of neutrality makes it tremendously compelling.

Indeed, in today's popular press, data is often called "the new oil"—a phrase meant to convey the potential of data to be converted into power and, in many cases, profit once it has been processed and refined (Garcia Martinez 2019). But unlike oil, which exists in a raw state inside the earth, there is no such thing as "raw data," even though that phrase is used by data analysts both inside and outside the university. In each of those settings, the phrase is intended to describe data that has not yet been standardized or otherwise prepared for analysis. But the trouble is that all data must be created by people before it can be analyzed or displayed. Information theorist Geoffrey Bowker puts it most memorably: "'Raw data' is an oxymoron" (2005, 184). Or in the words of Lisa Gitelman and Virginia Jackson, "Data are always already 'cooked' and never entirely 'raw'" (2013, 2).

Of course, people are not only responsible for creating data; they are also responsible for imagining what and who can constitute data in the first place. The indelible example of Atlantic world slavery, in which human lives were reduced to numbers and names, endures as evidence of the violence that comes with transforming people into data. "There is no bloodless data in slavery's archive," historian Jessica Marie Johnson observes. "The idea of data as fundamental and objective information . . . obscures rather than reveals the scene of the crime" (2018, 70). More recently, the concept of "Black data" has emerged as a response to "the historical and contemporary ways black queer people, like other people of African descent and people of color more broadly, are hailed by big data," as performance studies scholar Shaka McGlotten puts it, appearing as "commodities, revenue streams, statistical deviations, or vectors of risk" (2016, 262).

Other work by the Colored Conventions Project and members of its project team has called attention to how Black Americans in the nineteenth century were already aware of the vexed relation of data and blackness and attempted to intervene in their own time. The meeting minutes of the 1843 National Colored Convention included "statistical and qualitative reports that could reframe readers' understanding of Black communities' progress in America" (S. Patterson 2015). This tradition

of wielding data in support of Black welfare, especially in the social sciences, would be continued throughout the nineteenth and twentieth centuries and into the present. The quantitative work undertaken by Black sociologist, leader, and activist W. E. B Du Bois around the turn of the twentieth century can be understood as an example of socially oriented data visualization (Battle-Baptiste and Russert 2018). Invoking this history, Yeshimabeit Milner and the team associated with Data for Black Lives has sought to explore new ways to "use data science to create concrete and measurable change in the lives of Black people" (2018b).

At the same time, the present moment is rife with examples of the destructive potential of reducing lived experience to data devoid of context or absent from critique. We know that racism is encoded into Google's search algorithms (Noble 2018), just as other algorithms determine everything from which neighborhoods to police (O'Neill 2016) to which children to place into foster care (Eubanks 2018), amplifying the effects of already discriminatory systems. Meanwhile, the National Security Administration (NSA) uses data about our identities to track and classify us (Cheney-Lippold 2017). The entire edifice of computation, as Ruha Benjamin argues, has resulted in the "New Jim Code," for which we need a new set of abolitionist tools—both technical and critical—that can counter the negative impact of systems that employ data without first interrogating their sources or considering their effects (2019).

As we observe the increasingly pervasive effects of these algorithms on ours and others' everyday lives, we find ourselves struggling with even the most basic questions of what data are. Commentators often speak of data as though they share a common understanding of the term, but locating the essential criteria of data is enormously challenging. What are data to the literary scholar? To the meteorologist? To the historian? To the medical student? Are there features these data share? One response is to argue that there is no inherent property that distinguishes data as such or that connects certain forms of data to others. Rather, observations, information, or experience become data only at the moment that they are used as such (Borgman 2015). Perhaps, as Willard McCarty has argued, all data are in some way computationally "tractable," meaning that they are stored and structured in a way that it is amenable to classification, reordering, and manipulation (2005). Or perhaps data are above all "local," indissociable from the specific time, place, and people that created them (Loukissas 2019). Another inflection of the term, drawn from media studies, emphasizes data's ability to travel, communicating information across widely disparate locations and populations (Posner and Klein 2017).

These far-ranging articulations of the term help explain the appeal of the concept of "data" in the twenty-first century; at a time when we are besieged with digital information from every corner, the idea of data promises to provide order across time and space. We know from scholars of slavery and of marginalized communities that data's purported universality or neutrality is a mirage; every act of categorization annihilates other possibilities. We also know, from scholars of these same communities, that data has a world-building potential—that all forms of data collection and data visualization carry with them an ethics, either implicit or explicit. This ethics can be transformative, as proponents of the movement for data justice have claimed (Costanza-Chock 2020). Just as data can be used to erase or subordinate marginalized people, they can also be wielded by those same people as a tool to write themselves back into the historical record and to imagine alternate futures.

2020

21

Debt
Andrew Ross

In everyday speech, "debt" describes an economic relationship and typically applies to the money or assets owed to creditors by individuals, households, governments, and nation-states. But it has long been used metaphorically to refer to noneconomic moral obligations as well. A good deed done on someone's behalf is often said to be owed a similar response, in repayment of a debt. Incarceration and other forms of punishment for wrongful acts are similarly cast as the method by which the accused pay their "debt to society."

In most cultures, the moral injunction behind this expectation of reciprocity is so strong that its violation is akin to a taboo; in German, the word for debt is *schuld*, the same as that used for "guilt." For bankers and other lenders, payback morality is a primary deterrent against default, more powerful than the prospect of a ruined credit score. At the same time, many cultures regard moneylending itself as immoral and synonymous with the word "usury," excessive profiteering, or the taking of something for nothing. Christian scripture explains marital relations as involving duties owed by spouses to each other, which Augustine, in *De Bono Coniugali*, described as a condition of "mutual servitude." Accordingly, the Middle English phrase "debt of the body" evokes the responsibility to provide conjugal sex, though the long-enduring marital exemption from rape laws illustrates just how one-sided this mutual understanding was in practice and how forced taking without consent or any expectation of reciprocity was sanctioned under the legal system of gender subordination known as "coverture." As these examples illustrate, formations of social inequality have determined the use of debt to reinforce and magnify power relations, while variations in the enforcement of repayment through threats and discipline have meant that indebtedness, at almost all times, has been a component of subjecthood.

The imposition of debt on persons who cannot pay it back has long been tied to the curtailment of legal freedoms. In precapitalist societies, and especially in classical antiquity, nonchattel bondage for indebtedness was common. Those unable to settle their obligations were forced to place themselves or their children into bonded labor as a form of debt payment. Such pledges might also be made as surety or collateral for a new loan. Conversely, freedom was (and continues to be) manifested by liberation from debt obligations. In ancient Near Eastern societies, this practice was observed in a year known as the Jubilee, on a regular sabbatical basis (every forty-nine or fifty years, as outlined in the book of Leviticus), or when a new ruler came to power; debts were forgiven, debt slaves were freed, and land appropriated for debt settlement was returned to its original owners (Hudson 2018; Graeber 2011). The Bible provides a powerful transhistorical message of forgiveness for Christians—"Forgive us our debts, as we forgive our debtors" (Matthew 6:12 New King James Version)—from the Greek *opheilēmata* for "things that are owed." Some denominational versions (Catholic, Methodist, Episcopalian) of the Lord's Prayer use "trespasses" instead of "debts" (stemming from a choice made by William Tyndale, the first translator of the Bible into English), while ecumenical versions tend to prefer "sins." Both of these substitutions suggest a nonfinancial interpretation of the Greek original and reflect the complex, and often contradictory, character of Christian morality surrounding debt. More forthrightly, the Qur'an encourages the avoidance of debt and advocates for forgiveness if the debtor is in hardship, while, in general, Islamic societies proscribe usury (*riba*) in the form of interest-bearing loans.

Debt has almost always been used to deepen labor exploitation. For example, the Spanish term *peon*, referring to the forced labor of indigenous populations under the *conquistadores*, was used more exclusively in the United States to describe indebted workers compelled to labor for their creditors. Debt peonage was often lifelong, whereas in colonial regimes, bonded labor under a contract of indenture was generally for a fixed term. Indentured laborers did not surrender all their rights, unlike under the more systematic conditions of chattel slavery and serfdom. Although debt bondage was abolished in most societies and is outlawed by United Nations conventions on slavery, its institutions survive formally today in South Asia and sub-Saharan Africa and in the recruitment and transit debt incurred by migrant workers all over the world. Less formal versions are legion in the historical record: under the Black Codes of the US South, which led to the widespread practices of convict leasing and sharecropping; or in the North in the form of company scrip (where workers are paid in credit at the company store); or in loan sharking today. Debt has never lost its association with servitude, which survives in the more neutral phrase "debt service." So too the connection with a voluntary bond has been revived in the usage of some commentators today who refer to student loans as a form of indenture, since they involve a contractual pledge of repayment through future labor (Williams 2008).

In capitalist economies, economic debts can either be beneficial or injurious. For those with social standing, "good debt" comes in the form of credit that ensures returns to the debtor through advantageous investments, whether through property, enterprise, or financial speculation. By contrast, for those who rely on loans for subsistence, debt service is a more onerous obligation, and default is met with legal discipline: fines, forfeiture of assets, imprisonment, and in colonial societies, penal transportation and contracted labor migration (the "coolie trade"). A creditor is said to be holding "bad debt" if the borrower is in default—the loans in question are "nonperforming." Given the high risk of default with impunity on the part of royal rulers, the creditor class generally favored the transition from monarchic to mercantile societies. The growth of democratic state bureaucracies ensured that citizen taxes, rather than royal treasuries, could be used for the service of what would become known as sovereign—or (in the US) federal—debt. Representative governments of nation-states proved to be more reliable clients—that is, more efficient debt collectors. Even so, nation-states have regularly defaulted on their sovereign debts—more than 250 times since 1800, according to one estimate (Reinhardt and Rogoff 2009).

In the last half century, the inability of many postcolonial countries to repay external loans, either to Global North banks or to the International Monetary Fund, has often been summarized by the phrase "debt trap." The suggestion that their independent development paths were being intentionally arrested through the neocolonial recapture of their economies reinforced the association of debt with manipulation and forced constraints. Many of these countries sought relief from oppressive debt burdens through default or cancellation under the banner of the Jubilee South movement (Millet and Toussaint 2004, 2010; Jones 2013). In line with internationally recognized legal norms, external loans contracted by despotic rulers were sometimes treated as illegitimate—"odious debts" is the term of choice—and thus unenforceable by their more democratic successors. In the wake of the 2008 financial crash, the "debt trap" has migrated to northern countries, breaking its semantic association with the Global South. Peripheral states in the European Union such as Greece have been forced to prioritize the rights of foreign creditors over the needs of their citizenry, passing on the cost of debt service in the form of austerity policies.

Historically, taxpayers have often been unwilling to foot the bill for such public debts. In keeping with the antifeudal sentiment of their revolutionary rhetoric, founders of the US fulminated against what Jefferson called "the English career of debt, corruption, and rottenness" as the root of Old World tyranny. Indeed, he considered it a natural right to be freed of the debts of a previous generation, arguing that "the modern theory of the perpetuation of debt has drenched the earth with blood and crushed its inhabitants under burdens ever accumulating" (Jefferson 1905, 221). Yet the new republic's first order of business was to figure out how to make whole the creditors who funded the costs of the Revolutionary War. Efforts were made, in some states, to pass on these debts in the form of taxes on the yeoman farmers who had fought the war. This provoked the nation's first armed uprising in Shays's Rebellion in central and western Massachusetts (and echoed a few years later in the Whiskey Rebellion in eastern Pennsylvania), where state-appointed judges were imprisoning those who could not pay. The insurgents closed courts, liberated debtors from prisons, and vowed, in Shays's words, to "march directly to Boston, plunder it, and . . . destroy the nest of devils, who by their influence make the Court enact what they please, burn it and lay the town of Boston in ashes" (qtd. in Szatmary 1980, 100).

The specter of Shays's insurrectionary farmer-debtors was one of the reasons the framers hastened to adopt a constitution that limited democracy and enshrined property protection as the overriding function of government. In response to the perceived weakness of indebted states to collect from their citizenry, Article 6 established the more powerful federal responsibility to assume "debts contracted" from the war. In the course of the nineteenth century, the US ideal of civic republicanism, rooted in appeals to (debt-free) fee-simple land ownership, was further undercut by the experience of farmers' mass indebtedness to Wall Street banks, insolvency in the face of exorbitant and unpayable demands, and imprisonment at the dictate of creditors. The lopsided creditor-debtor relationship, reinforced by bankruptcy laws that still overwhelmingly favor lenders, illustrates the gulf between belief in the republican birthright of political freedom and the grisly substance of American capitalist reality, redolent of Jefferson's "perpetuation of debt" in the Old World.

Beginning in the 1920s, a concerted effort to jumpstart a consumer economy assailed the credo of Protestant thrift that preached against household debt as a vice. The introduction of the "installment loan" for consumer goods dissolved the distinction between "productive" and "consumptive" debt, but US bankers were generally reluctant to make noncommercial loans, especially for home buyers. As part of the recovery effort from the Depression, the US government made bankers an offer they could not refuse—in the form of federally backed security for homeowner loans (Hyman 2012). The subsequent introduction of the long-term amortized "mortgage" (literally, a death pledge) revolutionized consumer economics and breathed new life into the ideology of the American dream. The FHA (Federal Housing Administration) loans cemented the association of homeownership with republican liberty and proved key to middle-class stability for a select population of white, native-born employees in primary manufacturing and service sectors. However, since debt also functions as a form of social control, the long-term

payment schedule acted as a restraint on the social and political conduct of the mortgage holder. As William Levitt, the postwar kingpin of mass suburban housing, put it, "No man who owns a house and lot can be a Communist" (Hayden 2006, 276).

Redlining (the denial of credit to people based on their neighborhood, race, and marital status), deed restrictions, and racial covenants often meant that only white male borrowers qualified for government-backed mortgages; minorities and single women had to pay much more for homeownership and for all kinds of credit. Well into the 1970s, installment credit was still the retail norm in minority-dominated urban areas, where storeowners kept customers' debt ledgers, and studies showed that low-income urbanites were being charged more in their neighborhood stores for the same goods sold to middle-class consumers in suburban department stores (Caplowitz 1967). Accordingly, much of the anger incited by the urban uprisings of the 1960s was directed against retail outlets owned by white outsiders. To this day, inner-city neighborhoods host a disproportionate number of unbanked residents—as much as 12 percent of the US population—who cannot afford, or do not qualify for, accounts at accredited banks and are forced to use alternative or "fringe" lenders whose storefront outlets abound in low-income areas. "Predatory debt" is the colorful term often used by critics to describe loans targeted at the working poor that carry astronomical rates of interest: check cashing, rent-to-own finance, auto title lending, refund anticipation loans, pawnshops, prepaid credit cards, and payday loans (Rivlin 2010). Low-income and minority households were also targeted by subprime lenders in the frenzy of housing speculation that precipitated the financial crash in 2008 when African Americans lost half their overall household wealth as a result of the collapse in housing values.

Legislation passed in the wake of the 1960s urban uprisings broadened credit access and banned discrimination on the basis of race, gender, religion, national origin, and age. The Community Reinvestment Act (1977) legislated the principle that banks should return (or reinvest) monies extracted from their (previously redlined) service areas in the form of loans. The civil rights movement also sought to open the doors of higher education to Native Americans, African Americans, and Latinx excluded from the GI Bill of Rights (Servicemen's Readjustment Act of 1944), the program that gave free college access to more than eight million predominantly white war veterans and, along with its low-cost mortgage component, a promise of middle-class security to their families. After the 1965 Higher Education Act introduced federal loans for low-income students, eligibility was gradually expanded under pressure from the banks, and in 1978, the program was opened to all students regardless of income. In this way, the right to education morphed into the right to access education loans in much the same way that the right to housing was replaced by expanding the right to access mortgages.

Starting in the 1990s, the word "debt" was increasingly associated with student loans. Taxpayer revolts began to take a heavy toll on state budgets, slicing deeply into support for public colleges. In some states, the cuts were politically motivated. As early as the 1960s, California's governor Ronald Reagan had pushed for a fiscally-based clampdown on student activism, arguing that "the state should not subsidize intellectual curiosity." His ideas came to fruition over the coming decades with measures such as Proposition 13, which capped property taxes and thus constrained state spending on higher education. By mid-2018, aggregate student debt had passed the $1.5 trillion mark, with debt on graduation averaging $40,000, and more than a million debtors were defaulting annually. As with other debt classes, minority households shoulder the largest burden, and enrollees at for-profit colleges—the most unscrupulous exploiters of federal loan programs—account for the largest share per capita (Samuels 2013). Uniquely, student debt cannot be discharged through bankruptcy, and the now widespread requirement for parents or grandparents to cosign loan contracts has led to a marked generational shift in the household debt burden, leaving more and more retirees on the hook. The threat posed by lifelong student debt service to sustained consumer spending has prompted bipartisan support for reforms. In left-wing quarters, calls for the reinstatement of tuition-free public college have emerged alongside single-payer health care as the primary rallying cry of a generation whose relationship to indebtedness (generation debt) has become paradigmatic (Kamenetz 2006; Quart 2018). "You Are Not a Loan," the slogan of the Occupy Student Debt campaign, Strike Debt, and the Debt Collective (grassroots activist groups formed to combat education debt through collective action), captures the spirit of resistance to a financialized society where individuals are isolated and prepped as income streams. In addition to inspiring political action, the existential condition of debt—"indebted man"—has attracted philosophical attention (Lazzarato 2012).

In the wake of the 2008 financial crash, debt became a byword for risk and ruin, but efforts on the part of economic and political elites to restore its standing proved successful. By the end of 2017, aggregate household debt had climbed to $13.15 trillion, surpassing pre-2008 heights, and student loans, despite their disrepute as a generational ball and chain, increased their share of overall debt, from 5 percent to 10 percent. Globally, gross debt—combining public and private liabilities—reached $247 trillion in 2018, or 318 percent of the world's gross domestic product (GDP). No longer a symptom of uneven development, the daily obligation of nations, businesses, and private households to service a high volume of loans is now central to capitalist profit taking. Lifelong financial extraction—with debt at the center—has become the new model for twenty-first-century capital accumulation, with the so-called golden years of debt-free retirement a thing of the past.

This near universal condition of indebtedness has given rise to the kind of creditocracy where almost everybody is up to their neck in debt that can never be repaid (Ross 2014). Creditors don't want these debts to be paid off entirely—for the same reason that credit card issuers don't want credit card balances to be paid every month. The ideal citizens in a creditocracy are "revolvers" who cannot make ends meet and who pay the minimum along with interest and other finance fees and penalties, rolling over their credit from month to month. In this type of polity, every social good can be turned into a transactional commodity. A creditocracy emerges when the cost of access to each of these goods, no matter how staple, has to be debt financed and when indebtedness becomes the precondition not just for material improvements in the quality of life but for the basic requirements of life. Financiers seek to wrap debt around every possible asset and income stream, placing a tollbooth on every revenue source, ensuring a flow of interest from each. The primary source of accumulation for the wealthiest 1 percent now comes in the form of economic rents—from debt leveraging, capital gains, speculation through derivatives, and other forms of financial engineering. Today's advanced financialization is a far cry from the vision of the "euthanasia of the rentier" (whose income derives from property or investments), which was Keynes's remedy for the dysfunctional capitalist system in 1936 (Piketty 2014).

Managing the lifelong burden of debt service is now an existential condition for the majority, but what about its political impact? How can a democracy survive when it cannot check the power of a creditor class? The right of creditors to be made whole now routinely overrides the responsibility of elected representatives to carry out the popular will, resulting in "failed democracies" all over the world. In response, advocates have pushed for "citizen debt audits" to distinguish between "legitimate debts," which ought to be repaid, and "illegitimate debts" taken on by corrupt officials, which should be refused. Wherever governments cannot protect the citizenry from economic harms inflicted by rent extractors, the refusal to pay is cited as a defensible act of civil disobedience (Strike Debt 2014). Related calls for "debt jubilee" or "debt abolition" stem from a social justice tradition that defines debt quite differently from the spirit of religious charity through which debt "forgiveness" is offered as an act of moral benevolence. Another approach promotes the need for a new kind of nonextractive economy (Albert 2003; Alperovitz 2011; Wolff 2012). Pursuing that alternative path—to a cooperative economy guided by the socially productive use of credit—is increasingly touted as the only way of salvaging democracy from the ruinous impact of debt, increasingly conceived as a rapacious, systemic threat to the survival of basic freedoms and rights. In this kind of postcapitalist world, the keyword "debt" would be understood as a form of *mutual aid*, exemplified by community skill sharing, in contrast to the current usage of the term to signal a hierarchy of financial obligations, heavily wrapped in moral packaging.

2020

22

Digital

Tara McPherson

In the twenty-first century, we tend to associate the word "digital" with computation, but its origins hark back to ancient times. The term derives from *digitus* in classical Latin, meaning "finger," and later from *digit*, which refers both to whole numbers less than ten and to fingers or toes. Digital procedures long predate the development of electronic computers, and we might understand a number of earlier devices or systems to operate by digital principles. For instance, the abacus is a simple digital calculator dating from 300 BCE, while Morse code and Braille represent more recent digital practices. What each of these examples has in common—from fingers to digital computers—is a particular use of the digital to refer to discrete elements or to separate numbers. This focus on the discrete and the separate is central to the functioning of today's digital electronics, which, at a basic level, operate by distinguishing between two values, zero and one.

While the digital predates computation, today the two terms are closely linked, and the adjective "digital" is typically a shorthand for the binary systems that underpin computation. Thus we are living through a "digital revolution," are at risk of an increasing "digital divide," and are plugged into "digital devices" that play "digital audio" and store our "digital photographs." Some of us practice the "digital humanities," a term that replaced the "computational humanities" as part of a rebranding that both broadened the field's appeal and erased various complex debates about the role of computers within humanities disciplines (Martha Smith 2007). The slippage between the digital and computation seems so complete that it is easy to assume that the two terms are synonymous.

Computers have not always been digital. In the early decades of modern computation from the 1940s through the 1960s (and as we moved from mechanical to electrical machines), scientists were developing both analog and digital computers. Analog computers derived from earlier devices such as the slide rule. While the abacus used discrete beads to represent individual digits, the slide rule displayed a continuous scale. On an analog clock, time sweeps smoothly around a circular face; a digital clock represents time via discrete numbers, not as a continuous flow. Electronic analog computers functioned by analogy; that is to say, they built models of the problem to be solved and usually worked with continuous values rather than with the discrete binary states of digital computation. They converted the relationships between a problem's variables into analogous relationships between electrical qualities (such as current and voltage). They were often used (and still are) to simulate dynamic processes such as air flight and to model the physical world. Digital computers work differently. They process digital data as discrete units called bits, the zeroes and ones of binary code. A transistor in a digital computer has two states, on or off; a capacitor in an analog computer represents a continuous variable. The digital privileges the discrete and the modular; the analog represents continuity. As humans, we perceive the world analogically, as a series of continuous gradations of color, sound, and tastes.

Historians of computation typically narrate the transition from analog to digital computing as a story of efficiency and progress. Such evolutionary accounts suggest that digital machines win out because they are more precise, have greater storage capacities, and are better general-purpose machines. These teleological schemes can make it hard to understand the many cultural, economic, and historical forces that are in play during periods of technological change. Much recent scholarship has attended to the specificity of the digital, defining its key features (Wardrip-Fruin and Monfort 2003). Lev Manovich observes in his important *The Language of New Media* (2001) that digital media can be described mathematically, are modular, and are programmable—that is, are subject to algorithmic manipulation. He proposes that media and cultural studies should turn to computer science to understand the digital. General histories of computers and much of new media theory tend toward evolutionary or formalist explanations for the emergence of the digital as the dominant computational paradigm, but we might also understand the shift as cultural and historical along a number of registers.

Instead of posing the question "What is the digital?" American studies and cultural studies might instead ask, "How did the digital emerge as a dominant paradigm within contemporary culture?" Why, if we experience the world analogically, did we privilege machines that represent the world through very different methods? Scholars have begun to answer this question by highlighting how the move from analog to digital computing promoted notions of "universal" disembodied information while also concealing the computer's own operations from view (Chun 2011; Fuller 2008; Galloway 2004, 2014; Hayles 2012; Lanier 2010). The ascendancy of digital computation exists in tight feedback loops with the rise of new forms of political organization post–World War II—including neoliberalism, a mode of economic organization that encourages strong private property rights, expansive free markets, and corporate deregulation—as well as with the rise of modern genetics (Halpern 2015; Chun 2011).

During this period, early developments in digital computing were also intertwined with shifting racial codes. The introduction of digital computer operating systems at midcentury installed an extreme logic of modularity and seriality that "black-boxed" knowledge in a manner quite similar to emerging logics of racial visibility and racism, the covert modes of racial formation described by sociologists Michael Omi and Howard Winant ([1986] 1994). An operating system such as UNIX (an OS crucial to the development of digital computers) works by removing context and decreasing complexity; it privileges the modular and the discrete. Early computers from 1940 to 1960 had complex, interdependent designs that were premodular. But the development of digital computers and software depended on the modularity of UNIX and languages such as C and C++. We can see at work here the basic contours of an approach to the world that separates object from subject, cause from effect, context from code. We move from measuring to counting and from infinite variation to discrete digit. We move from the slide rule, which allowed the user to see problem, process, and answer all at once, to the digital calculator, which separated input from output, problem from answer. There is something particular *to the very forms* of the digital that encourages just such a separation (McPherson 2018).

We may live in a digital age, and the privileged among us might feel closely connected to our digital devices, but the sensations we feel as we touch our keyboards and screens are analog feelings, rich in continuous input and gradations of the sensory. We must remember that the digital is embedded in an analog world even as it increasingly shapes what is possible within that world. "Digital" emerges from and references particular histories, and these histories have consequences. By examining how these histories came to be, we will better understand and, perhaps, shape our present.

2014/2020

23

Diversity

Jodi Melamed

What is the best way to manage unlike human capacities in the name of human progress and improvement? This deceptively simple question has preoccupied Western political modernity, especially in the United States. The positive connotations often adhering to the keyword "diversity"—a term commonly used to reference human differences broadly considered—arise from its importance in high-status discourses that have sought to discern the best management of human differences, including eighteenth-century liberal political philosophy, nineteenth- and twentieth-century natural science (especially the so-called race sciences), and twentieth- and twenty-first-century law and education policy. In contrast, research in American studies and cultural studies has come to look on the endeavor of managing human differences in a suspicious light (Ferguson 2012b). It recognizes that ideologies of progress and development from Manifest Destiny to multiculturalism have consistently—and sometimes in surprising ways—divided people into good (desirable) and bad (undesirable) forms of human diversity, creating hierarchies that evaluate groups as more or less civilized, capable, advanced, or valuable according to a shifting catalog of criteria (Horsman 1981; Cacho 2012; Melamed 2011). This research suggests that these attempts to divide humanity are symptomatic of a fundamental contradiction between political democracy, which defines citizens as equal and working cooperatively for collective well-being, and capitalism,

in which individuals of unequal material means and social advantages compete with one another for profit (Lowe 1996).

Viewed in this light, discourses of diversity are a form of crisis management; they portray the inequality that capitalism requires as the result of differing human capacities, inaccurately representing groups dispossessed by and for capital accumulation as being in need of the improvements of civilization, education, or freedom. The result is that "diversity" has come to be seen as an ambiguous term that endows its referent—human differences—with only an indistinct and opaque legibility, making it easier to displace the causes of capitalism's structural unevenness onto naturalized fictions of human differences. Karl Marx's example of the nursery tale told by bourgeois political economists to explain the origin of capitalist wealth speaks to this cultural process ([1867] 1976). The tale involves two kinds of people who lived long ago: diligent, frugal elites who conserved the fruits of their labor so their progeny could become capitalists, and lazy, spendthrift masses who burned through their substance in riotous living so their heirs (wage laborers) have nothing to sell but themselves. This fable about the origins of human diversity (versions of which are still told every day) substitutes for the real acts of force that have expanded capital flows, including conquest, enslavement, land grabbing, and accumulation through dispossession (Harvey 2003). Diversity operates here as a ruse that naturalizes social inequality by inverting cause and effect.

The intertwined usage histories of the keywords "diversity" and "race" are central to this ruse. They appear together first across two disparate yet interrelated domains that influenced the organization of US modernity in the eighteenth and nineteenth centuries: liberal political philosophy and the race sciences. Both of these discourses were concerned with discerning and cultivating human differences, though to very different ends. Liberal political philosophers ranging from Jean-Jacques Rousseau ([1762] 1968) to John Stuart Mill ([1859] 1869) advocated the free play of the "good" diversity of European talents, interests, and beliefs as the means and end of a free society. In contrast, the race sciences of the period were concerned with controlling "bad" diversity, conceived as the biological inferiority of nonwhite races, through sterilization, termination, incarceration, and exclusion. Harry Laughlin, for example, America's leading eugenicist in the first half of the twentieth century, argued in the context of debates over the passage of the Johnson-Reed Act in 1924 that "progress cannot be built on mongrel melting-pots, but it is based on organized diversity of relatively pure racial types" (Laughlin and Trevor 1939, 18). The naturalization of race in relation to the category of diversity is what made credible these otherwise contradictory frameworks for understanding human difference. Concepts of diversity and race worked together to define "the white race" as so superior to others that freedom and self-cultivation were only beneficial and available to its members, thus assuaging conflicts between philosophical commitments to individual liberty and the realities of economic systems dependent on the coercions of slavery, poverty, and industrialization.

During and after World War II, white supremacy and biological concepts of race were discredited by an accumulation of sociopolitical forces including worldwide rejection of German National Socialist (Nazi) racism and antisemitism, anticolonial and antiracist struggles, and global labor migrations from the rural South to the metropolitan North (Winant 2001). As a result, the usages of the terms "diversity" and "race" became even more complexly related. The geopolitical context shaping their new meanings and relationship was the rise of the United States to the position of Cold War superpower and leading force for the expansion of transnational capitalism. In order to accomplish these postwar leadership goals, the United States began to sanction and promote a specific kind of liberal antiracism. The intent of this form of antiracism was to modernize and extend freedoms once reserved for white/European Americans to all US inhabitants regardless of race. These liberal freedoms became the meaning and goal of antiracism: possessive individualism, the right to self-cultivation, abstract legal equality, and access to the field of economic competition. Yet strengthening political democracy by ending white monopolies on liberal freedoms could not serve as an antidote for the structurally uneven relationships developed within global capitalism. The problem was and is that the conceptual framework for liberal antiracism overlapped with the knowledge architecture of global capitalism through the promotion of individualism and economic competition as foundational for racial equality and capitalist development.

As conflicts between democratic ideology and capitalist economy continued to emerge under new conditions, questions of how to best manage unlike human capacities in the name of progress, reform, and improvement continued to provide cover for the next phases of global capitalism. The ruse of racialization lives on: forms of humanity are valued and devalued in ways that fit the needs of reigning political-economic orders. Conventional understandings of race as skin color or phenotype no longer dominate the process. Instead, criteria of class, culture, religion, and citizenship status assume the role that race has played historically, positioning individuals who benefit from differential power arrangements as "fit" for success (good diversity) and those who are structurally exploited or excluded by power arrangements as "unfit" (bad diversity). As "racial difference" gets redefined as "cultural," the language of diversity takes on the burden previously borne by race. Though race never vanished as a means of managing difference, the emphasis on culture creates a situation that is both flexible and productive, allowing new categories of difference and diversity to evolve in relation to the crises perpetrated by global capital.

Beginning in the 1970s, law and educational policy became the dominant domains for these discussions of how to manage human differences in the name of progress and reform, with affirmative action law being most prominent. Beginning with Supreme Court Justice William Powell's watershed decision, *Regents of the University of California v. Bakke* (438 U.S. 265 (1978)), affirmative action discourse has conditioned the meaning of diversity and, in the process, redefined how the state can recognize and act on racial inequality. In his decision, Justice Powell deployed the keyword "diversity" no fewer than thirty times. His point was to invalidate all but one of the reasons offered by the University of California–Davis School of Medicine for reserving a few admission slots for students identified as "economically and/or educationally disadvantaged" or members of "minority groups" (*Regents*, 438 U.S. at 274). He found it unconstitutional to use race in admissions to counter discrimination, to break up white monopolies on medical training, or to increase the well-being of communities of color (by training more physicians of color). The only admissible ground for taking race into consideration was "obtaining the educational benefits that flow from a diverse student body" (*Regents*, 438 U.S. at 306). By ruling that "educational diversity" is protected under the free speech clause of the First Amendment, Powell negated material social change as a racial justice goal, replacing it with consideration for higher education's mission to provide all students with opportunities for self-cultivation through exposure to diversity. The decision rests on the capacity of diversity to abstract and generalize human differences in a way that forestalls more precise and relational analysis. It positions "racial justice" as anathema to "genuine diversity," defined only vaguely as "a far broader array of qualifications and characteristics" (*Regents*, 438 U.S. at 315).

Twenty-five years later, the next wave of Supreme Court affirmative action cases (*Grutter v. Bollinger*, 539 U.S. 306 (2003), and *Gratz v. Bollinger*, 539 U.S. 244 (2003)) were decided in a context where universities, corporations, and government agencies had all adapted to this definition of diversity by hiring an array of diversity managers, diversity consultants, and diversity directors, most of whom were assigned the task of finding the most efficient and profitable way to manage human differences of race, ethnicity, gender, culture, and national origin. Sandra Day O'Connor makes this logic apparent in her findings for *Grutter v. Bollinger*: "Diversity [in education] promotes learning outcomes and better prepares students for an increasingly diverse workforce," since "major American businesses have made clear that the skills needed in today's increasingly global marketplace can only be developed through exposure to widely diverse peoples, cultures, ideas, and viewpoints" (*Grutter*, 539 U.S. at 330). O'Connor's reasoning reflects a new common sense developed within multinational corporate capitalism. Bestsellers such as *The Diversity Toolkit: How You Can Build and Benefit from a Diverse Workforce* (Sonnenschein 1999) and *Managing Diversity: People Skills for a Multicultural Workplace* (Carr-Ruffino 1996) promised to teach corporate managers, in the words of the World Bank's Human Resources website, "to value [human] differences and use them as strategic business assets" (Office of Diversity and Inclusion 2013). One might argue that more is at stake than hiring multiracial; female; and lesbian, gay, bisexual, transgender, and queer/questioning (LGBTQ) employees to rainbow-wash corporate agendas. Corporate diversity's deeper violence is to claim all differences (material, cultural, communal, and epistemological) for capital management—that is, to recognize no difference that makes a difference, no knowledges, values, social forms, or associations that defer or displace capitalist globalization.

In the first decades of the twenty-first century, diversity's referent tends to slip back and forth, indexing with equal frequency both human differences in general *and* idealized attributes of the global economy. This slippage corresponds to the rise of neoliberal ideology and its mantra that competitive markets are the best way to manage unlike human capacities and other resources in the name of growth and improvement. Within the vocabulary of neoliberalism, diversity affirms the goodness of values such as "freedom" and "openness" and helps these values penetrate previously anti- or noncapitalist domains of social life, including education, religion, family, nonprofit organizations, and social services. As early as 1962, Milton Friedman argued in *Capitalism and Freedom* that truly free and prosperous societies arise only beside an unregulated market, which has "the great advantage" that it "permits wide diversity" ([1962] 2002, 15). This argument has become mainstream, in part as a result of the work done by the term "diversity" in portraying access to all the world's goods and services as the key to entry into a postracist world of freedom and opportunity.

Are there alternatives to this yoking of discussions of human difference to the goal of capital accumulation? One countervocabulary that emerges alongside the rise of diversity as a form of corporate management involves an alternative keyword: "difference." In contrast to "diversity," the roots of the term "difference" are found in the Afro-Asian solidarity movements of the 1950s and 1960s and the social movement activism of the 1970s. These movements sought to evade the contradictions

of the Cold War by arguing that the different experiences of postcolonial societies—differences grounded in the history of having undergone and defeated white supremacist colonization, in cultural epistemologies unlike those of the West, and in indigenous and non-Christian religious practices—meant that they should not have to fit into either capitalist or communist frameworks, with their shared values of productivity and geopolitical dominance (R. Wright [1956] 1995; Von Eschen 1997). The term thus valorized nonnormative and marginalized social subjects as agents of change, insisting that cultures and communities forged by people calling themselves Black, Brown, American Indian, Asian, militant, radical, lesbian, feminist, and queer were too valuable to be lost to assimilationist versions of "global diversity." "Difference" pointed toward economic justice, based on an understanding of the racialized, gendered, and sexualized nature of political economy, such as that developed in women of color feminism (Moraga and Anzaldúa 1981; Hong 2006; I. Young 1990).

Since the 1970s, American studies and cultural studies scholarship has been caught up in the conflict encapsulated by this struggle between discourses of diversity and difference. The stakes of the struggle are large. Whereas discourses of diversity suggest that group-differentiated vulnerability to premature death is a problem *for* democratic capitalist society and resolvable within its political-economic structures, discourses of difference insist that the globalization of capitalism and its compatibility with only weak forms of political democracy *is* the problem. "Diversity" consequently appears in American studies and cultural studies scholarship with both positive and negative connotations. Sometimes, as in the groundbreaking *Heath Anthology of American Literature*, the term "diversity" appears in a positive light, signifying the belief that a politics of multicultural recognition can dramatically increase racial democracy in the United States (Lauter 1994). At other times, the category of diversity is itself the problem. Often, this skepticism about the term is accompanied by commitments to support social movement knowledges, ranging from women of color feminism to diasporic queer activism, whose critical interventions demand a reckoning with material relations of enduring structural inequality propped up by liberal-democratic and multicultural norms. The result is that much scholarly effort has gone into preventing critical knowledge interventions—such as intersectional analysis, subaltern studies, Indigenous studies, and queer of color analysis—from being subsumed within the generalizing rhetoric of diversity.

As market rationality saturates the usage of "diversity" within universities today, this scholarship draws on the genealogy of difference to point to the limits of diversity discourse as a means of advancing democratizing projects. In sharp contrast to the vague manner in which diversity discourse presents human differences, it cultivates new ways of thinking about the structural, historical, and material relations that determine who can relate to whom and under what conditions (Hong 2006; Manalansan 2003; Nguyen 2012; Reddy 2011). Innovating new comparative analytics, such scholarship replaces "diversity" with terms such as "partition," "transit," "affinities," "assemblage," and "intimacies" to expose and imagine otherwise the connections and relations that sustain capital accumulation at the cost of generalized well-being (R. Gilmore 2012; Byrd 2011; Puar 2007; Lowe 2006; Hong and Ferguson 2011; Chuh 2003).

2014

24

Economy
Timothy Mitchell

The term "economy" in its contemporary sense came into use only quite recently. It is often assumed that the idea of the economy, defined as the relations of material production and exchange in a given territory and understood as an object of expert knowledge and government administration, was introduced by political economists such as William Petty, François Quesnay, and Adam Smith in the seventeenth and eighteenth centuries, or even by Aristotle. In fact, however, this use of the term developed only in the 1930s and 1940s and was well established only by the 1950s (T. Mitchell 2005).

In earlier periods, "economy" (usually with no definite article) referred to a way of acting and to the forms of knowledge required for effective action. It was the term for the proper husbanding of material resources or the proper management of a lord's estate or a sovereign's realm. "Political economy" came to mean the knowledge and practice required for governing the state and managing its population and resources (Tribe 1978; Poovey 1998). Michel Foucault (1991) connects the development of this expertise to the wider range of practices known as "government" in an older sense of that term, referring not to the official institutions of rule but to a variety of forms of knowledge and technique concerned with governing personal conduct, managing the health and livelihoods of a population, and controlling the circulation of material and political resources.

What is the difference between the older meaning of "economy," understood as a way of exercising power and accumulating knowledge, and the contemporary idea of "the economy," understood as an object of power and knowledge? Foucault (1991, 92) does not address this question but simply relates the two meanings by suggesting that "the very essence of government—that is the art of exercising power in the form of economy—is to have as its main object that which we are today accustomed to call 'the economy.'" This conflation has led several scholars to argue that the economy emerged as a distinct object in the late eighteenth or early nineteenth century. Others read Karl Polanyi's ([1944] 2001) argument that in the same period, market relations were "disembedded" from society as another version of this idea. Polanyi, however, is describing the emergence not of the economy but of society, formed as an object of political discourse in response to the increasingly unrestrained relations of what he calls "market economy."

The emergence of the economy in the mid-twentieth century differs from the era of nineteenth-century governmentality in at least three important senses. First, economists and government agencies defined the economy in a way that enabled them to claim new powers to measure it, manage it, and make it grow. They defined it not in terms of human labor, the management of resources, or the accumulation of national wealth but as the circulation of money. The economy is the sum of all those transactions in which money changes hands, and its size and growth are calculated by estimating this sum. Second, the idea of the economy belongs to the post-imperial era of nation-states, in which human sociality is understood as a series of equivalent national units. Each of these units claims the right to its own national state, replacing the earlier system of European colonial empires, and each is thought to be composed of a series of distinct sociotechnical spaces: a society, an economy, and a culture (T. Mitchell 2002). Third, the emergence of the idea that state, society, economy, and culture exist

as separate spheres, which collectively fill the space of the nation-state, coincided with the twentieth-century development of the social and cultural sciences as distinct professional and academic fields. Political science, sociology, economics, and anthropology (and the study of national literatures and histories in the case of Western societies) each contributed to the making of its respective object, providing it with concepts, calculations, agents, and methods of evaluation. Portrayed as merely an object of knowledge, the economy, along with these other spheres, was in fact enmeshed in the new forms of academic expertise and professional knowledge.

Acknowledging the role of economics and other professional expertise in making the economy does not mean that the economy is just a "representation" or merely a "social construction." Making the economy involved a wide range of sociotechnical projects that embedded people and things in new machineries of calculation, new techniques of accounting, and new impulsions of discipline and desire. The development of marketing and brand identity, the management of the flow of money by corporate and national banks, New Deal programs such as electrification and the building of dams, and colonial development schemes and the postwar projects of development agencies and the World Bank all contributed to the organization of worlds that could now be described and measured as the economy.

Firmly established by the 1950s, the modern idea of the economy was soon subject to criticism. Researchers pointed out that its measurement does not take proper account of unpaid labor, especially the work of maintaining and reproducing households, which is performed largely by women. It cannot measure illegal, unreported, or unregistered economic activity, such as the global arms trade or the informal, small-scale farming, manufacturing, and commerce that play a large role in many countries. It treats the natural world only as resources to be consumed and cannot express the cost of the exhaustion of nonrenewable resources, the destruction of species, or irreversible changes in the global climate.

These criticisms were made by writers and researchers mostly operating outside the academic discipline of economics. But even economists began to acknowledge the increasing difficulty of accurately measuring or describing the economy. The growth in the production of film and music, tourism and information, telecommunications and the internet, legal and consulting services, health care, and other forms of expertise and culture created economies whose products seem increasingly ethereal. Even in the case of consumer goods such as food, clothing, cars, and electronics, the creation of value through brand identity and through the shaping of fashion and taste has made the economic world seem less material and more difficult to measure or predict.

These changes in the economy have sometimes been described in American studies, as in cultural studies more broadly, as marking the transition to a postmodern stage of capitalism (Jameson 1991; Lowe and Lloyd 1997). Such accounts homogenize the changes and attribute them to the force of an underlying logic of the development of capital. They also invoke an earlier era, modernity, in which representations were more firmly anchored to material realities. The genealogy of the concept of the economy cautions against this view. There was never an era in which a simple, material reality could be captured and represented as the economy. The possibility of representing the economy as the object of economic knowledge rested on the proliferation of sociotechnical processes of representation. It was the spread of new forms of representational practice that made it possible to attempt the social-scientific representation of that world. The economy, the new object

of economics, was constructed out of not only numerical quantifications but an entire process of branding, product development, information production, and image making that formed both the possibility of the modern economy and the increasing impossibility of its representation.

The contemporary idea of the economy has also been affected by the rise of neoliberal economics, which has turned attention away from the economy and back toward the seemingly simpler idea of the "market." The trouble is that markets, like economies, must be made. They are produced not by the natural working of self-interest but by the complex organization of desire, agency, price, ownership, and dispossession. Economics (especially in a wider sense of the term, encompassing fields such as accounting and management) helps produce these arrangements by providing instruments of calculation and other necessary equipment (Callon 1998) just as it helped produce the economy. However, while the idea of the economy refers to a specific territory, usually the nation-state, the market has no particular spatial connotation. It can refer to the trading floor of a futures exchange or a transnational network. Unlike the economy, therefore, it does not invoke the role of the state as the power that governs economic space and defines its task as the management and growth of the economy and the nurturing and regulation of economic actors. The regulation of markets and the forming and governing of market agencies are dispersed at numerous levels.

The idea of the economy survives today as much as a political concept as an object of economic theory. A sign taped to the wall in the Democratic Party campaign headquarters for the 1992 US presidential election proclaimed, "It's the economy, stupid!" Placed there, it is said, as a reminder of where the campaign should keep its focus, it reminds us today of the work that is done to make the existence of the economy appear obvious and its truths uncontestable. President Trump's tweeted boast, a quarter century later, that he had helped engineer "the greatest economy in the HISTORY of America" (@realDonaldTrump, June 4, 2018) could be criticized for its poor understanding of economic history. But its effectiveness lies in having us continue to measure collective well-being, social justice, and the planetary future in terms of so narrow and uncontroversial an object.

While the field of cultural studies, American and otherwise, has paid much attention to other organizing concepts, such as nation, class, gender, society, and of course culture itself, it has often left the idea of the economy untouched. There have been a number of interesting studies of different "representations" of the economy. These usually assume, however, that the economy itself remains as a kind of underlying material reality, somehow independent of the intellectual equipment and machinery of representation with which it is set up and managed. In the same way, academic economics is often criticized for misrepresenting the "true nature" of the economy. The task now is to account for the great success of economics and related forms of expertise in helping make the economy in the first place.

2007/2020

25

Engagement
Erica Kohl-Arenas and George J. Sanchez

In everyday usage, the keyword "engagement" means several different things. To be engaged can mean that you have agreed to get married, or that you are in an armed battle, or that you are participating in a political process, or simply that you have arranged to do something or go somewhere. Students and scholars in American studies and cultural studies most often encounter this term within the diverse institutions that circulate under another keyword: "university." Those institutions often use "engagement" to reference efforts to partner with the "communities" they claim to serve. Like other large institutions that form these types of partnerships (hospitals, financial institutions, major employers), universities often link the two terms by using the phrase "community engagement" to name the practice of building relationships for the purposes of research, teaching, outreach, or development.

This more specific use of the term is common but seldom consistently defined, since it has multiple genealogies. One can be traced directly to discussions of publicly engaged scholarship in higher education. Referencing activities ranging from outreach efforts to engage regional stakeholders in large-scale university development projects to undergraduate service-learning classes, from collaborative action research to student organizing efforts, community engagement means different things to different people. One of the most common uses of the term, alternately called "service learning" or "civic engagement," describes projects that aim to get students involved in work with an off-campus "community"—often a local nonprofit organization or specific marginalized group of people who are believed to benefit from student volunteerism and service. In this usage of the term, the goal is for a community to be helped or even "empowered" by the experience of working with students and faculty while students gain knowledge about public issues in the world firsthand, a heightened sense of civic responsibility, and new collaborative skills through learning by doing (Dolgon, Mitchell, and Eatman 2017).

This usage emerges from what some scholars and institutional change agents call the civic engagement "movement" in higher education (Saltmarsh and Hartley 2016). This movement has roots in the early 1980s as a response to the critique of higher education as an elitist ivory tower where specialized knowledge is produced in isolation. This critique was a direct response to the increasing "technical rationalization" of knowledge during the cold war period that, through scientific funding and priorities, facilitated a fragmentation of research into a hierarchy of scientific disciplines, marginalizing both the liberal arts and civic or engaged forms of learning. With the goals of promoting experiential learning and inspiring civic agency among students, many advocates of the early civic engagement movement drew directly upon the ideas of progressive and radical educational theorists, most notably the democratic learning theories of John Dewey (Rhoads 2003).

Outside of the institutional context of higher education, similar practices were often referred to as "community action," a term that gained popularity as a poverty alleviation strategy in the 1960s. This usage history can be traced to the US War on Poverty, when social scientists and federal policy makers proposed that, in order to address cycles of intergenerational poverty, poor people themselves must be involved in analyzing local problems and building leadership to confront and reform unequal opportunity structures. Frequently referencing both the "culture of poverty" theory (O. Lewis 1959) and the rising demands for equal representation of the civil rights movement, these programs encouraged low-income residents in neighborhoods and regions across the United States to join federally funded community action projects (CAPs). While the War on Poverty most frequently used the terms "participation" and "action," the purpose of CAPs was described as increasing "political engagement" among the poor. Despite its stated aims and resulting achievements, including the founding of the national Head Start preschool programs, the War on Poverty has been widely critiqued for curtailing and defunding local CAPs whose efforts were deemed too confrontational, usually along the lines of racial and economic justice (Katz 2013; O'Connor 2002).

Like community action in the War on Poverty, community engagement in higher education has been criticized as embracing practices that can be both inauthentic (using a rhetoric of empowerment while failing to address local problems) and neglectful (ignoring structural inequalities amplified or produced by universities themselves; Boyle and Silver 2005). These critiques point out that the growing focus on university-community partnerships coincided with the rise of neoliberal ideologies and policies that called for disinvestment in programs that promote public welfare and a reorganization of public institutions toward bottom-line business logics and volunteerism in place of social welfare. Some proponents of civic engagement and service learning in higher education have addressed these critiques by using the term "community engagement" to mean co-organization and coleadership by university and community stakeholders, placing a high value on outcomes that privilege community concerns and issues over the short-term engagement and learning of students (Stoeker 2016; Boyte 2018).

The critique of community engagement in higher education is mirrored by scholars who study a parallel trend in global development. In their aptly titled book, *Participation: The New Tyranny* (2001), Bill Cooke and Uma Kothari use the term "participatory development" to describe how international development projects in the Global South often generate consent among local stakeholders during a time of neoliberal reorganizing and downsizing of the state, paving the way for development organizations like the World Bank to cement new relationships with transnational global capital. Despite the critique of "participatory development" as co-optive, the term was also used by proponents of the radical anticolonial theory of scholars such as Paulo Freire, Franz Fanon, and Amilcar Cabral. The *Training for Transformation* series is one example (Hope and Timmel 2000). Produced by nuns exiled from South Africa for their radical education work during the apartheid regime, the series uses the terms "participatory development" and "engagement" to translate Paolo Freire's pedagogy—aimed at liberating oppressed and colonized peoples through critical reflection and action on the world—into hands-on training tools for development workers. In global development circles, the liberatory use of the terms "participation" and "engagement" have been reclaimed in the book *From Tyranny to Transformation* (Hickey and Mohan 2005) in response to Cooke and Kothari's critique.

This use of the term "engagement" to describe liberatory pedagogy and practice also has roots in US-based third world liberation struggles for ethnic studies and other movements for justice and liberation on behalf of communities of color; women; and lesbian, gay, bisexual, transgender, and queer/questioning (LGBTQ) people during the 1960s and '70s. Inspired by international anticolonial movements, the freedom schools of the US civil rights movement, and the growing body of scholarship of faculty of color, artists, poets, and organizers during the 1960s, the Third World Liberation Front made demands for the first ethnic studies programs in the United States. One example is *El Plan de Santa Bárbara*, a manifesto that established direct links between academic departments and broader communities outside of the university. It concluded with a call for Chicano studies programming that would be "of the community, for the community," and a warning that those for whom engagement with "the barrio" is "merely a cathartic experience" should "stay out" (Chicano Coordinating Council 1969, 61; Jackson 2018). Today, the term "community-engaged scholar" is often used interchangeably with or alongside the term "activist scholar," which has roots in these movements (Kezar, Drivalas, and Kitchen 2018). The use of these terms is sometimes connected back to the historic battles for ethnic studies and in service to movements marginalized in academia and the exclusionary cultures and disciplinary divides of the university (Hale 2009; Collins 2012).

In the 1990s, the term "public scholarship" became another common way to describe these forms of engagement, with the modifier "public" doing the work of validating research undervalued in formal institutional rewards and recognition systems (Post et al. 2016). However, publicly engaged or public scholarship is not a new phenomenon. In many ways, the career of W. E. B. Du Bois exemplifies a model currently used by many academics who might describe themselves as "community engaged" or "public scholars." As the first African American to get a PhD in the United States, Du Bois became a public scholar by virtue of both his desire to serve the needs of the "Negro community" of his era and his rejection by traditional departments for a regular faculty position that likely would have blocked his public mission. This "enforced" freedom pushed him to take on projects such as *The Philadelphia Negro* and the Atlanta series of essays that uncovered aspects of the Black urban experience, not of interest in traditional history or sociology departments. Later in his life, Du Bois would develop his public voice as the editor of *The Crisis*, the organ of the NAACP, and as a spokesperson for black transnationalism and diasporic thought (Lewis 2009). Today, we see a robust and growing network of public and community-engaged scholars of this Black freedom struggles tradition, including Ruth Wilson Gilmore, Barbara Ransby, Angela Davis, Robin Kelley, and Keeanga-Yamahtta Taylor.

Other groundbreaking public scholars who focused on marginalized US communities of color also had varied careers that led them to what we now call community-engaged scholarship. Carey McWilliams inspired the first generation of Chicano scholars of the 1960s as the author of *North from Mexico*, the only available volume of Mexican American history at the time, and spent his career as a writer, government official, and major leftist editor. In the 1930s, he served the state of California as commissioner of immigration and housing, and after World War II, he became the editor of the *Nation*, where he raised critical questions during a particularly anti-communist era. Likewise, Américo Paredes moved into academia after editing the newspaper *Stars and Stripes* for US servicemen in postwar Japan. At the University of Texas, he had to confront the reach and power of William Prescott Webb, the dean of Texas historians and author and promoter of *The Texas Rangers*, in order to get his own work published and acknowledged. Paredes's *With a Pistol in His Hand*, about the rebel Gregorio Cortez, was pathbreaking scholarship as ethnomusicology and anthropology, and like Du Bois, Paredes would go on to also produce novels, poetry, and all forms of academic humanistic writings (Saldivar

2006). All these scholars worked at the boundaries of higher education and the wider public.

The scholars who make up this genealogy of the term "engagement" are noteworthy in that they charted a path for a public-facing and community-engaged scholarship that blurred disciplinary, methodological, and community-university boundaries. They catalyzed and provided new scholarly platforms, inspiring new models of academic writing and public engagement. In this way, the activist organizers, students of color, movement scholars, and public intellectuals who use the tools of popular media, op-eds, radio programs, blogs, and zines and who lend data to movement organizing are quite different from the advocates for more traditional community or civic engagement who have focused on getting students and faculty members involved in communities not of their own origin. In recent years, the civic engagement and service-learning movements have begun to learn from these organizing approaches and recognize their value for the many students who come from the very neighborhoods and populations that institutional engagement efforts aim to serve (Sanchez 2012). These lessons are increasingly important as universities seek to diversify and to engage students who bring with them knowledge and concerns from the surrounding region that is also often their community and home.

2020

26

Environment

Vermonja R. Alston

The term "environment" in its broadest sense indexes contested terrains located at the intersections of political, social, cultural, ecological, and economic systems. In its narrowest sense, it refers to the place of nature in human history. In each of these usages, representations of the natural world are understood as having a decisive force in shaping environmental policy and the environmental imagination. In *Keywords*, Raymond Williams ([1976] 1983, 219, 223) notes, "Nature is perhaps the most complex word in the language. . . . Nature has meant the 'countryside,' the 'unspoiled places,' plants and creatures other than man . . . : nature is what man has not made." At the heart of this conception of nature lies the sense that there exists inherent, universal, and primary law beyond the corrupt societies of "man." Conservation politics were inspired by this understanding of particular places as untouched by the industrial revolutions of the nineteenth century.

Much twentieth-century ecological thought inherited this preoccupation with wilderness traditions, pastoralism, and the eighteenth-century Romantic impulse of nature writing. In contrast, indigenous and postcolonial scholars point out that imaginative writing about "nature" has a long tradition among colonial settlers attempting to mythologize and indigenize their relationships to place. In the twenty-first century, many of these competing voices have coalesced around an analysis of the "Anthropocene," a term coined in 2000 by atmospheric chemist Paul J. Crutzen to name a geological era in which human activity has become the dominant influence on climate and the environment (Zalasiewicz, Williams, and Waters 2016, 14). At the same time, planet-altering events have come to dominate popular and academic ecological discourses: global climate change, rising sea levels, the loss of land, and sources of potable water.

While "environment" is not one of Williams's keywords, "ecology" does make an appearance, even though the term was not common in the English language until the middle of the twentieth century. "Ecology," defined as the "study of the relations of plants and animals with each other and their habitat," replaced "environment," a word in use since the early nineteenth century but derived from the mid-fourteenth century, borrowing from the Old French *environ*, meaning "to surround or enclose" ([1976] 1983, 111). In American studies and cultural studies, "environment" has undergone a renewal among scholars and activists, owing in part to resistance to the bracketing of "nature" and "wilderness" as privileged sites of national identity and its acceptance as a shorthand for research on ecosystems and diverse environmental movements. Though now used less often in popular culture, the term "ecology" has been condensed to a three-letter prefix, "eco," in the names of social and intellectual movements, such as ecocriticism and ecofeminism.

In the late eighteenth century, a transatlantic Romantic movement coincided with US independence to produce a form of settler colonialism in which nature, understood as "wilderness," came to underwrite a new national identity. A harmonious relationship with sublime, wild nature became a way of articulating civilized US American purity against the perceived decadence of Europe. With Henry David Thoreau's version of transcendentalism, "wildness" came to symbolize absolute freedom (R. Nash 1982, 84). Lawrence Buell

(1995) locates the "American environmental imagination" in the canonization of Thoreau as a naturalist by late nineteenth-century ecologists such as John Muir. Nevertheless, Muir's ecological ethos dispenses with Thoreau's eighteenth-century romanticism in two ways: by arguing that abuse of nature is wrong and by asserting that "nature has intrinsic value and consequently possesses at least the right to exist" (D. Payne 1996, 5).

The narrow sense of "environment" as a discourse on wilderness protection has fueled criticism by ecofeminists, urban ecologists, and environmental and climate justice thinkers. Ecofeminists suggest that human relationships with the natural world have been engendered by a masculinist impulse to imagine and experience the land as feminine (Kolodny 1975, 58). In response, ecofeminism attempts to deconstruct the nature/culture dualism that situates nature, women, and ethnic minorities as passive "others" against which the Anglo-American male constructs himself. By linking the salvation of the planet Earth to issues of social equality, ecofeminism contributes to our understanding of the place of human structures of domination and power in environmental change.

Perhaps no environmentalist of the twentieth century was better able to bridge the divide among Muir's ecological thinking, Thoreau's pastoralism, ecofeminism, and eventually, environmental justice theory than Rachel Carson. *Silent Spring* (1962), her best-known book, brought attention to the damage to an ecosystem—consisting of rivers, streams, birds, and fish—as a consequence of widespread use of pesticides (particularly DDT). Carson understood that toxic fish and birds would eventually enter the human food chain, poisoning human animals as well as wildlife. Carson's book inspired a bipartisan environmental movement culminating in the establishment of the Environmental Protection Agency (EPA) on December 2, 1970, by executive order of President Richard M. Nixon.

Building on the work of Carson, theorists of environmental justice and environmental racism point out that the antiurban bias of preservation politics has often resulted in the creation of toxic ghettos in cities while cordoning off scenic wonderlands. As Jim Tarter (2002, 213) notes, "some live more downstream than others," and those people tend to be poorer and darker and to have little or no access to environmental policymakers. For Robert D. Bullard (2002), the term "environmental racism" more accurately describes environmental policies and industry practices that provide benefits to whites while shifting costs to people of color. Environmental justice movements, including the "environmentalism of the poor" and climate justice activism in developing countries, place the survival of poor and marginalized people at the center of environmental activism.

In recent years, there have been no greater demonstrations of the concerns of scholars like Tarter and Bullard than the Flint water crisis and the Dakota Access Pipeline protests. The first was a product of state and municipal decisions to switch to untreated drinking water from the Detroit River, but with roots in the widespread dumping of industrial waste into the waterways by automobile manufacturers and other heavy industries as well as municipalities over the course of the twentieth century. The second united diverse constituencies—Sioux, delegations of other Indigenous peoples, traditional conservationists, veterans, farmers, and ranchers—who shared a fear that the pipeline, passing beneath the Missouri River, would imperil drinking water along the entire 2,341-mile stretch of the longest river in North America and related waterways. These two events show how movements for environmental preservation have shifted from a focus on bounded wilderness landscapes to one that centers on water and the way that water navigates and links vast networks of communities. In neither case was the keyword environment as central as it might have been in earlier decades, perhaps because it had become associated with left-leaning partisanship in the intervening years. The Flint water crisis is frequently framed as a public health issue, and the activists at Standing Rock saw themselves as water protectors. Veterans, in particular, understood the protest as part of their mission to defend the land and waterways against corporate greed (Erdrich 2016).

Contemporary activists and thinkers are questioning relations of power, agency, and responsibility to human and nonhuman systems, allowing the keyword "environment" to intersect with other terms, most notably "climate change," "global warming," and "Anthropocene." Jan Zalasiewicz, Mark Williams, and Colin N. Waters point out that "we are now living in the Anthropocene because of the scale of human-driven chemical, physical, and biological changes to the earth's atmosphere, land surface, and oceans" (2016, 14), while others fault capitalism and modernity for the failure to grapple with climate change (Ghosh 2016) and call attention to the relationship between climate change and the history of race, colonialism, and slavery (Yusoff 2018). The unequal impact of rising sea levels, desertification, droughts, record heat patterns, and the melting of polar ice caps have already resulted in challenges to those identities as more people become climate-change migrants, crossing social, cultural, and geopolitical borders in search of environmental and climate justice. As the focus on water and the health of the oceans has broadened the appeal of activism, it has simultaneously forced a more critical rethinking of the use of the term "environment" in the context of the specific and uneven threats to life posed by global climate change.

2007/2020

27

Ethnicity
Henry Yu

The term "ethnicity" gained widespread currency in the mid- to late twentieth century, naming a process by which individuals or groups came to be understood, or to understand themselves, as separate or different from others. This meaning of "ethnicity" commonly referred to the consciousness of exclusion or subordination, though it also indexed social practices—language, religion, rituals, and other patterns of behavior—that define the content of a group's culture. The spread of this theory of ethnic culture created two mutually exclusive, analytically separate categories: "ethnicity," defined as cultural traits, was utterly divorced from the workings of the physical body, defined as "race." When anthropologists such as Franz Boas (1940) of Columbia University and sociologists and anthropologists from the University of Chicago began to teach students in the early twentieth century that cultural characteristics were the most interesting social phenomena for study, they spread at the same time the idea that any attention to physical characteristics was intellectually inappropriate. Attacking justifications for racial hierarchy grounded in biology, social scientists used the concept of ethnicity as a weapon against racial thinking.

"Ethnicity" thus became the term that named an alternative to the earlier biological emphases of racial hierarchy. In *Man's Most Dangerous Myth: The Fallacy of Race* (1942), one of the most significant antiracist books published in the twentieth century, the anthropologist Ashley Montagu argued that race as a category of analysis should be dropped as a dangerous invention and that "ethnic group" was a more neutral term. "Ethnicity" became synonymous with cultural difference, and any theory dependent on physical characteristics was dismissed as racist. Similarly, the attempt by anthropologists such as Ruth Benedict (1934) to array societies in a spectrum of cultures aided this flattening of all human distinction into a matter of cultural or ethnic difference. Possibilities for the elimination of racial prejudice (defined specifically as the expression of conscious attitudes about a group of people considered racially different) depended on a very specific definition of race as a form of consciousness. Race was a myth because it had no basis in biology, yet race as a consciousness about the importance of a set of physical attributes could still exist. Because consciousness of race was claimed to be merely one form of ethnic consciousness, race and ethnicity were concepts simultaneously distinct and indistinct from each other.

The subsuming of race under the broader category of ethnicity was both a significant attempt at offering a solution to racial conflict and a sign of the persistent difficulties with distinguishing between the two. As a matter of consciousness, the racial culture of "Negro Americans" was no different in kind than the ethnic culture of "Polish Americans," and purely cultural processes of assimilation could eliminate all differences between them. However, there were chronic difficulties with the distinction between race and ethnicity. W. Lloyd Warner and Leo Srole's widely read *Social Systems of American Ethnic Groups* (1945) exemplified the paradox inherent in this distinction. According to them, the host society accepted some groups more easily than others. Class differences tended to fragment ethnic groups, and the class mobility of some members of ethnic groups was the major determinant of acceptance within the host society. Most difficult to accept,

however, were those groups seen to be racially different. Although Warner and Srole argued that group conflict was a matter of ethnic identification (in the sense that the host society viewed a group as different and the group viewed themselves as different), they also assumed that there was some characteristic that set apart ethnic groups that were racially defined. The "future of American ethnic groups seems to be limited," Warner and Srole concluded; "it is likely that they will be quickly absorbed. When this happens one of the great epochs of American history will have ended and another, that of race, will begin" (295).

This sense that a great epoch of ethnicity was about to end at midcentury was a product of a crucial social transformation in the decades following the explicitly racialized immigration exclusion policies of the late nineteenth and early twentieth centuries. By the 1920s, US social scientists (some of whom were themselves either migrants or children of migrants) had created a body of theories of race and culture that had grown out of studying mass migration (Yu 2001). The most significant of these studies were associated with sociologists such as William I. Thomas (Thomas and Znanieki 1918–20) and Robert E. Park (1950) at the University of Chicago. Park and Thomas were at the forefront of an attempt to advance a new theory about social interaction based on the concept of culture. In opposition to earlier theories about the importance of inherited characteristics and physical bodies in determining human behavior, cultural theories emphasized the centrality of consciousness, of the mental attitudes and forms of self-understanding that people communicated through writing, speech, and other media. One of the most important of these theories concerned what Park and Thomas labeled "cultural assimilation," the process by which two groups communicated with each other and came to share common experiences, memories, and histories. Applied specifically to US immigrants, the theory of assimilation promised that any migrant, no matter how different in language, religion, or other social practices at the moment of arrival, could learn to assimilate national cultural norms. This historically progressive vision of the United States became the foundation for later arguments about ethnic consciousness, self-identity, and group identity.

At the same time, the twentieth-century "alchemy of race" (Jacobson 1998) had its origins in the mechanisms by which European immigrants who were defined at the beginning of the century as racially different came to be seen as "white" ethnics by the end of the century (Brodkin 1998). Along with the intellectual transformation wrought by cultural theory, popular writers such as Louis Adamic, who was himself of recent immigrant ancestry, pushed for an overcoming of the nativist divide between old and new US Americans. In books such as *From Many Lands* (1940) and *Nation of Nations* (1944), Adamic reconceived the United States as a land of immigrants, subsuming what had earlier been major dividing lines such as religion and language into mere differences of ethnic culture. At the same time (and with Adamic's assistance), organizations such as the National Council of Christians and Jews, founded in 1928, were striving to unify Protestants, Catholics, Orthodox Christians, and Jews into a so-called Judeo-Christian tradition. This period also saw widespread mass-cultural arguments for the end of religious discrimination, perhaps most visibly in 1950s Hollywood motion pictures such as *The Ten Commandments* (1956) and *Ben-Hur* (1959). The focus on the assimilation of religious differences, powerfully propelled by wartime propaganda against the genocidal science of Nazism, helped label antisemitism and anti-Catholicism as un-American. By the end of the 1950s, class mobility fueled by the postwar Montgomery GI Bill and federal subsidies of suburban housing had made Adamic's dream of an amalgamation of new and old seem viable.

The truth is that such programs of social engineering were predominantly focused on men able to pass as white. Immigrants who had been treated in the period between 1890 and 1920 as racially different (Slavs, Jews, and southern Europeans such as Italians, Greeks, and Armenians) were now transformed into white ethnics, mere varieties of white people. Just as dividing lines over religion, which had seemed intractable a generation before, were now reduced to mere denominational differences, all such culturally defined elements of difference had disappeared into a generic whiteness marked only superficially by vestiges of ethnic culture. Ironically, the civil rights movement of the 1950s helped reinforce this process of ethnic transformation. Jewish American intellectuals of the 1930s and 1940s had been at the forefront of political coalitions with African Americans seeking civil rights. Similarities in discrimination and exclusion at work and in the legal segregation of housing and public facilities had drawn Jewish and African Americans together to fight for civil rights. However, paralleling the larger transformation of white ethnics, Jewish Americans by the end of the civil rights era had become solidly white, even if antisemitism remained in vestigial and virulent forms. The civil rights movement for blacks ended up helping immigrant groups that previously had been the targets of racial nativism to amalgamate into a new ethnic "whiteness."

Despite these formidable intellectual and political problems, "ethnicity" has continued to be used widely as a description of and prescription for social life. Indeed, the acceptance and eventual celebration of ethnic difference was one of the most significant transitions of the twentieth century. Coincident with the increasing awareness of migration at the beginning of the century, a cosmopolitan appreciation of exotic difference arose.

Writing in the days before World War I, a number of New York intellectuals embraced the rich diversity of the city, forecasting that the eclectic mix of global migrants was the future of US society. Randolph Bourne's vision of a "transnational America" (1916) and Horace Kallen's description of "cultural pluralism" (1915) argued against the xenophobia that fueled the immigration exclusion acts of the same period, replacing it with an embrace of the exotic. The consumption by elite whites of the music and art of the Harlem Renaissance in the 1920s, along with periodic fads for "Oriental" art and so-called primitive tribal objects, reflected an embrace of the different as valuable. The celebration of exoticism in theories about the cosmopolitan self laid the groundwork for two major developments concerning ethnicity. The first was the theoretical foundation for the commercialization of ethnic difference; the second was the creation of a new definition of elite, enlightened whiteness.

Beginning with the fascination with exotic art forms in modernism but also embodied in the hunger for ethnic food and objects, a tasteful appreciation of the exotic became part of an educational program to combat racism and ignorance in the 1960s. At the same time that education was touted as the answer to race relations, ethnic music and other forms of exotic art and entertainment were offered at first as alternatives to the mass productions of popular culture and by the 1990s as important commodities distributed and consumed in the marketplace. Interestingly, the rise and spread of a cosmopolitan embrace of exotic difference helped expand the boundaries of whiteness. One of the ways in which those individuals formerly excluded as racially or ethnically suspect could "whiten" themselves was by embracing cosmopolitan ideas. Those who continued to express racist opinions were subsumed under the newly enlarged rubric of white racists (a category

that "whitened" former ethnics at the same time that it tarred them as ignorant bigots of the lower classes). The embrace of cosmopolitan ideals offered a way of becoming an elite, enlightened white. Whether it was black music or Chinese food, an appreciation of exotic difference signaled one's aspiration to a higher class status. These ideas were spread through advertising and by an education system that began in the 1940s to promote this outlook on ethnicity and class.

By the end of the twentieth century, objects associated with ethnicity enjoyed a popular boom as commercial goods. Ethnic objects that had assumed the status of collectible art (such as African tribal masks and Native American totem poles), items of everyday use (such as Chinese woks and chopsticks or Scottish tartan kilts), and performances of identity that could be consumed (ethnic music and dance) were packaged as desirable objects of consumption. Ethnicity was something to be collected by a tasteful consumer able to appreciate an array of objects. This commercialization of ethnicity also allowed those who were identified as different to turn that identification into an object with value. Musical styles such as rhythm and blues, rock 'n' roll, soul, rap, and hip-hop were marketed through an association with their black origins. By the 1970s, the commercialization of ethnicity extended to those ethnics who had been targets of xenophobia but were now comfortably white. White ethnics could continue to express cosmopolitan appreciation for the exoticism of nonwhites, but they could also embrace signs of their own ethnicity without fear of exclusion from the privileges of whiteness. White ethnicity was thus securely different from nonwhite racial ethnicity, and white ethnics drew on a history as victims of discrimination in ways that attenuated their own enjoyment of the privileges of being white, even as it evoked parallels to the historical suffering of nonwhites.

There are many long-term legacies of this history of ethnicity, including the rise of "whiteness studies" and the current use of the term "ethnicity" in the US media to describe a wide array of subnational and transnational conflicts. The ethnic cultural theory that underwrites these legacies derived its popular appeal from the combination of two elements. One was the description of how European immigrants were transformed into white ethnics during the mid-twentieth century; the other was the hope that this social process would also work for US Americans subordinated as nonwhite. However, the extension of what Nathan Glazer (1983, 92) called the "ethnic analogy" to the problems of racial hierarchy has often foundered because of a widespread belief that ethnicity is a matter of choice. This mistake is a direct result of the way the concept was modeled on the extension of the privileges of white supremacy to those who could voluntarily erase signs of their foreign origins and the withholding of those privileges from those who could not. The process of forgetting the historical origins of ethnicity in white supremacy continues today in arguments about its definition.

2007

28

Fascism
Rebecca Hill

The Italian *fascio* is best translated as "band" or "league," a term shared by a variety of Italian activist groups in the early twentieth century. Benito Mussolini bound the "Fasci" indelibly to the modern understanding of "fascism" when he and about a hundred radical nationalists and syndicalists formed the Fasci Italiani de Combattimento in 1919 to "declare war against socialism" (Paxton 2005; S. Payne 1996). Starting with an attack on the office of the Socialist Party newspaper, the fascists grew in power as, backed by landowners, they attacked socialists across Italy, killing as many as nine hundred people between 1920 and 1922. After this violent campaign, Italy's king invited Mussolini to lead the government, ultimately disbanding parliament and criminalizing opposition parties.

During the same era, the antisemitic German National Socialist (Nazi) party also attacked socialists and communists in the streets while forming political alliances with existing conservative nationalists, finally coming to state power in 1933. As uniformed groups spread across Europe, "fascism" became the generic term used to describe an international phenomenon of nationalist authoritarian mass movements, leaders, and states. Although the word "fascism" originated with Mussolini, it was and still is used to refer to multiple movements and states, the most catastrophic version of which was the Nazi regime. For this reason, the words "Nazism" and "fascism" and references to Hitler often are used interchangeably. This usage suggests that the end result of unchecked fascism is aggressive war and genocide.

The first people in the United States to write about fascism were Italian, German, and Jewish immigrant socialists. Closely following events in European socialist newspapers, they shifted the meaning of the term by linking it to their own experiences of legal repression, antiunion thuggery, nativism, and racism in the United States. This experience, as well as the Marxist theory that class conflict is the driving force of history, led these socialist intellectuals to argue that fascism is an extreme version of capitalist repression. The Communist International of the Soviet Union (Comintern) codified a similar analysis with the statement that "fascism in power is the open, terroristic dictatorship of the most reactionary, most chauvinistic, the most imperialistic elements of finance capitalism" (Passmore 2006).

This understanding of fascism has remained central to Marxist analysis, which emphasizes continuities among fascism, capitalism, and imperialism. Whether Marxist or not, African Americans who had previously compared Eastern European pogroms against Jews to American lynching also saw continuity between the US racial regime and Nazi Germany (Gilmore 2008, 167; Whitman 2017). Both usages link racism, anticommunism, and fascism in ways that question the degree to which fascism can be seen as an aberration in the history of capitalist governments. Anticolonialist thinker and activist Aimé Césaire commented in 1950 that Hitler had "applied to Europe colonialist procedures which until then had been reserved exclusively for the Arabs of Algeria, the coolies of India, and the blacks of Africa" ([1950] 2001, 36). Since the Vietnam War, a generation of anti-imperialist activists has continued this usage, criticizing US support for brutally repressive authoritarian or "fascist" client states (Chomsky and Herman 1979).

At the same time, dissident leftists and right-wing commentators used the word "fascism" to describe tendencies within both the conventional left and anticolonialist nationalist movements. Trinidadian Marxist C. L. R. James saw fascist tendencies in Marcus Garvey's Universal Negro Improvement Association (UNIA), noting the use of military uniforms, the language of racial solidarity, and especially Garvey's own claim in 1938 that "we were the first fascists" (Gilroy 2000). Fascism also became a weapon in sectarian left conflict; the Soviet Communist Party described the Social Democrats as "social fascists" during the Weimar era, and Socialist leader Norman Thomas and others deemed Stalinism "red fascism" during the Cold War (Weitz 1997; Adler and Paterson 1970). Today, many argue that India's radical nationalist movement "Hindutva" is a form of "fascism wearing clerical garb, and speaking the language of religious fundamentalism" (Nanda 2003). Since the 9/11 attack on the United States by al-Qaeda, some commenters have described radical Islamic movements opposed to the West with the term "Islamofascism" (Hitchens 2007).

These varied uses of the term "fascism" indicate that with the exception of self-proclaimed fascists, nearly every political tendency—anarchists, liberals, communists, socialists, anti-imperialist nationalists, conservatives, and members of the Far Right—has described their opponents at some point as fascist and themselves as antifascist while using the word to mean different things. Antifascism was one of the few shared principles on both sides of the Cold War, as the United States and the USSR both deployed the term to define their national identities through the great war against Nazism. US leftists continue to describe police actions, antilabor laws, white racism, and Far-Right organizations as paving a road to fascism (Denning 1998; Hill 1998, 2014; Vials 2014). Early neoliberal thinkers identified a road to fascism by linking it to socialism, communism, and welfare states whose bureaucracy and collectivism they saw as limiting individual freedom (Hayek 1944; Von Mises 1944). Conservatives argued that fascism should be seen as just one form of "totalitarianism," a word that also originating in fascist Italy, then came into common usage for both liberals and conservatives in comparisons of Stalinism and Nazism, both of which were depicted as forms of government that sought to penetrate every aspect of individual life (Arendt [1950] 1973; Geyer and Fitzpatrick 2008; T. Snyder 2010). In one such example, Republican Howard Smith of Ohio argued during a congressional debate in 1939 that "bureaucracy, fascism, Nazism, and communism are one and the same with slight variations" (Hill 2014). Libertarians and conservatives continue to define fascism in this way, often claiming that it originated on the left rather than the right (J. Goldberg 2008; Gregor 2000). The majority of historians dispute this argument (Paxton 2010).

One reason for the wide application of the word "fascism" to myriad aspects of politics, culture, and daily life is that the social and political movements it names arose from within democratic states in ways that seem to have caught much of the West by surprise. To prevent such a recurrence, activists and scholars have sought to identify the seeds of fascism growing in ordinary places. Mid-twentieth-century critical theorists blended Marxism and psychoanalysis to locate the unconscious roots of fascism in the bourgeois family structure, sexual repression, conventional masculinity, and traditional conservatism (W. Reich [1933] 1980; Adorno 1950; Pick 2012). New Left and liberal scholars critical of historical communist parties and conformist society in the late 1960s saw fascism as based in bureaucracy and imperialism. Fascism, they argued, was driven by a form of scientific rationality that lacked any ethical core,

sometimes called "instrumental reason" (Adorno and Horkheimer 1947; Arendt 1963; Deleuze and Guattari 1987). In contrast, another group of thinkers argued that irrationalism was the seed of fascism in the form of an anti-Enlightenment reaction influenced by Nietzschean philosophy. Such scholars feared that New Left critics of Enlightenment reason, far from preventing fascism, were unwittingly drawing from the same well as the early fascists whom they argued had formed their ideology by mixing left- and right-wing critiques of liberal capitalist modernity (Sternhell 1995; Wolin, 2006; Beiner 2018). In both cases, identifying ideas as seeds of future fascism raised the stakes of any debate, suggesting that each side was protecting the culture at large from an accidental slide into fascism.

Historians and political scientists have suggested that these philosophical arguments are so broad as to render the word "fascism" meaningless. In contrast, they seek a definition of "generic fascism" based on comparisons of interwar fascist movements. One influential definition describes fascism as "a political ideology whose mythic core in its various permutations is a palingenetic form of populist ultra-nationalism," with "palingenetic" referencing a revolutionary "myth of national rebirth" that calls for the overthrow of existing state institutions (Griffin 1993, 26). Another argues that "fascism" exists in actions rather than ideology: an attack on the bourgeoisie as decadent or corrupt, followed by a compromise with the bourgeoisie to gain power. Fascism is understood in this framing not as a coherent ideology but as a movement of "mobilizing passions," preoccupied with "community decline, humiliation and victimhood." Fascism, in this account, is typically built on a mass-based militant party allied with conservative elites in pursuing "with redemptive violence and without ethical or legal restraints goals of internal cleansing and external expansion" (Paxton 2005, 41, 218).

Activist scholars have applied these definitions to a number of organizations in the United States, including the Ku Klux Klan, racist skinheads, right-wing political parties and religious organizations, militant white supremacist antigovernment groups, and the "alt-right" (Niewert 1999; Zeskind 2009; Lyons 2018). While some refer to politician David Duke or French intellectual Alain De Benoist as "suit and tie Nazis," others argue that it is more accurate to describe them as "right wing populist," "far right," or "white nationalist" (Griffin, Loh, and Umland 2006; Berlet and Lyons 2000). Key to these debates is fascism's relationship to capitalism and the extent to which a right-wing movement must include both paramilitary violence and a revolutionary vision of a new society in order to be truly fascist. Since the Cold War, many scholars have argued that contemporary groups seeking to represent a "third position" between capitalism and communism are fascists. While claiming to be "beyond left and right," these groups confound traditional left and right categories by mixing ultranationalism, mysticism, left-wing economic theories, environmentalism, and opposition to US imperialism (Griffin 2004; Bale 2004; Lyons 2019). The most influential political group to adopt the language of the Left in a battle against liberal democracy is the European New Right, whose US acolytes include former Donald Trump advisor Steve Bannon and avowed white supremacist Richard Spencer (Bar-On 2007; Shekhovstovm 2017; Eco 1995). Responding to such appeals by the Right to the Left, activists have begun to warn against a "red-brown alliance" of the Left (red) and Far Right (brown) in the context of antiwar, anticapitalist, and antiglobalization organizing (Sunshine 2014; Reid-Ross 2017; Lyons 2019). The growth in the early twenty-first century of "Antifa" (short for the German Antifascistisk Aktion) is another sign of the concern about the revival of fascism as a result of neoliberal globalization.

A decentralized global movement originating in opposition to racist skinheads in punk rock subcultures in the 1980s, Antifa groups do not share a single definition of fascism, though they share an anticapitalist orientation (Bray 2017).

These definitional debates inform the discussion about whether US president Donald Trump himself should be called a fascist rather than a populist or a conservative. Those who deem that term appropriate note Trump's disregard for truth and legality, support of violence against opponents at rallies, promotion of economic nationalism, and popularity among white nationalists, as well as his praise of international strongmen such as Vladimir Putin (Russia), Jair Bolsonaro (Brazil), Kim Jong Un (North Korea), Recip Erdogan (Turkey), Rodrigo Duterte (Philippines), and Viktor Orban (Hungary). While scholars of fascism have resisted using the "F-word" to describe Trump, they have nonetheless identified many uncomfortable similarities between Trumpism and interwar fascist movements (Browning 2018; Paxton 2017). This debate points toward fascism's own internally contradictory nature as well as the political force that it continues to wield as an accusation. Both populist and authoritarian, it is grandiose in its claims to heroism, cynical in its rejection of truth, sentimental in its descriptions of victimization, and ruthless in its praise of strength—as were the Italians who wrote on their own bandages, *Me Ne Frego* ("I don't care"). It may be that we have used the word "fascism" for so long to describe so many things that when we see an avowed fascist who also happens to have a job, watch TV, and even play video games—like Tony Hovater, interviewed by Richard Forest for the *New York Times* in 2017—we refuse to believe what is happening because it is all too normal, not at all like what we expect.

2020

29

Freedom
Stephanie Smallwood

"Freedom" is a keyword with a genealogy and range of meanings that extend far beyond the history and geographical boundaries of the United States, even as it names values that are at the core of US national history and identity. From the Declaration of Independence to Operation Enduring Freedom (the name given to the post-9/11 US military intervention in Afghanistan), the term is at the root of US claims to being not only exceptional among the world's nations but a model that others should follow. The *Oxford English Dictionary* defines "freedom" in abstract terms as "the state or fact of being free from servitude, constraint, [or] inhibition." But dictionary definitions cannot reveal the materiality of the specific contests through which freedom has attained its central place in modern Western understandings of self and society. While the term's etymological roots and core attributes date to the classical societies of ancient Greece and Rome, "freedom" gained its contemporary significance in the context of western Europe's transition from an ancien régime (comprising passive subjects over whom monarchs claimed divinely sanctioned absolute rule) to the era of the secular state (comprising citizen-subjects who consent to be governed through social contract).

Against the divinely ordained absolute rule of a singular sovereign in the seventeenth and eighteenth centuries, the discourse of freedom posited the popular sovereignty of the civic collective—a plurality composed of autonomous individuals possessed of purportedly natural, and therefore primordial, rights. This rights-bearing individual was the newly ascendant being around whom the core tenets of political freedom took shape—liberalism's claim that government exists to protect and guarantee the rights of the individual, the republican celebration of representative rule, and the leveling discourse of equality. Two related features that powerfully shaped this individualist understanding of freedom in the early modern West were its possessive quality and its universalist rhetoric. "Every man has a property in his own person," John Locke wrote in his highly influential *Second Treatise of Government* ([1690] 1988). Reflecting the penetration of market relations across northwest Europe in the seventeenth century, Locke's framing meant that freedom was conceptualized as something that resulted from an individual's ability to possess things and as something one experienced as though it was a possession itself (Macpherson 1962).

This understanding of freedom is paradoxical. The individual celebrated by the modern Western theory of freedom was male, and his purportedly self-produced economic independence derived at least in part from the labor of wives, children, servants, and other dependents whose political subjectivity was subsumed under his patriarchal authority. Shifting discourses of gender, race, and class, among others, rendered these relations of appropriation natural and self-evident elements of freedom's core conditions of possibility (K. Brown 1996; G. Brown 2001; J. Morgan 2004). By the end of the eighteenth century, the ideal of an expanding horizon of self-possessed (male) individuals was nowhere more fully realized than in British North America, where white men enjoyed lives remarkably independent of traditional institutions such as the family, church, or state, making them "the freest individuals the Western world had ever known" (Appleby 1992, 155). At the same time, the independent state that emerged out of the American Revolution gave the doctrine of possessive individualist freedom its ultimate expression with its institutionalization of racial slavery (D. Davis 1975; Blackburn 1988; Berlin 1998). Although the triumvirate of "life, liberty, and property" (or generalized "pursuit of happiness") was a commonly deployed phrase across the eighteenth-century Anglo-Atlantic world, these abstractions took materialized form for Thomas Jefferson, Patrick Henry, and other slaveholding architects of the radical American experiment in political freedom through the transmutation of property in one's "own person" into property in the full personhood of others.

Numerous writers of the period recognized that holding property in the personhood of others while waging a war for freedom defined as universal individual autonomy charted a path of logical inconsistency. "Would any one believe," Patrick Henry wrote in private correspondence, "that I am Master of Slaves of my own purchase! I am drawn along by ye general inconvenience of living without them, I will not, I cannot justify it" ([1773] 1957, 300). That a "people who have been struggling so earnestly to save *themselves* from slavery" were nonetheless "very ready to enslave *others*" was a problem put before Jefferson by his friend Richard Price ([1785] 1953, 259). Henry's admission that slavery produced "conveniences" that he would not relinquish offered an answer to Price's concern.

Among the most trenchant interpretive interventions regarding the relationship of freedom to slavery has been the suggestion that the former was produced by the latter. It was no accident that the leading authors of a North American revolutionary theory of freedom were men whose experience of individual autonomy derived from slavery. Put simply, the North American theory of freedom used racial exclusion to solve the problem posed by its egalitarian rhetoric. The

elite planter, middling proprietor, and poor tenant were "equal in not being slaves"—equal, that is, in being white. The new republic's universal freedom was marked by color from its inception (E. Morgan 1975, 381; Fields 1990; C. Harris 1993; Dain 2002; Waldstreicher 2010). Jefferson gave voice to this racialized and racializing freedom in his *Notes on the State of Virginia* when he concluded a lengthy exegesis on slavery and race with the opinion that black inferiority troubled the prospect of slave emancipation. For Jefferson, granting freedom to enslaved African Americans introduced the "second" and "necessary" step of forced exile: once freed, the emancipated African American would have to be "removed beyond the reach of mixture" ([1787] 2002, 181). Half a century later, Abraham Lincoln likewise gave voice to the mainstream white sentiment that black freedom within the space of the US nation-state was unthinkable ([1854] 1953).

The understanding of freedom produced by the founding and early maturation of the US nation-state thus turned on an understanding of possessive individualist freedom whose purported expansiveness was from the start circumscribed by gendered and racialized structures of exclusion and domination (Saxton 1990; Roediger 1991, 1999; Bederman 1995; Zagarri 2007). Because it relied on the theory that some humans were categorically superior to others, its universalist rhetoric worked not to realize individual autonomy for all humans but to secure the particular interests of propertied white men by naturalizing those interests and the relations of subordination required to produce and sustain them (Trouillot 1995; Lowe 2006; Welke 2010). But these dominant understandings of freedom did not emerge without contestation. From the antislavery movement of the antebellum period through subsequent "rights" movements on behalf of women, African Americans, workers, Chicanos, Native Americans, homosexuals, and Asian, Latino, and other immigrant communities, the boundaries of freedom have been redrawn and stretched beyond anything that its propertied white male architects would recognize or condone (V. Deloria [1969] 1988; Okihiro 1994; Foner 1998; Mariscal 2005; MacLean 2006).

Explaining these contestations of the meaning and practice of freedom has been one of the most important interpretive challenges for scholars. At stake in this question are two problems: how to tell the story of the expansion of freedom and how to assign responsibility for the positive transformations of freedom in US society. The mainstream response to these questions, generally associated with liberalism, understands the universalist rhetoric of the founding discourse of North American freedom as predestining freedom's expansion across time and space. It positions events such as the Emancipation Proclamation, the ratification of the Nineteenth Amendment to the US Constitution, the 1964 Civil Rights Act, and the *Roe v. Wade* Supreme Court decision as signposts along the march toward an ever-more-true expression of the nation's ideals. This narrative tends to locate the nation's founding patriarchs at its center, making their genius the catalyst that sets freedom's expansion in motion. The underlying logic produces the claim that to fault the nation's founders for what they did not do (their failure to extend freedom to nonwhites and women) is to miss the larger and more important point—namely, that it was their revolution that "made possible the eventual strivings of others—black slaves and women—for their own freedom, independence, and prosperity" (Wood 1992, 368).

Countering this narrative, a diverse body of scholarship has argued that the problem with this liberal approach to the paradox of freedom is that it represents the movement from past to present teleologically—as an already known eventuality. By figuring historical outcomes as evidence to support characterizations of the past as we wish it to have been, it disavows the lives and stories of those whose subjugation produced the very conditions for modern freedom's emergence and whose own freedom was a dream made real only by their revolutionary initiative. At stake here is not just recognition of agency for its own sake but an accounting for the material politics of insurgent agency in pursuit of more radical understandings of freedom. One of the key achievements of this scholarship has been to illuminate the politics of freedom's expansions and transformations across US history (Du Bois [1935] 1998; Hartman 1997; Linebaugh and Rediker 2000; Smallwood 2004; Bruyneel 2007). This work, which is varied in its subjects, methods, and conceptual approaches, shares an understanding of the expansion of freedom not as inevitable but as produced by the radical organizing and activism of those for whom freedom was never intended. Their struggles have generated understandings that run counter to the liberal progressive narrative of freedom's inevitable expansion, reflecting what one scholar has called the "historical politics of time-making" (W. Johnson 2002, 152).

The theory and practice of the black freedom struggles of the twentieth century provide one illustrative instance of a sense of temporality at odds with the liberal progressive narrative. Half a century after legal emancipation, the Great Migration carried millions of black southerners to cities such as New York, Chicago, and Los Angeles "looking for a free state to live in" and was characterized as a "second emancipation" (Foner 1998, 174; Grossman 1989; F. Griffin 1995; Hunter 1997; Sernett 1997; P. Ortiz 2005). Civil rights activists in the South likewise understood their struggle to make real the freedoms promised a century earlier by such Reconstruction measures as the Fourteenth and Fifteenth Amendments to the US Constitution as a "second reconstruction"

(Woodward 1955; Kennedy 1963). This lexicon of serial repetition suggests that the passage of time marks not the steady, linear progression from slavery to freedom but rather the crisis and (dis)orientation of being stuck in the time and place of slavery. Unable to move into a reliably free present, one cannot confidently assign slavery to the past. This circular temporality is captured in the metaphor used by Rev. Willie David Whiting, a black Floridian who was initially rejected at the polls in the 2000 US presidential election on the false charge that he was a convicted felon, when he described his experience in testimony before a US Civil Rights Commission: "I felt like I was sling-shotted back into slavery" (Adam C. Smith 2003). The same insight is expressed by the protagonist of Ralph Ellison's *Invisible Man*, who warns of history's "boomerang" effect (R. Ellison [1952] 1995, 6; Singh 2004, 55).

Meaningful analysis of such a lexicon of freedom and archive of struggle requires a willingness to take seriously its alternate understanding of the social conditions from which its temporality derives. Following the murder of James Chaney, the black civil rights activist killed along with white coworkers Andrew Goodman and Michael Schwerner during the "Freedom Summer" campaign to register black voters in Mississippi in 1964, Ella Baker decried the fact that Chaney's was not the only black body desecrated in the region's muddy waters. "Until the killing of black mothers' sons is as important as the killing of white mothers' sons, we who believe in freedom cannot rest," she famously proclaimed (qtd. in Ransby 2003, 335). The refrain "we who believe in freedom cannot rest" was revived by protesters in 2013 when a Florida court found that George Zimmerman was not criminally responsible for the death of Trayvon Martin, the unarmed black teenager he pursued and shot in "self-defense" (McGrory 2013; M. Edelman 2013). The mass incarceration of black men, the

Supreme Court's gutting of the 1965 Voting Rights Act, and the Zimmerman verdict can all be taken to indicate that time need not march forward in lockstep with freedom's steady expansion. Rather, the temporality of black freedom always threatens to carry the unfreedoms of the past forward into the present (A. Davis 2003, 2012; R. Gilmore 2007; Blackmon 2008; Michelle Alexander 2010). Replete with phrases and terms such as "turn back the clock," "rollback," and "reversal," discussion of current legal challenges to women's health and reproductive rights suggests another domain in which freedom's temporality does not conform to the steady forward progression posited by the liberal narrative (Roberts 1998; Stolberg 2009; Sanders 2012).

We must also recognize that as the dominant liberal understanding of freedom produces its subject through bourgeois, heteronormative, and patriarchal regimes of social control, it renders all who do not fit within those norms as deviant and subject to disciplinary regulation (Foucault [1975] 1995; Wendy Brown 1995). To the extent that historical projects to expand the boundaries of freedom have reified and benefited from such regulatory regimes rather than questioning and troubling them, they have served to (re)produce barriers to emancipation for women of color, homosexuals, transgendered persons, differently abled persons, and other nonnormative subjects. Bringing otherwise-unaccounted-for experiences and practices of these groups into view reveals the intersectional politics of freedom's meanings and illuminates some of the most radical (and also most easily silenced) understandings of freedom. Whether rejecting the "freedom" to marry, refusing reformist agendas of rescue and uplift, or critiquing the "free labor" regimes of global capitalism, these alternative understandings foreground the disciplinary structures of hierarchy and control on which the normative liberal discourse of freedom turns and question whether winning membership in the circle of possessive individualist freedom is a viable strategy for effective emancipation (L. Davis 1995; Stanley 1998; Byrd 2011; Lowe 2009; Ferguson 2004; Hong 2006).

International and transnational frameworks offer equally important critiques of liberal understandings of freedom. From the seventeenth century to our present moment, the concept of freedom has been instrumental in authorizing colonial violence and has underwritten US imperial agendas (Kaplan and Pease 1993; Von Eschen 1997; Renda 2001; Jung 2006; Smith-Rosenberg 2010). On the receiving end of US foreign-policy initiatives, the concept of freedom has also served to render peoples "liberated" by US interventions as indebted beneficiaries of the purported "gift" of freedom (Rodríguez-Silva 2005; Yoneyama 2005; Nguyen 2012). The disturbing imbrications of this "gift" have come to be especially evident in the post-9/11 era of the US security state. In 2010, the Matthew Shepard and James Byrd Jr. Hate Crimes Prevention Act was signed into law by being tethered to the National Defense Authorization Act. Pairing civil rights with national security, this legislation extends federal protection against hate crime to actual or perceived members of the lesbian, gay, bisexual, transgender, and queer/questioning (LGBTQ) community through the mechanism of the largest-ever appropriation of funds to the nation's military. That such a coupling has not drawn critique suggests a contemporary political culture in which freedom is produced with and through violence. What does it mean, we must ask, to pursue "homosexual emancipation" through the "sustenance and growth of the military," particularly when victims of unmanned drone strikes are increasingly the target of US military action undertaken under the banner of "freedom" (Reddy 2011, 5; Melamed 2011; Randall Williams 2010)?

A growing body of American studies and cultural studies scholarship suggests that the duality of freedom and various unfreedoms is best understood not as a paradox awaiting resolution by the teleological unfolding of the United States' ever-more-perfect and self-correcting expression of its destiny. Rather, it should be seen as evidence that the possessive individualist freedom enshrined in US modernity depends on and requires the unfreedom of some category of fellow humans. Given this long and complex history, it may be that the pressing question today is whether a fully universal human liberation is thinkable through normative logics of freedom in the United States.

2014

30

Futurity

Rebecca Wanzo

"Futurity" connotes not just what will happen or a time that is not yet. It is laden with affective attachments such as hope and fear. But it is best understood in relationship to the other words that are often proximate to it, such as "time," "horizon," "utopia," and "dystopia." Throughout North America, futurity is consistently associated with identity, linking ideas of what the future will look like with the belief that various groups can build a new space or, in our worst imaginings, be injured by an impending world that disavows or has no place for them. Futurities are simultaneous and sometimes competing with the idea of the future always contained within another project related to nation or identity. Theorists of futurity in American studies and cultural studies have thus focused on this nexus of identity and imagined world building.

One of the earliest deployments of futurity in the Americas was related to what Indigenous scholars frame as "settler futurity," most famously exemplified in the United States by the concept of "manifest destiny." Six years before he coined this phrase, John L. O'Sullivan argued in the *United States Democratic Review* that the United States was *destined* to be "the great nation of futurity," suggesting that what set the nation apart was that European colonists never sought to "depopulate the land" by "wicked ambition" (1839, 427). The violent takeover of Indian lands belies this claim, but this form of settler futurity demands crafting fictions about the past to justify visions of the future.

This belief that the United States was the great nation of futurity informed O'Sullivan's invention of the term "manifest destiny" in 1845 to advocate for the United States' expansion. A belief in the supremacy of the US experiment gave the nation "the right" to possess the continent. This construction of national futurity was deeply tied to a racist logic that understood white supremacy as foundational to the country's future, and discourse that tied futurity to whiteness would increase throughout the nineteenth century (Horsman 1981).

Sullivan's essay is illustrative of the ways in which settler colonialists and imperialist discourse crafted fantastic fictions that they masked as fact. As Eve Tuck and Ruben A. Gaztambide-Fernandez (2013) explain in their deconstruction of history curricula, settler colonialists in North America have constantly circulated stories that erase or romanticize violent histories and imagine a future in which there are only white inhabitants. North American settler colonialists construct a future for their countries that continuously depends on seeing the relationship between indigenous people and settlers as in the past because the former were allegedly a "vanishing race" (Dippie 1991).

Theories of "indigenous futurity" provide a counter-narrative to settler-colonial fantasies that indigenous people had and have no future. From public policy to frontier novels and westerns, settler-colonial fantasies have for centuries involved constructing white settlers as inheritors of land and Indian-ness (Tuck and Yang 2012, 14). Coined by Grace Dillon (2012), the term "indigenous futurisms" speaks to the ways in which indigenous people speak back to their spatial and temporal location in ongoing colonialist fantasies. Given the long history of cultural productions that displace and erase indigenous subjects, works that craft and theorize "indigenous media futures" explore the relationship between indigenous people and technology, pushing against the idea that they are always outside of scientific literacies (Lempert 2018; Roanhorse et al. 2017). Indigenous futurities resist these narratives through activism and media that refuse the erasure of indigenous people and imagine a future where various tribal nations thrive (Skawennati 2014). As Karen Recollet argues, "Indigenous futurity decolonizes the Indigenous imaginary" (2016, 91).

Indigenous writers and artists have often made use of the science fiction genre to show that they have a future, but the project of imagining a future for other identity categories has sometimes been more contested. The phrase "the future is female" is one example. It emerged out of lesbian separatist spaces and spoke to a larger cultural feminist project that believed women offered better ways of being than patriarchy. On the one hand, the phrase affirms the belief in the category of woman and a specificity to what women can offer in framing "feminist futures" (Hogan 2016). On the other hand, destabilization of gender and sexual binaries has been a mainstay of feminist and queer dystopias and utopias (LeGuin 1969; Russ 1975). Is an ideal feminist future one in which gender categories are eradicated or one in which people see women as offering unique perspectives as women? Do articulations of "woman" attentive to intersectionality and understandings of *trans futures* complicate some desired futures for "women" (K. Keeling 2009)? Feminist science fiction has offered an opportunity for imagining "future females" and exploring possibilities and anxieties about reproductive, sexual, and political futures (Barr 1981, 2000). But what it means for the future to be female is opaque.

The phrase would be taken up later by the popular "girl power" pop group the Spice Girls in the 1990s and presidential candidate Hillary Clinton in 2017, usages that emptied it of its original radical content. Clinton's attempt to mobilize the phrase in her campaign is illustrative of the long-standing belief that women can craft better political futures. But both she and the Spice Girls model a neoliberal future more attached to individualism, markets, and self-fulfillment (as in the use of the supposedly inspiring slogan for Clinton that it was "*her* turn") than to the collective utopian and radical possibilities others have originally evoked by the phrase (Rottenberg 2017).

For feminist philosopher Elizabeth Grosz, who has made a case for incorporating more science in feminist theorizing about change over time, futurity is fertile ground for imagining new models of gender and sexuality because bodies can be reevaluated and framed differently in the instability of the not yet (2005). Grosz makes the case that thinking about temporality and the future should be more explicitly critical to feminist theorizing. In contrast, these concepts have long been at the center of queer theory. While many feminist theoretical and fictional texts are an indictment of male domination more broadly, some of them are somewhat normatively concerned with what Lee Edelman has characterized as "reproductive futurism." Pointing to the clichéd idea that children are our future, Edelman criticizes the representation of the child as the ideal object of all politics (2004, 3). It is not enough to talk about what injures us now; it must also be about what "our" children will inherit. For Edelman, queer subjects can and should ethically stand outside reproductive futurism, because that notion of futurity never imagined a place for queer subjects. In contrast to Edelman, who sees giving up hope in politics as shaping a kind of ethical subject who resists normative discursive practices that make fantastic figurations the ground for what matters to everyone, José Estaban Muñoz imagines "queer futurity" as *all* about hope and politics. Because queerness is an ideality that is not here yet, he sees it "as a temporal arrangement in the present in the service of a new futurity" (2009, 16). Queer people are often constructed as not having a future; thus Muñoz highlights the art and performance practices that build utopia in the now and work to imagine queer worlds and bring them into being.

Edelman and Muñoz have been touchstones for many scholars attentive to the normative and political work of futurities. Following Muñoz, Alison Kafer resists Edelman's "fuck the future" framework in *Feminist, Queer, Crip* (2013), in which she describes a "crip futurity." Preventing and even eliminating disability are often seen as an ethical good in an ideal future, a notion modeled by the naturalized mandate that women abort fetuses that test positive for Down syndrome. While the decision to carry a fetus to term is and should be a personal one, some of the logic used in relation to disability and reproductive technologies adheres to a neoliberal agenda that requires every subject to be autonomous and self-supporting (Roberts 2009). Since people often have "felt and acted on the belief that disability destroys the future, or that a future with disability must be avoided at all costs," one could argue that crip and queer futurity should, as Edelman suggests, adopt a "fuck the future" position, indicting the ways in which social lives and policies are constructed to deny the viability of a future for disabled people (2004, 31). But like Muñoz, Kafer makes a case for hope and the ethical practice of envisioning that crip futures are possible and that multiple kinds of bodies and ways of being have a place in the world that we wish to inhabit (2013, 45).

The ethical mandate of imagining and demanding alternative futures is at the heart of social justice projects crafted by those who have been erased from hegemonic futurist visions of the nation-state. Like indigenous groups and disabled people, black people have been displaced from futurist constructions in the West. In the United States, this displacement has involved moving them outside of the country, white flight, incarceration, or gentrification efforts. Thus the primary question undergirding "Afrofuturism" in fiction by writers such as Samuel Delany, Octavia Butler, and proto-Afrofuturists such as W. E. B. Du Bois is this: "Can a community whose past has been deliberately rubbed out, and whose energies have subsequently been consumed by the search for legible traces of its history, imagine possible futures?" (Dery 1994, 180).

The answer is yes, in a futurity project that arguably has circulated more widely in the popular imagination than any of the other identity "futurities." Sun Ra's album and film *Space Is the Place* (1972) are considered early progenitors of Afrofuturism, modeling the blending of aesthetics and political vision that would predominate in many Afrofuturist visions. Emerging from the United States, the term "Afrofuturism" grew in use in the 1990s following Mark Dery's interview with Delany in the essay "Black to the Future" (1994). Sociologist Alondra Nelson founded an online community of scholars and artists in 1998 that explored issues of Afrofuturism, and this community was one of the inspirations for Grace Dillon's notion of indigenous futurisms. While always interested in Africa and the larger diaspora, Afrofuturism gradually became more of a transnational project. And while feminist, queer, and disability scholars more consistently trouble the past as something to escape from, Afrofuturism is shaped by the dialectic of breaking free of discriminatory pasts and an attachment to aesthetics and practices from Africa and the diaspora that can shape the future (Anderson and Jones 2016; Eshun 2003; Y. Womack 2013). As Nelson explains, Afrofuturism "looks backward and forward in seeking to provide insights about identity" by asking "what was and what if" (2002, 4). When a highly successful film adaptation of the comic book *Black Panther* hit the screens in 2018, discussions of Afrofuturism became widespread and moved beyond science fiction fans, artists, and academics and into mainstream news outlets. Like many other black speculative texts, the Hollywood film combined a pan-African aesthetic with speculative renderings of future technologies and debates about the best path for global black liberation.

One criticism of the sort of Afrofuturism portrayed in *Black Panther* is that it models neoliberalism, privileging individualism, economic competition, and state power; the hero believes he can build a better future for young African American men by showing them his country's superior technology and culture as opposed to participating in revolutionary action. The question of what liberation looks like outside a neoliberal model may best be articulated in what Aimee Bahng (2017) describes as speculative "migrant futures," which pushes against the imperialist violence of economic speculation and investment that is posited as the path to a better future. As Bahng notes, economic speculation has historically practiced both abstract and material violence on the subaltern in the name of progress. Thus a counterpoetics of migrant futures uses speculative fiction to resist the stories put forth by those who believe in capitalist utopias and craft new progress narratives that center those whose futurity has been most harmed by economic exploitation.

But of course, this battle of competing futurities in which people struggle to have a place in the ever-evolving world may not matter if there is no future for humanity or other species at all. The struggle to have a future, to be in the future, is not only an act of imagination and a power struggle over the stories we tell about who will belong in the future we imagine for ourselves; it is also a struggle with the seeming impending apocalypse brought about by humanity's cataclysmic impact on the environment—known as the Anthropocene—and the belief that the end of capitalism would be worse than the earth's destruction (Szeman 2007). And yet hope lies in competing futurities here too, in attempts to both decolonize the Anthropocene and imagine an ethical responsibility to future generations (Whyte 2017; Streeby 2018). Speculation about possible futures has had real effects on the world we inhabit, and part of the critical work of theorizing futurity has been about imagining the inevitable failure of US imperialism and capitalism to build a better world. By framing futurity in ways that recognize historical injuries and deromanticize narratives of progress, many theorists of the future work to imagine worlds in which justice—and survival itself—is possible.

2020

31

Gender

Jack Halberstam

In American studies and cultural studies, as in the humanities more broadly, scholars use the term "gender" when they wish to expose a seemingly neutral analysis as male oriented and when they wish to turn critical attention from men to women. In this way, a gender analysis exposes the false universalization of male subjectivity and remarks on the differences produced by the social marking we call "sex" or "sexual difference." Poststructuralist feminist theory queries this common usage by suggesting that the critique of male bias or gender neutrality comes with its own set of problems—namely, a premature and problematic stabilization of the meaning of "woman" and "female." In 1990, Judith Butler famously named and theorized the "trouble" that "gender" both performs and covers up. In doing so, she consolidated a new form of gender theory focused on what is now widely (and variably) referred to as "performativity." This focus on gender as something that is performed has enabled new modes of thinking about how the transgendered body is (and can be) inhabited, about the emergence of queer subcultures, and about practices that promise to radically destabilize the meaning of all social genders.

As a term, "gender" comes to cultural studies from sexology, most explicitly from the work of psychologist John Money (Money and Ehrhardt 1972). Money is credited with (and readily claimed) the invention of the term in 1955 to describe the social enactment of sex roles; he used the term to formalize the distinction between bodily sex (male and female) and social roles (masculinity and femininity) and to note the frequent discontinuities between sex and role. Since sex neither predicts nor guarantees gender role, there is some flexibility built into the sex-gender system. This reasoning led Money to recommend sex reassignment in a now-infamous case in which a young boy lost his penis during circumcision. Given the boy's young age, Money proposed to the parents that they raise him as a girl and predicted that there would be no ill effects. Money's prediction proved disastrously wrong, as the young girl grew up troubled and eventually committed suicide after being told about the decisions that had been made on his/her behalf as a baby.

This case has reanimated claims that gender is a biological fact rather than a cultural invention and has led some medical practitioners to reinvest in the essential relationship between sex and gender. It has also been used by some gender theorists to argue that the gendering of the sexed body begins immediately, as soon as the child is born, and that this sociobiological process is every bit as rigid and immutable as a genetic code. The latter claim (concerning the immutability of socialization) has been critiqued by poststructuralist thinkers who suggest that our understanding of the relation between sex and gender ought to be reversed: gender ideology produces the epistemological framework within which sex takes on meaning rather than the other way around (Laqueur 1990; Fausto-Sterling 1993).

All these arguments about how we ought to talk and think about sex and gender assume a related question about how the modern sex-gender system came into being in the first place. Different disciplines answer this question differently. In anthropology, Gayle Rubin's work on "the traffic in women" (1975) builds on Claude Lévi-Strauss's structuralist analysis of kinship (1971) to locate the roots of the hierarchical organization of a binary gender system in precapitalist societies in which kinship relied on incest taboos and the exchange of women between men. Esther Newton's (1972) ethnographic research on drag queens in Chicago in the 1960s and 1970s finds gender to be an interlocking system of performances and forms of self-knowing that only become visible as such when we see them theatricalized in the drag queen's cabaret act. In sociology, Suzanne Kessler and Wendy McKenna (1990) have produced a brilliant handbook on the production of gendered bodies, providing readers with a vocabulary and a set of definitions for the study of gender as a system of norms.

Working across these disciplinary formations, American studies and cultural studies scholarship on gender continues under numerous headings and rubrics. Researchers studying the effects of globalization have paid particular attention to transformations in the labor of women under new phases of capitalism (Enloe 1989; Kempadoo and Doezema 1998). Scholars working on race have traced very specific histories of gender formation in relation to racial projects that attribute gender and sexual pathology to oppressed groups. In African American contexts, for example, black femininity has often been represented as vexed by the idealization of white femininity on the one hand and the cultural stereotyping of black women as strong, physical, and tough on the other (Hammonds 1997). Other scholars seeking to denaturalize cultural conceptions of manhood have examined masculinity in terms of new forms of work, new roles for men in the home, the function of racialized masculinities, new styles of classed masculinity, the impact of immigrant masculinities on national manhood, and the influence of minority and nonmale masculinities on gender norms (Bederman 1995; Sinha 1995; Harper 1996). Queer theorists have detached gender from the sexed body, often documenting the productive nature of gender variance and its impact on the way gender is understood and lived.

In all of these research contexts, gender is understood as a marker of social difference: a bodily performance of normativity and the challenges made to it. It names a social relation that subjects often experience as organic, ingrained, "real," invisible, and immutable; it also names a primary mode of oppression that sorts human bodies into binary categories in order to assign labor, responsibilities, moral attributes, and emotional styles. In recent years, cultural work dedicated to shifting and rearticulating the signifying field of gender has been ongoing in queer and transgender subcultures. Drag-king shows, for example, have developed along very different lines than their drag-queen counterparts (including those documented by Newton). While drag queens tend to embody and enact an explicitly ironic relation to gender that has come to be called "camp," drag kings often apply pressure to the notion of natural genders by imitating, inhabiting, and performing masculinity in intensely sincere modes. Whereas camp formulations of gender by gay men have relied heavily on the idea that the viewer knows and can see the intense disidentifications between the drag queen and femininity, drag-king acts more often depend on the sedimented and earnest investments made by the dyke and trans performers in their masculinities. Drag-king acts disorient spectators and make them unsure of the proper markings of sex, gender, desire, and attraction. In the process, such performances produce potent new constellations of sex and theater (Halberstam 1998).

Understood as queer interventions into gender deconstruction, drag-king performances emerge quite specifically from feminist critiques of dominant masculinities. In this sense, they can be viewed as growing out of earlier practices of feminist theory and activism. Consider Valerie Solanas's infamous and outrageous 1968 *SCUM Manifesto* (SCUM stood for "Society for Cutting Up Men"), in which she argued that we should do away with men and attach all the positive attributes that are currently assigned to males to females. As long as we have sperm banks and the means for artificial reproduction, she argued, men have become irrelevant. While Solanas's manifesto is hard to read as anything more than a Swiftian modest proposal, her hilarious conclusions about the redundancy of the male sex ("he is a half-dead, unresponsive lump, incapable of giving or receiving pleasure or happiness; consequently he is an utter bore, an inoffensive blob," etc. [(1968) 2004, 36]) take a refreshingly extreme approach to the gender question. The performative work of the manifesto (its theatricalization of refusal, failure, and female anger and resentment; its combination of seriousness and humor) links it to contemporary queer and transgender theaters of gender. Like Solanas's manifesto, drag-king cultures offer a vision of the ways in which subcultural groups and theorists busily reinvent the meaning of gender even as the culture at large confirms its stability.

It is revealing, then, that Solanas is at once the most utopian and dystopian of gender theorists. While Butler, in her commitment to deconstructive undecidability, cannot possibly foretell any of gender's possible futures (even as she describes how gender is "done" and "undone"), Solanas is quite happy to make grand predictions about endings. Many academic and nonacademic gender theorists after Solanas have also called for the end of gender, noted the redundancy of the category, and argued for new and alternative systems of making sense of bodily difference (Bornstein 1994; Kessler 1998). But socially sedimented categories are hard to erase, and efforts to do so often have more toxic effects than the decision to inhabit them. Other theorists, therefore, have responded by calling for more categories, a wider range of possible identifications, and a more eclectic and open-ended understanding of the meanings of those categories (Fausto-Sterling 2000). It seems, then,

that we are probably not quite ready to do away with gender—or with one gender, in particular—but we can at least begin to imagine other genders.

Whether by manifesto or reasoned argumentation, scholars in the fields of American studies and cultural studies have made gender into a primary lens of intellectual inquiry, and the evolution of gender studies marks one of the more successful versions of interdisciplinarity in the academy. Indeed, as US universities continue to experience the dissolution of disciplinarity, a critical gender studies paradigm could well surge to the forefront of new arrangements of knowledge production. At a time when both students and administrators are questioning the usefulness and relevance of fields such as English and comparative literature, gender studies may provide a better way of framing, asking, and even answering hard questions about ideology, social formations, political movements, and shifts in perceptions of embodiment and community. Gender studies programs and departments, many of which emerged out of women's studies initiatives in the 1970s, are poised to make the transition into the next era of knowledge production in ways that less interdisciplinary areas are not. The quarrels and struggles that have made gender studies such a difficult place to be are also the building blocks of change. While the traditional disciplines often lack the institutional and intellectual flexibility to transform quickly, gender studies is and has always been an evolving project, one that can provide a particularly generative site for new work that, at its best, responds creatively and dynamically to emerging research questions and cultural forms while also entering into dialogue with other (more or less established) interdisciplinary projects, including cultural studies, American studies, film studies, science studies, ethnic studies, postcolonial studies, and queer studies.

2007

32

Globalization

Lisa Lowe

"Globalization" is a contemporary term used in academic and nonacademic contexts to describe a late twentieth- and early twenty-first-century condition of economic, social, and political interdependence across cultures, societies, nations, and regions precipitated by an unprecedented expansion of capitalism on a global scale. One problem with this usage is that it obscures a much longer history of global contacts and connections. In the ancient world, there were empires, conquests, slavery, and diasporas; in medieval and early modern times, Asian, Arab, and European civilizations mingled through trade, travel, and settlement. Only with European colonial expansion, beginning in the sixteenth century and reaching its height in the nineteenth, did global contacts involve Western European and North American dominance; the rise of Western industrialized modernity made possible by labor and resources in the "new world" of the Americas was, in this sense, a relatively recent global interconnection. Yet today, the term "globalization" is used to name a specific set of transformations that occurred in the late twentieth century: changes in world political structure after World War II that included the ascendancy of the United States and the decolonization of the formerly colonized world; a shift from the concept of the modern nation-state as bounded and independent toward a range of economic, social, and political links that articulate interdependencies across nations; and an acceleration in the scale, mode, and volume of exchange and interdependency in nearly all spheres of human activity.

Even with this caveat, "globalization" is not a self-evident phenomenon, and the debates to which it gives rise in American studies, cultural studies, and elsewhere mark it as a problem of knowledge. For economists, political scientists, sociologists, historians, and cultural critics, globalization is a phenomenon that exceeds existing means of explanation and representation. It involves processes and transformations that bring pressure upon the paradigms formerly used to study their privileged objects—whether society, the sovereign nation-state, national economy, history, or culture—the meanings of which have shifted and changed. Globalization is both celebrated by free-market advocates as fulfilling the promises of neoliberalism and free trade and criticized by scholars, policymakers, and activists as a world economic program aggressively commanded by the United States, enacted directly through US foreign policies and indirectly through institutions such as the World Bank, the International Monetary Fund, and the World Trade Organization, exacerbating economic divides with devastating effects for the poor in "developing" countries and in systematically "underdeveloped" ones (Amin 2014; Stiglitz 2002; Pollin 2003).

Political scientists argued in the 1980s that the global expansion of the economy had created asymmetries among nations and regions that provided sources of "complex interdependence" (Keohane and Nye 1989). Adherents of their "neoliberal" school of political science, dominant for nearly two decades, agreed that international laws and institutions, global commerce, and diplomatic networks of cooperation had lessened the need for war and militarism. Yet since 2001 and the unilateral US invasions of Afghanistan and Iraq, the US government has embraced "neoconservative" political thinking, reviving "neorealist" arguments from the

Cold War period to contend that despite economic or social links between nations, "national security" has never ceased to be the most important issue and that war constitutes a viable, "rational," and effective instrument of policy and of wielding power (Kagan and Kagan 2000). Such lethal contentions about the nature of global conditions have demonstrated that the epistemological problem of what can be known about "globalization" is never distant from ethical or political issues of life and death.

Sociologists adopted Max Weber's (1968) early twentieth-century observations about the contradictions of rationalizing modernity within a single society to study globalization as an acceleration and expansion of capitalist bureaucracy through transnational corporations (Sklair 1991), or a "disembedding" and "reembedding" of local context and knowledge, mediating the familiar through technologies that are themselves estranging (Giddens 1990). In this view, globalization both deepens interconnection *and* widens dissymmetries represented as "core" and "periphery" in an earlier "world-system" (Wallerstein 1976). With respect to culture, critics observe that flexible accumulation and mixed production fragment subjectivities and collectivities according to a "cultural logic of postmodernism" (Jameson 1991), an apparent shrinking or elimination of distances, and a general reduction of time spent (Harvey 1989). The rise of a new "global" culture composed of cross-border communities, multilingual immigrants, and syncretic religions revises the earlier anthropological presumption that place, culture, language, and identity could be mapped onto one another (Gupta and Ferguson 1992; Sassen 1998; Fregoso 2003). The coexistence of transnational diasporas and indigenous peoples creates material imaginaries dictated less by citizenship and national sovereignty than by new social identities and overlapping affinities (Appadurai 1996; Clifford 1997).

Yet some contend that globalization is a form of cultural imperialism and extractivism that erodes nation-state and indigenous sovereignties, and threatens to flatten cultural differences (Lavinas-Picq 2014; Gomez-Barris 2017), while others emphasize that global encounter, migration, and contact produce hybrid forms of cultural complexity (Hannerz 1992; Escobar 2011). To study "culture" within globalization is to understand it neither as merely commodified nor as simply the inert effects or ideological correlative of transnational capitalism. Rather, contemporary culture as the "structure of feeling" (Raymond Williams [1977] 1997) of globalization mediates uneven spaces linked through geohistorical, political, economic, and social logics (P. Taylor 1999). Whether the medium through which groups are persuaded to live and die as patriotic subjects or the inspiration for their dissent, "culture" expresses dynamic contradictions precisely at those intersections, borders, and zones where normative regimes enlist, restrict, or coerce. Critical cultural studies of the United States within global processes demonstrate that normative modes differentiate as they regulate and discipline as they include and assimilate.

The study of cultural production (literature, music, art, mass, and popular cultures) and cultural practices (the organization of cities, public spaces, schooling, religion) demonstrate that the US-global relation is increasingly yet unevenly mediated through electronic information technologies. Manuel Castells (2000) suggested that state, military, and economic processes are entirely coordinated, in real time across distances, through the vast reach of global information networks. Cultures of globalization now include social media platforms and information technologies that promise liberation from social restrictions yet may reproduce dispossessions and differences of race, class, gender, and nationality in new digital forms (Chun 2006; Nakamura 2008; Atanasoski and Vora 2019).

Even as some herald the creation of new social identities, others place them within the longer history of social differences produced by colonialism and racial capitalism (Goldstein 2014). From settler colonization of the Americas and transatlantic slavery through Manifest Destiny, the Cold War, and the "war on terror," the longer history of the United States has included the occupation, enclosure, and assault on peoples racialized and alleged as threats (Singh 2017). Theorists and practitioners of counterinsurgency justify this history of detention by arguing that such actions are necessary to protect "national security" (Khalili 2012). Whether the vilification of Native peoples, the policing of fugitive slaves, the internment of Japanese and Japanese Americans in World War II, the surveillance or banning of immigrants from Muslim-majority nations, or the exacerbated detention of migrants during the Trump era, "foreign" others have been targets of asymmetric wars over the course of the history of the United States.

The restructuring of the US economy by globalization has entailed a shift from vertically integrated national industries to transnational finance capitalism, a conversion of traditionally male jobs in manufacturing to more feminized forms of service operations, and an unsettling of historical neighborhoods by the influx of new immigrants. Communities of color in deindustrializing US cities of the 1980s were hit hard by the loss of jobs as manufacturing moved to export-processing zones in Asia and Latin America, even as the urban poor suffered from the simultaneous reduction of social welfare and buildup of the US prison system (R. Gilmore 1998; Hinton 2016). Transnational immigration that appears to bring more racial and ethnic diversity often renders these worsening inequalities more complex and certainly more difficult to decipher. New comparative work on race relations considers US cities as locations for understanding the history of racial inequalities and its rearticulation within neoliberal political and economic policies from the 1980s onward (J. Lee 2004; Ho-Sang 2010). Urban geographers have noted the colossal increase of impoverished dispossessed populations in cities around the world, disconnected from industrialization or economic growth (M. Davis 2007b), while political theorists have observed the consolidation of US capitalism through explicit war and covert military operations in East and Central Asia, the Pacific, Central America, and the Middle East (Mamdani 2004; Shigematsu and Camacho 2010).

For some observers of US society and culture, globalization signifies the "end" of many things: of modern US myths of purity; of "man" as the white race, redeemed by the authenticity of rural life; of the US as leader of the "free world" and "the American century." For others, it is a "crisis," a "chaos of governance," and the "end" of Enlightenment liberal humanism or civil society. Noting the weakening of states and waning social power of subordinated groups, some suggest that globalization changes the balance of power between "civilizations." Projected apocalyptically, it appears as a "clash of civilizations" between Western modernity and the Confucian-Islamic East (Huntington 1996). Others interpret Chinese modernization as a probable sign of emerging Asian economic supremacy (Krugman 1997). Still others herald the impact of antiglobalization movements, transnational feminism, global environmentalism, and international human rights activism and evaluate the possibilities for countering poverty and creating sustainable growth (Lowe and Lloyd 1997; Alexander and Mohanty 1997; Sen 1999). Some observe that transnational capitalism not only effects a "denationalization" of corporate power but also draws new workforces that express themselves in movements articulated in terms other than the "national"—for example, in transnational feminist work by US and UK women of color and immigrant women from the formerly colonized world (Sudbury 1998; Mohanty 2003; Hong 2006). Globalization not only "unbundles" territorial definitions of sovereignty, defying earlier maps of "core" and "periphery"; it also changes the means, agents, and strategies employed in contesting the "new world order." Global cities like New York, London, Tokyo, or São Paolo gather both the infrastructure to coordinate global finance and the transnational migrant workers who perform the service labors for these operations (Sassen 1991; Eade 1997), while a range of contemporary movements responding to globalization defy statist definitions of sovereignty: from Indigenous "water protectors" at Standing Rock to the Movement for Black Lives to Palestine solidarity movements. Migrants, prisoners, refugees, squatters, and other non–state subjects are among the important new social actors who are transforming how we conceive of ethics, justice, and change in conditions of globalization.

2007/2020

33

Government
Leerom Medovoi

In common usage, the word "government" often refers to the individuals or parties that operate the state (as in "I support this government"). But it can equally refer to the institutional features of the state (as in a "constitutional" or "aristocratic" form of government). One result of this dual usage is that the practices of governance and the institution of the state are often treated as the same thing, even though their implications are quite different. The modern state, as a form of governance, is typically bound to the idea of the nation and its popular sovereignty. By contrast, government understood as an act of governing originally referred to such diverse activities as moral self-control, household management, or even the sailing of a ship (*Oxford English Dictionary*). One can today still talk about "governing" one's behavior, a budget, or an organization. "Government" thus refers first and foremost to the regulation of activity. The fact that the term has become so closely tied to the state, despite these broader meanings, reveals much about the path taken by modern strategies of power.

One influential approach to this paradox begins in a series of famous lectures by the French historian and philosopher Michel Foucault (2009). Foucault argues that government first emerged as a political idea during the sixteenth century, as an explicit alternative to the rule of the Machiavellian prince, whose goal was simply to stay in power. Foucault then points out that the prince's sovereign power was essentially circular, a force that sought only to maintain itself. In contrast, early advocates of government emphasized how a state might best mobilize people and things toward such concrete ends as wealth, health, or trade. With this new conception of government, the modern state for the first time began to regulate ordinary people's everyday lives. This shift from sovereign authority to governmental power initially meant greater efficiency in achieving various ends as defined by the state, but it gradually came to delineate a newly specified domain of human action (the economy) that the state would be specially tasked with governing, particularly through its management of populations. Both Foucault and Mitchell Dean have described this process as the "governmentalization" of the state or as the rise of "governmentality" (Foucault 2009; Dean 2009).

Some scholars have suggested that governmentality actually finds its practical origins in the histories of early modern slavery and colonization, both of which sought early on to regulate the labor, health, sexuality, and docility of subjected populations with the aim of increasing their productivity (Stoler 1995; D. Scott 1995; Lowe 2006). During the eighteenth century, these goals of colonial governmentality began to infiltrate the political projects of popular sovereignty in Britain, France, and the early United States, where the ideal of a democratic state presupposed a citizenry whose conduct made it capable of regulating itself. Governmentality thus helped to produce a modern distinction between the normal citizen, who is capable of self-governance, and abnormal subjects, against whom the ends of self-government must be secured and defended, often violently: blacks, queers, rebellious workers, criminals, or otherwise "unhealthy" populations. The resulting policing practices reveal important continuities between colonial governmentality and the modern state's deployments of race, sexuality, and other markers of population (Reddy 2011).

Viewing government as a new kind of political logic or rationality helps us think about the rise of the modern state. It also allows us to consider the governmental dimension of social and cultural life. The policing of a population's conduct, after all, is hardly limited to state action. It has historically come to involve such disparate phenomena as fashion, education, public opinion, sexuality, and media arts. The range of venues where governmentality is enacted suggests that the political science approach to government—one that focuses on the state as a separate sphere of power and influence—could be fruitfully linked to humanistic and historical studies of the various cultural techniques through which the conduct of modern populations is regulated. The Australian cultural theorist Tony Bennett (1992) argues that we can best combine studies of government and culture by focusing on questions of cultural policy. Since culture is not simply a system of signifying practices or a way of life but also a "domain of morals, manners, codes of conduct" (26), it can be approached as both the object of government (what it seeks to change) and its instrument (how government seeks to intervene).

This proposition has begun to receive serious reflection in American studies (Bratich, Packer, and McCarthy 2003) and has been put to work by individual scholars. In recent years, it has resulted in a wide range of promising studies, including ones that explore the rise of demography in the nineteenth century in the United States as a spatial strategy of power (Hannah 2000), the uses of race making in administering post-9/11 "homeland security" (Grewal 2003), and the capacity of consumer niche marketing to regulate the social life of populations (Binkey 2007). Perhaps the most sustained investigations into

US cultural governmentality, however, are to be found in the historiography on US sexuality, which has long studied the strategies of power served by the regulation of sexual conduct. John D'Emilio and Estelle Freedman ([1988] 1997), for instance, have explored how the ethos of sexual freedom motored twentieth-century consumption imperatives, while Julian Carter (2007) has shown how protocols of sexual heteronormativity worked to justify and maintain white supremacy after emancipation.

The origins of a non-state-based governmentality date back to the rise of classical liberalism in the eighteenth century. Classical liberalism differs greatly from what we mean by liberalism today (a welfare-state approach to the population's well-being, associated with John Maynard Keynes). As enshrined in such texts as the Declaration of Independence, classical liberalism is an ancestor of both modern liberalism and modern conservatism, advocating a political vision of personal liberty and human rights. Yet classical liberalism was no mere ideology; it was also a practical strategy of using indirect means to govern "at a distance," as Nikolas Rose and Peter Miller have put it (2008, 173–85). Liberalism rejects sovereign power—the direct state intervention into the life of the population—as an effective strategy of government. The colonial rebels thereby rejected the rule of the British monarch not on the grounds of sovereign right (he should not be ruling over this people) but on the grounds of poor government: he failed to secure the ends of "Life, Liberty, and the Pursuit of Happiness," which the Declaration presents as the sole reason that "governments are instituted among men." Likewise for Thomas Paine (*Oxford English Dictionary Online* 2018), while a state simply *was*, a government could be better or worse at achieving its proper ends: security and freedom.

Liberal governmentality gained special impetus in the United States, where the word "state" came to refer to the thirteen (and now fifty) states, each of which retained its status as a quasi-sovereign entity. "Government," meanwhile, became the only available word to describe the federal system by which these states would be constitutionally bound together for the sake of improved commerce, self-defense, and other economic ends. Liberalism advocates a minimal state as a means of achieving increased human freedom from government. The trouble is that not everyone is seen as suited to freedom, and against those populations, sovereign power has often been exercised by way of incarceration in prisons, asylums, or military camps. But for the "normative" population that can regulate itself, it turns out that freedom is actually the means to achieving a minimal state. By "freeing" us from state-run health care, we are made individually responsible for monitoring and arranging our own medical needs. By "freeing" us from state media "propaganda," we make consumer choices that actually pay a culture industry to regulate our opinions, tastes, and behavior. And by having us perform such governmental work ourselves, the cost of operating the state can be reduced and government made more "efficient." This is why, to paraphrase Nikolas Rose, freedom is not the antithesis of government but in fact one of its key inventions (1999).

For this project of a self-governing population, it turns out that culture and older definitions of "government" (moral conduct, household management) still matter. When conservative antitax activist Grover Norquist (2001) said that he wanted to reduce government to the size that he could "drown it in the bathtub," he was expressing in particularly blunt terms the liberal dream of good government: the population takes on its own shoulders (through notions of personal responsibility, community service, proper sexual conduct, work habits, consumer activity) all the regulatory objectives of the state. This idea is also reflected in more radical traditions, as in Henry David Thoreau's opening creed in "On Civil Disobedience," where he asserts that not only does he accept the slogan "that government is best which governs least" but even that "that government is best which governs not at all" ([1849] 1966, 277). Is this not, in effect, the fantasy of an exercise of power so efficient that it requires no exertion of force whatsoever?

The more recent orthodoxy about politics and economics that is referred to as "neoliberalism" represents the latest permutation in liberal governmentality. Under neoliberalism, as political theorist Wendy Brown (2003) explains, social life is reorganized in ways that subject it to game theory rationality. The exercise of freedom is framed as the maximization of personal strategic investment in our own human capital, thereby encouraging choices that might serve governmental ends. The US right wing claims to hate big government, but seen in this way, the freedom they espouse is simply a displacement of the technologies of government from the state to the scene of civil society. They prefer their government in homes, supermarkets, and neighborhood associations, understood as sites of competition, rather than through the agency of the state bureau.

The theory of governmentality, in all its forms, expands our notion of what government is or has been. Above all, it calls our attention to the self-serving and indeed misleading account of power that classic liberal governmentality propagates when it draws distinctions between the state (allegedly the unique seat of government) and civil society (the domain of personal freedom). Liberalism conveniently indicts the state as a force of repressive political power, even while it quietly insinuates the regulation of the populace ever deeper into civil society. This process only continues under neoliberal governmentality, which actively reshapes society as well as the state in the image of the market. In so doing, neoliberalism simply extends a longer tradition of governmentality here described. Whether acting as social individuals, cultural consumers, sexual agents, or citizens of the state, we have come to build the political order that governs us by exercising our freedoms.

2014

34

History

Matthew Frye Jacobson

"History" names both the terrain of past human experience and the discipline that aspires to access, survey, and plot that terrain. As such, the word is used with staggering imprecision, even by thoughtful speakers (consider the phrase "history teaches us . . ."). According to modern etymologies, the word "history" traces its passage into late Middle English via the Old French *estoire* (story; chronicle) and from the Latin *historia* (account; tale; story), and originating in the Greek *historia* (a learning or knowing by inquiry; an account of one's inquiries; a record; a narrative). "Human beings participate in history both as actors and as narrators," writes Michel-Rolph Trouillot; "the inherent ambivalence of the word 'history' in many modern languages, including English, suggests this dual participation" (1995, 2). The full definition ranges from all-encompassing notions of *the past, former times, time gone by*, and *the days of old*, to notions that connote curation, such as *a series of past events connected with someone or something*, as in "the history of warfare." Who does this *connecting*? To what end? There is history-as-past, and then there is history-as-narrative (which masquerades as "past"). "History is Philosophy teaching by examples," as Thucydides had it. A given chronicler's guiding "philosophy" is bound to be selective of examples and may also distort, embellish, invent, or reify them.

Historical narratives have thus been vexed by questions of factuality or fidelity versus fantasy or romance from the very beginning, pressed into the service of this political project or that. History is a story told by the victors, enjoined and contested by the vanquished wherever possible. It is always *partial* in both meanings of that word: *incomplete* where one seeks a comprehensive account, and *biased* toward one perspective or faction where one wishes for neutrality. This partiality is as powerful in its patterns of forgetting and silencing as it is in its enforcement of remembering and retelling. Many who have sworn to forever remember the Alamo, Pearl Harbor, the Holocaust, or 9/11 have comfortably forgotten King Philip's War or the Sand Creek massacre, and they may even wonder aloud why African Americans cannot seem to forget slavery. The social order itself depends on certain patterns of remembering and forgetting. When the Italian theorist of hegemony Antonio Gramsci wrote that history has "deposited in you an infinity of traces, without leaving an inventory" (1971, 325), he intended history-as-past but could just as easily have been speaking of the framing powers of history-as-narrative.

This chimera of objective "truth" is worth returning to, but in the US setting, a second, equally pressing question has to do with the culture's disregard for the past altogether—what is sometimes referred to as its ahistoricism or even *anti*historicism—the tendency toward not just misrepresentation, but full-on collective amnesia. US culture places little value on serious historical reflection, occasionally generating a serious collective reverie along the lines of Ava DuVernay's epic Civil Rights film, *Selma*, but more often running in the registers of Hollywood fantasy or television hokum—*Gone with the Wind, Stagecoach, Davy Crockett, McHale's Navy*—rather than sustained reflection of the sort that enhances understanding or roots the present meaningfully in the soil of the past. The United States has developed a mild taste for history as adventure, as romance, as tragedy, as nostalgia or escapism, as farce, even as nonsense. But history as an instrument for analyzing the contours and meaning of present conditions? Generally no, not even in the context of policy debates or political oratory. The culture has a woefully short memory to begin with, but as the basic unit of public discourse has contracted—first to the tiny morsel of the television sound bite, then to the one hundred forty characters of a tweet—historical reflection has become an unwanted extravagance, and the nation goes careening ever onward.

In such a context the very word "history" has come to connote that which is absent, gone, irrelevant, forgotten, of no concern. Dust—as in "dustbin." To say *you're history* is both a swearing off and a curse. "I like the dreams of the future better than the history of the past," said Thomas Jefferson (1816). Centuries later, Henry Ford concurred: "History is more or less bunk. . . . We want to live in the present and the only history that is worth a tinker's dam is the history we make today" (1916). To make history is one thing; to *be* history is quite another. If "presentism" (the imposition of present-day assumptions on the past) is a sin to the historian, then *historicism* (the theory that present-day phenomena are determined by history) is like a pesky glob of gum on the sidewalk to the culture at large. But gum from the sidewalk does stick to the sole, and "history," too, will stick to the soul, whether we like it or not. A contending vernacular locution turns us back to history's staying power: *and the rest is history*—meaning that the story is well known and what accounts for where we are. History's great force, cautioned James Baldwin, "comes from the fact that we carry it within us, are unconsciously controlled by it in many ways, and history is literally present in all that we do" (1985, 410). History is what the present is made of.

We have to reckon, then, that just like any other object of study, "history" has its own *historicity*, its own

rooting in conditions once present and now past, its own time-specific "frames of reference, identities, and aspirations," to take Baldwin's formulation in that same passage. This is of immense portent to American studies and cultural studies, both of which have been animated by history's historicity. The American Historical Association (AHA), founded in 1884, marked the juncture at which history in the United States became professionalized, evolving from the intellectual pursuit of a leisured class of white patrician men to the full rigors of a credentialed and credentialing university discipline. The self-proclaimed hallmarks of this understanding of history, according to Peter Novick, were its "scientific method" and its "objectivity," even if still issuing from that class of patricians (1988, 21). Early AHA presidents included figures like George Bancroft, John Jay, Alfred Thayer Mahan, and Theodore Roosevelt, all representing a class of US military or government officials. Dominant historical narratives belonged to that class too—the victors. "The most ultimately righteous of all wars is a war with savages," wrote Roosevelt in *The Winning of the West*, placing all "civilized mankind" in debt to "the rude, fierce settler who drives the savage from the land"—"American and Indian, Boer and Zulu, Cossack and Tartar, New Zealander and Maori,—in each case the victor, horrible though many of his deeds are, has laid deep the foundations for the future greatness of a mighty people" ([1889] 2016, 353). Such was the nature of objective historical "fact," as victors built visions of a future on their own very particular understandings of "history," whatever else one wants to say about the professionalized methods and protocols that were emerging in the discipline.

The analysis and deployments of "history" in the interdisciplinary fields of American studies and cultural studies required two distinct but overlapping revolutions: one raised the question of who speaks and whose "history" receives a hearing; the other entailed an emerging methodology by which culture, ideas, ideology, and expression became a proper ambit of the scholar's concern, meaning that conceptions like "civilization" and "savagery" might themselves become objects of study rather than modes of historical description. The first revolution had been in motion for generations before it made a mark on the profession, largely through the work of figures like W. E. B. Du Bois (*The Souls of Black Folk*), Anna Julia Cooper (*The Voice of the South: By a Woman of the South*), and Charles Beard (*An Economic Interpretation of the Constitution*), all of whom challenged patrician historiographic traditions. AHA president Carl Bridenbaugh sounded the academic death knell of the old patrician order only at the remarkably late date of 1962, when he decried a rising "democratic urge for equality and the disappearance of the traditional social ranks." One object of Bridenbaugh's worry was the postwar democratization of the US university and a rising generation of students "of lower middle-class or foreign origins" who would be unable to reconstruct and communicate the past as Bridenbaugh himself understood it (1963). The post–World War II democratization of higher education proved one of the most important forces in redirecting and recomposing "history" as both discipline and accepted narrative. By the end of the 1960s, students and younger faculty had fought for and won the institutionalization of Black Studies, Ethnic Studies, and Women's Studies. The "culture wars" of the 1980s were at once a barometer of social change and a means of fighting out these turf battles over how best to "reconstruct and communicate" the US past.

The second revolution cut a longer path through the US curriculum. Well before Bridenbaugh's hand wringing at the AHA over the *who* of history, a series of diverse figures had challenged the discipline's standard practices on another front—the *what* of history.

What constitutes a proper question? What constitutes a proper source? What kinds of stories are worth telling? Turning away from wars, treaties, and tariffs, this line of inquiry took up structures of feeling; the dance of ideas; popular pursuits, entertainments, and media; the common coin of vernacular belief. Two distinct but gradually merging tributaries fed this stream: an interdisciplinary American studies tradition and a neo-Marxist theoretical tradition. The American studies genealogy began with interdisciplinary scholars in the early twentieth century, whose efforts to broaden "literary" study ended by mobilizing a number of contiguous disciplines toward an analysis of nothing less than "American civilization." "We may begin as critics but we end as historians," wrote Vernon Parrington, indicating a portentous and newly dynamic understanding of "texts" and "contexts" ([1917] 1953, 98–99). This movement produced two generations and more of holistic renderings of American Puritanism (Perry Miller, *The New England Mind*), expansionism (Henry Nash Smith, *Virgin Land*), sectionalism (William Taylor, *Cavalier and Yankee*), and technological change (Leo Marx, *The Machine in the Garden*)—a "myth and symbol" approach that sought to root history in human consciousness and vice versa. Subsequent work of New Left scholars like Annette Kolodny's *Lay of the Land: Metaphor as Experience and History in American Life and Letters* (1975) and Ronald Takaki's *Iron Cages: Race and Culture in 19th-Century America* (1978) retained a recognizable kernel of the myth and symbol approach.

These tendencies were extended by a historiography that engaged more explicitly with debates in the fields of philosophy and literature as well as the interdisciplines of ethnic studies and gender studies. The result was an understanding of history as both a set of social processes with a historicity of their own *and* an incubator of historical artifacts that included the shared narratives and icons of the sort that the social movements of the 1960s had so vigorously contested (Teddy Roosevelt's "civilized" settlers and "savages," for example, and his conception of militarized "manliness" too). How history *moves* had been an enduring philosophical and political concern from G. W. F. Hegel and Karl Marx on down, and a range of late twentieth-century writers and theorists discovered in that tradition a historical materialism that located the impetus of history in the interests, collectivities, and social relations generated by modes of production. Drawing on the work of the Frankfurt School, Gramsci, and Stuart Hall, among others, these forms of historical inquiry sought to delineate dominant and liberatory forces of power, to explore the nature of political "legitimacy" and "consent" in social equilibrium, and to breathe new life into the idea of resistance as a means of studying history's underdogs. Michel Foucault is a particularly important figure in this tradition due to his insistence on contingency, rupture, discontinuity, and multiplicity rather than historical "traditions" or "periods." There is no one past, he asserted, but "several pasts, several forms of connexion, several hierarchies of importance, several networks of determination, several teleologies" ([1969] 1982, 5).

All these theoretical approaches spoke in compelling ways to the concerns of that post–civil rights, post-second-wave feminist generation of scholars, for whom questions of power, consent, consciousness, and resistance in the United States posed a set of post-1960s riddles. Not least, feminist scholars of gender and sexuality like Joan Scott and Eve Kosofsky Sedgwick demonstrated the mutability, fluidity, and constructedness of social categories that had been written about as fixed and "natural" (if they weren't overlooked altogether), at one glance reframing the "social" and redefining the building blocks of "history" in the retelling. These approaches informed (and were informed by) the emergence of "new historicism" in the literary studies of the 1980s and 1990s, as well as the "cultural turn" in history departments in the same era. In each case, inquiry into neglected cultural forms such as popular entertainment, sports, advertising, and leisure and consumption focused explicitly on the constitution and workings of *power* in history-as-past. The "new historicism" as a method and "cultural history" as a subfield were more or less conjoined in the aim of exposing and analyzing the invisible mechanisms of power by deploying new tools of history-as-narrative. Both represented an evolution of older intellectual currents traced to neo-Marxist social theory and to early American studies and cultural studies paradigms.

The result in the twenty-first century has been a generation of scholars across the disciplines who are no less committed to "getting it right" than their predecessors but who are more comfortable with the constructedness of historical narratives, just as they are warier of the archive's biases and more skeptical of anything presented with a claim to objectivity. This generation has taken up—sometimes explicitly, sometimes only tacitly—Hayden White's charge "to expose the historically conditioned character of the historical discipline [itself] . . ." (1978, 29). They see creatures of history everywhere they look. They live happily with *tendencies* but reject historical *laws*; they accept contingency and are allergic to ironbound inevitability. Their historical writing is more self-reflexive and self-critical than that of their elders, and they are mostly at ease with the presentism of the historian's craft, assuming that the questions we ask can *only* be fashioned in present conditions, and so in that respect, we are all presentists now. They are also more drawn than their forebears to the interrogation of structural abstractions like "race" and "gender" and "sexuality" in the impetus of history—as opposed to great deeds and great men. They know that history is grist or ammunition for an argument that somebody or another is trying to advance or, as the French philosopher Jacques Derrida put it, that "there is no political power without control of the archive" ([1996] 2017, 4). Their use of the keyword "history" teaches us that the archiving and narration of the past is politics by other means and that if we do not play the role of the past's tenacious archivists and witnesses, we are destined to be its victims.

2020

35

Indigenous
J. Kēhaulani Kauanui

The keyword "indigenous" has varied genealogies in the fields of American studies and cultural studies. American studies scholarship has tended to use the terms "Indian" and "Native" to refer to indigenous peoples of North America, whereas the field of cultural studies has typically used the terms "Native," "Indigenous," and, in some contexts, "Aboriginal" interchangeably. "Indigenous" peoples in what is regarded by most people as the United States (although the very boundaries of the nation-state are contested by enduring indigenous presence and assertions of sovereignty) include American Indians and Alaska Natives (including Inuits and Aleutians) who constitute 573 federally recognized tribal nations and villages (Schilling 2018). From the island Pacific and Caribbean, there are also Native Hawaiians, American Samoans, Chamorros (Guam and the Northern Mariana Islands), and Taino/Jibara-identified people (Puerto Rico). While all of these peoples can make cases for distinct political statuses based on their indigeneity, four historical and political realities set American Indians apart: they were the original inhabitants of what is now considered the United States; their existence necessitated the negotiation of political compacts, treaties, and alliances with European nations and the United States; they are recognized sovereigns and subject to the US trust doctrine, a unique legal relationship with the US federal government that entails protection; the United States asserts plenary power over tribal nations that is exclusive and preemptive (Wilkins and Stark 2011, 33–37).

In both scholarly and political discussions today, usages of the terms "indigenous" and "indigeneity" emerge from this colonial history and as critical responses to it. One result is that the question of who and what counts as "Indigenous" seems to cause anxiety for just about everyone. The *Oxford English Dictionary* traces the etymology of the adjective "indigenous" to late Latin—*indigen-us*, meaning "born in a country, native" (< *indigen-a*, "a native")—and defines the term as "born or produced naturally in a land or region; native or belonging naturally *to* (the soil, region, etc.)," as well as "inborn, innate, native" and "of, relating to, or intended for the native inhabitants." This emphasis on nativity or birth often leads to assertions such as "everyone is indigenous to *some* place," a universalizing commonplace that makes the term meaningless by erasing the political history of specific indigenous struggles over land claims. Well into the twentieth century, white, Anglo-Saxon "nativists" used this logic to claim land within and beyond the borders of the United States. They dismissed the presence of a wide range of indigenous peoples (along with newly arrived migrants) by claiming, themselves, to be "native-born."

For these reasons, the general definition of "indigeneity" as "born or produced naturally in a land or region" is far too simple. It cannot account for the wide range of relations to region and nation of the more than 370 million indigenous people who are spread across seventy countries worldwide (United Nations 2005). Some indigenous peoples define themselves by their historical continuity with precolonial and presettler societies; others by ties to territories and surrounding natural resources; others in relation to distinct social, economic, or political systems; and still others by their distinct languages, cultures, and beliefs. A 1986–87 definition proposed by UN special rapporteur José Martínez Cobo remains most influential today: indigenous peoples are "those which, having a historical continuity with pre-invasion and pre-colonial societies that have developed on their territories, consider themselves distinct from other sectors of the societies now prevailing in those territories, or parts of them" (United Nations 2009, 5). The UN Permanent Forum on Indigenous Issues suggests that "the most fruitful approach is to identify, rather than define indigenous peoples" on the basis of the fundamental criterion of self-identification rather than by a single set of shared characteristics (United Nations 2005).

The principle of self-identification functions to rebut counterfactual claims that indigenous peoples are either entirely extinct due to genocide or diluted due to racial and cultural mixing. Histories of genocide within the legacy of conquest are pervasive, as settler-colonial societies—those built through permanent settlement of a foreign population to another land, where land is the central resource targeted for seizure—have typically expanded their territory by waging wars against indigenous peoples (Stannard 1992; Wolfe 2006). Jean M. O'Brien (2010) traces the genealogy of the myth of indigenous extinction to white settler ideologies that required that there be no "natives" who could trump their own nativist claims to land or country. In order to assert that the Indians had vanished, nineteenth-century US historians and their readers embraced notions of racial purity rooted in the period's scientific racism—the belief that races were organized in an evolutionary hierarchy that began with savagery, moved through barbarism, and ended with Christian civilization. One result was that most living Indians were cast as "mixed" and thus no longer truly Indian. The erasure and subsequent memorialization of indigenous peoples served the colonial goal of refuting Indian claims to land and rights and became a primary means by which European

Americans asserted their own "modernity" while denying it to putatively "primitive" Indian peoples. One effect of this history is that indigenous peoples have been subject to standards of authenticity based on a colonial logic of biological and cultural purity—notions undergirded by succeeding schools of physical and cultural anthropology.

Within the field of American studies, "indigenous"—as opposed to "native" or "Indian"—has only recently become an important keyword, largely because of interventions by Native American studies scholars (Deloria 2003; Warrior 2003; J. O'Brien 2003). "Indigenous" has increased its prominence for several reasons: it links US movements to the global political struggle to press for the right of self-determination for indigenous peoples, and it offers a more inclusive category with less derogatory baggage than "Indian"—which, as indigenous peoples in the Americas have pointed out, is itself a misnomer. The growing field of settler-colonial studies has also led to more engagement with the concept of indigeneity.

The relatively wider circulation of the term "indigenous" within cultural studies may result from that field's more extensive engagement with postcolonial studies, especially in the British Commonwealth states of Canada, Australia, and Aotearoa / New Zealand, all of which acknowledge that they are settler-colonial societies (and, along with Palestine, are the most frequent focus of settler-colonial studies). In contrast, cultural studies in the United Kingdom has tended to focus on how postcolonial migrant subjects from South Asia, the Middle East, Africa, and the Caribbean have reshaped British society and the United States. As a result, the concept of diaspora has been valorized over and above indigeneity within UK cultural studies (Diaz and Kauanui 2001). There have been some provocative exceptions to this generalization in research that has troubled the false binary between diaspora and indigeneity by teasing out

differences between these two approaches to postcolonial politics and theory (Diaz 1987, 1989, 1994, 1995; Clifford 1997, 2001; Teaiwa 1998, 2005; Kauanui 2007).

The emphasis in both American studies and cultural studies on the constructed as well as the contested nature of identities—the insistence that culture and identity are neither innocent nor pure—has too often and too quickly led scholars in those fields to dismiss assertions of indigenous identity as essentialist (Diaz and Kauanui 2001). They have assumed that claims to "indigeneity" are necessarily grounded in a belief in an underlying and unchanging "essence." While scholarship in cultural studies has offered nuanced critiques of power from the political and historical experiences of failed (or ongoing) revolutions in the First World (critiques of race, ethnicity, class, gender, sexuality, and science), indigeneity has rarely been taken up as a category of analysis. While there has been some productive work in this area on the way indigenous peoples have been racialized (Sturm 2003; Garroutte 2003), the concept of race does not map so neatly onto American Indians or any other indigenous peoples, since the question of indigeneity is rooted in a distinct relationship to land and territory that has consequences for sovereignty (Wilkins and Stark 2011). And while postcolonial studies (a field that responds to and analyzes the cultural legacy of colonialism and imperialism) has offered sustained criticism on the unfinished nationalist liberation movements in the "Third World," it rarely addresses the still-colonized "Fourth World"—a term coined in 1974 by George Manuel and Michael Posluns to name the "indigenous peoples descended from a country's aboriginal population and who today are completely or partly deprived of the right to their own territories and its riches" (Manuel and Posluns 1974, 40; see also Shohat 1992).

The strategies used by dominant groups to undercut indigenous claims to sovereignty vary and are deeply rooted. Consider as an example the contemporary contestation over the discovery doctrine, a concept that originated in a 1493 papal bull written to legitimate Columbus's second voyage to the Americas and subsequently used to justify colonial powers' claims to lands belonging to sovereign indigenous nations. The doctrine established Christian dominion and subjugated non-Christian peoples by invalidating or ignoring aboriginal possession of land in favor of the government whose subjects explored and occupied a territory whose inhabitants were not subjects of a European Christian monarch. Today, there is a widespread movement among indigenous peoples to demand that the Vatican revoke the 1493 edict, especially since European and Euro-settler nations continue to use the doctrine to rationalize the conquest of indigenous lands in order to perpetuate the legal fiction of land possession.

Contestations over issues such as the discovery doctrine are further complicated by the fact that conceptions of indigenous sovereignty tend to be framed by indigenous peoples themselves as a responsibility rather than as a right. This philosophy is reflected in a common saying heard throughout Native America—"the land does not belong to us; we belong to the land"—and serves to counter hegemonic claims made by settler-colonial regimes. For instance, US federal Indian law and policy have long been premised on Old Testament narratives of the "chosen people" and the "promised land," as exemplified in the 1823 Supreme Court ruling *Johnson v. M'Intosh* (21 U.S. (8 Wheat.) 543 (1823)), a landmark decision that held that private citizens could not purchase lands from Indian tribes. The foundations of the court's opinion lay in the discovery doctrine (Robert Williams 2005). Since this ruling has never been struck down, the US government considers tribal nations as mere occupants with use rights. Those who are indigenous are not even allowed collective property

rights of ownership over land—as is the case for domestic dependent nations (federally recognized tribes) with regard to their reservations. This legal imposition can also be traced to the eighteenth-century view that indigenous peoples' lifeways were incommensurate with civic life—that they were living in a "state of nature," the supposedly "natural condition" of humankind before the rule of man-made law and a state of society with an established government.

Today, states continue to impose this notion of the "premodern" savage as a mechanism of control in their negotiations with indigenous peoples' legal status and land rights. One result is that there is no global consensus that indigenous peoples have the right to full self-determination under international law—which would allow for the development of fourth world nation-states independent of their former colonizers, like the states of the postcolonial third world. Because the basic criteria defining colonies under international law include foreign domination and geographical separation from the colonizer, indigenous peoples have been at a disadvantage in the application of decolonization protocols to indigenous nations. This limitation reflects the long-term battle over whether indigenous peoples should be considered "peoples" in the context of chapter 11 of the UN Charter of 1945, which includes the Declaration Regarding Non-Self-Governing Peoples in article 73, and within UN General Assembly resolution 1514, which reads, "All peoples have the right to self-determination; by virtue of that right they freely determine their political status and freely pursue their economic, social and cultural development."

Even after the UN General Assembly's passage of the Declaration on the Rights of Indigenous Peoples in 2007, there is still no consensus. The declaration—a nonbinding, aspirational document—came after decades of global indigenous activism that led to the 1982 establishment of the Working Group on Indigenous Populations (WGIP) under the UN Economic and Social Council. The declaration was stalled for many years due to concerns by states with regard to some of its core statements—namely, the right to self-determination of indigenous peoples and the control over natural resources existing on indigenous peoples' traditional lands. Numerous African and Asian states also took exception to the term "indigenous," suggesting that their entire populations counted as such (even though many of those same states have indigenous minorities within their borders), while Anglo settler states opposed the use of the plural noun "peoples," which signifies collective legal rights under international law.

This difference in legal interpretation over the concepts of "self-determination" and "peoples" was reflected in the 2007 proposal presented to the General Assembly, in which the four votes against the declaration came from white settler states, all with a strong indigenous presence: Australia, Canada, New Zealand, and the United States. Article 46 continues to limit claims of secession and independence by indigenous peoples: "Nothing in this Declaration may be interpreted as implying for any State, people, group or person any right to engage in any activity or to perform any act contrary to the Charter of the United Nations or construed as authorizing or encouraging any action which would dismember or impair totally or in part, the territorial integrity or political unity of sovereign and independent States." Despite this limitation, the declaration is the most comprehensive international instrument addressing the rights of indigenous peoples. It calls for the maintenance and strengthening of indigenous cultural identities and emphasizes the right to pursue development in keeping with indigenous peoples' respective needs and aspirations. It states that indigenous peoples have the right "to the recognition, observance and enforcement of treaties" concluded with states or their successors. It also contains a number of provisions that stipulate "free, prior and informed consent"—the right of indigenous peoples to approve or reject proposed actions or projects that may affect them or their lands, territories, or resources (United Nations 2007).

Looking toward the future, the fields of American studies and cultural studies will need to engage the keyword "indigenous" in ways that acknowledge and interact with this global political history. This necessity is particularly pressing as both fields turn away from nation-based approaches and toward transnational modes of understanding politics, power, and culture. The problem and paradox are that the transnational approach of American studies and, to a lesser degree, cultural studies rarely includes indigenous peoples *as nations* in the first place because they are not nation-states. And yet states are legally (as well as morally) accountable to indigenous peoples *as peoples*. The emergence of the field of Native American and Indigenous studies (as exemplified by the Native American and Indigenous Studies Association, established in 2008) can be instructive for American studies and cultural studies in providing models of scholarly work that takes up this problematic relation between "nation," "state," and "people." One risk is that this lesson will be undercut by the rise of a separate field of settler-colonial studies that does not foreground indigeneity (Kauanui 2017). The promise lies in an inquiry that views settler colonialism as an analytic that is the counterpart—a corresponding keyword—to the indigenous.

2014/2020

36

Intersectionality

Daniel Martinez HoSang

In 1976, five black women who labored on the assembly line at General Motors in St. Louis sued their employer, alleging that the auto giant's seniority-based layoff system, in which the last workers hired were the first to be fired, discriminated against them on the basis of both race and sex. In the subsequent *DeGraffenreid v. General Motors* ruling, the court rejected their claim, arguing that protections of the Civil Rights Act of 1964 permitted them to bring forth a complaint either of race-based discrimination or of sex-based discrimination, but in the court's terms, "not a combination of both." Because the company could prove that it had hired some women (who were all white) who did not face the same seniority-based layoffs experienced by the black women plaintiffs as well as some African Americans (who were all men) who also did not lose their jobs, the *DeGraffenreid* plaintiffs found little protection under the prevailing interpretation of the law.

In a landmark law review article in 1989, the legal scholar Kimberlé Crenshaw introduced the term "intersectionality" to name the complex and uneven ways that the law and social power operated to render the experiences of the *DeGraffenreid* plaintiffs illegible within dominant legal and political discourse. The keyword posits an analogy between the discrimination faced by black women in the workplace and traffic at a four-way intersection. When an accident takes place there involving cars converging from different directions, it is not always possible to assign liability to a single source. In the

DeGraffenreid opinion and a series of similar rulings, the courts effectively denied black women the recognition and standing to seek protections against the simultaneous and intersecting forces of race and gender discrimination, in part because a definitive and single source of the harm they experienced allegedly could not be identified. The dominant "single-axis" conceptualization of discrimination not only tended to "treat race and gender as mutually exclusive categories of experience and analysis" but also legitimated a "paradigm of sex discrimination [that] tends to be based on the experiences of white women . . . [and a] model of race discrimination [that] tends to be based on the experiences" of black men (Crenshaw 1989, 139).

"Intersectionality," as introduced and deployed by Crenshaw in the analysis of *DeGraffenreid* and her decades-long body of work, names both a structural account of black women's experiences of race and gender discrimination and a political argument about the limitations of prevailing modes of feminism and antiracism (Crenshaw 1991). As developed in a body of scholarship and analysis known as critical race theory, intersectionality disrupts "single-axis" conceptualizations of domination that are a hallmark of liberal legal thought. Such conceptualizations assume that "but for" a singular form of discrimination (i.e., "but for racial discrimination"), individuated subjects could exercise their rights within otherwise neutral civil society and markets (Crenshaw 1989, 1995; Spade 2013). In contrast, intersectionality provides a means of naming and making legible forms of harm, violence, and exploitation experienced by subordinated groups that are often hidden by a "single-axis" framework, offering a much more robust and sophisticated understanding of the ways power operates through multiple and mutually constitutive forms of social difference. The keyword thus signifies a practice of analysis, study, and collective social action rather than a totalizing social theory of identity. Intersectionality names something one does rather than something one is (2015, 2).

Understood as this kind of "critical praxis" grounded in black feminism (Collins and Blige 2016, 2), intersectionality has a long collective genealogy, even if it has been defined and identified through alternative terms and signifiers (King 1988). Abolitionist Sojourner Truth's 1851 declaration "Ar'n't I a Woman?" at the Women's Rights Conference in Akron, Ohio, not only contested patriarchal assumptions used to dismiss women's fitness for public and political life; it also challenged white feminists to relinquish their interests and investments in white supremacy in their demands for gender equality (154). Anna Julia Cooper's late nineteenth-century essays, collected in *A Voice from the South*, similarly cautioned against a mode of antiracism in which the status and rights of black men stood in for the status of black people writ large, asserting, "Only the BLACK WOMAN can say 'when and where I enter . . . then and there the whole *Negro race enters with me*" (1998, 63). Truth and Cooper interrogate the dominant suppositions of feminism and antiracism and imagine more expansive alternatives rooted in the specificities of black women's experiences.

When the path-blazing legal scholar Pauli Murray used the word "conjunction" in the 1940s and 1950s to describe the race and sex discrimination faced by black women under what she described as the "Jane Crow" system (Murray and Eastwood 1965), she too was analyzing the "intersection" of seemingly singular modes of domination. "Special oppression" was the term used by the Trinidad and Tobago–born journalist and Communist Claudia Jones in 1949 to describe conditions black women faced "as Negro, as woman, as worker." Frances Beal used the formulation *Black Women's Manifesto; Double Jeopardy: To Be Black and Female* in a 1969

political pamphlet that insisted that antiracist and anticapitalist social movements had to center the gendered experiences of black women and that gender-based liberation could not be an afterthought to these struggles. When Beal and other women of color founded the Third World Women's Alliance soon after, they titled their journal *Triple Jeopardy* to name the ways that imperialism also shaped and produced race and gender oppression. And in the 1970s, groups ranging from the Boston-based Black feminist Combahee River Collective to the panindigenous Women of All Red Nations (WARN) to the Chicana feminists who edited the groundbreaking anthology *This Bridge Called My Back* (1981) were attentive to understanding what Evelyn Nakano Glenn describes as the "interacting, interlocking structures" of race, gender, and class (Glenn 2004, 6).

All these intersectional analyses and practices emerged from within working-class women of color formations as part of their political and analytic responses to material structures of subordination. Indeed, in another foundational law review article, Crenshaw drew explicitly on this tradition in demonstrating that Latina, Asian American, and indigenous women are subject to intersectional institutional regimes and logics in relation to sex- and gender-based violence (1991). Thus intersectionality should be understood *both* as a practice developed specifically from Black feminist organizing and experience *and* as an analytic that helps analyze and interpret relations of power experienced by many other groups.

When the term entered the academy in the late 1980s and early 1990s, scholars within a range of disciplines began using it to describe particular research methodologies and theoretical frameworks. In the social sciences, an intersectional analysis examines the interaction between different social categories, whether in a social movement analysis, the interpretation of survey data, or the development of research protocols (Lykke

2011; McCall 2005; Hancock 2007). As used by literary theorists and other humanists, intersectionality names a reading practice that encourages attention to simultaneity, mutability, and multiplicity and to variable modes of power in ways that reject such fixed categorical meanings (Ferguson 2012a).

The 2015 addition of "intersectionality" to the *Oxford English Dictionary* (*OED*) signaled the term's incorporation within popular media and political discourse. But the *OED*'s definition of the term as "the interconnected nature of social categorizations such as race, class, and gender" distances it both from its theorization and instantiation within Black and women of color feminist praxis and from its circulation within the law (Alexander-Floyd 2012). The term soon found its way into social media postings and speeches by prominent politicians and candidates (including by Hillary Clinton's campaign during the 2016 election) and within a growing number of popular culture references in film and television from *The Chilling Adventures of Sabrina* to HBO's *True Detective*, suggesting an emptying of its movement-building and oppositional political commitments (African American Policy Forum 2019).

As the term has circulated with greater visibly in public discourse, it has come under sharper criticism from cultural studies scholars and political commentators. In the words of Robin D. G. Kelley, "Intersectionality oscillates between a punching bag and a magic wand" (forthcoming). Some critics eschew Crenshaw's theorizing of the term and instead argue that intersectionality is too rooted in fixed conceptions of social identity, implicitly stabilizing the meanings of such identities (distilled into their constituent components of race, gender, or class) rather than understanding such meanings as ongoing processes of social contestation that resist permanent notions of linearity and coherence. These scholars argue that static taxonomies and discrete identity categories can lend themselves to the diversity management imperatives of the state and the forms of administrative violence and regulation undergirding such regimes (B. Cooper 2016).

Similarly, some detractors on the left have critiqued intersectionality as "the opiate of the professional managerial class," claiming that it individuates and fetishizes discreet and bounded differences of social identity at the expense of an analysis of structure, class antagonism, and collective struggle (Michaels 2016). To some extent, this critique mirrors the political Right's dismissal of intersectionality as rooted in rigid and derivative investments in identities of race, gender, and sexuality that refuse the allegedly universal categories of national citizenship and liberal subjectivity (Gonzalez 2018).

These criticisms share an understanding of intersectionality as referencing a *status*, presuming that some individuals possess or experience an "intersectional identity" while others do not. In this way, they elide the term's use as a political heuristic and practice that name and call attention to multiple vectors of power and oppression simultaneously. That is, intersectionality is better understood as a "how" of antisubordination rather than a "what" of identity, as an *analytic* of structures of power and modes of social categorization rather than a totalizing or dogmatic theory of personhood (Carbado 2013; Tomlinson 2019).

This "bottom-up" and open-ended way of posing questions about social relations and power has generated the most compelling uses of the term within contemporary social movements. For example, scholar-activists affiliated with the Oakland-based Asian Immigrant Women Advocates (AIWA) explain that "intersectionality primarily concerns the way things work rather than who people are" (Chun, Lipsitz, and Shin 2013, 923). Groups like AIWA have deployed intersectionality to analyze the particular conditions that immigrant women of color face in contesting their exploitation as low-wage workers rather than to make their identity positions more legible or differentiated. Similarly, the Center for Intersectional Justice in Berlin deploys intersectionality to engage lawmakers at the national and European levels about new horizons of antidiscrimination law and practice. The African American Policy Forum, cofounded by Crenshaw, uses the term to surface the often hidden ways that Black girls have been harmed by heavy-handed school discipline policies (2015). Civil rights attorneys have mobilized the term to build more complex legal cases challenging employment discrimination faced by trans people (E. Young, forthcoming).

All of these usages of the keyword call attention to the particular forms of analysis, solidarity, and collective action that can be produced through its deployment. They do not presume that intersectionality constitutes a singular or grand social theory that can be uniformly applied to all contexts, structures, and dynamics or abstracted from a particular social location and condition. Used in this way, intersectionality affords a necessary optic on the uneven ways that power operates across social groups as well as a set of practices to collectively contest these distinct forms of domination.

As a practice and prism, intersectionality conceptualizes social identities as collective registers of power relations that are always unstable, interconnected, variable, and contradictory (Cho, Crenshaw, and McCall 2013). The keyword in this context becomes essential to understanding how oppositional political practices such as antiracism and feminism can unintentionally occlude some forms of subordination, exploitation, and violence. It thus names one component of a broader political practice that can contest and transform oppressive structures of power.

2020

37

Islam
Brian T. Edwards

The arrival of Islam as a religion in the United States is far from new, yet neither the religion nor its adherents received much attention in American studies or cultural studies until Islam became a media and popular fixation, especially after September 11, 2001. In this sense, scholarly interest in Islam has responded to the obsessions of the US public sphere, where the religion is poorly understood and often defined in imprecise or fallacious ways, resulting in inaccurate references to and representations of both Islam and the "Muslim" or "Arab" worlds. Locating "Islam" as a keyword for American studies and cultural studies thus requires an exploration of related terms such as "Muslim" and "Arab." While not all Arabs are Muslim, and only about one-quarter of all Muslims are Arab, US public discourse has often collapsed the religion and the ethnicity through the logics of Orientalism, wherein the inscription of a unified Other located in the "Orient" buttresses the equally fictitious sense that there is a unified West or "Occident" (Said 1978; Prashad 2007).

Anyone studying US culture therefore needs to consider how "Islam" has at least three different referents. First, it designates a poorly understood and massively misrepresented global religion. Second, it is a catchall term that US Americans have used to describe a variety of intertwined religious, ethnic, or racial others, some of them Muslim but not all. Third, it names a complex sociological reality that includes waves of migration and large-scale religious conversions that have brought millions of Muslims to the United States. In the key-word "Islam," these three referents become intertwined.

The monotheistic religion now called Islam first emerged in the Arabian Peninsula when, in 610 CE, during the month called Ramadan, an Arab businessman named Muhammad received the first of a series of revelations from God. Two years later, Muhammad began to preach to others. Muhammad did not at first think of himself as founding a new religion but as bringing an older faith in the One God to the Arabs, who had not had their own prophet before (K. Armstrong 2002). The God of the Arabs (al-Lah, which in Arabic means, simply, "the God") before Muhammad was a single deity whom many Arabs considered the same as the one worshipped by Jews and Christians in the neighboring Byzantine and Persian Empires. When Muhammad began to recognize himself as a prophet for the Arabs, he saw his message as extending that of a line of prophets from Abraham, Moses, David, and Solomon to Jesus, all of whom are mentioned in the Qur'an and considered prophets by Muslims. The Qur'an calls Jews and Christians ahl al-kitab, or People of the Book, and commands Muslims to say to them, "Our God and your God is one, and to Him we have submitted" (Qur'an 29:46, trans. Muhsin Khan).

Muhammad's preaching focused on the creation of a just society and the sharing and distribution of wealth, a message that resonated in the city of Mecca, where he lived. For the following two decades, Muhammad continued to receive revelations in the form of verses of Arabic. Though Muhammad was illiterate, the Qur'an (which means "recitation" in Arabic) as received or revealed to him was considered a masterpiece of the use of language and poetry. Indeed, its sophistication and beauty were so immediate and overwhelming that it convinced even some of the most skeptical and resistant in Muhammad's day to convert to the new religion.

To the present, versions of the Qur'an translated into other languages are considered secondary and not to be the Qur'an at all. The title of the English translation, for instance, is often rendered as "The Meaning of the Holy Qur'an," to indicate the secondary status of the translation. While Islam has become the second-largest religion in the world, with an estimated 1.5 billion adherents (about one-fifth of the population of the world), the vast majority of whom do not speak Arabic, the Qur'an in Arabic is its centerpiece.

The word "Islam" appears eight times in the Qur'an, while the word Muslimun, the Arabic plural form of Muslim, is much more common (Gardet 1978). Both words derive from the trilateral Arabic root s–l–m, meaning "to surrender" and also "to prostrate oneself." A "Muslim," understood etymologically, is thus someone who surrenders to God. This trilateral root also gives us the Arabic word salaam, meaning "peace." Of course, etymology only goes so far in explaining the history of the word and its uses. Gardet, in the widely respected Encyclopedia of Islam, notes that though the word "Islam" is relatively rare in the Qur'an, it was increasingly used to designate the faith in the titles of Arabic-language works during the classical period (i.e., the Middle Ages in Europe), far surpassing the word iman (or "faith"), a word that earlier scholars had often erroneously equated with it. Scholars of Islam note the centrality of the idea of a community (umma) of believers whose submission and surrender to God, beyond merely following God's commandments, grant them admission to the umma of Muslims.

Muhammad was an influential figure, both while he was alive and after his death. While alive, he was a charismatic individual, a great preacher, and an extremely talented political and military leader. In 622, Muhammad, along with roughly seventy Muslim families living alongside him in Mecca, departed for the city of

Medina. This migration (or *hijra*) represented Muhammad's breaking with the tribe and the creation of a new community, a just society in which politics and religion intermingle (K. Armstrong 2002). After the death of Muhammad in 632, three *khalifa* (or caliphs, meaning "representatives") were chosen to lead the Muslims, each succeeding another, all of them close associates of Muhammad. However, when the third caliph, Uthman, was assassinated, a contest over succession emerged, leading to a period called a *fitna* (or "confusion"), as different communities of Muslims rallied around two possible successors. These two different lines became the basis for the major division between the Shi'a and Sunni denominations or branches of Islam. Both Shi'a and Sunni denominations, and variants on them such as the Isma'ili branch of Shi'a Islam and the Nation of Islam, which affiliates with the Sunni branch, are prevalent in the United States today (Curtis 2009).

Those who eventually called themselves the Shi'a (from *Shi'at Ali*, meaning "followers or partisans of Ali") support Muhammad's son-in-law and cousin Ali ibn Abi Talib. Ali became the fourth caliph in 656 but was assassinated five years later. His followers consider him the first imam of the Islamic community. His murder and the eventual slaughter of his second son, Husain, the grandson of Muhammad, by the troops of the rival Umayyad caliph as Husain marched to Iraq to take up leadership, are considered by Shi'a as symbols of the perpetual injustice pervading human life. The response to the killings of Ali and Husain established patterns that carried forward in time: "[They] seemed to show the impossibility of integrating the religious imperative in the harsh world of politics, which seemed murderously antagonistic to it" (K. Armstrong 2002, 43). For a long time, Shi'a tended not to be invested in practical affairs of state (postrevolutionary Iran, a Shi'a majority state, is a recent exception). In contrast, in

most Arab countries, the Sunni (whose name refers to the *sunna*, or "customs"—namely, the religious practice of Muhammad himself) have been more numerous and more concerned with politics and are in the majority (roughly 85–90 percent of Muslims globally, though in the Middle East, the divide is roughly 60–40 Sunni-Shi'a). Still, the differences between Shi'a and Sunni—which many observers argue are primarily political, not spiritual—have in many cases been overstated in Western discourse, and there are numerous examples of peaceful cohabitation between adherents of the two branches (Mamdani 2004).

Today, with 1.5 billion Muslims, six different schools of *fiqh* (jurisprudence) between the Sunni and Shi'a branches, and variations among nationally or locally inflected traditions and customs, "Islam" could hardly be considered the monolith that mainstream commentators in Western media have sometimes claimed it is. What many scholars consider fundamental to contemporary Islam is the practice of its five central tenets or pillars (though Shi'a do not call them pillars of Islam)—namely, the *shahada* (profession of faith), prayers five times per day, fasting during the month of Ramadan, the giving of charity or alms (*zakat*), and taking a *hajj* or pilgrimage to Mecca at least once in a lifetime. But given the diversity of the religion as practiced globally, Islam's tolerance of the interruption of day-to-day affairs, and a much greater secular impulse in many of the Muslim-majority countries than is generally appreciated in the West (so-called cultural Muslims), these are often ideals rather than practices.

While the origins of Islam were far from the United States in place and time, Islam has long fascinated people in the United States. In recent years, scholars in American studies have investigated the history of this interest and key moments when US culture engaged the global religion from a distance or when US international projects led individuals from the United States to a closer encounter with lands where Islam was the majority religion. A point of debate in such scholarship is whether there is a prevailing continuity in US representations of Islam—thus a continuation of what Edward Said called the "fabric" of Orientalism (1978, 24) and transposition of French and British traditions into US discourse—or whether discontinuities and persistent historical amnesia have led different generations to redefine and recharacterize Islam and Muslim lands and peoples without cognizance of previous generations' patterns of so doing (see McAlister 2001; Brian Edwards 2005; Marr 2006; Makdisi 2007; Nance 2009; Berman 2012).

Scholars trace the US preoccupation with Islam as far back as the seventeenth-century European settlement in North America. Timothy Marr has called this persistent obsession "American Islamicism," which he describes as motivated by the "need to acknowledge Islam as an important world phenomenon" and the "desire to incorporate its exotic power within national genealogies" (2006, 1–2). In early and antebellum North America, there was a surprising diversity of images of Islam that exhibit an ambivalent response to the religion and to Muslims: both revulsion and attraction. The former is represented by Captain John Smith, who had violently fought Turks in the Ottoman Europe prior to his arrival at Jamestown, Virginia; the latter can be seen in the missionary impulse of Mary Fisher, an important Quaker who left New England in 1658 to preach the Christian gospel in Turkey (Marr 2006). In either case, early concerns with Islam were more international (or "planetary") than we have traditionally understood.

In the early eighteenth century, West African Muslims arrived on North American shores as slaves. Their prompt and forced conversion to Christianity did not free them from bondage but was a condition of it. In the late eighteenth century, during the popular fascination with white slavery and the Barbary pirates of North Africa, this point was highlighted by novelist Royall Tyler (1797) and satirized by Benjamin Franklin (1790), both of whom made readers aware of the paradox that US citizens held captive in North Africa who converted to Islam were immediately freed by their captors, while African slaves who were forced to convert to Christianity in the United States were not. This intriguing connection in what can be seen as eighteenth-century comparative accounts of captivity was, along with the more general obsession with white captivity in Muslim lands, a moment when Islam seemed to matter immediately to the United States (Sayre 2010).

Through the nineteenth century and into the early twentieth, there were other occasions when individuals living in the United States were fascinated with Islam and Muslims. Islam figured in antebellum antislavery and temperance movements, played a large role in Herman Melville's and Washington Irving's cosmopolitan literary engagements, and ran through Ralph Waldo Emerson's deep interest in classical Persian poetry (Marr 2006; Dimock 2006). In popular culture, the rise of the Shriners, belly dancers, and mystics domesticated Muslim iconography and forms, and the Nation of Islam emerged from the African American community in Detroit in 1930, innovating a starkly different understanding of the religion practiced in the Arab world (Nance 2009). Scholars in American studies have plumbed these overlooked archives. To be sure, present concerns have deeply infected popular and scholarly understandings of the history of US engagement with the Arab Muslim world (Brian Edwards 2010, 2016).

Across this complex history, there is a tension between Islam as signifier of the *foreign* and Islam as *domestic* practice and sociological phenomenon. As a domestic practice and phenomenon, Islam existed in North America earlier than commonly recognized and is more prevalent in the United States than generally known. Despite its arrival with West African slaves in the eighteenth century, Islam did not survive with substantial numbers (the forced conversion of Muslim slaves to Christianity had a major effect). With the decline and dissolution of the Ottoman Empire in the late nineteenth and early twentieth centuries, a second wave of Muslims arrived in the United States, many of them from Syria, Lebanon, and Turkey. A third major wave of Muslim migration to the United States followed the easing of restrictions on immigration after the passage of the Immigration Act of 1965. Numbers are always contested and difficult to know because the US Census does not collect data on religion. A recent credible estimate of the current Muslim population in the United States was 3.45 million in 2017, according to the Pew Research Center, which also predicted a significant growth in the coming years (a higher estimate, of six million, was made by Cainkar in 2010). The major communities of Muslims are South Asian, Arab, and African American. Among African American Muslims, conversion to Islam has been an important factor, and the Nation of Islam continues to play a major role and to demonstrate that there is a significant disparity among practices of Islam in the United States and abroad (Abdo 2006; Curtis 2009).

After 2001, the experience of Muslims in the United States became especially fraught and difficult because of a popular obsession with Islam as a source of global terrorism and the misapprehension and misrepresentation of the global religion as scapegoat for the actions of individuals. If nothing else, the history of the Western fascination with Islam teaches us that American Orientalism or American Islamicism has for centuries generalized and collapsed a multiplicity of Muslim sects, schools, and practices (including secular nonpractice)

into a monolithic or misrepresented symbol of foreignness. In the first decade of the twenty-first century, anxieties about the waning of US cultural and economic hegemony—the advent of what has been called the "post-American world" (Zakaria 2008)—often were channeled into simplistic and single-minded accounts of the second-largest religion in the world, using as evidence details from tiny minorities. Books such as Dave Eggers's nonfiction work *Zeitoun* (2009), set in New Orleans during Hurricane Katrina; Moustafa Bayoumi's academic reportage *How Does It Feel to Be a Problem?* (2008), based on interviews in Brooklyn in the wake of 9/11, and essays collected in *This Muslim American Life* (2016); and Amaney Jamal and Nadine Naber's collection *Race and Arab Americans before and after 9/11* (2008) showed how anti-Muslim and anti-Arab stereotyping threatened to repeat the worst aspects of US racism and to extend the Orientalism of past centuries into the present.

More recently, the venomous expressions of hatred toward Islam unleashed during the 2016 presidential campaign and Donald Trump presidency represents a new, dark chapter. Candidate Trump's 2015 call for a halt on Muslims entering the US provoked both domestic and international outcry (Brian Edwards 2015), which led to public demonstrations after President Trump attempted to put a so-called Muslim ban into effect during the first year of his administration. Fueled by alternative media and digital communication technologies, resurgent white nationalist discourse in the late 2010s collapses anti-immigrant, antisemitic, and anti-Muslim rhetoric. The slippage between categories demonstrates the persistence and resilience of a long tradition in which the keyword "Islam" structures discourse about racial, ethnic, and national difference in and beyond the United States.

2014/2020

38

Labor

Marc Bousquet

In April 1968, Martin Luther King Jr. was assassinated while organizing mass protests in support of an illegal strike by Memphis sanitation workers. Like many activists of his day, he saw a series of connections among discrimination by race, sex, and workplace exploitation. He asked, "What does it profit a man to be able to eat at an integrated lunch counter if he doesn't earn enough money to buy a hamburger and a cup of coffee?" (1968). In response to intersecting modes of oppression, King and others believed that liberatory social movements needed to pursue shared goals. The long tradition of such intersectional labor analysis includes the oratory of Frederick Douglass (2000) and the sociology of W. E. B. Du Bois (1995a, 1995b); the feminist anarchism of Lucy Parsons (2004) and Emma Goldman (1969); the revolutionary communist poetry of Langston Hughes (1973) and Amiri Baraka (1999); and the socialist feminism of Roxanne Dunbar-Ortiz (2006), Donna Haraway (1985), Angela Davis (1983), Barbara Ehrenreich (2001), and Leslie Feinberg (1993), among countless others.

The intersectional view of power exists in significant tension with common uses of the term "labor" to name a distinct or "special" interest group. In mainstream journalism and school curricula, the word most commonly refers to organized labor, especially politically influential trade-union membership. For many people, this mainstream usage calls up images of sweat and industrial grime, especially the meatpackers, miners, and autoworkers in films such as Paul Schrader's *Blue Collar* (1978) or Barbara Kopple's Oscar-winning documentaries *Harlan County, U.S.A.* (1976) and *American Dream* (1990). The problem with this usage is that it obscures a far more diverse reality. At present, the most unionized US occupations are education and civil service (about 40 percent), as compared to 10 percent of miners and factory workers (US Bureau of Labor Statistics 2011). If image reflected reality, our notion of a typical union member might be fiftyish and female, an Inuit teacher, a Puerto Rican corrections officer, or a Korean American clerk at the Department of Motor Vehicles. The gulf between simplistic media imagery and diverse reality raises critical questions regarding the tendency to stereotype labor as a chiefly white and male, well-organized, "blue-collar" special interest group characterized by a culture of rough, manly, almost effortless solidarity.

Associated with agricultural or mechanical toil and modest social standing in earlier usages dating from the Middle Ages, "labor" emerged as a keyword in the nineteenth century for critical theorists and social reformers addressing questions of political and economic modernity. Along with the democratic revolutions and emergence of a capitalist economy, the rising self-organization and social consciousness of individuals who worked in order to live produced a new social category: "laborers." This category—and the lived experience that enabled it—led to the recognition by social theorists that organized workers constituted a powerful, socially transformative class of persons. A wide array of theorists, both radical and conservative, recognized that this class embodied interests that were clearly distinguished from those of people whose incomes derived from ownership rather than their own efforts (the possessors of capital, or the capitalist class; Blanc 1839; Marx and Engels [1848] 1976).

Critical to understanding any deployment of the term "labor" during this period is the revolutionary "labor theory of value." Plainly put, this theory is based on the idea that the value of goods derives from the labor necessary to their production (Adam Smith [1776] 1937; Ricardo 1817; Marx 1844, [1867] 1976; Mandel 1974). Karl Marx praised capitalism for its "constant revolutionizing of production" and agreed that it was generally an improvement for many ordinary workers over previous forms of economic organization. But he also observed, drawing on the sensationalist working-class literature of the period, that the system operated vampirically; it diverted a large fraction of labor-generated value to persons who owned the industrial means of production (i.e., the investing class that purchases machinery and factories, hires the brainpower of inventors and engineers, pays workers in advance of sales, and so on). In this sense, capital is nothing more than dead labor, as Marx put it, thriving and accumulating "by sucking living labor, and lives the more, the more labor it sucks" (1848).

This usage by Marx and other early social theorists emerged in connection with labor's militant self-organization in the nineteenth century. The labor movement's understanding of itself as a socially transformative class or group is broadly evident in the newspapers, essays, dialogues, and plays produced by workers in labor fraternities and working women's associations. Women in New England mills built some of the earliest and most militant working-class organizations in the country and, like their male counterparts, produced a countercultural literature of dissent, provocation, and solidarity ("Women Working, 1800–1930" n.d.). This literature-from-below described a profound antagonism between labor and capital, describing laborers' working conditions as the return of slavery, the end of democracy, and the return by stealth of aristocracy to North American soil. Between the middle of the nineteenth and the middle of the twentieth century, countless workers drew on this literature as they developed that "one big union" model of industrial unionism, as practiced by the Industrial Workers of the World (IWW, or Wobblies), the Congress of Industrial Organizations (CIO), and the pioneering Knights of Labor.

Influenced by E. P. Thompson and the Birmingham school of cultural studies, US scholars such as Stanley Aronowitz (1974), Sean Wilentz (1984b), David Montgomery (1987), and Paul Buhle (1987) aligned themselves with these activists and reformers as they produced a "new labor history." What was new about this history was its understanding of working people as cultural producers, not merely the consumers of cultural artifacts produced for them by others. Extending this legacy, the cultural historian Michael Denning (1997) chronicles how the rich and complex culture produced by and for union members—often dissident or radical union members seeking to change the culture of their unions for the better—shaped the broader culture and its politics, most notably in the left-wing popular art of the 1930s and '40s. Until the campaign of repression launched by McCarthyism, most unions, mainstream and radical, had significant membership crossover with socialist, communist, or anarchist movements aimed at revolutionary working-class liberation, typically adopting an intersectional view toward oppression by race and sex (Maxwell 1999; Rabinowitz 1991; Coiner 1995; Kelley 1994).

Largely as a result of feminist activism and research, the activities that we understand as labor have expanded enormously since the early 1970s. Pointing out that the creation, training, and care of (traditionally) male wage workers depends, all over the globe, on the often unwaged, traditionally female "labor of reproduction," Selma James and Mariarosa Dalla Costa (1972) led an innovative "Wages for Housework" campaign and radicalized our understanding of the labor process. James and Dalla Costa objected to the common understanding of "reproductive labor" as referring to the generally unwaged activities of child rearing by parents and other caregivers in the family and community. Instead, they usefully expanded the insight that capitalism's visibly waged activities depend on an elaborate supporting network of unwaged effort. This insight altered a long-standing agreement between radical and conservative nineteenth-century theorists that the political-economic analysis of capitalism should focus only on wage labor, particularly labor that led directly to the employer's profit, such as factory work.

As a result of this feminist intervention into labor history and politics, new areas of analysis came into focus: unwaged labor, as in child rearing and housework; donated labor, as in volunteerism or internship; waged labor in the nonprofit sector, such as teaching, policing, and civil service; free creative or intellectual work; subsistence labor in small agriculture; forms of forced labor such as slavery, indenture, and prison labor; labor in illegal or unregulated circumstances, as in sweatshops or sex work; and working "off the books" in otherwise legal activities such as babysitting and food service. Underscoring all the teaching, feeding, nursing, transportation, clothing, and training involved in "producing" an industrial worker, feminists and analysts in the Italian autonomist tradition, such as Paolo Virno and Tiziana Terranova, argued that the value represented by consumer goods is produced in a "social factory," a vast web of effort that intersects at the point of assembly but is not limited to it (Virno 2010).

This is not just a critical or theoretical observation. As any college student or recent graduate can attest, nearly all forms of contemporary enterprise are restructuring the labor process to maximize the contributions of unwaged, underwaged, or donated "labor": from volunteers, students, apprentices, and interns; from regular wage workers who communicate by email and take phone calls at home or in transit; from local government, which pays for worker training and security services; from permanently "temporary" workers who are not entitled to benefits; or from outsourced workers who are superexploited by contractors, often in another country. The persons who contribute much of this unaccounted-for labor include women, students and teachers, migrants, guest workers, the undocumented, workers in the service economy, clergy, and civil servants. Many of them are seduced into donating or discounting their labor by canny management that portrays the discount as a fair exchange for workplaces that are perceived as fun, creative, or satisfying (Ross 2004, 2009). Persons in all of these intensely racialized laboring groups played a leading role in the worldwide revolutionary ferment of the 1960s. While they often intersected with each other in both planned and spontaneous ways, the new social movements they participated in were largely independent (or "autonomous") of traditional sources of power to shape the course of the state, such as political parties and the dominant trade unions. The school of thought that came to be known as autonomism emphasizes their power independent of organized political parties and trade unions and the intersection of workers' interests across economic sectors and national borders.

Grasping labor as social productivity includes the crucial understanding that contemporary capitalism captures profit from many activities not generally understood as labor. Consider social media as an example. Many kinds of businesses directly monetize recreational or self-expressive social activity, as in the social sourcing of revenue-producing content on YouTube, the Huffington Post, and other media-sharing sites. Users also make a second, less obvious gift of countless related activities—the labor of rating content, publicizing it (by passing links along), and surrounding the content with entertaining commentary. This phenomenon was notably described by Maurizio Lazzarato (1996) as "immaterial labor," a kind of labor previously reserved to privileged or professional tastemakers such as professors, critics, public-relations and advertising workers, and journalists. The breadth of this social productivity includes students' low-wage, underwaged, and donated labor in work-study or internship arrangements. But that is only the tip of the iceberg. Students create value for campuses in myriad ways, from athletics and performance to donated journalism, service learning, running extracurriculars for other students, and so on. Facebooking one's social life or working out in the fitness center can be understood as making a donation to the campus brand (Bousquet 2008, 2009).

Where capital cannot seduce labor, it seeks to rule by other means. The capitalist reaction to labor insurrection worldwide has been state adoption of economic neoliberalism and the steady globalization of the production process (Harvey 1989). This means that much of the work involved in producing goods consumed in the United States—even putatively "American" brands such as Apple, Levi's, and Harley-Davidson—is the labor of Chinese, Mexican, Indonesian, African, and Indian workers. Organizations such as China Labor Watch and films such as *China Blue* (2005) document, across industries, persistent patterns in Chinese manufacture: typically hiring primarily young, single, female workers between the ages of sixteen and twenty-five, who will burn out or be fired because of worker abuse ranging from violence and toxic chemical exposure to eighty- and ninety-hour workweeks, often with net salaries (after deductions for employer-provided dormitory housing, food, and other necessities) of less than thirty cents an hour. In response to the domination that many workers experience in capital's globalization-from-above, it seems inevitable that laborers will have to build a worldwide solidarity in self-defense—a visionary workers' globalization-from-below.

2014

39

Latino/a/x

Juana María Rodríguez

The oldest and most conventional of this keyword's variants, "Latino," is commonly used as an ethnic designation that distinguishes Latin Americans living in the United States from those living in their countries of origin. Even this seemingly straightforward variant sustains a hefty set of internal contradictions and has a decidedly blurry genealogy. While commonly used as an adjective modifying everything from voting blocs to musical categories, neighborhoods, and foodways, the exact referent of the term remains indeterminate even as it seems to imply specific populations, geographies, histories, colonialisms, languages, and cultural practices. The problem is that each of these potential referents carries significant contradictions and erasures. The gendered nature of the Spanish language presents its own stylistic challenges. In Spanish, the masculine form—for example, *Latino*—is intended to be applied universally, a convention that has carried over to English-language usage of these terms. To counteract this masculinist imposition, writers in both languages have developed a range of rhetorical strategies in order to be more inclusive. These have included a slash between an *o* and *a* meant to register two possible gendered possibilities, as in "Latino/a," and the spelling out of both gendered articulations, such as "Latina" and "Latino." However, feminist and queer Spanish-language communities have criticized how these reinscribe a gender binary and exclude those who identify outside the binary. While in the 1990s, queer

online communities took up the *arroba*—intended to mark where someone is "at" in terms of gender—to create terms such as *latin@* or *amig@s*, difficulties in pronunciation and objections to the appearance of the *a* seemingly engulfed by a larger *O* stalled its widespread usage. In contrast, the use of the letter *x* in *latinx* (and other gendered nouns in Spanish) seeks to be more gender inclusive and more radical in its gesture toward incorporating other elements of difference. These usages have gained significant traction and are currently being taken up by a range of universities, research centers, community groups, and initiatives (Milian 2017). In 2018, "Latinx" was added to the Merriam-Webster Dictionary.

Whether written as Latino, Latino/a, or Latinx, the most widespread meaning of these terms is as a geographic reference to peoples in the United States who originate from Latin America. This definition immediately invokes cartographic debates about the precise borders of Latin America, where Latin America as a specific cultural and historical construct is understood as distinct from both South America and North America. Mexico is, of course, in North America, and prior to the 1848 Treaty of Guadalupe Hidalgo, it included 525,000 square miles of what is now US territory, including California, Utah, and Nevada along with parts of Colorado, Wyoming, New Mexico, and Arizona. This history of annexation disrupts the commonplace association of Latinx populations with immigration or "foreign" origin. The terms "Chicano" and "Chicana" (often spelled "Xicano" and "Xicana") emerged in the 1960s as politically inflected alternatives to "Mexican American" to mark the distinct cultural and political characteristics of people of Mexican ancestry living in the United States, to differentiate these populations from more recent immigrants, and to reclaim an imagined historical past rooted in *Aztlán*, a constructed designation used to name the lands annexed by the United States (Rosales 1997; Noriega and Sandoval 2011). These occupied territories contained sizable indigenous communities that have remained culturally, linguistically, and legally distinct from their Mexican, Chicanx, and US neighbors and serve as a caution against collapsing distinctions between Latinxs and Native Americans in the region (Saldaña-Portillo 2016). Broad attempts to imagine Latin America as beginning at the Rio Grande and ending at the southernmost tip of Chile elide the various nation-states that do not share a Spanish or even Iberian colonial history. As the numbers of Brazilians in the United States have grown, they are increasingly being included in the designation "Latinx." However, populations that immigrate to the United States from countries historically associated as French, Dutch, or English colonies in South and Central America, such as Belize, Suriname, Guyana, French Guiana, and the Falkland Islands, most of which have Black-majority populations, are often excluded from forming part of what is imagined as Latinx.

The various countries, cultures, and colonies of the Caribbean also press on attempts to categorize "Latinx" through recourse to geography. Puerto Ricans are certainly a visible and recognizable portion of what is termed "US Latinxs," yet the island's current colonial status as an unincorporated territory of the United States adds an additional consideration. The tendency to understand "Latinx" as implying a migratory relationship to the United States differentiates it from the term "Latin American," with the effect that Puerto Ricans both on and off the island are implicated in its usage. Despite their US passports, many Puerto Ricans living on the mainland (often termed "Nuyoricans" to signal their significant presence in New York or "Diasporicans" to mark broader migratory trajectories) are stigmatized as foreign or ethnic others in relation to an imagined Anglo-Saxon populace. In contrast, Puerto

Ricans on the island experience their relationship to the mainland through the legal, economic, militaristic, linguistic, and cultural force of US colonial power. The lived consequences of their colonial status include being US citizens who cannot vote in US presidential elections and have no vote in Congress. Other islands such as Hispaniola, which is shared by both the Dominican Republic and Haiti, create additional problems of categorization. While Dominicans, as Spanish speakers, might more easily self-identify as Latinxs, French- and Creole-speaking Haitians are more likely to use the geographic referent "Caribbean" if they wish to stake a claim to a pannational, regionally situated, ethnic identity. The numerous nations and islands of the Caribbean, with their messy tangle of serial colonialism, multilingualism, and interregional migration, create particular challenges for a geographic understanding of the term. Similarly, recourse to shared Iberian conquest fails to bring clarity to our understanding of Latinx—after all, Spain and Portugal have had colonial investments in the Philippines, Cape Verde, Macao, Mozambique, Morocco, Guinea Bissau, Angola, and elsewhere. Upon migration to the United States, these populations have rarely been viewed as Latinx.

Questions of race—as a categorical designation separate from ethnicity, geography, or nationality—further complicate attempts to define Latinx. Colonialism, slavery, migration, and interracial reproduction through state-sanctioned rape, concubinage, and marriage have produced phenotypically diverse and racially stratified Latin American and Latinx populations. Centuries of racialized slavery throughout the hemisphere have resulted in numerically larger populations of African Americans in South American than in North America. In the United States, the "one-drop" rule historically designated anyone with African heritage as black. In Latin America, understandings of race generally allow any mixture that includes European to be defined as something *other* than black or indigenous, thus producing a much wider range of terms designating specific racial mixtures, including terms such as *mulato, mestiza, pardo*, and *trigeño*. Some Latin American countries have linked their national identities to concepts such as *mestizaje* (which has also been taken up widely in US Latinx discourse), attempting to indicate a racially mixed and nationally unified population. The risk of these universalizing gestures is that they can erase or marginalize specific racial, ethnic, and religious minorities, particularly indigenous, African, and immigrant populations. Despite the discourse of racial multiplicity and coexistence that is often associated with Latinx communities, antiblack, anti-indigenous, and colorist racial hierarchies that privilege whiteness remain the norm throughout the hemisphere (Dávila 2008; Román and Flores 2010).

Reflecting these categorical ambiguities and in response to shifting political pressures, the US Census has used a range of criteria in its efforts to enumerate these populations (C. Rodríguez 2000). In 1940, the census collected data on "persons of Spanish mother tongue"; in 1950 and 1960, the criteria shifted to "persons of Spanish surname"; in 1970, the census asked if "this person's origin or descent was Mexican, Puerto Rican, Cuban, Central or South American or Other Spanish"; and in 1980, it used the phrase "Spanish/Hispanic origin or descent," identifying individuals as racially white unless they specifically indicated otherwise. These early uses of "Hispanic" included immigrants from Spain, emphasized the "Spanish" roots of Latin America, and promoted an identification with whiteness. Politically and culturally, the term "Latino," which was first adopted in the 2000 census, shifted the focus to origins in Latin America. The 2000 census also marked the first time that individuals who identified themselves as "Latino

or Hispanic" were also asked to indicate their race and the first time an individual could check multiple boxes for race. This effort to refute an assumed whiteness on behalf of Latinxs is significant as a means to enumerate the presence of Afro-Latinxs, Asian-Latinxs, and those with mixed racial identifications, even as these hyphenated terms can likewise perpetuate a definition of "Latinx" that exists separate from these racial currents.

Throughout the second half of the twentieth century, US studies of these diverse populations participated in the politics of these naming practices. The field was divided between Chicano studies on the West Coast and Puerto Rican studies on the East Coast. These scholarly explorations emerged from the civil rights movements of the late sixties and early seventies and were generally centered on questions of identity, language, history, community, and lived experiences of discrimination. In early Chicanx cultural production and activism, the labor conditions of farmworkers figured centrally, as did protests against police violence and political demands for expanding educational access and diversifying existing curricula (Rosales 1997). Puerto Rican cultural and political projects tackled more broadly the daily realities of urban poverty, street violence, racial discrimination in the United States, and the cultural complexities brought about by the *guagua aérea*, or "air bus," of circular migration between San Juan and New York City (Flores 2000; Laó-Montes and Dávila 2001). On both coasts, much of the political writing of the civil rights era was formed through heterosexist and masculinist concepts of nationalism that stressed patriarchal dominance in familial and activist hierarchies, often using cultural narratives of "tradition" to buttress binary gender distinctions and social roles (Blackwell 2011; R. Rodríguez 2009). These gendered critiques of nationalist politics were not unique to Latinxs, but they were forcefully given voice in the breakthrough cultural phenomenon that was *This Bridge Called My Back*, edited by Chicana lesbians Cherríe Moraga and Gloria Anzaldúa (1981). Moraga (1983) and Anzaldúa (1987) became leading figures in feminist of color movements and pushed forward efforts to address heterosexism in Latinx communities and white ethnocentrism in US feminist and gay and lesbian communities of the era. Since then, significant critical work produced at the intersection of Latinx studies and queer theory has intervened in both streams of inquiry, complicating the political and performative function of identity (Muñoz 1999, 2009; Quiroga 2000; J. Rodríguez 2003, 2014; Soto 2010).

In the early twenty-first century, issues surrounding immigration have dominated public discourse on Latinxs and have resulted in crucial investigations into education, public health, law, public policy, and voting patterns (Beltrán 2010; Dávila 2008; García Bedolla 2009). As migration patterns have shifted, regionalism and site-specific investigations within urban centers such as Los Angeles, Miami, New York, Hartford, and Chicago and within different areas of the Southwest, particularly border towns, have gained prominence as a means of interrogating the implications of the localized diversity of Latinx populations, often in relation to other racialized communities (Fernandez 2012; Laó-Montes and Dávila 2001; Schmidt Camacho 2008). Scholarly investigations of Latinx art, literature, and more recently, music and dance have dominated humanistic investigations within Latinx studies. This work has highlighted themes related to gender roles and family; home, cultural belonging, loss, and displacement; colonial histories and processes of racialization; and the complexities involved in translating languages and cultures across borders, regions, and bodies (Aparicio 1998; Fiol-Matta 2017; Flores 2000; Lima 2007; Parédez 2009; Pérez 2007; Rivera 2003; Rivera-Servera 2012; Vazquez

2013). Increasingly, the multinational and generationally differentiated nature of Latinx communities has shifted scholarly attention to investigate how *latinidad*, a term used to highlight the constructed nature and political possibilities of pan-Latinx expression, gets deployed. This turn has also prompted some scholars to critique the term "Latino," suggesting that it functions most effectively as a marketing strategy, a way to designate diverse but aggregated populations in order to better serve the economic needs of specific local, regional, national, and transnational markets (Dávila 2001). Others have shifted away from identitarian accounts of racialized subjectivity in order to linger in the aesthetics, politicized affects, and ephemeral modes of expression that also circulate around the signifier Latinx (Guzmán and León 2015; Muñoz 2000, 2006a, 2006b; Rodríguez 2014; Vargas 2012; Viego 2007). Future directions in the fields of Latino/a/x studies are poised to make productive use of the complexity of these terms by fully interrogating historical and regional specificity alongside transnational currents, drawing on the interdisciplinary history of the field in order to interrogate how bodies, gestures, ideas, language, popular culture, and forms of social connection circulate across disciplinary, regional, and imaginary borders.

2014/2020

40

Law

Dean Spade

The word "law" is most commonly used with reference to what the *Oxford English Dictionary* calls "the body of rules . . . which a particular state or community recognizes as binding on its members." It also refers to statements of fact or truth that are based on observable patterns of physical behavior, as in the "law of gravity" and other "scientific laws." These two uses of the term—a body of rules and an established scientific truth—are related. Liberal legal systems, including US law, claim to be grounded in universal truths, even as they create bodies of rules specific to a particular society or community. The dominant story about the US legal system, as told from the perspective of its founders and those who govern, is that it exists to establish and preserve freedom, equality, and certain individual rights. Law, in this account, is the neutral arbiter of fairness and justice. The background assumption is that law codifies a set of agreed-upon reasonable limits on human violence or disorderly behavior and that citizens freely submit to the legal system in order to be protected from the violence that would occur without enforcement of rules.

The concept of "the rule of law" supports this commonsense understanding of the law by asserting the legitimacy of legal rules that apply to all, are created through clear and consistent procedures, and are enforced by an independent judiciary (Hart 1961; Raz [1977] 1999). In this framework, the rule of law refers to the technical application of neutral principles, and

courts are cast as autonomous from the political pressures that influence the elected branches of government; they are the accessible place for parties experiencing unfairness, inequality, or impediments to freedom to assert their rights (Sarat 1982). For example, the case *Brown v. Board of Education* (347 U.S. 483 (1954)), in which the US Supreme Court declared that race segregation in public schooling was unconstitutional, is often said to demonstrate the promise of US law to resolve injustice and promote universal fairness and equal rights. This case is a critical part of a widely disseminated national narrative about how the white supremacist and patriarchal norms codified in the founding documents of the country were eventually eradicated through proper interpretation and enforcement of neutral constitutional principles. From this vantage point, white supremacy was a problem of law resolved through law; the rule of law thus appears to be a seamless and self-correcting system.

Scholars and activists have critiqued this image of US law (and liberal legalism more generally), questioning the assumption that law is a neutral set of universal principles analogous to scientific laws. The alternative account points out that the founding of the United States and the establishment of a system of participatory democracy raised great anxieties among the wealthy colonial elites authoring its legal structure. They identified a need to prevent the potential redistribution of wealth that might be demanded by less wealthy white men who were newly entitled to political representation. For this reason, the key rights protected by the new legal system were property rights (Mensch 1982). Important critiques of this system emerged in the 1920s when a group of theorists known as the legal realists suggested that an awareness of social conditions should inform purportedly neutral legal reasoning. Supreme Court Justice Oliver Wendell Holmes argued that the legal system used the pretense of neutral principles to promote laissez-faire economic theory for the benefit of those groups with the most economic and social power. He noted that judicial decisions striking down laws passed to protect workers in the name of enforcing the liberty of contract in *theory*, as in the famous case *Lochner v. New York* (198 U.S. 45 (1905)), ignored the *reality* of the contexts in which workers contract with employers and cast as neutral conditions that actually benefited wealthy people and perpetuated the exploitation of everyone else (G. White 1986).

The realists were neither the first nor the last to argue that US law was founded to protect and preserve the concentration of wealth and property. The critical legal studies movement that emerged in the 1970s, the critical race theory movement of the 1980s, and the various social movements that engage with the law (including indigenous mobilizations, antiracist movements, and various strains of feminism) all have contributed to an analysis of the US system of property law as securing racialized and gendered property statuses from the start. The legal rules governing indigenous and enslaved people articulated their subjection through the imposition of violent gender norms, such as the enforcement of natal alienation among slaves and European binary gender categories and gendered legal statuses among indigenous people (C. Harris 1993; Andrea Smith 2005; Roberts 1993). The statuses and norms established by these systems were (and are) racializing and gendering at the same time. They do not create rules for all women or all men or all white people or all native people or all black people; instead, they reproduce intersectional social hierarchies by inscribing within the law specific subject positions that are simultaneously racialized and gendered.

Contemporary writers influenced by these overlapping critical traditions and social movements continue to argue that the purported universality of the freedom, equality, and rights established in US law operates in ways that perpetuate the theft of land and labor by a very small group at the expense of the majority. Feminists have deconstructed the legal distinction between private and public spheres, observing that this division has relegated the violence and harm that women experience routinely (often in unregulated, unpaid or underpaid domestic labor) to the private sphere in a way that precludes relief under the law (Taub and Schneider 1982). Critical race theorists have pointed out how the idea that certain choices are private, such as the decision by white parents to move away from jurisdictions where public schools have been integrated, has been used by courts to declare that law cannot be used to remedy de facto racial segregation in education (*Miliken v. Bradley*, 418 U.S. 717 (1974); A. Freeman 1995). From this perspective, US law has established processes of racialization and gendering from the outset, since the purportedly universal categories of citizenship that it deploys were operationalized in ways that secured colonial, racial, wealth, and gender hierarchies (Burns 1982; Gómez 2007; Ngai 2004; Valverde 2007).

These types of analyses cast doubt on the idea that the legal system is a place where those who are left out can and should assert their rights. Representations of the law as a vehicle for delivering freedom and equality are commonplace in the United States. Yet venues of potential rights enforcement such as voting, litigation, and legislation are not accessible to all people because of wealth concentration, campaign finance rules, gerrymandering, voter suppression practices, media consolidation, and the reality that the legal profession and judiciary are dominated by white, wealthy people. Formal legal equality has been established on some fronts, but material inequality is still in place and, for many populations, expanding. During the "post–civil rights" period when we have all supposedly become equal under the law, we have witnessed a growing wealth gap and the drastic expansion of racially targeted criminalization and immigration enforcement systems. This contradiction is particularly striking in relation to a legal system that declares itself "color-blind" and claims to have overcome white supremacy. The trouble with these assertions is that legal reform comprehends discrimination very narrowly, primarily forbidding intentional discrimination against individuals on the basis of race (and other categories such as sex and disability) in areas such as employment, public accommodations, and housing. The ongoing conditions facing marginalized groups—widespread disparity in access to education, health care, and employment; overexposure to poisonous pollution and police violence and imprisonment—cannot be traced to the intentional actions of individual discriminators (A. Freeman 1995). Due to the logic of "color blindness" advanced by discrimination law, programs aimed at remedying these widespread conditions of maldistribution, such as affirmative action initiatives that use race as a factor in distributing life chances in university admissions or job applications, can be declared unlawfully discriminatory and prohibited (*Parents Involved in Community Schools v. Seattle School District No. 1*, 551 U.S. 701 (2007); Gotanda 1991; *Fisher v. University of Texas at Austin*, 132 S. Ct. 1536 (2012)).

A focus on legal reform as the site of social and political transformation also misrecognizes and misrepresents demands of populations facing marginalization and maldistribution. It fails to comprehend how the violences of white supremacy, patriarchy, ableism, and other systems of meaning and control work together to produce particular vulnerabilities. Critical race theorist Kimberlé Crenshaw famously describes this phenomenon as "intersectionality" (1995). Crenshaw asserts that political resistance mobilized to fight racism *or* sexism

frequently disregards intragroup differences. She demonstrates that single-axis strategies tend to address only the harms facing the privileged subject of that specific axis, leaving those who are facing intersecting forces of oppression outside the scope of the remedies. For instance, when white feminist activists advocate increased criminal punishment as a solution to sexual and domestic violence, women of color who live in communities terrorized by policing and immigrant women who fear that police contact might lead to deportation for themselves, their loved ones, or neighbors are marginalized. In response, women of color activists have critiqued white feminists for focusing their analysis exclusively on gender and failing to understand that expanding punishment systems will not make women of color and immigrant women safer. They have also exposed how anticriminalization campaigns, when they focus only on the concerns of men of color, can ignore problems of sexual and gender violence that women of color face (Critical Resistance and INCITE! Women of Color against Violence 2006).

These critical inquiries into the politics of legal reform and the US legal system have raised significant questions for scholars and activists operating across a wide range of social movement contexts. The debate about hate crime legislation in queer and trans politics is an example. Some advocates of lesbian, gay, bisexual, transgender, and queer/questioning (LGBTQ) rights have worked to pass legislation designed to increase the penalties for people convicted of crimes motivated by bias and to require criminal punishment agencies to collect data about such crimes. They argue that hate crimes perpetrated against queer and transgender people are common and often underprosecuted and that these laws will help establish that this kind of violence will not be tolerated. In response, queer and trans scholars and activists who oppose hate crime laws as a method of addressing the problem of violence point out that these laws do nothing to prevent homophobic or transphobic violence. Rather, they provide increased resources to a criminal punishment system that targets queer and trans people, people of color, and poor people (Spade 2011). They point out that the United States currently imprisons 25 percent of the world's prisoners while having only 5 percent of the world's population and that over 60 percent of people in US prisons are people of color, with one in three black men experiencing imprisonment during their lifetimes (Bonczar 2003; Sabol and Couture 2008). Viewed within this context, hate crime laws use violence against queer and trans people to rationalize further expansion of a system that is actually one of the leading perpetrators of violence against them (Whitlock 2001; Mogul, Ritchie, and Whitlock 2011; Sylvia Rivera Law Project 2009; Sylvia Rivera Law Project et al. 2009). Debates about whether to seek access to institutions long understood by feminist, antiracist, and anticapitalist critics as fundamentally violent and harmful, such as legal marriage and military service, have similarly divided queer and trans social movements (Farrow 2005; Kandaswamy, Richardson, and Bailey 2006; Bassichis, Lee, and Spade 2011; Queers for Economic Justice 2010).

Embedded in the keyword "law," then, is a series of questions about the location and efficacy of legal reform within social movement activism. Do legal reform projects necessarily legitimize and expand violent and coercive systems, or can they be used to dismantle such systems? Can US law or particular legal and administrative systems in the United States (criminal punishment systems, immigration systems, tax systems) be redeemed and reformed in ways that reduce violence and create a fairer distribution of wealth and life chances, or do such efforts merely co-opt and neutralize resistance formations? Are the key categories and concepts of legal liberalism (individual freedom, equality, citizenship) ultimately about exclusion and the maintenance of racialized and gendered systems of maldistribution, or can they be mobilized to transform those systems? There can be no doubt that the language of "rights" and "equality" has come to have deep emotional meaning for people in struggle. The trouble is that this language shifts the transformative demands of social movements into legal reform strategies that do not deliver sufficient change. Given this contradiction, what relationship should change seekers have to law-based rights and equality rhetoric? These questions are important entry points for exploring what law means, inquiring into structural matters of governance and power, and crafting new cultural and political narratives about difference, progress, and redemption.

2014

41

Literature

Sandra M. Gustafson

Derived from the Latin *littera*, or "letter," "literature" for many centuries referred to a personal quality ("having literature") that meant possessing polite learning through reading. To call someone "illiterate" in the seventeenth century did not mean that the person could not read; it meant that the individual was not possessed of learning, notably knowledge of the classics. Any formal written work—for instance, a scientific treatise, a sermon text, a work of philosophy, or an ethnographic narrative—counted as "literature." Then around 1750, the historical associations of literature with literacy and polite learning began to change. Literacy rates rose, printing presses became more common, and the products of those presses grew increasingly varied. Reading styles slowly shifted from intensive reading of a few works to wide reading of many works. Authorship emerged as a distinct profession, while printed works were increasingly treated as intellectual property. All these factors undermined the association of literacy with polite learning and affected the definition of literature, until eventually it was restricted primarily to works of imaginative literature, notably poetry, drama, and fiction (Kernan 1990; Amory and Hall 2000; McGill 2003).

This account of the emerging conception of literature summarizes developments in Europe and in creole communities in the Americas. In 1539, the first printing press in the Americas was established in Mexico City. It issued mainly religious works, including many in indigenous languages. Britain was a latecomer to the competition for empire, and a full century passed before Boston became home to the first press in British North America. The British colonies were among the most literate societies of their day. The Protestant tradition, which stresses the authority of scripture and the priesthood of all believers, justified the extension of literacy as a tool of spiritual enlightenment and of redemption from bondage to sin. Literacy contributed as well to the religious community, uniting like-minded people around the reading of the Bible (Amory and Hall 2000). A parallel but secular narrative that links literacy, enlightenment, political freedom, and the body politic emerged somewhat later, gaining prominence in the age of revolution (D. Hall 1996). Often entwined, these two liberationist narratives promoted high rates of literacy, particularly in New England, where the common schools movement joined other efforts to expand access to education during the antebellum period.

Even as literacy came to be understood as the basis for an informed citizenry and an essential component of democratic civic responsibility in the early United States, the expanding array of reading materials available to the literate was a matter of concern to guardians of social order. From the beginning of the nineteenth century, when ministers and cultural elites fretted over the potential of the novel to distract women and the lower classes from their prescribed tasks and roles, to Anthony Comstock's campaign against "dangerous books" at the end of the century, to current debates about "banned books" and the internet, the increasing availability of cheap and often sensational or politically charged texts produced a backlash from those who believed that literature should function primarily as a tool of social discipline (Davidson [1986] 2004).

Works of literature could also be used to encourage imaginative self-extension and nurture social critique. The idea that fiction can expand reader sympathies arose along with the novel in the eighteenth century (Nussbaum 1995; Hunt 2007). Among those who identified critique as a central function of literature were the writers now associated with the project of creating a US national literature, notably Ralph Waldo Emerson, Henry David Thoreau, Margaret Fuller, Walt Whitman, and Herman Melville. As European national identities coalesced around distinct literatures constituted by a shared language and allegedly bearing the marks of the genius of the "race" that produced them, writers associated with the transcendentalist and Young America movements began in the 1830s to create what they considered to be a distinctively "American literature" (Matthiessen 1941; Widmer 1999) that manifested a uniquely "American spirit" through its subject matter and form. Some writers and reformers argued that the uniqueness of "American literature" could be found in its use of critique to nurture social progress (M. Gilmore 1985).

Such overtly nationalistic literary efforts were more the exception than the rule on the literary scene of the United States, however. Until 1891, when an international copyright law was passed giving foreign authors intellectual property in their works, the US book and periodical markets were dominated by reprints, many of them works by English writers. Moreover, in contrast to the more centralized publishing institutions of Europe, the US book market was regional and heterogeneous until after the Civil War. This market was often multilingual, with regional presses publishing works in a wide range of languages, particularly German, Spanish, and French. Indigenous writers had increasing access to the press as well (Round 2010). The

multilingual nature of the US market grew with the acquisition of formerly French and Mexican territories and with the enormous influx of immigrants after the Civil War (Sollors 1998; Shell 2002; McGill 2003; Loughran 2007).

The consolidation of a mass book market in the twentieth century tempered but did not eliminate the heterogeneity of the literary marketplace in the United States. For many decades, literature was defined by its representative and inclusive nature. The consolidation of a more exclusive, more narrowly "literary" canon during the Cold War was soon challenged, first by the democratization of universities that began in the 1950s and later through the canon-busting movements of the 1960s through the 1980s. The rise of ethnic literatures and the emergence of performance art contributed to these broadening trends as well. Other factors influencing the expanded notion of the "literary" include the development of interdisciplinary methodologies and programs; the rise of theory within English departments; and the impact of British cultural studies, with its emphasis on social forms, media, and "communication." Debates about "cultural literacy" led to the conceptualization of multiple literacies (Graff 1987; Kernan 1990).

The challenges that these social, cultural, and intellectual movements pose to a narrow conception of literature are not novel features of a debased modern mass culture, as is sometimes argued. Manuscript, performance, and now electronic forms of verbal expression complicate and resist the consolidation of a restrictive, print-based sense of the literary. For instance, the circulation of poetry in manuscript form had an important vogue in the middle of the nineteenth century, at the height of what is often called "print culture," a trend most famously associated with the fascicles of Emily Dickinson (Cameron 1992; Howe 1993; Martha Smith 1998; Gustafson and Sloat 2010). Beginning in the late nineteenth century and with growing vigor during the following century, artists' books reflected a vital interest in visual elements and nonprint modes of literary production (Drucker 1995).

Oral genres have a special place in understandings of the literary, from the roots of lyric poetry in song to the delivery of lines in dramatic performances. For much of the nineteenth century, political and religious forms of oratory were central to the world of letters. Oratory was perceived as a consummate republican form and so well suited to the United States. Even as US writers suffered the contempt of English reviewers and the competition of foreign reprints, the nation's orators were celebrated (not always without irony) as peers of Demosthenes and Cicero. Elocution was a popular subject of study, compilations of "great American speeches" circulated widely, and critics wrote books analyzing the qualities and strengths of various public speakers. The central place of oratory is visible in the essays, fiction, and poetry of the antebellum period, constituting an important element in the era's literary culture. Performance art, poetry readings, stand-up comedy, and other verbal arts are all heirs of the spoken word from this earlier era (Gustafson 2000, 2011).

US literary history cannot be fully understood without reference to the forms that modern critics call "orature," a term invented by the Ugandan linguist Pio Zirimu and developed by Ngũgĩ wa Thiong'o (Lauter 1990; Ngũgĩ 1998; Gustafson 2000). The continued influence of oral genres has been particularly important for US ethnic writers. Alphabetic literacy not only was in some instances prohibited to African Americans and Native Americans, as in the slave codes outlawing literacy training. It also came with the added burden of being identified as a skill derived from and properly belonging to whites and often used to advance white interests through false treaties and unjust laws. For some ethnic-minority verbal artists, literacy was a tool of oppression and, at times, of self-division, separating an individual from a community distinguished by oral forms of verbal art. In the twentieth century, writers and other artists associated with the Black Arts Movement, as well as many Native American writers, reflected on the paradoxes of oppression and liberation intrinsic to alphabetic literacy.

Today the rise of electronic media poses important challenges to print culture. Beginning in 1990, a series of books and studies has tracked the impending "death of literature," linking its demise to social trends and, increasingly, to technological developments, notably the rise of the World Wide Web and the proliferation of social media. These critics characteristically employ the most restrictive definition of "literature," limiting it to poetry, drama (in a book, not on the stage), and, above all, the novel. The novel has a special status for these writers, who often take it to be the paradigmatic literary form because of its length, the "linear" reading that it encourages, and the solitude and consequent richness of subjectivity that novel reading is supposed to produce. They trace certain forms of social order and cultural organization to widespread engagement with "the literary," in this narrow definition (Birkerts 1994; Edmundson 2004).

These claims for and about literature have not gone unchallenged. One of the most striking recent developments in American studies and cultural studies is the emergence of a critical discourse focused on the range of textual media and their varied modalities of creative verbal and visual expression. Studies of new media and digital humanities demand that scholars

LITERATURE   SANDRA M. GUSTAFSON

rethink the heterogeneous nature of textuality and the varied forms of reading that these textualities produce (McGann 2001; Hayles 2008). This expansive approach opens new avenues for interpreting older textual forms, including "Aboriginal oral, glyphic, artefactual modes, and conceptualizations of communication" (Battiste 2004, 121; M. Cohen 2009; Cohen and Glover 2014). Such a capacious framing of "literature" enables scholars to engage a broader archive in order to consider the diverse institutions and practices organized by alphabetic literacy.

2007/2020

42

Media
Lisa Nakamura

"Media" is a word with unusual weight in the United States. The keyword appears in the name of a discipline—media studies—as well as numerous subfields, such as media industry studies, feminist media studies, comparative and transnational media studies, and most recently, digital media studies. "Participatory media," "interactive media," and "social media" are all relatively new terms that describe the production and consumption of digital texts, images, and sounds through the World Wide Web and mobile applications that use social networks such as YouTube, Pandora, Facebook, and Twitter. The quick uptake and incorporation of these new media into everyday life in the United States and globally have resulted in a proliferation of usages of the keyword "media."

Though "media" is the grammatical plural of the singular "medium," the word is most often used in the singular. It is easy to portray "the media" in negative terms as "addictive" and socially isolating, as a purveyor of harmful stereotypes and violent images, yet media scholars working in the cultural studies tradition have tended to focus less on this preoccupation and more on the ways that the media creates a sense of identity and practices of social belonging for its users. Some of the earliest thinkers to take the media as an object of critical analysis were Continental philosophers such as Theodor Adorno (2001) and Walter Benjamin (1968), who worked in a mostly German tradition known as "critical theory" or the Frankfurt school. Like the later French writer Jean Baudrillard (1994), they were deeply interested in the increasing ubiquity, cheapness, and profusion of printed images, recorded sounds, and moving image sequences. They saw these new media technologies as signaling a profound social shift. Technological advances starting with the printing press and moving on to photography, film, and digital devices and networks enabled copies to circulate more widely than ever before, bathing individuals in a constant flow of images that had meant something very different when they were singular and traveled less freely. In the foundational 1936 essay "The Work of Art in the Age of Mechanical Reproduction" ([1936] 1968), Benjamin both mourns the loss of the unique "aura" that original artworks possessed and ushers in the study of the media as an academic discipline. Benjamin's focus on the automation of media production has inflected media studies in the United States and elsewhere with an abiding concern with the technology, politics, and economics of media as well as its content.

Members of the Frankfurt school shared Benjamin's interest in mechanically reproduced or "mass" media, and their stance toward it was fundamentally suspicious. At the same time, this group, particularly Adorno, was among the first to take the power of the "mass media" seriously and to recognize it as a cultural apparatus deserving of its own set of theories. In his 1963 essay "The Culture Industry Reconsidered" ([1963] 2001), Adorno argued eloquently for a critical and pessimistic view of "monopolistic mass culture," or the sale of culture for profit, a phenomenon that he considered fundamentally at odds with aesthetic quality and the public good. Adorno reserved special scorn for news magazines and television, particularly genres such as Westerns and musicals, which not only were full of empty spectacle and numbing repetition but earned enormous sums for companies that exploited both workers *and* audiences. He is careful to note that his objection to "mass media" and "mass culture" has nothing to do with his moral judgments of its audience and its taste preferences. Indeed, his critique of mass media is that it is not popular *enough*, meaning it does not "arise spontaneously from the masses themselves" but is rather a commodity, a product "tailored for consumption by masses" (98).

In sharp contrast to Adorno, Marshall McLuhan had a sunnier, even utopian attitude toward the role of media in society. In *Understanding Media: The Extensions of Man* ([1964] 2003), he was eager to consider electronic media forms such as television, radio, and film as specific forms of technological practice. While we no longer envision television as "hot" or radio as "cool," as McLuhan advocated, digital media scholars have taken up his work after a period of neglect during the eighties. What they find useful is McLuhan's envisioning of electronic media forms such as television and radio not just as ways to get information and entertainment but also as having distinctive affective qualities and as extensions of the human body and brain. Benedict Anderson's influential 1983 *Imagined Communities*, for instance, found a new and receptive audience in the 2000s and beyond because it explained national identity and nationalism as artifacts of a particular medium—print—and the sociocultural formation he called "print capitalism." Drawing on historical materials from diverse anticolonial movements (beginning with the American Revolution), Anderson found that newspapers did far more than report happenings in a particular regional locale. They also brought the nation into being by creating a readership that came to view or imagined itself as sharing a common identity. Media, in this account, do more than convey information or even ideology. They create communities. Anderson

MEDIA   LISA NAKAMURA

claimed that national identity was less a function of birthplace or legal standing within a citizenry than it was an "imagined" or virtual state—called into being by the process of mediation itself. A form of media such as print, in this account, functions as a space or medium of cultural interpellation.

One trouble with this account is that not everyone uses or is positioned by the media in the same way. The postcolonial response to this line of argument emphasizes the ways that unequal access to media power and the tools of media production results in the exclusion of specific populations from the nation on both a symbolic and a very real level. People of color, women, sexual minorities, and other subaltern individuals possess less power within the media system, which has often represented them in stereotyped, limited ways. In other words, mass media do not hail all bodies equally (Loomba 2005). When the internet and the World Wide Web were adopted more widely in the mid-1990s, the so-called Web 1.0 period, it seemed that McLuhan's dream of an intimate democratic community through media—what he called the "global village"—had come true. However, it quickly became clear that the internet was far from radically democratic. Not everybody had an equal or voluntary relation to it in terms of access or authorship. The feminist philosopher Donna Haraway argued eloquently that the computer age has made it impossible to separate the body from technology (1991). Biotechnologies enabled by computing devices entangle us in webs and assemblages of human and machine, since the human body *is* literally a form of media—informational technologies are interwoven with and inform our bodily existence. Haraway's critique of these technologies, particularly the military and commercial technologies that gave rise to our current media system, has proven very influential to science and technology studies scholars as well as to feminist media scholars. Her work also draws attention to the systemic role that gendered and raced labor plays in building the integrated circuits needed in electronic and, later, digital media devices.

Consider as an example of this system the deep and often unacknowledged connections between internal colonization, settler colonialism, and computing hardware. From 1965 to 1975, the Fairchild Corporation's Semiconductor Division operated a large integrated-circuit manufacturing plant in Shiprock, New Mexico, on a Navajo reservation. During this period, the corporation was the largest private employer of Indian workers in the United States. The circuits that the almost entirely female Navajo workforce produced were used in devices such as calculators, missile guidance systems, and other early computing devices. To address this type of history, media criticism and analysis will have to turn away from a narrow focus on representations of stereotypes as the most central form of media influence and toward an attention to the intersections of design, implementation, and production of media technologies themselves. This materialist or archaeological approach to media, digital or otherwise, urges us to examine not just how media represent or interpellate different cultures, genders, and identities but also how media devices are produced and marketed. Mobile media such as cell phones, for instance, require rare metals such as coltan, which is extracted from the Congo and finds its way to the rest of the world in a system that echoes earlier forms of resource extraction under colonialism. These practices, along with technological constraints and affordances and less known histories behind the screen, are inseparable from the way that digital media mean (Ernst 2013). Recent scholarship focused on materialist media archaeologies in the digital realm has contributed greatly to the fields of American studies and cultural studies by mapping the links between media infrastructures' origins, design cultures, and informing principles, as well as the hidden or neglected histories of marginalized groups in computing (Chun 2011; McPherson 2012b; Sandvig 2012).

Earlier digital media scholarship tended to represent new forms of media production and distribution as tools for liberation. Recent scholarship adopts a more critical stance, stressing the ways in which mass media are often fundamentally at odds with the aesthetic and economic needs of the people they claim to liberate. This critical stance has become increasingly important with the rise of digital "participatory media." For the past twenty years, digital media have been posited as a way for individuals to exert more control over their own identities through media making and distribution. The advent of social media such as Facebook, Twitter, blogging, and other forms of user-generated content management and distribution have ushered us into the age of Web 2.0, the "participatory web." It is true that more and more of us are "participating" by contributing our content, images, location information, and "likes" and "dislikes" in exchange for these services. And the production of mash-ups, amateur videos, and sampled sound recordings can indeed enable users to create countercultural and critical new messages (Jenkins 2006). Yet to observe that users make and distribute certain types of digital media content such as memes, mash-ups, and videos is not to erase the rampant racial, gender, and sexual misrepresentation and exclusion that are characteristic of mass media. Women and people of color have not been well served by the mass media, which has thrived on the circulation of racist and sexist ideologies as a means of marketing commodities (Banta 1987; McClintock 1995; Ewen and Ewen 2006). Digital media have given users new opportunities to exploit images of race and gender as part of memetic culture (Nakamura 2008; Nakamura and Chow-White 2012). Whether scholars of media choose to focus on neglected histories of media forms; the way that media represents bodies, identities, sexualities, or genders; or other aspects of media altogether, the everydayness of digital media will require us to pay more attention to the media platforms and communities, digital and otherwise, where so many of us live our lives.

2014

43

Migration

Alyshia Gálvez

"Migration" was initially used in early sixteenth-century French to refer to human movement across space. These early usages date to the initial period of European conquest and colonization of the Americas, arguably the first phase of what is today referred to as globalization (Wolf 1982). The contexts of these usages were largely historical and literary, referring to the expulsion of Adam and Eve from Eden or the travel of a person from one town to another. A century later, "migration" was deployed by natural scientists in reference to the migration of birds, salmon, and butterflies. This naturalistic use of the term predominated into the twentieth century, as the natural and social sciences came to view animal and human actions, relations, and movements in an empiricist light, as objective and apolitical (Foucault [1976] 1990, [1975] 1995). Human migration was thus dehumanized, reduced to a mechanistic response to the availability of resources. Whether nomadic groups crossing the ice bridge in the Bering Sea twenty thousand years ago or Canada geese flying south for the winter, humans and animals can be expected to move to where they find the necessities of life. Pioneering studies of human migration in the fields of geography and demography were influenced by this orientation, charting "laws of migration" and the "push" and "pull" factors that expelled migrants from their homes and attracted them to new lands (Ravenstein 1885; Everett Lee 1966).

As this usage history indicates, "migration" is a general term, encompassing many different kinds of movement, including immigration (migration *to* a nation) and emigration (migration *from* a nation), as well as flows *within* a nation such as rural-to-urban migration (urbanization) and urban-to-suburban migration (suburbanization). Globally, the magnitude of movement is greater now than at any other point in human history: as many as a billion people are migrants, a quarter of them transnational and three-quarters internal or domestic migrants (Suárez-Orozco, Suárez-Orozco, and Sattin-Bajaj 2010). At present, there are two main ways that the term "migration" is deployed in relation to these movements. First, "migration" refers to any movement of populations in space. While this usage is less common in the United States, it continues to be dominant in some international and supranational contexts. The Migration Policy Institute (n.d.), for instance, dedicates itself to "the study of the movement of people worldwide," while Migrant Rights International (n.d.) describes itself as a "global alliance of migrant associations and migrant rights, human rights, labor, religious, and other organizations that operate at the local, national, regional or international level."

The second usage of the term occurs when the topic of interest is a specific subset of the phenomena encompassed by migration: when migrants cross national borders. This selective emphasis has been dominant in the field of American studies and, to a lesser extent, cultural studies. It typically excludes other meanings, including forms of involuntary migration that are categorized under headings such as human trafficking and refugee policy. While refugee and asylum issues are addressed in many industrialized nations as part of foreign aid and humanitarian assistance, they are typically distinguished from the desire of people to relocate to such nations for economic or social reasons. In short, nation-states and institutions make distinctions between different kinds of migration—between "immigrants" and "refugees"—that are in many ways arbitrary but can have life-and-death consequences for those who receive these designations. In the United States, unauthorized flows of newcomers, who are classified generally as "economic migrants" and often referred to as "illegal immigrants," fall into the bureaucratic jurisdiction of law enforcement agencies such as Immigration and Customs Enforcement, or ICE, which was created in the period following September 11, 2001.

Since the mid-twentieth century, "migration" has been used most often in US contexts only with modifiers or prefixes: "transnational migration," "emigration," and "immigration." Arguably, terms like "emigration" and "immigration" center on the perspective of the state: movement is implicitly categorized as inward or outward with respect to the nation-state and teleological, rather than neutral, circular, or indeterminate. "Migration" is thus made specific in everyday usage in ways that privilege the nation-state and its borders over the motivations of those moving. In American studies and cultural studies, these usages shape both fields of inquiry. In the mid-twentieth century, it was still common to use "migration" as a general term referring to both "foreign" immigration and "internal" migration, as in Sidney Goldstein's "Migration: Dynamic of the American City" (1954). It is almost unthinkable to imagine a study such as Goldstein's today: comprehensive of both immigration and internal migration trends in the United States. The same is true in less scholarly contexts. Discussions of the contemporary movement of African Americans to the South, a reversal of earlier flows usually referred to as the "Great Migration," are described in a 2011 New York Times article as a movement, an exodus, a return, and only once as a "migration" (Bilefsky 2011).

"Migration" in popular usage signifies more narrowly than it once did; it has become almost synonymous with "immigration."

This selective use and semantic narrowing of the terminology reflects the preoccupation in the United States with national security, borders, and their regulation. Only the circulation of people across US borders is cast as relevant to public policy and debate about migration. This limited use of the term is prevalent not only in the United States but also in other countries classifiable as "immigrant receiving" such as the United Kingdom, Italy, Spain, France, and Chile. In these national contexts, the use of the term to refer primarily to the specific phenomenon of cross-border migration has the effect of making migrants and their movements seem a thing of the past. In a time of unprecedented militarization of US borders, migration becomes, at best, a quaint remnant of more innocent times and, at worst, an aggressive act of defiance against the rule of law. From the normative viewpoint of receiving nations, *im*migration is a problem to be regulated through the orderly flow of those who respect the sovereignty of nations, while migration remains an unregulated, unplanned movement of populations ignorant or defiant of the borders they cross and the states that seek to regulate those borders.

Applied to the history of migration in the United States, these assumptions mean that Europeans passing through Ellis Island in the early twentieth century were *immigrants*, subject to the nation's interest in regulating admission, while Mexican workers traveling to pick crops were *migrants*, their movement pegged to a natural cycle of the cultivation, ripening, and harvest of fruits and vegetables; their entry not always controlled by bureaucracy; and their return assumed. Even when the work was industrial, not agricultural, and regulated, the term "migrant worker" was used, with time limits and return implied. In the early to mid-twentieth century, regular migrant flows across the border, even without authorization, were not viewed as terribly controversial because workers were thought likely to return from where they came at the conclusion of the season. Policies such as the Bracero Program (a guest-worker program in existence from 1942 to 1964) were premised on the notion of cyclical flows. Like migratory birds, migrant workers were thought to respond to instinctual rhythms of labor supply and scarcity. Cyclical movement, not settlement, continues to be implied in the ever more limited use of the term "migration" in the United States today.

The distinction between immigration as a regulated, bureaucratic, and legal process and the more naturalistic usages of the term "migration" legitimizes the flows of some people and delegitimizes others. Contemporary social life is thought to be governed by "the rule of law," borders, and state sovereignty. Migration becomes a political issue to be regulated and managed by nation-states. No longer are there large-scale guest-worker programs with temporary visas for seasonal work in the United States. Even the relationship between agriculture and seasonality has been obscured as supermarkets are filled with fruits and vegetables imported as often from another hemisphere as from local agricultural regions. In the context of globalization, the notion of the seasonality of labor supply and demand and the right of human beings to move across borders to seek a living (upheld in the United Nations' Universal Declaration of Human Rights) are increasingly viewed as threats to national sovereignty, while migrants themselves are less tolerated than ever and viewed as anachronistic and even insufficiently civilized. The most frequently cited argument for withholding legalization from undocumented immigrants is the notion that they must "show respect for the law" at the same time that the law has shifted, becoming ever more stringent and restrictive over time. In this way, the term "migration" does the semantic work of dehumanizing people who travel across borders of various kinds, depicting them as out of step with current modes and juridical structures of citizenship and belonging.

The category of immigrants is reserved for those who do not need to migrate but are highly skilled and highly mobile individuals who stand patiently at the door, awaiting the clearance of legal and bureaucratic obstacles to entry. By the same logic, "illegal immigrants" are the inverse, imagined as those who are not skilled or educated and certainly not patient, viewed as "cutting the line" or "jumping the fence." Even when viewed charitably, as "economic" migrants, they are denied the status of *im*migrants due to unauthorized entry or impermanent visa status, their complex array of motivations for movement reduced to simple self-interest. The power of this distinction increased in the early twenty-first century, as Presidents G. W. Bush and Obama militarized and fortified the border more than at any prior point in history. Donald J. Trump's campaign and policies in office—the supposedly impenetrable wall; the widespread expulsions of border crossers, detainees, and deportees (including lawful permanent residents); punitive detention procedures including family separations—depend on the ongoing process of framing some kinds of migration as unlawful and illegitimate and some kinds of migrants as undeserving of legal rights and protection. Another result of this expansion of the category of "illegal" is that asylum-seeking migrants are often assumed both in popular discourse and by border patrol officers to have illegitimate or fraudulent claims.

Rather than a unidirectional, authorized, and regulated flow, migrants are framed not as part of the polity but as usurpers, sojourners, a fleeting presence, soon to return or, if not, subject to forcible return or deportation (G. Chang 2000; Chavez 1988; De Genova 2005; Hondagneu-Sotelo 1995). Given the vast diversity of reasons people relocate, both internally and transnationally (see M. García 2006; Swinth 2005), greater awareness of how the term "migration" is used to dehumanize and delegitimize migrants and their motivations is more critical than ever.

2014/2020

44

Nation

Alys Eve Weinbaum

"Nation" has been in use in the English language since the fourteenth century, when it was first deployed to designate groups and populations. Although the concept of "race" was not well defined in this period, the *Oxford English Dictionary* (*OED*) retrospectively refers to such groups and populations as "racial" in character. In the modern period, the *OED* continues, the meaning of "nation" came to refer to large aggregates of people closely associated through a combination of additional factors, including common language, politics, culture, history, and occupation of the same territory. Though it appears that an initial racial connection among nationals was later supplanted by a widened range of associating factors, the early understanding of "nation" as based in race and "common descent" remains central to discussions of the term to this day, either as a retrospective imposition of the sort orchestrated by the *OED* or as a "natural" grounding. An important contribution of American studies and cultural studies has been to interrogate race as a description and sometimes a synecdoche for "nation" and to insist that an uncritical conflation of race and nation constitutes a pressing political and theoretical problem. Indeed, as numerous scholars argue, ideas of race and racist ideologies continue to subtend the expression of nationalism in the United States, which is unsurprising given that the founding and consolidation of the nation was pursued as a project of racial nationalism that arrogated full belonging (if not citizenship) to whites or, in nineteenth-century parlance, to people of Anglo-Saxon descent.

Beginning in the late eighteenth century, when "nation" first accrued consistent political usage and "national" became a routine noun used to designate individual subjects, the constitution of political units (nation-states) composed of so-called nationals began to center on the identification of the factors that would ideally cohere large aggregates and bestow belonging on individual members of such groups. During the nineteenth century, generally referred to as the century of modern nationalism, principles of inclusion and exclusion were hotly debated by political pundits favoring immigration restriction or curtailment and various population-control measures that, over time, profoundly shaped the racial, ethnic, and class composition of nations by designating those who could rightfully belong and by circumscribing that belonging through restriction on the reproductive pool and designation of the progeny of "mixed" unions as "illegitimate" or "foreign." Such nineteenth-century debates exposed nation formation as deeply ideological—as involving processes of self-definition and self-consolidation as often dependent on the embrace as on the persecution of differences, especially those construed as racial in character.

Even as nationalization centers on the construction of a people, it also raises questions of land and territory. In the case of settler-colonial nations such as the United States, South Africa, and Israel, nationalization has depended on the transformation of a territory into a "homeland"; on the defeat, enslavement, and genocidal destruction of "natives"; and on the subsequent expropriation of land from people already inhabiting it. In this sense, nation building and imperialism ought to be seen as closely and historically allied. As Seamus Deane (1990, 360) eloquently explains, "Nationalism's opposition to imperialism is . . . nothing more than a continuation of imperialism by other means." Imperialism arises contemporaneously with modern nationalism because the two forms of power have needed each other. The ideology of racial, cultural, and often moral superiority that is used to justify imperialism is also always at least in part national, and vice versa. Like imperialism, nation building is an ideological and material project that involves continuing reorganization of space, bodies, and identities. It is at once individual and collective, internally and externally oriented, destructive and productive, and all too often brutally violent.

Although philosophers and political scientists writing in the transatlantic context tend to agree on the range of factors that may be used to identify nations and the nationals belonging to them, they continue to argue over the nature of the elusive glue that binds individuals into nations. Ernest Renan ([1882] 1990) suggests in his famous lecture "What Is a Nation?," first delivered at the Sorbonne and often regarded as the gambit that inaugurated contemporary debate, that language, culture, and territory are not in and of themselves enough to constitute a nation. Rather, to all these must be added a common substance capable of binding disparate individuals into a people. And yet, paradoxically, this substance is far too ephemeral to be readily or decisively distilled. Approximating religious faith or spirituality but not reducible to either, nationalism, Renan suggests, is nothing more or less than an inchoate feeling, albeit an extremely consequential one. By contrast with citizenship, a set of political and civil rights guaranteed to nationals on the basis of their legal belonging within the nation, "nationness" and feelings of national belonging are far harder to pin down.

This vexing question of what binds nationals to one another has led contemporary theorists to argue that nations are fictions given solidity through political and juridical processes that transform them into material practices, including population control and eugenic containment, immigration restriction and curtailment, and full-scale genocide. As a materialized fiction, national belonging may thus be understood as what Raymond Williams ([1977] 1997, 128–35) has labeled, in a different context, a "structure of feeling": an emergent sentiment not easily articulated but so deeply and fully inhabited by individuals and collectivities that it appears to them as primordial, inevitable, and enduring. Thus on the one side (commonly denoted as uncritically nationalist, often jingoistic), we find the nation discussed as a "natural" formation. On the other side (which holds itself above nationalism or opposes it in the form, for instance, of socialist internationalism or Enlightenment cosmopolitanism), we find the nation posited as a harmful construction. In this latter view, nationalism is seen as fomenting dangerously partisan solidarities, and the nation is seen as a fiction that is made to cohere through ideological pressures that masquerade as "natural" but are in fact self-interested, self-consolidating, and ultimately driven by capitalist and imperialist imperatives. As world-systems theorists such as Immanuel Wallerstein (2004) argue, nations can be regarded as racialized economic and political units that compete within a world marketplace composed of other similar units. As the globe divided into core and periphery, into regions made up of those who labor and those who exploit such labor, nations located in the core often rationalized their economic exploitation of those of the periphery by racializing it.

Although individuals may move from one nation to another, thus losing or being forced by law to forgo one form of citizenship for another, feelings of national belonging cannot be forcibly stripped away. Indeed, such feelings are often willfully carried with individuals and groups as they migrate. In the United States, the bipartite, sometimes hyphenated, identities of some

nationals—Italian Americans, Irish Americans, Polish Americans—express such national retention or carry-over. In these instances, which must be contextualized within a framework of voluntary migration, the designations "Italian," "Irish," and "Polish" indicate a desire to retain a previous national identity now regarded as cultural or ethnic. In other instances, self-constituting invocations of national identity have been transformed into a critique of dominant nationalism or into an alternative imagination of "nation," as with the forms of insurgent third world nationalism examined by the theorist of decolonization Frantz Fanon (1963). In such instances, the new or invented nationalism competes either to exist alongside or to displace the dominant national identity, which is viewed as a violent imposition. In the Americas, this is perhaps most evident in movements for Native sovereignty that work to build tribal nations or in the form of Chicano nationalism that claims Aztlán as both a mythical homeland and a name for the portion of Mexico taken by the United States after the US-Mexico War of 1846–48.

In the case of modern diasporas, we witness yet another form of oppositional nationalism, one occasioned by forced displacement and shared oppression. In those instances in which a homeland no longer exists or has never existed, or in which a diasporic people seek to constitute a new nation unconstrained by the dictates of geography, ideas of nation and national belonging come into sharp focus. Consider the black nationalism that had its heyday in the United States and the decolonizing world in the 1970s, or Queer Nation, an activist organization that gained prominence in the United States during the 1980s and early 1990s. Although very different in political orientation, both movements appropriated the idea of the nation to contest dominant forms of nationalism and to reveal the constitutive exclusions that enable national hegemony. Somewhat paradoxically, the imaginative creation of these collectivities revealed, even as it mimicked, the constructed nature of hegemonic nations formally recognized as political states.

This idea of hegemonic nations as ideologically constructed or "imagined communities" is most famously elaborated by Benedict Anderson, who, in the early 1980s, theorized the emergence of the modern nation out of the nationalist revolutions that took place throughout the Americas in the late eighteenth and early nineteenth centuries. As Anderson (1983, 19) argues, nations are brought into being by peoples whose access to print culture enables collective imagination of involvement in a political and cultural project that extends back into an "immemorial past" and "glides into a limitless future." Anderson built his theory on modern European historiography (especially Eric Hobsbawm's work; 1983) that argued that nations produced themselves by inventing traditions that enabled them to constitute populations as historical and cultural entities meaningfully joined over time and in space. Anderson is also indebted to critical theorist Walter Benjamin ([1950] 1968, 262), who theorized the "homogeneous, empty time" characteristic of modernity—a temporality that Anderson regards as necessary to national imagining and that he calibrates to a set of technological developments, principally the invention of the printing press and the tabloid newspaper. Together, print culture and the thinking of "nation time" that it enabled allowed people living in a given territory and speaking and reading a similar language to materialize connections to one another in a synchronic and cohesive manner that was previously unthinkable.

Numerous scholars of third world nationalisms have taken issue with Anderson's Eurocentric and teleological view of national development and have called attention to his overemphasis on print culture, thus exposing his theory's dependence on the application of European-style nationalism throughout the world and on the presupposition of universal literacy as a requirement of national development. Yet others have used the idea of the nation as an "imagined community" to argue for the special relationship between nationalism and print culture and between nation and narration more generally. As postcolonial theorist Homi Bhabha (1990b, 1) avers in a formulation self-consciously indebted to both Renan and Anderson, "Nations, like narratives, lose their origins in the myths of time and only fully realize their horizons in the mind's eye. Such an image of the nation—or narration—might seem impossibly romantic and excessively metaphorical, but it is from . . . political thought and literary language that the nation emerges . . . in the west."

The idea that nations need narratives to exist—that they need to be narrated into being—has resonated for an entire generation of American studies scholars. Their research suggests that elite and popular cultural texts, including public spectacle and performance, are and have been used to consolidate and contest various nationalist projects. Some of these scholars focus on texts manifestly intent on nation building (e.g., the *Federalist Papers*) or on offering alternatives to hegemonic nationalism (e.g., W. E. B. Du Bois's *The Souls of Black Folk* [(1903) 1997]), while others dwell on those that are less transparent in their ideological commitments but that may be read against the grain to expose the processes through which nationalist sensibilities are generated and torn apart (e.g., Gertrude Stein's *The Making of Americans* [(1925) 1995] and Américo Paredes's *George Washington Gómez* [1990]). Literary scholars working on US culture from the Revolutionary War through the present have been at the forefront of such inquiry, focusing on canonized traditions and on texts authored by those who have been historically minoritized within the nation. Such writings frequently expose the ideologies of racism, sexism, and heterosexism that lie at the heart of US nationalism (Berlant 1991, 1997; D. Nelson 1992, 1998; Wald 1995; Lowe 1996).

Central to this scholarship is an understanding that, in the United States and elsewhere, the relationship between nationalism and racism can be characterized as one of historical reciprocity in that modern nationalism expresses itself as racial (Balibar 1994). With the centrality of this relationship in mind, researchers have focused on histories of Native American genocide, African American enslavement, and immigration to the United States over the past three centuries. As such work attests, westward expansion of the frontier in the eighteenth and nineteenth centuries was facilitated by racist ideologies that viewed Indians as "lesser breeds" whose removal or extermination was necessary to the establishment of Anglo-Saxon civilization (Horsman 1981; Hietala 1985; Rogin 1996). Four hundred years of enslavement and disenfranchisement of Africans was the steep price paid for the creation of whiteness as a form of "status property" (C. Harris 1993, 1714) that functioned as a guarantor of national belonging and citizenship rights. After the Civil War and well into the twentieth century, the nativist and restrictionist policies toward immigrants from southern and eastern Europe and Asia allowed for further consolidation of the United States as a white nation whose population could be imagined as principally Anglo-Saxon and thus as free of the taint of "foreign blood." As detailed case studies have demonstrated, ethnicized immigrant groups have shed the taint of their otherness through expressions of various forms of racism. Indeed, entrance into the national fold has invariably depended on a group's ability to differentiate and distinguish itself as white and free (Roediger 1991; Theodore Allen 1994; Jacobson 1998). Central here are both internally directed racism, responsible for keeping the national body "pure" by separating "true" nationals (free whites) from nonnationals (slaves and natives), and externally directed racism, or xenophobia, which clearly defines the nation's borders and keeps "undesirable" immigrant populations (those deemed "unassimilable") out.

Feminist and queer scholarship has further complicated our understanding of the dialectic between race and nation by demonstrating that men and women participate differently in nation building and that reproductive heterosexuality plays a decisive role in the creation of nationalist ideologies, which are, in turn, deeply gendered and heteronormative. As such scholarship makes plain, it is misguided to study nations and nationalism without bringing to bear a theory of gender power and an understanding of the historically sedimented relationship of nation building to reproductive politics (A. Parker et al. 1992; McClintock 1995; Kaplan, Alarcón, and Moallem 1999). Women commit themselves to and are either implicitly or explicitly implicated by others in the production of nations, nationals, and nationalism in a number of ways: as active participants in nationalist struggles for liberation; as mothers, the biological reproducers of subjects and national populations; as upholders of the boundaries of nations through restrictions on reproductive sexuality and the circumscription of marriage within ethnic and racial groups; as teachers and transmitters of national culture; and as symbolic signifiers of nations (Yuval-Davis and Anthias 1989).

Though often overlooked, the reproductive dimensions of the idea of nation are embedded within the term (derived as it is from the Latin root *natio*, "to be born"). Likewise, the idea that nationals are literally reproduced has been naturalized and rendered invisible within many national cultures. In the United States, birth to a national is one of the principal bases on which both national belonging and citizenship are granted (Stevens 1999). In practice, the idea that national populations are reproduced by racially "fit" or "superior" mothers has been used to justify a range of eugenic policies that allow some women to reproduce while restricting others. Nazi Germany is the most glaring example of such eugenic celebration of national motherhood and of the control of reproductive sexuality. However, it is too seldom acknowledged, particularly when the Nazi example is invoked, that the mainstream eugenics movement of the early part of the twentieth century emerged not in Europe but in the United States, where it was widely celebrated as a means to "strengthen" the national populace by "breeding out" so-called degenerate members of society, including immigrants, people of color, homosexuals, and the "feeble-minded" (Ordover 2003).

The idea that nationals and nations are reproduced is not only or simply a material reality but also an elaborate ideology positing that the essence of nationality is itself reproducible. Within this ideology, protection of the "naturalness" of heterosexual reproduction becomes central, as does the construction of women's wombs as repositories of racial identity (Weinbaum 2004). Buried within the ideology of national reproduction is a concept of the female body as the source from which nationals spring and the related idea that national populations are racially homogeneous and can be maintained as such only if sexual unions that cross racial and ethnic lines are carefully monitored and even more carefully represented. Significantly, in the United States, it was not during the antebellum period that interracial sex was most forcefully legislated against and a mixed nation (a so-called miscege*nation*) vociferously denounced but, rather, after the Civil War, emancipation, and the incorporation of African Americans as citizens. In other words, although master-and-slave sex was routine, it was only after black people began to be regarded as nationals and were granted at least some of the rights held by other (white) citizens that sexuality across racial lines was deemed threatening to the national body.

The continuous policing of reproductive sexuality that is characteristic of most forms of modern nationalism ought to lead us to the realization that just as nationalism is an ideology inextricably intertwined with racism, so too are racism and nationalism bound together with sexist and heterosexist reproductive imperatives. From this perspective, it becomes clear that in order to fully limn the idea of nation, it is necessary to refocus the study of the keyword on discussions of the ideological and material processes that exploit existing racial, gender, and sexual hierarchies in the production of nations, nationals, and feelings of national belonging. Such a reorientation ideally should begin with the idea that the nation is differently produced in each instantiation and historical conjuncture and within the context of each raced, gendered, and sexualized social and political formation.

2007

45

Nature

Julie Sze and June Wayee Chau

In everyday speech, the meaning of the term "nature" may seem self-evident. Nature is the opposite of culture: the outdoors, the untamed, the wild, the timeless. It is what lies before and beyond society and civilization. Toddlers use the term in this way when they say that they "collect nature" when gathering sticks and leaves in the backyard or park. Yet as Raymond Williams observes, "Nature is perhaps the most complex word in the language," and any effort to fix or define its meaning is a fraught venture (1983, 219). This danger arises because definitions of nature are historically specific and culturally embedded in ideological systems. The *nature of nature* under Western modernity was (and remains) marked by violent and racializing processes of European colonialism and global capitalism, just as contestation over the *nature of nature* is central to efforts to dismantle that legacy today.

In Europe, Enlightenment uses of the term "nature" were built on an older system of hierarchical classification known as the Great Chain of Being. This system consigned nonhuman nature (such as animals and plants) to the lowest rungs of "a fixed and vertical hierarchy stretching from God down to the lowliest sentient beings" (Schiebinger 1993, 145). The chain codified a set of binaries between nature and culture. Nature was associated with the body, the feminine, the nonwhite, and the primitive. Culture was associated with the mind, the masculine, the white, and the civilized. These associations perpetuated and justified social hierarchies that placed whiteness over blackness, man over woman, mind over body, and human over nonhuman (Ogunnaike 2016; Merchant 1980).

As this understanding of nature was taken up by the Enlightenment, ideologies of nature were divided. For some, nature served as a "guarantor of hierarchy and tradition" (Purdy 2015, 11–12); for others, nature was less benign. Life was "solitary, poor, nasty, brutish, and short" (Hobbes 1994, 76) in what Thomas Hobbes and others called "the state of nature." In each case, nature served as an abstraction, a fundamental organizing principle for liberal philosophy and political discourse that was instrumental to the expansion of colonialism and capitalism (Meyer 2001). While Europeans generally imagined themselves as using rationality and reason to leave the state of nature behind, they saw Asia, Africa, and the Americas as defined by this state and, as a result, "defective in a way that requires external intervention to be redeemed" (Mills 1997, 42). Non-Europeans were "savages," a word rooted in the Latin *silva*, or "wood": untamed and uncivilized (43). Their excessive closeness to nature, paradoxically, placed them outside "human nature." As such, they could be excluded from the category of the human itself.

This opposition between (untamed) nature and (civilized) culture provided European powers with an ideological rationale for conquest and a material basis for capitalist and extractive forms of growth. Asia, Africa, and the Americas would provide emergent capitalist systems with the land, labor, and raw materials—the "natural resources"—necessary for the expansion of markets and production. Colonial powers drew on ideologies of nature alongside arsenals of power and violence to justify their actions. "Cheap nature" was the foundational category that enabled the cheapening of money, work, care, food, energy, and lives central to the organization and reproduction of capitalist societies (Patel and

Moore 2018, 19). Because they saw Native peoples in the Americas as living in a "state of nature," European settler colonists could see North America as *terra nullius*: uninhabited and undeveloped land. Unable to see Indigenous knowledges, systems, and practices as "cultural" or "developed," European settlers exercised their providential right to take that which was underutilized and underdeveloped. The rivers, oceans, and forests were seen to be untamed and therefore fit for settler "recovery" and "improvement," with slave and indentured labor transforming the land into "Euroscapes" (Haymes 2018, 43; Gilio-Whitaker 2019; Merchant 1996).

US usages of the term "nature" followed European and settler-colonial antecedents. That the US Constitution calls the process of gaining formal legal citizenship "naturalization" shows how boundaries and conceptions of national and political belonging are connected to ideologies of "nature." US environmental imaginaries in the seventeenth and eighteenth centuries constructed indigenous peoples and chattel slaves as the degraded half of the nature/culture binary, closer to a "state of nature." These groups were viewed as uncivilized and thus unfit to hold rights associated with political citizenship (Native Americans did not have US citizenship rights until 1924). In turn, this understanding of nature underwrote the nation's westward expansion and territorial acquisitions as the imperial ambitions of Christianity and white settler agriculture led to the Indian Wars and genocide (Dunbar-Ortiz 2015). The US West and its epic landscapes were seen as holy or sublime, rivaling the soaring cathedrals of Europe's Old World (Cronon 1996b).

After the Indian Wars, dominant US views of nature centered on settler nostalgia. In 1893, historian Frederick Jackson Turner set forth the "Frontier Thesis," asserting that US democracy was forged through a frontier that was a thing of the past (the 1890 census stated that the frontier was "closed"). Both nature and the Native came to be understood through a romantic primitivism that revived Enlightenment understandings of nature as powerful and sublime. These views of wilderness as sacred nature became sanctioned and expanded in the National Park System. Representations of the jewels of that system—Yosemite, Glacier, Yellowstone—drew upon mythologies of wilderness as pristine nature to justify Native expulsion from those lands (Spence 1999). At the same time, cultural anxieties about the disappearing frontier, alongside high rates of immigration and urbanization, generated a masculinity crisis that took political form (Cronon 1996b). Political figures like President Theodore Roosevelt brought together obsessions with manhood, nature, eugenics, conquest, imperialism, and hunting, exemplified through the 1898 Spanish-American War. New institutions such as the Boy Scouts emerged to respond to the boyhood and masculinity crisis by "going back to nature," understood as a return to a precivilized (but not Native) state that lays the basis for maturation into (white, male) adulthood (Ray 2013).

Hierarchical understandings of "nature" similarly underwrite a range of cultural and political projects that have sought to order the "races of man" (Kim 2015). When slaves are compared to apes, when youth gangs are constructed as "wolfpacks," and when undocumented people are depicted as "pests and animals," racism is drawing on ideologies of nature. In the early twentieth century in California's agricultural fields, Japanese farmers were conflated with Japanese beetles (Shinozuka 2013). In the US-Mexico borderlands, fencing that was initially used to prevent livestock from spreading foot-and-mouth disease was later repurposed as a tool to deter and constrict Mexican and Central American immigrants (Mendoza 2019). The ongoing use of fences, barbed wire, and cages continues this history of US dehumanization of (nonwhite) immigrants,

African Americans, and Native Americans, who are treated as closer to animals than humans.

Given this contested history of "nature" in the United States and across the world, why use the term at all? Why not abandon a language and politics of nature? There are at least two compelling reasons nature remains important and useful as a concept. First, a subaltern and subversive deployment of the term can enable human freedom. This usage can be seen in environmental justice movements and calls for more equitable social ecologies. Nature remains that which is abused and made cheap under the shifting conditions of an extractive capitalism. It is a critical element in the protest against the exploitation of land, labor, and life, both locally and globally (Gómez-Barris 2017). The second reason to continue to engage with the term is its deployment in discussions of global climate change in the era of the Anthropocene—the period when human impacts (carbon emissions and deforestation, among others) have shaped geologic time (Crutzen and Stoermer 2000; Purdy 2015). Both usages are critical for the contemporary environmental justice movement, particularly in its attempts to challenge the use of the term "nature" as a category unmarked by race, class, or gender and to reconnect discussions of nature to question of community, urban, and racial justice (Sze 2017; Di Chiro 1996).

Consider as an instance of these usages the deployment of the term "nature" in one of the founding documents of the environmental justice movement in the 1980s and '90s. The Principles of Environmental Justice were articulated at the First National People of Color Environmental Leadership Summit in 1991 with a preamble that affirms, among other principles, the need to "re-establish our spiritual interdependence to the sacredness of our Mother Earth" and to "respect and celebrate each of our cultures, languages, and beliefs about the natural world and our roles in healing ourselves." These principles use the concepts of nature and the natural world to suggest how colonialism and capitalism have devalued and abstracted the cultures of people of color and indigenous people. The environmental justice movement thus calls for political, economic, and cultural liberation from these systems to ground actions and policies that affirm environmental protection for all peoples. "Environment" and "nature" are names for those places where people of color and Native peoples live, work, and play (later movement slogans add places where people learn, transit, rest, pray, and are imprisoned; Global Environmental Justice Project 2018). Even when the term "nature" is not invoked explicitly (or when it is actively resisted as a colonizing abstraction), environmental justice posits a nature that matters in the lives and environments of historically marginalized and politically disenfranchised populations. It traces the ways in which historical layers of injustice create and compound environmental extraction, exposures, and pollution, creating forms of environmental racism that are a result of a "'sedimentation' of racism over time" (Voyles 2015, 23). Examples include the disproportionate pollution exposures of communities of color, which reflect and reinforce inequalities that are inextricably connected with historically racialized policy decisions (residential segregation), resource and labor extractions, and intergenerational dispossessions and wealth transfers (Taylor 2014).

This redefinition of the *nature of nature* in movements for environmental justice is particularly important in the context of climate crisis. The term "Anthropocene" has been critiqued in various ways: for its masking of political power and social difference; for its failure to note different levels of responsibility for climate change across nations, their colonial histories, and their postcolonial trajectories; for its skirting of questions concerning the unequal human agency and impacts of climate change; and for its avoidance of naming extractive capitalism as the systemic context within which climate change has taken place (Haraway 2016; Nixon n.d.; Moore 2015; Yusoff 2018; Davis and Todd 2017; Whyte 2014). But it is also useful when linked to analyses that take these factors into account. Calls for "climate justice" have emerged across various global fora, including the Environmental and Climate Justice Hub. These calls reconceptualize the terms of the "climate crisis" in a historically relevant manner. One instance is the analytical concept of climate debt, which requires countries that have, in the past, emitted levels in excess of an equal per-capita allocation to receive less than their equal per-capita allocation in the future and allows those that have emitted levels lower than their equal per-capita contribution to be considered carbon creditors (Friends of the Earth International 2005).

This type of accounting suggests that understandings of nature focused on those who are most affected by extractive forms of economic development may be the only way out of the crisis of climate and capitalism. Indigenous land rights activists seek to protect their lands from oil pipelines and as biodiverse places rather than viewing them as "natural resources" to be developed. Indigenous activism prioritizes historical and cultural ties to the land as a justification for its protection, insisting in the words of Julian Brave NoiseCat (Canim Lake Band Tsq'escen) and Anne Spice (Tlingint) that "Indigenous peoples are more than cameo extras. They are central protagonists in the fight against the forces of capitalist expansion, which would destroy the land and water, and trample indigenous sovereignty, all for the purposes of resource extraction" (n.d.). Countermovements to extractive capitalism include the material alternatives proposed by indigenous, feminist, and anarchist artists and activists (Gómez-Barris 2017), including iconic fights by the Standing Rock Sioux around the Dakota Access Pipeline (Estes 2019). Internationally, extrajudicial killings of those who oppose economic development (oil and dam construction) and deforestation have accelerated, with the death rate rising rapidly to an average of two activists a week (Global Environmental Justice Project 2018). In these contexts, the linkage of nature and justice is necessary, now more than ever, because climate change and economic inequality exacerbate the lived impacts of natural disasters. Such natural disasters are also social disasters that hurt the poor and powerless more intensely. Estimates are that climate change alone will cause between two hundred million and one billion people to become migrants by the year 2050 (Laczko and Aghazarm 2009).

In a contemporary political landscape that is virulently anti-immigrant, antirefugee, and probusiness, discourses and policies that demand the extraction and continued abuse of nature remain dominant and destructive to communities, peoples, and ecosystems. The keyword "nature" matters only if it can be used in ways that recognize the unequal responsibility for the present state of a world characterized by environmental racism, injustice, and climate disasters. The United States has unique culpability and responsibility in a range of environmental and social inequalities that rely on the abuse and cheapening of nature and peoples. With only 4 percent of the world's population, the United States is responsible for 33 percent of the excess carbon dioxide in the atmosphere. Even as the current US president calls climate change a "hoax" and announces the nation's withdrawal from the Paris Climate Accords, young people globally are demonstrating their frustration with the status quo through creative means such as school climate strikes (Fridays for the Future) and direct action groups (Extinction Rebellion). Speeches, lawsuits, and protests are tactics that environmental activists, frontline communities, and tribal groups who want to protect nature are using in their fight against global and carbon-based extractive capitalism. Nature continues to matter, now more than ever. But what nature means—with all its fraught and liberatory possibilities—is still contested, as it always has been.

2020

46

Neoliberalism
Lisa Duggan

The word "neoliberalism," first used during the 1930s, came into widespread circulation in the 1990s to name a utopian ideology of "free markets" and minimal state interference, a set of policies slashing state social services and supporting global corporate interests, a process (neoliberalization) proceeding in company with procorporate globalization and financialization, and a cultural project of building consent for the upward redistributions of wealth and power that have occurred since the 1970s. But neoliberalism might best be understood as a global social movement encompassing all these political goals. In American studies and cultural studies, the concept has gathered force as a description of current tendencies in global politics and a critique of those tendencies, even as its meanings have dispersed.

Though the term tends to be used differently across the social sciences and the humanities, there is wide agreement that neoliberalism is a radicalized form of capitalist imperialism, centered in the United States and Anglo-Europe, that has developed unevenly across the globe since the 1970s. Most scholars trace its intellectual genealogy to the Mont Pelerin Society and the ideas of Friedrich Hayek (1944), Ludwig von Mises (1949) and economists of the Austrian school, and the writing and activities of Milton Friedman ([1962] 2002) and the Chicago school, developed and circulated since the 1940s. These economists defended classical liberalism and market-based economies grounded in individualism and published scathing critiques of the centralized government regulation and redistributive social benefits provided by capitalist welfare states as well as socialist societies.

These minority views moved toward centers of power during the 1970s, beginning with the overthrow of the democratically elected socialist government of Salvador Allende in Chile by the Chilean military and internal elites, with the assistance of the CIA and the advice of the University of Chicago–based economists surrounding Milton Friedman, often called the "Chicago Boys." Neoliberal reforms—privatization of state enterprises, opening up to foreign business ownership and expatriation of profits, cuts to social services—were accomplished along with violent suppression of dissent. When these policies were later modified to meet the challenges of economic stagnation in the mid-1970s, neoliberalism as state policy (rather than a utopian theory opposed to the state) began to appear as a practical set of strategies for maintaining capitalism in the face of global social movement challenges and for reinforcing or installing elites with access to an increasing share of economic and political power. As David Harvey (2005) and Naomi Klein (2007) describe the genealogy of neoliberalism since the Chilean coup, successive experiments developed means of extracting resources on the US imperial model (as had occurred in earlier interventions in Nicaragua and Iran, among many others), the installation of unaccountable governing structures, the transfer of profits out of social services supported by progressive taxation, and the maintenance of widening inequalities.

These events and tactics function as experiments by creating or exploiting crisis conditions to test key economic hypotheses central to the theory of neoliberalism, as political institutions and modes of decision-making are simultaneously reshaped to entrench neoliberal power brokers. Such experiments include the 1975 New York City fiscal crisis that slashed social services and gave bankers and bondholders unprecedented control over the city's finances; the 1980s "structural adjustment" programs forced on Latin American economies through the practices of the International Monetary Fund (IMF) that created and exploited sovereign debt to enforce investor domination of the political process; and the 2003 US invasion of Iraq, where the administrator of the US-controlled Coalition Provisional Authority of Iraq, Paul Bremer, presided over massive privatization of state enterprises opened to foreign control. These experiments developed policies in localities at the periphery of US imperial power that might then be generalized for use in the center, both nationally, as in the rebuilding of New Orleans after Hurricane Katrina, and transnationally, as in the imposition of austerity policies in the European Union after the 2008 economic crisis and recession. By the 1990s, such policies had been fittingly labeled the Washington Consensus.

Within the imperial purview of the United States and the policies of US-dominated global institutions including the IMF, the World Bank, and the World Trade Organization, these neoliberal policies express ongoing tensions and contradictions. As an ideological revival of classical liberalism in radicalized form, neoliberalism constitutes an attack on the twentieth-century capitalist welfare state, with its modest redistributions and state regulation of corporate power. Critiques of the theories of John Maynard Keynes (1936), the welfare-state liberal capitalism that he championed during the Great Depression of the 1930s, and the Keynesian economic policies dominant in the United States and Anglo-Europe from the 1940s to the 1980s have been a crucial focus of neoliberal intellectual and policy elites. As a set of strategies, set in place over time through trial and error, via both force and consent, neoliberalism in practice has often deviated from the theories of the intellectuals. Overlapping at times with neoconservative security-state policies that deploy centralized military power for imperial violence and war, neoliberalism has functioned historically less as a clearly defined set of ideas and theories and more as an internally contradictory mode of upward redistribution of wealth and power and an extension of the practices of imperial extraction of resources from economies of the Global South.

But US imperial power has not been the sole source of global neoliberal reform. From the "opening" of China to world capitalist markets in the 1980s, through the new business and trade policies of post-Soviet Russia and postapartheid South Africa in the 1990s, to the policies enacted via the 1992 Maastricht Treaty on European Union, many global, local, and national forces have produced the uneven spatial and temporal landscape of neoliberalism. Some scholars acknowledge this unevenness but emphasize the hegemonic force of global neoliberalism since 1980. These writers focus on the power of the dominant economic system in reshaping global societies and politics (Harvey 2010). Others acknowledge global neoliberalism's historical power but emphasize the highly variable landscape of exceptions to neoliberalism and of neoliberalism as an exception under other economic regimes around the globe. This group includes many researchers who are as interested in tracking the limitations of neoliberalism's influence as in documenting its power (Ong 2006).

Despite these differences, there is wide agreement among scholars on the foundational causes and enduring effects of global neoliberalism. As a response to the economic and political challenges to capitalist dominance in the mid-twentieth century, neoliberalism organized the uneven, contradictory efforts of global corporate and political elites to maintain and concentrate power. The effect of widening global inequalities is indisputable (Galbraith 2012; Stiglitz 2013). But within this consensus, approaches to the study of neoliberalism

within American studies and cultural studies are broadly various. Sociologists, geographers, and urbanists tend to take a structural approach, emphasizing the overall logic and force of neoliberal policies as they spread over time and space (N. Smith 1983; N. Brenner 2004). Anthropologists are more likely to point to the contingencies of those policies and to the power of resistance to them, especially in the Global South (Sawyer 2004; Tsing 2011). Scholars located in the literary humanities tend to analyze the cultural project of neoliberalism, its modes of subject formation, along with its affective traces (G. Harkins 2009; Berlant 2011). Layered alongside these divisions are other theoretical differences. Marxist scholars offer narratives of political-economic conflict and change, focused on the class conflicts that shape the shifting forms of capitalism and the state (Harvey 2005; N. Smith 1983; N. Brenner 2004). Writers influenced by Michel Foucault examine the broad dispersion of power among institutions that regulate populations, including schools, prisons, health care industries, popular culture, the media, and the ways that self-disciplining subjects who comply with neoliberal expectations are produced (N. Rose 1999; Povinelli 2011).

Across all these fields, postcolonial and transnational studies scholars have offered the most pointed set of challenges to the standard narratives of spreading neoliberal hegemonies since the 1970s. Rather than focus primarily on the structural impact of late capitalism, procorporate globalization, and financialization on states, economies, cultures, and everyday lives, these scholars have noted the myriad ways in which challenges to Western colonial modernity have shaped, rather than simply resisted, the ideas and practices of neoliberalism. These scholars expand on postcolonial and decolonial studies of the cultural work of racial taxonomies, gendered narratives, and sexual discourses in producing dominant forms of Western modernity and empire since the sixteenth century (McClintock 1995; Stoler 2010; M. Jacqui Alexander 2005). They have noted the role of decolonization and of feminist, queer, and ecological social movements, as well as of class and labor politics, in producing constantly morphing responses to and from ruling institutions (Grewal 2005; Reddy 2011).

This group of scholars enables expansive ways of thinking about social change. If we follow their lead in going beyond notions of neoliberal hegemony, uneven developments, or dominance and resistance, we can begin to trace the interactions among complexly intertwined axes of power. The global landscape of social movements contesting the impact of neoliberalism today—all of which treat the boundaries between state, economy, and culture, public and private, as dynamic and fluid—might be best understood as an ongoing set of dispersed yet interconnected efforts at achieving more just forms of globalization (Duggan 2003).

2014

47

Normal
Robert McRuer

"Normal," because of its easy associations with typical, ordinary, or unremarkable, appears to many people as a benign word, nothing more than a neutral descriptor of certain groups, bodies, or behaviors that are more common than others. Yet more than almost any other keyword in American studies and cultural studies, "normal" carries with it a history of discursive and literal violence against those who could never hope to be described by the term. Sexual minorities, disabled people, racialized populations, immigrants, and many others have at times found themselves among the motley group that the Chicana lesbian feminist Gloria Anzaldúa terms *los atravesados*: "those who cross over, pass over, or go through the confines of the 'normal'" (1987, 3). For Anzaldúa and innumerable other critics of normal, this border crossing has consequences. Lives lived beyond the confines of the normal have been marked as illegitimate and targeted for surveillance, control, correction, confinement, and even elimination.

The history of the keyword "normal" is relatively short compared to that of most words in the English language, despite the fact that the term structures contemporary cultures in powerful and nearly ubiquitous ways. The *Oxford English Dictionary* (*OED*) notes that the idea of "normal" as "constituting or conforming to a type or standard; regular, usual, typical; ordinary, conventional" was not in common usage until 1840. This usage roughly coincides with the French statistician Adolphe Quetelet's (1835) widely influential notion of *l'homme moyen*, or the average man, an abstract human being with particular qualities that could be measured and graphed. Characteristics that were "abnormal," according to the new understandings of statistics developed by Quetelet and others, were those located outside a "normal" bell-shaped curve. Over the course of the nineteenth century, statistical measurement became an imperative: not only *could* human characteristics be observed and plotted on graphs and charts, but they *should* be, in order to identify (and potentially correct) that which was abnormal (L. Davis 1995).

By the end of the century, this imperative produced a second usage traced in the *OED* of "normal" as descriptive of a person "physically and mentally sound; free from any disorder; healthy." Here, the word's appearance of carrying mere statistical meaning (as average or mean) masks its ability to bear moral judgment and to privilege certain groups (as normal) while subordinating others (as deviant). Only at the beginning of the twentieth century did the term begin to name a person who might be understood as "heterosexual" (a term that itself was coined only in 1868; J. Katz 1995). In less than a century, then, a word with a Latin etymology that meant "conforming to or organized by a rule" began to carry, in most European languages, dominant meanings that Anzaldúa and other scholars of American studies and cultural studies now critique.

Across this history, the normal was not simply being identified and described; rather, as the philosopher Michel Foucault makes clear, an entire culture and machinery of "normalization" were emerging. Normalization entailed the widespread production of knowledge and discourse about those who were "abnormal." Technologies of normalization developed over the nineteenth century. These technologies, ranging from medical or psychiatric charts to judicial records, targeted "dangerous individuals" who deviated from a standard, or

"norm," and on whom corrective power thus needed to be exercised (Foucault [1999] 2003). Normalizing power, in these contexts, is not simply repressive; it works by producing ways of knowing, recognizing, and categorizing individuals. Power is therefore best understood as a relation, as something always in motion, rather than an inert substance or property. Put differently, power is not simply *held* by one privileged group and *exercised* on another, weaker or "disempowered," group. Instead, power is at work everywhere, constructing—literally, materializing—normal and abnormal subjects.

Discourses of normalcy and abnormalcy were generated in, and traveled through, institutions such as schools, prisons, asylums, and hospitals and were codified by the "expert opinion" of people authorized by such institutions. Enforcing normalcy and identifying and containing abnormalcy were particularly important for an emerging industrial capitalist order, which needed the majority of people to function as able-bodied laborers in a "work-based" rather than a "need-based" system. Tests, measurements, questionnaires, and other "validating devices" shaped by a range of authorities (doctors, psychiatrists, government officials, insurance agents) were developed both to keep the majority of normal people in the work-based system and to stigmatize those sorted, through a newly invented "clinical concept of disability," into the need-based system (D. Stone 1984). These processes did more than make the association of "normal" and "able-bodied" appear to be completely natural. Over the nineteenth and twentieth centuries, they required that disabled people—those forced to appeal to the very institutions that had deemed them abnormal and dependent—had to pass through "ceremonies of social degradation" to demonstrate their eligibility for the work-based system (L. Davis 1995; Longmore 2003).

Flourishing throughout the nineteenth century and into the twentieth, freak shows, which put on display people with congenital disabilities and racialized groups, made abnormalcy spectacular in a somewhat different way. Freaks were constructed through a discursive transformation of individual (and otherwise unremarkable) characteristics: William Henry Johnson, an African American man with a cognitive disability, became the "What Is It?" exhibit; Charles Tripp, performing everyday tasks with his toes, became the "Armless Wonder" (Bogdan 1988). Attendees at freak shows could reassure themselves of their own normalcy as they observed the display of freakish others (Garland-Thomson 1997; Clare 1999). The complex web of power relations staged by freak shows generated that which was abnormal, delineated that which was normal, and depended on embodied "evidence." Here and elsewhere, the project of enforcing normalcy had particularly profound ramifications for disabled people, who were increasingly positioned by experts and laypeople alike as having abnormal bodies (L. Davis 1995).

The emergence of "unsightly beggar laws" in urban areas in the late nineteenth and early twentieth centuries (laws that prohibited "diseased, maimed, or unsightly" bodies from being in public spaces) likewise functioned to spatialize a distinction between normal citizens and those whose bodies or behavior marked them as deviant and in need of correction. Disability activists later termed these ordinances "ugly laws," recognizing the extent to which they could be, or had been, deployed to control or contain people with disabilities (Schweik 2009). Such containment was often quite literal, as the rate of institutionalization of disabled people skyrocketed as the nineteenth century ended (Trent 1994). The move to displace individuals and populations deemed abnormal reached its most lethal conclusion in eugenic policies that flourished at the turn of the twentieth century. In both Europe and the United States, these policies encouraged the sterilization of disabled people, with the explicit goal and justification of extending normalcy for future generations (Snyder and Mitchell 2006). In Nazi Germany, the phrase "life unworthy of life" was eventually used to describe disabled people, and thousands were killed alongside millions of Jewish people and others (homosexuals, gypsies, religious minorities, political dissidents) who went beyond the confines of the new eugenic normal (Garland-Thomson 2007).

By the mid-twentieth century, scholars had begun to map and critique the contours of normal and abnormal and the mechanisms used to divide one from the other. Foucault's former teacher Georges Canguilhem, a philosopher and historian of science, traced the ways that the biological, scientific, and statistical division of the world into "normal" and "pathological" was always saturated with political and ideological concerns and never entailed simple or neutral measurement ([1966] 1989). Erving Goffman studied the workings of stigma and argued that people with "spoiled identities," outside the realm of the normal, had to manage, fastidiously, their encounters with others (1963). This management might be what Goffman called "stigmaphobic" (if one essentially insisted on one's normalcy and distanced oneself from more deviant others) or "stigmaphilic" (if one embraced, or even reveled in, one's outsider status), but it was constant.

Anzaldúa and other feminists, particularly feminists of color in the 1970s and 1980s, extended these early efforts toward a critical understanding of normalization, focusing on how regimes of normalcy were constructed through overlapping and mutually reinforcing systems of age, race, class, gender, and embodiment (Moraga and Anzaldúa 1981; B. Smith 1982; Ferguson 2004). "Somewhere on the edge of consciousness," Audre Lorde wrote, "there is what I call a *mythical norm*, which each one of us within our hearts knows 'that is not me.' In america, this norm is usually defined as white, thin, male, young, heterosexual, christian, and financially secure" (1984a, 116). Disability studies scholars surveyed the uneven and unequal ways that bodies had been cast as normal and abnormal, and perhaps most famously, the interdisciplinary field of queer studies began to excavate the ways that normal was both naturalized as "heterosexual" and made compulsory (Rich [1980] 1983; de Lauretis 1991; M. Warner 1999). By the end of the century, queer disability studies began to posit that "compulsory heterosexuality" was thoroughly interwoven with "compulsory able-bodiedness" (McRuer 2006; McRuer and Wilkerson 2003).

In the same period, feminist and queer theory more generally began to rename "compulsory heterosexuality" as "heteronormativity" in order to convey the ways in which technologies of normalization operate not simply through logics of repression or compulsion but through forms of power that privilege, naturalize, and institutionalize heterosexuality (Berlant and Warner 1998). Eventually, queer theory moved from a textured delineation of the workings of "heteronormativity" to accounts of the ways in which gay men and lesbians themselves participate in what was dubbed "homonormativity," especially as the organizations running the mainstream movement began to seem more and more like corporations and to emphasize disproportionately integrationist issues such as the right to marry or serve in the military (Duggan 2002). Transgender theorists, in turn, insisted that homonormativity consisted not only in contemporary gay and lesbian desires for normalcy and assimilation but also in a privileging of normative masculine and feminine experiences and embodiments (Stryker 2008; Spade 2011).

Normal ways of being and living have generally been accorded a privacy denied to abnormal lives. That privacy has been secured through social forms such as the heterosexual (and reproductive) couple. Resistant alternatives to regimes of the normal thus argue for forms of being-in-common that are public, accessible, and collective. This expansive sense of public culture, which might be comprehended as both queer and disabled (or "crip," as some scholars have begun to theorize it), are particularly vital now, because conceptualizations of "normal" have shifted during an era of neoliberal capitalism. Brian Massumi (2002a), Slavoj Žižek (2010), and other critical theorists have argued that contemporary capitalism no longer deploys a logic of "totalizing normality"; instead, neoliberal capitalism focuses on and markets constant change, flexibility, "difference," and, indeed, freakiness. Put differently, neoliberal capitalism arguably embraces the freaky or abnormal, domesticating or taming it as it sells it back to us. The more expansive and accessible public cultures offered by feminist, queer, and disability theorists seek to recognize and resist this embrace as just one more form of normalization (and indeed privatization), blocking a more democratic materialization of queer, freaky, and crip public cultures.

2014

48

Politics

Kandice Chuh

"Politics," in its most common usage, refers to the activities of governance, including efforts to attain or retain the power to control those activities. In this sense, the term refers to an interest in how the state (the regulating structures and governing practices of the nation) works and under what or whose authority. This understanding of "politics" is clearly present in both American studies and cultural studies, most markedly in the work of political scientists and legal scholars. However, both fields have long had a broader interest in how and with what consequences the power to govern operates. How and why are resources distributed as they are and to the benefit or disadvantage of which populations? Who gets to be represented in, and who is excluded from, participation in governance? What ideas and institutions legitimize the exercise of authority, and how can existing practices and structures be transformed? In what ways do cultural products and practices shape the relationship of individuals and groups to power and authority? How is life itself regulated as a matter of power and authority? Answers to these questions draw on a different meaning of the term "politics," one that stresses contestation over the power to define legitimate authority and recognizes that politics shape everything from the organization and activities of educational and legal institutions to the valuing of some aesthetic practices over others. It is for this reason that phrases such as the "politics of knowledge," "the politics of culture," "the politics

of gender," and so on commonly frame the work undertaken in American studies and cultural studies.

The term is most often used in the phrase "the politics *of*" or as the nominalized adjective "the political," and its significance in American studies and cultural studies may be seen in two ways: first, as marking an awareness of the historical conditions of the emergence of these fields and, second, as pointing toward an inquiry into the kind of work that critics in these fields undertake. Common narratives explain the establishment of American studies within US universities as closely related to the global politics of the Cold War era—what may be understood as Cold War *geo*politics. These narratives suggest that, alongside other area studies (e.g., Asian studies), American studies was institutionally legitimated because of the interests of the US nation-state in having detailed knowledge about other nations and regions as it entered into empire-building activities globally (Kaplan and Pease 1993). These stories of the field's establishment closely align it with the politics of US national interests. American studies today, however, tends to be defined by its difference from such nationalist inclinations. What had been a heavy reliance on empirical studies designed to provide information about the United States and its populations has given way to a much richer and more diverse critical sensibility. This transformation echoes the changes to the historical contexts and corollary politics of the movement from the Cold War to the post–Cold War era and reflects the impact of the globally dispersed social movements of the post–civil rights era.

The shift to a more diversified field of study also reflects the influence of academic discourses and theoretical insights of the late part of the twentieth century, including cultural studies. The field of cultural studies is generally understood to have been established in the 1970s and '80s, with roots in the British class struggles of that era. Key figures such as Simon During ([1993] 2007), Stuart Hall (1980), and Lawrence Grossberg (Grossberg, Nelson, and Treichler 1992), in accord with the demands of the social movements of the late twentieth century, argued for attention to the ways in which universities play a significant role in the organization of society into different classes. Universities and their dominant ways of producing and disseminating knowledge—their dominant epistemologies and pedagogies—have historically contributed to the uneven distribution of power and resources. Debates over what gets studied and taught, by whom, and how were framed in these founding texts of cultural studies as a politics of knowledge. These debates changed the landscape of what could be taken up and taught as legitimate objects of knowledge. For example, the legitimation of the study of popular culture is an effect of the struggles over the politics of knowledge of this time. Politics, then, are one way of understanding the history of the fields themselves.

Feminist, queer, postcolonial, and ethnic studies politics, theories, and traditions have been driving forces in the kinds of questions that animate these fields. Not all of the work undertaken in American studies or cultural studies attends to matters of power and difference, which is a central concern of these discourses and the social movements with which they are intimately connected. But it is arguable that the most compelling work draws on the energies that issue from thinking through race, sex, gender, sexuality, empire, and bodily norms, along with class, as intersecting axes of analysis. In these ways, American studies and cultural studies are largely organized by questions that are at once political (they address matters of authority and power) and epistemological (they ask how knowledge is produced and what value it is given).

The politics of the field formations of American studies and cultural studies thus draw attention to the boundary between the realms of politics and culture, knowledge and society. What is American studies? What is cultural studies? What are their stakes and objectives? Persistently and deeply concerned with these foundational questions, both fields have made it possible to recognize the role of politics in the ways that culture is shaped and expressed, the role of culture in giving meaning to political processes, and the role of academic discourses and institutions in making it possible to attend to questions of power and authority. Engagement with these kinds of issues often draws on political theorists and philosophers associated closely with Marxist thinking and related theories of ideology and hegemony, which have had enormous impacts on the ways that power and its relationships to the people are conceptualized (Althusser [1971] 2001; Gramsci 1971) and on the material aspects of art and culture (Benjamin [1936] 1968; Raymond Williams [1976] 1983). The theorization of power in terms of *biopolitics* has enabled a crucial understanding of politics as a mechanism by which life is given or taken (Foucault [1975] 1995). Other critics have generated key insights into the affective dimensions of life, culture, and politics (Berlant 1991, 2011); the rise of neoliberalism as an ideology of governance (Duggan 2003; Wendy Brown 2005); the ways in which sex and race shape knowledge production (Ferguson 2012b); the history of popular culture and social movements (Lipsitz 1990b, [1998] 2006); the interrelation of race and gender, capitalism and national identity formation (Lowe 1996); and the performative dimensions of racial and sexual embodiment and identification (J. Butler 1993; Muñoz 1999, 2009).

At the same time, contemporary scholarship in American studies and cultural studies also focuses critical attention on the boundaries of "the political" itself. Partly in response to the dominance of the kinds of critiques associated with the politics of identity and representation, recent work has encouraged an expansion of the topics, sites, and methods of cultural studies analyses in American studies. Identity and representation in this context refer to sociopolitical identities—those of race, gender, age, and so on—and how they are constructed and with what effects. Enormously powerful in showing how such identities matter to the lives, cultures, and histories of the United States—powerful, that is, in showing that there *is* a politics of identity—these approaches have been criticized for defining the objectives of politically engaged work in terms of dominant representational politics. For instance, analyses of the history of racism in the United States that focus primarily on the objective of attaining citizenship and the rights that accompany it operate within the nation's normative framework by promoting identity understood in nationalist terms as the achievement of social justice. A critique of that type of analysis encourages questioning the adequacy of national identity as the solution to social and economic problems rather than encouraging identification with it (Moten 2003; Reddy 2011).

This emphasis on the boundaries of the political has made it clear that politics are too narrowly defined when attached to the frameworks of identity and representation that are sanctioned by the nation-state. These critiques have led to efforts to expand and theorize "the political" itself. Partly, these efforts can be observed in the variety of "turns" that cultural studies and American studies have taken—toward the transnational, the hemispheric, the global, the aesthetic, the ethical, the affective, and so on—with each named "turn" attempting to generate paradigms for critical inquiry that are better able to apprehend the complexity of power structures and dynamics and their effects. Likewise, the currency and traction of terms such as "indigeneity," "sovereignty," "disability," "the commons," and "ecocriticism"

reflect the changing critical and political landscape of both American studies and cultural studies. Some of these moves attempt to alter the spatial protocols by which "Americanness" is conceptualized and studied, to illuminate the politics of the nation and of citizenship. Others may be better understood as more explicitly rewriting "the political" itself. One example is the increased interest in the cultural and material significance of affect. Driven largely by feminist and queer theorists, this attention to "the politics of affect" inverts the usual association of politics with reason and the public sphere and of feeling with sentiment and domesticity (Berlant 1991, 2011; Clough and Halley 2007; Cvetkovich 1992, 2003; S. Ngai 2005).

In these ways, the space of American cultural studies—the overlap between American studies and cultural studies—is a site through which the complexity and breadth of both "politics" and "the political" can be apprehended as an aspect of world-making ideologies (such as imperialism and nationalism) and ordinary lives, of ways of knowing and of sorting knowledge, and of the distribution of life and death. By insisting on asking what constitutes "the political," this vein of scholarship importantly necessitates awareness of how its definition delimits what can be studied, known, and potentially transformed.

2014

49

Populism

Joseph Lowndes

"Populism" is an unusual political term in that its meanings vary widely, both for those who claim the label and those who use it as a term of derision. It is rooted in the republican notion that all legitimate political authority is grounded in the people as such. Yet populism has never meant the same thing as popular sovereignty. It describes not a type of regime but an active demand for political power. To those who claim it as a political identity, it is meant to describe a struggle for majoritarian rule against threats from above, below, or within. To those for whom it is a term of derision, populism describes an antiliberal desire for mob or authoritarian rule.

The term was first used by reporters and by members of the US People's Party in the late nineteenth century to denote its claim to speak and act in the name of the common people against powerful banking and railroad interests and corrupt government officials in both major parties. Its origins are also found in the Russian Narodniki, a movement of left-wing intellectuals in the 1860s and 1870s to ground anticzarism in the supposed authenticity and communal practices of agrarian life. Usages of the term have been the subject of continual historical and political argument since then. One important debate concerns the political content of populism. One influential view of populism sees it as reactionary (Hofstadter 1955), while another defines it as democratic and egalitarian (Goodwyn 1976). Disagreement over populism's basic political content has

led many scholars to debate what exactly populism is. While some scholars see it as an ideology (Canovan 1981; Mudde and Kaltwasser 2018), others see it as a discourse that constructs a notion of the people (Panizza 2005) and still others as a demagogic performance (Moffitt 2017; Ostiguy 2017).

One of the most influential accounts of populism was written by historian Richard Hofstadter during the era of Wisconsin senator Joseph McCarthy's anticommunist campaigns in the 1950s. Hofstadter ([1955] 2011) saw it as a provincial, moralistic form of agrarianism marked by anticosmopolitanism and atavism: "Somewhere along the way a large part of the Populist-Progressive tradition has turned sour, become illiberal and ill-tempered" (20–21). For Hofstader, the moral energies that split the world sharply into good and evil and the worldview that saw the common people as always vulnerable to elite conspiracies could all too easily shift far rightward. This potential was apparent early in the history of populism. A good example is Vice Presidential People's Party candidate Tom Watson, who campaigned on behalf of "the people" on a progressive platform in 1896 but later focused attacks on African Americans, immigrants, and Jews.

Contesting Hofstader's views two decades later, historian Lawrence Goodwyn (1976) saw in populism a revolt that created a rich culture of participatory democracy. For Goodwyn, a veteran of New Left political struggles, populism challenged the economic power of concentrated capital while breaking down racial barriers between black and white farmers. Viewed in this way, populism expressed not the outrage of paranoid moralists looking backward but a desire for collective self-determination that radically altered the consciousness of its participants. These two opposed interpretations continue to echo through how the term "populism" is understood and used today.

All populist projects, left or right, posit a majoritarian people in conflict with internal or external enemies. Left populists identify with the tradition of the nineteenth-century populists as political actors who formed cooperatives, printed newspapers, organized speaker's bureaus, and ran independent political campaigns to halt the power of monopolies and the political arrangements that enabled them. That tradition extended into early twentieth-century progressivism and shaped fundamental elements of Franklin Delano Roosevelt's New Deal. In the 1960s and 1970s, various political projects focused on grassroots organizing and cooperative building saw themselves as populist, although none had anything like the force of the People's Party. Today we find the word "populist" used to describe a wide range of campaigns and movements against corporate and financial power and global free trade agreements, including Occupy Wall Street and Bernie Sanders's insurgent presidential campaigns in the United States; numerous parties and regimes in Latin America; the Syriza Party in Greece; and the Podemos movement in Spain.

In recent years, right-wing populism has expanded rapidly, particularly in Europe and the United States. This rendering of popular sovereignty depicts cultural threats to the people as coming from nonwhite immigrants and Islam. Like left versions of populism, these movements oppose international trade alliances, such as the European Union or the North American Free Trade Agreement. There are numerous right-wing populist parties in Europe, such as Hungary's Jobbik Party, the Dutch Party for Freedom, the Danish Peoples Party, the National Front in France, or the UK Independence Party. In the United States, right-wing populism has been expressed episodically in and outside the Republican Party and powerfully in the presidency of Donald Trump. Right-wing populism draws on older discourses of racism, colonialism, antisemitism, traditionalism, and in some cases, variants of socialism.

The dramatic rise of right-wing populism has led many scholars to see populist attacks on liberal democratic institutions as a fundamental threat to democracy (Mounk 2018; Levitsky and Ziblatt 2018). In these contexts, usages of the word "populism" often conjure another contested term: "fascism." Some scholars see in both US and European forms of right-wing populism something resembling the rise of fascism (J. Stanley 2018; Steigmann-Gall 2016). Others argue that the distinction between populism and fascism is an important one. Chip Berlet and Matthew Lyons have suggested that while right-wing populism is a key element of fascism, the two differ in that fascism is ultimately expressed in the seizure of state power for a form of revolutionary nationalism that reorganizes society along rigid hierarchical lines (Berlet and Lyons 2000; Berlet 2016).

Against the claim that populism as such threatens democracy or that liberal democratic institutions must be defended against it, some have argued that populism is democracy's only hope (Riofrancos 2017; Mouffe 2018). In this view, liberal democratic institutions are not the bulwark against right-wing populism but the condition of its emergence, a response to the vast inequalities enabled and protected by those institutions in recent decades. Left populism, it is argued, can enlist the democratic energies of the people in broad-based social movements, people no longer served by liberal institutions and, in some cases, vulnerable to recruitment by the populist Right. This form of populism pits movements for popular democratic control from below against both antidemocratic state power and private capital.

In theory, it should be simple to distinguish right-wing populism understood as chauvinist, exclusionary, and authoritarian from left-wing populism understood as open, emancipatory, and radically democratic. Left-wing populism embraces a far more capacious version of the people than does right-wing populism. Thus does populism become the very definition of all struggles for hegemony in the work of Argentinian post-Marxist theorist Ernesto Laclau (2007). Yet all evocations of populism risk drawing exclusionary lines around those who count as the people or ignoring forms of difference and hierarchies within the people, such as those based on gender, sexuality, race, or colonial status (Ciccariello-Maher 2019). Indeed, some populist parties successfully merge left- and right-wing populism, such as the Italian Movimento 5 Stelle, which combines prowelfare and antirefugee positions.

Versions of populism also have been vehicles for anticolonial projects, such as the Movimiento al Socialismo in Bolivia, a national populist party rooted in land reform and indigenous rights struggles. Political theorist Laura Grattan (2016) has argued that principles and practices of resistance to elite power and an insistence on popular sovereignty always open the door to the pressing claims of subaltern subjects. Such was the case for the emergence of black populist organizations in the late nineteenth century US South (Ali 2010) or the struggles for collective self-determination by the undocumented today. Such possibilities for what Grattan calls "aspirational populism" require that the "populi" of populism remains an open, contested category. Stefano Harney and Fred Moten's influential invocation of the "undercommons" as a site and modality of black struggle and resistance is an extension of this thinking (2013).

Populism is likely to become an increasingly important political word in the coming years. The demise of the Cold War era's broad social contract between right and left (and capital and labor), the rise of an extreme wealth gap within and between countries, the thoroughgoing privatization of formerly public functions of the state, and the accelerated financialization of dominant economies all have corroded the institutions and norms of liberal democratic states and further destabilized governing regimes in the Global South. Under these conditions, along with rapid and profound ecological catastrophe, passionate new assertions in the name of the people against real and imagined foes may usher in a populist era worldwide. In this context, American studies and cultural studies have much to offer our understanding of populism as a political force that blurs the distinction between the affective, the performative, and the ideological.

2020

50

Prison

Caleb Smith

The United States now incarcerates more people than any other country in the world, both as a percentage of its own population and in absolute numbers. The federal government operates a far-reaching network of immigrant detention centers and war prisons. Like the domestic warehouses of mass incarceration, these are spaces where the boundaries of legal personhood and cultural identity are contested. While prisons have been expanding, many other public institutions have disappeared or withered; those that remain, such as schools and housing projects, seem increasingly prison-like. Critics have described the United States as a "prison nation," arguing that imprisonment, which serves various functions elsewhere, has become a core mission of the US, an end in itself (Herivel and Wright 2003). To claim that the United States, as a nation, is distinguished by its prisons is to pose a problem, not to resolve one, since prison stands for so many enduring contradictions—between assimilation and exclusion, deracination and racialization, subject formation and abjection.

"Prison" is an ancient word. The *Oxford English Dictionary* suggests an etymological link between "prisoner" and "prize," perhaps because captives taken (*pris*) in war, according to some customs and codes, could be sold into servitude or otherwise exploited by their captors. In the modern era, following the Atlantic revolutions, "prison" came to name an institution designed for the long-term incarceration of convicted criminals. Thus prisons were distinguished from jails, which are places of detention where inmates await trial or punishment. Led by reformers from the northeastern United States, many European and North American criminal justice systems gradually abandoned public punishments—hanging, whipping, branding, and other forms of disfigurement and shame—and established imprisonment as the new standard. The first wave of reform promised to rationalize and humanize the penal system, to re-create the prison as a scene of reflection and rehabilitation. To emphasize these new ideals, the reformers called their institutions "houses of correction" or "penitentiaries." Since the 1960s, scholars in American studies, cultural studies, and the interdisciplinary field of critical prison studies have excavated the causes and consequences of these transformations. Their research suggests that, even as the prison came to signify a revolution in punishment, it never fully severed its ties to the forms of captivity associated with empire, war, and slavery. Today, imprisonment's genealogical bonds to those kinds of large-scale violence seem more durable than its frayed connection to such concepts as justice and the rule of law.

Interdisciplinary and activist scholarship uses "prison" as a critical concept, analyzing the penal system in terms other than the official ones, which are used to justify that system or to improve it from within. Scholars have submitted the discourses of legitimation and reform to a dual critique, analyzing them from alternative theoretical perspectives and, at the same time, attending to inmates' own accounts of their experience. Some of this work promotes specific policy changes, such as an end to solitary confinement or life sentencing. Increasingly, though, critical prison studies has allied itself with the radical project of ending imprisonment altogether—a "new abolitionism" (J. James 2005). From the start, this critique confronted an institution so normalized that it was difficult to imagine any alternative. To make the prison visible as an object of controversy, Michel Foucault's influential *Discipline and Punish: The Birth of the Prison* took a genealogical approach, writing a "history of the present" ([1975] 1995, 31). With the rise of the penitentiary, according to the received wisdom, punishment ceased to wound the body and dedicated itself to rehabilitating the soul. Foucault rejected this narrative, arguing that the modern prison was a scene of unending struggle. It was "born" when techniques of disciplinary training, surveillance, and control that had first been developed elsewhere—in the military, the workshop, and the school—were used to reorganize the penal system. These disciplines produced prisoners as objects of specialized knowledge and as subjects responsible for the regulation of their own actions. Rather than releasing the state's hold on the body, the shift from spectacular torture to prison discipline actually tightened its grip.

Foucault's research focused on Western Europe, but the movements that produced the first penitentiaries were transatlantic in scope, and the boundary between torture and its civilized alternatives was drawn most vividly at the edges of empires (Asad 2003). In the United States, prison reform was aligned with other enlightened causes—temperance, antislavery, even democracy itself. By the 1830s, prison reformers had the support of powerful Protestant organizations, and two world-famous penitentiary systems were competing for prestige. Pennsylvania's "solitary system" placed every inmate in solitary confinement. New York's "congregate system" enforced group labor in factory-like workshops. The rivalry was the topic of a fierce pamphlet war, but it also obscured some deeper continuities; soon it was taken for granted, at least in the free states, that imprisonment would be the standard punishment for most serious crimes. Already, the penitentiary had become a key component in the international reputation of the United States. Charles Dickens (1842) and Harriet Martineau (1837) joined the debate, and Alexis de Tocqueville compiled his notes for *Democracy in America* ([1835] 2004) while he was studying US penitentiaries for the French government. These visitors suspected that the penitentiary systems would disclose something essential about the character of the new republic, where punishment had been reconceived as an implement of humanization and enlightened justice. In the solitary confinement cell, the United States fashioned its ideal citizens; in the prison workshop, it built its model of a well-regulated society.

Critical histories of the penitentiary have explored how the new institution, promising rationality and humanity, reinforced hierarchies of race and class and tightened social control (W. Lewis 1965; Rothman 1971; Dumm 1987; Meranze 1996). Seeing prison reform less as a humanitarian movement and more as a tactical shift in the exercise of power, this approach connects the penitentiary to other institutions designed for surveillance and training: the industrial factory, the asylum, the technical college, and the Indian school. Today, however, the penal system rarely promises rehabilitation, and historians have come to doubt that the genealogy of the prison can be traced exclusively to the nineteenth-century penitentiary. Studies of US war prisons, for instance, have situated contemporary torture and indefinite detention within far-reaching histories of imperialism (M. Brown 2005; A. Kaplan 2005; Dayan 2007). And new work on the highly racialized regime of mass incarceration has discovered precedents in the antebellum plantation and its successors, convict leasing, the prison farm, and Jim Crow segregation (Wacquant 2002; Oshinsky 2008; Michelle Alexander 2010). These new genealogies have tended to set aside the term "penitentiary," with its reformist and religious connotations, in favor of "prison," emphasizing that the object of critique is not a machine for remaking subjects but a scene of abjection, dehumanization, and death (C. Smith 2009).

Despite the rhetoric of reform, the true "uses of incarceration in the United States," Colin Dayan argues, have always been "to criminalize, exclude, and do such violence to persons that they are returned to their communities—when they are—diminished and harmed sometimes beyond repair, or redress" (2011, xiv). This sense of prison as a zone of exclusion and mortification undergirds an increasing scholarly interest in prison literature and in fieldwork that documents inmates' accounts of their own lives. Several studies and collections have emphasized imprisonment as a defining aspect of African American experience and expression, linking the project of prison abolition to the nineteenth-century abolitionists' antislavery campaigns (Philip 1973; H. Franklin 1978; T. Green 2008). Others have asked what modes of consciousness and resistance remain available within the conditions of disciplinary isolation and social death (Rhodes 2004; D. Rodríguez 2006; Guenther 2013). When the prison is understood as an implement of vengeance whose true aim is to annihilate, not to rehabilitate, the self, inmates' own documentary accounts and creative testimonials are of special value to a critical practice that identifies itself with the activist struggle to end imprisonment.

What does it mean to speak of the prison today? In recent decades, new developments have made the penal system an object of critical and popular controversy. The privatization of some facilities introduces a profit motive and allows corporations to screen their practices from public oversight by invoking the legal protections that guard trade secrets. The large-scale incarceration of undocumented immigrants is explained in terms of sovereignty and citizenship rather than correction. The same is true of indefinite detention (or internment) and torture in "the new war prison" at Guantánamo (J. Butler 2004a, 53). And solitary confinement, now euphemized as "administrative segregation" or "special housing," has been redefined as a strategy for system-internal securitization, imposed at the discretionary authority of bureaucratic officials. Hunger strikes, riots, and other acts of resistance by inmates have called attention to a human rights crisis. In the academy and in the public sphere, critics have pointed to the widening and scandalous gap between the actual functions of prisons and their traditional role as public institutions of criminal justice. Some of these scandals may seem to partake in the logic of the "exception," instances of sovereign power operating outside the ordinary rule of law (Agamben 2005). But they can also be connected to the normal functioning of a new kind of prison system, unlike any other in the world.

Between 1975 and 2000, the total number of inmates in US facilities jumped from just under 380,000 to almost 2 million, an increase of more than 500 percent, driven largely by harsh, racially targeted sentencing laws for drug-related offenses (Wacquant 2009). The result was imprisonment on a scale that is unprecedented in US history and unequaled anywhere else in the world. In an effort to understand and resist this dramatic turn, scholars have advanced several critiques, each with its own account of what the prison has become. One argument points to the decline of the ideal of rehabilitation and the resurgence of a vengeful popular attitude, accompanied by spectacular, sensationalized images of crime and punishment in mass culture (F. Allen 1981; J. Whitman 2003; M. Brown 2009). Another points to a thriving "prison industrial complex," a coalition of state and private interests that exerts such a strong influence on policy that the main business of criminal justice in the United States is simply to continue expanding the nation's prisons (Parenti 1999; A. Davis 2001).

A third argument, associated with critical legal studies, suggests a shift in the very nature of government. With deindustrialization, the welfare state gave way to the "penal" or "carceral" state. As neoliberal reforms dismantled the midcentury's institutions of welfare and public health, governments began using jails and prisons to manage forms of social insecurity—mental illness, drug addiction, and poverty—that had previously been addressed by other means (Simon 2007; Wacquant 2009; Dolovich 2011). Critical prison studies has begun to advance the radical proposition that the penal system no longer maintains *any* meaningful connection to popular conceptions of justice, whether reformist or retributive, but operates instead to identify disorderly groups and to redistribute bodies in geographic space, warehousing them in a state of *incapacitation* (Feeley and Simon 1992; R. Gilmore 2007). The prison, in these analyses, is the centerpiece of a penal system that has shifted its focus away from the offender and toward target populations, away from justice and toward security, away from rehabilitation and toward the smooth functioning of its own institutional machinery. Prison today names both the principal implement of domestic state violence and the object of an intensifying critical resistance.

2014/2020

51

Queer
Siobhan B. Somerville

"Queer" causes confusion, perhaps because two of its current meanings seem to be at odds. In both popular and academic usage in the United States, "queer" is sometimes used interchangeably with the terms "gay" and "lesbian" and occasionally "transgender," "bisexual," or "Two-Spirit." In this sense of the word, "queer" is understood as an umbrella term that refers to a range of sexual identities that are "not straight." In other political and academic contexts, "queer" is used in a very different way: as a term that calls into question the stability of any such categories of identity based on sexual orientation. In this second sense, "queer" is a *critique* of the tendency to organize political or theoretical questions around sexual orientation per se. To "queer" becomes a way to denaturalize categories such as "lesbian" and "gay" (not to mention "straight" and "heterosexual"), revealing them as socially and historically constructed identities that have often worked to establish and police the line between the "normal" and the "abnormal."

Fittingly, the word "queer" itself has refused to leave a clear trace of its own origins; its etymology is unknown. It may have been derived from the German word *quer* or the Middle High German *twer*, which meant "cross," "oblique," "squint," "perverse," or "wrongheaded," but these origins have been contested. The *Oxford English Dictionary* notes that while "queer" seems to have entered English in the sixteenth century, there are few examples of the word before 1700. From that time until the mid-twentieth century, "queer" tended to refer to anything "strange," "odd," or "peculiar," with additional negative connotations that suggested something "bad," "worthless," or even "counterfeit." In the late eighteenth and early nineteenth centuries, the word "queer" began to be used also as a verb, meaning "to quiz or ridicule," "to puzzle," "to cheat," or "to spoil." During this time, the adjectival form also began to refer to a condition that was "not normal," "out of sorts," "giddy, faint, or ill."

By the first two decades of the twentieth century, "queer" became linked to sexual practice and identity in the United States, particularly in urban sexual cultures. During the 1910s and 1920s in New York City, for example, men who called themselves "queer" used the term to refer to their sexual interest in other men (Chauncey 1994). Contemporaneous literary works by African American writers such as Nella Larsen (1929) and Jean Toomer ([1923] 1969) suggest that the term could also carry racialized meanings, particularly in the context of mixed-race identities that exposed the instability of divisions between "black" and "white." But it was not until the 1940s that "queer" began to be used in mainstream US culture primarily to refer to "sexual perverts" or "homosexuals," most often in a pejorative, stigmatizing way, a usage that reached its height during the Cold War era.

In the early twenty-first century, "queer" remains a volatile term; the *American Heritage Dictionary* even appends a warning label advising that the use of "queer" by "heterosexuals is often considered offensive," and therefore "extreme caution must be taken concerning [its] use when one is not a member of the group." The term has also carried specific class connotations in some periods and contexts. On the one hand, as one participant in a 2004 online forum put it, "'Queer' is a rebellion against those posh middle-class business owners who want to define gaydom as being their right to enjoy all the privileges

denied them just cos they like cock" (Isambard 2004). On the other hand, these class connotations are unstable. "If I have to pick an identity label in the English language," wrote poet and critic Gloria Anzaldúa, "I pick 'dyke' or 'queer,' though these working-class words . . . have been taken over by white middle-class lesbian theorists in the academy" (1998, 263–64).

The use of "queer" in academic and political contexts beginning in the late 1980s represented an attempt to reclaim this stigmatizing word and to defy those who have wielded it as a weapon. This usage is often traced to the context of AIDS activism that responded to the epidemic's devastating toll on gay men in US urban areas during the 1980s and 1990s. Queer Nation, an activist organization that grew out of ACT UP (AIDS Coalition to Unleash Power), became one of the most visible sites of a new politics that was "meant to be confrontational—opposed to gay assimilationists and straight oppressors while inclusive of people who have been marginalized by anyone in power" (Escoffier and Bérubé 1991, 14). In subsequent decades, queer political groups have not always achieved this goal of inclusiveness in practice, but they have sought to transform the homophobic ideologies of dominant US culture as well as strategies used by existing mainstream lesbian and gay rights movements, many of which have tended to construct lesbian and gay people as a viable "minority" group and to appeal to liberal models of inclusion (Duggan 1992).

The movement to gain legal rights to same-sex marriage demonstrated some of the key differences between a lesbian/gay rights approach and a queer activist strategy. While advocates for same-sex marriage argued that lesbians and gay men should not be excluded from the privileges of marriage accorded to straight couples, many queer activists and theorists questioned why marriage and the nuclear family should be the sites of legal and social privilege in the first place. Because same-sex marriage leaves intact a structure that disadvantages those who either cannot or choose not to marry (regardless of their sexual orientation), a more ethical project, queer activists argue, would seek to detach material and social privileges from the institution of marriage altogether (Ettelbrick 1989; Duggan 2004).

Sometimes in conversation with activist efforts and sometimes not, queer theory emerged as an academic field during the late 1980s and early 1990s. Drawing on the work of Michel Foucault, scholars who are now referred to as queer theorists argued that sexuality, especially the binary system of "homosexual" and "heterosexual" orientations, is a relatively modern production. As Foucault ([1976] 1990) argued, although certain acts between two people of the same sex had long been punishable through legal and religious sanctions, these practices did not necessarily define individuals as "homosexual" until the late nineteenth century. While historians have disagreed about the precise periods and historical contexts in which the notion of sexual identity emerged, Foucault's insistence that sexuality "must not be thought of as a kind of natural given" has been transformative, yielding an understanding of sexuality not as a "natural" psychic or physical drive but as a "set of effects produced in bodies, behaviors, and social relations by a certain deployment" of power (105, 127). Moving away from the underlying assumptions of identity politics and its tendency to locate stable sexual subjects, queer theory has focused on the very process of sexual subject formation. If much of the early work in lesbian and gay studies tended to be organized around an opposition between homosexuality and heterosexuality, the primary axis of queer studies shifted toward the distinction between normative and nonnormative sexualities as they have been produced in a range of historical and cultural contexts.

For this reason, a key concept in queer theory is the notion of "heteronormativity," a term that refers to "the institutions, structures of understanding, and practical orientations that make heterosexuality seem not only coherent—that is, organized as a sexuality—but also privileged" (Berlant and Warner 1998, 548n2). Heteronormativity, it is important to stress, is not the same thing as heterosexuality (though the two are not entirely separable); indeed, various forms of heterosexuality (adultery, polygamy, and interracial marriage, among others) and heterosexual practices (e.g., fornication, sodomy) have historically been proscribed in certain contexts rather than privileged (Rubin 1984; C. Cohen 1997; Burgett 2005).

Because queer critique has the potential to destabilize the ground on which any particular claim to identity can be made (though, importantly, not destroying or abandoning identity categories altogether), a significant body of queer scholarship has warned against anchoring the field primarily or exclusively to questions of sexuality. Instead, these scholars have argued, we should dislodge "the status of sexual orientation itself as the authentic and centrally governing category of queer practice, thus freeing up queer theory as a way of reconceiving not just the sexual, but the social in general" (Harper et al. 1997, 1). In local, national, and transnational contexts, such a formulation allows us to contest constructions of certain issues as "sexual" and others as "nonsexual," a distinction that has often been deployed by US neoconservatives and neoliberals alike to separate "lesbian and gay" movements from a whole range of interconnected struggles for social justice.

The field of queer studies has challenged this tendency by using intersectional approaches that begin from the assumption that sexuality cannot be separated from other categories of identity and social status. Whereas some early queer theorists found it necessary to insist on understanding sexuality as a distinct category of analysis, one that could not be fully accounted for by feminist theories of gender, it is now clear that sexuality and gender can never be completely isolated from each other (Rubin 1984; Sedgwick 1990). Indeed, Judith Butler (1990, 5) has shown that our very notions of sexual difference (male/female) are an effect of a "heterosexual matrix." A significant body of scholarship, largely generated out of questions raised by transgender identity and politics, has productively revisited and scrutinized the relationships among sex, gender, and sexuality, with an emphasis on recalibrating theories of performativity in light of materialist accounts of gender (S. Stone 1991; Prosser 1998; Valentine 2007; Spade 2011).

If queer theory's project is understood, in part, as an attempt to challenge identity categories that are presented as stable, transhistorical, or authentic, then critiques of naturalized racial categories are also crucial to its antinormative project. As a number of critics have shown, heteronormativity derives much of its power from the ways in which it (often silently) shores up as well as depends on naturalized categories of racial difference in contexts ranging from sexology and psychoanalysis to fiction and cinema (Somerville 2000; Eng 2001). Heteronormativity itself must be understood, then, as a racialized concept, since "[racially] marginal group members, lacking power and privilege although engaged in heterosexual behavior, have often found themselves defined as outside the norms and values of dominant society" (C. Cohen 1997, 454). This insistence on putting questions of race at the center of queer approaches has been vigorously argued in a body of scholarship identified as "queer of color critique" (Muñoz 1999; Ferguson 2004; Reddy 2011; Rivera-Servera 2012). An allied body of scholarship has asked how queer theory and indigenous studies might be brought together both to address the specificities of Indigenous gay,

lesbian, bisexual, transgender, queer, and Two-Spirit (GLBTQ2) lives and communities and to develop new critical accounts of gender and sexual normativity that take into account the workings of settler colonialism (Justice, Rifkin, and Schneider 2010; Morgensen 2011a; Driskill et al. 2011; Kauanui 2017).

Related work in queer studies has examined the dynamics of globalization, imperialism, and colonialism. Scholars have interrogated both the possibilities and the limitations of queer theory for understanding the movement of desires, bodies, and identities within a transnational frame as well as the necessity of attending to the relationship between the methods of queer theory and colonial structures of knowledge and power (Manalansan 2003; Gopinath 2005; Mendoza 2015; Pérez 2015). A growing body of work in queer critique has brought greater attention to settler colonialism, a specific form of power organized around seizing land, eliminating indigenous peoples, and replacing them with settler populations on a permanent basis. These studies have interrogated how the field of queer studies has inadvertently naturalized certain settler-colonial assumptions as well as how discourses of normative gender, sexuality, and race have been entwined with the histories and ongoing violences of US settler projects (Kauanui 2017; Morgensen 2011b; Rifkin 2011; Byrd 2017).

If the origins of the term "queer" are elusive, its future horizons might be even more so. While the term itself has a contested and perhaps confusing history, one of the points of consensus among queer theorists has been that its parameters should not be prematurely (or ever) delimited (Sedgwick 1993; Berlant and Warner 1995). While the field of queer studies has made inroads in a number of different academic disciplines and debates, some critics have asserted that the term has lost its ability to create productive friction. Pointing to its seeming ubiquity in popular-cultural venues, others criticize the ways that the greater circulation of "queer" and its appropriation by the mainstream entertainment industries have emptied out its oppositional political potential. Whether we should be optimistic or pessimistic about the increasing visibility of "queer" culture remains an open question. Meanwhile, scholars continue to carefully interrogate the shortcomings and possibilities of "queer" approaches to a range of diverse issues, such as migration (Luibhéid and Cantú 2005; Chávez 2013), temporality (Edelman 2004; Halberstam 2005; E. Freeman 2010; Rohy 2009), region (Herring 2010; Gopinath 2007; Tongson 2011; Manalansan et al. 2014), disability (McRuer 2006; Kafer 2013); and environment (Chen 2012; Mortimer-Sandilands and Erickson 2010; Ahuja 2015). Whatever the future uses and contradictions of "queer," it seems likely that the word will productively refuse to settle down, demanding critical reflection in order to be understood in its varied and specific cultural, political, and historical contexts.

2007/2020

52

Racialization
Daniel Martinez HoSang and Oneka LaBennett

In contrast to keywords such as "race" and "racist," "racialization" is relatively new to American studies and cultural studies. The term has a diverse lineage but is most often associated with the work of Michael Omi and Howard Winant ([1986] 1994), who helped make the concept of racialization a central analytic within both fields. Omi and Winant utilize the term to "signify the extension of racial meaning to a previously racially unclassified relationship, social practice or group. Racialization is an ideological process, an historically specific one" (64). In contrast to static understandings of race as a universal category of analysis, racialization names a process that produces race within particular social and political conjunctures. That process constructs or represents race by fixing the significance of a "relationship, practice or group" within a broader interpretive framework. Working within this paradigm, scholars have investigated processes and practices of racialization across a wide range of fields, including electoral politics, music, literature, sports, aesthetics, religion, public policy, and social identity.

Any use of the term "racialization" requires some account of the theoretical status of race within popular culture and mainstream social science. Inherent in Omi and Winant's definition are three assumptions common to much of the critical scholarship on race in the United States since the 1970s: race functions as a signifier of social identity, power, and meaning rather than as a biological or hereditary characteristic; racial meaning is a dynamic, fluid, and historically situated *process* of social and political ascription (James Lee 2009); and race can be generative of diverse ideological frameworks that justify many forms of social hierarchy and power. Response to this definition has been varied. On the one hand, some sociologists and historians have questioned race as a theoretical concept and a category that can explain social outcomes, suggesting that any use of the term "race"—or "racialization"—as an explanatory category ultimately serves to reify or legitimate it as a fixed and stable category of human existence (Das Gupta et al. 2007; Fields 1990; Gilroy 2000; Loveman 1999; Miles and Torres 2007). On the other hand, scholars such as Cornel West (1994) and Kimberlé Crenshaw (1990) reason that race cannot be abandoned as an analytical concept, since, as Winant notes, "U.S. society is so thoroughly racialized that to be without racial identity is to be in danger of having no identity" (1994, 16).

All of these deployments of the term "racialization" draw on and diverge from earlier usages that carried different theoretical and normative assumptions regarding the basis of racial hierarchies. As early as 1899, one can find references to the term "deracialization," a process described as the removing or eradicating of racial characteristics from a person or population. A coinage that emerged from social Darwinism, this usage of the term locates parochial or retrogressive traits as expressions of racial difference that could be eliminated through education, acculturation, or the mixing of populations, thus rendering a "deracialized" group or subject. By the early 1930s, this notion of deracialization as a process of homogenization and incorporation gave way to uses of "racialization" that referenced a process of bodily differentiation capable of explaining the development of distinct "racial stocks" to which different groups of Europeans allegedly belonged. For example, Sir Arthur Keith, a prominent physical anthropologist,

conceptualized "race-feeling" as "part of the evolutionary machinery which safeguards the purity of race" (1928, 316). Keith and his colleagues theorized that nature embedded race within human populations as a means toward the betterment of humankind through differentiation. Racialization thus described a positive and necessary process by which Anglo and Nordic racial supremacy and biological purity could be sustained and reproduced (Barot and Bird 2001, 602–6).

As the scientific imprimatur to claims of white supremacy withered in the aftermath of World War II and the state racism of Nazi Germany, references to "racialization" receded from academic and popular discourse. The term then reemerged in Frantz Fanon's influential *The Wretched of the Earth* ([1963] 2004). Writing in the context of anticolonial struggles in North Africa, Fanon contrasted social conditions that were "racializing" against those that were "humanizing," demonstrating how racial oppression organizes and constrains a universal recognition of human capabilities (Essed and Goldberg 2000; Barot and Bird 2001; Fanon [1963] 2004). In Fanon's usage, racialization, or the hierarchical production of human difference through race, is posed as a necessary precondition for colonial domination and a hindrance to the process of internal self-making among Black subjects. The influence of Fanon's equation of racialization and dehumanization is apparent in a wide range of scholarly work that interrogates the social construction of race, especially in postcolonial scholarship (Said 1978; Bhabha 1994; Rabaka 2010). This work has exposed the legacies of racialized colonial discourses, noting the ways that racial meaning structures the construction of "the Orient" in western European artistic, literary, and political discourse and interrogating how the emergence of the United States as an empire has depended on an array of racial formations: the historical racialization of Asians as dangerous threats to the nation; the contemporary racialization of the same population as "model minorities"; and the post-9/11 racialization of the "uncivilized" Muslim/Arab as an object of racial terror and as a population requiring US intervention, supervision, and domination (Prashad 2007; Lee and Lutz 2005; Razack 2012).

In a parallel use of the term, scholars of social policy have examined the ways in which debates over issues such as welfare, immigration, crime, reproductive rights, and taxes in the United States have become thoroughly racialized since the 1960s. As the civil rights movement effectively challenged formal policies of race-based segregation and discrimination, the concept of racial "color blindness" became the dominant principle within official legal and political discourse (Gotanda 1991). Within this framework, discriminatory practices and ideals are supposedly inadmissible in policy debates and legal deliberations. But public controversies about whether the government should provide cash assistance to low-income families (Fujiwara 2008; Quadagno 1994) or militarize national borders or cover abortions in publicly financed health-insurance programs (E. Gutiérrez 2008; K. Baird 2009; Richie, Davis, and Traylor 2012) or raise property taxes to improve schools (Edsall and Edsall 1992) or prosecute a "War on Drugs" (Michelle Alexander 2010) all draw on and produce a dense set of racial meanings. The simultaneous withdrawal of public funding for social welfare programs, along with the systematic reduction of property and income taxes perceived to support those programs, is often tied to assumptions about the racial identities of the beneficiaries of those policies. In this sense, these debates are racialized.

Contemporary scholarship has also complicated our understanding of processes of racialization by attending to the intersections of gender, class, age, and sexuality and by venturing beyond the national boundaries and Black/white dichotomy that has long dominated the literature on race (Crenshaw 1995). Along these lines of inquiry, the meanings attached to the racialized body have led to wide-ranging questions. How can the concept of racialization challenge the double or triple vulnerability of Muslim immigrant women with disabilities (Dossa 2009)? What do the debates surrounding US immigration policies reveal about the racialization of the "illegal immigrant" as a displaced nonperson who embodies criminality (T. Sandoval 2008)? How has the racialization of Black women in the United States depended on notions of the pregnant Black woman's body as representative of the "undeserving poor" (Bridges 2011)? How does religion structure and articulate processes of racialization for followers of Islam and Judaism and for Hindus (Joshi 2006)? Comparative and intersectional analyses of the colonization of indigenous peoples in a number of regions and the colonization of nations in Africa and the Caribbean similarly link processes of racialization and globalization (Das Gupta et al. 2007). Work in this vein has focused on topics including the globalized production of knowledge about race, the cultural dimensions of globalization, transnational migration, feminism and the politics of decolonization, consumption, and global economies (M. Jacqui Alexander 2005; Appadurai 1996; De Genova 2005; Ferreira da Silva 2007; C. Freeman 2000; Gilroy 1993; Thomas and Clarke 2006).

A promising trajectory within the current scholarship on racialization explores the ways in which the hierarchies of humanity that the concept of race has historically signified increasingly become articulated through the logics of neoliberalism, militarism, and security. In a discussion of the post–World War II global shift toward official antiracisms, Jodi Melamed has argued that the "trick of racialization" is that it displaces differential valuations of humans into global ordering systems that yield new, more covert expressions for privileged racializations such as "liberal," "multicultural," and "global citizen," alongside stigmatized racializations such as "unpatriotic," "monocultural," and "illegal" (2011, 2). The state's formal antiracism becomes pressed into service to defend or justify unbridled US military occupation, widening economic inequalities, muscular immigration enforcement, and the expansion of prisons and police authority within the United States (Cacho 2012; De Genova 2012; Singh 2012). These diverse usages of the term "racialization" across a range of fields and disciplines—including sociology, ethnic studies, anthropology, cultural studies, and American studies—will continue to be foundational to conveying relations of power and authority within and beyond US political culture, even as its referents change and evolve.

2014

53

Rights
Crystal Parikh

Consider these two usages of the word "rights" from works of literature published nearly a century apart from one another. In F. Scott Fitzgerald's novel *The Great Gatsby* ([1925] 1992), the character Tom Buchanan and his secret lover, Myrtle Wilson, argue over whether the latter "had any right" to say the name of Tom's wife, Daisy. Tom feels so strongly that Myrtle lacks this "right" that he breaks her nose when she tries to exercise it (41). In Jhumpa Lahiri's short story "Year's End" from the collection *Unaccustomed Earth* (2008), the protagonist Kaushik angrily berates his two young step-sisters when he discovers them gazing admiringly at photographs of his dead mother: "You have no right to be looking at these. . . . They don't belong to you" (286).

The keyword "rights" most commonly references claims that are enforceable by law. But these two examples point toward the term's circulation in more intimate and nonjuridical contexts and with respect to seemingly arbitrary distinctions and privileges. The question of who can say a name or pore over a photograph cannot be answered by reference to the law. The deployment of the language of rights in these extralegal contexts suggests that more than one kind of authority polices hierarchies of obligation, freedom, and power in social life. It also points to how thoroughly legal or juridical concepts give form to the modern subject of liberalism—the private or autonomous self and its possessions. The social fictions that we tell about that subject in large part determine what types of substantive rights anyone might legitimately invoke, despite the law's conventional representation of itself as based in pure and abstract reason.

Because the first ten amendments to the US Constitution are called the "Bill of Rights," many consider rights to be an essential component of US national character and culture. The Bill of Rights addresses a citizenry assumed to be a community of reasonable, autonomous individuals who have entered into a "social contract," wherein they submit themselves to the authority of the state. Individuals thereby secure a peaceful, orderly coexistence through the rule of law by relinquishing some of the unlimited freedom they supposedly enjoyed in what Enlightenment philosophers such as John Locke ([1689] 2016) described as the "state of nature." The freedoms enumerated in the Bill of Rights were part of this exchange since they remain the dominion of the individual. The right to free speech, the right to bear arms, and the right to a speedy and public trial are a few of the better-known of these rights.

Liberal political philosophy, legal traditions, and social discourse define such rights as universal and neutral principles that theoretically apply equally to all humans. But the conception of the subject who enters the social contract as a fully formed and fully consenting being is very much ideological, a liberal fantasy of the modern person that serves well a specific set of economic, political, and social arrangements. As political theorist C. B. Macpherson pointed out in the 1960s, the liberal vision of society and government crucially depends on a laboring body, animated by reason and operating within a market economy, for its conception of the human person. In this tradition, also traceable back to Locke, rights are possessions and are hence linked to citizenship and property. In other words, human beings are presumed to be, first and foremost, in possession of their bodies and the body's capacity to labor and to think. From this perspective, the most valuable kinds of rights are property rights—the right to use, exclude, transfer, and dispose of one's possessions, which are earned through and are an extension of one's laboring body, as the owner sees fit. Macpherson called this doctrine "possessive individualism."

For this reason, many scholars and activists are skeptical of the term "rights," and especially of its centrality in the liberal tradition, as a means for delivering social, political, or economic *justice*. Subjects who do not meet the criteria of the self-possessed individual because they are considered incapable of self-sustaining bodily labor or independent rational thought and consciousness occupy diminished forms of citizenship or are excluded from it altogether. Such subjects lack, in Hannah Arendt's phrase, the "right to have rights," which amounts to full membership in a rights-bearing political community of liberalism (Arendt 1951, 376). In historical practice, these subjects have included women, children, persons with disabilities, and a host of racialized populations, among others. To the extent that citizenship secures "the right to have rights" in the modern system of liberal nation-states, the rights to which such marginalized subjects can lay claim—including to life, limb, property, and land—are likewise diminished (DeGooyer et al. 2018, 70–73). In any liberal system that construes rights as property and restricts justice to the protection of the individual's possessions, the right to have rights is limited, at the very least by national boundaries but also by other social hierarchies of difference such as race, gender, and ability.

Defined as the property of autonomous individuals, rights further fail to acknowledge either human beings' essential interdependency upon one another or their exposure to institutional, environmental, and structural conditions beyond their control. Recognizing this failure, critics of liberalism positioned across the political spectrum—ranging from the seventeenth-century political philosopher Robert Filmer ([1680] 2017), to twentieth-century sociologist Émile Durkheim (1957) and intellectual historian J. G. A. Pocock (1975), to feminist theorists of law and society (J. Butler 2004b, 2016; Turner 2006; Fineman and Grear 2013)—have challenged the construction of humanity as, in Filmer's words, "a company of men at the very first to have been created together without any dependency one of another" ([1680] 2017, 188). Instead, as Martha Fineman puts it in her formulation of the "vulnerability thesis," the human body's openness to injury, suffering, and pain proves a "universal, inevitable, enduring aspect of the human condition that must be at the heart of our concept of social and state responsibility" (2008, 8). The reality of human vulnerability entails a "dependency on infrastructure for a livable life," the many material, social, and cultural institutions and practices that shelter and sustain human beings (Butler 2016, 12). Rather than doing away with the language of rights altogether, these theorists emphasize enduring and shifting forms of vulnerability and interdependency and ask us to consider how *what* counts *as* rights undergoes change through social struggles and political processes.

The history of the dominant US usage of the term provides one example of these changes, since it differs strikingly from how rights are identified by other nations and by international organizations and treaties, including the United Nations International Bill of Rights. US law, culture, and politics have tended to treat *civil* rights, those claims that affect citizens' individual autonomy such as habeas corpus rights or the right to free expression, as natural and hallowed; their pride of place in the Constitution attests to and reproduces their paramount value. Many other US Constitutional amendments address what are known as *political* rights, the rights by which participation in the governance of

the nation proceeds, such as the granting of women's suffrage. Absent here are *social*, *economic*, or *cultural* rights. The resulting link between the autonomous individual's rights to the body politic by way of the social contract (to the exclusion of other kinds of claims) helps explain how a massive social movement for black liberation in the twentieth century came to be widely and reductively known in US political discourse as "the civil rights movement" and further, why many radical scholars and activists prefer the moniker "black freedom struggle," which highlights the broader visions of justice to which its members aspired (Lawson 2003, 4).

In contrast, the lexicon of international human rights law, first delineated in 1977 by Czech jurist Karel Vasak, offers a more expansive vocabulary for understanding different kinds of rights and the freedoms they support, including political and civil rights ("first-generation rights"); social and economic rights such as those that enable individuals to enjoy economic security and social welfare ("second-generation rights"); and cultural rights such as those that protect collective identity and cultural practices ("third-generation rights"). The fact that US political discourse focuses primarily on "first-generation rights" does not mean that individuals living in the United States enjoy no social, economic, or cultural rights. The public education system and the printing of official documents such as ballots in multiple languages are only two examples where social and cultural rights are honored. Tellingly, however, neither of these rights is federally recognized. While civil rights and liberties have proven durable elements in the construction of US national identity, social security and cultural life have regularly been regarded as private matters for the market, the family, or other nongovernmental institutions to address. As such, state provisions for social security, welfare, education, and health care have been vulnerable to attack by right-wing political and legal advocacy focused on limiting rather than expanding rights-based claims (Duggan 2003).

These political struggles in the United States over what counts as rights have had implications across the globe. The construction of the liberal rights-bearing and autonomous subject that has enjoyed nearly unwavering prominence in US national life has been exported as part and parcel of the "American dream" through both "hard" and "soft" forms of US power. Especially during the Cold War and the widespread reordering of nations and empires in the twentieth century, US dominance depended on a campaign to "win hearts and minds" with the transmission of US ideals and the "American way of life" around the globe, whether by Hollywood and commercial culture or by way of military intervention and economic policy (Normand and Zaidi 2007; Westad 2007; Sargent 2014).

A clear example of this campaign occurred during the struggles against the South African apartheid regime in the 1980s. US geopolitical and economic interests shaped the liberal commonsense by which Amnesty International, the erstwhile leading organization in the field of human rights during the twentieth century, revoked the South African activist and eventual president Nelson Mandela's status as "prisoner of conscience" due to his defense of armed struggle against the apartheid state. While the group did name Mandela as "one of the world's most visionary leaders in the fight to protect and promote human rights" upon his death in 2013 (Amnesty International 2013), the failure to recognize Mandela properly at the time reflected US policy, as the Reagan administration supported the murderous activities of anti-communist governments and insurgents in Latin America by employing a rhetoric of human rights. A State Department memo from the era hence stipulated that "'human rights'—meaning political rights and civil liberties—conveys what is ultimately at issue in our contest with the Soviet bloc," and assistant to the president for national security affairs Richard V. Allen insisted that "the notion of economic and social rights is a dilution and distortion of the original and proper meaning of human rights" (*New York Times* 1981). By the end of the century, with the United States functioning as the world's sole superpower, such limited conceptions of rights and freedom might have appeared to have won the day (Grandin 2010; Randall Williams 2010; Atanasoski 2013; Bradley 2016).

But that victory is not total. Challenges to the notion of rights and the possessive individualism of the rights-bearing subject of liberalism have come from a diverse range of political and theoretical perspectives. As scholars of law and politics explain, the functional practice of rights requires a corresponding "rectitude" from others who carry out their obligations in regards to those rights claims (Donnelly 2003, 7). In other words, for a subject to exercise his or her rights, others must "do right" by that person. The force of duty derives from the moral worth granted to rights holders within the social world in which subjects exercise their rights. While the state retains the most force in granting or denying rights in practice, rights claims both derive from and reproduce the *social* relations between the rights-bearing subject and others who are obligated to recognize and respect them. As such, those making rights claims sometimes transform our conception of the rights-bearing subject and the meaning of "rights." One example is the federal case *Gary B. v. Snyder*, where students from failing schools in Detroit brought suit against the State of Michigan for failing to uphold their federally guaranteed right to an education (especially given the woeful state of school buildings and class materials in the city), without which their civil and political rights become essentially meaningless. Not only did the students' legal argument expand the meaning of the right to an

RIGHTS CRYSTAL PARIKH

education by insisting upon the state's responsibility to foster the development of children, but the plaintiffs proposed that the individual autonomy of the rights-bearing subject is as much a *product* of social life and political decision-making as it is a starting point for them.

Precisely because there is no *necessary* link between liberalism's idealized subject and the practical functioning of rights as a legal and juridical mechanism, all sorts of subjects are invited by the vocabulary of rights to transform the political communities they inhabit by making claims on the state and on one another. The scenes from *The Great Gatsby* and *Unaccustomed Earth* provide examples in which the usage of the language of "rights" marks individuals' forceful *refusal* to grant standing to others, despite the reality that the characters in each narrative share a social and ethical world. When and where subjects *have* successfully laid public claims to rights that have been challenged or denied—such as when the civil rights movement led to court-ordered desegregation and the 1965 Voting Rights Act, when battles for the right to same-sex marriage led to the 2015 *Obergefell v. Hodges* decision, and when trans activism led in 2019 to the New York State legislation recognizing the right to gender expression—they have provoked considerable, sometimes even thoroughgoing, transformations in the meaning of the term rights, both within the legal system and beyond it.

Writing in the 1960s, Macpherson anticipated this possibility. He stressed that "a new equality of *insecurity* among individuals, not merely within one nation but *everywhere*," occasioned a need to rethink how we define the boundaries of rights, responsibility, and belonging in order to recognize a form of moral obligation to "humane society, cohabitation or being, . . . above all earthly things" (Macpherson 1962, 276–77; emphasis added). In the twenty-first century, the war on terror, the economic upheavals spawned by global capitalism,

and the planetary crisis of global climate change only amplifies this urgency. Millions of migrants have been put into motion across borders, impelled by economic necessity, environmental devastation, catastrophic warfare, and domestic and political violence. Those individuals not on the move find themselves subject to stepped-up surveillance, policing, detention, incarceration, precarity, and expulsion from their national communities, while increasing political power and freedom accrue to economic agents and corporate entities. Evolving definitions of rights as a form of recognition granted to persons "not merely within one nation but everywhere" shifts our attention toward competing social and political conceptions of human rights and away from citizenship rights that correspond to the sovereign authority enjoyed by national states. It may seem utopian to imagine a cosmopolitan ethical community that feels obligation to everyone "everywhere." But how we understand who and what counts as the human and what transnational institutions are able to enforce the claims of human rights remain open and vital political questions. In answering them, we do more than shift our usages of the term "rights." We also pose the possibility of transforming who and what we think the subject of contemporary rights—and thus of political life—ought to be.

2020

54

Rural

Scott Herring

The simple life often evoked by the keyword "rural" belies its extraordinary complexity. Across the centuries, many hands have wielded this term for contradictory purposes: to exalt and exhaust the nation's natural resources, to malign and glorify nonurban citizens, and to incite and squelch revolutions. As a word that invites and resists reduction, "rural" can signal a pastoral landscape on one hand and neglect the labor that cultivates it on the other. It can conjure a bucolic retreat at odds with dynamic histories of political, socioeconomic, and racial conflict. It can appear outdated in our postindustrial era of globalization and expansive megacities, yet it persists in the conservative rhetoric of small-town values as well as the radical manifestoes of eco-activism.

Some of these tensions originate from overlapping—and historically entrenched—uses of "rural" as a noun and as an adjective. As a noun, "rural" can refer to any geographic place (the countryside, the outskirts, the woods) distinct from a city. According to the *Oxford English Dictionary*, "rural" is "opposed to urban" and defined by its presumed contrast to the metropolis. This geography can, however, be material (clay soil, prairie wheatgrass), or it can be metaphoric (a poetic arcadia, a Delta blues folk song). As an adjective, "rural" applies to those who occupy these nonurban spaces as well as their everyday life practices. It has been used as a pejorative social category (a hayseed) as well as a positive one (a hardworking husbandman). These

distinctions collide and evolve across genres and historical periods.

It comes as no surprise, then, that the interlocking disciplines of American studies and cultural studies attend to the definitional intricacies of "rural." While a tendency to privilege urban-based phenomena persists in cultural studies, foundational works such as *The Country and the City* examine how meanings of "rural" contribute to understandings of capitalism, aesthetics, urbanization, and nationhood. In this centuries-spanning literature review, Raymond Williams assesses how "rural" accrues cultural and economic significance as he simultaneously reproaches those who cast nonurban inhabitants as "broken and ignorant" (1973, 190). Exploring links between "rural" and synonyms such as "country," Williams finds that a cultural hierarchy "between country and city, as fundamental ways of life, reaches back into classical times" (1). Yet while country/rural has often been subordinate to city/urban, the keyword remains an important resource for patriotic nationalism. "In its general use, for native land," Williams stresses in *Keywords*, "country has more positive associations than either nation or state" ([1976] 1983, 81).

Scholars in American studies have likewise explored how the term informs social belonging and nation building from the colonial era to the present. In the inaugural 1949 volume of *American Quarterly*, University of Minnesota sociologist Lowry Nelson published an essay titled "The American Rural Heritage" that discussed some of the keyword's overlapping applications. Nelson outlined the "material" and "nonmaterial" aspects of rural life in the United States, whereby "material culture" such as farmland and agricultural instruments could be found alongside "nonmaterial aspects, including especially the agrarian ideals" (1949, 225). Both characteristics, he felt, contributed to "laying the foundation of our society and its institutions," and Nelson's attempt to showcase the positive role played by agrarianism points to the centrality of the rural in scholarly accounts of national origins and the countryside (225).

This idealized vision of rural citizenry and native land had been prevalent for some time. Romantic depictions of rural life reach back to Thomas Jefferson's *Notes on the State of Virginia* ([1787] 1984), a commendation of yeomanry that paints agrarianism as a cornerstone of the new American republic: "Those who labor in the earth are the chosen people of God, if ever he had a chosen people" (197). Confirming Williams's observation regarding the metaphoric meaning of native land, this claim fuses the idea of rural with the ideal of the country. It finds echo in writings by French immigrant J. Hector St. John de Crèvecoeur, whose influential *Letters from an American Farmer* ([1782] 1981) praised rural living across the eastern-seaboard states even as the text lamented what Jefferson's condoned—the enslavement of Africans who toiled the earth. Scholars of American culture have shown that these idealizing portraits of country people—both evoking a pastoral tradition begun by Greek poet Theocritus—were accompanied by frequent dismissals of rural populations on behalf of urban elites across the late eighteenth and early nineteenth centuries (Bushman 1992). We may also recall that the slur "poor white trash" surfaced by the mid-nineteenth century to denigrate nonmetropolitan spaces and nonurban working-class whites alike (Wray 2006).

As this last link suggests, fraught connections between class, race, and other identity categories inform changing ideas of rural existence. The rise of sharecropping across the rural South after the US Civil War set the stage for the largest relocation in the nation's history—the Great Migration of largely rural African Americans to industrializing cities beyond the Mason-Dixon line starting in the early twentieth century (F. Griffin 1995). Many impoverished white farmers threw their weight behind the People's Party (Populist Party) in 1891 to protest the overreach of corporate interests, and the coalition both invited and abused relationships with African American agrarians throughout its various permutations (Goodwyn 1978). Occurring at a moment of escalating urbanization, these watershed events were matched by rural betterment programs such as Theodore Roosevelt's Country Life Commission (1908–9) that addressed the rural as a backward and unhygienic locale in desperate need of modernization (Roosevelt 1909). Such biases were aided by a newfound interest in racially degenerate "hill folk," an interest supported by proponents of eugenics (Danielson and Davenport 1912).

By the mid-twentieth century, many rural inhabitants in the United States did not consider themselves God's chosen people, yet some managed to improvise creative encounters with nonurban spaces. In 1942, the US government launched the Bracero Program, an exploitative agricultural guest-worker program for transnational Mexican migrants that lasted officially until 1964 (D. Cohen 2011). The shift to industrialized farming and the gradual dominance of monoculture crops made agriculture more efficient (Fitzgerald 2003), but it weakened the single-family farm unit. A round of rural white migration to industrialized cities such as Chicago stoked moral panics over metropolitan "hillbilly ghettoes" and cast a harsh light on these migratory laborers (A. Harkins 2005). In 1964, Lyndon B. Johnson pronounced a War on Poverty, his response to depressed living conditions in Appalachia and one that investigated the plights of impoverished rural Native and Hispanic populations across the Great Plains, the West Coast, and the Southwest.

Soon thereafter, countercultural back-to-the-land movements followed these ongoing geographic calamities. Extending long-standing traditions of US utopianism, hippies embraced the keyword to launch rural art colonies and small-scale farms across the nation. Sexual minorities also organized around the rural in hopes of finding spaces and mind-sets conducive to social and sexual experiments. Several of these communes—lesbian separatist collectives and radical faerie gatherings—flourish to this day and offer respite to a variety of queers across class, race, and generation (Povinelli 2006). As with earlier representational battles, country life remained a material and cultural space stocked with possibility and constriction. In pliable imaginaries that featured clashing themes of technological progress, geographic displacement, population decline, and agrarian idealism, the rural was at once a utopia to till and a place to leave behind.

In the twenty-first century, scholars continue to track how "rural" has been put to novel cross-purposes as the term surfaces across competing systems of knowledge and emergent forms of material culture. Food co-ops that support local agriculture struggle to vend alongside multinational agribusiness ventures that use countrified corporate logos. Once-pejorative identity markers such as "redneck" have become a questionable basis for regional race pride as theme parks such as Dollywood and culture industries such as Nashville's Music Row cater to white working-class nostalgia. Privileged exurbanites turn abandoned farmland outside the metropolis into rural retreats, and a conservative populism with little resemblance to its late nineteenth-century predecessor maintains prominent sway over voters with the fantasy of small-town America. Sexual minorities continue to occupy rural spaces that are both welcoming and inhospitable (John Howard 2001; E. Johnson 2008; Herring 2010), and transborder migrants create social networks that connect nonurban US spaces to larger communities within and beyond the hemisphere (Stephen 2007). Millions who will never own a shovel tend to their virtual farms with online games. Frozen only in stereotype, the rural exists in a state of perpetual development and decline.

These recent innovations counter the idea of nonurban environments as uncomplicated geographies, and scholarship continues to trace the cultural richness inherent in the unfolding idea of rural life. Across anthropology, religious studies, gender studies, and critical race/ethnic studies (to name but four), scholars have investigated impoverished West Virginia hollers (Stewart 1996), African American return migration to the rural South (Stack 1996), sexual liberation and small-town campus life in Kansas (B. Bailey 1999), and the global rise of the Ozarks as the crown jewel of Christian-based capitalist endeavors (Moreton 2009). The intellectual vistas of these wide-ranging inquiries suggest that the rural offers a productive means of grappling with—and working through—contemporary issues of social welfare, leisure, labor, consumption, mobility, and sexual citizenship that are both particular to rural populations and shared by other geographic locales. This is especially true for those who have historically experienced a tortuous relationship to the land—the minority populations who continue to feel the material and nonmaterial unevenness of agrarian ideals cited by Nelson in his *American Quarterly* essay.

Hence even as the metropolis may appear ascendant since the start of the twentieth century, thinking with "rural" offers a rich vocabulary for articulating the aspirations and the injustices faced by many people in what counts for present-day modernity. As a symbolic space that is all too real, the rural remains an enduring theme in the wake of the global city and in conversation with it. Both reactionary and radical, the countryside continues to provide rich soil for mobilization and quietism. Its heritage is to remain a problem area for American studies and cultural studies.

2014

55

Safe

Christina B. Hanhardt

The word "safe" is both a noun and an adjective. As a noun, it names an object, a locked box, often containing valuables; as an adjective, it describes the property of a subject or object, its value being a condition or a feeling. Like many affective attributes, to be safe is relational and often defined by what it is not: one is *safe from* a specific harm or makes a *safe* choice rather than a risky bet. In this way, the word "safe" can index something fixed in place (have you ever tried to lift a safe?) or difficult to pin down (feelings are often undermined by their lack of surety). But insofar as the word suggests a desired good, it offers a helpful vantage point to analyze aspirational ideals that respond to danger, uncertainty, and inequality.

The word "safe" is often attached to locations, from safe houses to safe neighborhoods to safe spaces. The concept of "safe spaces" has been polarizing in recent years, especially on college campuses and in the press coverage of them, where they are most often associated with the use of trigger warnings on syllabi (statements warning of disturbing images or text, especially of sexual violence) and the removal of the names and images of racist figures from institutional markers. In these contexts, advocates of safe spaces point to being safe as a shared, common good and as a way to name efforts at greater inclusion; critics of the concept tend to emphasize the more tenuous or contradictory aspects of the ideal of safety, sometimes suggesting that there is no such thing as a "safe space" and that the role of

educators is to disrupt a sense of comfort with what we think we already feel and know.

Scholars have described a heightened concern with safety as symptomatic of broad political and economic changes during the latter half of the twentieth century. Sociologists Ulrich Beck (1992) and Anthony Giddens (1998) describe the emergence during that period of a postindustrial "risk society" to signal both the heightened vulnerability of some to the harms, often environmental, of commodity production and a growing obsession with managing risk in new legal, social, and economic forms. "Risk," in this usage, is opposed to "safe": its uncertainty attached to undesirable, rather than affirmative, outcomes. That said, risk taking can be stigmatized or celebrated: it is often cast as an irresponsible choice when adopted by those without resources and as a bold or entrepreneurial move that might bring high returns to those who can afford to lose.

This ideal of safety is by no means new; what has changed is what the word signifies and how it is assumed to be achieved. The Declaration of Independence paired "Safety and Happiness" as the just grounds to "alter or to abolish [a 'Form of Government']" and to build a system anew. Yet the Constitution also affirmed that "when in Cases of Rebellion or Invasion the public Safety may require it," the state may take away bodily freedom without a writ of *habeas corpus*. Nearly one hundred years later, the Homestead Act of 1862 encouraged settlement of indigenous lands by European immigrants. The historian Frederick Turner's famed frontier thesis argued that the "pioneer ideals" of US democracy were built on the "free land" and "abundant resources" of the US West and that they provided a "safety valve" from the dangers of urban density and poverty in the East (F. Turner [1893] 1920; Von Nardroff 1962).

Starting in the 1950s, American studies scholars of the "myth and symbol school" identified Turner's thesis as a "myth" that has had significant power in shaping policy and action (H. Smith 1950). More recently scholars—especially those identified with ethnic studies, indigenous studies, cultural studies, and carceral studies—have deepened our understanding of what it means to claim safety by examining the violence of settler colonialism, the definition of and response to supposed threats against the nation; the social construction of urban danger and disorder, and the implications of law-and-order solutions to vulnerability. Throughout US history, debates about freedom, borders, and bodies have been framed in terms of *being safe* from violence, harm, and the unknown. From waging war to providing health insurance, from policing city streets to planning academic curricula, the concept of safety has justified both a demand for sovereignty and the punitive limits set upon that claim.

War has provided one of the most common contexts for promoting the ideal of being *safe* in the United States, both as a promise exported elsewhere (in 1917 President Woodrow Wilson called for US entry into World War I in order to make the world "safe for democracy") and as that which must be protected within US borders. While "safety" denotes protection from danger in general, the related word "security" is most often used to describe freedom from intended threats. Soon after the 2001 attack on the World Trade Center in New York, the US declared a global War on Terror and established a new cabinet department called Homeland Security. Almost twenty years into the War on Terror, the United States and many of its allies continue to pursue military activity and policy in the name of keeping women, children, and sexual minorities *safe* in other regions and to *secure* borders, markets, and citizens at "home" (Grewal 2017; Puar 2007). This has been the case not only for US wars waged abroad; the writer of *The Wonderful Wizard of Oz* editorialized in response to the 1890 massacre at Wounded Knee that "the best safety of the frontier settlements will be secured by the total annihilation of the few remaining Indians" (Baum 1890). This "logic of elimination" has also been used to justify Australian settler colonialism and the Israeli settlement of Palestine in the name of safety (Wolfe 2006).

Though they have different connotations, "security" and "safety" are often used interchangeably, especially when the threats they supposedly protect against are treated as ever present and self-evident, be that communism during the Cold War or Islam in the global War on Terror. In this way, the ideal of making a place safe for some is often used to justify security strategies that can undermine safety for others. In the years following World War II, policies like the GI Bill and redlining practices cultivated a standard of living for white middle-class US families that was celebrated as a safe haven from the ravages of wars and from the crime, drugs, and disorder associated with—but also produced by the simultaneous disinvestment in—cities (Lipsitz 2006). In 1965, in the thick of the Vietnam War, President Lyndon B. Johnson declared a War on Crime, describing uprisings against the war and against the poverty and racism of US cities as part of a broad problem of urban violence. Three years later, Johnson signed into law the Omnibus Crime Control and Safe Streets Act of 1968. The act established the federal agency known as the Law Enforcement Assistance Administration (LEAA), which provided state-based support to prevent and reduce crime. The law's emphasis on the role of local communities in policing and the importance of research about the causes and prevention of crime were central to its avowed goal of achieving *safe* city streets (Hinton 2016).

One safe-streets theory that has had particular weight is best known as "broken windows." Its architects, James Q. Wilson and George L. Kelling, argued in 1982 that signs of social disorder (such as broken windows) lead to more serious crime and that residents' "sense of safety" was paramount, regardless of actual rates of crime. This theory has been instrumental to the justification of crime-control strategies adopted around the globe and has found support across the political spectrum; the liberal urbanist Jane Jacobs (1961) had famously declared that familiar "eyes on the street"—everyday characters—were essential to neighborhood safety and more effective than top-down city planning or policing. Its broad uptake is due in large part because the ideal of being or feeling *safe* is assumed to be a non-ideological good. Safety is understood as an affective state, but one that might be empirically measured, predicted, and controlled—and marketed to both homeowners and city managers (Low and Maguire 2019). At the same time, the more conservative criminology research driving the broken-windows theory was informed by theories of rational choice that assume risk calculations based on market-place ideals of self-interest and a naturalized fear of "others" (Garland 2001).

The history of local community involvement in policing initiatives and the assumption that there might be a common perception of what it means to be safe helped the War on Terror draw a seamless connection between global threat and daily domestic life. Popular mantras like "See Something, Say Something" suggest that everyone knows what, or who, is out of place and might pose a threat to being safe. These strategies draw on a long history of assumptions about race, gender, and sexuality, from the history of the lynching of black men in the name of protecting white women to the disproportionate ascription of homophobia to Muslim identification. In fact, throughout the twentieth and into the twenty-first centuries, gender and sexuality-based activism has often been framed in the terms of safety from violence, and the outcomes have been greater forms of protection for some and greater risks of

violence for others (Feimster 2009; Haritaworn 2015). In the 1970s, feminist activists extended and revised these arguments by demonstrating that the privacy of home was far from a safe space for many women, and the anti-rape and antiviolence movement exposed the structural forms of violence hidden within the domestic sphere (Bevacqua 2000). During these very same years, lesbian, gay, bisexual, transgender, and queer/questioning (LGBTQ) people also began to organize in the name of their safety, in this case highlighting their vulnerability to anti-LGBTQ violence brought by visibility and most often meted out on the street (Herek and Berrill 1992).

By the 1980s and 1990s, national feminist and LGBTQ antiviolence movements were essential to the passage of the Violence against Women Act of 1994 as well as local and federal hate crime laws that heighten penalties for crimes based on bias (Jenness and Grattet 2001). Although these laws target unlawful acts motivated by actual or perceived race, gender, gender identity, sexual orientation, religion, national origin, and ability, scholars and activists have highlighted how different understandings of safety have meant that such measures have not always delivered what they promise. For example, increasing criminal penalties—from longer prison sentences to the application of the death penalty—offers state violence as a solution to individual violence. Insofar as criminal penalties are disproportionately levied against people of color, especially African Americans who are also often racially profiled and wrongly convicted, solutions to violence based in anticrime strategies risk making some less safe in the name of making others safer (Bumiller 2008; Hanhardt 2013; Spade 2015; Whitlock and Bronski 2015). Critics of this approach have drawn on more intersectional forms of analysis to articulate solutions to violence beyond crime control and the expansion of the carceral state (Richie 2012). In 1979, the black feminist Combahee River Collective joined the Coalition for Women's Safety, which adopted strategies of education and mutual aid to organize in response to the unsolved murders of black women in Boston (Thuma 2019); this is also the approach of the New York activist organization Audre Lorde Project's "Safe outside the System" campaign, founded over thirty years later.

Nonetheless, the words "safe" and "safety" often have adhered to debates about gender and sexuality in isolation from other vectors of power and difference. Calls for safe spaces on college campuses are again instructive here: many campaigns address labor issues and institutional racism, but the popular press tends to focus attention only on sexual violence, sexual harassment, and accessibility for transgender students. This association is a result of the history of antiviolence movements, but it is also because safe space stickers have been familiar icons on university doors, intended to mark those inside as accepting of LGBTQ students. In many ways, this confusion about claims for safe space is not unlike responses to the 1960s phrase "The personal is political," which is associated with one strand of feminism despite the broad New Left politics from which it emerged. Many activists of the period pushed against the in loco parentis ("in place of the parent") policies governing universities at the time—policies that dictated student behavior and set limits on sexual and political activity. This approach was designed to assure parents of students' *safety* and a nation that they were *safe* from student activism. Years later, this approach was replaced by policies designed to protect colleges from personal injury claims based on negligence. While the end of in loco parentis was a response to social movements, the rise of liability models was based on tort law (Lee 2011). In the twenty-first-century university, students, staff, faculty, and administrators continue to debate to what degree university policies should be motivated by

a quest for student safety versus the avoidance of institutional liability (Doyle 2015).

The invocation of safety to protect against liability is an outcome of the privatization of resources and services, from access to nature to the provision of housing, health, and care. In the face of negligent government research and care in the late 1980s, HIV/AIDS activists developed practices to promote safe sex—or *safer* sex, noting that no sex is without risk—and transformed a public health call for responsible individual choices into a strategy of shared community protection (Crimp 1987). The effect of industrial toxins has also provided a salient cultural flashpoint for debating whether a heightened concern with safety is an atomized response of individuals who imagine themselves as always vulnerable or a necessary collective response to deregulated industrial practices (Haynes 1995; Soderbergh 2000a). Be it fear about lead paint in toys from China or the unproven link between vaccines and autism, the call for safety can sometimes cloud the distinction between the demand for private or governmental accountability and more protectionist claims for individual choice (Chen 2012; Jain 2006, 2013). As a result, issues of health and environmental safety provide a link between the management of bodies and the activities of empire (Ahuja 2016).

Across these various uses of the term "safe," one related keyword is often if silently invoked: "fear." Like safety, fear is relational and subjective. Claims about the objects of fear can drive calls for heightened safety and can be used to undermine group safety in favor of individual security. This use of fear has a long political history, with roots traceable to the founding of the United States (Robin 2004). It has become a contested tool in the twenty-first century, especially around issues of immigration. Sanctuary cities, for instance, were initially founded in the 1980s to protect undocumented Central

American migrants from anti-immigrant federal policies that were, in turn, justified by often constructed and manipulated fears about the supposedly negative effects of migration on the quality of life of a protected category called "US citizens." In the first decades of the twenty-first century, those same cities are cast as unsafe by right-wing politicians and pundits precisely because they are (somewhat) safer for migrants who can live (a bit) less fearfully there. These usages demonstrate that keywords like "safety" and "fear" always have an unstable referent: they name an affect ("I feel unsafe" or "I am afraid") and a claim about an affect ("You are at risk" or "You should feel scared") while rarely clarifying the experiences or contexts that give these feelings meaning. They gain their power when the two usages meet and set a goal or action, enabling the development of both policies that exclude others from promised protection and alternative strategies for building a safer and freer future for all.

2020

56

Science
Laura Briggs

To speak of science is to deploy a deceptively simple word whose use confers the mantle of authority. As Raymond Williams ([1976] 1983, 276–80) and the *Oxford English Dictionary* tell us, the word came into English from the Latin *scientia*, meaning simply "knowledge." In the fourteenth century, "science" signified theoretical knowledge and was distinguished from "conscience," which referred to knowing something with conviction and passion. In the seventeenth century, it began to denote that which was learned through theoretical—as opposed to practical—knowledge: in short, what we might now call philosophy. Already, the term "science" was making hierarchical distinctions in kinds of learning, favoring the abstract and the dispassionate. In the nineteenth century, "science" came to distinguish the experimental from the metaphysical, that which was known as truth as from what is asserted. Science's slow and incomplete divorce from Christian theology in the nineteenth and twentieth centuries provoked fireworks in some corners, most famously over the emergence of a battle between Darwinian and "fundamentalist" accounts of creation. More broadly, science offered a secularized and human-centered way of understanding the world that did gradually replace religious accounts as foundational and authoritative. As religion became belief, science referenced an alternative experimental and materialist way of knowing.

In its current configuration, the struggle over which kinds of knowledge could be accorded the higher status of being known as "science" is carried out through adjectives; the word, with no modifier, most often refers to the "natural sciences," or "physical sciences," but seldom the "social sciences" and never to work in the arts and humanities. Science is not *a* knowledge, in this usage, but *the* knowledge, that which can speak truthfully about the real. Its heyday as truth in the United States was produced through its alliance with defense funding during the post–World War II period. This period may now be in decline as the internet, social media, and polarization of public opinion through alliances between capital and politics have produced multiple and diverse centers of power and knowledge.

The long history of the understanding of science as *the* authoritative knowledge emerges, at least in part, from practices of European colonialism. As Gyan Prakash and others have suggested, natural science was first and foremost a colonial imposition that took the place of alternative, indigenous ways of knowing (which, they argue, are just as aptly described as "sciences"), often absorbing their knowledges and renaming them as European science (Prakash 1999; Fanon 1967a; Harding 1998). They have shown how the practices known as science made colonialism imaginable and reasonable to imperial countries by elaborating a theory of race that sought to explain colonized and enslaved peoples' differences from Europeans. The science of craniometry compared skull sizes of different "races," presuming to measure racial intelligence; pelvimetry identified "race pelves," looking for smaller pelvic openings that supposedly corresponded to smaller crania in offspring in the "lower" races; phrenology identified criminality (particularly in the lower classes) from head shape; polygeny, the theory of multiple, separate "creations" of the world by God, provided a religiously heretical account (favored by many US slaveholders) in which the "lower races" were separate, inferior species (Gould 1981; Briggs 2000). Each of these nineteenth-century "sciences" validated the colonial enterprise, even as they leaned on colonialism's immense funding and prestige to produce new knowledge that in turn authorized science as a necessary and important way of knowing.

A few decades later, after Charles Darwin's *Origin of Species* (1859) had taken the world by storm, evolution provided a new grammar of human difference that cemented the break with religion. Evolution—and the notion that some people were further along its track than others—provided social Darwinists and eugenicists with ways of explaining why women should not vote; why immigration should be restricted; why "overcivilization" and "degeneration" were dangerous; and how homosexuals, immigrants, professional women, labor-union members, and even children were like primitives (Newman 1999; Stern 1999a; Shah 2001). At the end of the twentieth century, with the collapse of old-style colonialism and the rise of the United States as an international military superpower that insisted (however implausibly) that it was not an imperial power, science continued its role as the language of global dominance, taken up by an emergent international development bureaucracy focused on population control and agriculture.

This dominance is not unchallenged, however. In the 1960s in the United States, movements demanding an end to US imperialism, militarism, and rapacious capitalist exploitation emerged to counter the simple equation of science with authoritative knowledge and began asking questions about the conditions of its emergence and its effects. In 1962, Thomas Kuhn published his widely read book, *The Structure of Scientific Revolutions*, which suggested that scientific knowledge was produced through the communal, purposeful knowledge-making efforts of scientists, conditioned by the social context in which they worked, not just a set of experimental procedures that allowed us to know the truth about nature. This analysis, in turn, opened up space for a sociology of science and the controversies that had emerged sharply since the creation of the atomic bomb and the use of napalm in Vietnam: the role of science in furthering the ends of the military and business (Schmalzer, Chard, and Bothelo 2018). Groups like Science for the People! challenged the funding and priorities of science, and many called for a democratization of science—its procedures, practitioners, and funding structures. In a similar spirit, marine biologist Rachel Carson's 1962 book, *Silent Spring*, demanded an end to the chemical industry's promotion of pesticides because of their role in environmental degradation and is credited with launching the modern environmental movement.

Science became an object of study for cultural studies and American studies in relation to these political developments, often with a focus on struggles over gender, sexuality, race, and reproduction. In the 1970s, it became conventional for feminists to clear space for their politics over and against a "biology is destiny" argument—which insisted that women were *by nature* doing reproductive labor or working in underpaid "caring professions" such as teaching and nursing—by explaining that there were two things at play culturally: sex, which referred to biology, and gender, which was a social system open to criticism and change. Pursuing this logic further, some began to ask whether we have to agree that women's sex is what they say it is—flaky hormones, weak anatomy. As Judith Butler wrote, "Perhaps this construct called 'sex' is as culturally constructed as gender; indeed, perhaps it was always already gender" (1990, 7). Feminist scientists like Anne Fausto-Sterling challenged the basis in the natural sciences for

suggesting that women could not hold some jobs (from police work to the presidency); that they were unfit for higher education, at least in math and science; and that menstrual cycles made them dangerously unreliable (Fausto-Sterling 1985; Hubbard, Henifin, and Fried 1979). Others such as Evelyn Fox Keller went further, arguing that the epistemology of the natural sciences was intrinsically dominative and hence patriarchal and militaristic (Keller 1985; S. Griffin 1978).

At about the same time, another battle was being fought over race, ostensibly over the concept of IQ measurements but more generally about African Americans and public school desegregation, admission to higher education, equality of opportunity to win good jobs, and civil rights. Physicist Arthur Jensen wrote a *Harvard Educational Review* article in 1969 arguing that black children's lower IQs meant they could never achieve equal success in school alongside white children. It generated furious rebuttal, captured most enduringly in biologist Stephen Jay Gould's *The Mismeasure of Man* (1981), which examined the history of the scientific production of supposed racial differences in intelligence and launched a parallel study of the social and natural science of race. This entire controversy was reproduced almost without change two decades later, in response to *The Bell Curve*, Richard Herrnstein and Charles Murray's nasty 1994 polemic against welfare reform and affirmative action, replete with charts and graphs about African Americans' supposedly lower intelligence. Another struggle that cast science into question concerned the sterilization of people with disabilities and African American, Latinx, and Native American people in the 1960s and '70s, often under the authority of eugenics laws enacted in the early twentieth century. Civil rights and feminist groups opposed these sterilizations through lawsuits, Senate hearings, and public fights to stop new legislation from being enacted (J. Nelson 2003).

These scholarly and activist struggles intersected with the analysis of science by students of sexuality influenced by Michel Foucault's genealogy of late nineteenth-century European sexology—what he referred to as the long history of *scientia sexualis*. Jennifer Terry (1999) showed how sexology migrated from Europe to the United States, where it functioned simultaneously to contain, define, and make possible queer identities and practices. More recently, transgender scholars and activists have drawn on the same type of analysis to make two types of claims on science, medicine, and psychiatry. They have challenged the pathologizing and gatekeeping function of the mental health system and its diagnoses of gender identity disorder, and they have drawn on advances in biomedical technology to modify bodies through hormones and/or surgery. Those who have sought to affirm or transform their trans or nonbinary identities without biomedical intervention—by changing their birth certificate, driver's license, passport, or other state documents—have often found that *only* a doctor's statement will suffice to authorize that change, underscoring again the power of (medical) science in pronouncing one male or female (Bornstein 1994; Halberstam 1998, 2005; J. Butler 2004b; Spade 2006, 2007; Hausman 1995; Meyerowitz 2004). C. Riley Snorton has argued brilliantly that cultural debates over trans bodies are also haunted by the specter of race science and its account of the gendered indeterminacy of Black bodies (Snorton 2017).

While some of these critiques concluded with a rejection of science, others focused on the need for more and better science. Donna Haraway (2003) has argued influentially that we are all "naturecultural" or "cyborgs" and that any utopian, back-to-nature fantasies—whether by radical feminists or others—do not make sense in a world where virtually all forms of power, authority, economy, and family are shaped in relationship to science. AIDS activists in the 1990s and beyond embraced the terms of public health and science but contested the organization of AIDS research, struggling to shift the content of public health education, the quantity of funding overall, the kinds of research, and the conduct of clinical trials (Patton 1985, 1996; Epstein 1996; Treichler 1999). Even earlier, women's health activists in the 1970s transformed doctor-patient relationships and, ultimately, scientific research on women by putting information in women's hands through popular books such as *Our Bodies, Ourselves* (Boston Women's Health Book Collective 1973, 1976, 1996). Each of these movements negotiated a tension over how much to engage with organized "science" as such, asking whether the highly funded, academic, and commercially organized set of procedures that operates under the name of "science" was something to be opposed or embraced and transformed.

This tension continues into the present. By the early twenty-first century, the political Right began to attack both science and its funding. In this context, some cultural studies scholars suggested that their fields' critiques of science had gone too far or been misunderstood. Feminist theorists and philosophers began to argue for a "new materialism," which insisted that cultural studies practitioners need to take the biological body and natural world seriously rather than engage in knee-jerk rejection of scientific inquiry into gendered or raced difference (e.g., Grosz 1994; E. Wilson 2004; Squier 2004). Critics of this move countered that this account of (feminist) cultural studies is a straw horse—that there never was any sustained corpus of poststructuralist, antiracist, or feminist work that simply dismissed the materiality or reality of the body. On the contrary, much scholarship engaged knowledge within the biological sciences directly (Ahmed 2008; Franklin 2003; Haraway 1989, 2003; Fausto-Sterling 1985). Still others wondered whether this debate itself was a product of the continued confounding of the sciences with the "nature" they study, including the fact that "biology" could stand for both a scientific field and matter or the body itself (Willey 2016), noting how science once again comes to stand for the fact of the real.

It is clear that a great deal is at stake when scientific authority is disputed or appropriated, particularly as oil companies, tobacco companies, and antivaccine activists have been imitating left strategies and funding politically interested science. Defending the importance of scientific research on such phenomena as environmental degradation, evolution, and vaccines and refuting unproven claims such as the linkage between abortions and breast cancer have become critical tasks (Latour 2004). This dynamic is clearly present in early twenty-first-century debates over climate change. As well-established scientific consensuses about the human causes of transformations in climate come under attack by industry and right-wing religious groups and antisex, antifeminist, and homophobic conservatives in government debate banning birth control, abortion, and research on sexual minorities, "social construction" has come to seem like a tool that can be used effectively against many of the same groups it was initially developed to defend.

Ironically, the very academics who called for a reduced role of military research in universities have reaped the whirlwind by winning. In the post–Cold War university, scientists have seen a sharp decline in government funding (often from military sources) for research and its replacement with corporate money—and with it, corporate organization and management styles—as well as an undervaluing of nonscientific and nonprofessional education and research (Newfield

2008). One strategy, of agglomerating "STEM" as a field (science, technology, engineering, math), has joined science to the theoretical world of math, its deployment for high finance and digital encryption, and the military-intelligence-business funding for computing and other technologies. STEM is now marketed less as a mode of understanding or producing truth or knowledge and more as a means of creating a better return on investment for students and funders in creating wealth. Together, corporate funding and STEM seem to be building a new center of power in higher education, understood now as a private good, though still not rivaling a Cold War level of prestige and funding.

From an emergent ethnonationalist right, the early decades of the twenty-first century saw a raft of new books and articles quite unapologetically bringing back a science of racial, sex/gender, and queer/trans difference embedded in brains and genes—a renewed effort to naturalize inequalities through the authority of science. For example, a kerfuffle at internet giant Google renewed debate about whether women and people of color in the aggregate had the intelligence to be hired as coders or for other well-paying jobs in the information economy. In contrast to earlier years, those who said they did *not* generated the most activist attention, this time from the Right. Misogynists and racists like Milo Yiannopoulos and Ann Coulter have bought public platforms at universities through funding for very small student groups from a network of right-wing political donors to advance claims about science. Specifically, they have insisted on the natural, hormonal, and neurological inferiority of women and transfolk and the danger of "white genocide" from low white birth rates. They have been turned into a symbol by the right-wing and mainstream press of intolerance for *conservative* ideas when students and others challenge their legitimacy in university contexts (Wade 2015; Baron-Cohen

2003; Damore 2017; Murray 2008; for critics, see, e.g., Jordan-Young 2011; Roberts 2011; Stern 2019).

As Haraway has been arguing for many years, perhaps what we need are simply more modest claims for science, acknowledging that it is not *the* knowledge but *a* knowledge. We can take seriously the value of replicable, empirical, evidence-based claims while avoiding the hubris of the "god's-eye view." Above all, perhaps we should mistrust researchers of any political stripe who invoke the authority of "science" to make invidious comparisons between groups of people or see in biology a theory of limits rather than of human possibility.

2007/2020

57

Slavery
Walter Johnson

"Slavery has never been represented, slavery never can be represented," said the novelist, antislavery lecturer, and former slave William Wells Brown in 1847 ([1847] 1969, 82). Brown referred, in the first instance, to the world-making violence of the system of kidnapping, dispossession, and labor extraction that emerged in the fifteenth century and persisted almost to the dawn of the twentieth. But he referred in the second instance to a sort of epistemological violence, a murderous, forcible forgetting of the history of slavery. Only slavery's victims—if it is possible to use the word "only" in the context of so many millions of stolen lives—might have truly told the story he wanted to tell. Brown reminds us that we approach the history of slavery by way of whispers and shadows, where truth has often been hidden in half truth in order to be saved away for the future. We approach it, that is to say, across a field of argument in which the history of slavery has often been conscripted to the economic, political, and imperial purposes that have hidden inside the word "freedom."

Over the four centuries of Atlantic slavery, millions of Africans and their descendants were turned into profits, fancies, sensations, and possessions of New World whites. The vast majority of the enslaved were agricultural workers whose lives were devoted to the production of staple crops (sugar, tobacco, indigo, coffee, and cotton). Their labor provided the agricultural base of European mercantile capitalism and much of the surplus capital that, by the late eighteenth century, was being invested in the development of European industry. North America was alone among New World slave societies in having a self-reproducing slave population. Elsewhere, particularly in the Caribbean and Brazil, the murderous character of the slaveholding regime (the life expectancy of Africans put to work cultivating sugar in the Americas was seven years from the time they stepped ashore) meant that slaveholders depended on the Atlantic slave trade as a replacement for biological reproduction.

The history of New World slavery was characterized by daily resistance on the part of the enslaved, terrific brutality on the part of the enslaving, and frequent military conflict between the two. Daily forms of resistance took the form of everything from mouthing off and shamming sickness to flight, arson, and assault. The slaveholders' violent responses, which seem at first to emblematize the license of unchecked power, upon closer inspection reveal the brittleness of their control; mastery had constantly to be—could only be—shored up through brutality. Everyday forms of resistance helped slaves come to trust one another enough to plan a hemisphere-wide series of insurgencies—some on a very small scale, some mobilizing thousands at a time—which varied widely in their ideology and aspiration but which continually presented the possibility that the "Atlantic World" might be remade as a "Black Atlantic" (C. James [1938] 1989; Genovese 1979; Stuckey 1987; Gwendolyn Hall 1992; Gilroy 1993; da Costa 1994; Sidbury 1997; Berlin 1998; W. Johnson 2002; Dubois 2004; Jennifer Morgan 2004). Indeed, the military and diplomatic history of the New World was distilled in the alembic of black revolt. From the Maroon Wars in Jamaica to the Haitian Revolution to the American Revolution, the Civil War, and the Cuban Revolution, armed and insurgent blacks (and the almost unspeakable threat they represented to white leaders) decisively shaped the course of European and American history.

The foundational role of African and African American labor and resistance in the history of European imperialism and the economic growth of the Atlantic economy was reflected in the institution's role in shaping Atlantic culture. Institutions of law and governance, structures and styles of authority, religious faith and medical knowledge, cultural forms ranging from popular amusements to sentimental novels and autobiographies: all of these emergent forms of European modernity bore the stamp (often forcibly obscured) of slavery. So, too, did the ongoing identification of blackness with the condition of dispossession and the disposition to insurgency.

The long nineteenth century, beginning with the Haitian Revolution in 1792 and culminating with the legislative emancipation in Brazil in 1888, marked the passing of slavery from the governing institutional solution to problems of labor, empire, and difference, to a residual social form (persisting to this day, it should be said) with tremendous discursive power. The end began with the idea that the opposite of slavery was neither redemption (as the Christian emphasis on sin as a form of slavery would have it) nor mastery (as the idea of history as a sort of race war would have it) but "freedom." The emergent antislavery version of enslavement was one that tried to demonstrate the ways in which slavery deformed the course of right and history by specifying its evils: its epochal barbarities and quotidian tortures, its corruptive tyranny and degrading license, its economic and moral backwardness, its unfreedom. And over the course of the nineteenth century, this new view increasingly contested a proslavery argument that slavery itself represented the unfolding course of "freedom": the alignment of social institutions with natural (racial) history, the propagation of the earth for the benefit of its masters, the temporal manifestation of an institution that was both ancient in provenance and providential in design. Beginning with the Haitian Revolution, it was the antislavery argument about slavery that won: African American slavery came to be seen as the antithesis of "freedom."

Though the term "slavery" referred over the course of that century-long argument to a condition that was historically specific to black people, it came to serve as a sort of switchboard through which arguments over the character of "freedom" could be routed and defined: the archaic pendant to the emergent future. By using the word "slavery" to describe institutions ranging from wage labor and marriage to prostitution and peonage, nineteenth-century reformers sought to extend the moral force of the argument against African American slavery to other sorts of social relations. Their efforts were generally met with an insistence that slavery was a condition that was (or had been) unique to African Americans, who were, with emancipation, presumed to be experiencing "freedom."

The framing of slavery as archaic and freedom as emergent has a complex history in Western political economy. In both Smithian and Marxian thought, slavery remained an almost wholly unthought backdrop to the unfolding history of capitalism in Europe. For Adam Smith, slavery was destined to fall away before the superior capacity of wage labor to motivate workers through their own self-interest; the inferior motivation of bonded labor was in the Smithian tradition taken as a given rather than recognized (and theorized) as the result of the resistance of enslaved people (Oakes 2003). For Karl Marx, slavery was a moment in the history of primitive accumulation—the initial process of dispossession out of which capitalist social relations were subsequently built. It was the past to the present of "capitalism" (understood here as that system of social relations characterized by "free" labor and the factory mode of production) with which he was primarily concerned (Marx [1867] 1976, 1:667–712; W. Johnson 2004). To this

day, much of the scholarship on slavery done in each of these traditions—so radically opposed in so many other ways—shares the common metanarrative shape of outlining a "transition" from slavery to capitalism.

The marking of slavery as an archaism, destined to be superseded by the emergent history of freedom, even as it provided the term with enormous critical potential, made it (and the history of the millions of martyrs it contains) useful to those who defined freedom in terms of national belonging or economic license. In this usage, as found in nineteenth-century reform and political economy, the relationship between slavery and freedom is figured as one of temporal supersession. The United States is no longer figured as a place where the contest between the two is to be fought out but as a place where it has been uniformly and once and for all completed. As George W. Bush put it in his 2001 inaugural address, the history of the United States is "the story of a slaveholding society that became a servant of freedom." He went on to elaborate this claim, asserting that "the very people traded into slavery helped to set America free" through their struggle against injustice (2003). In the historical vision expressed by (but certainly not limited to) Bush's addresses, the history of slavery has been turned into a cliché, a set of images that have been emptied of any authentic historical meaning through their sheer repetition in connection with their supposed extinction at the hands of "freedom." The history of slavery in this usage exists in a state of civil servitude to the idea of "American freedom."

A countercurrent within mostly Marxist and black radical thought—notably W. E. B. Du Bois ([1935] 1998), C. L. R. James ([1938] 1989), Eric Williams ([1944] 1994), Stuart Hall (2002), Sidney Mintz (1985), David Brion Davis (1975), and Cedric Robinson ([1983] 2000)—has insistently contested the temporal framing of the relationship of slavery to freedom as one of linear progress.

By insisting on the place of slavery in the history of European and American capitalism—on the way that the palpable experiences of freedom in Europe and the Americas and the narrowness of an idea of freedom defined as the ability to work for a wage both depended on slavery—they have framed the relationship between the two terms as being one of dynamic simultaneity. They have, that is to say, insistently pointed out practices of servitude at the heart of the history of freedom, a set of insights that gives new and subversive meaning to Bush's phrase "servant of freedom."

The idea of the simultaneous coproduction of slavery and freedom lies at the heart of the case for reparations for slavery. This ongoing case has a history in the United States that dates to Reconstruction, and it represents a powerful (if also powerfully stigmatized by the intellectual and cultural mainstream) refiguration of the relationship of capitalism, slavery, freedom, past, and present. By reworking the history of the exploitation of Africans in the Americas—by whatever means, under whatever mode of production, mystified by whatever Western category of analysis—as a single extended and ongoing moment of time, the heterodox historiography of reparations calls on us to recognize slavery as an element not of the national (or hemispheric) past but of the global present.

2007

58

Sound
Josh Kun

The final moments of President Ronald Reagan's second inaugural address took a decidedly sonic turn. Standing inside the rotunda of the Capitol building, Reagan said that he could hear "echoes" of the "American" past and then proceeded to list them off as if he were doing a voice-over for the trailer to a new History Channel miniseries: "A general falls to his knees in the hard snow of Valley Forge; a lonely President paces the darkened halls, and ponders his struggle to preserve the Union; the men of the Alamo call out encouragement to each other; a settler pushes west and sings a song, and the song echoes out forever and fills the unknowing air. It is the American sound. It is hopeful, big-hearted, idealistic, daring, decent, and fair. That's our heritage; that is our song. We sing it still" (Reagan 1985). For Reagan, the arc of US history is an arc of sound: the crunch of knees on snow, the click of pacing heels, the shouts of soldiers, the songs of cowboys. A sound is "American" if it is "hopeful, big-hearted, idealistic, daring, decent, and fair," and if a sound is "American," then it is also a song, a song that reaches back to an imagined collective heritage and resonates through the throats and mouths of the living present. The "American" sound is the song "we" sing.

For practitioners of American studies and cultural studies, these broadly nationalist claims raise questions that are worth asking whenever one is formulating methodologies of listening around the keyword "sound." Can a sound be a song? Can a sound have a national character? What is the relationship between a sound, its echo, and the walls of the building they bounce off? What are the sounds of settlement, of colonialism? What are the sounds of decolonialism—the audible rebuttals of empire, the screams of freedom, the murmurs of rebellion? And perhaps most importantly for all the references to the "sound" of "America," the "singing of America" and the "song of America" (references that have been repeated along the long arc of the US political and cultural imagination from the sonic cauldron of the melting pot to Dr. Martin Luther King Jr. urging us to "let freedom ring" with a remix of "My Country, 'Tis of Thee") are sonic metaphors traces of actual sounds? Answers to these questions were once the domain of acousticians, sound artists, experimental composers, and a small cadre of ear-obsessed scholars, mostly located in the disciplines of history, anthropology, and ethnomusicology. They were united by a collective sense of marginalization by the nagging dominance of sound's alleged antithesis—the visual—largely due to what Martin Jay once dubbed the "ocularcentrism" of Western thought (Jay 1994, 3; Howes 2005; Attali 1985).

Over the past two decades, a broader palette of sound criticism and analysis has emerged as scholars across a range of disciplines have turned their attention to the audible world (Keeling and Kun 2011). The ethnomusicologist Veit Erlmann (2004) has put hearing and listening at the center of the study of modernity; the historian Emily Thompson (2004) has listened closely to the acoustic impacts of concert halls and skyscrapers on the formation of modern subjectivity; the media studies scholar Kate Lacey (2013) has turned to listening's role in the making of media audiences and media citizenship. Both Karin Bijsterveld (2008) and Jonathan Sterne (2003) have reckoned with sound's impact on society by focusing on technologies of sound and their role in brokering distinctions among sound, music, and noise. This critical focus on sound technologies has led to an expansive scholarly interest in sound's relationship to the media that store, transmit, and distribute it and the recordings of sound that are produced and consumed through formal and informal industries of culture (Stadler 2010; Bijsterveld 2008; Brady 2009; Suisman and Strasser 2009; Hilmes 2005). The depth and breadth of this scholarship may mean that the visual focus of the En*light*enment has been displaced by the sonic possibilities of what Sterne playfully calls the "En*soni*ment," referencing the period between 1750 and 1925 when the world became audible in new ways, and new listening practices and sonic bodies of knowledge were born through the advent of sound reproduction technologies such as the stethoscope, the telephone, and the phonograph (2003, 2).

For all the intellectual breadth and diversity of these approaches to sound studies, they all share a common jumping-off point. Sound is not treated as something that exists objectively and is then heard. It is contingent on an object that moves and a body that receives and translates the vibrations caused by that movement. Sound can be studied scientifically (as acoustic physicists do), but it also needs to be addressed humanistically (as literary scholars might), precisely because there is no sound without a mind and a body to create it. As Sterne has put it, "The hearing of sound is what makes it" (2003, 11). Sound is social and experiential, "a modality of knowing and being in the world" (Feld 2003). The social uses and experiences of sound imbue it with materiality and politics. Not all sounds are treated equally, nor is any sound universal. Yet all sounds have histories rooted in the layered bedrocks of culture, economy, territory, and identity.

To study sound is to track its trajectories while it exists, to follow it from source to listener, and to analyze its geographies and networks, asking both where sounds come from and where they go (LaBelle 2010). These geographical referents and frameworks mean that sound needs to be theorized as spatial. All sounds originate in space and move across territories, making sound a primary site for the study of political and cultural geography and for the mapping of identity and society. The most prominent and influential early work on sound and space emerged out of the World Soundscape Project at Canada's Simon Fraser University under the leadership of R. Murray Schafer in the 1970s. It was Schafer who introduced into critical and artistic vocabularies the term "soundscape," his shorthand for a grand theory of the world as sound, and the practice of "sonography," the acoustic field of study and composition that aims to preserve that world (Schafer 1977; Hirschkind 2006).

Schafer's neologisms echoed earlier invocations in US culture of an "American" soundscape. Walt Whitman focused *Leaves of Grass* ([1855] 1965) on the sounds of the spaces around him, sounds such as autumn winds, church organ pipes, sounds of the city, chattering children, the cries of the sick, the shouts of dockworkers, the ring of alarm bells, and the whirr of steam engines. Henry David Thoreau believed there was something he called "the broad, flapping American ear" ([1854] 1966, 43). In *Walden*, he listened for the sounds that, as Leo Marx ([1964] 2000) later argued, were active in shaping "the pastoral ideal" of "America." Thoreau heard the train's whistle—a signal "that many restless city merchants are arriving within the circle of town" ([1854] 1966, 96)—the rattling of the cattle train, and all the natural sounds he praised above all else: the chanting of the whippoorwills, the wailing of the owls. Schafer's "soundscape" was more apt to tune into the physical properties of sound and the sound environment, while Thoreau conceived of the soundscape of Walden Pond as the product of both the environment and the listener.

It was closer to the "acoustic communication" approach that Schafer's own colleague Barry Truax advocated decades later (1984). Sound could not be abstracted from the social; sound is a social network with the listener as the central node.

In all these instances, there is a politics to audibility, to what is heard and what is not heard, what is listened for and what is ignored, what is accepted as sound and what is policed as noise, and what is silenced and what is amplified. In current work in American studies and cultural studies, the story of sound is both the story of the powerful silences that sound can cover up and a push for new methods of listening—a close listening, a listening differently, a more just listening, a listening anew (Lipsitz 1990a). The assumption is that any organization of sounds is, as Jacques Attali notes, a "tool for the creation or consolidation of a community, a totality. It is what links a power center to its subjects, and more generally, it is an attribute of power in all its forms" (1985, 6). Democracy, for example, rests on the utopia of all voices being heard, the oratory of leadership, the rhetorical promise of freedom, the *declaration* of independence (Fliegelman 1993). Yet the distinct sound of the founding of the United States as a nation was one that excluded African Americans, Native Americans, and women. "Americans" made "American" sounds; blacks and Indians made noise. As listeners, the founders of the United States were strategically hard of hearing, selective listeners who used sound to shape an exclusionary auditory politics of self, citizen, and Other.

The sound of the "free American" was built on rendering sonically incomprehensible or silent the Others that freedom refused. The Ohio abolitionist Sara G. Stanley framed it this way in 1860: "As the song of freedom verberates and reverberates through the northern hills, and the lingering symphony quivers on the still air and then sinks away into silence, a low deep wail, heavy with anguish and despair, rises from the southern plains, and the clank of chains on human limbs mingles with the mournful cadence" ([1860] 1977, 286). Stanley's nineteenth-century commentary reminds us that the sonic character of US conceptions of race and racial equality is not a new idea. W. E. B. Du Bois does the same in *The Soul of Black Folks* ([1903] 1997), his pioneering study of African American identity and culture. Using transcriptions of the sorrow songs of slaves as chapter preludes, Du Bois shaped the entire book through the sonic imagination of the black freedom struggle, making it a "singing book" (Baker 1987b, 68).

Sounds are constitutive of national imaginaries and national possibilities, each of which is interwoven with racial formations, racial identities, and racial imaginations. Studying sound helps us put an ear to "the audio-racial imagination," which refers to the aurality of racial meanings, and to sound's role in systems and institutions of racialization and racial formation within and across the borders of the United States (Kun 2005, 26; Vaillant 2002; Tahmahkera 2011; Lott 2011; Eidsheim 2011). Scholars in American studies and ethnomusicology have called our attention to the profound ways in which the US racial imagination is a sonic formation and how the famous problem of "the color line" once envisaged by Du Bois is also a "sonic color-line" (Stoever-Ackerman 2010, 54; Radano and Bohlman 2000). Others have highlighted the interweaving of sound with gender and sexuality, with particular attention to the gendering of certain sounds as masculine or feminine (bodily noises, pitches of voice, decibels of speech, "soft" versus "hard" sounds) and the management and regulation of listening practices along gender and sexuality lines (K. Brown 1996; Norton 1996; Karpf 2006; Koestenbaum [1994] 2001; P. Bailey 2004; Rodgers 2010).

Across all of this scholarship, a methodological question remains: How do we study certain sonic formations from a historical perspective when no recorded audio evidence exists? "The world of unrecorded sound is irreclaimable," writes the historian Leigh Eric Schmidt (2000, 15). The emergence of "historical soundscape studies" has gone a long way to foreground listening as a historical methodology, allowing us to trace sounds in literature, historical documents, memoirs, political texts, and visual art in order to construct sonic portraits of social formations before the advent of recorded sound. Mark M. Smith, for example, has shown how nineteenth-century ideas of progress were linked to sounds of work and industry (the cadence of hammers), how plantations ran according to an aural social order of managed sound and noise, and how racial and ethnic otherness, while traditionally rooted in visual terrains of exclusion and biological racism, were also aurally constructed, from the "whoops" and "peals" of Native American "savagery" to the incomprehensible "noise" of black speech and black song (2000). Present and future work will continue to listen for the mechanisms of power and injustice and to listen for sound as a battlefield over which struggles for community, subjectivity, and citizenship are waged.

What is the song of twenty-first-century "America"? Is there such a thing as "the American sound" in the age of twenty-first-century economic globalization and mass international migration? What will sound studies of future audile techniques—Spotify playlists, SoundCloud embeds, musical discovery and sharing applications, sonic surveillance, and YouTube streams—reveal about the new cultures and technologies of sound? The echoes of the past reverberate all around us, but so do the emergent sound cultures of the future, which we can now engage with a critical toolbox that is better equipped than ever before.

2014

59

Space
George Lipsitz

In order for history to take place, it takes places. American studies and cultural studies scholars have drawn on the ideas and insights of critical geographers Henri Lefebvre (1991), David Harvey (2000), Yi-fu Tuan (1977), Cindy Katz (2004), Ruth Wilson Gilmore (2007), Laura Pulido (1996), and many others to explore the creative possibilities and the moral meanings attributed to particular spaces and places. The politics and poetics of space permeate the culture of the United States as a nation through moral values that get attached to the open ranges of the western frontier and the far reaches of empire overseas; that contrast the barrio, the ghetto, and the reservation with the propertied and properly gendered suburban home; that juxtapose the finite limits of social space with the infinite possibilities of cyberspace and outer space. In both scholarly research and everyday life, the moral meanings attributed to these spaces and places have often been resolutely and creatively contested.

For European political philosophers during the Renaissance, corruption came from time—from the particularity of historical events—while the universality of space was presumed to promote virtue and morality. After the discovery and conquest of the Americas, these ideas helped fuel the hope that the virtues of the ideal space they associated with what they called "America" could provide escape from the corruptions of European time. As historian David W. Noble argues, idealized fantasies about pure and virtuous space have

permeated the political and expressive cultures of the United States from the era of colonization and conquest up to the present day. The idea of a free "America" especially excited European thinkers because they had come to believe that free nations needed to be composed of homogeneous populations with strong ties to the national landscape, to "timeless spaces" where citizens could dwell in harmony with one another. European Americans who imagined that the purity of "American" space might offer them a refuge from the corruptions of European time developed what Noble calls "the metaphor of two worlds"—the idea that the territory of the United States would be an island of virtue in a global sea of corruption (2002, xxxiv). Later institutionalized inside US national culture, this metaphor depends on binary oppositions between the pure spaces of New World freedom and their contamination by despised and demonized groups overseas or at home marked as "other." In order to have pure and homogeneous spaces, "impure" populations have to be removed or marginalized, destroyed or dominated. Noble argues that belief in a redemptive national landscape performed important cultural work in constituting the United States as an imagined community grounded in white masculine property and power.

Imagined utopian spaces have long served as idealized escapes from the problems of real places. Images of the pastoral rural landscape and the rugged western frontier permeate works of expressive culture by writers, painters, and composers (H. Smith 1950; Kolodny 1984; L. Marx [1964] 2000). In the nineteenth century, literary and philosophical works by transcendentalists and paintings of the Hudson River school imbued the national landscape with democratic possibility. In the twentieth century, musical compositions by Virgil Thompson and Aaron Copland echoed writings by historians Frederick Jackson Turner ([1893] 1920) and

William Prescott Webb ([1931] 1981) that identified the open spaces of the western frontier as unique sources of democratic regeneration. These imagined free spaces were constructed discursively in opposition to the constraints that settled society seemed to impose on freedom-seeking US Americans. Herman Melville's Ishmael in *Moby-Dick* in 1851 and Mark Twain's Huck Finn in 1885 may be the best known of many fictional heroes who have been eager to take to sea or to "light out for the territory" to avoid facing the contradictions of settled society (Melville [1851] 1971; Twain [1885] 1985).

Of course, neither Ishmael nor Huck fled "civilized" space alone. Both were accompanied by people of color on whom they depended for moral instruction and guidance. People from communities of color could not access the metaphor of two worlds because it required their subordination, humiliation, exclusion, sometimes even their annihilation. The putatively empty and timeless North American discursive space that settler colonists expected to serve as a space of refuge from the corruptions of European time was actually a physical place inhabited by indigenous people with long histories and distinct customs. The heroism of conquest, settlement, and westward expansion depended on genocidal wars against Native Americans, slavery imposed on Africans, lands seized from Mexicans, and the exploitation of laborers in and from Asia and Latin America. Rather than imagining the national landscape as common ground to be shared, the moral geography of settler colonialism required conquest, slavery, and empire. As white civilization and its corruptions penetrated the West, it became increasingly difficult for people in the United States to believe that they inhabited the democratic landscape of their dreams. The end of slavery, the rise of the interracial egalitarian coalition formed around what W. E. B. Du Bois ([1935] 1998, 184) called "abolition-democracy," mass immigration from Europe, and working-class mobilizations for justice all challenged the homogeneity and harmony central to the dominant national spatial and social imaginary.

Rather than reckon honestly and openly with the internal contradictions and conflicts that rendered domestic society unable to produce the freedom and democracy that had been promised, many white US Americans looked outward, seeking in the global marketplace the perfect harmony and happiness they had failed to produce in the national landscape. If the United States of America could not be an island of virtue in a global sea of corruption, the sea had to be transformed to be like it (D. W. Noble 2002). But the United States itself also had to be made more homogeneous. In the face of the increasing public presence and growing power of communities of color, the imagined free spaces of the frontier had to be fabricated in the segregated suburb, in the normative, properly gendered, and prosperous household (E. May 1988; Massey 1994; Marsh 1990) A distinct spatial imaginary propelled the creation of subdivisions designed to secure comparative advantages from what political economist Robert Reich (1991) calls "the secession of the successful" into gated exclusive communities governed by ever smaller subunits of government set up to hoard amenities and advantages for their residents (McKenzie 1994). Just as pastoral North American space was once viewed as the ideal escape from the corruptions of European time, the rewards and privileges of whiteness have configured US suburbs as the means of escape from the responsibilities and obligations of national citizenship. In segregated white communities, the intersection of race and space produced a radically restricted spatial imaginary, one that reinforced the rewards, privileges, and structured advantages of whiteness through commitments to hostile privatism and defensive localism (Lipsitz 2011).

Because aggrieved communities of color could not access for themselves the amenities and advantages of places shaped by the white spatial imaginary, they have often manifested a different approach to discursive space and physical place that has had enormous cultural and political appeal for people of all races. As the philosopher Charles Mills notes, the white spatial imaginary tells people of color that they belong "somewhere else," that "you are what you are in part because you originate from a certain kind of space, and that space has those properties in part because it is inhabited by creatures like yourself" (1997, 42). Yet populations living in ghettos, barrios, and reservations have turned segregation into congregation through social movements that depict space as valuable and finite, as a public resource for which all must take responsibility. The competing spatial imaginaries of the national political culture have influenced a variety of works of expressive culture. The art of John Biggers and Betye Saar, the fiction of Paule Marshall, plays and essays by Lorraine Hansberry, and the creation of collectives of musicians by Horace Tapscott and Sun Ra all exemplify this alternative to the dominant spatial imaginary (Lipsitz 2011). The American studies and ethnic studies scholars Robert Alvarez (2005), Arlene Dávila (2004), Raul Villa (2000), and Mary Pat Brady (2002) have delineated the complex cultural consequences of racialized space for Latinos, while Linda Trinh Vo (2004), Leland Saito (2009), and Chiou-ling Yeh (2008) have produced similar studies of Asian American communities.

The Black spatial imaginary has been a particularly generative force for new spatial and racial ideas exemplified in the work of the jazz pianist, composer, bandleader, and political visionary Sun Ra. The dual meaning of "space" as both a continuous empty expanse of territory and the physical universe beyond the Earth's atmosphere enabled Sun Ra to expose how

relations among races in the United States are also relations among spaces. In the early 1970s, he picked the phrase "space is the place" as the title for a song, an album, and a feature film. As part of a long-standing effort on his part to use flamboyant self-dramatization and performance to make a serious point, Sun Ra presented himself as a visitor from outer space appalled by the racism he discovered on the planet Earth. The jazz musician's mischievous play with the words "space" and "place" contained obvious implications about race. In these works, Sun Ra imagined utopian travels in space as a direct contrast to and a direct rebuke of "Earthy" spatial imaginaries: housing segregation based on a long history of restrictive covenants, racial zoning, mortgage redlining, steering, blockbusting, and mob violence that relegated people of different races to different spaces. Sun Ra's target audience had firsthand experience with the more than sixteen hundred urban renewal projects starting in the 1930s that destroyed the economic and emotional ecosystems of minority communities (Fullilove 2004, 20). The spatial imaginary that guided Sun Ra's eccentric art and public persona had more to do with the problems of segregated spaces on the planet Earth than with the utopian possibilities of travel through the universe. His artistry emerged from and spoke to a Black spatial imaginary based on mutuality and solidarity that developed over decades in Black communities where residents turned divisive segregation into celebratory congregation.

Like other artists, activists, and intellectuals from aggrieved communities, Sun Ra attempted to make the familiar realities of racialized space appear unnatural and therefore unnecessary. His adopted public persona as a purported interplanetary traveler from Saturn blended long-standing strains of Afro-diasporic tricksterism with emerging currents of Afrofuturism. He invoked the cosmos to contrast an imagined freedom in outer space with the confinements confronting Black people on the planet Earth (Szwed 1998; Kilgore 2003). Similarly important spatial imaginaries have been developed through political mobilizations to forge new spaces of inclusion and opportunity. The Chicano movement of the 1960s and 1970s united citizens and noncitizens through brilliant deployments of the mythic and poetic "land of Aztlán" as a discursive space uniquely suited to positioning group struggle within and across borders. This spatial imaginary recruited people of Mexican origin in both Mexico and the United States without condoning the conquest and suppression of indigenous peoples by both nations. It positioned Chicano activists to battle for both national civil rights and global human rights (Bebout 2011). The intercommunalism of the Black Panther Party leader Huey P. Newton created a cognitive mapping that connected Black struggles for self-determination in Oakland, California, to peasant resistance to imperialism in Vietnam. In Newton's view, the United States was not a nation into which Blacks should assimilate but rather an empire that they should oppose (Singh 2004). Queer Latina activists mobilizing in San Francisco's Mission District in the 1990s in response to official indifference to the AIDS epidemic converted a storefront on a busy street into a welcoming space for progressive and culturally sensitive political education and organizing among people from different national-origin groups (J. Rodríguez 2003).

Insurgent struggles have often made history take place by seizing space and deploying it for unexpected purposes. On Thanksgiving Day in 1969, activists identifying themselves as Indians of All Nations seized and occupied the abandoned prison on Alcatraz Island. The name Indians of All Nations turned aggregate anti-Indian racism into a new form of solidarity by asserting a unified panethnic identity. The activists cited a provision of a treaty between the Lakota nation and the federal government as a guarantee that members of all tribes had the right to seize unused government land (Smith and Warrior 1996). They used the sentimental appropriation of Indian history in this national holiday to call attention to the original seizure and occupation of North America by white settler colonialists that preceded the first Thanksgiving. They dramatized the desperate situation facing indigenous people by becoming the first people in history to break *into* jail. The action underscored the culpability of the federal government by seizing national park property as reparations for lands confiscated from Indians elsewhere. Similarly, the American Indian Movement desacralized the physical places of westward expansion through the Trail of Broken Treaties caravan from Alcatraz to Washington, DC, in 1972. Signifying on the forced removal of the Cherokee and Choctaw people to Oklahoma on the brutal Trail of Tears in 1831, the caravan traveled in the opposite direction of westward expansion, foregrounding white duplicity in the title of the march. It stopped along the way in the racialized spaces of reservations and urban ghettos, turning them from forgotten and abandoned places into spaces supplying new recruits for the campaign.

There are lessons to be learned from these activist mobilizations. By organizing in actual locations over the discursive meanings of space and place, they have drawn attention to the ways in which new relations among races require the renegotiation of relations among places. They signal that space is not merely a barren expanse, the universe around the Earth, or an empty temporal interval. It is a dynamic place where important discursive and political work can be done when people recognize that space is the place in which to do it.

2014

60

Subject

Tavia Nyong'o

Hey you! Yes . . . you! Now that I have your attention, let me ask you a question. How did you know it was you I was addressing? I didn't call you by your name, after all. In fact, I don't know your name or any of your other distinguishing characteristics. Nonetheless, I called out, and you turned your attention to me. There is a lot of power in what just happened, more than you might initially suspect. Or maybe you *do* already suspect. Perhaps you are already conscious of the coercion in my addressing you in this abrupt and unceremonious manner. Maybe you rankle a little at my interruption of what you intended to be doing, my disruption of what you were expecting to find here in this essay. Who am I, you may be asking, to presume to command your attention as I have just done?

"Subject" first emerged as a keyword in the fields of cultural studies and American studies as an effort to understand situations just like this one: situations in which a subjective response emerges out of a seemingly impersonal call or hail. What "subject"—or the closely related term "subjective"—means in such situations is anything but clear. A subject (from the Latin verb for "to throw under") is something that comes under the influence of an external authority or force. Some examples may suggest the breadth and subtlety of the concept.

In the colonial era, North American settlers were "loyal subjects" of the British Crown. When, in the course of human events, revolutionary white men felt obliged to throw off their imperial yoke, they felt "a decent respect to the opinions of mankind" required them to justify this act through an open declaration of independence. Even in revolutionizing themselves, they continued to guide their conduct and speech in relation to an abstract, external authority (Fliegelman 1993).

During the notorious Tuskegee syphilis experiment, conducted by the US government from the 1930s to the 1970s, hundreds of impoverished black men were "experimental subjects" of an inhumane medical study in which they were denied treatment in order to track the "natural" progress of their disease. More recently, a historian discovered prior tests conducted by the US Public Health Service in Guatemala, in which humans were *deliberately* infected with syphilis (Reverby 2009). These medical crimes resulted in the creation of institutional review boards (IRBs) that now govern research on what are called "human subjects."

The standardized test you probably took to qualify you for the college-level course in which you may be reading this essay made you a "psychological subject." Your aptitude or capacity for reasoning was assessed, and the results affected which educational opportunities would be open or closed to you. The legitimacy of such assessments in organizing economic and educational opportunity in a democratic society has been intensely researched and debated since the test was first invented (Lemann 2000). Many people argue that they are illegitimate in a democratic society and lie on the discredited foundations of eugenic science.

In each of these examples, the *political* character of subjectification—the process of becoming a subject—should be clear. In each case, the *historical* character of the subjectifying power that precedes and makes the subject may not be obvious. Subjectification bears a history, but it is a history that is often masked. One is seemingly "born" owing allegiance to the British monarch or to the opinions of humankind. One "happens" to be a black sharecropper in the Jim Crow South or a Guatemalan prostitute and therefore available for use in a government experiment on the efficacy of penicillin. One is simply "gifted" with the ability to achieve in school, as "revealed" by the SAT or other tests, and thus merits more or better education than someone who is less highly ranked.

The hidden history of these processes of subjectification allows their results to appear impersonal and objective. This *naturalizes* the structural effects that subjectification has on how we are formed as subjects—how we live or die, what rights we possess or lack, what we know or are kept ignorant of. Subject positions are not merely a set of "boxes" or "labels" with no real substance to them; they are not something we can elect to freely "identify with" or not. They inform who we feel ourselves to be in our "innermost selves" and how we are entangled in our most objective and immediate environment. They form the ground on which we stand, when and if we take a stand. Even when we refuse or rebel against our subjectification, we do so *as* subjects.

Scholars who use the term "subject" to explore processes of subjectification draw on a variety of theoretical traditions, ranging from Marxism and psychoanalysis to Foucauldianism and feminism. A common theme in many of these traditions is the observation that subjectification works most powerfully when it is felt most consensually. Of course, brute force, or the realistic fear of it, can also be subjectifying. But so can the protection from violence, the provision of medical care, the granting of legal rights, the enlightenment of the mind with education or knowledge (Hartman 1997). American studies has long been interested in the terrain of "soft power" and "tender violence": it has tracked the winning of "hearts and minds" and the "rites of assent" through which the formerly excluded are incorporated

into the fabric of society (Abel 1997; Bercovitch 1993; Wexler 2000). Such processes are stories of subjectification. If violence tends to render humans as objects, power turns them into subjects (Scarry 1985). But the power that subjects us does not emanate from a single mythical source, like the sovereign body of the king (Kantorowicz 1957). It is continuously reproduced in moments of hailing such as the one with which this essay began, the hail that made you, however temporarily, into a "learning subject," a subject to my expertise and scholarly authority.

To be sure, my authority in this scene of instruction is tenuous. For one, it is mediated by my own ongoing subjectification. In order to teach you about the keyword "subject," I rely on your ongoing cooperation and comprehension, however partial or skeptical. The pedagogic power that renders you a learning subject is a negotiation in which I attempt to anticipate and provide for your instruction, while you "follow along" in hopes of "mastering" the subject. At least this is what happens in one ideal scenario, which may not resemble yours or mine. Perhaps we decide to read against the grain, to wrest this essay away from its seeming intent, to employ it for different purposes.

As a democratic educator, I should welcome such creativity as a sign of the consensual nature of our negotiation, as proof that you are a *free* subject in this learning scenario and not any kind of conscript. But who am "I" in this case? I am not the "grammatical subject" of this sentence, psychoanalysis has argued, but the *split* between that grammatical "I" and the body that speaks through the "I" (Fink 1995). That speaking body is forever finding, losing, and dispersing itself in the grammatical subject "I" that ostensibly secures and stabilizes its authority. According to the psychoanalytic view of the subject, I am not the master of the discourse I would pass along to you—especially not when I claim to speak in the first person. Rather than imagine a power-free context for the subject, situations in which we are somehow free to be who we really are independent of others, we might do better to seek fuller accounts of *intersubjectivity*, that is, to better understand the *relations of power* at work—whether behind the scenes or quite openly on the surface—in our various scenes of subjectification.

Cultural studies, including the traditions of critical theory on which it draws, has trained scholars to be suspicious of situations that present themselves as free of coercion or constraint (Horkheimer and Adorno [1944] 2002). This suspicion raises the important question of whether knowledge about the subject implies power over the subject. To answer that question, let us return to the scene with which I began, one that I have borrowed from the Marxist philosopher Louis Althusser ([1971] 2001). In Althusser's example, it is not an author but a police officer yelling, "Hey you!" Althusser wanted to know why we turn when we hear this hail (he called it an "interpellation") and what happens when we do. Althusser was searching for a critical account of how and why working people "consent" to their domination and exploitation in capitalist societies. Integrating the insights of Marxism and psychoanalysis, Althusser developed an account of a subject who was given a *forced choice* to belong to the capitalist order (as enforced by schools, police, and other "apparatuses" of the state). Since "you" could refer to anyone, in deciding that it nonetheless is "me" whom the police officer is addressing, "I" become a subject *for* the police. The resulting analysis emphasizes both the relations of production in society and the institutions that hold those relations in place despite our possible wishes otherwise.

If I am "stopped and frisked" by the New York Police Department because I am a young black or Latino male or have to show my papers in Arizona because I fit another racial profile, I may understand that this interpellation by the state is in violation of rights conveyed by the US Constitution. But knowing this does not in itself give me choice. "You" *could* mean me, and so I turn. I am structurally—"always already"—hailed by the police officer. In Althusser's account, my subjectivity is in a crucial sense an *effect* of the policeman's power. Other critical theorists contest this point: Slavoj Žižek (1999) argues that there is always an inextricable core of irrationality to subjectivity that interpellation cannot reach (although neither can the individual subject). And the philosopher and historian Michel Foucault famously argued that "where there is power, there is resistance": the hail that produces the subject is also the swerve of the subject against its power or authority ([1976] 1990, 95). There is a minimum of momentum always available for escape.

You may have already noticed an ambiguity running throughout these usages of the term "subject" to denote the process of being hailed by an external power. You may suppose that it is better, all other things being equal, to be a "subject" than to be an "object." But this common usage of the term smuggles into language the confusing assumption that subjects always possess agency and objects always lack it. When feminists critique the objectification of women or antiracists critique the stereotyping of people of color, they do not always rely on the liberal humanism that privileges subjects over objects. Scholars have begun to question the underlying assumptions regarding subjective agency and even to argue that it is distributed more broadly and unpredictably across "subjects" and "objects" than we may expect (J. Bennett 2010). They have asked how and in what ways objects also resist (Moten 2003). And they have shown how the norms that the subject cites can be subverted through the very act of citation, which can expose their natural self-evidence as a fiction (Butler 1990).

If objectification is a problem, subjectification is no straightforward solution. It may be better understood as a beneficial harm or poisonous cure since the results of subjectification are indeterminate and ambiguous with regard to the goals of greater agency and more capacious identity (Derrida 1981). Foucault illustrates this point through the powerful example of modern sexuality. Most modern subjects feel themselves to possess an innate sexuality and sexual orientation. The struggle for women's rights and lesbian, gay, bisexual, transgender, and queer/questioning (LGBTQ) rights in the United States has been waged, in large part, over this idea of sexuality as central to who we are as subjects, especially as it pertains to the freedom to dispose of one's body as one wills, to enter and exit sexual relationships, to choose to reproduce or not, and to create families and communities of our choosing. Foucault, himself a gay man, certainly supported feminism and LGBTQ rights as political tactics with efficacy in the contemporary historical moment. But he also pointed out that sexuality, seen as an innate or personal "thing" that we discover, accept, and express, is itself a relatively recent invention, not a human invariant. Prior to the nineteenth century, when categories such as "heterosexual" and "homosexual" came into being, both reproductive and nonreproductive sex could be organized quite differently than they are today and could have quite different ramifications for subjectivity (Foucault [1976] 1990). This history should make us particularly suspicious of our conviction that our sexuality is a secret we somehow repress or an orientation we need to speak openly in order to be liberated. Even as the concept of sexual orientation has been a vehicle for the liberation of queer and transgender people, it has also produced new knowledges about subjects that can be dangerous for them (Epstein 1996; Massad 2007). This risk may not lead us to abandon either the use of the term "sexual orientation" or the feeling that we possess one, but it may keep us wary about the ambiguous nature of the concepts we use regarding the subject.

As the example of sexuality indicates, an awareness of these relations of power at work in processes of subjectification can make it tricky to approach history as a narrative in which we progress from coercion to freedom. The trouble is that any narrative about the making of subjects will lack an external point of view from which we speak, since there is no objective standpoint from which we might talk about subjectivity. Put differently, objectivity is one of many ruses through which the relations of power that produce subjectification are sustained (Novick 1988). Rather than narrate history as a process of the gradual liberation of humans from various forms of prejudice and domination, we might want instead to tell a story of the emergence, layering, and gradual erosion of different practices of subject formation. These practices, in turn, reflect different regimes of knowledge-power—that is, different ways of knowing about and managing subjectivity. The resulting tale may not be one of liberation; rather, it may be a *genealogy of the subject* (Foucault 1994). The resulting politics may involve a drive not to "be who we are" but to "refuse who we are." The critical commitment to a genealogical approach to the study of subject formation is important because it immerses us in a critical understanding of how power hails, solicits, empowers, debilitates, chooses, and abandons subjects. Genealogy also calls for our ethical commitment to those who, while historically subjugated, have not vanished but still crowd our consciousness, hungry ghosts if only we would hear (A. Gordon 2008).

Thank you for your attention. This lesson is concluded. You're free to go.

2014

61

Technology

Jentery Sayers

When used today in everyday speech, the keyword "technology" refers primarily to physical devices. Yet this usage was not common until the second half of the twentieth century. During the seventeenth century, "technology" was either a systematic study of the arts or the specific terminology of an art (Casaubon 1612; Bentham 1827; Carlyle 1858). An encyclopedia, dictionary, or publication like *Keywords for American Cultural Studies* would have been called a technology. Related terms such as "tool," "instrument," and "machine" described physical devices (Sutherland 1717; Hanway 1753). In the nineteenth century, "technology" became the practical application of science, a system of methods to execute knowledge (Horne 1825; Raymond Williams [1976] 1983), or a discipline of the "industrial arts" focused on the use of hand and power tools to fabricate objects (G. Wilson 1855; Burton 1864). During the twentieth century, the meaning of "technology" gradually expanded to include both the processes of a system and the physical devices required of that system (D. F. Noble 1977). By midcentury, it was used as a modifier to characterize socioeconomic developments, as in the use of "high technology" or "high tech" to describe complex applications of specialized machines in industrialized economies.

Practitioners of American studies and cultural studies have emphasized technology's social, cultural, and economic dimensions. They have tended to resist complicity with technological determinism (technology as the sole cause of cultural change), technological instrumentalism (technology as value-neutral), technological positivism (technological progress as social progress), and technological essentialism (technology as having some intrinsic nature or essence). In fact, prevalent approaches to technology in American studies and cultural studies are best described as "nonessentialist." The central premise of nonessentialism is that technologies cannot be divorced from the contexts of their production (Ross 1990). American studies and cultural studies approaches begin with the claim that technologies can be made, interpreted, and used in multiple and often contradictory ways (Ihde 1990; Feenberg 1999; Haraway 1985). They share with "constructivist" approaches a focus on how social conditions and meanings shape how people create, perceive, and understand technologies. But they also underscore why technologies are not immaterial concepts. Technologies actively turn this into that (Fuller 2005; Galloway 2006; Gitelman 2006; Bogost 2007; Kirschenbaum 2008). They can, for instance, articulate complex relations between nodes in networks, rendering decisions for people without their awareness or even their consent (Latour 1987; Kittler 1999; Galloway 2004; Aneesh 2006; Chun 2011; Noble 2018). From a nonessentialist perspective, technologies are thus never "extensions" of human beings or human rationality (McLuhan [1964] 2003). They are entanglements involving vulnerabilities too, and they must be understood as material processes, not just products.

To better understand a nonessentialist approach, consider a key moment in the history of technology: the Luddite rebellions that started in Nottingham, England, in 1811. Composed largely of experienced artisans in the hosiery and lace trades, the Luddites broke wide-frame looms—a new technology of the moment—because looms threatened their livelihood by automating their craft and reducing the costs of hosiery and lace production. The rebellions spread beyond Nottingham (to Derby, Yorkshire, and elsewhere) and to other industries (cotton, cropping, and wool). They ultimately failed to stop the proliferation of wide-frame looms, and their legitimacy was undermined by the Luddites' violent attacks on magistrates, merchants, and other townspeople. Yet the rebellions are historically relevant because the Luddites anticipated technology's gradual shift from "the theory and accurate description of useful arts and manufactures" (Zimmermann 1787, iii) to the material application of science in industries such as textile manufacturing. To adapt a metaphor from Karl Marx ([1867] 1976), the Luddites understood how technology was becoming "frozen labor" or, put differently, "work and its values embedded and inscribed in transportable form" (Bowker and Star 1999, 135).

A nonessentialist approach to technologies such as wide-frame looms suggests that machines contributed to the shift toward frozen labor during the nineteenth century, but they were not its sole cause. Instead, machines represented and even enabled forces of industrial capitalism: the rise of factories (L. Klein 2008); the alienation, systemization, and automation of handicraft; the widespread investment in efficiency; and the decrease of human error through scientific management and standardization (F. Taylor [1911] 2010). Nonessentialist approaches also recognize how technology's implications are interpreted differently across settings and populations. For working-class Luddites, the wide-frame loom deskilled craftwork and rendered obsolete various forms of manual labor; for engineers such as Charles Babbage (1832), it pointed toward innovation, heightened productivity, decreased costs, and increased accuracy in manufacturing. Such differing perspectives reproduced asymmetrical relations of class and power.

These class and power differences are important to remember when observing how industrialization corresponded with the formation of technology as an academic discipline during the mid-nineteenth century. At that time, the word began to appear in university names, such as the Massachusetts Institute of Technology, which opened in 1865. As a discipline, technology was associated with the humble and economically useful "industrial arts" rather than the noble and aesthetically useful "fine arts" (G. Wilson 1855). It was also a set of technical skills possessed by an individual: "His technology consists of weaving, cutting canoes, [and] making rude weapons" (Burton 1864, 437). In many universities, such skills were deemed inferior to the mental labor of science and literature. During debates with biologist T. H. Huxley, the nineteenth-century poet and critic Matthew Arnold defined technology as mere "instrument-knowledge" ([1882] 1885, 107), peripheral to culture and the civilizing pursuits of spiritual and intellectual life (Mactavish and Rockwell 2006). Although Huxley and Arnold disagreed about the role that science should play in education, neither considered technology to be a discipline worthy of the ideal university. Weaving, cutting canoes, and making rude weapons were routines delegated to the working class, not the late nineteenth century's educated elite.

The nineteenth-century definition of "technology" as a practical application of science persisted well into the twentieth century, especially through the proliferation of phonography, photography, cinema, radio, and other modes of mechanical reproduction (T. Armstrong 1998). The effects of this proliferation were perceived variously across contexts, but a common question during the first half of the twentieth century was how politics were aestheticized and aesthetics were politicized through technology (Benjamin [1936] 1968). The totalitarian regimes of fascism and Nazism aestheticized their politics through references to technological innovation. They presented automobiles, airplanes, cameras, radios, and typewriters as beautiful objects: symbols of progress, modernity, efficiency, and mastery over nature (Marinetti [1909] 2006; Riefenstahl 1935). Once aestheticized, technologies such as cinema helped mask totalitarian violence through commodity culture and mass distribution, prompting Frankfurt school philosopher Herbert Marcuse to write, "The established technology has become an instrument of destructive politics" ([1964] 2002, 232).

Like the Luddites, Marcuse and other neo-Marxists were critical of the tendency to reify politics and labor through technologies and aesthetics (Horkheimer and Adorno [1944] 2002; Dyer-Witheford 1999). Their response required the politicization of aesthetics through the same modes of mechanical reproduction. For example, early cinema was used for purposes other than formalizing and disseminating totalitarian ideology. It also fostered shared experiences in the theater, the collective witnessing of narratives and moving images, and a better understanding how consciousness and perception are socially produced (Benjamin [1936] 1968; Kracauer [1960] 1997; Hansen 2011). This response did not reduce technology to an instrument of positivism. It instead positioned technology as one cultural form or practice in a complex system of processes and conditions (Williams [1974] 2000). The more practical this system appears, the more determinist it becomes (Postman 1993). In this sense, "practical" is nearly synonymous with a "natural," "intuitive," or "invisible" technology (Heidegger [1977] 1993; Weiser 1991; Norman 1998).

This common affiliation of technology with practicality explains why nonessentialist approaches are central to American studies and cultural studies: they resist the tendency to either give technologies too much authority or relegate people to unconscious consumers, who are incapable of intervening in systems of oppression, extraction, and injustice (Braverman [1974]

1998; D. F. Noble 1995). They also highlight the fact that technology becomes gendered, sexualized, and racialized through its naturalization or routinization. Historically, technology has been coded as masculine (Wajcman 1991; Balsamo 1996; Rodgers 2010), and it has consistently served the interests of ableism, colonialism, whiteness, and cisheteropatriarchy (Haraway 1985; A. Stone 1996; Nakamura 2002, 2008; Sterne 2003; T. Foster 2005; E. Chang 2008; Browne 2010). Technology is therefore not a "cure" or solution to problems. As frozen labor, it is entangled with contexts and conditions, which must also change.

In response to this recognition, some practitioners of American studies and cultural studies encourage a "technoliteracy" influenced by hacking and prototyping (Wark 2004; Hertz 2009; Ratto 2011; Losh 2012; McPherson 2012a). Andrew Ross (1990) defines "technoliteracy" as "a hacker's knowledge, capable of reskilling, and therefore of rewriting the cultural programs and reprogramming the social values that make room for new technologies" (para. 43). Technoliteracy complicates Matthew Arnold's reduction of technology to mere instrument knowledge since it refuses to draw a neat division between devices and values. More important, it intervenes actively in technologies—at the level of systems and applications—as key ingredients in the everyday production of knowledge and culture (Sayers 2018). Thus nonessentialist technoliteracy asks this fundamental question: "Technology, but for whom, by whom, under what assumptions, how, and to what effects?"

Today, many people would assume that interventions in technological processes are accessible to more people than ever before. After all, the internet has been depicted as a decentralized, democratizing, and even immaterial "cyberspace" of radical freedom—a hacker's paradise of do-it-yourself performance and publication

(Gibson 1982; Barlow [1996] 2001; Hayles 1999). But proliferation should not be conflated with access or intervention. As the very word "technology" is subsumed by industry terms such as "iPad," "Twitter," "Droid," and "Facebook," not to mention the ubiquity of verbs such as "Bing," "Zoom," and "Google" (Vaidhyanathan 2011), the values and procedures of high-technology platforms grow increasingly opaque or invisible to most people, who are deemed to be mere "users." On the one hand, strategies for social control and regulation both persist and expand through algorithms, which exceed the knowledge of any given individual (Galloway 2004; Beller 2006; Chun 2006, 2011). On the other hand, people are reimagining the implications of technoliteracy through collaboration, experimental media, social justice, and decolonization (Daniel and Loyer 2007; Juhasz 2011; Anthropy 2012; Cárdenas 2012; Goldberg and Marciano 2012; Women Who Rock 2012; Cong-Huyen 2013; Cushman 2013; Lothian and Phillips 2013).

Collaborative work around technologies allows people to build alternative infrastructures and projects that are difficult (if not impossible) to construct alone (Davidson 2008; Sayers 2011). And experimental media afford multimodal approaches to expression, anchored in not only text but also video, audio, images, code, and visualizations (McPherson 2009). Such expression is central to many social justice and decolonization initiatives that rely on witnessing, interviews, process documentation, community protocols, intercultural dialogue, and participatory action research (Ang and Pothen 2009). These initiatives suggest an exciting and necessary trajectory for American studies and cultural studies, one that invites people to engage the histories and futures of technologies through thinking and doing, critiquing and making, immersion and self-reflexivity.

2014/2020

62

Terror
Junaid Rana

"Terror" is a complex word that refers both to physical violence and to the emotional response produced by that violence. While this dual meaning has persisted for centuries, the term's connotations have shifted in the modern era in relation to the perceived source of such force. In contrast to earlier usages that reference punitive measures of the state, such as political violence and persecution, terror is now used to name threats posed by nonstate actors. Though amplified in the United States after 9/11, this shift began in the context of conflict with militant left and liberation struggles throughout the nineteenth and twentieth centuries, the rearticulation of radicalism with anti-Americanism and terrorism during the 1970s, and the advent of wars on drugs, crime, and terror in recent decades. The result is a notion of terror that is shorthand for an abstract, state-sanctioned war against a multivalent idea (terrorism) and an ambiguous actor (the terrorist). This meaning obscures the history of state violence administered in the United States, and increasingly across the globe, to control and dominate particular populations. As such, the rhetoric of terror narrows the discourse of dissent and debate toward state-sanctioned ideologies and otherwise permissible views, beliefs, and actions.

The origin of this concept of terror is often attributed to revolutionary France in the 1790s. The Jacobin state led by Maximilien Robespierre conceived of terror as a means of enforcing state justice and patriotic duty. Targeting internal and foreign enemies for mass executions by guillotine, the Reign of Terror, as this period of state repression came to be known, created a populist notion of state virtue and public service that imposed a swift and severe form of justice (Robespierre 2007). Of particular importance was the idea that citizen-led policing through surveillance and open persecution expressed one's patriotic duty to the sovereign nation. This development in modern citizenship, along with an emphasis on abstract rights, led Edmund Burke, in his classic of modern conservatism, *Reflections on the Revolution in France* ([1790] 2009), to conclude that revolutionary France would devolve into tyrannical rule and state-imposed violence on its citizens. Replies to this position came from Thomas Paine in his *Rights of Man* (*Oxford English Dictionary Online* 2018) and Mary Wollstonecraft's *A Vindication of the Rights of Man* ([1790] 2009) and *A Vindication of the Rights of Women* ([1792] 2009). Both argued against Burke's promotion of hereditary rights and for individual liberties based in an equal society. The importance of these dueling positions to the debate on relations among terror, liberalism, and modern statecraft continues in the present era.

In the nineteenth and early twentieth centuries, the term "terror" continued to evolve. In Europe, governments associated terror with the strand of revolutionaries identified with anarchism, a varied antiauthoritarian political philosophy that sought to end fascism and, in some cases, to overthrow the state through political violence, including bombings and targeted assassinations. These ideas quickly traveled to North American shores and contributed to a range of radical politics. Key moments in the history of violence involving anarchist struggles in the United States include the 1886 Haymarket affair at a labor demonstration in Chicago, in which a bomb exploded, meant for the police, who then opened fire and wounded over sixty protestors (Avrich 1984; J. Green 2006); the 1901 assassination of President William McKinley; and the 1920 Wall Street bombing by a horse-drawn wagon, considered the precursor to modern car bombing (M. Davis 2007a). In the twentieth century, the convergence of violent militancy with the labor movement led to two periods often referred to as Red Scares in which the US government imposed far-reaching and severe measures of control to prevent the spread of terror. The first, beginning in the 1900s and lasting through the 1920s, targeted alleged anarchist and communist activity, most notably in the infamous raids of Attorney General A. Mitchell Palmer. The second, in the late 1940s and 1950s, was led by Senator Joseph McCarthy, as he attempted to expand and exploit popular fears of communism as a means of discrediting a variety of leftist and progressive political ideologies.

In the second half of the twentieth century, the meaning of "terror" in the United States continued to shift in ways that served to control domestic populations and to shape foreign policy. Richard Nixon's "law and order" platform of the late 1960s took the institutional form in 1972 of the Committee to Combat Terrorism, which sought to purge and eliminate domestic political and ideological opponents (Collins 2002). In the 1970s, terrorist studies took off as an intellectual field, as a special brand of political science and public policy, creating a form of expertise based in public service and political experience (Herman and O'Sullivan 1989). The study of terrorism became a cottage industry, as the same experts who researched and reported on terrorism were largely responsible for crafting US domestic and foreign policy as elected or appointed officials or political lobbyists. Later, in the 1980s, Ronald Reagan expanded this policy approach as part of a battle against foreign and domestic communism and the alleged support of international terrorism, using the term "evil empire" to describe the Soviet Union for the first time in a speech to the National Association of Evangelicals in 1983. Under Reagan, counterterrorism, widespread surveillance, and covert operations increased, as did the power of intelligence experts groomed in the academy and independently funded think tanks.

Over the same period, the sociological and geographical referent of terror began to shift to Islam and the Arab and Muslim world. As many scholars have demonstrated, the discourse of terror is part of an image and information war that is waged through representational meanings and popular consent (Alsultany 2012; W. Mitchell 2011). The association of terrorism with the strategy of targeted hijackings and the Palestinian struggle for self-determination were linked in US mass media and popular culture throughout the 1970s (Said 1981; Shaheen 2001). Associated with a wide array of stereotypes concerning oil and terrorism, these representations positioned the origins of terror as foreign, ignoring domestic and right-wing militant groups in the United States. The gap in policy analysis blindsided government officials and the news media in the 1995 bombing of the federal building in Oklahoma City by Timothy McVeigh, an attack first attributed to Islamic militants rather than domestic groups associated with the white supremacy movement (Linenthal 2001). Since 9/11, terrorism has become inseparable from the idea of Islamic radicalism—a phrasing that combines Islamic militancy with antileft sentiments. This rhetorical strategy resurrects and repurposes the Red Scares of the early and mid-twentieth century, linking radicalism, Islam, and terror. Reminiscent of the McCarthy hearings, the congressional hearings in 2011 launched by Representative Peter King to examine the supposed radicalization of Muslims in the United States epitomize the establishment and widespread reach of Islamophobia (Kumar 2012; Lean 2012; Sheehi 2011).

For all these reasons, popular understandings of terror and terrorism conceal a longer history of state terror in the United States and beyond its borders. The US government has sought to control a wide array of militant organizations on the right and left, including the Communist Party USA, the Ku Klux Klan, the American Nazi Party, and the Nation of Islam, by labeling them terrorists. In relation to these and other organizations, terror is associated with militancy and branded as anti-American and unpatriotic activity. This association neutralizes arguments about inequality and ongoing forms of social and economic violence while making racists equivalent to antiracists. Such governmental scrutiny has overwhelmingly focused on progressive social movements, including antinuclear and environmental groups, the labor movement, queer activists, radical intellectuals, feminist groups, and other liberation struggles and solidarity groups. During the 1960s and 1970s, for example, the Black Panther Party and the American Indian Movement were subjected to forms of surveillance, infiltration, and systematic repression that included alleged murders and assassinations by the FBI's counterintelligence program known as COINTELPRO (Churchill and Vander Wall [1990] 2001). More recently, the tactics and strategies of covert intelligence gathering by local, state, and federal authorities have expanded to focus on Muslims, especially since 9/11; they have also been applied to political groups such as the Occupy movement (Aaronson 2013; Apuzzo and Goldman 2013).

After 9/11, the War on Terror established under the presidency of George W. Bush extended counterintelligence tactics by mobilizing military operations in global wars across the Middle East, Central Asia, and South Asia in places such as Iraq, Afghanistan, and Pakistan while also reinforcing a domestic security apparatus built on an expanded system of policing, surveillance, detention, and deportation (De Genova and Peutz 2010; Shiekh 2011; Rana 2011). The War on Terror draws on previous campaigns of the US government, including the War on

Crime and the War on Drugs, that marked the inner city of the United States and international locations largely in the Global South as racialized sites in need of regulation and control. Despite the popular understanding of terror as a form of destruction by nonstate actors in the contemporary era, modern state violence through overt and covert means overwhelmingly surpasses that of so-called terrorists (Asad 2007). The impact of such violence is apparent in the media representations and emergent social structures associated with the US government and military. Iconic representations such as those of the 2004 Abu Ghraib torture scandal reveal the complex social relations of US imperial discourses (Danner 2004; Eisenman 2007; Puar 2005; Sontag 2003). The image of tortured Iraqis not only represents the horror of dehumanization at the site of carceral subjugation, but also visualizes enemies of the state as racialized bodies and positions them within the social hierarchies of the US nation-state. In the administration of President Barack Obama, the War on Terror intensified through the proliferation of covert intelligence and the use of drone strikes to eliminate so-called terror targets, including US citizens, on foreign soil.

These tactics of the US government follow a history of state control and regulation that employs the terms "terror," "terrorist," and "terrorism" to curb dissent, to manufacture state enemies as terrorists, to obtain popular consent, and to hide state violence while further shifting the meaning of citizenship, fundamental rights, autonomy, and self-determination. Given this complex history, the challenge of critically engaging the concept of terror is to understand how it is deployed and for what purposes, particularly as the right to protest state uses of power become increasingly limited and curtailed.

2014

63

Time

Valerie Rohy

A child can learn to "tell time," but telling time in American studies and cultural studies is anything but simple—not least because time is crucial to the act of telling, the work of narration. The *Oxford English Dictionary* defines "time" tautologically, as "a space or extent of time" and "a system of measuring or reckoning the passage of time." It eventually suggests that "time" can signify a "period or duration," but after a lengthy entry including "time out" and "time after time," the *concept* of time remains unspecified. As these circular definitions indicate, time often seems self-evident—it either needs no explanation or has no explanation, perhaps because its meanings are so prolific and so various.

Scholars in American studies and cultural studies have sought to unpack some of these meanings, starting with the distinction between time understood as a natural phenomenon and time recognized as a social construction. If you have a clock, you can determine how long it takes you to read this page, understanding time as a quantifiable physical reality. But when you reset your clock for daylight saving time, you join a collective, state-sanctioned agreement that what was three o'clock yesterday is four o'clock today. Here time is not an empirical fact but a social fiction, an idea, or a system of ideas. In a very real sense, "all time is social time" (Adam 1990, 45).

The term "temporality" recognizes time as a product of social negotiation that may seem natural or self-evident to those who have internalized its logic and assumptions. This concept has enabled scholars to denaturalize time and to expose the heterogeneous temporalities operating in US culture and beyond: psychic time, historical time, narrative time, reproductive time, hour and day, duration, time as commodity, modernism, memory and nostalgia, anachronism, musical tempos such as syncopation, time and hegemony, sequence, futurity, synchronization, timekeeping technologies, progress and teleology, anticipation, grammatical tenses such as the future anterior, childhood and aging, continuity and discontinuity, belatedness, and retroaction, each with its own ideological burden.

As these diverse temporalities indicate, time itself is subject to time—that is, to alterations brought by changing cultural, economic, and political circumstances. For example, the capitalist commodification of time ("time is money") is a relatively recent development. In a groundbreaking article, the British historian E. P. Thompson traced the eighteenth- and nineteenth-century shift from agrarian, task-oriented time to industrial clock time. Once employers purchased the time of laborers, particularly in factory settings, "time is now currency: it is not passed but spent," and the lesson of how properly to spend this commodity is taught to children at school (E. P. Thompson 1967, 61, 84). Benjamin Franklin's late eighteenth-century autobiography stressed the monetary value of time well spent, offering a daily schedule meant to ensure that "every part" of one's business has "its allotted time" through all "twenty-four hours of the natural day" (1895, 155). That this "natural day" is wholly unnatural—that is, invented and contingent—hardly impedes the commodification of time throughout the United States, from North to South and city to farm.

This temporality was critical to the rise of modern capitalism, in which "time enters into the calculative application of administrative authority" (Giddens 1984, 135). Even the slaveholding, agrarian US South, which might seem exempt from industrial clock time, adopted northern concepts of temporality, not merely in urban wage labor but also in rural slave labor (Mark Smith 1997, 8). Spending time in this way required a standardization of timekeeping, which in turn supported common notions of time as neutral and homogeneous. From the seventeenth century on, new technologies allowed more affordable and more accurate clocks and watches, even as other mechanical innovations changed time on a larger scale. In Great Britain, Greenwich mean time was adopted in 1847 to facilitate railroad schedules, and in the United States, what we now call standard time was instituted, again by the railroads, in 1883 (Bartky 2000).

This regularization of time not only promoted new kinds of social discipline but also produced new forms of national identity, as historian Benedict Anderson argues. Modern nationalism was enabled by the nineteenth-century rise of print culture and organized by what Anderson calls, borrowing from Walter Benjamin, "homogeneous, empty time": a shared sense of standardized, linear temporality and with it a national identity founded on continuous history (1991, 24). In contrast to Anderson, the postcolonial theorist Homi Bhabha suggests that national time is anything but homogeneous; rather, tensions between dominant and minority cultures create a disjunctive "double-time," which sets the "continuist, accumulative temporality" of progress against the nonlinear, recursive temporality that disrupts nationalist histories (1990a, 294). Other responses to Anderson have emphasized the heterogeneity of national time in the nineteenth-century United States, where the plurality of temporalities or ideas about time, including the particular temporality of the feminine domestic sphere, resists national consolidation (Pratt 2010; Thomas Allen 2008).

Time is always political, and its politics extend beyond the nation-state; indeed, matters of time inevitably engage with questions of space. Wai Chi Dimock, for example, argues that accounts of US literature and culture can be limited by the short historical reach attendant on their national scope and proposes instead a larger temporal scale, an awareness of the *longue durée*, or "deep time," that would also expand the boundaries of American studies beyond the borders of the nation (2006, 3–4). While Dimock takes issue with Anderson's monolithic sense of national modernity, the notion that different cultures occupy different temporalities is itself problematic. The rhetoric of racism and colonialism often places the Other outside the time of the observer or outside of time as such. It renders "difference as *distance*," temporal as well as geographical, rather than acknowledging different cultures as coeval—that is, contemporaneous and linked by that temporal commonality (Fabian 2002, 16).

There is danger, then, both in universalizing time and in overparticularizing it. While we cannot assume that different cultures occupy different temporalities, we must also acknowledge that time is not identical for all; at every juncture, diachronic aspects of temporality—changes in time over time—are complicated by synchronic differences among different subjects in a particular moment. As Rita Felski explains, "The peaks and valleys of historical time may appear in very different places, depending on who is looking and whose fortunes are being tracked across centuries" (2000, 2). Like other feminist scholars, she notes the ways in which women's time differs from men's time, from the masculine bias of conventional historical periodization to the distinct rhythms of women's work in the home. Where sexuality is concerned, there is again no universal time. Queer approaches critique the heteronormative timeline of psychic development, which equates maturity with genital, reproductive

sexuality; conventions of narrative temporality and teleology; and historicist methods that cordon off past from present. Alternatively, Lee Edelman (2004) exposes reproductive futurism, in which homosexuality seemingly threatens to foreclose futurity by replacing temporal progress with an unproductive force of monstrous repetition.

If time itself changes over time, so too do its representations, not least in accounts of the past. The rise of historicist methodologies in American studies and cultural studies over the past quarter century has been challenged by poststructuralist and postmodern views of history. The latter approaches not only recognize time as heterogeneous; they also resist totalizing metanarratives, claims of "objective" mastery, and the very possibility of a stable, positivist historical knowledge. Instead, we find accounts of US culture that acknowledge the contingency of "history" and underscore the plurality of past and present. One such account is Jonathan Goldberg's (1995) reading of the temporality invoked by Thomas Harriot's chronicle of Virginia and other colonial discourses in the Americas, which strangely combine recounting the past and predicting the future, the history that is yet to come.

There is a certain irony, therefore, in any effort to historicize time, for history is always a construction of yesterday in today's terms; its chronology can only be anachronistic because it is relational, the past of a particular present. In a well-known argument, Fredric Jameson describes this postmodern insight as a "crisis in historicity": if modernity means linear, continuous time, postmodernity is the loss of that temporality (1991, 71). Yet he does so in classically historical terms, accepting the Marxist model of linear, teleological time and presuming the knowable facticity of the past (Hutcheon 2002, 61). The paradox is hardly unique to Jameson. While the project of historicizing time seeks to address the contingency of any chronology, old ideas of time inevitably return within it, reasserting conventional periodization and familiar narratives of sequential change. Indeed, any effort to theorize temporality is marked by its particular era. When Walt Whitman declared in *Leaves of Grass* that "these are really the thoughts of all men in all ages and lands," his claim echoed nineteenth-century notions of universal, homogeneous time despite his effort to transcend his historical moment ([1855] 1965, 45). There is no place outside time from which we can observe time.

2014/2020

64

University
Erin Manning

Maybe you always knew. Your parents presumed you would go to university. They told you often that they were saving for your future. Thinking back, "future" and "university" were one and the same. It was simply expected, and so here you are.

Maybe university felt like it was out of reach. You just don't come from a place where people go to university. As you were growing up, you often heard the arts were a waste of time. Real jobs don't come from literature, or history, or philosophy. But somehow you've arrived here, in a literature department, in studio arts, in philosophy, and you feel caught in between. No one at home really understands what you're up to. They want to know where it will lead.

Maybe growing up, it was a dream. You just couldn't wait to have the opportunity to spend hours reading, learning, exploring. But once you got to university, it was hard to concentrate. Working at night and studying in the early morning before class, you increasingly found you just couldn't take it in. So much of what was being taught was not about you, about your history, about your culture. Still, you persisted. After a while it felt like they weren't teaching you so much as making sure you moved from step to step on a ladder. You don't read for pleasure the way you used to. Maybe that will come back. For now, you mostly try to figure out what the teacher wants you to know.

Maybe no one thought you could do it. You are a classical autistic who types to communicate in language.

You have a lot to say, but not in the way people expect, and in any case, no one expects much from you (Savarese 2017). Or you are DeafBlind. So few in your community have ever completed university—indeed, it took you nineteen years (Clark 2014)! It's not just that accommodations are not there—it's that there is a fundamental lack of imagination as regards facilitation (Manning 2016). "No one believed that a nonspeaking [autistic] could really get into, let alone go to, college" (Savarese 2017). Your body is always considered too complicated, too much, not enough. "University faculty and administrators are not skilled when it comes to thinking about diverse learning styles or needs. In historical terms, the university is built on a model of exclusion, a narrow model, one which suggests quite openly that only certain bodies and minds need apply" (Kuusisto 2019).

The term *universitas*, Latin for university, is defined as "the whole, the universe, the world." This sounds like a great promise, but whose world exactly does the university foster? What modes of existence are facilitated by the knowledge it bestows? What universes are composed?

The promise of the university is often allied to a particular account of democracy: Thomas Jefferson claimed that education was for all, proposing the university as the great equalizer of existence. It's a nice story, but very few women graduated from university in the United States for the first two hundred years of its existence, and full formal inclusion didn't occur until well into the twentieth century. Lucy Sessions, the first black woman to graduate in 1850, was followed by Mary Jane Patterson in 1862, both at Oberlin College. This despite the fact that prior to the Civil Rights Act of 1964, most colleges and universities prohibited African Americans from attending.

And now there is talk of the corporate university—the turn, in the university, toward business interests. Maybe you've noticed it: the focus on "innovation" or "entrepreneurship" or "return on investment" (Williams 2016; Davidson 2017; Murphie 2008). Or you might have heard the university compared to a market (Readings 1997; Bousquet 2008; Newfield 2008, 2016; Massumi 2015)? Maybe you've noticed how tired your professors are. Many may have mentioned that they are not employed by the university on the tenure track. In fact, you now realize that most of your undergraduate degree has been taught by professors who have studied for as long as the others but get paid a third as much or less. Maybe you've noticed that they don't have an office and are always out of breath, running to their next class. You might not have realized that they teach twice or three times more than those on the tenure track. When you ask them for a reference letter, they will tell you, though. Their conditions of overwork do not bestow prestige.

It's February. You're tired of trying to navigate the morass. You want to just have a bit of time to think, but four papers are due. You haven't finished the books yet, but probably you can do some quick scanning. There's just not enough time, and they've changed your shifts at the restaurant.

But there are things you love: you met some great students who have started a reading group. You know you shouldn't add more reading to your already busy schedule, but it's nice to sit with them and get close to the text. You can almost taste the thinking! And you've heard talk about setting up a collective project. Maybe you'll drop that class you're having trouble getting up for. Just focus for a while on the reading and then, when it seems more feasible, get back to the degree.

The Undercommons is the book you've been reading collectively. Here, you've learned about study. Stefano Harney and Fred Moten also call it "black study." Study, as you now understand it, exceeds the frame of the classroom. Study is an occasion for thinking, a sociality in the making: "We enter into the social world of study, which is one in which you start to lose track of your debts and begin to see that the whole point is to lose track of them and just build them in a way that allows for everyone to feel that she or he can contribute or not contribute to being in a space" (Harney and Moten 2013, 109). The more you create occasions for thinking, the clearer it is that study is not limited to the bounds of a given text. Study is the way of entering, the way of being in relation with thought while moving with others: "When I think about the way we use the term 'study,' I think we are committed to the idea that study is what you do with other people. It's talking and walking around with other people, working, dancing, suffering, some irreducible convergence of all three, held under the name of speculative practice" (110).

Now Fred Moten and Stefano Harney's statement that "the only possible relationship to the university is a criminal one" is beginning to make sense (2013, 26). You find yourself returning to this one complex thought: "In the face of these conditions one can only sneak into the university and steal what one can. To abuse its hospitality, to spite its mission, to join its refugee colony, its gypsy encampment, to be in but not of—this is the path of the subversive intellectual in the modern university" (2009, 145).

To steal from the university begins to feel like the only option. Suddenly you want not only to survive but to thrive! It's taking longer to get through the degree, but you're learning! Sites are growing around the thinking. These sites that emerge sporadically, sites that make thinking possible, that feel like a subterranean web, are what Moten and Harney call undercommons, commons operative at the interstices, emergent in the coming into relation. You might think of them as qualitative intensities for thought in the act (Manning and Massumi 2014).

When Moten and Harney admit that the university can be "a place of refuge" but that it "cannot be accepted that the university is a place of enlightenment," they are gesturing toward these emergent undercommons (2013, 26). Your aim is no longer to compete to be part of "the whole, the universe, the world" of the universitas but to imagine worlds into being, to catch them in the making. Gilles Deleuze calls this activity of revaluing value "belief in the world," reminding us that all living carries within itself the germs of what remains unthinkable, that quality of life living itself outside the dimensions of preexisting forms of value (1989, 166). Study attends to these germs of unthinkability not to resolve them but to give them space to grow. Belief in the world is an attunement to the excess that moves through a thinking in the act, to thinking's understory, to life's exquisite ineffability.

Study is changing you. You are thinking a lot about the necessity to know otherwise. An enclave has grown in resistance to all the universitas values.

Sometimes study finds its way into a classroom, and briefly there is a sense of what else a university could do. Might the crafting of undercommons for a thinking in the act decolonize the university? You feel vitalized. Learning begins to carry a sense of scope that moves beyond evaluation. But you worry: Can the colonial institution really move beyond its originary vision (Simpson 2014; Battiste 2013; Coulthard 2014)?

You feel aligned to Robin D. G Kelley when he calls for taking a suspicious stance with respect to any reform of the university. Refusing to situate the university as an "engine of transformation," he asks why we would commit to the reform of what is fundamentally exclusive. Integration is not the answer for Kelley: "The fully racialized social and epistemological architecture upon which the modern university is built cannot be radically transformed by 'simply' adding darker faces, safer spaces, better training, and a curriculum that acknowledges historical and contemporary oppressions" (2016). Inclusion, after all—whether in the name of race, or gender, or disability—assumes a normative center: accommodations remain tethered to existing systems of value (Manning 2018).

Maybe you find yourself drawn to the concept of deschooling and the "deinstitutionalization of value" (Illich 1970). Deschooling, after all, is never a call to stop learning. Quite the opposite: to deschool is to decouple thought from the market of knowledge.

This is what you now know: study does not involve measuring value according to the yardstick of the *universitas*. Study multiplies the thinking in the act that already moves across the interstices where the studying has always already begun. In the amplification of undercommon resistance, what is proposed is not a return. For what resists has never stopped resisting.

2020

65

Whiteness
Lee Bebout

In everyday speech, the word "whiteness" often names an identity, one marking people of European descent and their shared cultural attributes. "Whiteness," then, functions as demographic descriptor: a category to mark on government forms, a means of identifying common ground with others of European ancestry. Used in these ways, "whiteness" is often naturalized and treated as transhistorical. This familiar usage evades the actual history of the term, both as an identity category and as a keyword. Within and beyond the United States, "whiteness" has meant different things at different times since it has been fabricated through the erasure of specific European ethnic heritages and the negation of racialized others (Baldwin 1985; Ignatiev 1995). At least since current understandings of race and ethnicity were established in the 1920s, when a person has claimed whiteness in the United States, it has meant that they need not say that they are not Italian, Irish, or English, but that they *could* trace such a lineage. To say one is white is also to say that one is in no way black, Asian, or mestiza/o. In this way, whiteness both signals and silences a double negation.

As a keyword and critical concept in American studies and cultural studies, "whiteness" has been used by scholars and activists less as an identity category and more as a means of naming everyday systems and cultures of white supremacy. Rather than treating white supremacy as an extreme and aberrant position, embodied in the violence and rhetoric of paramilitary groups and right-wing politicians, critical race scholars and antiracist activists underscore that white supremacy is instantiated in everyday life and identity as an ideology, a discourse, and a set of policies. Whiteness describes the ideology through which people of European descent are positioned as both the norm and the ideal of human life, a position against which others can be measured and found lacking (Mills 1997; Dyer 1997). The discourse of whiteness ranges from the explicit racialist thinking of David Duke and other white supremacists to the subtler rhetorical practices of calling unarmed subjects of police violence "thugs" and using color-blind slogans such as "Blue Lives Matter" (Haney López 2014, 4; Bonilla-Silva 2017). In terms of policy, whiteness has its roots in the enslavement of African peoples, the expropriation of Indigenous lands, and restrictive immigration and naturalization laws, but it can also be found in the legally enforced school and housing segregation of the early to mid-twentieth century and the intergenerational transfer of wealth and school choice initiatives that disproportionately negatively impact families of color today (Lipsitz 2018). In essence, the term "whiteness" makes legible complex systems of ideology, language, and policies that have long produced an identity built upon the double negation of European ethnic heritage and communities of color.

Though the use of the term was not widespread until the late eighteenth century, the prehistory of US whiteness can be traced back to the seventeenth century, the arrival of enslaved Africans, and the emergence of the slave codes. The fear among colonial elites of slave uprisings like those in Barbados and Virginia spurred the creation of slave codes that codified whiteness as a racial identity against blackness; whites regardless of class could marry, own weapons, and travel freely and were afforded other rights, but unfree black people could not.

Since its inception, however, whiteness has expanded who could be counted within its ranks even as it has been constituted by an exclusion of others. During the nineteenth century, virulent anti-Catholic nativists attacked Irish immigrants and Irish Americans, particularly within the eastern US cities. People of Irish descent were cast as nonwhite and compared to black US Americans and other communities of color. By adopting the identity label "white," ethnic European workers in the US aligned themselves with white elites and spurned common cause with black workers (Roediger 2007). In the US Southwest, Mexican Americans also faced the exclusive and expansive dynamics of whiteness. Legally identified as white, Mexican Americans were often socially ascribed a nonwhite status, facing segregated schools and businesses as well as civic disenfranchisement in many parts of the Southwest (García 2009; Gómez 2018). As a legal strategy, Mexican Americans used "whiteness" to identify and lay claim to civil rights goals of equality with Anglo-Americans (García 2009).

Since the first appearance of "white" in US law, the term has been closely related to both "immigration" and "citizenship." The Naturalization Act of 1790 limited naturalized citizenship to "free white persons," thus excluding Indigenous and Asian peoples as well as indentured servants and free blacks. The 1868 ratification of the Fourteenth Amendment opened up birthright citizenship for people of African descent, while subsequent laws and legal findings allowed for birthright citizenship and naturalization for Latin Americans who could claim whiteness via European heritage. However, the meaning of whiteness in immigration law was often under contestation. In 1923, the Supreme Court denied Bhagat Singh's claim to US citizenship on the grounds that he was a "high caste Aryan, of full Indian blood." Singh's claims to citizenship vis-à-vis the label and identity of "white" were rejected and the boundaries of whiteness and citizenship were fortified. It was not until the Immigration Act of 1965 that naturalized citizenship was legally disentangled from claims to whiteness as an identity. Indeed, today the terms "white," "citizen," and "American" are often conflated in US popular and political culture with dangerous and devastating consequences.

In the past four decades, "whiteness" has become a much more frequently used word in academic scholarship. There is even a field of study, "critical whiteness studies," which initially emerged from the black intellectual tradition. Throughout the twentieth century, major black intellectuals such as W. E. B. Du Bois, Ida B. Wells, James Weldon Johnson, and James Baldwin wrote about whiteness as a means of naming, understanding, and contesting enduring systems of racial inequality. During the late 1980s and 1990s, critical whiteness studies exploded in US race scholarship, particularly in the fields of history, literature, philosophy, and media studies. In this scholarship, "whiteness" was often framed in relation to other terms of analysis. Drawing on the work of Du Bois, David Roediger examined how white workers in the nineteenth century received social and psychological benefits—the "wages of whiteness"—by asserting their whiteness against the marginalization of black laborers (2007). Others advanced the term "white privilege" to describe how whiteness was built upon a system of unearned advantages that often went unrecognized by its recipients (McIntosh 1988); deployed whiteness along with "racial contract" to describe an epistemic dysfunction wherein whites may be unable to see the structural inequalities of the racial world their ancestors fashioned and that contemporary whites have maintained (Mills 1997, 18); linked whiteness to the legal category of "property" (Harris 1993; Lipsitz 2018); and excavated the role that whiteness has played in the constitution of literature, culture, and national identity

(Dyer 1997; Morrison 1992). Notably, because critical whiteness studies originated in the black intellectual tradition, some of these scholars relied upon a black/white binary, using "whiteness" to describe primarily an opposition to and a rejection of "blackness."

After this intellectual surge, explicit use of whiteness as a term of analysis briefly receded as other frameworks garnered attention. At the beginning of the third decade of the twenty-first century, whiteness scholarship is experiencing a resurgence, in part due to the ways in which whiteness has returned to the foreground of popular and political culture in the United States. The twenty-first-century rise in Islamophobia, anti-Latinx nativism, and antiblackness (particularly surrounding the election of Barack Obama to the US presidency) coalesced with the creation of online social network communities that spawned more public, widespread interrogations of whiteness, white privilege, systemic racism, and other related concepts. The candidacy and election of Donald J. Trump to the US presidency were also grounded in the rise and articulation of an identity politics defined by the grievances and injuries felt by whites, white nationalism, and campaigns of harassment based on perceived threats to whiteness. This constellation of circumstances has fostered greater mainstream media coverage of whiteness. The *New York Times* is one example. It mentioned "whiteness" 153 times between 2010 and 2014 and 1,745 times between 2015 and 2019, an increase of 1,040 percent. Within American studies and cultural studies, "whiteness" has also experienced a revival through the impact earlier writers have had on a new generation of scholars. In the past fifteen years, the keyword "whiteness" and the analytical possibilities that it opens up have found a strong footing in rhetoric (Ratcliffe 2006; Kennedy, Middleton, Ratcliffe 2017), psychology (Spanierman, Todd, and Anderson 2009; Fryberg and Watts 2010), and education (Castagno 2014; Matias 2016; Cabrera 2018), in addition to the fields within which it took root during the 1990s.

Recognizing that in a multiracial society, whiteness's relationship to various marginalized communities gives it dynamic shape, recent scholarship has explored the keyword "whiteness" and its relationship to communities of color beyond the black/white binary. At the intersection of psychology and Indigenous studies, the term has been used to identify the boost white people receive to their self-image when primed by the imagery of Native peoples as sports mascots (Fryberg and Watts 2010). The field of Chicanx studies offers an even more complex path for interrogating whiteness. Some scholars have illustrated how people of Mexican descent have at times claimed a form of whiteness and belonging in the US through the mythos of Spanish ancestry or legal definitions of the term (Nieto-Phillips 2004; García 2009), while others have demonstrated how popular and political representations of Mexican-descent people are deployed to construct whiteness as coterminous with (Anglo-)Americanness (Bebout 2016). These are but a few exciting trajectories for how the term "whiteness" has propelled scholarship within American studies and cultural studies that demonstrate its emergence from the black intellectual tradition and its movement beyond a black/white binary.

In part because of a shift in disciplinary grounding, recent scholarship has deployed the word "whiteness" to draw attention to previously underrecognized attributes. Some have identified the ways in which whiteness shapes everyday discourse and understandings of race (Bonilla-Silva 2017; Feagin 2013; Hill 2008). These rhetorical and interpretive strategies create a buffer so that white people may be protected from confronting the system of white supremacy that benefits them and is foundational to the identity of whiteness. Others have noted that "white fragility" erupts in emotional outbursts when these strategies fail to insulate them from discomforting truths (DiAngelo 2018) and explored the way oppression and hierarchies can come to be treated as a naturalized good, a move that both relies on the vilification of racialized others and simultaneously legitimizes "white saviorism" that may range from volunteer work to US military intervention (Mills 1997; Martinot 2010). Conflating "whiteness" with "goodness" has allowed many to distance themselves not just from people of color but also from aberrant and abhorrent racists, fashioning themselves as "good white people" (Sullivan 2014) and occluding their participation in systemic racism. Alongside this critique of notions of white goodness, scholars have also theorized articulations of "white victimhood" (Mike King 2017; Bebout 2019). Although this articulation has a long history, "white victimhood" has become a dominant cultural narrative since the late 1970s. White folks are cast as an aggrieved community who are facing the challenges of deindustrialization and reverse discrimination vis-à-vis affirmative action. The discourse of white victimhood and resentment appears in the popular, political media to legitimate anti-immigrant fervor, the support of monuments to white supremacy, and the election of Trump, who ran on a campaign rooted in the belief in widespread white victimization.

At first glance, goodness and victimhood may appear contradictory. How can whiteness be imagined as a heroic and messianic as well as a victimized position? Here one must recognize that whiteness is not a stable identity; "whiteness" refers to a constellation of strategies, often in flux, that works in tandem to maintain power and domination in the guises of normalcy, fairness, and benevolence. One of the key attributes of whiteness is its lability (Carroll 2011). That is, whiteness can change, shift, and emphasize different, seemingly contradictory elements at a moment's notice, depending on the exigency of the situation. US whiteness can support English-only initiatives and, in the next moment, deploy mock Spanish to deride Latinxs in the guise of multicultural inclusion. Whiteness can imagine itself as heroic savior and oppressed victim without seeing the potential of contradiction. For scholars and activists, tremendous power comes from a term that can name and make visible this complex nexus of racial power.

Since its origins in the black intellectual tradition, the term "whiteness" has been used to make legible the everyday practices, ideologies, and identity investments that structure racial inequality to denaturalize the norm. This move is designed to propel white folks to choose between the comfort of oppressing others and the value of racial justice and equity. Whiteness has been key in doing this work because it names this everyday system of white supremacy and makes it recognizable. In the words of Richard Dyer, "Whiteness needs to be made strange" (1997, 10). For George Yancy, this constitutes a gesture that renders the normal visible: "Look, a white!" (2012). Making whiteness legible in this way requires more than pointing out white racial identity. It requires close attention to the practices, ideologies, and identity investments that structure racial inequality vis-à-vis whiteness. While "whiteness," "white privilege," and "white fragility" are now part of the popular lexicon in a way that they were not in the late twentieth century, public discussions rarely go beyond an understanding of whiteness as an identity framework, and critiques of whiteness remain a taboo for mainstream politicians. There is work to be done in maintaining these critiques, and scholars and activists committed to racial justice will need to continue to lead the way.

2020

66

Youth
Sunaina Maira

The keyword "youth" bears a powerful and overdetermined symbolism that has made it both central to cultural studies and potent, if relatively marginal, in American studies. Critical conversations about youth span anthropology, sociology, psychology, education, history, and geography and cross over into interdisciplinary areas such as cultural studies, American studies, feminist studies, queer studies, and ethnic studies. Across these fields, the word "youth" is used in myriad ways, generally as a signifier of a developmental stage, a transition to adulthood, or a moment of socialization into or rejection of social norms. A universalizing notion of youth as a period of development that everyone experiences coexists with a particularized understanding of youth as subjects-in-the-making who are always embedded in specific historical and social contexts. This tension underlies the significance of the keyword and its appearance and disappearance in scholarly and political debates.

The most common definition of "youth" in the United States is a transitional period or stage of development between childhood and adulthood. It is associated with a condition of liminality—an uneasy location between one social space or political status and another. Youth are not yet adults and not quite citizens, so they must be shepherded into proper adulthood and, as they acquire that status, the social order. As such, "youth" is a signifier that is fraught with meaning. Discussions of youth in the United

States tend to be preoccupied with "youth in crisis" (or "youth at risk" of crisis), concerns that young people are particularly susceptible to behaviors and lifestyles deemed criminal, subversive, or radical (Giroux 1996). Media-induced panics about youth—the gang banger, the mass killer, or the "homegrown" terrorist—are generally linked to deeper anxieties about social, political, or economic transformation that are displaced onto young people. Immigrant and second-generation youth are viewed as being caught in a "clash of cultures," neither authentically ethnic nor sufficiently "American" (Maira 2002). A perceived crisis in culture or civilization thus gets projected onto a generational category viewed as being inherently unstable. Youth are perceived by adults as being in need of protection, even when those adults question the social control and surveillance of youth by technologies of classification, policing, and imprisonment. Across the political spectrum, "youth" names an appealing site for narrating particular cultural anxieties and for evading or erasing other social problems.

The cultural construction of youth as in crisis or at risk is embedded in the evolving debate about how, where, and when to study youth. Until the 1960s or 1970s, the word "adolescence" was used much more commonly than "youth" to describe the idea of a transition into adulthood when social identities and political allegiances are formed. In 1904, G. Stanley Hall, a US psychologist and the founding president of the American Psychological Association, published the first study to propose adolescence as a unique period in individual development, laying the groundwork for the now familiar association of youth with a universal developmental trajectory leading to autonomy and individuality. This notion of adolescence as a passage into adulthood was tied to economic and social shifts in the United States that produced the "teenager" and, later, "youth" after World War II. In the 1950s, the emerging leisure industries began to target a marketing niche—"teenagers"—who had new levels of disposable income and were located between compulsory childhood education (ages five to sixteen) and the adult labor force (generally ages twenty and above), helping to consolidate this generational category. New social and material conditions, including extended educational demands, diminishing economic opportunities, and shifts in child bearing and rearing practices, led to a prolongation of adolescence and a deferral of adulthood.

Even as the understanding of adolescence as a universal developmental stage gained traction in mainstream social science and popular culture, more critical approaches stressed the cultural and historical specificity of the concept. The anthropologist Margaret Mead argued persuasively in her pioneering, if controversial, ethnography *Coming of Age in Samoa* ([1928] 1961) that the notion of adolescence as a period of "storm and stress" was a peculiarly Western and US view. At a time when the nature/nurture debate was raging and cultural relativists were challenging racist theories of individual and group development, Mead suggested that adolescence was shaped by culturally distinct views of the relationship of the individual to community, gender, sexuality, and labor. Psychosocial theories, particularly those influenced by the work of Erik Erikson ([1944] 1968), similarly defined adolescence as a period of identity development and the crystallization of ethical and political beliefs, shaped by a culturally specific set of rituals.

This debate about adolescence as a cultural or ideological framework is ongoing in various disciplines. A significant critique of developmental theories of youth was offered by feminist psychologists, such as Carol Gilligan (1982), who focused on the crisis facing white, middle-class girls and argued for a gendered rethinking of US adolescence. Subsequently, Nancy Lesko (2001) argued that adolescence is shaped by a dominant belief in a "civilizing" process for young individuals. She observed that the notion of adolescence emerged from an assumption that the teenage years were the proper age during which to instill in (white) boys a desire for "a particular national and international order," which was their responsibility to uphold (Lesko 2001, 41). The codification of adolescence and, later, youth in the United States has always been intertwined with fears about loss of racial privilege, male dominance, and national unity—the various cultural "crises" that "youth" embody. The compulsion to classify young people's behaviors highlights the ways in which the trope of "youth as transition"—like youth in crisis or at risk—serves as a justification for the surveillance, incarceration, and management of young bodies in modern state systems, through educational, social welfare, labor, military, and prison regimes (Mizen 2002).

The preoccupation with youthful transgression resonates with early twentieth-century research on "deviant" adolescents and young adults by sociologists at the University of Chicago. From the 1920s through the 1950s, ethnographers focused on issues of social status, collective problem solving, and urban subcultures. The "delinquent" behaviors of young people were understood as responses to problems of social (class or racial) status in urban environments (J. Young 1971). The Chicago school paved the way for cultural studies work on youth cultures at the University of Birmingham. These scholars focused on youth at a time of social transition in postwar Britain, drawing on Marxist analyses of culture and resistance by the Frankfurt school and theorists such as Antonio Gramsci to develop youth subculture theory. The Birmingham school's research diverged from earlier studies of adolescence by focusing on the resources that mass culture could provide youth in responding to shifts in labor and leisure patterns (McRobbie and Garber 1976; Willis 1977; Hebdige 1979). This work helped crystallize what could be described as a shift from social science research on "adolescence" to cultural studies scholarship on "youth," youth subcultures, and youth cultures.

Seminal texts, such as Stuart Hall and Tony Jefferson's *Resistance through Rituals: Youth Subcultures in Postwar Britain* (1976), signaled the ambivalent assessment of the politics of youth culture typical of the Birmingham school scholars and their interest in the concept of "resistance," particularly in relation to class. Their analyses suggested that the youth subcultures of the 1960s and '70s, such as mod or punk culture, provided symbolic resolutions to the dilemmas facing the urban working class but also that they were not structural solutions to the crisis of class. Youth had to be situated within the larger economic and social contradictions that these subcultural rituals were invented to address but that they were unable, ultimately, to transform. This subculture theory focused on the production of youth itself, through ethnographic research that interrogated the articulation of class with generation, nation, and gender. The Birmingham school's work has been very influential even as it has been critiqued for overinterpreting subcultural possibilities of "resistance" and focusing primarily on the spectacular cultural practices of white, working-class young men (Gelder and Thornton 1997).

British subcultural theory has informed subsequent work on youth in cultural studies and American studies, much of which has inherited the preoccupation with and ambivalence about youth and resistance. While some of this scholarship in the United States has focused on the representational aspects of youth culture, generally relying on textual rather than ethnographic analysis, there is a growing body of work that has grappled with the politics of gender, sexuality, class, and race in young people's everyday lives. Influential studies such as those by Penelope Eckert (1989) and Douglas Foley (1994) have interrogated the reproduction of social inequalities through schooling, while other research has investigated the contradictory political meanings and spatial dimensions of youth subcultures and of oppositionality (Kelley 1997; LaBennett 2011; T. Rose 1994; Austin and Willard 1998; Skelton and Valentine 1998). Work in cultural studies and American studies has built on the Birmingham school's legacy to explore the work of "youth" as an expression of political crises or cultural anxieties. Catherine Driscoll, for instance, suggests that girlhood and the notion of adolescence in general define "the ideal coherence of the modern subject—individuality, agency, and adult (genital) sexuality" (2002, 53). Driscoll argues that "the role of adolescence . . . as psychosocial crucible for becoming a Subject" is embedded in late modernity and in the narrative of maturing nationalism (50).

The lingering association of youth with liminality and with subjects that are not quite formed means that there are key questions about nationalism, the state, and citizenship that remain unaddressed in relation to youth in American studies. At the same time, there seems to be an easy reaching for the notion of youth in studies of cultural production and consumption. Cultural studies has claimed youth as a key analytic category due to the association of young people with popular culture's—and now digital media's—possibilities and pitfalls in the wake of theories developed by scholars of the Frankfurt, Chicago, and Birmingham schools. Youth signifies both the romance of resistance and the tragedy of consumerist conformity. As such, it names the ambiguity lying between these primary tropes in cultural studies. Recent work on "youthscapes" (Maira and Soep 2005) responds to this ambiguity by integrating an analysis of the material realities and social practices of young people with that of cultural representations of youth. This analysis moves beyond the romantic/tragic binary of resistance/conformity that is so often pinned onto youth. The framework of youthscapes situates youth in relation to debates about transnationalism, the nation-state, and empire. In doing so, it provides an epistemological and methodological intervention in interdisciplinary studies of youth, a category that is not bound to the nation-state and that travels across disciplinary borders.

The simultaneous invisibility and dramatic visibility of young people in both public debates and scholarly work is the key to the puzzle of the appearance and disappearance of the keyword "youth." The developmental narrative of youth as not-yet-adults underlies the assumption that young people are incomplete citizens or social actors. This assumption intensifies the deeper fantasies about and fears of social change or stasis embodied by the specter of youth. The traditional investment of cultural studies in the heuristic of resistance means that youth continue to appear as a site where battles over status quo forms of national culture are fought. Across American studies and cultural studies, the category of youth continues to be central to debates about the making of national subjects, but it should also be considered when discussing crucial questions of rights, belonging, and the remaking of the social order in a globalized world and at a late moment of US empire.

2014

Acknowledgments

A project that spans fourteen years accrues a lot of debts. As we did in previous editions, we want to start out by thanking all our contributors. We rushed them, then we delayed, then we rushed again and brought new contributors on board with very little lead time. The intellectual and pedagogical work this volume does is due to their brilliance but also to their patience with us as we requested revision after revision. Whether you joined the volume in the month before it was completed or have been in it since the 2007 first edition, we thank you.

The idea for this publication emerged, developed, and was tested through interactions with a series of collaborators, interlocutors, and audiences, including the American Cultures workshop at the University of Chicago; the Americanist Workshop at the University of Notre Dame; the Columbia American Studies Seminar; the Simpson Center for the Humanities at the University of Washington; the Clinton Institute at University College Dublin; the Futures of American Studies Institute at Dartmouth College; the Cultural Studies Now Conference at the University of East London; the Mobility Shifts Learning Summit at the New School for Social Research; the Graduate Center at the City University of New York; Evergreen State College; St. John's University; the University of Wisconsin–Milwaukee; Yale University; the University of Ljubljana; and the annual conferences of the American Studies Association, the Cultural Studies Association, and the Modern Language Association, among others.

Thanks to everyone who participated in and attended those events and specifically to Carla Peterson and Sandy Zagarell for sharing their concept early on for a keywords conference panel, to Chandan Reddy and Nikhil Singh for offering advice at various points along the way, and to Kathy Woodward for being a catalyst for the digital aspects of the publication. Generous support for the development of the second and third editions and, especially, their digital components was provided by the Simpson Center for the Humanities at the University of Washington and by the Graduate School of Arts and Sciences, Instructional Technology and Academic Computing, the Office of Research, and the Deans of Arts and Sciences at Fordham University. Thanks also to the University of Washington Whiteley Center for its support of the editing of the third edition through a summer fellowship. What a fabulous place to copyedit!

One thing those institutions funded was the labor of a series of brilliant and efficient graduate students. Brooke Cameron was absolutely central to the production of the first edition, working tirelessly to correspond with contributors, to maintain files on all the essays, to check and recheck bibliographical citations, and to generate an increasingly baroque spreadsheet of deadlines, revisions, and addresses. Liz Porter and then Julia Cosacchi played similar roles in the second edition, tracking a dizzying array of citations across more than ninety essays and putting them in their proper places. Deborah Kimmey was critical to the launch of the first iteration of the *Keywords* website, including the management of the Keywords Collaboratory at the University of Washington. It would not have happened without her. Elizabeth Cornell followed ably in Deborah's place when the Collaboratory moved from the University of Washington to Fordham University and was equally central to its subsequent success and further development.

Speaking of students, one of the reasons we produced *Keywords* in the first place, and even more so the reason we keep updating it, is because we wanted it to be useful in classrooms and needed it for our own courses. For more than a decade now, a series of lively, engaging undergraduates in Fordham's American Studies program and both undergraduates and grad students in the English department have tested out both editions of the volume, as well as individual keyword essays, sometimes in draft form. Of course, *Keywords* is widely taught beyond our own institutions. We hope it is rewarding and useful for all students and their instructors. And we thank everyone who has sent us syllabi, sample assignments, and other materials over the years. You make *Keywords* generative and productive.

Eric Zinner deserves credit for looking at lists of words and names and seeing the idea not for one or two publications but for a growing series. Thanks as well to New York University Press's production team, including Adam Bohannon, Charles Boyd Hames, and Martin Coleman, and to Dolma Ombadykow for all her help. In addition, Jonathan Greenberg and Furqan Sayeed deserve thanks for their work on the *Keywords* website.

Thanks to Nina for putting aside the *Weltchroniken* long enough to let Glenn travel for keywords to faraway places like Slovenia and San Juan Island and to Ezra for providing a great piano soundtrack for the editing process. Thanks to Miriam, whose keyword is still "skill"—though accompanied by "balance," "reciprocity," and "wisdom"—and to Sputnik, whose keyword

is "fluffiness." Thanks, finally, to our readers and users, past and future, who treat the *Keywords for American Cultural Studies* not as summative of work completed but as generative of future projects. You are the reason we undertook it.

References

Aaronson, Trevor. 2013. *The Terror Factory: Inside the FBI's Manufactured War on Terrorism*. Brooklyn, NY: Ig.

Abdel Malek, Anwar. 1963. "Orientalism en crise." *Diogenes* 44:107–8.

Abdo, Genieve. 2006. *Mecca and Main Street: Muslim Life in America after 9/11*. New York: Oxford University Press.

Abel, Elizabeth, ed. 1997. *Female Subjects in Black and White: Race, Psychoanalysis, Feminism*. Berkeley: University of California Press.

Abolition Collective. 2018. *Abolishing Carceral Society*. Vol. 1 of *Abolition: A Journal of Insurgent Politics*. Brooklyn: Common Notions.

Abrams, M. H. 1971. *Natural Supernaturalism: Tradition and Revolution in Romantic Literature*. New York: Norton.

Abu-Lughod, Lila. 1991. "Writing against Culture." In *Recapturing Anthropology: Working in the Present*, edited by Richard G. Fox, 137–62. Santa Fe, NM: School of American Research Press.

ACLU. 2017. "How the Israel Anti-Boycott Act Threatens First Amendment Rights." July 26, 2017. www.aclu.org.

Adam, Barbara. 1990. *Time and Social Theory*. Philadelphia: Temple University Press.

Adamic, Louis. 1940. *From Many Lands*. New York: Harper.

———. 1944. *Nation of Nations*. New York: Harper.

Adams, Abigail. (1776) 1988. "Letter to John Adams, March 31, 1776." In *The Feminist Papers: From Adams to de Beauvoir*, edited by Alice Rossi, 10–11. Boston: Northeastern University Press.

Adams, Katelyn. 2019. "Playing Favorites: Challenging Denials of U.S. Citizenship to Children Born Abroad to U.S. Same-Sex Parents." *Georgetown Law Journal* 107:747–65.

Adams, Rachel. 2001. *Sideshow U.S.A.: Freaks and the American Cultural Imagination*. Chicago: University of Chicago Press.

Adams, Rachel, Benjamin Reiss, and David Serlin. Forthcoming. *Keywords for Disability Studies*. New York: New York University Press.

Adamson, Joni, William Gleason, and David N. Pellow. Forthcoming. *Keywords for Environmental Studies*. New York: New York University Press.

Adler, Les K., and Thomas G. Paterson. 1970. "Red Fascism: The Merger of Nazi Germany and Soviet Russia in the American Image of Totalitarianism 1930s–1950s." *American Historical Review* 75 (4): 1046–64.

Adorno, Theodor. (1970) 1984. *Aesthetic Theory*. Translated by C. Lenhardt. Edited by Gretel Adorno and Rolf Tiedemann. London: Routledge and Kegan Paul.

———. 2001. *The Culture Industry: Selected Essays on Mass Culture*. Edited by J. M. Bernstein. London: Routledge.

Adorno, Theodor, and Max Horkheimer. (1947) 2007. *The Dialectic of Enlightenment: Philosophical Fragments*. Palo Alto, CA: Stanford University Press.

Adorno, Theodor, Else Frenkel-Brunswik, Daniel J. Levinson, and R. Nevitt Sanford. (1950) 1967. *The Authoritarian Personality*. John Wiley and Sons.

African American Policy Forum. 2015. *"Black Girls Matter: Pushed Out, Overpoliced, and Underprotected."* Panel forum, African American Policy Forum, New York.

———. 2019. "Mythbusting Intersectionality." Public forum moderated by Kimberlé Crenshaw, Columbia Law School.

Afzal-Khan, Fawzia, and Kalpana Rahita Seshadri, eds. 2000. *The Pre-occupation of Postcolonial Studies*. Durham, NC: Duke University Press.

Agamben, Giorgio. 1993. *The Coming Community*. Translated by Michael Hardt. Minneapolis: University of Minnesota Press.

———. 1998. *Homo Sacer: Sovereign Power and Bare Life*. Stanford, CA: Stanford University Press.

———. 2005. *State of Exception*. Translated by Kevin Attell. Chicago: University of Chicago Press.

Agarwal, Arun, and K. Sivaramakrisnan. 2003. *Regional Modernities: The Cultural Politics of Development in India*. Stanford, CA: Stanford University Press.

Agnew, Jean-Christophe. 1986. *Worlds Apart: The Market and the Theater in Anglo-American Thought, 1550–1750*. New York: Cambridge University Press.

Ahmad, Aijaz. 1992. *In Theory: Classes, Nations, Literature.* London: Verso.

Ahmed, Sara. 2006. *Queer Phenomenology: Orientations, Objects, Others.* Durham, NC: Duke University Press.

———. 2008. "Open Forum Imaginary Prohibitions: Some Preliminary Remarks on the Founding Gestures of the 'New Materialism.'" *European Journal of Women's Studies* 15 (1): 23–39.

Ahuja, Neel. 2015. "Intimate Atmospheres: Queer Theory in a Time of Extinctions." *GLQ* 21 (2–3): 365–85.

———. 2016. *Bioinsecurities: Disease Interventions, Empire, and the Government of Species.* Durham, NC: Duke University Press.

Akcigit, Ufuk, and Sina T. Ates. 2019. "What Happened to U.S. Business Dynamism?" Working Paper 25756, National Bureau of Economic Research. www.nber.org.

Alaimo, Stacy. 2016. *Exposed: Environmental Pleasures and Politics in Posthuman Times.* Minneapolis: University of Minnesota Press.

Alarcón, Norma. 1996. "Anzaldúa's *Frontera*: Inscribing Gynetics." In *Displacement, Diaspora, and Geographies of Identity,* edited by Smadar Lavie and Ted Sweedenburg, 41–54. Durham, NC: Duke University Press.

Albert, Michael. 2003. *Parecon: Life after Capitalism.* New York: Verso.

"Alcatraz Reclaimed." (1970) 1971. *Newsletter of the Indian Tribes of All Nations.* Reprinted in *Chronicles of American Indian Protest,* edited by Council on Interracial Books for Children. Greenwich, CT: Fawcett.

Alcoff, Linda Martín. 2000. "Who's Afraid of Identity Politics?" In *Reclaiming Identity: Realist Theory and the Predicament of Postmodernism,* edited by Paula M. L. Moya and Michael Hames-García, 312–44. Berkeley: University of California Press.

Alemán, Jesse. 2006. "The Other Country: Mexico, the United States, and the Gothic History of Conquest." *American Literary History* 18 (3): 406–26.

Alexander, J. Robert. 1981. *The Right Opposition: The Lovestoneites and the International Communist Opposition of the 1930s.* Westport, CT: Greenwood.

Alexander, M. Jacqui. 1991. "Redrafting Morality: The Postcolonial State and the Sexual Offences Bill of Trinidad and Tobago." In *Third World Women and the Politics of Feminism,* edited by Chandra Talpade Mohanty, Ann Russo, and Lourdes Torres, 133–52. Bloomington: Indiana University Press.

———. 1994. "Not Just Any Body Can Be a Citizen." *Feminist Review* 48:5–23.

———. 2005. *Pedagogies of Crossings: Meditations on Feminism, Sexual Politics, Memory, and the Sacred.* Durham, NC: Duke University Press.

Alexander, M. Jacqui, and Chandra Talpade Mohanty, eds. 1997. *Feminist Genealogies, Colonial Legacies, Democratic Futures.* New York: Routledge.

Alexander, Michelle. 2010. *The New Jim Crow: Mass Incarceration in the Age of Colorblindness.* New York: New Press.

Alexander-Floyd, Nikol G. 2012. "Disappearing Acts: Reclaiming Intersectionality in the Social Sciences in a Post–Black Feminist Era." *Feminist Formations* 24 (1): 1–25.

Ali, Omar. 2010. *In the Lion's Mouth: Black Populism in the New South, 1886–1900.* Jackson: University Press of Mississippi.

Allen, Chadwick. 2002. *Blood Narrative: Indigenous Identity in American Indian and Maori Literary and Activist Texts.* Durham, NC: Duke University Press.

———. 2012. *Trans-indigenous: Methodologies for Global Native Literary Studies.* Minneapolis: University of Minnesota Press.

Allen, Francis. 1981. *The Decline of the Rehabilitative Ideal: Penal Policy and Social Purpose.* New Haven: Yale University Press.

Allen, Theodore. 1994. *The Invention of the White Race.* Vol. 1, *Racial Oppression and Social Control.* London: Verso.

Allen, Thomas M. 2008. *A Republic in Time: Temporality and Social Imagination in Nineteenth-Century America.* Chapel Hill: University of North Carolina Press.

Alperovitz, Gar. 2011. *America beyond Capitalism: Reclaiming Our Wealth, Our Liberty, and Our Democracy.* 2nd ed. Boston: Democracy Collaborative Press and Dollars and Sense.

Alsultany, Evelyn. 2012. *Arabs and Muslims in the Media: Race and Representation after 9/11.* New York: New York University Press.

Althusser, Louis. (1971) 2001. "Ideology and Ideological State Apparatuses." In *Lenin and Philosophy and Other Essays,* 85–126. New York: Monthly Review Press.

Alvarez, Robert R., Jr. 2005. *Mangos, Chiles, and Truckers: The Business of Transnationalism.* Minneapolis: University of Minnesota Press.

Amariglio, Jack, and Antonio Callari. 1993. "Marxian Value Theory and the Problem of the Subject: The Role of Commodity Fetishism." In *Fetishism as Cultural Discourse,* edited by Emily Apter and William Pietz, 186–216. Ithaca, NY: Cornell University Press.

Ambrose, Stephen E. 1984. *Eisenhower, the President.* Vol. 2. New York: Simon & Schuster.

American Studies Association. 2013. "ASA National Council Votes Unanimously to Endorse Academic Boycott of Israel." Accessed September 30, 2018. http://theasa.net.

——. 2016. "A Statement by the Council of the American Studies Association." Accessed September 30, 2018. http://theasa.net.

Amin, Samir. 1976. *Unequal Development: An Essay on the Social Formations of Peripheral Capitalism*. Translated by Brian Pearce. New York: Monthly Review Press.

——. 1997. *Capitalism in the Age of Globalization: The Management of Contemporary Society*. London: Zed Books.

——. 2014. *Capitalism in the Age of Globalization: The Management of Contemporary Society*. 2nd ed. London: Zed.

Ammerman, David. 1974. *In the Common Cause: American Response to the Coercive Acts of 1774*. Charlottesville: University of Virginia Press.

Amnesty International. 2013. "Nelson Mandela 1918–2013." December 5, 2013. www.amnesty.org.

Amory, Hugh, and David D. Hall. 2000. *The Colonial Book in the Atlantic World*. Cambridge: Cambridge University Press.

Amott, Teresa, and Julie Matthaei. 1996. *Race, Gender, and Work: A Multi-cultural Economic History of Women in the United States*. Rev. ed. Boston: South End.

Andersen, Margaret. 2003. "Whitewashing Race: A Critical Perspective on Whiteness." In *White Out: The Continuing Significance of Racism*, edited by Ashley Doane and Eduardo Bonilla-Silva, 21–34. New York: Routledge.

Anderson, Benedict. 1983. *Imagined Communities: Reflections on the Origin and Spread of Nationalism*. London: Verso.

——. 1991. *Imagined Communities: Reflections on the Origin and Spread of Nationalism*. Rev. ed. London: Verso.

Anderson, Reynaldo, and Charles E. Jones. 2016. *The Rise of Astro-Blackness*. Lanham, MD: Lexington Books.

Anderson, Warwick. 2006. *Colonial Pathologies: American Tropical Medicine, Race, and Hygiene in the Philippines*. Durham, NC: Duke University Press.

Andrews, Lori B. 2012. *I Know Who You Are and I Saw What You Did: Social Networks and the Death of Privacy*. New York: Free Press.

Aneesh, A. 2006. *Virtual Migration: The Programming of Globalization*. Durham, NC: Duke University Press.

Ang, Ien. 2006. "From Cultural Studies to Cultural Research: Engaged Scholarship in the 21st Century." *Cultural Studies Review* 12 (2).

Ang, Ien, and Nayantara Pothen. 2009. "Between Promise and Practice: Web 2.0, Intercultural Dialogue and Digital Scholarship." *Fibreculture Journal* 14. http://fourteen.fibreculturejournal.org.

Angwin, Julia, Jeff Larson, Surya Mattu, and Lauren Kirchner. 2016. "Machine Bias." *ProPublica*, May 23, 2016. www.propublica.org.

Anonymous. 1579. *Of Cyvile and Uncyvile Life: A Discourse Where Is Disputed What Order of Lyfe Best Beseemeth a Gentleman*. London: S.T.C. 15589.

——. 1820. *Zelica, the Creole, a Novel by an American*. 3 vols. London: William Fearman.

Anthropy, Anna. 2012. *Rise of the Videogame Zinesters: How Freaks, Normals, Amateurs, Artists, Dreamers, Drop-Outs, Queers, Housewives, and People like You Are Taking Back an Art Form*. New York: Seven Stories.

Anti-Eviction Mapping Project. 2018. www.antievictionmap.com.

Anzaldúa, Gloria. 1987. *Borderlands / La Frontera: The New Mestiza*. San Francisco: Spinsters / Aunt Lute Books.

——. 1998. "To(o) Queer the Writer—Loca, escritora y chicana." In *Living Chicana Theory*, edited by Carla Trujillo, 263–76. Berkeley: University of California Press.

——. 1999. *Borderlands / La Frontera: The New Mestiza*. Rev. ed. New York: Aunt Lute Books.

Anzillotti, Eillie. 2018. "For Young People, Socialism Is Now More Popular Than Capitalism." *Fast Company*, August 13, 2018. www.fastcompany.com.

Aparicio, Frances R. 1998. *Listening to Salsa: Gender, Latin Popular Music, and Puerto Rican Cultures*. Hanover, NH: University Press of New England.

——. 2003. "Latino Cultural Studies." In *Critical Latin American and Latino Studies*, edited by Juan Poblete, 3–31. Minneapolis: University of Minnesota Press.

Apess, William. (1833) 1992. "The Experiences of Five Christian Indians" ["An Indian's Looking-Glass for the White Man"]. In *On Our Own Ground: The Complete Writings of William Apess, a Pequot*, edited by Barry O'Connell, 117–62. Amherst: University of Massachusetts Press.

——. (1836) 1992. "Eulogy on King Philip, as Pronounced at the Odeon, in Federal Street, Boston." In *On Our Own Ground: The Complete Writings of William Apess, a Pequot*, edited by Barry O'Connell, 275–310. Amherst: University of Massachusetts Press.

Appadurai, Arjun. 1996. *Modernity at Large: Cultural Dimensions of Globalization*. Minneapolis: University of Minnesota Press.

Appleby, Joyce. 1992. *Liberalism and Republicanism in the Historical Imagination*. Cambridge, MA: Harvard University Press.

Apuzzo, Matt, and Adam Goldman. 2013. *Enemies Within: Inside the NYPD's Secret Spying Unit and Bin Laden's Final Plot against America*. New York: Touchstone.

Aranda, José. 2016. "When Archives Collide: Recovering Modernity in Early Mexican American Literature." In *The Latino Nineteenth Century: Archival Encounters in American*

Literary History, edited by Rodrigo Lazo and Jesse Alemán, 146–67. New York: New York University Press.

Arendell, Telory Davies. 2015. *The Autistic Stage: How Cognitive Disability Changed 20th-Century Performance Paperback*. New Milford, CT: Sense.

Arendt, Hannah. (1950) 1973. *The Origins of Totalitarianism*. New York: Mariner Books.

———. 1951. "The Decline of the Nation-State and the End of the Rights of Man." In *The Origins of Totalitarianism*, 341–84. New York: Schocken Books.

———. (1963) 2006. *Eichmann in Jerusalem: A Report on the Banality of Evil*. New York: Penguin.

Aristide, Jean-Bertrand. 2001. "Ten Commandments of Democracy in Haiti." In *Theories of Democracy: A Reader*, edited by Ronald J. Terchek and Thomas C. Conte, 308–14. Boston: Rowman & Littlefield.

Armstrong, David F., William C. Stokoe, and Sherman E. Wilcox. 1995. *Gesture and the Nature of Language*. Cambridge: Cambridge University Press.

Armstrong, Elisabeth, and Vijay Prashad. 2005. "Solidarity: War Rites and Women's Rights." *CR: The Centennial Review* 5 (1): 213–53.

Armstrong, Karen. 2002. *Islam: A Short History*. Rev. ed. New York: Modern Library.

Armstrong, Tim. 1998. *Modernism, Technology, and the Body: A Cultural Study*. Cambridge: Cambridge University Press.

Arnold, Matthew. (1869) 1994. *Culture and Anarchy*. Edited by Samuel Lipman. New Haven: Yale University Press.

———. (1882) 1885. "Literature and Science." In *Discourses in America*, 72–137. London: Macmillan.

Aronowitz, Stanley. 1974. *False Promises: The Shaping of American Working Class Consciousness*. New York: McGraw-Hill.

———. 2003. *How Class Works: Power and Social Movement*. New Haven: Yale University Press.

Arrhenius, Svante. 1896. "On the Influence of Carbonic Acid in the Air upon the Temperature of the Ground." *Philosophical Magazine and Journal of Science* 5 (41): 237–76.

Arrighi, Giovanni. 1994. *The Long Twentieth Century: Money, Power and the Origins of Our Times*. London: Verso.

———. 2009. "The Winding Paths of Capital: Interview by David Harvey." *New Left Review* 56:61–94.

Asad, Talal. 1993. *Genealogies of Religion: Discipline and Reasons of Power in Christianity and Islam*. Baltimore: Johns Hopkins University Press.

———. 2003. *Formations of the Secular: Christianity, Islam, Modernity*. Stanford, CA: Stanford University Press.

———. 2007. *On Suicide Bombing*. New York: Columbia University Press.

Asante, Molefi. 1987. *Afrocentric Idea*. Philadelphia: Temple University Press.

Asch, Adrienne, and Michelle Fine, eds. 1988. *Women with Disabilities: Essays in Psychology, Culture, and Politics*. Philadelphia: Temple University Press.

Asch, Adrienne, and Erik Parens, eds. 2000. *Prenatal Testing and Disability Rights*. Washington, DC: Georgetown University Press.

Ashcroft, Bill, Gareth Griffiths, and Helen Tiffin. 1989. *The Empire Writes Back: Theory and Practice in Post-colonial Literatures*. London: Routledge.

Asher, R. E., and J. M. Y. Simpson, eds. 1994. *The Encyclopedia of Language and Linguistics*. 10 vols. New York: Pergamon.

Atanasoski, Neda. 2013. *Humanitarian Violence: The U.S. Deployment of Diversity*. Minneapolis: University of Minnesota Press.

Atanasoski, Neda, and Kalindi Vora. 2019. *Surrogate Humanity: Race, Technoliberalism, and the Engineering of Contested Futures*. Durham, NC: Duke University Press.

Attali, Jacques. 1985. *Noise: The Political Economy of Music*. Minneapolis: University of Minnesota Press.

Aufderheidi, Patricia, and Peter Jaszi. 2011. *Reclaiming Fair Use: How to Put Balance Back in Copyright*. Chicago: University of Chicago Press.

Ausick, Paul. 2019. "Student Debt Repayment Is Completely Different for White and Black Americans." *USA Today*, July 30, 2019.

Austin, J. L. 1962. *How to Do Things with Words*. Cambridge, MA: Harvard University Press.

Austin, Joe, and Michael Willard, eds. 1998. *Generations of Youth: Youth Cultures and History in Twentieth-Century America*. New York: New York University Press.

Avrich, Paul. 1984. *The Haymarket Tragedy*. Princeton, NJ: Princeton University Press.

Babbage, Charles. 1832. *On the Economy of Machinery and Manufactures*. Philadelphia: Carey and Lea.

Bacevich, Andrew. 2006. *The New American Militarism: How Americans Are Seduced by War*. New York: Oxford University Press.

Bahng, Aimee. 2017. *Migrant Futures: Decolonizing Speculation in Financial Times*. Durham, NC: Duke University Press.

Bailey, Beth. 1999. *Sex in the Heartland*. Cambridge, MA: Harvard University Press.

Bailey, Peter. 2004. "Breaking the Sound Barrier." In *Hearing History: A Reader*, edited by Mark M. Smith, 23–35. Athens: University of Georgia Press.

Baird, Karen L., ed. 2009. *Beyond Reproduction: Women's Health, Activism, and Public Policy*. Madison, NJ: Fairleigh Dickinson University Press.

Baird, Robert. 2000. "Late Secularism." *Social Text* 64 (18:3): 123–36.

Baker, Houston, Jr. 1986. "Belief, Theory, and Blues: Notes for a Post-structuralist Criticism of Afro-American Literature." In *Belief vs. Theory in Black American Literary Criticism*, edited by Joe Weixlmann and Chester J. Fontenot, 5–30. Greenwood, FL: Penkeville.

———. 1987a. "In Dubious Battle." *New Literary History* 18:363–69.

———. 1987b. *Modernism and the Harlem Renaissance*. Chicago: University of Chicago Press.

Baker, Houston, Jr., Manthia Diawara, and Ruth Lindeborg. 1996. *Black British Cultural Studies: A Reader*. Chicago: University of Chicago Press.

Baldwin, Davarian L. 2007. *Chicago's New Negroes: Modernity, the Great Migration, and Black Urban Life*. Chapel Hill: University of North Carolina Press.

Baldwin, James. 1985. *The Price of the Ticket: Non-Fiction 1948–1985*. New York: St. Martin's.

Bale, Jeffrey. 2004. "National Revolutionary Groupuscules and the Resurgence of 'Left Wing' Fascism: The Case of France's Nouvelle Resistance." In *Fascism: Critical Concepts in Political Science*, edited by Roger Griffin with Matthew Feldman, 267–94. Vol. 5. Routledge.

Balibar, Etienne. 1994. *Masses, Classes, Ideas: Studies on Politics and Philosophy before and after Marx*. New York: Routledge.

Balsamo, Anne. 1996. *Technologies of the Gendered Body: Reading Cyborg Women*. Durham, NC: Duke University Press.

Baltzly, Vaughn Bryan. 2014. "Two Models of Disestablished Marriage." *Public Affairs Quarterly* 28 (1): 41–69.

Bamberger, Bill, and Cathy N. Davidson. 1999. *Closing: The Life and Death of an American Factory*. New York: Norton.

Banta, Martha. 1987. *Imaging American Women: Idea and Ideals in Cultural History*. New York: Columbia University Press.

Baptist, Edward E. 2002. *Creating an Old South: Middle Florida's Plantation Frontier before the Civil War*. Chapel Hill: University of North Carolina Press.

———. 2014. *The Half Has Never Been Told: Slavery and the Making of American Capitalism*. New York: Basic Books.

Baraka, Amiri. 1999. *The LeRoi Jones / Amiri Baraka Reader*. New York: Basic Books.

Barghouti, Omar. 2011. *Boycott, Divestment, Sanctions: The Global Struggle for Palestinian Rights*. Chicago: Haymarket Books.

Barker, Joanne. 2008. "Gender, Sovereignty, Rights: Native Women's Activism against Social Inequality and Violence in Canada." *American Quarterly* 60 (2): 259–66.

Barlow, Joel. (1807) 2006. *The Columbiad: A Poem*. Michigan Historical Reprint Series. Ann Arbor: Scholarly Publishing Office, University of Michigan Library.

Barlow, John Perry. (1996) 2001. "A Declaration of the Independence of Cyberspace." In *Crypto Anarchy, Cyberstates, and Pirate Utopias*, edited by Peter Ludlow, 27–30. Cambridge: MIT Press.

Barnes, Elizabeth. 1997. *States of Sympathy: Seduction and Democracy in the American Novel*. New York: Columbia University Press.

Bar-On, Tamir. 2007. *Where Have All the Fascists Gone?* London: Ashgate.

Baron-Cohen, Simon. 2003. *The Essential Difference: The Truth about the Male and Female Brain*. New York: Basic Books.

Barot, Rohit, and John Bird. 2001. "Racialization: The Genealogy and Critique of a Concept." *Ethnic and Racial Studies* 24 (4): 601–18.

Barr, Marleen, ed. 1981. *Future Females: A Critical Anthology*. Bowling Green, OH: Bowling Green University Press.

———. 2000. *Future Females, the Next Generation: New Voices and Velocities in Feminist Science Fiction*. Lanham, MD: Rowman & Littlefield.

Barrett, Michèle, and Mary McIntosh. 1982. *The Anti-social Family*. London: Verso.

Bartelson, Jens. 2001. *The Critique of the State*. Cambridge: Cambridge University Press.

Bartha, Miriam, and Bruce Burgett. 2014. "Why Public Scholarship Matters for Graduate Education." In *Pedagogy: Critical Approaches to Teaching Language, Literature, Composition, and Culture*, 31–43. Vol. 15.1. Duke University Press.

Barthes, Roland. 1977. "Rhetoric of the Image." In *Image, Music, Text*, edited and translated by Stephen Heath, 32–51. New York: Hill and Wang.

Bartky, Ian R. 2000. *Selling the True Time: Nineteenth-Century Timekeeping in America*. Stanford, CA: Stanford University Press.

Bassichis, Morgan, Alexander Lee, and Dean Spade. 2011. "Building an Abolitionist Trans and Queer Movement with Everything We've Got." In *Captive Genders: Trans Embodiment and the Prison Industrial Complex*, edited by Nat Smith and Eric Stanley, 15–40. Oakland, CA: AK.

Battiste, Marie. 2004. "Print Culture and Decolonizing the University: Indigenizing the Page: Part 1." In *The Future of the Page*, edited by Peter Stoicheff and Andrew Taylor, 111–23. Toronto: University of Toronto Press.

———. 2013. *Decolonizing Education: Nourishing the Learning Spirit*. Saskatoon, Canada: Purich.

Battle-Baptiste, Whitney, and Brit Russert. 2018. *Du Bois's*

Data Portraits: Visualizing Black America. Princeton, NJ: Princeton University Press.

Baucom, Ian. 2005. *Specters of the Atlantic World: Finance Capital, Slavery, and the Philosophy of History*. Durham, NC: Duke University Press.

Baudrillard, Jean. 1994. *Simulacra and Simulation*. Translated by Sheila Faria Glaser. Ann Arbor: University of Michigan Press.

Bauer, Ralph. 2014. "Writing as 'Khipu.'" In *Colonial Mediascapes: Sensory Worlds of the Early Americas*, edited by Matt Cohen and J. Glover, 325–56. Lincoln: University of Nebraska Press.

Baum, L. Frank. 1890. "Editorial." *Aberdeen Saturday Pioneer*, December 20, 1890.

Bauman, H-Dirksen L., ed. 2007. *Open Your Eyes: Deaf Studies Talking*. Minneapolis: University of Minnesota Press.

Bayer, Patrick, and Kerwin Kofi Charles. 2016. "Divergent Paths: Structural Change, Economic Rank, and the Evolution of Black-White Earnings Differences, 1940–2014." Working Paper 22797, National Bureau of Economic Research. www.nber.org.

Baym, Nina. 1985. "Melodramas of Beset Manhood." In *The New Feminist Criticism: Essays on Women, Literature, and Theory*, edited by Elaine Showalter, 63–80. New York: Pantheon.

Baynton, Douglas. 1998. *Forbidden Signs: American Culture and the Campaign against Sign Language*. Chicago: University of Chicago Press.

———. 2016. *Defectives in the Land: Disability and Immigration in the Age of Eugenics*. Chicago: University of Chicago Press.

Bayoumi, Moustafa. 2008. *How Does It Feel to Be a Problem? Being Young and Arab in America*. New York: Penguin.

———. 2016. *This Muslim American Life*. New York: New York University Press.

Beal, Frances M. 1969. *Black Women's Manifesto; Double Jeopardy: To Be Black and Female*. New York: Third World Women's Alliance.

Beaumont, Gustave de. (1835) 1958. *Marie, or Slavery in the United States*. Translated by Barbara Chapman. Baltimore: Johns Hopkins University Press.

Bebout, Lee. 2011. *Mythohistorical Interventions: The Chicano Movement and Its Legacies*. Minneapolis: University of Minnesota Press.

———. 2016. *Whiteness on the Border: Mapping the US Racial Imagination in Brown in White*. New York: New York University Press.

———. 2019. "Weaponizing Victimhood: Discourses of Oppression and the Maintenance of Supremacy on the Right." In *News on the Right: Studying Conservative News Cultures*, edited by Anthony Nadler and A. J. Bauer, 64–83. Oxford: Oxford University Press.

Beck, Scott H., and Kenneth, J. Mijeski. 2000. "Indigena Self-Identity in Ecuador and the Rejection of Mestizaje." *Latin American Research Review* 35 (1): 119–37.

Beck, Ulrich. 1992. *Risk Society: Towards a New Modernity*. London: Sage.

Becker, Carl. 1932. *The Heavenly City of the Eighteenth-Century Philosophers*. New Haven: Yale University Press.

Beckert, S. 2014. *Empire of Cotton: A Global History*. New York: Knopf.

Bederman, Gail. 1995. *Manliness and Civilization: A Cultural History of Gender and Race in the United States, 1880–1917*. Chicago: University of Chicago Press.

Beecher, Catherine. 1841. *A Treatise on Domestic Economy for the Use of Young Ladies at Home and at School*. Boston: Marsh, Capen, Lyon, and Webb.

Beecher, Catherine, and Harriet Beecher Stowe. 1869. *The American Woman's Home; or, Principles of Domestic Science*. New York: J. B. Ford.

Beiner, Ronald. 2018. *Dangerous Minds: Nietzsche, Heidegger, and the Return of the Far Right*. Philadelphia: University of Pennsylvania Press.

Bell, Daniel, ed. 1955. *The New American Right*. New York: Criterion.

———. 1960. *The End of Ideology: On the Exhaustion of Political Ideas in the Fifties*. Glencoe, IL: Free Press.

Bellah, Robert. 1970. *Beyond Belief: Essays on Religion in a Posttraditional World*. Berkeley: University of California Press.

———. 1975. *The Broken Covenant: American Civil Religion in Time of Trial*. New York: Seabury.

Bellah, Robert, Richard Madsen, William M. Sullivan, Ann Swidler, and Steven M. Tipton. 1985. *Habits of the Heart: Individualism and Commitment in American Life*. New York: Harper & Row.

Beller, Jonathan. 2006. *The Cinematic Mode of Production: Attention Economy and the Society of the Spectacle*. Lebanon, NH: Dartmouth University Press.

Bellion, Wendy. 2011. *Citizen Spectator: Art, Illusion, and Visual Perception in Early National America*. Chapel Hill: University of North Carolina Press.

Beltrán, Cristina. 2010. *The Trouble with Unity: Latino Politics and the Creation of Identity*. Oxford: Oxford University Press.

Bender, Thomas. 1978. *Community and Social Change in America*. Baltimore: Johns Hopkins University Press.

———, ed. 1992. *The Antislavery Debate: Capitalism and Abolition as a Problem in Historical Interpretation*. Berkeley: University of California Press.

Benedict, Ruth. 1934. *Patterns of Culture*. Boston: Houghton.

Benjamin, Ruha. 2019. *Race after Technology: Abolitionist Tools for the New Jim Code*. New York: Polity.

Benjamin, Walter. (1936) 1968. "The Work of Art in the Age of Mechanical Reproduction." In *Illuminations: Essays and Reflections*, edited by Hannah Arendt, translated by Harry Zohn, 217–51. New York: Schocken Books.

———. (1950) 1968. "Theses on the Philosophy of History." In *Illuminations: Essays and Reflections*, edited by Hannah Arendt, translated by Harry Zohn, 253–66. New York: Schocken Books.

———. 1968. *Illuminations: Essays and Reflections*. Edited by Hannah Arendt. Translated by Harry Zohn. New York: Schocken Books.

———. 1998. *Understanding Brecht*. Translated by Anna Bostock. London: Verso.

Bennett, Dan. 2016. "If Skills Are the New Canon, Are Colleges Teaching Them?" *Chronicle of Higher Education*, April 3, 2016.

Bennett, Jane. 2010. *Vibrant Matter: A Political Ecology of Things*. Durham, NC: Duke University Press.

Bennett, Tony. 1992. "Putting Policy into Cultural Studies." In *Cultural Studies*, edited by Cary Nelson, Paula Treichler, and Lawrence Grossberg, 23–37. New York: Routledge.

———. 1995. *The Birth of the Museum: History, Theory, and Politics*. London: Routledge.

Bennett, Tony, Lawrence Grossberg, and Meaghan Morris, eds. 2005. *New Keywords: A Revised Vocabulary of Culture and Society*. Oxford, UK: Blackwell.

Ben-Sasson, Haim Hillel. 1971. "Galut." In *Encyclopaedia Judaica*, edited by Cecil Roth and Geoffrey Wigoder, 275–94. Vol. 7. Jerusalem: Encyclopaedia Judaica.

Bensel, Richard Franklin. 2000. *The Political Economy of American Industrialization, 1877–1900*. New York: Cambridge University Press.

Benston, Kimberly. 2000. *Performing Blackness: Enactments of African-American Modernism*. New York: Routledge.

Bentham, Jeremy. 1827. *Rationale of Judicial Evidence: Specially Applied to English Practice*. London: Hunt and Clarke.

Bercovitch, Sacvan. 1993. *The Rites of Assent: Transformations in the Symbolic Construction of America*. New York: Routledge.

Bercovitch, Sacvan, and Myra Jehlen, eds. 1986. *Ideology and Classic American Literature*. Cambridge: Cambridge University Press.

Berestein, Leslie. 2005. "Border Desert Nearing Grim Record." *San Diego Union-Tribune*, August 10, 2005.

Berger, John. 1972. *Ways of Seeing*. London: British Broadcasting Corporation / Penguin.

———. 2006. "We Must Speak Out." *Guardian*, December 15, 2006. http://theguardian.com.

Berger, Peter. 1963. "A Market Model for the Analysis of Ecumenicity." *Social Research* 30 (1): 77–93.

———. 1969. *The Sacred Canopy*. Garden City, NY: Doubleday.

Berger, Peter, and Thomas Luckmann. 1966. *The Social Construction of Reality*. New York: Doubleday.

Bergman, Jill, and Debra Bernardi, eds. 2005. *Our Sisters' Keepers: Nineteenth-Century Benevolence Literature by American Women*. Tuscaloosa: University of Alabama Press.

Berkhofer, Robert, Jr. 1979. *The White Man's Indian: Images of the American Indian from Columbus to the Present*. New York: Vintage Books.

Berlant, Lauren, ed. 1991. *The Anatomy of National Fantasy: Hawthorne, Utopia, and Everyday Life*. Chicago: University of Chicago Press.

———. 1997. *The Queen of America Goes to Washington City: Essays on Sex and Citizenship*. Durham, NC: Duke University Press.

———. 2002. "Uncle Sam Needs a Wife: Citizenship and Denegation." In *Materializing Democracy: Toward a Revitalized Cultural Politics*, edited by Dana D. Nelson and Russ Castronovo, 144–74. Durham, NC: Duke University Press.

———. 2004. *Compassion: The Culture and Politics of an Emotion*. New York: Routledge.

———. 2008. *The Female Complaint: The Unfinished Business of Sentimentality in American Culture*. Durham, NC: Duke University Press.

———. 2011. *Cruel Optimism*. Durham, NC: Duke University Press.

Berlant, Lauren, and Lee Edelman. 2013. *Sex, or the Unbearable*. Durham, NC: Duke University Press.

Berlant, Lauren, and Jordan Greenwald. 2012. "Affect in the End Times: A Conversation with Lauren Berlant." *Qui Parle* 20 (2): 71–89.

Berlant, Lauren, and Michael Warner. 1995. "What Does Queer Theory Teach Us about X?" *PMLA* 110 (3): 343–49.

———. 1998. "Sex in Public." *Critical Inquiry* 24 (2): 547–66.

———. 2000. *Intimacy*. Chicago: University of Chicago Press.

Berle, Adolf A., and Gardiner C. Means. 1932. *The Modern Corporation and Private Property*. New York: Macmillan.

Berlet, Chip. 2016. "Populism Is a Core Element of Fascism." Political Research Associates. www.politicalresearch.org.

Berlet, Chip, and Matthew Lyons. 2000. *Right-Wing Populism in America: Too Close for Comfort*. Boston: Guilford.

Berlin, Ira. 1998. *Many Thousands Gone: The First Two Centuries of Slavery in North America*. Cambridge, MA: Harvard University Press.

Berman, Jacob Rama. 2012. *American Arabesque: Arabs, Islam, and the 19th-Century Imaginary*. New York: New York University Press.

Bernabé, Jean, et al. 1990. "In Praise of Creoleness." Translated by Mohamed B. Taleb Khyar. *Callaloo* 3 (4): 886–909.

Bernal, Martin. 1995. "Greece: Aryan or Mediterranean? Two Contending Historiographical Models." In *Enduring Western Civilization: The Constructions of the Concept of Western Civilization and Its "Others,"* edited by Silvia Federici, 3–11. Westport, CT: Praeger.

Bernardin, Susan, and Krista Comer. 2018. "Introduction: Pasts, Presents, Futures." Edited by Krista Comer and Susan Bernardin. *On the Occasion of the 50th Anniversary of the Western Literature Association*. Special issue, *Western American Literature* 53 (1): xi–xix.

———. 2007. "The Authenticity Game: 'Getting Real' in Contemporary American Indian Literature." In *True West: Authenticity and the American West*, edited by William R. Handley and Nathaniel Lewis, 155–78. Lincoln: University of Nebraska Press.

Bernstein, Robin. 2011. *Racial Innocence: Performing American Childhood from Slavery to Civil Rights*. New York: New York University Press.

Berthele, Raphael. 2000. "Translating African American Vernacular English into German: The Problem of 'Jim' in Mark Twain's *Huckleberry Finn*." *Journal of Sociolinguistics* 4 (4): 588–613.

Bethman, Brenda, and C. Shaun Longstreet. 2013. "The Alt-Ac Track." Inside Higher Ed. www.insidehighered.com.

Bettie, Julie. 2003. *Women without Class: Girls, Race, and Identity*. Berkeley: University of California Press.

Bevacqua, Maria. 2000. *Rape on the Public Agenda: Feminism and the Politics of Sexual Assault*. Boston: Northeastern University Press.

Bhabha, Homi K. 1983. "The Other Question . . . Homi K. Bhabha Reconsiders the Stereotype and Colonial Discourse." *Screen* 24 (6): 18–36.

———. 1990a. "DissemiNation: Time, Narrative, and the Margins of the Modern Nation." In *Nation and Narration*, edited by Homi K. Bhabha, 291–322. New York: Routledge.

———. 1990b. "Introduction: Narrating the Nation." In *Nation and Narration*, edited by Homi K. Bhabha, 1–7. New York: Routledge.

———. 1994. *The Location of Culture*. New York: Routledge.

Bhagwati, Jagdish. 2003. *Free Trade Today*. Princeton, NJ: Princeton University Press.

Bhargava, Rajeev, ed. 1998. *Secularism and Its Critics*. Delhi: Oxford University Press.

Bierce, Ambrose. 1911. *Devil's Dictionary*. New York: Albert and Charles Boni.

Bijsterveld, Karin. 2008. *Mechanical Sound: Technology, Culture, and Public Problems of Noise in the Twentieth Century*. Cambridge: MIT Press.

Bilefsky, Dan. 2011. "For New Life, Blacks in City Head South." *New York Times*, June 21, 2011.

Binkey, Sam. 2007. "Governmentality and Lifestyle Studies." *Sociology Compass* 1 (1): 111–26.

Birkerts, Sven. 1994. *The Gutenberg Elegies: The Fate of Reading in an Electronic Age*. New York: Fawcett Columbine.

Black, Edwin. 2003. *War against the Weak: Eugenics and America's Campaign to Create a Master Race*. Berkeley, CA: Four Walls Eight Windows.

Blackburn, Robin. 1988. *The Overthrow of Colonial Slavery*. London: Verso.

Black Hawk. (1833) 2008. *Life of Black Hawk, or Ma-ka-tai-me-she-kia-kiak: Dictated by Himself*. New York: Penguin.

Blackhawk, Ned. 2006. *Violence over the Land: Indians and Empires in the Early American West*. Boston: Harvard.

Blackmon, Douglas A. 2008. *Slavery by Another Name: The Reenslavement of Black Americans from the Civil War to World War II*. New York: Doubleday.

Blackstone, William. (1765–69) 1979. *Commentaries on the Laws of England*. Vol. 1, *1765–69*. Chicago: University of Chicago Press.

Blackwell, Maylei. 2011. *Chicana Power! Contested Histories of Feminism in the Chicano Movement*. Austin: University of Texas Press.

Blanc, Louis. 1839. "The Organization of Labour." Available in part at www.fordham.edu.

Bledstein, Burton. 1976. *The Culture of Professionalism: The Middle Class and the Development of Higher Education in America*. New York: Norton.

Blee, Kathleen. 1992. *Women of the Klan: Racism and Gender in the 1920s*. Berkeley: University of California Press.

Bleichmar, Daniela, and Barbara E. Mundy. 2013. "Vistas: Visual Culture in Spanish America, 1520–1820." Smith College. www.smith.edu.

Blencowe, Claire. 2010. "Foucault's and Arendt's 'Insider View' of Biopolitics: A Critique of Agamben." *History of the Human Sciences* 23 (5): 113–30.

Blight, David W., and Robert Gooding-Williams. 1997. "The Strange Meaning of Being Black: Du Bois's American Tragedy." Introduction to *The Souls of Black Folk*, by W. E. B. Du Bois, edited by David W. Blight and Robert Gooding-Williams, 1–30. New York: Bedford Books.

Blumenberg, Hans. 1983. *The Legitimacy of the Modern Age*. Translated by Robert M. Wallace. Cambridge: MIT Press.

Blumin, Stuart M. 1989. *The Emergence of the Middle Class: Social Experience in the American City, 1760–1900*. New York: Cambridge University Press.

Blyden, Edward W. (1887) 1967. *Christianity, Islam and the Negro Race*. Edinburgh: Edinburgh University Press.

Boas, Franz. 1911. *The Mind of Primitive Man*. New York: Macmillan.

———. 1928. *Anthropology and Modern Life*. New York: Norton.

———. 1940. *Race, Language, and Culture*. New York: Macmillan.

Bogdan, Robert. 1988. *Freak Show: Presenting Human Oddities for Amusement and Profit*. Chicago: University of Chicago Press.

Boggs, Abigail, Eli Meyerhoff, Nick Mitchell, and Zach Schwartz-Weinstein. 2019. "Abolitionist University Studies: An Invitation." Abolition University. https://abolition.university.

Boggs, Colleen. 2013. *Animalia Americana: Animal Representations and Biopolitical Subjectivity*. New York: Columbia University Press.

Bogost, Ian. 2007. *Persuasive Games: The Expressive Power of Videogames*. Cambridge: MIT Press.

Bogues, Anthony. 2003. *Black Heretics, Black Prophets: Radical Political Intellectuals*. New York: Routledge.

Boime, Albert. 1991. *The Magisterial Gaze: Manifest Destiny and the American Landscape Painting, c. 1830–1865*. Washington, DC: Smithsonian Institution Press.

Bolton, Herbert Eugene. 1921. *The Spanish Borderlands: A Chronicle of Old Florida and the Southwest*. New Haven: Yale University Press.

Bonczar, Thomas P. 2003. *Prevalence of Imprisonment in the US Population, 1974–2001*. NCJ197976. Washington, DC: US Department of Justice, Bureau of Justice Statistics.

Bonilla, Yarimar. 2017. "Unsettling Sovereignty." *Cultural Anthropology* 32 (3): 330–39.

Bonilla-Silva, Eduardo. 2003. *Racism without Racists: Color-Blind Racism and the Persistence of Racial Inequality in the United States*. Lanham, MD: Rowman & Littlefield.

———. 2017. *Racism without Racists: Color-Blind Racism and Racial Inequality in Contemporary America*. 5th ed. New York: Rowman & Littlefield.

Bonneuil, C., and J. Fressoz. 2015. *The Shock of the Anthropocene*. New York: Verso.

Bonus, Rick. 2000. *Locating Filipino Americans: Ethnicity and Cultural Politics of Space*. Philadelphia: Temple University Press.

Boon, Marcus. 2010. *In Praise of Copying*. Cambridge, MA: Harvard University Press.

Borgman, Christine L. 2015. *Big Data, Little Data, No Data: Scholarship in the Networked World*. Cambridge: MIT Press.

Boris, Eileen. 1993. "Beyond Dichotomy: Recent Books in North American Women's Labor History." *Journal of Women's History* 4 (3): 162–79.

Bornstein, Kate. 1994. *Gender Outlaw: On Men, Women, and the Rest of Us*. New York: Routledge.

Borsuk, Amaranth, and Brad Bouse. 2016. *Between Page and Screen*. Denver: SpringGun.

Borsuk, Amaranth, Kate Durbin, and Ian Hatcher. 2015. *Abra: A Living Text*. Center for Book and Paper Arts. iOS 8.0 or later.

Bosniak, Linda. 1998. "The Citizenship of Aliens." *Social Text*, no. 56, 29–35.

Boston Women's Health Book Collective. 1973. *Our Bodies, Ourselves*. New York: Simon & Schuster.

———. 1976. *Our Bodies, Ourselves*. Rev. ed. New York: Simon & Schuster.

———. 1996. *The New Our Bodies, Ourselves*. New York: Simon & Schuster.

Bourdieu, Pierre. 1973. "Cultural Reproduction and Social Reproduction." In *Knowledge, Education, and Cultural Change: Papers in the Sociology of Education*, edited by Richard K. Brown, 71–84. London: Tavistock.

———. 1977. *Outline of a Theory of Practice*. Cambridge: Cambridge University Press.

———. 1987. *Distinction: A Social Critique of the Judgment of Taste*. Cambridge, MA: Harvard University Press.

Bourne, Randolph. 1916. "Trans-national America." *Atlantic Monthly* 118:86–97.

Bousquet, Marc. 2008. *How the University Works: Higher Education and the Low-Wage Nation*. New York: New York University Press.

———. 2009. "Take Your Ritalin and Shut Up." *South Atlantic Quarterly* 1084:623–49.

Bowker, Geoffrey. 2005. *Memory Practices in the Sciences*. Cambridge: MIT Press.

Bowker, Geoffrey C., and Susan Leigh Star. 1999. *Sorting Things Out: Classification and Its Consequences*. Cambridge: MIT Press.

Bowlby, Rachel. 1995. "Domestication." In *Feminism beside Itself*, edited by Diane Elam and Robyn Wiegman, 71–92. New York: Routledge.

Boyarin, Jonathan, and Daniel Boyarin. 2002. *Powers of Diaspora: Two Essays on the Relevance of Jewish Culture*. Minneapolis: University of Minnesota Press.

Boyce Davies, Carole, and Babacar M'Bow. 2007. "Towards African Diaspora Citizenship: Politicizing an Existing Global

Geography." In *Black Geographies and the Politics of Place*, edited by Katherine McKittrick and Clyde Woods, 14–45. Boston: South End.

Boydston, Jeanne. 1990. *Home and Work: Housework, Wages, and the Ideology of Labor in the Early Republic*. New York: Oxford University Press.

Boyle, James. 2010. *The Public Domain: Enclosing the Commons of the Mind*. New Haven: Yale University Press.

Boyle, Mary-Ellen, and Ira Silver. 2005. "Poverty, Partnerships, Elite Institutions and Community Empowerment." *City and Community* 4 (3).

Boyte, Harry. 2018. *Awakening Democracy through Public Work: Pedagogies of Empowerment*. Nashville: Vanderbilt University Press.

Bradley, Mark Philip. 2016. *The World Reimagined: Americans and Human Rights in the Twentieth Century*. New York: Cambridge University Press.

Brady, Erika. 2009. *A Spiral Way: How the Phonograph Changed Ethnography*. Jackson: University Press of Mississippi.

Brady, Mary Pat. 2000. "The Fungibility of Borders." *Nepantla: Views from South* 1 (1): 171–90.

———. 2002. *Extinct Lands, Temporal Geographies: Chicana Literature and the Urgency of Space*. Durham, NC: Duke University Press.

Brake, Elizabeth. 2012. *Minimizing Marriage: Marriage, Morality, and the Law*. New York: Oxford University Press.

Bramen, Carrie Tirado. 2001. *The Uses of Variety: Modern Americanism and the Quest for National Distinctiveness*. Cambridge, MA: Harvard University Press.

Branham, Robert J. 1996. "'Of Thee I Sing': Contesting 'America.'" *American Quarterly* 48 (4): 623–52.

Brathwaite, Edward Kamau. 1971. *The Development of Creole Society in Jamaica*. Oxford University Press.

Bratich, Jack Z., Jeremy Packer, and Cameron McCarthy, eds. 2003. *Foucault, Cultural Studies, and Governmentality*. Albany: State University of New York Press.

Braudel, Fernand. (1981–84) 1992. *Civilization and Capitalism*. 3 vols. Translated by Siân Reynold. New York: Harper & Row.

Braverman, Harry. (1974) 1998. *Labor and Monopoly Capital: The Degradation of Work in the Twentieth Century*. Foreword by Paul M. Sweezy. New York: Monthly Review Press.

Bray, Mark. 2017. *Antifa: The Anti-fascist Handbook*. New York: Melville House.

Brecht, Bertolt. (1957) 1992. "On Gestic Music." Reprinted in *Brecht on Theater: The Development of an Aesthetic*, edited and translated by John Willetta, 104–6. New York: Hill and Wang.

Brennan, Denise. 2004. *What's Love Got to Do with It? Transnational Desires and Sex Tourism in the Dominican Republic*. Durham, NC: Duke University Press.

Brenner, Neil. 2004. *New State Spaces: Urban Governance and the Rescaling of Statehood*. New York: Oxford University Press.

Brenner, Robert. 2003. *The Boom and the Bubble: The U.S. in the World Economy*. London: Verso.

Bridenbaugh, Carl. 1963. "AHA Presidential Address, 1962." Reprinted in *American Historical Review*, January 1963. www.historians.org.

Bridges, Khiara M. 2011. *Reproducing Race: An Ethnography of Pregnancy as a Site of Racialization*. Berkeley: University of California Press.

Briffault, Richard. 2012. "Super PACS." Columbia Public Law Research Paper WP 12–298. April 16, 2012.

Briggs, Laura. 2000. "The Race of Hysteria: 'Overcivilization' and the 'Savage' Woman in Late Nineteenth-Century Obstetrics and Gynecology." *American Quarterly* 52 (2): 246–73.

Brisbane, Albert. 1846. "The American Associationists." *United States Magazine, and Democratic Review*, February 1846.

Brodhead, Richard. 1993. *Cultures of Letters: Scenes of Reading and Writing in Nineteenth-Century America*. Chicago: University of Chicago Press.

Brodkin, Karen. 1998. *How Jews Became White Folks and What That Says about America*. New Brunswick, NJ: Rutgers University Press.

Broecker, Walter. 1975. "Climate Change: Are We on the Brink of a Pronounced Global Warming?" *Science* 189:460–63.

Brooks, Daphne. 2006. *Bodies in Dissent: Spectacular Performances of Race and Freedom*. Durham, NC: Duke University Press.

Broome, Richard. 2010. *Aboriginal Australians: A History since 1788*. 4th rev. ed. New York: Allen and Unwin.

Brown, Dona. 1995. *Inventing New England: Regional Tourism in the Nineteenth Century*. Washington, DC: Smithsonian Institution Press.

Brown, Elspeth H., and Thy Phu, eds. 2014. *Feeling Photography*. Durham, NC: Duke University Press.

Brown, Gillian. 1990. *Domestic Individualism: Imagining Self in Nineteenth-Century America*. Berkeley: University of California Press.

———. 2001. *The Consent of the Governed: The Lockean Legacy in Early American Culture*. Cambridge, MA: Harvard University Press.

Brown, Joshua. 2002. *Beyond the Lines: Pictorial Reporting, Everyday Life, and the Crisis of Gilded Age America*. Berkeley: University of California Press.

Brown, Kathleen M. 1996. *Good Wives, Nasty Wenches, and Anxious Patriarchs: Gender, Race, and Power in Colonial Virginia*. Chapel Hill: University of North Carolina Press.

Brown, Kirby. "Sovereignty." *Western American Literature* 53:1, 81–89.

Brown, Michelle. 2005. "'Setting the Conditions' for Abu Ghraib: The Prison Nation Abroad." *American Quarterly* 57 (3): 973–94.

———. 2009. *The Culture of Punishment: Prison, Society, and Spectacle*. New York: New York University Press.

Brown, Wendy. 1995. *States of Injury: Power and Freedom in Late Modernity*. Princeton, NJ: Princeton University Press.

———. 2003. "Neo-liberalism and the End of Liberal Democracy." *Theory and Event* 7 (1): 1–43.

———. 2005. *Edgework: Critical Essays on Knowledge and Politics*. Princeton, NJ: Princeton University Press.

Brown, William Hill. (1789) 1996. *The Power of Sympathy: "The Power of Sympathy" and "The Coquette."* New York: Penguin.

Brown, William Wells. (1847) 1969. "Lecture." In *Four Fugitive Slave Narratives*, 81–98. Reading, MA: Addison-Wesley.

Browne, Simone. 2010. "Digital Epidermalization: Race, Identity and Biometrics." *Critical Sociology* 36:131–50.

Browning, Christopher. 2018. "The Suffocation of Democracy." *New York Review of Books*, October 25, 2018.

Bruce, Steve, and David Voas. 2004. "The Resilience of the Nation-State: Religion and Polities in the Modern Era." *Sociology* 38 (5): 1025–34.

Bruce-Novoa, Juan. 2004. "Twenty Years of Transatlantic Usonianism." In *The United States in Global Contexts: American Studies after 9/11 and Iraq*, edited by Walter Grünzweig, 23. Münster, Germany: LIT.

Brueggemann, Brenda. 2009. *Deaf Subjects: Between Identities and Places*. New York: New York University Press.

Bruyneel, Kevin. 2007. *The Third Space of Sovereignty: The Postcolonial Politics of U.S.-Indigenous Relations*. Minneapolis: University of Minnesota Press.

Bryan, Dick, and Mike Rafferty. 2006. *Capitalism with Derivatives: A Political Economy of Financial Derivatives, Capital and Class*. Basingstoke, UK: Palgrave Macmillan.

Buck-Morss, Susan. 1992. "Aesthetics and Anaesthetics: Walter Benjamin's Artwork Essay Reconsidered." *October* 62:3–41.

Buell, Lawrence. 1995. *The Environmental Imagination: Thoreau, Nature Writing, and the Formation of American Culture*. Cambridge, MA: Harvard University Press.

Buff, Rachel Ida, ed. 2008. *Immigrant Rights in the Shadow of Citizenship*. New York: New York University Press.

Buffon, Georges-Louis Leclerc, Count de. 1749–89. *L'histoire naturelle, générale et particulière, avec la description du cabinet du roi*. 36 vols. Paris: L'Imprimerie Royale.

Buhle, Paul. 1987. *Marxism in the United States: Remapping the History of the American Left*. London: Verso.

Bullard, Robert D. 2000. *Dumping in Dixie: Race, Class, and Environmental Quality*. Routledge.

———. 2002. "Confronting Environmental Racism in the Twenty-First Century." In *The Colors of Nature: Culture, Identity, and the Natural World*, edited by Alison H. Deming and Lauret E. Savoy, 90–97. Minneapolis: Milkweed.

Bullard, Robert, and Beverly Wright. 2009. *Race, Place, and Environmental Justice after Hurricane Katrina: Struggles to Reclaim, Rebuild, and Revitalize New Orleans and the Gulf Coast*. Westview Press.

Bülow-Jacobsen, Adam. 2011. "Writing Materials in the Ancient World." In *Oxford Handbook of Papyrology*. Oxford: Oxford University Press. https://doi.org/10.1093/oxfordhb/9780199843695.013.0001.

Bumiller, Elisabeth. 2002. "Bush, Calling U.S. 'a Nation Guided by Faith,' Urges Freedom of Worship in China." *New York Times*, February 22, 2002. www.nytimes.com.

———. 2003. "After Cheney's Private Hunt, Others Take Their Shots." *New York Times*, December 15, 2003. www.nytimes.com.

Bumiller, Kristin. 2008. *In an Abusive State: How Neoliberalism Appropriated the Feminist Movement against Sexual Violence*. Durham, NC: Duke University Press.

Burawoy, Michael. 1985. *The Politics of Production: Factory Regimes under Capitalism and Socialism*. London: Verso.

Burch, Susan. 2004. *Signs of Resistance: American Deaf Cultural History, 1900 to World War II*. New York: New York University Press.

Bureau of Indian Affairs. "What We Do." Accessed August 16, 2012. www.bia.gov.

Burgett, Bruce. 1998. *Sentimental Bodies: Sex, Gender, and Citizenship in the Early Republic*. Princeton, NJ: Princeton University Press.

———. 2005. "On the Mormon Question: Race, Sex, and Polygamy in the 1850s and the 1990s." *American Quarterly* 57 (1): 75–102.

Burke, Edmund. (1790) 2009. *Reflections on the Revolution in France*. Oxford: Oxford University Press.

Burke, Kenneth. 1957. *The Philosophy of Literary Form*. New York: Vintage.

Burns, W. Haywood. 1982. "Law and Race in Early America." In *The Politics of Law: A Progressive Critique*, edited by David Kairys, 279–84. New York: Basic Books.

Burton, Richard Francis. 1864. *A Mission to Gelele, King of Dahome*. Vol. 2. London: Tinsley Brothers.

Bush, Adam Seth. 2014. "Passing Notes in Class: Listening to Pedagogical Improvisation in Jazz History." PhD diss., University of Southern California. http://digitallibrary.usc.edu.

Bush, George W. 2001a. "An Address to a Joint Session of Congress and the American People." White House Archives. http://georgewbush-whitehouse.archives.gov.

———. 2001b. "President George W. Bush's Inaugural Address." White House Archives. http://georgewbush-whitehouse.archives.gov.

———. 2003. "Remarks by the President on Goree Island, Senegal." White House Archives. http://georgewbush-whitehouse.archives.gov.

Bushman, Richard L. 1992. *The Refinement of America: Persons, Houses, Cities*. New York: Vintage.

Butler, Judith. 1988. "Performative Acts and Gender Constitution: An Essay in Phenomenology and Feminist Theory." *Theater Journal* 40 (4): 519–31.

———. 1990. *Gender Trouble: Feminism and the Subversion of Identity*. New York: Routledge.

———. 1993. *Bodies That Matter: On the Discursive Limits of "Sex."* New York: Routledge.

———. 2000. *Antigone's Claim*. New York: Columbia University Press.

———. 2004a. *Precarious Life: The Powers of Mourning and Violence*. London: Verso.

———. 2004b. *Undoing Gender*. New York: Routledge.

———. 2013. "Interview with Cihan Aksan and Jon Bailes." *Counterpunch*, October 11, 2013. http://counterpunch.org.

———. 2016. "Rethinking Vulnerability and Resistance." In *Vulnerability in Resistance*, edited by Judith Butler et al., 12–27. Durham, NC: Duke University Press.

Butler, Kim. 2001. "Defining Diaspora, Refining a Discourse." *Diaspora* 10 (2): 189–219.

Byrd, Jodi A. 2011. *The Transit of Empire: Indigenous Critiques of Colonialism*. Minneapolis: University of Minnesota Press.

———. 2017. "*Loving* Unbecoming: The Queer Politics of the Transitive Native." In *Critically Sovereign: Indigenous Gender, Sexuality, and Feminist Studies*, edited by Joanne Barker, 207–27. Durham, NC: Duke University Press.

Cabrera, Nolan. 2018. *White Guys on Campus: Racism, White Immunity, and the Myth of "Post-racial" Higher Education*. New Brunswick, NJ: Rutgers University Press.

Cacho, Lisa M. 2012. *Social Death: Racialized Rightlessness and the Criminalization of the Unprotected*. New York: New York University Press.

Cainkar, Louise. 2010. "American Muslims at the Dawn of the 21st Century." In *Muslims in the West after 9/11: Religion, Politics and Law*, edited by Jocelyne Cesari, 176–97. New York: Routledge.

Callison, Candis. 2014. *How Climate Change Comes to Matter: The Communal Life of Facts*. Duke University Press.

Callon, Michel. 1998. *The Laws of the Markets*. Oxford, UK: Blackwell.

Cameron, Sharon. 1992. *Choosing Not Choosing: Dickinson's Fascicles*. Chicago: University of Chicago Press.

Camp, Stephanie. 2003. *Closer to Freedom: Enslaved Women and Everyday Resistance in the Plantation South*. Chapel Hill: University of North Carolina Press.

Campbell, James. 1995. *Songs of Zion: The African Methodist Episcopal Church in the United States and South Africa*. Chapel Hill: University of North Carolina Press.

Campbell, Neil. 2000. *The Cultures of the American New West*. London: Fitzroy.

———. 2008. *The Rhizomatic West: Representing the West in a Transnational, Global, Media Age*. Lincoln: University of Nebraska Press.

———. 2011. "Post-Westerns." In *A Companion to the Literature and Culture of the American West*, edited by Nicolas Witschi, 409–25. London: Blackwell.

———. 2013. *Post-Westerns: Cinema, Region, West*. Lincoln: University of Nebraska Press.

———. 2016. *Affective Critical Regionality: Place, Memory, Affect*. London: Rowman & Littlefield International.

Canguilhem, Georges. (1966) 1989. *The Normal and the Pathological*. Translated by Carolyn R. Fawcett. New York: Zone Books.

Cannizzaro, Danny, and Samantha Gorman. 2014. *Pry*. Tender Claws. iOS 6.0 or later.

Canovan, Margaret. 1981. *Populism*. New York: Houghton Mifflin.

Caplowitz, David. 1967. *The Poor Pay More: Consumer Practices of Low-Income Families*. New York: Free Press.

Carbado, Devon W. 2013. "Colorblind Intersectionality." *Signs* 38 (4): 811–13.

Carby, Hazel. 1987. *Reconstructing Womanhood: The Emergence of the Afro-American Woman Novelist*. New York: Oxford University Press.

Cárdenas, Micha. 2012. *The Transreal: Political Aesthetics of Crossing Realities*. New York: Atropos.

Carey, Henry Charles. 1967. *The Past, the Present, and the Future*. New York: Augustus M. Kelley.

Carlson, Elof Axel. 2001. *The Unfit: A History of a Bad Idea*. Cold Spring Harbor, NY: Cold Spring Harbor Laboratory Press.

Carlyle, Thomas. 1858. *The History of Friedrich II of Prussia, Called Frederick the Great*. Vol. 1. London: Chapman and Hall.

Carmichael, Stokely, and Charles Hamilton. 1967. *Black Power: The Politics of Liberation in America*. New York: Vintage.

Carr, Nicholas. 2013. "Don't Burn Your Books—Print Is Here to Stay." *Wall Street Journal*, January 5, 2013.

Carrera, Magali M. 2003. *Imagining Identity in New Spain*. Austin: University of Texas Press.

Carroll, Hamilton. 2011. *Affirmative Reaction: New Formations of White Masculinity*. New Americanists. Durham, NC: Duke University Press.

Carr-Ruffino, Norma. 1996. *Managing Diversity: People Skills for a Multicultural Workplace*. Upper Saddle River, NJ: Pearson.

Carson, Rachel. 1962. *Silent Spring*. New York: Crest Books.

———. (1962) 2002. *Silent Spring*. New York: Houghton Mifflin Harcourt.

Carter, Dan T. 1995. *The Politics of Rage: George Wallace, the Origins of the New Conservatism, and the Transformation of American Politics*. Baton Rouge: Louisiana State University Press.

———. (1995) 2000. *The Politics of Rage: George Wallace, the Origins of the New Conservatism, and the Transformation of American Politics*. 2nd ed. Baton Rouge: Louisiana State University Press.

Carter, Julian B. 2007. *The Heart of Whiteness: Normal Sexuality and Race in America, 1880–1940*. Durham, NC: Duke University Press.

Carter, Prudence. 2005. *Keepin' It Real: School Success beyond Black and White*. New York: Oxford University Press.

Casaubon, Isaac. 1612. *The Ansvvere of Master Isaac Casaubon to the Epistle of the Most Reuerend Cardinall Peron: Translated out of Latin into English*. London: Felix Kyngston.

Castagno, Angelina E. 2014. *Educated in Whiteness: Good Intentions and Diversity in School*. Minneapolis: University of Minnesota Press.

Castells, Manuel. 2000. *The Rise of Network Society*. Oxford, UK: Blackwell.

Castiglia, Christopher. 2008. *Interior States: Institutional Consciousness and the Inner Life of Democracy in the Antebellum United States*. Durham, NC: Duke University Press.

Castoriadis, Cornelius. 1987. "The Social Imaginary and the Institution." In *The Castoriadis Reader*, edited by David Ames Curtis, 196–217. Oxford, UK: Blackwell.

Castronovo, Russ. 2007. *Beautiful Democracy: Aesthetics and Anarchy in a Global Era*. Chicago: University of Chicago Press.

Cavallo, Guglielmo, and Roger Chartier, eds. 1999. *A History of Reading in the West*. Translated by Lydia G. Cochrane. Amherst: University of Massachusetts Press.

Caves, Richard E. 2000. *Creative Industries: Contracts between Arts and Commerce*. Cambridge, MA: Harvard University Press.

Cavicchi, Daniel. 2011. *Listening and Longing: Music Lovers in the Age of Barnum*. Lebanon, NH: University Press of New England.

Centre for Contemporary Cultural Studies. 1982. *The Empire Strikes Back: Race and Racism in 70s Britain*. London: Taylor and Francis.

Césaire, Aimé. (1950) 2001. *Discourse on Colonialism*. Translated by Joan Pinkham. New York: Monthly Review Press.

Chakkalakal, Tess. 2011. *Novel Bondage: Slavery, Marriage, and Freedom in Nineteenth Century America*. Urbana-Champaign: University of Illinois Press.

Chakrabarty, Dipesh. 2000. *Provincializing Europe: Postcolonial Thought and Historical Difference*. Princeton, NJ: Princeton University Press.

Chambers, Clare. 2017. *Against Marriage: An Egalitarian Defense of the Marriage-Free State*. New York: Oxford University Press.

Chamfort, Sébastien-Roch-Nicolas. 1984. *Products of the Perfected Civilization*. Translated by W. S. Merwin. San Francisco: North Point.

Chan, Jeffrey Paul, and Frank Chin. 1972. "Racist Love." In *Seeing through Schuck*, edited by Richard Kostelanetz, 65–79. New York: Ballantine.

Chandra, Bipan. 1980. "Colonialism, Stages of Colonialism, and the Colonial State." *Journal of Contemporary South Asia* 10 (3): 272–85.

Chang, Edmond Y. 2008. "Gaming as Writing, or, World of Warcraft as World of Wordcraft." *Computers and Composition Online*, August–September 2008. www2.bgsu.edu.

Chang, Grace. 2000. *Disposable Domestics: Immigrant Women Workers in the Global Economy*. Boston: South End.

Chang, Jiat-Hwee. 2016. *A Genealogy of Tropical Architecture: Colonial Networks, Nature, and Technoscience*. New York: Routledge.

Chanlatte, Juste. 1818. *L'Entrée du Roi en sa capitale*. Cap-Henry.

Chapman, Mary, and Glenn Hendler, eds. 1999. *Sentimental Men: Masculinity and the Politics of Affect in American Culture*. Berkeley: University of California Press.

Chappell, David. 2004. *A Stone of Hope: Prophetic Religion and the Death of Jim Crow*. Chapel Hill: University of North Carolina Press.

Charles, Ray. 1972. "America the Beautiful." In *A Message from the People . . . by the People . . . and for the People*. Los Angeles: Tangerine Records.

Chase, Richard. 1949. *Quest for Myth*. Baton Rouge: Louisiana State University Press.

Chateaubriand, François-René de. 1848. *Mémoires d'outre-tombe*. Vol. 1. Philadelphia: Carey and Hart.

Chauncey, George. 1994. *Gay New York: Gender, Urban Culture, and the Making of the Gay Male World, 1890–1940*. New York: Basic Books.

Chavez, Cesar. 1970. "A Conversation with Cesar Chavez." Interview by John Moyer. *Journal of Current Social Issues* 9 (3). http://libraries.ucsd.edu.

Chávez, Karma R. 2013. *Queer Migration Politics: Activist Rhetoric and Coalitional Possibilities*. Urbana: University of Illinois Press.

Chavez, Leo R. 1988. "Settlers and Sojourners: The Case of Mexicans in the United States." *Human Organization* 47 (2): 95–108.

———. 2008. *The Latino Threat: Constructing Immigrants, Citizens, and the Nation*. Stanford, CA: Stanford University Press.

Chen, Mel. 2012. *Animacies: Biopolitics, Racial Mattering, and Queer Affect*. Durham, NC: Duke University Press.

Cheney-Lippold, John. 2017. *We Are Data: Algorithms and the Making of Our Digital Selves*. New York: New York University Press.

Chevigny, Bell Gale, and Gari Laguardia. 1986. Preface to *Reinventing the Americas: Comparative Studies of Literature of the United States and Spanish America*, edited by Bell Gale Chevigny and Gari Laguardia, vii–xiv. New York: Cambridge University Press.

Chicano Coordinating Council on Higher Education. 1969. *El Plan de Santa Bárbara: A Chicano Plan for Higher Education*. Oakland, CA: La Causa.

Chidester, David. 1996. *Savage Systems: Colonialism and Comparative Religion in Southern Africa*. Charlottesville: University of Virginia Press.

Cho, S., K. W. Crenshaw, and L. McCall. 2013. "Toward a Field of Intersectionality Studies: Theory, Applications, and Praxis." *Signs* 38 (4): 785–810.

Cho, Yu-Fang. 2013. *Uncoupling American Empire: Cultural Politics of Deviance and Unequal Difference, 1890–1910*. Albany: State University of New York Press.

Chomsky, Noam. 2005. "The Non-election of 2004." *Z Magazine*, January 2005.

Chomsky, Noam, and Edward S. Herman. 1979. *The Washington Connection and Third World Fascism*. Boston: South End.

Chomsky, Noam, and Robert W. McChesney. 2011. *Profit over People: Neoliberalism and Global Order*. New York: Seven Stories.

Christian, Barbara. 1987. "The Race for Theory." *Cultural Critique* 6:51–63.

Christiansen, John, and Sharon Barnartt. 2002. *Deaf President Now! The 1988 Revolution at Gallaudet University*. Washington, DC: Gallaudet University Press.

Chuh, Kandice. 2003. *Imagine Otherwise: On Asian Americanist Critique*. Durham, NC: Duke University Press.

Chun, Jennifer Jihye, George Lipsitz, and Young Shin. 2013. "Intersectionality as a Social Movement Strategy: Asian Immigrant Women Advocates." *Signs* 38 (4): 917–40.

Chun, Wendy Hui Kyong. 2006. *Control and Freedom: Power and Paranoia in the Age of Fiber Optics*. Cambridge: MIT Press.

———. 2011. *Programmed Visions: Software and Memory*. Cambridge: MIT Press.

Churchill, Ward, and John Vander Wall. (1990) 2001. *The COINTELPRO Papers: Documents from the FBI's Secret Wars against Dissent in the United States*. Boston: South End.

Ciccariello-Maher, George. 2019. "Populism, Universalism, and Democracy in Latin America." In *Oxford Handbook of Comparative Political Theory*, edited by M. Idris, L. Jenco, and M. Thomas, 504–24. Oxford: Oxford University Press.

Clare, Eli. 1999. *Exile and Pride: Disability, Queerness, and Liberation*. Boston: South End.

———. 2017. *Brilliant Imperfection: Grappling with Cure*. Durham, NC: Duke University Press.

Clark, John Lee. 2014. *Where I Stand: On the Signing Community and My Deaf Blind Experience*. Handtype.

Clarke, Cheryl. 1983. "The Failure to Transform: Homophobia in the Black Community." In *Home Girls: A Black Feminist Anthology*, edited by Barbara Smith, 197–208. New York: Kitchen Table / Women of Color.

Clarke, John. 2010. "After Neo-liberalism." *Cultural Studies* 24 (3): 375–94.

Cleaver, Eldridge. 1968. *Soul on Ice*. New York: Laurel.

Clifford, James. 1997. . . . *Routes: Travel and Translation in the Late Twentieth Century*. Cambridge, MA: Harvard University Press.

———. 2000. "Taking Identity Politics Seriously: 'The Contradictory, Stony Ground . . .'" In *Without Guarantees: In Honour of Stuart Hall*, edited by Paul Gilroy, Lawrence Grossberg, and Angela McRobbie, 94–112. New York: Verso.

———. 2001. "Indigenous Articulations." *Contemporary Pacific* 13 (2): 468–90.

Clifford, James, and George Marcus, eds. 1986. *Writing Culture: The Poetics and Politics of Ethnography*. Berkeley: University of California Press.

Clough, Patricia, and Jean Halley, eds. 2007. *The Affective Turn: Theorizing the Social*. Durham, NC: Duke University Press.

Cohen, Cathy J. 1997. "Punks, Bulldaggers, and Welfare

Queens: The Radical Potential of Queer Politics?" *GLQ* 3:437–65.

Cohen, Deborah. 2011. *Braceros: Migrant Citizens and Transnational Subjects in the Postwar United States and Mexico*. Chapel Hill: University of North Carolina Press.

Cohen, Ed. 2009. *A Body Worth Defending: Immunity, Biopolitics, and the Apotheosis of the Modern Body*. Durham, NC: Duke University Press.

Cohen, Jean L. 2002. *Regulating Intimacy: A New Legal Paradigm*. Princeton, NJ: Princeton University Press.

Cohen, Jean L., and Andrew Arato. 1992. *Civil Society and Political Theory*. Cambridge: MIT Press.

Cohen, Jonathan. 2004. "The Naming of America: Fragments We've Shored against Ourselves." Jonathan Cohen's website. www.uhmc.sunysb.edu.

Cohen, Lizabeth. 2003. *A Consumer's Republic: The Politics of Mass Consumption in Postwar America*. New York: Knopf.

Cohen, Matt. 2009. *The Networked Wilderness: Communicating in Early New England*. Minneapolis: University of Minnesota Press.

Cohen, Matt, and Jeffrey Glover, eds. 2014. *Colonial Mediascapes: Sensory Worlds of the Early Americas*. Lincoln: University of Nebraska Press.

Cohen, Patricia Cline. 1982. *A Calculating People: The Spread of Numeracy in Early America*. Chicago: University of Chicago Press.

Cohn, Deborah N. 1999. *History and Memory in the Two Souths: Recent Southern and Spanish American Fiction*. Nashville: Vanderbilt University Press.

Coiner, Constance. 1995. *Better Red: The Writing and Resistance of Tillie Olsen and Meridel Le Sueur*. Urbana: University of Illinois Press.

Coldewey, Devin. 2010. "It's Futurists versus Consumers as the Death of the Book Is Prophesied." *TechCrunch*, August 7, 2010.

Collingwood, R. G. 1971. *The New Leviathan*. New York: Crowell.

Collins, Jane L., Micaela di Leonardo, and Brett Williams, eds. 2008. *New Landscapes of Inequality: Neoliberalism and the Erosion of Democracy in America*. Santa Fe, NM: School of Advanced Research Press.

Collins, John. 2002. "Terrorism." In *Collateral Language: A User's Guide to America's New War*, edited by John Collins and Ross Glover, 155–74. New York: New York University Press.

Collins, M. E. 1993. *History in the Making—Ireland 1868–1966*. Dublin: Educational Company of Ireland.

Collins, Patricia Hill. 2012. *On Intellectual Activism*. Philadelphia: Temple University Press.

Collins, Patricia Hill, and Sirma Bilge. 2016. *Intersectionality*. Cambridge, UK: Polity.

Combahee River Collective. 1983. "The Combahee River Collective Statement." In *Home Girls: A Black Feminist Anthology*, edited by Barbara Smith, 264–74. New York: Kitchen Table / Women of Color.

Comer, Krista. 1999. *Landscapes of the New West: Gender and Geography in Contemporary Women's Writing*. Chapel Hill: University of North Carolina Press.

———. 2010a. "Exceptionalisms, Other Wests, Critical Regionalism." *American Literary History* 23 (1): 159–73.

———. 2010b. *Surfer Girls in the New World Order*. Durham, NC: Duke University Press.

———. 2013. "Introduction: Assessing the Postwestern." *Western American Literature* 48 (1–2): 3–15.

———. 2014. "Thinking Otherwise across Global Wests: Issues of Mobility and Feminist Critical Regionalism." Edited by Aaron Nyerges and Golnar Nabizadeh. PopWest. *Occasion: Interdisciplinary Studies in the Humanities*, no. 10, 1–18. http://arcade.stanford.edu.

———. 2015. "The Problem of the Critical in Global Wests." In *A History of Western American Literature*, edited by Susan Kollin, 205–21. New York: Cambridge University Press.

———. "Place and Worlding: Feminist States of Critical Regionalism." Edited by Ángel Chaparro Sainz and Amaia Ibarraran.

Commager, Henry Steele, ed. 1947. *America in Perspective: The United States through Foreign Eyes*. New York: Random House.

Common Dreams. 2010. Accessed September 30, 2018. http://commondreams.org.

Comte, August. 1858. *The Positive Philosophy of August Comte*. Translated by Harriet Martineau. London: Chapman.

Condé, Maryse. 1998. "Créolité without the Creole Language?" In *Caribbean Creolization: Reflections on the Cultural Dynamics of Language, Literature, and Identity*, translated by Kathleen M. Balutansky, edited by Kathleen M. Balutansky and Mari-Agnès Soureau, 101–9. University Press of Florida.

———. 2013. "Literature and Globalization." *The Encyclopedia of Global Human Migration*, edited by I. Ness. https://doi.org/10.1002/9781444351071.wbeghm34.

Condorcet, Jean-Antoine-Nicolas de Caritat de. 1795. *Esquisse d'un tableau historique des progrès de l'esprit humain*. Paris: Chez Agasse.

Cong-Huyen, Anne. 2013. "'Dark Mass,' or the Problems with Creative Cloud Labor." *E-Media Studies* 3 (1). http://journals.dartmouth.edu.

Conley, Dalton. 1999. *Being Black, Living in the Red: Race,*

Wealth, and Social Policy in America. Berkeley: University of California Press.

Connerton, Paul. 1989. *How Societies Remember.* Cambridge: Cambridge University Press.

Connolly, William. 2000. *Why I Am Not a Secularist.* Minneapolis: University of Minnesota Press.

Consortium of Professional and Academic Associations Condemns Arizona Immigration Law 2010.

Constable, Nicole. 2012. "International Marriage Brokers, Cross-Border Marriages, and the U.S. Anti-trafficking Campaign." *Journal of Ethnic and Migration Studies* 38 (7): 1137–54.

Cooke, Bill, and Uma Kothari. 2001. *Participation the New Tyranny.* Chicago: University of Chicago Press.

Cook-Lynn, Elizabeth. 1996. *Why I Can't Read Wallace Stegner and Other Essays: A Tribal Voice.* Madison: University of Wisconsin Press.

Coombe, Rosemary. 1998. *The Cultural Life of Intellectual Properties: Authorship, Appropriation, and the Law.* Cambridge, MA: Harvard University Press.

Coontz, Stephanie. 1988. *The Social Origins of Private Life: A History of American Families, 1600–1900.* New York: Verso.

———. 1992. *The Way We Never Were: American Families and the Nostalgia Trap.* New York: Basic Books.

———. 1998. *The Way We Really Are: Coming to Terms with America's Changing Families.* New York: Basic Books.

———. 2006. *Marriage, a History: How Love Conquered Marriage.* New York: Penguin Books.

Cooper, Anna Julia. 1998. *The Voice of Anna Julia Cooper: Including a Voice from the South and Other Important Essays, Papers, and Letters.* New York: Rowman & Littlefield.

Cooper, Brittany. 2016. "Intersectionality." In *The Oxford Handbook of Feminist Theory,* edited by Lisa Disch and Mary Hawkesworth. Oxford: Oxford University Press.

Cooper, Melinda. 2008. *Life as Surplus: Biotechnology and Capitalism in the Neoliberal Era.* Seattle: University of Washington Press.

Corker, Mairian. 2001. "Sensing Disability." *Hypatia* 16 (4): 34–52.

Corrigan, Paul T. 2018. "Jobs Will Save the Humanities." *Chronicle of Higher Education,* June 28, 2018.

Costa, Robert. 2010. "Gingrich: Obama's 'Kenyan, Anti-colonial' Worldview." *National Review Online,* September 11, 2010. www.nationalreview.com.

Costanza-Chock, Sasha. 2020. *Design Justice: Community-Led Practices to Build the Worlds We Need.* Cambridge: MIT Press.

Cott, Nancy. 2000. *Public Vows: A History of Marriage and the Nation.* Cambridge, MA: Harvard University Press.

Coulthard, Glen Sean. 2014. *Red Skin, White Masks: Rejecting the Colonial Politics of Recognition.* Minneapolis: University of Minnesota Press.

Courbe, M. J. de la. 1913. *Premier voyage du sieur de La Courbe fait à la coste d'Afrique en 1685.* Paris: E. Champion.

Crary, Jonathan. 1992. *Techniques of the Observer: On Vision and Modernity in the Nineteenth Century.* Cambridge: MIT Press.

Crawford, Matthew. 2009. *Shop Class as Soulcraft: An Inquiry into the Value of Work.* New York: Penguin.

Creed, Gerald, ed. 2006. *The Seductions of Community.* Santa Fe, NM: SAR Press.

Crenshaw, Kimberlé W. 1989. "Demarginalizing the Intersection of Race and Sex: A Black Feminist Critique of Antidiscrimination Doctrine, Feminist Theory and Antiracist Politics." *University of Chicago Legal Forum* 1989, article 8.

———. 1990. "A Black Feminist Critique of Antidiscrimination Law and Politics." In *The Politics of Law: A Progressive Critique,* edited by David Kairys, 356–80. New York: Basic Books.

———. 1991. "Mapping the Margins: Intersectionality, Identity Politics, and Violence against Women of Color." *Stanford Law Review* 43 (6).

———. 1995. "Mapping the Margins: Intersectionality, Identity Politics, and Violence against Women of Color." In *Critical Race Theory: The Key Writings That Formed the Movement,* edited by Kimberlé Crenshaw, Neil Gotanda, Gary Peller, and Kendall Thomas, 357–83. New York: New Press.

"Créole." n.d. Accessed September 25, 2018. www.littre.org.

Crèvecoeur, J. Hector St. John de. (1782) 1981. *Letters from an American Farmer: "Letters from an American Farmer" and "Sketches of Eighteenth-Century America."* New York: Penguin.

Crimp, Douglas. 1987. "How to Have Promiscuity in an Epidemic." *October* 43, AIDS: Cultural Analysis/Cultural Activism: 237–71.

———. 2002. *Melancholia and Moralism: Essays on AIDS and Queer Politics.* Cambridge: MIT Press.

Critical Resistance and INCITE! Women of Color against Violence. 2006. "Gender Violence and the Prison-Industrial Complex." In *Color of Violence: The INCITE! Anthology,* edited by INCITE! Women of Color against Violence, 223–26. Boston: South End.

Cronin, Ann. 2000. *Advertising and Consumer Citizenship: Gender, Images, and Rights.* London: Routledge.

Cronon, William. 1996a. "Introduction: In Search of Nature." In *Uncommon Ground: Rethinking the Human Place in Nature,* edited by William Cronon, 23–56. New York: Norton.

———. 1996b. "The Trouble with Wilderness: Or, Getting Back

to the Wrong Nature." In *Uncommon Ground: Rethinking the Human Place in Nature*, edited by William Cronon, 69–90. New York: Norton.

Crozier, Michael, Samuel Huntington, and Joji Watanuki. 1975. *The Crisis of Democracy: Report on the Governability of Democracies to the Trilateral Commission*. New York: New York University Press.

Cruikshank, Barbara. 1994. "The Will to Empower: Technologies of Citizenship and the War on Poverty." *Socialist Review* 23 (4): 29–55.

Crutzen, Paul J., and Eugene F. Stoermer. 2000. "The 'Anthropocene.'" *Global Change Newsletter*, no. 41, 17–18.

Cuarón, Jonás, dir. 2015. *Desierto*. StxFilms.

Cugoano, Quobna Ottobah. (1787) 1999. *Thoughts and Sentiments on the Evils of Slavery*. Edited by Vincent Carretta. New York: Penguin.

Cumings, Bruce. 2005. *Korea's Place in the Sun: A Modern History*. New York: Norton.

Cummins, Maria Susanna. (1854) 1988. *The Lamplighter*. New Brunswick, NJ: Rutgers University Press.

Curtis, Edward E., IV. 2009. *Muslims in America: A Short History*. New York: Oxford University Press.

Cushman, Ellen. 2013. "Wampum, Sequoyan, and Story: Decolonizing the Digital Archive." *College English* 76 (2): 115–35.

Cvetkovich, Ann. 1992. *Mixed Feelings: Feminism, Mass Culture, and Victorian Sensationalism*. New Brunswick, NJ: Rutgers University Press.

———. 2003. *An Archive of Feelings: Trauma, Sexuality, and Lesbian Public Cultures*. Durham, NC: Duke University Press.

da Costa, Emilia Viotti. 1994. *Crowns of Glory, Tears of Blood: The Demerara Slave Rebellion of 1823*. New York: Columbia University Press.

Dahlberg, Lincoln. 2001. "Democracy via Cyberspace: Mapping the Rhetorics and Practices of Three Prominent Camps." *New Media and Society* 3 (2): 157–77.

Dain, Bruce. 2002. *A Hideous Monster of the Mind: American Race Theory in the Early Republic*. Cambridge, MA: Harvard University Press.

Damasio, Antonio R. 1994. *Descartes' Error: Emotion, Reason, and the Human Brain*. New York: Putnam.

Daminois, Adèle. 1824. *Lydie; ou la créole*. Leterrier.

Damore, James. 2017. "Google's Ideological Echo Chamber." https://web.archive.org.

Daniel, Carter A. 1998. *MBA: The First Century*. Lewiston, PA: Bucknell University Press.

Daniel, Sharon, and Erik Loyer. 2007. "Public Secrets." *Vectors* 2 (2). http://vectorsjournal.org.

Danielson, Florence H., and Charles B. Davenport. 1912. *The Hill Folk: Report on a Rural Community of Hereditary Defectives*. Lancaster, PA: New Era.

Danner, Mark. 2004. *Torture and Truth: America, Abu Ghraib, and the War on Terror*. New York: New York Review of Books.

Darnton, Robert. 2009. *The Case for Books*. New York: Public Affairs.

Darwin, Charles. 1872. *The Expression of the Emotions in Man and Animals*. London: John Murray.

———. 1909. *The Voyage of the Beagle*. New York: Collier.

Das Gupta, Monisha. 2006. *Unruly Immigrants: Rights, Activism, and South Asian Politics in the United States*. Durham, NC: Duke University Press.

Das Gupta, Tania, Carl L. James, Roger C. A. Maaka, Grace-Edward Galabuzi, and Chris Andersen, eds. 2007. *Race and Racialization: Essential Readings*. Toronto: Canadian Scholars Press.

Davidson, Cathy N. (1986) 2004. *Revolution and the Word: The Rise of the Novel in America*. Exp. ed. New York: Oxford University Press.

———. 2008. "Humanities 2.0: Promise, Perils, Predictions." *PMLA* 123 (3): 707–17.

———. 2017. *The New Education: How to Revolutionize the University to Prepare Students for a World in Flux* New York: Basic Books.

Davidson, Cathy N., and Jessamyn Hatcher, eds. 2002. *No More Separate Spheres!* Durham, NC: Duke University Press.

Davies, W. D. 1982. *The Territorial Dimension of Judaism*. Berkeley: University of California Press.

Dávila, Arlene M. 2001. *Latinos, Inc.: The Marketing and Making of a People*. Berkeley: University of California Press.

———. 2004. *Barrio Dreams: Puerto Ricans, Latinos, and the Neoliberal City*. Berkeley: University of California Press.

———. 2008. *Latino Spin: Public Image and the Whitewashing of Race*. New York: New York University Press.

Davis, Angela. 1983. *Women, Race, and Class*. New York: Vintage.

———. 1997. "Reflections on Race, Class, and Gender in the USA." Interview with Lisa Lowe in *The Politics of Culture in the Shadow of Capital*, edited by Lisa Lowe and David Lloyd, 303–23. Durham, NC: Duke University Press.

———. 2001. *The Prison-Industrial Complex*. Oakland, CA: AK.

———. 2003. *Are Prisons Obsolete?* New York: Seven Stories.

———. 2005. *Abolition Democracy beyond Empire, Prisons, and Torture: Interviews with Angela Y. Davis*. New York: Seven Stories.

———. 2012. *The Meaning of Freedom and Other Difficult Dialogues*. San Francisco: City Lights Books.

———. 2016. *Freedom Is a Constant Struggle: Ferguson, Palestine, and the Foundations of a Movement*, edited by Frank Barat and Cornel West. Chicago: Haymarket Books.

Davis, David Brion. 1975. *The Problem of Slavery in the Age of Revolution, 1770–1823*. Ithaca, NY: Cornell University Press.

Davis, Heather, and Zoe Todd. 2017. "On the Importance of a Date, or, Decolonizing the Anthropocene." *ACME: An International Journal for Critical Geographies* 16 (4): 761–80. www.acme-journal.org.

Davis, Lennard. 1995. *Enforcing Normalcy: Disability, Deafness, and the Body*. New York: Verso.

Davis, M. 2018. *Old Gods, New Enigmas: Marx's Lost Theory*. London: Verso.

Davis, Mike. 1990. *City of Quartz: Excavating the Future in Los Angeles*. London: Verso.

———. 2007a. *Buda's Wagon: A Brief History of the Car Bomb*. New York: Verso.

———. 2007b. *Planet of Slums*. London: Verso.

Davis, Natalie Zemon. 2009. "Creole Languages and Their Uses: The Example of Colonial Suriname." *Historical Research* 82 (216). https://onlinelibrary.wiley.com.

Dawson, Ashley. 2010. "Climate Justice: The Emerging Movement against Green Capitalism." *South Atlantic Quarterly* 109 (2): 313–38.

Dawson, Ashley, and Bill Mullen, eds. 2015. *Against Apartheid: The Case for Boycotting Israeli Universities*. Haymarket.

Dawson, Melanie. 2015. *Emotional Reinventions: Realist-Era Representations beyond Sympathy*. Ann Arbor: University of Michigan Press.

Dawson, Michael G. 2001. *Black Visions: The Roots of Contemporary African-American Political Ideologies*. Chicago: University of Chicago Press.

Dayan, Colin. 2007. *The Story of Cruel and Unusual*. Boston: Boston Review Books and MIT Press.

———. 2011. *The Law Is a White Dog: How Legal Rituals Make and Unmake Persons*. Princeton, NJ: Princeton University Press.

Dean, Mitchell. 2009. *Governmentality: Power and Rule in Modern Society*. New York: Sage.

Dean, Robert. 2001. *Imperial Brotherhood: Gender and the Making of Cold War Foreign Policy*. Amherst: University of Massachusetts Press.

Deane, Seamus. 1990. "Imperialism/Nationalism." In *Critical Terms for Literary Study*, edited by Frank Lentricchia and Thomas McLaughlin, 354–68. Chicago: University of Chicago Press.

de Certeau, Michel. 1984. *The Practice of Everyday Life*. Berkeley: University of California Press.

De Genova, Nicholas. 2002. "Migrant 'Illegality' and Deportability in Everyday Life." *Annual Review of Anthropology* 31:419–47.

———. 2005. *Working the Boundaries: Race, Space, and "Illegality" in Mexican Chicago*. Durham, NC: Duke University Press.

———. 2012. "The 'War on Terror' as Racial Crisis: Homeland Security, Obama, and Racial (Trans)Formations." In *Racial Formation in the Twenty-First Century*, edited by Daniel Martinez HoSang, Oneka LaBennett, and Laura Pulido, 246–75. Berkeley: University of California Press.

De Genova, Nicholas, and Nathalie Mae Peutz, eds. 2010. *The Deportation Regime: Sovereignty, Space, and the Freedom of Movement*. Durham, NC: Duke University Press.

de Gobineau, Arthur. (1853–55) 1967. *The Inequality of Human Races, 1853–55*. Translated by Adrian H. Collins. New York: H. Fertig.

DeGooyer, Stephanie, et al. 2018. *The Right to Have Rights*. New York: Verso.

DeGraff, Michel. 2016. "Demystifying the Creolization/Decolonizing Creole Studies." In *Different Spaces, Different Voices: A Rendez-Vous with Decoloniality*, edited by Sayan Dey, 64–92. Accessed August 1, 2019. http://lingphil.scripts.mit.edu.

DeGraffenreid v. General Motors Assembly Div., etc., 413 F. Supp. 142 (E.D. Mo. 1976).

De Hart, Jane Sherron. 1991. "Gender on the Right: Meaning behind the Existential Scream." *Gender and History* 3:246–67.

de Kock, Leon. 2001. "Sitting for the Civilization Test: The Making(s) of a Civil Imaginary in Colonial South Africa." *Poetics Today* 22 (2): 391–412.

Delacotte, Philippe. 2009. "On the Sources of Consumer Boycotts Ineffectiveness." *Journal of*.

Delany, Samuel R. 1994. *Return to Nevèrÿon*. Middletown, CT: Wesleyan University Press.

———. 2001. *Times Square Red, Times Square Blue*. Rev. ed. New York: New York University Press.

de Lauretis, Teresa. 1991. "Queer Theory: Lesbian and Gay Sexualities (an Introduction)." *differences: A Journal of Feminist Cultural Studies* 3 (2): iii–xviii.

Delay, Brian. 2009. *War of a Thousand Deserts: Indian Raids and the U.S.-Mexican War*. New Haven: Yale University Press.

Deleuze, Gilles. 1989. *Cinema 2: The Time-Image*. Translated by Hugh Tomlinson and Robert Galeta. Minneapolis: University of Minnesota Press.

Deleuze, Gilles, and Felix Guattari. 1983. *Anti-Oedipus: Capitalism and Schizophrenia*. Minneapolis: University of Minnesota Press.

———. 1987. *A Thousand Plateaus: Capitalism and Schizophrenia.* Translated by Brian Massumi. Minneapolis: University of Minnesota Press.

Delgado Bernal, Dolores. 1998. "Using a Chicana Feminist Epistemology in Educational Research." *Harvard Educational Review* 68 (4): 555–82.

Delgado, Richard, and Jean Stefancic, eds. 1995. *Critical Race Theory: The Cutting Edge.* Philadelphia: Temple University Press.

Deloria, Philip J. 1998. *Playing Indian.* New Haven: Yale University Press.

———. 2003. "American Indians, American Studies, and the ASA." *American Quarterly* 55 (4): 669–80.

Deloria, Vine, Jr. (1969) 1988. *Custer Died for Your Sins: An Indian Manifesto.* Norman: University of Oklahoma Press.

Delphy, Christine. 1977. *The Main Enemy: A Materialist Analysis of Women's Oppression.* London: Women's Resources and Research Centre.

Delpit, Lisa. 1995. *Other People's Children: Cultural Conflict in the Classroom.* New York: New Press.

Demers, Joanna. 2006. *Steal This Book: How Intellectual Property Law Affects Musical Creativity.* Athens: University of Georgia Press.

D'Emilio, John, and Estelle Freedman. (1988) 1997. *Intimate Matters: A History of Sexuality in America.* 2nd ed. Chicago: University of Chicago Press.

DeMille, Cecil B., dir. 1956. *The Ten Commandments.* Paramount Pictures / Motion Picture Associates.

Denning, Michael. 1997. *The Cultural Front: The Laboring of American Culture in the 20th Century.* London: Verso.

———. 1998. *The Cultural Front.* New York: Verso.

———. 2004. *Culture in the Age of Three Worlds.* London: Verso.

Derrida, Jacques. 1981. "Plato's Pharmacy." In *Dissemination,* translated by Barbara Johnson, 61–119. Chicago: University of Chicago Press.

———. 1993. *Aporias.* Stanford, CA: Stanford University Press.

———. (1996) 2017. *Archive Fever: A Freudian Impression.* Translated by Eric Prenowitz. Chicago: University of Chicago Press.

Dery, Mark. 1994. "Black to the Future: Interviews with Samuel R. Delany, Greg Tate, and Tricia Rose." In *Flame Wars: The Discourse of Cyberculture,* edited by Mark Dery. Durham, NC: Duke University Press.

De Voe, Thomas. 1862. *The Market Book.* New York.

Dewey, John. 1927. *The Public and Its Problems.* New York: Holt.

———. (1934) 1980. *Art as Experience.* New York: Perigree.

———. 1935. *Liberalism and Social Action.* New York: Putnam.

Diamond, Elin. 1988. "Brechtian Theory/Feminist Theory: Towards a Gestic Feminist Criticism." *TDR* 32 (1): 82–94.

DiAngelo, Robin J. 2018. *White Fragility: Why It's so Hard for White People to Talk about Racism.* Boston: Beacon.

Diaz, Vicente M. 1987. "Disturbing the Horizon." *Horizons: Journal of the East West Center Participants Association* 2:100–107.

———. 1989. "Restless Na(rra)tives." *Inscriptions* 5:165–75.

———. 1994. "Canoes of Micronesia: Navigating Tradition into the Future." *Pacific Daily News,* April 28, 1994.

———. 1995. "Grounding Flux in Guam's Cultural History." In *Work in Flux,* edited by Emma Greenwood, Andrew Sartori, and Klaus Neumann, 159–71. Melbourne: University of Melbourne, History Department.

Diaz, Vicente M., and J. Kēhaulani Kauanui. 2001. "Native Pacific Cultural Studies on the Edge." *Contemporary Pacific* 13 (2): 315–42.

Di Chiro, Giovanna. 1996. "Nature as Community: The Convergence of Environment and Social Justice." In *Uncommon Ground: Rethinking the Human Place in Nature,* edited by William Cronon, 298–320. New York: Norton.

Dickens, Charles. 1842. *American Notes, for General Circulation.* London: Chapman and Hall.

Dickinson, Laura A. 2011. *Outsourcing War and Peace: Preserving Public Values in a World of Privatized Foreign Affairs.* New Haven: Yale University Press.

Dienst, Richard. 2011. *The Bonds of Debt.* New York: Verso.

di Leonardo, Micaela. 1998. *Exotics at Home: Anthropologies, Otherness, and American Modernity.* Chicago: University of Chicago Press.

———. 2008. "Introduction: New Global and American Landscapes of Inequality" and "The Neoliberalization of Minds, Space and Bodies: Rising Global Inequality and the Shifting American Public Sphere." In *New Landscapes of Inequality: Neoliberalism and the Erosion of Democracy in America,* edited by Jane Collins, Micaela di Leonardo, and Brett Williams, 3–20, 191–208. Santa Fe, NM: School for Advanced Research Press.

Dillard, Angela D. 2001. *Guess Who's Coming to Dinner Now? Multicultural Conservatism in America.* New York: New York University Press.

Dillon, Elizabeth Maddock. 2004. "Sentimental Aesthetics." *American Literature* 76:495–523.

———. 2014. *New World Drama: The Performative Commons in the Atlantic World, 1649–1849.* Durham, NC: Duke University Press.

———. 2019. "Zombie Biopolitics." *American Quarterly* 71 (3): 221–44.

Dillon, Grace. 2012. "Imagining Indigenous Futurisms." In *Walking the Clouds: An Anthology of Indigenous Science Fiction*. Tucson: University of Arizona Press.

Dimock, Wai Chee. 2006. *Through Other Continents: American Literature across Deep Time*. Princeton, NJ: Princeton University Press.

Dionne, E. J., Jr., ed. 1998. *Community Works*. Washington, DC: Brookings Institution Press.

Dippie, Brian W. 1991. *The Vanishing American: White Attitudes and U.S. Indian Policy*. Lawrence: University of Kansas Press.

"Diskou Aristide, Asanble Jeneral Nasyonzini." Duke University Libraries Repository.

Dolby, Nadine. 2000. "The Shifting Ground of Race: The Role of Taste in Youth's Production of Identities." *Race, Ethnicity, and Education* 3 (1): 7–23.

Dolgon, Cory, Tania Mitchell, and Timothy Eatman. 2017. *The Cambridge Handbook of Service Learning and Community Engagement*. Cambridge: Cambridge University Press.

Dolmage, Jay Timothy. 2018. *Disabled upon Arrival: Eugenics, Immigration, and the Construction of Race and Disability*. Columbus: Ohio State University Press.

Dolovich, Sharon. 2011. "Exclusion and Control in the Carceral State." *Berkeley Journal of Criminal Law* 16 (2): 259–339.

Dominguez, Virginia R. 1986. *White by Definition: Social Classification in Louisiana*. New Brunswick, NJ: Rutgers University Press.

Donnelly, Jack. 2003. *Universal Human Rights in Theory and Practice*. 2nd ed. Ithaca, NY: Cornell.

Dorsey, Bruce. 2002. *Reforming Men and Women: Gender in the Antebellum City*. Ithaca, NY: Cornell University Press.

Dossa, Parin. 2009. *Racialized Bodies, Disabling Worlds: Stories in the Lives of Immigrant Muslim Women*. Toronto: University of Toronto Press.

Douglas, Ann. 1977. *The Feminization of American Culture*. New York: Knopf.

Douglass, Frederick. 2000. *Selected Speeches and Writings*, edited by Philip S. Foner and Yuval Taylor. Chicago: Lawrence Hill Books.

Dowd, Douglas Fitzgerald. 1977. *The Twisted Dream: Capitalist Development in the United States since 1776*. 2nd ed. Cambridge, MA: Winthrop.

Dower, John. 1986. *War without Mercy: Race and Power in the Pacific War*. New York: Pantheon.

Doyle, Jennifer. 2015. *Campus Sex, Campus Security*. Los Angeles: Semiotext(e).

Drescher, Seymour. 2009. *Abolition: A History of Slavery and Antislavery*. New York: Cambridge University Press.

Driscoll, Catherine. 2002. *Girls*. New York: Columbia University Press.

Driskill, Qwo-Li, Chris Finley, Brian Joseph Gilley, and Scott Lauria Morgensen. 2011. *Queer Indigenous Studies: Critical Interventions in Theory, Politics, and Literature*. Tucson: University of Arizona Press.

Drucker, Johanna. 1995. *The Century of Artists' Books*. New York: Granary.

———. 2011. "Humanities Approaches to Graphical Display." *Digital Humanities Quarterly* 5 (1).

———. 2013. "Performative Materiality and Theoretical Approaches to Interface." *Digital Humanities Quarterly* 7:1.

Duboff, Richard B. 1989. *Accumulation and Power: An Economic History of the United States*. Armonk, NY: M. E. Sharpe.

Dubois, Laurent. 2004. *Avengers of the New World: The Story of the Haitian Revolution*. Cambridge, MA: Harvard University Press.

Du Bois, W. E. B. (1900) 1978. "The Twelfth Census and the Negro Problem." In *W. E. B. Du Bois: On Sociology and the Black Community*, edited by Dan S. Green and Edwin D. Driver, 65–69. Chicago: University of Chicago Press.

———. (1903) 1986. *The Souls of Black Folk: W. E. B. Du Bois: Writings*. Edited by Nathan Huggins. New York: Library of America.

———. (1903) 1997. *The Souls of Black Folk*. Edited by David W. Blight and Robert Gooding-Williams. New York: Bedford Books.

———. (1903) 2016. *The Souls of Black Folk*. London: Dover Publications.

———. (1935) 1998. *Black Reconstruction in America, 1860–1880*. New York: Free Press.

———. 1995a. "The African Roots of the War." In *W. E. B. Du Bois: A Reader*, edited by David Levering Lewis, 642–51. New York: Holt.

———. 1995b. *The Philadelphia Negro: A Social Study*. Edited by Elijah Anderson. Philadelphia: University of Pennsylvania Press.

DuCille, Ann. 1993. *The Coupling Convention: Sex, Text, and Tradition in Black Women's Fiction*. New York: Oxford University Press.

Dudden, Faye. 1994. *Women in the American Theatre: Actresses and Audiences 1790–1870*. New Haven: Yale University Press.

Duggan, Lisa. 1992. "Making It Perfectly Queer." *Socialist Review* 22:11–31.

———. 2002. "The New Homonormativity: The Sexual Politics of Neoliberalism." In *Materializing Democracy: Toward a Revitalized Cultural Politics*, edited by Russ Castronovo and

Dana D. Nelson, 175–94. Durham, NC: Duke University Press.

———. 2003. *The Twilight of Equality? Neoliberalism, Cultural Politics, and the Attack on Democracy*. Boston: Beacon.

———. 2004. "Holy Matrimony!" *Nation Online*, February 26, 2004. www.thenation.com.

Dumm, Thomas. 1987. *Democracy and Punishment: Disciplinary Origins of the United States*. Madison: University of Wisconsin Press.

Dunbar, Paul Laurence. 1993. *The Collected Poetry of Paul Laurence Dunbar*, edited by Joanne Braxton. Charlottesville: University of Virginia Press.

———. 2005. *Sport of the Gods and Other Essential Writing by Paul Laurence Dunbar*, edited by Shelley Fisher Fishkin and David Bradley. New York: Random House / Modern Library.

Dunbar-Ortiz, Roxanne. 2006. *Red Dirt: Growing Up Okie*. Norman: University of Oklahoma Press.

———. 2015. *An Indigenous Peoples' History of the United States*. Boston: Beacon.

Duncan, Johnny. 2010. "Afr-i-can Amer-i-can Turns Twenty-Three." *Community Audio*, January 2, 2010.

Dunn, Christopher. 2001. *Brutality Garden*. Chapel Hill: University of North Carolina Press.

During, Simon, ed. (1993) 2007. *The Cultural Studies Reader*. 3rd ed. New York: Routledge.

Durkheim, Emile. (1957) 2003. *Professional Ethics and Civic Morals*. London: Routledge.

Durkheim, Émile, and Marcel Mauss. (1913) 1971. "Note on the Notion of Civilization." Translated by Benjamin Nelson. *Social Research* 38:808–13.

Duthu, N. Bruce. 2008. *American Indians and the Law*. New York: Viking.

Dworkin, Craig. 2013. *No Medium*. Cambridge: MIT Press.

Dyer, Richard. 1988. "White." *Screen* 29 (4): 44–64.

———. 1997. *White*. New York: Routledge.

Dyer-Witheford, Nick. 1999. *Cyber-Marx: Cycles and Circuits of Struggle in High-Technology Capitalism*. Urbana: University of Illinois Press.

Eade, John, ed. 1997. *Living the Global City: Globalization as a Local Process*. London: Routledge.

Eagleton, Terry. 1990. *The Ideology of the Aesthetic*. Oxford, UK: Blackwell.

———. 2000. *The Idea of Culture*. Malden, MA: Blackwell.

Eckel, Jan, and Samuel Moyn, eds. 2014. *Breakthrough: Human Rights in the 1970s*. Philadelphia: University of Pennsylvania Press.

Eckert, Penelope. 1989. *Jocks and Burnouts: Social Categories and Identities in High School*. New York: Teachers College Press.

Eco, Umberto. 1995. "Ur-Fascism." *New York Review of Books*, June 22, 1995.

Edelman, Lee. 2004. *No Future: Queer Theory and the Death Drive*. Durham, NC: Duke University Press.

Edelman, Marian Wright. 2013. "Justice Denied." Child Watch Column, Children's Defense Fund. www.childrensdefense.org.

Edmondson, Locksley. 1986. "Black America as a Mobilizing Diaspora: Some International Implications." In *Modern Diasporas in International Politics*, edited by Gabriel Sheffer, 164–211. London: Croom Helm.

Edmundson, Mark. 2004. *Why Read?* New York: Bloomsbury.

Edsall, Thomas Byrne, and Mary D. Edsall. 1992. *Chain Reaction: The Impact of Race, Rights, and Taxes on American Politics*. New York: Norton.

Edwards, Brent Hayes. 2001. "The Uses of Diaspora." *Social Text* 66:45–73.

———. 2003a. *The Practice of Diaspora: Literature, Translation, and the Rise of Black Internationalism*. Cambridge, MA: Harvard University Press.

———. 2003b. "The Shadow of Shadows." *Positions* 11 (1): 11–49.

Edwards, Brian T. 2005. *Morocco Bound: Disorienting America's Maghreb, from Casablanca to the Marrakech Express*. Durham, NC: Duke University Press.

———. 2010. "Disorienting Captivity: A Response to Gordon Sayre." *American Literary History* 22 (2): 360–67.

———. 2015. "'Why Islam? Why Are Muslims Considered the Worst by Americans?' The Questions Young Muslims Ask Me about Donald Trump and America." Salon. https://salon.com.

———. 2016. *After the American Century: The Ends of U.S. Culture in the Middle East*. New York: Columbia University Press.

Eggers, Dave. 2009. *Zeitoun*. San Francisco: McSweeney's Books.

Ehrenreich, Barbara. 2001. *Nickel and Dimed: On (Not) Getting By in America*. New York: Metropolitan Books.

Eidsheim, Nina Sun. 2011. "Marian Anderson and 'Sonic Blackness' in American Opera." In *Sound Clash: Listening to American Studies*, edited by Kara Keeling and Josh Kun, 197–228. Baltimore: Johns Hopkins University Press.

Eisenhower, Dwight D. 1961. "Farewell Address." www.ourdocuments.gov.

Eisenman, Stephen. 2007. *The Abu Ghraib Effect*. London: Reaktion Books.

Elam, Harry Justin, and Kennell Jackson, eds. 2005. *Black Cultural Traffic: Crossroads in Global Performance and Popular Culture*. Ann Arbor: University of Michigan Press.

Elam, Michelle. 2011. *The Souls of Mixed Folk: Race, Politics, and*

Aesthetics in the New Millennium. Stanford, CA: Stanford University Press.

Elias, Norbert. (1939) 1969. *Über den Prozess der Zivilisation*. Munich: Franke Verlag Bern.

Eliot, T. S. 1949. "Notes towards the Definition of Culture." In *Christianity and Culture*, 79–186. New York: Harcourt, Brace and World.

Elizondo, Virgilio. 2000. *The Future Is Mestizo: Life Where Culture Meets*. Boulder: University Press of Colorado.

Elkins, James, ed. 2007. *Visual Literacy*. New York: Routledge.

Ellis, Kate, and Stephen Smith. 2017. "Shackled Legacy." *APM Reports*, September 4, 2017. www.apmreports.org.

Ellison, Julie. 1999. *Cato's Tears and the Making of Anglo-American Emotion*. Chicago: University of Chicago Press.

Ellison, Ralph. (1952) 1995. *Invisible Man*. New York: Vintage.

Emerson, Ralph Waldo. (1837) 1990. "The American Scholar." In *Selected Lectures and Poems*, edited by Robert D. Richardson Jr., 82–100. New York: Bantam.

———. (1841) 1983. "Man the Reformer." In *Essays and Lectures*, 135–50. New York: Library of America New York.

———. (1841) 1990. "Self-Reliance." In *Selected Essays, Lectures, and Poems*, edited by Robert D. Richardson Jr., 148–71. New York: Bantam.

———. 1983. "Art." In *Essays and Lectures*, 429–40. New York: Library of America.

Emmanuel, Arghiri. 1972. "White-Settler Colonialism and the Myth of Investment Imperialism." *New Left Review* 73:35–57.

Eng, David. 2001. *Racial Castration: Managing Masculinity in Asian America*. Durham, NC: Duke University Press.

Eng, David, Judith Halberstam, and José Muñoz. 2005. "Introduction: What's Queer about Queer Studies Now?" *Social Text* 84–85:1–17.

Eng, David, and David Kazanjian, eds. 2002. *Loss*. Berkeley: University of California Press.

Engels, Friedrich. (1884) 1972. *The Origins of the Family, Private Property, and the State*. New York: Pathfinder.

Enloe, Cynthia. 1989. *Bananas, Beaches, and Bases: Making Feminist Sense of International Politics*. Berkeley: University of California Press.

Entwistle, Joanne. 2000. *The Fashioned Body: Fashion, Dress, and Modern Social Theory*. Malden, MA: Polity.

Environment & Development. 2009. 18 (3): 306–22.

Environmental Justice and Climate Justice Hub, Orfalea Center. Accessed September 15, 2018. http://ejcj.orfaleacenter.ucsb.edu.

Epstein, Steven. 1996. *Impure Science: AIDS, Activism, and the Politics of Knowledge, Medicine and Society*. Berkeley: University of California Press.

Equiano, Olaudah. (1789) 2003. *The Interesting Narrative and Other Writings*. Edited by Vincent Carretta. New York: Penguin.

Erdrich, Louise. 2016. "Holy Rage: Lessons from Standing Rock." *New Yorker*, December 22, 2016. www.newyorker.com.

Erikson, Erik H. (1944) 1968. *Identity: Youth and Crisis*. New York: Norton.

Erlmann, Viet, ed. 2004. *Hearing Cultures: Essays on Sound, Listening, and Modernity*. Oxford, UK: Berg.

Ernst, Wolfgang. 2013. *Digital Memory and the Archive*. Minneapolis: University of Minnesota Press.

Escobar, Arturo. 1995. *Encountering Development: The Making and Unmaking of the Third World*. Princeton, NJ: Princeton University Press.

———. 2011. *Encountering Development: The Making and Unmaking of the Third World*. Princeton, NJ: Princeton University Press.

Escoffier, Jeffrey, and Allan Bérubé. 1991. "Queer/Nation." *OUT/LOOK: National Lesbian and Gay Quarterly* 11:14–16.

Eshun, Kevin. 2003. "Further Considerations on Afrofuturism." *CR: The New Centennial Review* 3 (2): 287–302.

Essed, Philomena, and David Theo Goldberg, eds. 2000. *Race Critical Theories*. Malden, MA: Blackwell.

Estes, Nick. 2019. *Our History Is the Future: Standing Rock versus the Dakota Access Pipeline, and the Long Tradition of Indigenous Resistance*. Verso: New York.

Ettelbrick, Paula. 1989. "Since When Is Marriage the Path to Liberation?" *OUT/LOOK: National Lesbian and Gay Quarterly* 2:14–16.

Etzioni, Amitai. 1993. *The Spirit of Community: Rights, Responsibilities, and the Communitarian Agenda*. New York: Crown.

Eubanks, Virgina. 2018. *Automating Inequality: How High-Tech Tools Profile, Police, and Punish the Poor*. New York: St. Martin's Press.

Ewen, Elizabeth, and Stuart Ewen. 2006. *Typecasting: On the Arts and Sciences of Human Inequality; A History of Dominant Ideas*. New York: Seven Stories.

Fabella, Yvonne. 2010. "Redeeming the Character of the Creoles: Whiteness, Gender, and Creolization in Pre-Revolutionary Saint-Domingue." *Journal of Historical Sociology* 23 (1): 40–72.

Fabian, Johannes. 2002. *Time and the Other: How Anthropology Makes Its Object*. New York: Columbia University Press.

Falk, Richard. 1994. "The Making of Global Citizenship." In *The Condition of Citizenship*, edited by Bart Van Steenbergen, 127–40. London: Sage.

Faludi, Susan. 1991. *Backlash: The Undeclared War against American Women*. New York: Crown.

Fanon, Frantz. (1963) 2004. *The Wretched of the Earth*. Translated by Richard Philcox. New York: Grove.

———. 1967a. *Black Skin, White Masks*. Translated by Charles Lam Markmann. New York: Grove.

———. 1967b. *A Dying Colonialism*. Translated by Haakon Chevalier. New York: Grove.

Fanuzzi, Robert. 2003. *Abolition's Public Sphere*. Minneapolis: University of Minnesota Press.

Farrow, Kenyon. 2005. "Is Gay Marriage Anti-black?" *Kenyon Farrow* (blog). http://kenyonfarrow.com.

Fausto-Sterling, Anne. 1985. *Myths of Gender: Biological Theories about Women and Men*. New York: Basic Books.

———. 1993. "The Five Sexes: Why Male and Female Are Not Enough." *Sciences*, March–April 1993.

———. 2000. *Sexing the Body: Gender Politics and the Construction of Sexuality*. New York: Basic Books.

Favor, Martin J. 1999. *Authentic Blackness: The Folk in the New Negro Renaissance*. Durham, NC: Duke University Press.

Feagin, Joe R. 2013. *The White Racial Frame: Centuries of Racial Framing and Counter-framing*. 2nd ed. New York: Routledge.

Feeley, Malcolm, and Jonathan Simon. 1992. "The New Penology: Notes on the Emerging Strategy of Corrections and Its Implications." *Criminology* 30 (4): 449–74.

Feenberg, Andrew. 1999. *Questioning Technology*. New York: Routledge.

Feher, Michel. 2018. *Rated Agency: Investee Politics in a Speculative Age*. Zone Books.

Feimster, Crystal N. 2009. *Southern Horrors: Women and the Politics of Rape and Lynching*. Cambridge, MA: Harvard University Press.

Feinberg, Leslie. 1993. *Stone Butch Blues*. Ithaca, NY: Firebrand Books.

Feld, Steven. 2003. "A Rainforest Acoustemology." In *The Auditory Culture Reader*, edited by Michael Bull and Les Back, 223–40. New York: Berg.

Felski, Rita. 2000. *Doing Time: Feminist Theory and Postmodern Culture*. New York: New York University Press.

Ferguson, Roderick A. 2004. *Aberrations in Black: Toward a Queer of Color Critique*. Minneapolis: University of Minnesota Press.

———. 2005. "The Stratifications of Normativity." *Rhizomes* 10. www.rhizomes.net.

———. 2012a. "Reading Intersectionality." *Trans-Scripts* 2:91–99.

———. 2012b. *The Reorder of Things: On the Institutionalization of Difference*. Minneapolis: University of Minnesota Press.

Fernandez, Lilia. 2012. *Brown in the Windy City: Mexicans and Puerto Ricans in Postwar Chicago*. Chicago: University of Chicago Press.

Ferreira da Silva, Denise. 2007. *Toward a Global Idea of Race*. Minneapolis: University of Minnesota Press.

Fetterley, Judith, and Marjorie Pryse. 2003. *Writing Out of Place: Regionalism, Women, and American Literary Culture*. Urbana: University of Illinois Press.

Fields, Barbara. 1990. "Slavery, Race, and Ideology in the United States of America." *New Left Review* 181:95–118.

Fields, Barbara, and Karen E. Fields. 2012. *Racecraft: The Soul of Inequality in American Life*. London: Verso.

Filmer, Sir Robert. (1680) 2017. *Patriarcha and Other Political Works of Sir Robert Filmer*. Edited by Peter Laslett. London: Routledge.

Fine, Michelle. 1989. "Silencing and Nurturing Voice in an Improbable Context: Urban Adolescents in Public School." In *Critical Pedagogy, the State, and Cultural Struggle*, edited by Henry A. Giroux and Peter McLaren, 152–73. New York: State University of New York Press.

Fine, Michelle, Lois Weis, Linda C. Powell, and L. Mun Wong, eds. 1997. *Off White: Readings on Race, Power, and Society*. New York: Routledge.

Fineman, Martha Albertson. 2008. "The Vulnerable Subject: Anchoring Equality in the Human Condition." *Yale Journal of Law and Feminism* 20 (1): 1–23.

Fineman, Martha Albertson, and Anna Grear. 2013. *Vulnerability: Reflections on a New Ethical Foundations for Law and Politics*. Farnham: Ashgate.

Fink, Bruce. 1995. *The Lacanian Subject: Between Language and Jouissance*. Princeton, NJ: Princeton University Press.

Fiol-Matta, Licia. 2017. *The Great Woman Singer: Gender and Voice in Puerto Rican Music*. Durham, NC: Duke University Press.

Fischer, Sibylle. 2003. *Haiti and the Cultures of Slavery in the Age of Revolution*. Durham, NC: Duke University Press.

Fish, Stanley. 1996. "Professor Sokal's Bad Joke." *New York Times*, May 21, 1996.

———. 2018. "Stop Trying to Sell the Humanities." *Chronicle of Higher Education*, June 17, 2018.

Fisk, Clinton B. 1866. *Plain Counsels for Freedmen: In Sixteen Brief Lectures*. Boston.

Fitzgerald, Deborah. 2003. *Every Farm a Factory: The Industrial Ideal in American Agriculture*. New Haven: Yale University Press.

Fitzgerald, F. Scott. (1925) 1992. *The Great Gatsby*. New York: Collier Books.

Fitzhugh, George. 1854. *Sociology for the South; or, The Failure of Free Society*. Richmond, VA: A. Morris.

———. (1857) 2006. *Cannibals All! Or, Slaves without Masters.* Cambridge, MA: Belknap.

Fleming, J. R. 2005. *Historical Perspectives on Climate Change.* New York: Oxford University Press.

Fliegelman, Jay. 1982. *Prodigals and Pilgrims: The American Revolution against Patriarchal Authority, 1750–1800.* New York: Cambridge University Press.

———. 1993. *Declaring Independence: Jefferson, Natural Language, and the Culture of Performance.* Stanford, CA: Stanford University Press.

Flores, Juan. 2000. *From Bomba to Hip-Hop: Puerto Rican Culture and Latino Identity.* New York: Columbia University Press.

Florida, Richard. 2002. *The Rise of the Creative Class.* New York: Basic Books.

Foley, Douglas. 1994. *Learning Capitalist Culture: Deep in the Heart of Tejas.* Philadelphia: University of Pennsylvania Press.

Foner, Eric. 1998. *The Story of American Freedom.* New York: Norton.

Foote, Stephanie. 2001. *Regional Fictions: Culture and Identity in Nineteenth-Century American Literature.* Madison: University of Wisconsin Press.

———. 2003. "The Cultural Work of American Regionalism." In *A Companion to the Regional Literatures of America*, edited by Charles L. Crow, 25–41. Malden, MA: Blackwell.

Forbes, Jack D. 1992. *Africans and Native Americans: The Language of Race and the Evolution of Red-Black Peoples.* 2nd ed. Urbana: University of Illinois Press.

Ford, Henry. 1916. *Chicago Tribune*, May 25, 1916.

Fordham, Signithia. 1996. *Blacked Out: Dilemmas of Race, Identity, and Success at Capital High.* Chicago: University of Chicago Press.

Forrest, Richard. 2017. "A Voice of Hate in America's Heartland." *New York Times*, November 25, 2017. www.nytimes.com.

Foster, Frances Smith. 2005. "A Narrative of the Interesting Origins and (Somewhat) Surprising Developments of African-American Print Culture." *American Literary History* 17 (4): 714–40.

Foster, Hal. 1988. Preface to *Vision and Visuality (Dia Art Foundation Discussions in Contemporary Culture, no. 2)*. Seattle: Bay.

Foster, John Bellamy, and Fred Magdoff. 2009. *The Great Financial Crisis: Causes and Consequences.* New York: Monthly Review Press.

Foster, Thomas. 1999. "'The Souls of Cyberfolk': Performativity, Virtual Embodiment, and Racial Histories." In *Cyberspace Textualities: Computer Technology and Literary Theory*, edited by Marie-Laure Ryan, 137–63. Bloomington: Indiana University Press.

———. 2005. *The Souls of Cyberfolk: Posthumanism as Vernacular Theory.* Minneapolis: University of Minnesota Press.

Foucault, Michel. (1969) 1982. *The Archaeology of Knowledge: And the Discourse on Language.* New York: Vintage.

———. (1975) 1995. *Discipline and Punish: The Birth of the Prison.* Translated by Alan Sheridan. New York: Vintage.

———. (1976) 1990. *The History of Sexuality.* Vol. 1, *An Introduction*, translated by Robert Hurley. New York: Vintage.

———. 1977. "Panopticism." In *Discipline and Punish: The Birth of the Prison*, 195–228. New York: Pantheon Books.

———. 1980. *Power/Knowledge: Selected Interviews and Other Writings, 1972–1977.* New York: Pantheon Books.

———. 1982. "Afterword: The Subject and Power." In *Michel Foucault: Beyond Structuralism and Hermeneutics*, edited by Hubert L. Dreyfus and Paul Rabinow, 208–26. Chicago: University of Chicago Press.

———. 1991. "Governmentality." In *The Foucault Effect: Studies in Governmentality*, edited by Graham Burchell, Colin Gordon, and Peter Miller, 87–104. Chicago: University of Chicago Press.

———. 1994. *The Order of Things: An Archaeology of the Human Sciences.* New York: Vintage.

———. (1999) 2003. *Abnormal: Lectures at the Collège de France, 1974–1975.* Translated by Graham Burchell. New York: Picador.

———. 2003. *"Society Must Be Defended": Lectures at the Collège de France, 1975–1976.* Translated by David Macey. New York: Picador.

———. 2006. *Essential Works of Foucault, 1954–1984.* Vol. 1, *Ethics.* New York: New Press.

———. 2009. *Security, Territory, Population: Lectures at the Collège de France, 1977–1978.* Translated by Graham Burchell. New York: Picador.

Fowler, O. S. 1844. *Education and Self-Improvement.* New York: O. S. and L. N. Fowler.

Fox, Claire. 1999. *The Fence and the River: Culture and Politics at the U.S.-Mexico Border.* Minneapolis: University of Minnesota Press.

Fox, Richard. 1995. "The Breakdown of Culture." *Current Anthropology* 36:1–2.

Frampton, Kenneth. 1983. "Towards a Critical Regionalism: Six Points for an Architecture of Resistance." In *The Anti-aesthetic: Essays on Postmodern Culture*, edited by Hal Foster, 16–30. Port Townsend, WA: Bay.

Frank, Thomas. 2004. *What's the Matter with Kansas? How*

Conservatives Won the Heart of America. New York: Henry Holt.

Franke, Andre Gunder. 1998. *ReOrient: Global Economy in the Asian Age*. Berkeley: University of California Press.

Franke, Katherine M. 1999. "Becoming a Citizen: Reconstruction-Era Regulation of African-American Marriages." *Yale Journal of Law and the Humanities* 11 (2): 251–309.

———. 2009. *Wedlocked: The Perils of Marriage Equality*. New York: New York University Press.

———. 2019. *Repair: Redeeming the Promise of Abolition*. Chicago: Haymarket Books.

Frankenberg, Ruth. 1993. *White Women, Race Matters: The Social Construction of Whiteness*. Minneapolis: University of Minnesota Press.

Franklin, Benjamin. 1790. "Sidi Mehemet Ibrahim on the Slave Trade." Letter to the *Federal Gazette*, March 23, 1790.

———. 1895. *The Autobiography of Benjamin Franklin*. Philadelphia: Henry Altemus.

Franklin, H. Bruce. 1978. *The Victim as Criminal and Artist: Literature from the American Prison*. New York: Oxford University Press.

Franklin, Sarah. 2003. "Rethinking Nature–Culture: Anthropology and the New Genetics." *Anthopological Theory* 3 (1): 65–85.

Fredrickson, George. 1981. *White Supremacy: A Comparative Study in American and South African History*. Oxford: Oxford University Press.

Freeman, Alan David. 1995. "Legitimizing Racial Discrimination through Anti-discrimination Law: A Critical Review of Supreme Court Doctrine." In *Critical Race Theory: The Key Writings That Formed the Movement*, edited by Kimberlé Crenshaw, Neil Gotanda, Garry Peller, and Kendall Thomas, 29–45. New York: New Press.

Freeman, Carla. 2000. *High Tech and High Heels in the Global Economy: Women, Work, and Pink-Collar Economies in the Caribbean*. Durham, NC: Duke University Press.

Freeman, Elizabeth. 2010. *Time Binds: Queer Temporalities, Queer Histories*. Durham, NC: Duke University Press.

Fregoso, Rosa Linda. 2003. *MeXicana Encounters: The Making of Social Identities on the Borderlands*. Berkeley: University of California Press.

Freyre, Gilberto. (1933) 1956. *The Masters and the Slaves: A Study in the Development of Brazilian Civilization*. Translated by Samuel Putnam. New York: Knopf.

Friedan, Betty. 1963. *The Feminine Mystique*. New York: Dell.

Friedberg, Anne. 1993. *Window Shopping: Cinema and the Postmodern*. Berkeley: University of California Press.

Friedman, Lawrence M. 2002. *American Law in the Twentieth Century*. New Haven: Yale University Press.

Friedman, Milton. (1962) 2002. *Capitalism and Freedom*. Chicago: University of Chicago Press.

Friedman, Thomas L. 2000. *The Lexus and the Olive Tree: Understanding Globalization*. New York: Farrar, Straus and Giroux.

———. 2005. *The World Is Flat: A Brief History of the Twenty-First Century*. New York: Farrar, Straus and Giroux.

Friends of the Earth International. 2005. "Climate Debt: Making Historical Responsibility Part of the Solution." www.foei.org.

Fryberg, Stephanie A., and Alisha Watts. 2010. "We're Honoring You Dude: Myths, Mascots, and American Indians." In *Doing Race: 21 Essays for the 21st Century*, edited by Hazel Rose Markus and Paula M. Moya, 458–80. New York: W. W. Norton.

Fryd, Vivien Green. 1992. *Art and Empire: The Politics of Ethnicity in the United States Capitol, 1815–1860*. New Haven: Yale University Press.

Fuchs, Christian, Matthias Schafranek, David Hakken, and Marcus Breen. 2010. "Capitalist Crisis, Communication & Culture." Special issue, *tripleC: Communication, Capitalism & Critique* 8 (2): 193–309.

Fujitani, Takeshi. 2001. "*Go for Broke*, the Movie: Japanese American Soldiers in U.S. National, Military, and Racial Discourses." In *Perilous Memories: The Asian Pacific War(s)*, edited by Takeshi Fujitani, Geoffrey Wright, and Lisa Yoneyama, 239–66. Durham, NC: Duke University Press.

Fujitani, Takeshi, Geoffrey Wright, and Lisa Yoneyama, eds. 2001. *Perilous Memories: The Asian Pacific War(s)*. Durham, NC: Duke University Press.

Fujiwara, Lynn. 2008. *Mothers without Citizenship: Asian Immigrant Families and the Consequences of Welfare Reform*. Minneapolis: University of Minnesota Press.

Fukuyama, Francis. 1995. *Trust: The Social Virtues and the Creation of Prosperity*. New York: Free Press.

Fuller, Matthew. 2005. *Media Ecologies: Materialist Energies in Art and Technoculture*. Cambridge: MIT Press.

———. 2008. *Software Studies: A Lexicon*. Cambridge: MIT Press.

Fullilove, Mindy Thompson. 2004. *Root Shock: How Tearing Up City Neighborhoods Is Ruining America and What We Can Do about It*. New York: Ballantine Books.

Gaines, Kevin K. 2006. *American Africans in Ghana: Black Expatriates and the Civil Rights Era*. Chapel Hill: University of North Carolina Press.

Galbraith, James. 2012. *Inequality and Instability: A Study of the World Economy Just before the Great Crisis*. New York: Oxford University Press.

Galloway, Alex. 2004. *Protocol: How Control Exists after Decentralization*. Cambridge: MIT Press.

———. 2006. *Gaming: Essays on Algorithmic Culture*. Minneapolis: University of Minnesota Press.

———. 2012. *The Interface Effect*. New York: Polity.

Gallup. 2016. "Americans' Views of Socialism, Capitalism Are Little Changed." May 6, 2016.

Gamber, Wendy. 1997. *The Female Economy: The Millinery and Dressmaking Trades, 1860–1930*. Urbana: University of Illinois Press.

Garberoglio, Carrie, Stephanie Cawthon, and Adam Sales. "Deaf People and Educational Attainment, White Paper."

García, Ignacio M. 2009. *White but Not Equal: Mexican Americans, Jury Discrimination, and the Supreme Court*. Tucson: University of Arizona Press.

García, Maria Cristina. 2006. *Seeking Refuge: Central American Migration to Mexico, the United States, and Canada*. Berkeley: University of California Press.

García Bedolla, Lisa. 2009. *Latino Politics*. Malden, MA: Polity.

García Canclini, Néstor. 1995. *Hybrid Cultures: Strategies for Entering and Leaving Modernity*. Translated by Christopher L. Chippari and Silvia L. López. Minneapolis: University of Minnesota Press.

———. 2004. *Diferentes, desiguales y desconectados: Mapas de la interculturalidad*. Barcelona: Gedisa.

Garcia Martinez, David. 2019. "No, Data Is Not the New Oil." *Wired*, February 26, 2019.

Garcilaso de la Vega. 1704. *Le commentaire royal, ou l'histoire des Incas, roys du Perv; contenant leur origine, depuis le . . . leurs sacrifices . . . traduite de l'Espagnol de l'Ynca Garcillasso de la Vega*. Translated by J. Baudouin. 2 vols. Amsterdam: G. Kuyper.

Gardet, L[ouis]. 1978. "Islam." In *Encyclopedia of Islam* Edited by E. van Donzel, B. Lewis, and Ch. Pellat, 171–74. 2nd ed. Vol. 4. Leiden: Brill.

Gardner, Howard. 1983. *Frames of Mind: The Theory of Multiple Intelligences*. New York: Basic Books.

Garland, David. 2001. *The Culture of Control: Crime and Social Order in Contemporary Society*. Chicago: University of Chicago.

Garland-Thomson, Rosemarie. 1997. *Extraordinary Bodies: Figuring Physical Disability in American Culture and Literature*. New York: Columbia University Press.

———. 2007. "Cultural Commentary: 'Transferred to an Unknown Location . . .'" *Disability Studies Quarterly* 27 (4). http://dsq-sds.org.

Garraway, Doris. 2005. *Libertine Colony: Creolization in the Early French Caribbean*. Durham, NC: Duke University Press.

Garroutte, Eva. 2003. *Real Indians: Identity and the Survival of Native America*. Berkeley: University of California.

Garza, Monica. 1998. *Foto-Escultura: A Mexican Photographic Tradition*. Albuquerque: University of New Mexico Art Museum.

Gates, Henry Louis, Jr. 1978. "Preface to Blackness: Text and Pretext." In *Afro-American Literature: The Reconstruction of Instruction*, edited by Dexter Fisher and Robert B. Stepto, 44–69. New York: Modern Language Association.

———. 1987. "'What's Love Got to Do with It?': Critical Theory, Integrity, and Black Idiom." *New Literary History* 18:345–62.

Gayle, Addison, ed. 1971. *The Black Aesthetic*. New York: Doubleday.

Geertz, Clifford. (1966) 1983. "Religion as a Cultural System." In *The Interpretation of Cultures: Selected Essays*, 87–125. London: Fontana.

Geiger, Roger. 2014. *The History of American Higher Education*. Princeton, NJ: Princeton University Press.

Gelder, Ken, and Sarah Thornton, eds. 1997. *The Subcultures Reader*. London: Routledge.

Genovese, Eugene D. 1979. *From Revolution to Rebellion: Afro-American Slave Revolts in the Making of the Modern World*. Baton Rouge: Louisiana State University Press.

———. 1994. *The Southern Tradition: The Achievements and Limitations of an American Conservatism*. Cambridge, MA: Harvard University Press.

Georgacas, Demetrius J. 1969. "The Name *Asia* for the Continent: Its History and Origin." *Names* 17 (1): 1–90.

Geronimo. (1905) 1996. *Geronimo: His Own Story: The Autobiography of a Great Patriot Warrior; as Told to S. M. Barrett*. New York: Penguin.

Geyer, Michael, and Sheila Fitzpatrick, eds. 2008. *Beyond Totalitarianism: Stalinism and Nazism Compared*. Cambridge: Cambridge University Press.

Ghosh, Amitav. 2016. *The Great Derangement: Climate Change and the Unthinkable*. Chicago: University of Chicago Press.

Giberti, Bruno. 2002. *Designing the Centennial: A History of the 1876 International Exhibition in Philadelphia*. Lexington: University Press of Kentucky.

Gibson, William. 1982. "Burning Chrome." *Omni*, July 1982.

Gibson-Graham, J. K. 1996. *The End of Capitalism (as We Knew It): A Feminist Critique of Political Economy*. Cambridge, MA: Blackwell.

Gibson-Graham, J. K., Stephen Resnick, and Richard Wolff, eds. 2001. *Re/presenting Class: Essays in Postmodern Marxism*. Durham, NC: Duke University Press.

Giddens, Anthony. 1984. *Constitution of Society: Outline of the Theory of Structuration*. Berkeley: University of California Press.

———. 1990. *Consequences of Modernity*. Stanford, CA: Stanford University Press.

———. 1998. "Risk Society: The Context of British Politics." In *The Politics of Risk Society*, edited by J. Franklin. Cambridge, UK: Polity.

Giles, Paul. 2001. *Transatlantic Insurrections: British Culture and the Formation of American Literature, 1730–1860*. Philadelphia: University of Pennsylvania Press.

———. 2003. "Transnationalism and Classic American Literature." *PMLA* 118 (1): 62–77.

Gilio-Whitaker, Dina. 2019. *As Long as Grass Grows: The Indigenous Fight for Environmental Justice from Colonization to Standing Rock*. Boston: Beacon.

Gilligan, Carol. 1982. *In a Different Voice: Psychological Theory and Women's Development*. Cambridge, MA: Harvard University Press.

Gill-Peterson, Julian. 2018. *Histories of the Transgender Child*. Minneapolis: University of Minnesota Press.

Gilman, Nils. 2003. *Mandarins of the Future: Modernization Theory in Cold War America*. Baltimore: Johns Hopkins University Press.

Gilman, Sander. 1986. "Black Bodies, White Bodies: Toward an Iconography of Female Sexuality in Late Nineteenth Century Art, Medicine, and Literature." In *Race, Writing, and Difference*, edited by Henry Louis Jr., 223–61. Chicago: University of Chicago Press.

———. 1995. *Picturing Health and Illness: Images of Identity and Difference*. Baltimore: Johns Hopkins University Press.

Gilmore, Glenda. 2008. *Defying Dixie: The Radical Roots of Civil Rights 1919–1950*. New York: W. W. Norton.

Gilmore, Grant. 1974. *The Death of Contract*. Columbus: Ohio State University Press.

Gilmore, Michael T. 1985. *American Romanticism and the Marketplace*. Chicago: University of Chicago Press.

Gilmore, Ruth Wilson. 1998. "Globalisation and U.S. Prison Growth: From Military Keynesianism to Post-Keynesian Militarism." *Race and Class* 40 (2–3): 171–88.

———. 2007. *Golden Gulag: Prisons, Surplus, Crisis, and Opposition in Globalizing California*. Berkeley: University of California Press.

———. 2012. "Partition." Lecture at "Decolonize the City!," Rosa Luxemburg Foundation, Berlin, Germany, September 23, 2012.

Gilroy, Paul. 1987. *"There Ain't No Black in the Union Jack": The Cultural Politics of Race and Nation*. Chicago: University of Chicago Press.

———. 1991. *"There Ain't No Black in the Union Jack": The Cultural Politics of Race and Nation*. Rev. ed. Chicago: University of Chicago Press.

———. 1993. *The Black Atlantic: Modernity and Double Consciousness*. Cambridge, MA: Harvard University Press.

———. 2000. *Against Race: Imagining Political Culture beyond the Color Line*. Cambridge, MA: Belknap Press of Harvard University Press.

Ginsburg, Faye T. 1998. *Contested Lives: The Abortion Debate in an American Community*. Berkeley: University of California Press.

Giri, Ananta Kumar. 2004. "Rethinking the Politics and Ethics of Consumption: Dialogues with the."

Giroux, Henry. 1996. *Fugitive Cultures: Race, Violence, and Youth*. New York: Routledge.

Gitelman, Lisa. 2006. *Always Already New: Media, History, and the Data of Culture*. Cambridge: MIT Press.

Gitelman, Lisa, and Virginia Jackson. 2013. Introduction to *"Raw Data" Is an Oxymoron*, 1–14. Cambridge: MIT Press.

Glazer, Nathan. 1983. *Ethnic Dilemmas, 1964–1982*. Cambridge, MA: Harvard University Press.

Glenn, Evelyn Nakano. 2004. *Unequal Freedom: How Race and Gender Shaped American Citizenship and Labor*. Cambridge, MA: Harvard University Press.

Glenn, Susan. 2000. *Female Spectacle: The Theatrical Roots of American Feminism*. Cambridge, MA: Harvard University Press.

Glickman, Lawrence B. 1997. *A Living Wage: American Workers and the Making of Consumer Society*. Ithaca, NY: Cornell University Press.

Glissant, Édouard. 1989. *Caribbean Discourse: Selected Essays*. Translated by J. Michael Dash. Charlottesville: University Press of Virginia.

———. 2000. *Faulkner Mississippi*. Translated by Barbara Lewis and Thomas C. Spear. Chicago: University of Chicago Press.

Global Environmental Justice Project, Pellow, et al. 2018. *Environmental Injustice Behind Bars: Toxic Imprisonment in America*. UCSB. https://gejp.es.ucsb.edu.

Global Witness. n.d. "Deadly Environment." Last modified April 15, 2014.

Goffman, Erving. 1959. *The Presentation of Self in Everyday Life*. Garden City, NY: Doubleday.

———. 1963. *Stigma: Notes on the Management of Spoiled Identity*. New York: Touchstone / Simon & Schuster.

Goldberg, David Theo. 1993. *Racist Culture: Philosophy and the Politics of Meaning*. Cambridge, MA: Blackwell.

Goldberg, David Theo, and Richard Marciano. 2012. "T-RACES: Testbed for the Redlining Archives of

California's Exclusionary Spaces." *Vectors* 3 (2). http://vectors.usc.edu.

Goldberg, Jonah. 2008. *Liberal Fascism: The Secret History of the American Left from Mussolini to the Politics of Meaning*. New York: Doubleday.

Goldberg, Jonathan. 1992. *Sodometries: Renaissance Texts, Modern Sexualities*. Stanford, CA: Stanford University Press.

———. 1995. "The History That Will Be." *GLQ* 1 (4): 385–403.

Goldman, Emma. 1969. *Anarchism and Other Essays*. Mineola, NY: Dover.

Goldstein, Alyosha. 2012. *Poverty in Common: The Politics of Community Action during the American Century*. Durham, NC: Duke University Press.

———. 2014. *Formations of U.S. Colonialism*. Durham, NC: Duke University Press.

Goldstein, Alyosha, and Alex Lubin. 2008. "Settler Colonialism." Special issue, *South Atlantic Quarterly* 107 (4).

Goldstein, Sidney. 1954. "Migration: Dynamic of the American City." *American Quarterly* 6 (4): 337–48.

Golinski, J. 2007. "American Climate and the Civilization of Nature." In *Science and Empire in the Atlantic World*, edited by J. Delbourgo and N. Dew, 153–74. New York: Taylor and Francis.

Gombrich, E. H. 1969. *Art and Illusion: A Study in the Psychology of Pictorial Representation*. Princeton, NJ: Princeton University Press.

Gómez, Laura E. 2007. *Manifest Destinies: The Making of the Mexican American Race*. New York: New York University Press.

———. 2018. *Manifest Destinies: The Making of the Mexican American Race*. 2nd ed. New York: New York University Press.

Gómez-Barris, Macarena. 2017. *The Extractive Zone: Social Ecologies and Decolonial Perspectives*. Durham, NC: Duke University Press.

Gómez-Peña, Guillermo. 1990. *Border Brujo*. Videocassette recording. Cinewest Productions.

Gonzalez, Christian Alejandro. 2018. "Intersectionality—a Review." Quillette, August 14, 2018. https://quillette.com.

Goodman, Audrey. 2002. *Translating Southwestern Landscapes: The Making of an Anglo Literary Region*. Tucson: University of Arizona Press.

Goodman, Paul. 1998. *Of One Blood: Abolitionism and the Origins of Racial Equality*. Berkeley: University of California Press.

Goodwyn, Lawrence. 1976. *Democratic Promise: The Populist Movement in America*. Oxford: Oxford University Press.

———. 1978. *The Populist Moment: A Short History of the Agrarian Revolt in America*. Oxford: Oxford University Press.

Gopinath, Gayatri. 2005. *Impossible Desires: Queer Diasporas and South Asian Public Cultures*. Durham, NC: Duke University Press.

———. 2007. "Queer Regions: Locating Lesbians in *Sancharram*." In *A Companion to Lesbian, Gay, Bisexual, Transgender, and Queer Studies*, edited by George E. Haggerty and Molly McGarry, 341–54. Malden, MA: Blackwell.

Gordley, James. 1991. *The Philosophical Origins of Modern Contract Doctrine*. Oxford, UK: Clarendon.

Gordon, Avery. 2008. *Ghostly Matters: Haunting and the Sociological Imagination*. Minneapolis: University of Minnesota Press.

Gordon, David M. 1996. *Fat and Mean: The Corporate Squeeze of Working Americans and the Myth of Managerial "Downsizing."* New York: Free Press.

Gordon, Edmund T. 1998. *Disparate Diasporas: Identity and Politics in an African Nicaraguan Community*. Austin: University of Texas Press.

Gotanda, Neil. 1991. "A Critique of 'Our Constitution Is Color-Blind.'" *Stanford Law Review* 44 (1): 1–68.

Gotham, Kevin Fox, and Miriam Greenberg. 2014. *Crisis Cities: Disaster and Redevelopment in New York and New Orleans*. New York: Oxford University Press.

Goudie, Sean X. 2006. *Creole America: The West Indies and the Formation of Literature and Culture in the New Republic*. University of Pennsylvania Press.

Gould, Philip. 2003. *Barbaric Traffic: Commerce and Antislavery in the Eighteenth-Century Atlantic World*. Cambridge, MA: Harvard University Press.

Gould, Stephen Jay. 1981. *The Mismeasure of Man*. New York: Norton.

———. 1982. "The Hottentot Venus." *Natural History* 91 (10): 20–25.

Graeber, David. 2002. "The New Anarchists." *New Left Review* 13:61–73.

———. 2011. *Debt: The First 5000 Years*. New York: Melville.

Graff, E. J. 1999. *What Is Marriage For? The Strange Social History of Our Most Intimate Institution*. Boston: Beacon.

Graff, Gerald. 1987. *Professing Literature: An Institutional History*. Chicago: University of Chicago Press.

Gramsci, Antonio. 1929–35. *Selections from the Prison Notebooks*. New York.

———. 1971. *Selections from the Prison Notebooks*. Edited and translated by Quintin Hoare and Geoffrey Nowell Smith. New York: International.

Grandin, Greg. 2010. *Empire's Workshop: Latin America, the United States, and the Rise of the New Imperialism*. New York: Metropolitan Books.

———. 2014. *The Empire of Necessity: Slavery, Freedom, and Deception in the New World*. New York: Metropolitan Books.

Grant, Madison. 1916. *The Passing of the Great Race, or, the Racial Basis of European History*. New York: Scribner.

Grattan, Laura. 2016. *Populism's Power: Radical Grassroots Democracy in America*. New York: Oxford University Press.

Green, Adam. 2007. *Selling the Race: Culture, Community, and Black Chicago, 1940–1955* Chicago: University of Chicago Press.

Green, James. 2006. *Death in the Haymarket: A Story of Chicago, the First Labor Movement, and the Bombing That Divided Gilded Age America*. New York: Random House.

Green, Nancy L. 1997. *Ready-to-Wear and Ready-to-Work: A Century of Industry and Immigrants in Paris and New York*. Durham, NC: Duke University Press.

Green, Tara T. 2008. *From the Plantation to the Prison: African-American Confinement Literature*. Macon, GA: Mercer University Press.

Greenwald, Glenn. 2013. "NSA Collecting Phone Records of Millions of Verizon Customers Daily." *Guardian*, June 6, 2013. www.theguardian.com.

Greeson, Jennifer. 2010. *Our South: Geographic Fantasy and the Rise of National Literature*. Cambridge, MA: Harvard University Press.

Gregg, Melissa, and Gregory J. Seigworth, eds. 2010. *The Affect Theory Reader*. Durham, NC: Duke University Press.

Gregor, A. James. 2000. *The Faces of Janus: Marxism and Fascism in the Twentieth Century*. New Haven: Yale University Press.

Greiman, Jennifer. 2010. *Democracy's Spectacle: Sovereignty and Public Life in Antebellum America*. New York: Fordham University Press.

Grewal, Inderpal. 2003. "Transnational America: Race, Gender and Citizenship after 9/11." *Social Identities* 9 (4): 535–61.

———. 2005. *Transnational America: Feminisms, Diasporas, Neoliberalisms*. Durham, NC: Duke University Press.

———. 2017. *Saving the Security State: Exceptional Citizens in Twenty-First-Century America*. Durham, NC: Duke University Press.

Griffin, Farrah Jasmine. 1995. *"Who Set You Flowin'?" The African-American Migration Narrative*. New York: Oxford University Press.

Griffin, Roger. 1993. *The Nature of Fascism*. New York: New York: Routledge.

———. 2004. "Paper Tiger or Cheshire Cat? A Spotter's Guide to Fascism in the Post-fascist Era." In *Fascism: Critical Concepts in Political Science*, edited by Griffin, 386–93. Vol. 5. Routledge.

Griffin, Roger, Werner Loh, and Andreas Umland, eds. 2006. *Fascism Past and Present, West and East: An International Debate on Concepts and Cases in Comparative Study of the Extreme Right*. Stuttgart: Ibidem Verlag.

Griffin, Susan. 1978. *Woman and Nature: The Roaring inside Her*. New York: Harper & Row.

Griffiths, Alison. 2016. *Carceral Fantasies: Cinema and Prison in Early Twentieth-Century America*. New York: Columbia University Press.

Griggs, Richard. 1992. "Background on the Term 'Fourth World': An Excerpt from CWIS Occasional Paper #18, The Meaning of 'Nation' and 'State' in the Fourth World." University of Capetown, Center for World Indigenous Studies. http://cwis.org.

Grossberg, Lawrence. 2010a. *Cultural Studies in the Future Tense*. Durham, NC: Duke University Press.

———. 2010b. "Standing on a Bridge: Rescuing Economies from Economists." *Journal of Communication Inquiry* 34 (4): 316–36.

Grossberg, Lawrence, Cary Nelson, and Paula Treichler, eds. 1992. *Cultural Studies*. London: Routledge.

Grossman, Allen. 1985. "The Poetics of Union in Whitman and Lincoln: An Inquiry toward the Relationship of Art and Policy." In *The American Renaissance Reconsidered*, edited by Walter Benn Michaels and Donald E. Pease, 183–208. Baltimore: Johns Hopkins University Press.

Grossman, James R. 1989. *Land of Hope: Chicago, Black Southerners, and the Great Migration*. Chicago: University of Chicago Press.

Grossman, Lev. 2011. "From Scroll to Screen." *New York Times*, September 2, 2011.

Grosz, Elizabeth A. 1994. *Volatile Bodies: Toward a Corporeal Feminism*. Indiana University Press.

———. 2005. *Time Travels: Feminism, Nature, Power*. Durham, NC: Duke University Press.

———. 2011. *Becoming Undone: Darwinian Reflections on Life, Politics, and Art*. Durham, NC: Duke University Press.

Grove, Richard. 1996. *Green Imperialism: Colonial Expansion, Island Edens, and the Origins of Environmentalism, 1600–1860*. New York: Cambridge University Press.

Gruen, Erich S. 2002. "Diaspora and Homeland." In *Diasporas and Exiles: Varieties of Jewish Identity*, edited by Howard Wettstein, 18–46. Berkeley: University of California Press.

Gruesz, Kirsten Silva. 2002. *Ambassadors of Culture: The Transamerican Origins of Latino Writing*. Princeton, NJ: Princeton University Press.

Guenther, Lisa. 2013. *Social Death and Its Afterlives: A Critical*

Phenomenology of Solitary Confinement. Minneapolis: University of Minnesota Press.

Gulbenkian Commission. 1996. *Open the Social Sciences: Report of the Gulbenkian Commission on the Restructuring of the Social Sciences.* Stanford, CA: Stanford University Press.

Gunning, Tom. 1989. "An Aesthetic of Astonishment: Early Film and the (In)Credulous Spectator." *Art and Text* 34:31–45.

Gupta, Akhil, and James Ferguson. 1992. "Beyond 'Culture': Space, Identity and the Politics of Difference." *Cultural Anthropology* 7 (1): 6–23.

Gustafson, Sandra M. 2000. *Eloquence Is Power: Oratory and Performance in Early America.* Chapel Hill: University of North Carolina Press.

———. 2011. *Imagining Deliberative Democracy in the Early American Republic.* Chicago: University of Chicago Press.

Gustafson, Sandra M., and Caroline F. Sloat. 2010. *Cultural Narratives: Textuality and Performance in American Culture before 1900.* Notre Dame: University of Notre Dame Press.

Guterson, David. 1995. *Snow Falling on Cedars: A Novel.* New York: Vintage.

Gutiérrez, David G., and Pierette Hondagneu-Sotelo. 2008. Introduction to *American Quarterly* 60 (3): 503–21.

Gutiérrez, Elena R. 2008. *Fertile Matters: The Politics of Mexican-Origin Women's Reproduction.* Austin: University of Texas Press.

Gutiérrez-Jones, Carl. 1995. "Desiring B/orders." *diacritics* 25 (2): 99–112.

Gutman, Herbert G. 1976. *Work, Culture, and Society in Industrializing America.* New York: Vintage.

Guzmán, Joshua Javier, and Christina A. León, eds. 2015. *Lingering in Latinidad: Theory, Aesthetics, and Performance in Latina/o Studies.* Vol. 25.

Habermas, Jürgen. 1987. *The Philosophical Discourse of Modernity: Twelve Lectures.* Translated by Frederick Lawrence. Cambridge, UK: Polity.

———. 1999. *The Structural Transformation of the Public Sphere: An Inquiry into a Category of Bourgeois Society.* Translated by Thomas Burger. Cambridge: MIT Press.

Habitant d'Hayti. 1811. *Idylles et Chansons, ou Essais de Poësie Créole.* Philadelphia: Imprimerie J. Edwards.

Hacker, Jacob. 2006. *The Great Risk Shift: The Assault on American Jobs, Families, Health Care, and Retirement and How You Can Fight Back.* New York: Oxford University Press.

Haines, Christian. 2019. *A Desire Called America: Biopolitics, Utopia, and the Literary Commons.* New York: Fordham University Press.

Hakluyt, Richard. 1589. *The Principall Navigations, Voiages, and Discoveries of the English Nation.* London: George Bishop and Ralph Newberie, deputies to Christopher Barker.

Halberstam, Judith. 1995. *Skin Shows: Gothic Horror and the Technology of Monsters.* Durham, NC: Duke University Press.

———. 1998. *Female Masculinity.* Durham, NC: Duke University Press.

———. 2005. *In a Queer Time and Place: Transgender Bodies, Subcultural Lives.* New York: New York University Press.

Hale, Charles R. 1994. "Between Che Guevara and the Pachamama: Mestizos, Indians, and Identity Politics in the Anti-quincentenary Campaign." *Critique of Anthropology* 14 (1): 9–39.

———. 2008. *Engaging Contradictions: Theory, Politics, and Methods for Activist Scholarship.* Oakland: University of California Press.

Haley, Sarah. 2016. *No Mercy Here: Gender, Punishment, and the Making of Jim Crow Modernity.* Chapel Hill: University of North Carolina Press.

Hall, David. 1996. *Cultures of Print: Essays in the History of the Book.* Amherst: University of Massachusetts Press.

———. 2014. *A History of the Book in America.* Chapel Hill: University of North Carolina Press.

Hall, Edward. 1969. *The Hidden Dimension.* Garden City, NY: Doubleday.

Hall, G. Stanley. 1904. *Adolescence: Its Psychology and Its Relation to Physiology, Anthropology, Sex, Crime, Religion, and Education.* New York: Appleton-Century-Crofts.

Hall, Gwendolyn Midlo. 1992. *Africans in Colonial Louisiana: The Development of Afro-Creole Culture in the Eighteenth Century.* Baton Rouge: Louisiana State University Press.

Hall, Stuart. 1973. "Deviancy, Politics, and the Media." In *Deviance and Social Control*, edited by Paul Rock and Mary McIntosh, 261–305. London: Tavistock.

———. 1978. *Policing the Crisis: Mugging, the State, and Law and Order.* New York: Holmes and Meier.

———. 1980. "Cultural Studies: Two Paradigms." *Media, Culture and Society* 2 (1): 57–72.

———. 1988. "The Toad in the Garden: Thatcherism among the Theorists." In *Marxism and the Interpretation of Culture*, edited by Cary Nelson. Champaign: University of Illinois Press.

———. 1990. "Cultural Identity and Diaspora." In *Identity: Community, Culture, Difference*, edited by Jonathan Rutherford, 222–37. London: Lawrence and Wishart.

———. 1991. "Cultural Studies and Its Theoretical Legacies." In *Cultural Studies Reader*, edited by Lawrence Grossberg, Cary Nelson, and Paula Treichler, 277–94. New York: Routledge.

———. 1992a. "Race, Culture and Communications: Looking

Backward and Forward at Cultural Studies." *Rethinking Marxism* 5 (1): 10–18.

———. 1992b. "What Is This 'Black' in Black Popular Culture?" In *Black Popular Culture*, edited by Gina Dent, 21–36. Seattle: Bay.

———. 1993. "Culture, Community, Nation." *Cultural Studies* 7 (3): 349–63.

———. 2002. "Race, Articulation, and Societies Structured in Dominance." In *Race Critical Theories: Text and Context*, edited by Philomena Essed and David Theo Goldberg, 38–68. Malden, MA: Blackwell.

Hall, Stuart, and Bram Gieben, eds. 1992. *Formations of Modernity*. Cambridge, UK: Polity.

Hall, Stuart, and Tony Jefferson, eds. 1976. *Resistance through Rituals: Youth Subcultures in Post-war Britain*. London: Hutchinson / Centre for Contemporary Cultural Studies, University of Birmingham.

Halley, Janet E. 1999. *Don't: A Reader's Guide to the Military's Anti-gay Policy*. Durham, NC: Duke University Press.

Halpern, Orit. 2015. *Beautiful Data: A History of Vision and Reason since 1945*. Durham, NC: Duke University Press.

Hamburger, Philip. 2002. *Separation of Church and State*. Cambridge, MA: Harvard University Press.

Hames-García, Michael. 2000. "How to Tell a Mestizo from an Enchirito: Colonialism and National Culture in the Borderlands." *diacritics* 30 (4): 102–22.

Hammer, Michael, and James A. Champy. 1993. *Reengineering the Corporation: A Manifesto for Business Revolution*. New York: HarperCollins.

Hammonds, Evelynn. 1997. "Toward a Genealogy of Black Female Sexuality: The Problematic of Silence." In *Feminist Genealogies, Colonial Legacies, Democratic Futures*, edited by M. Jacqui Alexander and Chandra Talpade Mohanty, 170–82. New York: Routledge.

Hanchard, Michael. 2006. *Party/Politics: Horizons in Black Political Thought*. Oxford: Oxford University Press.

Hancock, Ange Marie. 2007. "When Multiplication Doesn't Equal Quick Addition: Examining Intersectionality as a Research Paradigm." *Perspectives on Politics* 5 (1): 63–79.

Haney López, Ian. 1996. *White by Law: The Legal Construction of Race*. New York: New York University Press.

———. 2014. *Dog Whistle Politics: How Coded Racial Appeals Have Reinvented Racism and Wrecked the Middle Class*. Oxford: Oxford University Press.

Hanhardt, Christina B. 2013. *Safe Space: Gay Neighborhood History and the Politics of Violence*. Durham, NC: Duke University Press.

Hannah, Matthew G. 2000. *Governmentality and the Mastery of Territory in Nineteenth-Century America*. New York: Cambridge University Press.

Hannerz, Ulf. 1992. *Cultural Complexity: Studies in the Social Organization of Meaning*. New York: Columbia University Press.

Hansen, Miriam. 2011. *Cinema and Experience: Siegfried Kracauer, Walter Benjamin, and Theodor W. Adorno*. Berkeley: University of California Press.

Hanway, Jonas. 1753. *An Historical Account of the British Trade over the Caspian Sea*. London.

Haraway, Donna. 1985. "A Cyborg Manifesto: Science, Technology, and Socialist-Feminism in the Late Twentieth Century." *Socialist Review* 80:65–108.

———. 1988. "Situated Knowledges: The Science Question in Feminism and the Privilege of Partial Perspective." *Feminist Studies* 14 (3): 575–99.

———. 1989. *Primate Visions: Gender, Race, and Nature in the World of Modern Science*. New York: Routledge.

———. 1991. *Simians, Cyborgs, and Women: The Re-invention of Nature*. New York: Routledge.

———. 2003. *The Haraway Reader*. New York: Routledge.

———. 2008. *When Species Meet*. Minneapolis: University of Minnesota Press.

———. 2016. *Staying with the Trouble: Making Kin in the Chthulucene*. Durham, NC: Duke University Press.

Hardin, Garrett. 1968. "The Tragedy of the Commons." *Science* 162 (3859): 1243–48.

Harding, Sandra G. 1998. *Is Science Multicultural? Postcolonialisms, Feminisms, and Epistemologies*. Indiana University Press.

Harding, Susan. 2001. *The Book of Jerry Falwell: Fundamentalist Language and Politics*. Princeton, NJ: Princeton University Press.

Hardt, Michael, and Antonio Negri. 2000. *Empire*. Cambridge, MA: Harvard University Press.

Haritaworn, Jin. 2015. *Queer Lovers and Hateful Others: Regenerating Violent Times and Places*. London: Pluto.

Harkins, Anthony. 2005. *Hillbilly: A Cultural History of an American Icon*. New York: Oxford University Press.

Harkins, Gillian. 2009. *Everybody's Family Romance: Reading Incest in Neoliberal America*. Minneapolis: University of Minnesota Press.

Harney, Stefano, and Fred Moten. 2009. "The University and the Undercommons." In *Toward a Global Autonomous University—the Edu-Factory Collective*. New York: Autonomedia.

———. 2013. *The Undercommons: Fugitive Planning and Black Study*. Minor Compositions.

Harper, Kristine. 2017. *Make It Rain: State Control of the Atmosphere in Twentieth-Century America*. Chicago: University of Chicago Press.

Harper, Philip Brian. 1994. *Framing the Margins: The Social Logic of Postmodern Culture*. New York: Oxford University Press.

———. 1996. *Are We Not Men? Masculine Anxiety and the Problem of African-American Identity*. Oxford: Oxford University Press.

Harper, Phillip Brian, Anne McClintock, José Esteban Muñoz, and Trish Rosen. 1997. Introduction to "Queer Transexions of Race, Nation, and Gender." Edited by Phillip Brian Harper, Anne McClintock, José Estaban Muñoz, and Trish Rosen. Special issue, *Social Text* 52–53:1–4.

Harris, Cheryl I. 1993. "Whiteness as Property." *Harvard Law Review* 106 (8): 1707–91.

Harris, Laura. 2005. "The Subjunctive Poetics of C. L. R. James's *American Civilization*." Unpublished manuscript.

Harris, Lee. 2004. *Civilization and Its Enemies: The Next Stage of History*. New York: Free Press.

Harris, Marvin. 1977. *Cannibals and Kings: The Origins of Cultures*. New York: Random House.

Harris, Neil. 1973. *Humbug: The Art of P. T. Barnum*. Boston: Little, Brown.

Harrison, Lawrence E., and Samuel P. Huntington, eds. 2000. *Culture Matters: How Values Shape Human Progress*. New York: Basic Books.

Hart, Albert Bushnell. 1910. *The Southern South*. New York: D. Appleton.

Hart, H. L. A. 1961. *The Concept of Law*. Oxford, UK: Clarendon.

Hartigan, John, Jr. 1997. "Objectifying 'Poor Whites' and 'White Trash' in Detroit." In *White Trash: Race and Class in America*, edited by Matt Wray and Annalee Newitz, 41–56. New York: Routledge.

———. 1999. *Racial Situations: Class Predicaments of Whiteness in Detroit*. Princeton, NJ: Princeton University Press.

Hartman, Andrew. 2015. *A War for the Soul of America: A History of the Culture Wars*. Chicago: University of Chicago Press.

Hartman, Saidiya. 1997. *Scenes of Subjection: Terror, Slavery, and Self-Making in Nineteenth-Century America*. New York: Oxford University Press.

Hartnell, Anna. 2017. *After Katrina: Race Neoliberalism, and the End of the American Century*. State University of New York Press.

Hartog, Hendrik. 2000. *Man and Wife in America: A History*. Cambridge, MA: Harvard University Press.

Hartz, Louis. 1955. *The Liberal Tradition in America: An Interpretation of American Political Thought since the Revolution*. New York: Harcourt Brace.

Harvey, David. 1989. *The Condition of Postmodernity: An Enquiry into the Origins of Cultural Change*. Oxford, UK: Blackwell.

———. 2000. *Spaces of Hope*. Berkeley: University of California Press.

———. 2003. *The New Imperialism*. Oxford: Oxford University Press.

———. 2005. *A Brief History of Neoliberalism*. New York: Oxford University Press.

———. 2010. *The Enigma of Capital and the Crises of Capitalism*. New York: Verso.

———. 2017. *Marx, Capital, and the Madness of Economic Reason*. New York: Oxford University Press.

Haskell, Thomas L., and Richard F. Teichgraeber III, eds. 1996. *The Culture of the Market: Historical Essays*. New York: Cambridge University Press.

Hausman, Bernice L. 1995. *Changing Sex: Transsexualism, Technology, and the Idea of Gender*. Duke University Press.

Hawthorne, Nathaniel. 1844. "Earth's Holocaust." *Graham's Lady's and Gentleman's Magazine*, March 1844.

———. (1855) 1987. "Letter to William Ticknor, January 19, 1855." In *Centenary Edition of the Works of Nathaniel Hawthorne*. Vol. 17, *The Letters, 1853–56*, 304. Columbus: Ohio State University Press.

Hay, Denys. 1957. *Europe: The Emergence of an Idea*. Edinburgh: Edinburgh University Press.

Hayden, Dolores. 2006. *A Field Guide to Sprawl*. New York: Norton.

Hayek, Friedrich A. 1944. *The Road to Serfdom*. Chicago: University of Chicago Press.

———. (1944) 2007. *The Road to Serfdom*. Chicago: University of Chicago Press.

Hayles, Katherine N. 1999. *How We Became Posthuman: Virtual Bodies in Cybernetics, Literature, and Informatics*. Chicago: University of Chicago Press.

———. 2002. *Writing Machines*. Cambridge: MIT Press.

———. 2008. *Electronic Literature: New Horizons for the Literary*. Notre Dame: University of Notre Dame Press.

———. 2012. *How We Think: Digital Media and Contemporary Technogenesis*. Chicago: University of Chicago Press.

Haymes, Stephen Nathan. 2018. "An Africana Studies Critique of Environmental Ethics." In *Racial Ecologies*, edited by Leilani Nishime and Kim D. Hester Williams, 34–49. Seattle: University of Washington Press.

Haynes, Todd, dir. 1995. *Safe*. New York: Sony Pictures.

Hearne, Joanna. 2013. *Native Recognition: Indigenous Cinema and the Western*. New York: State University of New York Press.

Hebdige, Dick. 1979. *Subculture: The Meaning of Style*. London: Methuen.

Hedges, Chris. 2002. *War Is a Force That Gives Us Meaning*. New York: PublicAffairs.

Hegel, G. W. F. (1821) 1979. *Hegel's Philosophy of Right*. Edited by and translated by T. M. Knox. Oxford, UK: Clarendon / Galaxy Books.

——. (1837) 1956. *The Philosophy of History*. Translated by J. Sibree. New York: Dover.

Heidegger, Martin. (1977) 1993. "The Question concerning Technology." In *Basic Writings*, edited by David Farrell Krell, 307–42. New York: Harper.

Henderson, Bruce, and Noam Ostrander, eds. 2010. *Understanding Disability Studies and Performance Studies*. New York: Routledge.

Henderson, Mae G. 1989. "Speaking in Tongues: Dialogics and Dialectics and the Black Woman Writer's Literary Tradition." In *Changing Our Own Words: Essays on Criticism, Theory, and Writing by Black Women*, edited by Cheryl Wall. New Brunswick, NJ: Rutgers University Press.

Henderson, Stephen. 1973. *Understanding the New Black Poetry: Black Speech and Black Music as Poetic References*. New York: Morrow.

Hendler, Glenn. 2001. *Public Sentiments: Structures of Feeling in Nineteenth-Century American Literature*. Chapel Hill: University of North Carolina Press.

Henry, Patrick. 1957. "Letter to Robert Pleasants, January 18, 1773." In *Patrick Henry: Patriot in the Making*, edited by Robert Douthat Meade. Vol. 1. Philadelphia: Lippincott.

——. 1981. "'And I Don't Care What It Is': The Tradition-History of a Civil Religion Proof-Text." *Journal of the American Academy of Religion* 49 (1): 35–47.

Herbert, James D. 2003. "Visual Culture / Visual Studies." In *Critical Terms for Art History*, edited by Robert S. Nelson and Richard Shiff, 452–64. 2nd ed. Chicago: University of Chicago Press.

Herder, Johann Gottfried von. (1766) 2002. "On the Change of Taste." In *Herder: Philosophical Writings*, 247–56. Cambridge: Cambridge University Press.

Herek, Gregory M., and Kevin T. Berrill, eds. 1992. *Hate Crimes: Confronting Violence against Lesbians and Gay Men*. Newbury Park, CA: Sage.

Herivel, Tara, and Paul Wright, eds. 2003. *Prison Nation: The Warehousing of America's Poor*. New York: Routledge.

Herman, Edward S., and Gerry O'Sullivan. 1989. *The "Terrorism" Industry: The Experts and Institutions That Shape Our View of Terror*. New York: Pantheon Books.

Herring, Scott. 2010. *Another Country: Queer Anti-urbanism*. New York: New York University Press.

Herrnstein, Richard J., and Charles Murray. 1994. *The Bell Curve: Intelligence and Class Structure in American Life*. New York: Free Press.

Hertz, Garnet. 2009. "Dead Media Research Lab." Concept Lab. www.conceptlab.com.

Hickey, Samuel, and Giles Mohan. 2005. *From Tyranny to Transformation: Exploring New Approaches to Participation in Development*. London: Zed Books.

Hietala, Thomas R. 1985. *Manifest Design: Anxious Aggrandizement in Late Jacksonian America*. Ithaca, NY: Cornell University Press.

Higham, John. 1963. *Strangers in the Land: Patterns of American Nativism, 1860–1925*. New York: Atheneum.

——. 1984. *Send These to Me: Immigrants in Urban America*. Rev. ed. Baltimore: Johns Hopkins University Press.

Hilderbrand, Lucas. 2009. *Inherent Vice: Bootleg Histories of Videotape and Copyright*. Durham, NC: Duke University Press.

Hill, Jane H. 2008. *The Everyday Language of White Racism*. Malden, MA: Wiley-Blackwell.

Hill, Rebecca. 1998. "Fosterites and Feminists, or 1950s Ultraleftists and the Invention of AmeriKKKa." *New Left Review* 228.

——. 2014. "The History of the Smith Act and the Hatch Act: Anti-communism and the Rise of the Conservative Coalition in Congress." In *Little Red Scares: Anti-communism and Political Repression in the United States 1921–1946*, edited by Goldstein, 315–46. London: Ashgate.

Hilmes, Michele. 2005. "Is There a Field Called Sound Culture Studies? And Does It Matter?" *American Quarterly* 57 (1): 249–59.

Hine, Darlene Clark. 1989. "Rape and the Inner Lives of Black Women in the Middle West: Preliminary Thoughts on the Culture of Dissemblance." *Signs* 14 (4): 912–20.

Hine, Darlene Clark, Trica Danielle Keaton, and Stephen Small, eds. 2009. *Black Europe and the African Diaspora*. Urbana: University of Illinois Press.

Hinks, Peter. 1997. *To Wake My Afflicted Brethren: David Walker and the Problem of Antebellum Slave Resistance*. University Park: Penn State University Press.

Hinton, Elizabeth. 2016. *From the War on Poverty to the War on Crime: The Making of Mass Incarceration in America*. Cambridge, MA: Harvard University Press.

Hirschkind, Charles. 2006. *The Ethical Soundscape: Cassette*

Sermons and Islamic Counterpublics. New York: Columbia University Press.

Hitchens, Christopher. 2007. "Defending the Term Islamofascism: It's a Valid Term. Here's Why." *Slate*, October 22, 2007. https://slate.com.

Ho, Fred, ed. 2000. *Legacy to Liberation: Politics and Culture of Revolutionary Asian/Pacific America*. San Francisco: AK.

Hobbes, Thomas. 1994. *Leviathan: With Selected Variants from the Latin Edition of 1668*. Edited by Edwin Curley. Indianapolis: Hackett.

Hobsbawm, Eric. 1983. "Introduction: Inventing Tradition." In *The Invention of Tradition*, edited by Eric Hobsbawm and Terence Ranger, 1–14. Cambridge: Cambridge University Press.

Hodgson, Godfrey. 2009. *The Myth of American Exceptionalism*. New Haven: Yale University Press.

Hofmeyr, Isabel. 2004. *The Portable Bunyan: A Transnational History of "The Pilgrim's Progress."* Princeton, NJ: Princeton University Press.

Hofstadter, Richard. (1955) 2011. *The Age of Reform*. New York: Vintage.

———. 1964. *The Paranoid Style in American Politics, and Other Essays*. New York: Vintage.

Hogan, Kristen. 2016. *The Feminist Bookstore Movement: Lesbian Antiracism and Feminist Accountability*. Durham, NC: Duke University Press.

Hogeland, Lisa Maria, et al., eds. 2004. *The Aunt Lute Anthology of U.S. Women Writers*. Vol. 1, *17th through 19th Centuries*. San Francisco: Aunt Lute Books.

Holcomb, Thomas K. 2012. *Introduction to American Deaf Culture*. Oxford: Oxford University Press.

Holyoake, George J. 1854. *Secularism, the Philosophy of the People*. London.

Hondagneu-Sotelo, Pierette. 1995. "Beyond 'the Longer They Stay' (and Say They Will Stay): Women and Mexican Immigrant Settlement." *Qualitative Sociology* 18 (1): 21–43.

Hong, Grace Kyungwon. 2006. *The Ruptures of American Capital: Women of Color Feminism and the Culture of Immigrant Labor*. Minneapolis: University of Minnesota Press.

Hong, Grace Kyungwon, and Roderick A. Ferguson. 2011. *Strange Affinities: The Gender and Sexual Politics of Comparative Racialization*. Durham, NC: Duke University Press.

Honig, Bonnie. 1998. "Immigrant America? How Foreignness 'Solves' Democracy's Problems." *Social Text* 56:1–27.

Hope, Ann, and Sue Timmel. 2000. *Training for Transformation: A Handbook for Community Workers*. Warwickshire, UK: Practical Action.

Hopfyl, Harro, and Martyn P. Thompson. 1979. "The History of the Contract as a Motif in Political Thought." *American Historical Review* 84 (4): 919–44.

Horkheimer, Max, and Theodor W. Adorno. (1944) 2002. *Dialectic of Enlightenment: Philosophical Fragments*. Edited by Gunzelin Schmid Noerr. Translated by Edmund Jephcott. Stanford, CA: Stanford University Press.

Horne, T. H. 1825. *Outlines for the Classification of a Library*. London: Woodfall and Court.

Hornung, Alfred. 1998. "George Washington Cable's Literary Reconstruction: Creole Civilization and Cultural Change." In *Creoles and Cajuns: French Louisiana—La Louisiane Française*, edited by Wolfgang Binder, 229–46. Frankfurt: Peter Lang.

Horowitz, Tony. 1999. *Confederates in the Attic: Dispatches from the Unfinished Civil War*. New York: Vintage.

Horsman, Reginald. 1981. *Race and Manifest Destiny: The Origins of American Racial Anglo-Saxonism*. Cambridge, MA: Harvard University Press.

Horwitz, Howard. 1987. "The Standard Oil Trust as Emersonian Hero." *Raritan* 6 (4): 97–119.

HoSang, Daniel. 2010. *Racial Propositions: Ballot Initiatives and the Making of Postwar California*. Berkeley: University of California Press.

Howard, John. 2001. *Men like That: A Southern Queer History*. Chicago: University of Chicago Press.

Howard, June. 1994. "Introduction: Sarah Orne Jewett and the Traffic in Words." In *New Essays on* The Country of the Pointed Firs, edited by June Howard, 1–38. Cambridge: Cambridge University Press.

———. 1999. "What Is Sentimentality?" *American Literary History* 11:63–81.

———. 2001. *Publishing the Family*. Durham, NC: Duke University Press.

———. 2018. *The Center of the World: Regional Writing and the Puzzles of Place-Time*. Oxford: Oxford University Press.

Howe, Susan. 1993. *The Birth-Mark: Unsettling the Wilderness in American Literary History*. Hanover, NH: Wesleyan University Press / University Press of New England.

Howes, David, ed. 2005. *Empire of the Senses: The Sensual Culture Reader*. Oxford, UK: Berg. www.aclu.org.

Hubbard, Ruth, Mary Sue Henifin, and Barbara Fried, eds. 1979. *Women Look at Biology Looking at Women: A Collection of Feminist Critiques*. Cambridge, MA: Schenkman.

Hudson, Michael. 2018. *"And Forgive Them Their Debts": Lending, Foreclosure and Redemption from Bronze Age Finance to the Jubilee Year*. New York: Islet.

Hughes, Langston. 1973. *Good Morning, Revolution: Uncollected*

Social Protest Writings. Edited by Faith Berry. Brooklyn, NY: Lawrence Hill.

Hugo, Victor. (1826) 1890. *Bug-Jargal*. Paris: Emile Testard.

Hume, David. (1757) 1993. *The Natural History of Religion: "Dialogues" and "Natural History of Religion."* Oxford: Oxford University Press.

Hunt, Lynn. 2007. *Inventing Human Rights: A History*. New York: Norton.

Hunter, Tera W. 1997. *To 'Joy My Freedom: Southern Black Women's Lives and Labors after the Civil War*. Cambridge, MA: Harvard University Press.

Huntington, Samuel P. 1996. *The Clash of Civilizations and the Remaking of World Order*. New York: Simon & Schuster.

———. 2004a. "The Hispanic Challenge." *Foreign Policy*, March–April 2004. www.foreignpolicy.com.

———. 2004b. *Who Are We? The Challenges to America's National Identity*. New York: Simon & Schuster.

Hurtado, Aída. 1989. "Relating to Privilege: Seduction and Rejection in the Subordination of White Women and Women of Color." *Signs* 14 (4): 833–55.

Hutcheon, Linda. 2002. *The Politics of Postmodernism*. 2nd ed. New York: Routledge.

Hutcheson, Frances. (1742) 2003. *An Essay on the Nature and Conduct of the Passions and Affections, with Illustrations on the Moral Sense*. Edited and introduction by Aaron Garrett. Indianapolis: Liberty Fund.

Hyman, Louis. 2012. *Debtor Nation: The History of America in Red Ink*. Princeton, NJ: Princeton University Press.

Ignatiev, Noel. 1995. *How the Irish Became White*. New York: Routledge.

Ignatiev, Noel, and John Garvey, eds. 1996. *Race Traitor*. New York: Routledge.

Ihde, Don. 1990. *Technology and the Lifeworld: From Garden to Earth*. Bloomington: Indiana University Press.

Illich, Ivan. 1970. *Deschooling Society*. New York: Harper & Row.

International Geosphere-Biosphere Programme (IGBP). 2015. "Planetary Dashboard Shows Great Acceleration in Human Activity since 1950." www.igbp.net.

Irick, Robert L. 1982. *Ch'ing Policy toward the Coolie Trade, 1847–1878*. Taipei: Chinese Materials Center.

Irvine, Janice. 1990. *Disorders of Desire: Sex and Gender in Modern American Sexology*. Philadelphia: Temple University Press.

Irving, Sarah, Rob Harrison, and Mary Rayner. 2002. "Ethical Consumerism: Democracy through the Wallet." *Journal of Research for Consumers*, 3. http://jrconsumers.com.

Isambard. 2004. "Would You Describe Yourself as Queer?" Urban75 Forums. www.urban75.net.

Isenberg, Nancy. 1998. *Sex and Citizenship in Antebellum America*. Chapel Hill: University of North Carolina Press.

Isham, Samuel. 1905. *History of American Painting*. New York: Macmillan.

Ishiguro, Laura. 2016a. "'Growing Up and Grown Up . . . in Our Future City': Discourses of Childhood and Settler Futurity in Colonial British Columbia." *BC Studies* 190:15–37.

———. 2016b. "Histories of Settler Colonialism: Considering New Currents." *BC Studies* (Summer): 5–13.

Jackson, Carlos. 2018. "Taller Arte Del Nuevo Amanacer: A Space Where Subjectivity Is Produced." *Public: A Journal of Imagining America* 5 (1).

Jackson, Jonathan David. 2002. "The Social World of Voguing." *Journal for the Anthropological Study of Human Movement* 12 (2): 26–42.

Jacobs, Harriet. (1861) 2001. *Incidents in the Life of a Slave Girl*. Edited by Nellie Y. McKay and Frances Smith Foster. New York: Norton.

Jacobs, Jane. 1961. "The Uses of Sidewalks: Safety." In *The Death and Life of Great American Cities*. New York: Random House.

Jacobson, Matthew Frye. 1998. *Whiteness of a Different Color: European Immigrants and the Alchemy of Race*. Cambridge, MA: Harvard University Press.

———. 2000. *Barbarian Virtues: The United States Encounters Foreign Peoples at Home and Abroad, 1876–1917*. New York: Hill and Wang.

Jacoby, Daniel. 1998. *Laboring for Freedom: A New Look at the History of Labor in America*. Armonk, NY: M. E. Sharpe.

Jain, Lochlann. 2006. *Injury: The Politics of Product Design and Safety Law in the United States*. Princeton, NJ: Princeton University Press.

———. 2013. *Malignant: How Cancer Becomes Us*. Berkeley: University of California Press.

Jamal, Amaney, and Nadine Naber, eds. 2008. *Race and Arab Americans before and after 9/11: From Invisible Citizens to Visible Subjects*. Syracuse: Syracuse University Press.

James, C. L. R. (1938) 1989. *The Black Jacobins: Toussaint L'Ouverture and the San Domingo Revolution*. New York: Dial. Reprint, New York: Vintage.

———. 1956. "Every Cook Can Govern: A Study of Democracy in Ancient Greece." In *The Future in the Present: Selected Writings*, 160–74. Westport, CT: Lawrence Hill.

James, Joy. 2005. *The New Abolitionists: (Neo)Slave Narratives and Contemporary Prison Writings*. Albany: State University of New York Press.

James, Lawrence. 2000. *Raj: The Making and Unmaking of British India*. New York: St. Martin's Griffin.

James, Selma, and Mariarosa Dalla Costa. 1972. *The Power of Women and the Subversion of Community: Wages for Housework*. Bristol, UK: Falling Wall.

Jameson, Fredric. 1991. *Postmodernism, or, the Cultural Logic of Late Capitalism*. Durham, NC: Duke University Press.

———. 1993. "On 'Cultural Studies.'" *Social Text* 36:17–52.

Janoski, Thomas. 2010. *The Ironies of Citizenship: Naturalization and Integration in Industrialized Countries*. New York: Cambridge University Press.

Jay, Gregory. 2011. "Hire Ed! Deconstructing the Crises in Academia" (book review). *American Quarterly*, March 2011.

Jay, Martin. 1994. *Downcast Eyes: The Denigration of Vision in Twentieth-Century French Thought*. Berkeley: University of California Press.

Jefferson, Thomas. (1776) 1984. "Declaration of Independence." In *Writings*, 19–24. New York: Library of America.

———. (1787) 1984. *Notes on the State of Virginia: Writings*. New York: Library of America.

———. (1787) 2002. *Notes on the State of Virginia: With Related Documents*. Edited by David Waldstreicher. Boston: Bedford / St. Martin's.

———. 1816. "Letter to John Adams." *Thomas Jefferson Encyclopedia*. Accessed August 4, 2018. www.monticello.org.

———. 1905. "Letter to John W. Eppes" (June 24, 1813). In *Letters and Addresses of Thomas Jefferson*, edited by William Parker and Jonas Viles. New York: Unit Books.

Jeffords, Susan. 1989. *The Remasculinization of America: Gender and the Vietnam War*. Bloomington: Indiana University Press.

Jehlen, Myra, and Michael Warner. 1997. *The English Literatures of America, 1500–1800*. New York: Routledge.

Jenkins, Henry. 2006. *Convergence Culture: Where Old and New Media Collide*. New York: New York University Press.

Jenness, Valerie, and Ryken Grattet. 2001. *Making Hate a Crime: From Social Movement to Law Enforcement*. New York: Russell Sage Foundation.

Jennings, Chris. 2016. *Paradise Now: The Story of American Utopianism*. New York: Random House.

Jensen, Arthur. 1969. "How Much Can We Boost IQ and Scholastic Achievement?" *Harvard Educational Review* 39:1–123.

Jenson, Deborah. 2007. "Fétichisme de la marchandise: la poésie créole des courtisanes noires de Saint-Domingue." In *Relire l'histoire et la littérature haïtiennes*, edited by Christiane Ndiaye, 27–56. Presses nationales d'Haïti.

Johns, Elizabeth. 1991. *American Genre Painting: The Politics of Everyday Life*. New Haven: Yale University Press.

Johnson, E. Patrick. 2003. *Appropriating Blackness: Performance and the Politics of Authenticity*. Durham, NC: Duke University Press.

———. 2008. *Sweet Tea: Black Gay Men of the South*. Chapel Hill: University of North Carolina Press.

Johnson, E. Patrick, and Mae G. Henderson. 2005. *Black Queer Studies: A Critical Anthology*. Durham, NC: Duke University Press.

Johnson, Jessica Marie. 2018. "Markup Bodies: Black [Life] Studies and Slavery [Death] Studies at the Digital Crossroads." *Social Text* 36 (4): 57–79.

Johnson, Lyndon Baines. 1965. "Annual Message to the Congress on the State of the Union, January 8, 1964." In *Public Papers of the Presidents, Lyndon Baines Johnson, 1963–64*. Vol. 1, entry 91, 112–18. Washington, DC: Government Printing Office.

Johnson, Samuel. 1755. *A Dictionary of the English Language*. London: W. Strahan.

Johnson, W., and R. G. D. Kelley, eds. 2017. *Race Capitalism Justice*. Boston: Boston Review.

Johnson, Walter. 1999. *Soul by Soul: Life inside the Antebellum Slave Market*. Cambridge, MA: Harvard University Press.

———. 2002. "Time and Revolution in African America: Temporality and the History of Atlantic Slavery." In *Rethinking American History in a Global Age*, edited by Thomas Bender, 148–67. Berkeley: University of California Press.

———. 2004. "The Pedestal and the Veil: Re-thinking the Capitalism/Slavery Question." *Journal of the Early Republic* 24:299–308.

Jonassaint, Jean. 2003. "Literatures in the Francophone Caribbean." *Yale French Studies* 103:55–63.

Jones, Gavin. 1999. *Strange Talk: The Politics of Dialect Literature in Gilded Age America*. Berkeley: University of California Press.

Jones, Tim. 2013. *Life and Debt: Global Studies of Debt and Resistance*. London: Jubilee Debt.

Jordan, Winthrop. 1969. *White over Black: American Attitudes toward the Negro, 1550–1812*. Baltimore: Pelican Books.

Jordan-Young, Rebecca M. 2011. *Brain Storm: The Flaws in the Science of Sex Differences*. Harvard University Press.

Joseph, Miranda. 2002. *Against the Romance of Community*. Minneapolis: University of Minnesota Press.

———. 2006. "A Debt to Society." In *The Seductions of Community*, edited by Gerald Creed, 199–226. Santa Fe, NM: SAR Press.

Joshi, Divya. 2002. *Ghandiji on Khadi*. Gandhi Book Centre. www.mkgandhi.org.

Joshi, Khyati Y. 2006. "The Racialization of Hinduism, Islam, and Sikhism in the United States." *Equity and Excellence in Education* 39:211–26.

Joyce, Joyce A. 1987a. "The Black Canon: Reconstructing Black American Literary Criticism." *New Literary History* 18:335–44.

———. 1987b. "'Who the Cap Fit': Unconsciousness and Unconscionableness in the Criticism of Houston A. Baker, Jr., and Henry Louis Gates, Jr." *New Literary History* 18:371–83.

J. T., Émilie. 1801. *Zorada; ou la Créole*. 2 vols. Vatar et Jouannet.

Juhasz, Alexandra. 2011. *Learning from YouTube*. Cambridge: MIT Press.

Jung, Moon-Ho. 2006. *Coolies and Cane: Race, Labor, and Sugar Production in the Age of Emancipation*. Baltimore: Johns Hopkins University Press.

Justice, Daniel Heath. 2005. *Kynship: The Way of Thorn and Thunder, Book One*. Neyaashiinigmiing, Nawash First Nation: Kegedonce.

Justice, Daniel Heath, Mark Rifkin, and Bethany Schneider, eds. 2010. "Sexuality, Nationality, Indigeneity." Special issue, *GLQ* 16 (1–2).

Kafer, Alison. 2013. *Feminist, Queer, Crip*. Bloomington: Indiana University Press.

Kagan, Donald, and Frederick W. Kagan. 2000. *While America Sleeps: Self-Delusion, Military Weakness, and the Threat to Peace Today*. New York: St. Martin's.

Kallen, Horace. 1915. "Democracy versus the Melting-Pot." *Nation* 100:190–94, 217–20.

Kallendorf, Craig. 2010. "The Ancient Book." In *Oxford Companion to the Book*, edited by Michael F. Suarez and H. R. Woudhuysen. Oxford University Press.

Kamenetz, Anya. 2006. *Generation Debt*. New York: Penguin Random House.

Kandaswamy, Priya, Mattie Eudora Richardson, and Marlon Bailey. 2006. "Is Gay Marriage Racist? A Conversation with Marlon M. Bailey, Priya Kandaswamy, and Mattie Eudora Richardson." In *That's Revolting: Queer Strategies for Resisting Assimilation*, edited by Mattilda Bernstein Sycamore, 87–93. Brooklyn, NY: Soft Skull.

Kant, Immanuel. (1790) 1952. *The Critique of Judgment*. Translated by James Creed Meredith. Oxford: Oxford University Press.

Kanter, Rosabeth Moss. 1990. *When Giants Learn to Dance*. New York: Free Press.

Kantorowicz, Ernst. 1957. *The King's Two Bodies*. Princeton, NJ: Princeton University Press.

Kaplan, Amy. 1991. "Nation, Region, Empire." In *The Columbia History of the American Novel*, edited by Emory Elliott, 240–66. New York: Columbia University Press.

———. 1993. "'Left Alone with America': The Absence of Empire in the Study of American Culture." In *Cultures of United States Imperialism*, edited by Amy Kaplan and Donald Pease, 3–21. Durham, NC: Duke University Press.

———. 1998. "Manifest Domesticity." *American Literature* 70:581–606.

———. 2002. *The Anarchy of Empire in the Making of U.S. Culture*. Cambridge, MA: Harvard University Press.

———. 2004. "Violent Belongings and the Question of Empire Today: Presidential Address to the American Studies Association, Hartford, Connecticut, October 17, 2003." *American Quarterly* 56 (1): 1–18.

———. 2005. "Where Is Guantanamo?" *American Quarterly* 57 (3): 831–54.

Kaplan, Amy, and Donald E. Pease, eds. 1993. *Cultures of United States Imperialism*. Durham, NC: Duke University Press.

Kaplan, Caren, Norma Alarcón, and Minoo Moallem, eds. 1999. *Between Women and Nation: Nationalisms, Transnational Feminisms, and the State*. Durham, NC: Duke University Press.

Kaplan, Carla. 1996. *The Erotics of Talk: Women's Writing and Feminist Paradigms*. New York: Oxford University Press.

Kaplan, Morris. 1997. *Sexual Justice: Democratic Citizenship and the Politics of Desire*. New York: Routledge.

Karpf, Anne. 2006. *The Human Voice*. London: Bloomsbury.

Katz, Cindi. 2004. *Growing Up Global: Restructuring and Children's Everyday Lives*. Minneapolis: University of Minnesota Press.

Katz, Jonathan Ned. 1995. *The Invention of Heterosexuality*. New York: Dutton/Penguin.

Katz, Michael. 2013. *The Undeserving Poor: America's Enduring Confrontation with Poverty*. Oxford: Oxford University Press.

Kauanui, J. Kēhaulani. 2004. "Asian American Studies and the 'Pacific Question.'" In *Asian American Studies after Critical Mass*, edited by Kent Ono, 123–243. Malden, MA: Blackwell.

———. 2007. "Diasporic Deracination and 'Off-Island' Hawaiians." *Contemporary Pacific* 19 (1): 137–60.

———. 2016. "'A Structure, Not an Event': Settler Colonialism and Enduring Indigeneity." *Lateral* 5 (1). https://doi.org/10.25158/L5.1.7.

———. 2017. "Indigenous Hawaiian Sexuality and the Politics of Nationalist Decolonization." In *Critically Sovereign: Indigenous Gender, Sexuality, and Feminist Studies*, edited by Joanne Barker, 45–68. Durham, NC: Duke University Press.

Kazanjian, David. 2003. *The Colonizing Trick: National Culture and Imperial Citizenship in Early America*. Minneapolis: University of Minnesota Press.

———. 2011. "The Speculative Freedom of Colonial Liberia." *American Quarterly* 63 (4): 863–93.

———. 2012. "Hegel, Liberia." *Diacritics* 40 (1): 6–39.

Keane, John. 2003. *Global Civil Society?* Cambridge: Cambridge University Press.

Keay, Douglas. 1987. "AIDS, Education, and the Year 2000: An Interview with Margaret Thatcher." *Woman's Own*, October 31, 1987.

Keegan, William F., and Corinne L. Hofman. 2017. *The Caribbean before Columbus.* Oxford University Press.

Keeling, Charles David. 1960. "The Concentration and Isotopic Abundances of Carbon Dioxide in the Atmosphere." *Tellus* 12 (2): 200–203.

Keeling, Kara. 2009. "Looking for M—Queer Temporality, Black Political Possibility, and Poetry from the Future." *GLQ* 15 (4): 565–82.

Keeling, Kara, and Josh Kun, eds. 2011. *Sound Clash: Listening to American Studies.* Baltimore: Johns Hopkins University Press.

Keith, Arthur. 1928. "The Evolution of the Human Races." *Journal of the Royal Anthropological Institute of Great Britain and Ireland* 58:305–21.

Keller, Evelyn Fox. 1985. *Reflections on Gender and Science.* New Haven: Yale University Press.

Kelley, Robin D. G. 1994. *Race Rebels: Culture, Politics, and the Black Working Class.* New York: Free Press.

———. 1997. *Yo Mama's DisFUNKtional: Fighting the Culture Wars in Urban America.* Boston: Beacon.

———. 2016. "Black Study, Black Struggle." *Boston Review*, March 7, 2016. http://bostonreview.net.

———. Forthcoming. Forward to *On Intersectionality: Essential Writings* by Kimberlé Crenshaw. New York: New Press.

Kelly, Alfred H., Winfred A. Harbison, and Herman Belz. 1983. *The American Constitution: Its Origins and Development.* 6th ed. New York: W. W. Norton.

Kempadoo, Kamala, and Jo Doezema, eds. 1998. *Global Sex Workers: Rights, Resistance, and Redefinition.* New York: Routledge.

Ken Burns's America. 1996. New York: PBS Home Video; Turner Home Entertainment.

Kendon, Adam. 2004. *Gesture: Visible Action as Utterance.* Cambridge: Cambridge University Press.

Kennedy, John F. 1963. "Report to the American People on Civil Rights, 11 June 1963." John F. Kennedy Presidential Library and Museum. www.jfklibrary.org.

Kennedy, Tammie M., Joyce Irene Middleton, and Krista Ratcliffe. 2017. *Rhetorics of Whiteness: Postracial Hauntings in Popular Culture, Social Media, and Education.* Carbondale: Southern Illinois University Press.

Kenny, Gale L. 2011. *Contentious Liberties: American Abolitionists in Post-emancipation Jamaica, 1834–1866.* Athens: University of Georgia Press.

Keohane, Robert O., and Joseph S. Nye Jr. 1989. *Power and Interdependence.* Glenview, IL: Scott, Foresman.

Kerber, Linda K. 1980. *Women of the Republic: Intellect and Ideology in Revolutionary America.* Chapel Hill: University of North Carolina Press.

Kerber, Linda K., and Jane Sherron De Hart. 2004. *Women's America: Refocusing the Past.* 5th ed. New York: Oxford University Press.

Kernan, Alvin. 1990. *The Death of Literature.* New Haven: Yale University Press.

Kerr, Clark. (1963) 1995. *The Uses of the University.* 5th ed. Cambridge, MA: Harvard University Press.

Kersten, Holger. 1996. "Using the Immigrant's Voice: Humor and Pathos in Nineteenth-Century 'Dutch' Dialect Texts." *MELUS* 21 (4): 3–18.

———. 2000. "The Creative Potential of Dialect Writing in Later Nineteenth-Century America." *Nineteenth-Century Literature* 55 (1): 92–117.

Kessler, Suzanne J. 1998. *Lessons from the Intersexed.* New Brunswick, NJ: Rutgers University Press.

Kessler, Suzanne J., and Wendy McKenna. 1990. *Gender: An Ethnomethodological Approach.* Chicago: University of Chicago Press.

Kessler-Harris, Alice. 1990. *A Woman's Wage: Historical Meanings and Social Consequence.* Lexington: University Press of Kentucky.

Kettner, James. 1978. *The Development of American Citizenship, 1608–1870.* Chapel Hill: University of North Carolina Press.

Keynes, John Maynard. 1936. *The General Theory of Employment, Interest and Money.* London: Macmillan.

Kezar, Adrianna, Yianna Drivalas, and Joseph Kitchen. 2018. *Envisioning Public Scholarship for Our Time: Models for Higher Education Researchers.* Sterling, VA: Stylus.

Khalili, Laleh. 2012. *Time in the Shadows: Confinement in Counterinsurgencies.* Stanford, CA: Stanford University Press.

Kilgore, DeWitt. 2003. *Afro-futurism: Science, Race, and Visions of Utopia in Space.* Philadelphia: University of Pennsylvania Press.

Kilgour, Frederick. 1998. *The Evolution of the Book.* New York: Oxford University Press.

Kim, Ahan. 2001. "Poll Finds Many Want Restrictions on Arab Americans." *Seattle Post-Intelligencer*, September 18, 2001.

Kim, Claire Jean. 2015. *Dangerous Crossings: Race, Species, and Nature in a Multicultural Age.* New York: Cambridge University Press.

King, Deborah. 1988. "Multiple Jeopardy, Multiple Consciousness: The Context of a Black Feminist Ideology." *Signs* 14 (1): 42–72.

King, Martin Luther, Jr. 1968. Speech to striking sanitation workers, Memphis, Tennessee, March 18, 1968. American Federation of Teachers. www.aft.org.

King, Mike. 2017. "Aggrieved Whiteness: White Identity Politics and Modern American Racial Formation." *Abolition: A Journal of Insurgent Politics*, May 4, 2017. https://abolitionjournal.org.

Kingston, Maxine Hong. 1989. *Tripmaster Monkey: His Fake Book*. New York: Knopf.

Kintz, Linda. 1997. *Between Jesus and the Market: Emotions That Matter in Right-Wing America*. Durham, NC: Duke University Press.

Kipling, Rudyard. 1899. "The White Man's Burden." *McClure's Magazine*, February 1899.

Kirschenbaum, Matthew G. 2008. *Mechanisms: New Media and the Forensic Imagination*. Cambridge: MIT Press.

Kittler, Friedrich A. 1999. *Gramophone, Film, Typewriter*. Translated by Geoffrey Winthrop-Young and Michael Wutz. Stanford, CA: Stanford University Press.

Klebnikov, Sergei. 2015. "Liberal Arts vs. STEM: The Right Degrees, the Wrong Debate." *Forbes*, June 19, 2015. Accessed September 22, 2018. www.forbes.com.

Klein, Julia Thompson. 2005. *Humanities, Culture, and Interdisciplinarity: The Changing American Academy*. Albany: State University of New York Press.

Klein, Kerwin Lee. 1996. "Reclaiming the 'F' Word: On Being and Becoming Postwestern." *Pacific Historical Review* 65 (12): 179–215.

Klein, Lisl. 2008. *The Meaning of Work: Papers on Work Organization and the Design of Jobs*. London: Karnac Books.

Klein, Naomi. 2007. *The Shock Doctrine*. New York: Metropolitan Books.

Knopp, Fay H., Barbara Howard, and Mark O. Morris. 1976. *Instead of Prisons: A Handbook for Abolitionists*. Syracuse, NY: Prison Research Education Action Project.

Kochhar-Lindgren, Kanta. 2006. *Hearing Difference: The Third Ear in Experimental, Deaf, and Multicultural Performance*. Washington, DC: Gallaudet University Press.

Koestenbaum, Wayne. (1994) 2001. *The Queen's Throat: Opera, Homosexuality, and the Mystery of Desire*. Cambridge, MA: Da Capo.

Kolchin, Peter. 2002. "Whiteness Studies: The New History of Race in America." *Journal of American History* 89:154–74.

Kollin, Susan, ed. 2007. *Postwestern Cultures: Literature, Theory, Space*. Lincoln: University of Nebraska Press.

———. 2015a. *Captivating Westerns: The Middle East in the American West*. Lincoln: University of Nebraska Press.

———. 2015b. *A History of Western American Literature*. New York: Cambridge University Press.

Kolodny, Annette. 1975. *The Lay of the Land: Metaphor as Experience and History in American Letters*. Chapel Hill: University of North Carolina Press.

———. 1984. *The Land before Her: Fantasy and Experience of the American Frontiers, 1630–1860*. Chapel Hill: University of North Carolina Press.

———. 2012. *In Search of First Contact: The Vikings of Vinland, the Peoples of the Dawnland, and the Anglo-American Anxiety of Discovery*. Duke University Press.

Kopple, Barbara, dir. 1976. *Harlan County, U.S.A.* FirstRun Features.

———, dir. 1990. *American Dream*. Prestige Films/HBO.

Koritz, Amy, and Paul Schadewald. 2016. "Civic Professionalism: A Pathway to Practical Wisdom for the Liberal Arts." Imagining America: Artists and Scholars in Public Life. https://imaginingamerica.org.

Koselleck, Reinhart. (1985) 2004. *Futures Past: On the Semantics of Historical Time*. Translated by Keith Tribe. New York: Columbia University Press.

Kotkin, Joel, and Erika Ozuna. 2002. *The Changing Face of the San Fernando Valley*. Davenport Institute Research Report. Malibu, CA: School of Public Policy, Pepperdine University.

Kozol, Wendy. 1988. "Madonnas of the Fields: Photography, Gender, and 1930s Farm Relief." *Genders* 2:1–23.

Kracauer, Siegfried. (1960) 1997. *Theory of Film: The Redemption of Physical Reality*. Princeton, NJ: Princeton University Press.

Krapp, George Philip. 1925. *The English Language in America*. 2 vols. New York: Century.

———. 1926. "The Psychology of Dialect Writing." *Bookman* 63:522–27.

Krentz, Christopher. 2007. *Writing Deafness: The Hearing Line in Nineteenth-Century American Literature*. Chapel Hill: University of North Carolina Press.

Kroeber, Alfred Louis. 1917. "The Superorganic." *American Anthropologist* 19:163–213.

Kroeber, Alfred Louis, and Clyde Kluckhohn. 1952. *Culture: A Critical Review of Concepts and Definitions*. New York: Vintage.

Krugman, Paul. 1997. *The Age of Diminished Expectations: U.S. Economic Policy in the 1990s*. Cambridge: MIT Press.

———. 2002. "Plutocracy and Politics." *New York Times*, June 14, 2002. www.nytimes.com.

Krugman, Paul, and Robin Wells. 2004. *Microeconomics*. North York: Worth.

———. 2017. *Economics*. 5th ed. New York: Worth.

Kruse, Kevin. 2005. *White Flight: Atlanta and the Making of Modern Conservatism*. Princeton, NJ: Princeton University Press.

Kuhn, Thomas. 1970. *The Structure of Scientific Revolutions*. 2nd ed. Chicago: University of Chicago Press.

Kulick, Bruce. 1972. "Myth and Symbol in American Studies." *American Quarterly* 24:435–50.

Kumar, Deepa. 2012. *Islamophobia and the Politics of Empire*. Chicago: Haymarket Books.

Kun, Josh. 2005. *Audiotopia: Music, Race, and America*. Berkeley: University of California Press.

Kuppers, Petra. 2003. *Disability and Contemporary Performance: Bodies on Edge*. New York: Routledge.

———. 2011. *Disability Culture and Community Performance: Find a Strange and Twisted Shape*. New York: Palgrave Macmillan.

———. 2014. *Studying Disability Arts and Culture: An Introduction*. New York: Palgrave Macmillan.

———. 2017. *Theatre and Disability*. New York: Red Globe.

Kushner, Rachel. 2019. "Is Prison Necessary? Ruth Wilson Gilmore Might Change Your Mind." *New York Times Magazine*, April 17, 2019. www.nytimes.com.

Kuusisto, Stephen. 2019. "Universal Design and Utopian Insistence." In *Planet of the Blind*. https://stephenkuusisto.com.

LaBelle, Brandon. 2010. *Acoustic Territories: Sound Culture and Everyday Life*. London: Continuum.

LaBennett, Oneka. 2011. *She's Mad Real: Popular Culture and West Indian Girls in Brooklyn*. New York: New York University Press.

Lacan, Jacques. (1963) 1978. *The Seminar of Jacques Lacan: The Four Fundamental Concepts of Psychoanalysis*. Translated by Alan Sheridan. New York: Norton.

Lacey, Kate. 2013. *Listening Publics: The Politics and Experience of Listening in the Media Age*. Cambridge, UK: Polity.

Lacey, Nicola. 1996. "Community in Legal Theory: Idea, Ideal or Ideology." *Studies in Law, Politics and Society* 15:105–46.

Lacey, Nicola, and Lucia Zedner. 1995. "Discourses of Community in Criminal Justice." *Journal of Law and Society* 22 (3): 301–25.

Laclau, Ernesto. 1990. *New Reflections on the Revolution of Our Time*. London: Verso.

———. 1994. Introduction to *The Making of Political Identities*, edited by Ernesto Laclau, 1–8. London: Verso.

———. 2007. *On Populist Reason*. London: Verso Books.

Laczko, F., and C. Aghazarm, eds. 2009. *Migration, Environment and Climate Change: Assessing the Evidence*. Geneva: International Organization for Migration.

LaFeber, Walter. 1963. *The New Empire: An Interpretation of American Expansion, 1860–1898*. Ithaca, NY: Cornell University Press.

Lahiri, Jhumpa. 2008. *Unaccustomed Earth*. New York: Alfred A. Knopf.

Lakoff, George. 1991. "Metaphor and War: The Metaphor System Used to Justify War in the Gulf." *Viet Nam Generation Journal & Newsletter* 3 (3). www2.iath.virginia.edu.

Landry, Charles. 2000. *The Creative City: A Toolkit for Urban Innovators*. London: Earthscan.

Lane, Harlan. 1989. *When the Mind Hears: A History of the Deaf*. New York: Vintage Books.

Lanier, Jaron. 2010. *You Are Not a Gadget: A Manifesto*. New York: Vintage Books.

Laó-Montes, Agustín, and Arlene M. Dávila, eds. 2001. *Mambo Montage: The Latinization of New York*. New York: Columbia University Press.

Laqueur, Thomas. 1990. *Making Sex: Body and Gender from the Greeks to Freud*. Cambridge, MA: Harvard University Press.

Laroche, Maximilen. 2001. *L'Avènement de la littérature haïtienne*. Port-au-Prince: Éd. Mémoire.

Larsen, Nella. 1929. *Passing*. New York: Knopf.

Latour, Bruno. 1987. *Science in Action: How to Follow Scientists and Engineers through Society*. Cambridge, MA: Harvard University Press.

———. 2004. "Why Has Critique Run Out of Steam? From Matters of Fact to Matters of Concern." *Critical Inquiry* 30 (2): 225–48.

Laughlin, Harry H., and John B. Trevor. 1939. *Immigration and Conquest: A Study of the United States as the Receiver of Old World Emigrants Who Become the Parents of Future-Born Americans; a Report of the Special Committee on Immigration and Naturalization of the Chamber of Commerce of the State of New York*. New York: Chamber of Commerce of the State of New York.

Lauter, Paul, ed. 1990. "The Literatures of America: A Comparative Discipline." In *Redefining American Literary History*, edited by A. La Vonne Brown Ruoff and Jerry W. Ward Jr., 9–34. New York: Modern Language Association.

———. 1994. *The Heath Anthology of American Literature*. 2 vols. Lexington, MA: Heath.

Lavinas-Picq, Manuela. 2014. "Self-Determination as Antiextractivism." In *Restoring Indigenous Self-Determination: Theoretical and Practical Approaches*, edited by Marc Woons, 26–33. Bristol, UK: E-International Relations Collections.

Lavoie, Judith. 2002. *Mark Twain et la parole noire*. Montréal: Les Presses de l'Université de Montréal.

Lawson, Steven F. 2003. *Civil Rights Crossroads: Nation, Community, and the Black Freedom Struggle*. Lexington: University Press of Kentucky.

Lazo, Rodrigo. 2005. *Writing to Cuba: Filibustering and Cuban Exiles in the United States*. Chapel Hill: University of North Carolina Press.

Lazzarato, Maurizio. 1996. "Immaterial Labour." In *Radical Thought in Italy: A Potential Politics*, edited by Paolo Virno and Michael Hardt, 132–46. Minneapolis: University of Minnesota Press.

———. 2012. *The Making of the Indebted Man*. Translated by J. D. Jordan. New York: Semiotexte.

Lean, Nathan. 2012. *The Islamophobia Industry: How the Right Manufactures Fear of Muslims*. New York: Pluto.

Lears, Jackson. 1981. *No Place of Grace: Antimodernism and the Transformation of American Culture, 1880–1920*. New York: Pantheon.

Lederer, Richard M. 1985. *Colonial American English: A Glossary*. Essex, CT: Verbatim.

Lee, Anthony. 2001. *Picturing Chinatown: Art and Orientalism in San Francisco*. Berkeley: University of California Press.

Lee, Erika. 2007. *At America's Gates during the Exclusion Era*. Chapel Hill: University of North Carolina Press.

Lee, Everett S. 1966. "A Theory of Migration." *Demography* 3 (1): 47–57.

Lee, James Kyung-Jin. 2004. *Urban Triage: Race and the Fictions of Multiculturalism*. Minneapolis: University of Minnesota Press.

———. 2009. "The Transitivity of Race and the Challenge of the Imagination." *PMLA* 123 (5): 1550–56.

Lee, Jo-Anne, and John Lutz. 2005. "Introduction: Toward a Critical Literacy of Racisms, Anti-racisms, and Racialization." In *Situating "Race" and Racisms in Space, Time, and Theory: Critical Essays for Activists and Scholars*, edited by Jo-Anne Lee and John Lutz, 3–29. Montreal: McGill-Queen's University Press.

Lee, Philip. 2011. "The Curious Life of in Loco Parentis at American Universities." *Higher Education in Review* 8:65–90.

Lee, Rachel. 2014. *The Exquisite Corpse of Asian America: Biopolitics, Biosociality and Posthuman Ecologies*. New York: New York University Press.

Lee, Stacy. 2005. *Up against Whiteness: Race, School, and Immigrant Youth*. New York: Teachers College Press.

———. 2009. *Unraveling the "Model Minority" Stereotype*. New York: Teachers College Press.

Lefebvre, Claire. 1998. *Creole Genesis and the Acquisition of Grammar: The Case of Haitian Creole*. New York: Cambridge University Press.

Lefebvre, Henry. 1991. *The Production of Space*. Cambridge, UK: Blackwell.

LeGuin, Ursula. 1969. *The Left Hand of Darkness*. New York: Walker.

Leja, Michael. 2004. *Looking Askance: Skepticism and American Art from Eakins to Duchamp*. Berkeley: University of California Press.

Lemann, Nicholas. 2000. *The Big Test: The Secret History of the American Meritocracy*. New York: Macmillan.

LeMenager, Stephanie. 2004. *Manifest and Other Destinies: Territorial Fictions of the Nineteenth-Century United States*. Lincoln: University of Nebraska Press.

Lemke, Thomas. 2011. *Biopolitics: An Advanced Introduction*. Preface by Monica J. Casper and Lisa Jean Moore. New York: New York University Press.

Lempert, William. 2018. "Indigenous Media Futures: An Introduction." *Cultural Anthropology* 33 (2): 173–79.

Lendhardt, R. A. 2015. "Marriage as Black Citizenship." *Hastings Law Journal* 66 (5): 1317–64.

Lesko, Nancy. 2001. *Act Your Age! A Cultural Construction of Adolescence*. New York: Routledge.

Lessig, Lawrence. 2002. *The Future of Ideas: The Fate of the Commons in a Connected World*. New York: Vintage.

Levander, Caroline F., and Robert S. Levine, eds. 2008a. *Hemispheric American Studies*. New Brunswick, NJ: Rutgers University Press.

———, eds. 2008b. "Introduction: Essays beyond the Nation." In *Hemispheric American Studies*, edited by Caroline F. Levander and Robert S. Levine, 1–17. New Brunswick, NJ: Rutgers University Press.

———, eds. 2011. *A Companion to American Literary Studies*. Malden, MA: John Wiley and Sons.

Levine, Lawrence. 1988. *Highbrow, Lowbrow: The Emergence of Cultural Hierarchy in America*. Cambridge, MA: Harvard University Press.

Levine, Robert. 1997. *Martin Delany, Frederick Douglass, and the Politics of Representative Identity*. Chapel Hill: University of North Carolina Press.

Lévi-Strauss, Claude. 1963. *Cultural Anthropology*. New York: Anchor Books.

———. 1971. *The Elementary Structures of Kinship*. Boston: Beacon.

Levitsky, Steven, and Daniel Ziblatt. 2018. *How Democracies Die*. New York: Penguin Random House.

Lewis, David Levering. 2009. *W. E. B. Du Bois: A Biography, 1868–1963*. New York: Henry Holt.

Lewis, Earl. 1995. "To Turn as on a Pivot: Writing African Americans into a History of Overlapping Diasporas." *American Historical Review* 100:765–87.

Lewis, Jason E., David DeGusta, Marc R. Meyer, Janet M. Monge, Alan E. Mann, et al. 2011. "The Mismeasure of Science: Stephen Jay Gould versus Samuel George Morton on Skulls and Bias." *PLoS Biol* 9 (6): e1001071. https://doi.org/10.1371/journal.pbio.1001071.

Lewis, Nathaniel. 2003. *Unsettling the Literary West: Authenticity and Authorship.* Lincoln: University of Nebraska Press.

Lewis, Oscar. 1959. *Five Families: Mexican Case Studies in the Culture of Poverty.* New York: Basic Books.

Lewis, R. W. B. 1955. *The American Adam: Innocence, Tradition, and Tragedy in the Nineteenth Century.* Chicago: University of Chicago Press.

Lewis, Simon, and Mark A. Maslin. 2015. "Defining the Anthropocene." *Nature* 519:171–80.

Lewis, Victoria Ann, ed. 2005. *Beyond Victims and Villains: Contemporary Plays by Disabled Playwrights.* New York: Theatre Communications Group.

Lewis, W. David. 1965. *From Newgate to Dannemora: The Rise of the Penitentiary in New York, 1796–1848.* Ithaca, NY: Cornell University Press.

Lichtenstein, Nelson. 2002. *State of the Union: A Century of American Labor.* Princeton, NJ: Princeton University Press.

Lima, Lázaro. 2007. *The Latino Body: Crisis Identities in American Literary and Cultural Memory.* New York: New York University Press.

Limerick, Patricia Nelson. 1991. "The Trail to Santa Fe, NM: The Unleashing of the Western Public Intellectual." In *Trails: Toward a New Western History*, edited by Patricia Nelson Limerick, Clyde A. Milner II, and Charles E. Rankin, 59–80. Lawrence: University Press of Kansas.

Limón, José. 1999. *American Encounters: Greater Mexico, the United States, and the Erotics of Culture.* Boston: Beacon.

Lincoln, Abraham. 1953. "Speech at Peoria, Illinois, October 16, 1854." In *The Collected Works of Abraham Lincoln*, edited by Roy P. Basler, 247–83. Vol. 2. New Brunswick, NJ: Rutgers University Press.

Linebaugh, Peter, and Marcus Rediker. 2000. *The Many-Headed Hydra: Sailors, Slaves, Commoners, and the Hidden History of the Revolutionary Atlantic.* Boston: Beacon.

Linenthal, Edward T. 2001. *The Unfinished Bombing: Oklahoma City in American Memory.* New York: Oxford University Press.

Linnaeus, Carolus. 1735. *Systema Naturae.* Leiden.

Linton, Simi. 1998. *Claiming Disability: Knowledge and Identity.* New York: New York University Press.

Lipietz, Alain. 1994. "Post-Fordism and Democracy." In *Post-Fordism: A Reader*, edited by Ash Amin, 338–57. Oxford, UK: Blackwell.

Lipovetsky, Gilles. 1994. *The Empire of Fashion: Dressing Modern Democracy.* Princeton, NJ: Princeton University Press.

Lippmann, Walter. 1927. *The Phantom Public.* New York: Macmillan.

Lipset, Seymour. 1963. *The First New Nation: The United States in Historical and Comparative Perspective.* New York: Basic Books.

Lipsitz, George. 1990a. "Listening to Learn and Learning to Listen: Popular Culture, Cultural Theory, and American Studies." *American Quarterly* 42 (4): 615–36.

———. 1990b. *Time Passages: Collective Memory and American Popular Culture.* Minneapolis: University of Minnesota Press.

———. 1995. "The Possessive Investment in Whiteness: Racialized Social Democracy and the 'White' Problem in American Studies." *American Quarterly* 47 (3): 369–87.

———. (1998) 2006. *The Possessive Investment in Whiteness: How White People Profit from Identity Politics.* Philadelphia: Temple University Press.

———. 2001. *American Studies in a Moment of Danger.* Minneapolis: University of Minnesota Press.

———. 2006. *The Possessive Investment in Whiteness: How White People Profit from Identity Politics.* Rev. ed. Philadelphia: Temple University Press.

———. 2011. *How Racism Takes Place.* Philadelphia: Temple University Press.

———. 2018. *The Possessive Investment in Whiteness: How White People Profit from Identity Politics.* 20th anniversary ed. Philadelphia: Temple University Press.

LiPuma, Edward, and Ben Lee. 2004. *Financial Derivatives and the Globalization of Risk.* Durham, NC: Duke University Press.

Litman, Jessica. 2001. *Digital Copyright.* Amherst, NY: Prometheus Books.

Littré, Émile. 1863–72. *Dictionnaire de la langue française.* Paris: Hachette.

Liu, Alan. 2004. *The Laws of Cool: Knowledge Work and the Culture of Information.* Chicago: University of Chicago Press.

Livingston, Jennie, dir. 1991. *Paris Is Burning.* Miramax.

Lloyd, David, and Paul Thomas. 1995. "Culture and Society or 'Culture and the State'?" In *Cultural Materialism: On Raymond Williams*, edited by Christopher Prendergast, 268–304. Minneapolis: University of Minnesota Press.

———. 1998. *Culture and the State.* New York: Routledge.

Locke, John. (1689) 2016. *Second Treatise of Government; And a*

Letter concerning Government. Edited by Mark Goldie. Oxford: Oxford University Press.

———. (1690) 1980. *Second Treatise of Government.* Edited by C. B. Macpherson. Indianapolis: Hackett.

———. (1690) 1988. *Two Treatises of Government.* Edited by Peter Laslett. New York: Cambridge University Press.

Lockwood, J. Samaine. 2015. *Archives of Desire: The Queer Historical Work of New England Regionalism.* Chapel Hill: University of North Carolina Press.

London, Jack. 1903. *The People of the Abyss.* New York: Lawrence Hill.

Longmore, Paul. 2003. *Why I Burned My Book and Other Essays on Disability.* Philadelphia: Temple University Press.

Longmore, Paul, and Lauri Umansky, eds. 2001. *The New Disability History: American Perspectives.* New York: New York University Press.

Loomba, Ania. 2005. *Colonialism/Postcolonialism.* 2nd ed. London: Routledge.

Loraux, Nicole. 1998. *Mothers in Mourning.* Ithaca, NY: Cornell University Press.

Lorde, Audre. 1984a. "Age, Race, Class, and Sex: Women Redefining Difference." In *Sister Outsider: Essays and Speeches,* 114–23. Trumansburg, NY: Crossing.

———. 1984b. "Poetry Is Not a Luxury." In *Sister Outsider: Essays and Speeches,* 36–39. Trumansburg, NY: Crossing.

Losh, Elizabeth. 2012. "Hacktivism and the Humanities: Programming Protest in the Era of the Digital University." In *Debates in the Digital Humanities,* edited by Matthew K. Gold, 161–86. Minneapolis: University of Minnesota Press.

Lothian, Alexis, and Amanda Phillips. 2013. "Can Digital Humanities Mean Transformative Critique?" *E-Media Studies* 3 (1). http://journals.dartmouth.edu.

Lott, Eric. 1993. *Love and Theft: Blackface Minstrelsy and the American Working Class.* New York: Oxford University Press.

———. 2011. "Back Door Man: Howlin' Wolf and the Sound of Jim Crow." In *Sound Clash: Listening to American Studies,* edited by Kara Keeling and Josh Kun, 253–66. Baltimore: Johns Hopkins University Press.

Loughran, Trish. 2007. *The Republic in Print: Print Culture in the Age of U.S. Nation Building, 1770–1870.* New York: Columbia University Press.

Louie, Miriam Ching Yoon. 2001. *Sweatshop Warriors: Immigrant Women Workers Take on the Global Factory.* Cambridge, MA: South End.

Loukissas, Yanni. 2019. *All Data Are Local: Thinking Critically in a Data-Driven World.* Cambridge: MIT Press.

Love, Heather. 2007. *Feeling Backward: Loss and the Politics of Queer History.* Cambridge, MA: Harvard University Press.

Loveman, Mara. 1999. "Is 'Race' Essential?" *American Sociological Review* 64:891–98.

Low, Setha, and Mark Maguire, eds. 2019. *Spaces of Security: Ethnographic of Securityscapes, Surveillance, and Control.* New York: New York University Press.

Lowe, Lisa. 1996. *Immigrant Acts: On Asian American Cultural Politics.* Durham, NC: Duke University Press.

———. 2006. "The Intimacies of Four Continents." In *Haunted by Empire: Geographies of Intimacy in North American History,* edited by Ann Laura Stoler, 191–212. Durham, NC: Duke University Press.

———. 2009. "Autobiography out of Empire." *small axe* 28:98–111.

———. 2015. *The Intimacies of Four Continents.* Durham, NC: Duke University Press.

Lowe, Lisa, and David Lloyd, eds. 1997. *The Politics of Culture in the Shadow of Capital.* Durham, NC: Duke University Press.

Loyd, Virgil. (1865) 1990. "Statement of a Louisiana Freedman." In *Freedom: A Documentary History of Emancipation, 1861–1867.* Ser. 1, vol. 3, *The Wartime Genesis of Free Labor: The Lower South,* edited by Ira Berlin, Steven F. Miller, Joseph P. Reidy, and Leslie S. Rowland, 614–16. New York: Cambridge University Press.

Loyer, Erik. 2010. *Strange Rain.* Opertoon. iOS 4.3 or later.

Luce, Henry R. 1941. "The American Century." *Life,* February 17, 1941.

Luibhéid, Eithne. 2002. *Entry Denied: Controlling Sexuality at the Border.* Minneapolis: University of Minnesota Press.

Luibhéid, Eithne, and Lionel Cantú, eds. 2005. *Queer Migrations: Sexuality, U.S. Citizenship, and Border Crossings.* Minneapolis: University of Minnesota Press.

Luker, Kristin. 1984. *Abortion and the Politics of Motherhood.* Berkeley: University of California Press.

Lye, Colleen. 2004. *America's Asia: Racial Forms and American Literature, 1893–1945.* Princeton, NJ: Princeton University Press.

Lykke, Nina. 2011. *Feminist Studies: A Guide to Intersectional Theory, Methodology and Writing.* New York: Routledge.

Lyman, Stanford M. 1990. *Civilization: Contents, Discontents, Malcontents, and Other Essays in Social Theory.* Fayetteville: University of Arkansas Press.

Lyons, Matthew. 2018. *Insurgent Supremacists: The U.S. Right's Challenge to State and Empire.* Montreal: Kersplebedeb.

———. 2019. "The Christchurch Massacre and Fascist Revolutionary Politics." threewayfight. http://threewayfight.blogspot.com.

MacLean, Nancy. 2006. *Freedom Is Not Enough: The Opening of the American Workplace*. Cambridge, MA: Harvard University Press.

———. 2017. *Democracy in Chains: The Deep History of the Radical Right's Stealth Plan for America*. New York: Viking.

Macpherson, C. B. 1962. *The Political Theory of Possessive Individualism: Hobbes to Locke*. New York: Oxford University Press.

Mactavish, Andrew, and Geoffrey Rockwell. 2006. "Multimedia Education in the Arts and Humanities." In *Mind Technologies: Humanities Computing and the Canadian Academic Community*, edited by Raymond Siemens and David Moorman, 225–43. Calgary: University of Calgary Press.

Maddox, Lucy. 1991. *Removals: Nineteenth-Century American Literature and the Politics of Indian Affairs*. New York: Oxford University Press.

———. 2005. *Citizen Indians: Native American Intellectuals, Race, and Reform*. Ithaca, NY: Cornell University Press.

Magnis, Nicholas E. 1999. "Thomas Jefferson and Slavery: An Analysis of His Racist Thinking as Revealed by His Writings and Political Behavior." *Journal of Black Studies* 29 (4): 491–509.

Maira, Sunaina. 2002. *Desis in the House: Indian American Youth Culture in New York City*. Philadelphia: Temple University Press.

———. 2018. *Boycott! The Academy and Justice for Palestine*. Berkeley: University of California Press.

Maira, Sunaina, and Elisabeth Soep. 2005. *Youthscapes: The Popular, the National, the Global*. Philadelphia: University of Pennsylvania Press.

Makdisi, Ussama S. 2007. *Artillery of Heaven: American Missionaries and the Failed Conversion of the Middle East*. Ithaca, NY: Cornell University Press.

Mamdani, Mahmood. 2004. *Good Muslim, Bad Muslim: America, the Cold War, and the Roots of Terror*. New York: Three Rivers.

Manalansan, Martin F. 2003. *Global Divas: Filipino Gay Men in the Diaspora*. Durham, NC: Duke University Press.

———. 2006. "Queer Intersections: Gender and Sexuality in Migration Studies." *International Migration Review* 40 (1): 224–49.

Manalansan, Martin F., Chantal Nadeau, Richard T. Rodríguez, and Siobhan B. Somerville. 2014. "Queering the Middle: Race, Region, and a Queer Midwest." Special issue, *GLQ* 20 (1–2).

Mandel, Ernest. 1974. "Marx's Labor Theory of Value." International Viewpoint. www.internationalviewpoint.org.

———. 1976. *Late Capitalism*. Rev. ed. New York: Schocken Books.

Mankiw, N. G. 2017. *Principles of Economics*. 8th ed. Boston: Cengage Learning.

Manning, Erin. 2016. *The Minor Gesture*. Durham, NC: Duke University Press.

———. 2018. "Me Lo Dijo un Pajarito: Neurodiversity, Black Life, and the University as We Know It." *Social Text* 36:1–24.

Manning, Erin, and Brian Massumi. 2014. *Thought in the Act: Passages in the Ecology of Experience*. Minneapolis: Minnesota University Press.

Manning, Susan. 2004. *Modern Dance, Negro Dance: Race in Motion*. Minneapolis: University of Minnesota Press.

Manovich, Lev. 2001. *The Language of New Media*. Cambridge: MIT Press.

Manuel, George, and Michael Posluns. 1974. *The Fourth World: An Indian Reality*. New York: Free Press.

Marable, Manning. 1999. *Black Liberation in Conservative America*. Boston: South End.

———. 2000. "Introduction: Black Studies and the Racial Mountain." In *Dispatches from the Ebony Tower: Intellectuals Confront the African American Experience*, edited by Manning Marable, 1–30. New York: Columbia University Press.

Marchand, Ronald. 1998. *Creating the Corporate Soul: The Rise of Public Relations and Corporate Imagery in American Big Business*. Berkeley: University of California Press.

Marcus, George E. 2002. *The Sentimental Citizen: Emotion in Democratic Politics*. University Park: Penn State University Press.

Marcus, George E., and Michael Fischer. 1986. *Anthropology as Cultural Critique: An Experimental Moment in the Human Sciences*. Chicago: University of Chicago Press.

Marcuse, Herbert. (1964) 2002. *One-Dimensional Man: Studies in the Ideology of Advanced Industrial Society*. New York: Routledge.

Marez, Curtis. 2014. "Seeing in the Red: Looking at Student Debt." *American Quarterly* 66 (2): 261–81.

Marinetti, F. T. (1909) 2006. "The Foundation and Manifesto of Futurism." In *Critical Writings: F. T. Marinetti*, edited by Günter Berghaus, 11–17. New York: Farrar, Straus and Giroux.

Mariscal, George. 2005. *Brown-Eyed Children of the Sun: Lessons from the Chicano Movement, 1965–1975*. Albuquerque: University of New Mexico Press.

Marlow, Joyce. 1973. *Captain Boycott and the Irish*. Saturday Review Press.

Marr, Timothy. 2006. *The Cultural Roots of American Islamicism*. New York: Cambridge University Press.

Marsden, George. 1980. *Fundamentalism and American Culture:*

The Shaping of Twentieth-Century Evangelicalism, 1879–1925. New York: Oxford University Press.

Marsh, Margaret. 1990. *Suburban Lives.* New Brunswick, NJ: Rutgers University Press.

Marshall, T. H. 1965. *Class, Citizenship, and Social Development.* New York: Doubleday Anchor.

Martí, José. (1891) 2002. "Our America." In *Selected Writings,* 288–95. New York: Penguin.

Martin, Biddy, and Chandra Mohanty. 1986. "Feminist Politics: What's Home Got to Do with It?" In *Feminist Studies, Critical Studies,* edited by Teresa de Lauretis, 191–212. Bloomington: Indiana University Press.

Martin, David. 1969. *The Religious and the Secular.* London: RK.

———. 1978. *A General Theory of Secularization.* New York: Harper & Row.

Martin, Randy. 2002. *Financialization of Daily Life.* Philadelphia: Temple University Press.

———. 2010. "The Good, the Bad and the Ugly: Economies of Parable." *Cultural Studies* 24 (3): 418–30.

———. 2011. *Under New Management: Universities, Administrative Labor, and the Professional Turn.* Philadelphia: Temple University Press.

Martin, Randy, with Miriam Bartha, Bruce Burgett, Diane Douglas, and Kanta Kochhar-Lindgren. 2017. "Lateral Moves—across Disciplines." *Public: The Journal of Imagining America* 4 (1). http://public.imaginingamerica.org.

Martineau, Harriet. 1837. *Society in America.* London: Sanders and Otley.

Martinez-San Miguel, Yolanda, and Sarah Tobias, eds. 2016. *Trans Studies: The Challenge to Hetero/Homo Normativities.* New Brunswick, NJ: Rutgers University Press.

Martinot, Steve. 2010. *The Machinery of Whiteness: Studies in the Structure of Racialization.* Philadelphia: Temple University Press.

Marx, Karl. 1844. "Estranged Labour." In *Economic and Philosophical Manuscripts of 1844.* www.marxists.org.

———. (1844) 1978. "On the Jewish Question." In *The Marx-Engels Reader,* edited by Robert Tucker, 26–52. 2nd ed. New York: Norton.

———. (1852) 1954. *The Eighteenth Brumaire of Louis Bonaparte.* Moscow: Progress.

———. (1858) 1993. *Grundrisse: Foundations of the Critique of Political Economy.* New York: Penguin.

———. (1867) 1990. *Capital.* Vol. 1. New York: Penguin.

———. (1867–94) 1976–81. *Capital.* 3 vols. Translated by Ben Fowkes and David Fernbach. New York: Vintage.

Marx, Karl, and Friedrich Engels. (1845) 1975. *The Holy Family.* In *Collected Works,* 5–211. Vol. 4. New York: International.

———. (1845–46) 1972. *The German Ideology.* Edited by C. J. Arthur. New York: International.

———. (1848) 1976. *Manifesto of the Communist Party: Collected Works.* Vol. 6. New York: International.

Marx, Leo. (1964) 2000. *The Machine in the Garden: Technology and the Pastoral Ideal in America.* New York: Oxford University Press.

Marzec, Robert. 2015. *Militarizing the Environment: Climate Change and the Security State.* Minneapolis: University of Minnesota Press.

Massad, Joseph. 2006. *The Persistence of the Palestinian Question: Essays on Zionism and the Palestinians.* New York: Routledge.

———. 2007. *Desiring Arabs.* Chicago: University of Chicago Press.

Massey, Doreen. 1994. *Space, Place, and Gender.* Minneapolis: University of Minnesota Press.

Massumi, Brian. 2002a. "Navigating Moments." In *Hope: New Philosophies for Change,* edited by Mary Zournazi, 210–43. New York: Routledge.

———. 2002b. *Parables for the Virtual: Movement, Affect, Sensation.* Durham, NC: Duke University Press.

———. 2015. *Power at the End of the Economy.* Durham, NC: Duke University Press.

Mather, Cotton. (1702) 1967. *Magnalia Christi Americana.* New York: Russell and Russell.

Mathias, Charles M., Jr. 1981. "Ethnic Groups and Foreign Policy." *Foreign Affairs* 59 (5): 975–98.

Matias, Cheryl. 2016. *Feeling White: Whiteness, Emotionality, and Education.* New York: Sense.

Matory, J. Lorand. 1999. "The English Professors of Brazil: On the Diasporic Roots of the Yorùbá Nation." *Comparative Studies in Social History* 41 (1): 72–103.

Matthews, Glenna. 1987. *"Just a Housewife": The Rise and Fall of Domesticity in America.* New York: Oxford University Press.

Matthiessen, F. O. 1941. *American Renaissance: Art and Expression in the Age of Emerson and Whitman.* New York: Oxford University Press.

Mauss, Marcel. (1934) 1992. "Techniques of the Body." Reprinted in *Incorporations,* edited by Jonathan Crary and Sanford Kwinter, 455–77. New York: Zone Books.

Maxwell, William. 1999. *New Negro, Old Left.* New York: Columbia University Press.

May, Elaine Tyler. 1988. *Homeward Bound: American Families in the Cold War Era.* New York: Basic Books.

May, Henry F. 1976. *The Enlightenment in America.* New York: Oxford University Press.

Mayer, Jane. 2016. *Dark Money: The Hidden Histories of the*

Billionaires behind the Rise of the Radical Right. New York: Doubleday.

Mayer, Margit. 1994. "Post-Fordist City Politics." In *Post-Fordism: A Reader*, edited by Ash Amin, 316–37. Oxford, UK: Blackwell.

Mbembe, Achille. 2003. "Necropolitics." *Public Culture* 15 (1): 11–40.

McAlister, Melani. 2001. *Epic Encounters: Culture, Media, and U.S. Interests in the Middle East, 1945–2000.* Berkeley: University of California Press.

———. 2005. *Epic Encounters: Culture, Media, and U.S. Interests in the Middle East, 1945–2000.* Updated ed., with a post-9/11 chapter. Berkeley: University of California Press.

McCall, Leslie. 2005. "The Complexity of Intersectionality." *Signs* 30 (3): 1771–1800.

McCann, Sean. 2015. "Structures of Feeling." *American Literary History* 27 (2): 321–30.

McCarthy, Cormac. 1992. *All the Pretty Horses.* New York: Vintage.

McCarthy, Kevin F., Elizabeth H. Ondaatje, Laura Zakaras, and Arthur C. Brooks. 2005. *Gifts of the Muse: Reframing the Debate about the Benefits of the Arts.* Santa Monica, CA: Rand.

McCarty, Willard. 2005. *Humanities Computing.* New York: Palgrave Macmillan.

McClintock, Anne. 1993. "Family Feuds: Gender, Nationalism and the Family." *Feminist Review* 44:61–80.

———. 1995. *Imperial Leather: Race and Gender in the Colonial Contest.* Durham, NC: Duke University Press.

McCullough, Kate. 1999. *Regions of Identity: The Construction of America in Women's Fiction, 1885–1914.* Stanford, CA: Stanford University Press.

McGann, Jerome. 2001. *Radiant Textuality: Literature after the World Wide Web.* New York: Palgrave Macmillan.

McGill, Meredith L. 2003. *American Literature and the Culture of Reprinting, 1834–1853.* Philadelphia: University of Pennsylvania Press.

McGlotten, Shaka. 2016. "Black Data." In *No Tea, No Shade: New Writings in Black Queer Studies*, edited by E. Patrick Johnson, 262–86. Durham, NC: Duke University Press.

McGregor, Jena. 2018. "Why 'Buycotts' Could Overtake Boycotts among Consumer Activists." *Washington Post*, February 28, 2018. Accessed November 25, 2018. www.washingtonpost.com.

McGrory, Kathleen. 2013. "At Florida's Capitol, Dream Defenders Are Determined to Make a Difference." *Miami Herald*, July 19, 2013. www.miamiherald.com.

McGurl, Mark. 2011. *The Program Era: Postwar Fiction and the Rise of Creative Writing.* Cambridge, MA: Harvard University Press.

McIntosh, Peggy. 1988. "White Privilege and Male Privilege: A Personal Account of Coming to See Correspondences through Work in Women's Studies." Working Paper 189, Wellesley College, MA, Center for Research on Women. Distributed by ERIC Clearinghouse.

McKenzie, Evan. 1994. *Privatopia: Homeowner Associations and the Rise of Residential Private Government.* New Haven: Yale University Press.

McLeod, Kembrew. 2007. *Freedom of Expression: Resistance and Repression in the Age of Intellectual Property.* Minneapolis: University of Minnesota Press.

McLeod, Kembrew, and Peter DiCola. 2011. *Creative License: The Law and Art of Digital Sampling.* Durham, NC: Duke University Press.

McLuhan, Marshall. (1964) 2003. *Understanding Media: The Extensions of Man.* Edited by W. Terrence Gordon. Corte Madera, CA: Gingko.

McPherson, Tara. 2003. *Reconstructing Dixie: Race, Gender, and Nostalgia in the Imagined South.* Durham, NC: Duke University Press.

———. 2009. "Media Studies and the Digital Humanities." *Cinema Journal* 48 (2): 119–23.

———. 2012a. "U.S. Operating Systems at Mid-century: The Intertwining of Race and UNIX." In *Race after the Internet*, edited by Lisa Nakamura, Peter Chow-White, and Alondra Nelson, 21–37. New York: Routledge.

———. 2012b. "Why Are the Digital Humanities So White? Or Thinking the Histories of Race and Computation." In *Debates in the Digital Humanities*, edited by Matthew K. Gold, 139–60. Minneapolis: University of Minneapolis Press.

———. 2018. *Feminist in a Software Lab: Difference + Design.* Cambridge, MA: Harvard University Press.

McRobbie, Angela. 1988. *British Fashion Design: Rag Trade or Image Industry?* London: Routledge.

McRobbie, Angela, and Jenny Garber. 1976. "Girls and Subcultures: An Exploration." In *Resistance through Rituals: Youth Subcultures in Post-war Britain*, edited by Stuart Hall and Tony Jefferson, 209–22. London: Hutchinson / Centre for Contemporary Cultural Studies, University of Birmingham.

McRuer, Robert. 2006. *Crip Theory: Cultural Signs of Queerness and Disability.* New York: New York University Press.

———. 2018. *Crip Times: Disability, Globalization, and Resistance.* New York: New York University Press.

McRuer, Robert, and Anna Mollow, eds. 2012. *Sex and Disability.* Durham, NC: Duke University Press.

McRuer, Robert, and Abby L. Wilkerson, eds. 2003. "Desiring Disability: Queer Theory Meets Disability Studies." Special issue, *GLQ* 9 (1–2): 1–23.

Mead, George Herbert. (1934) 1967. *Mind, Self, and Society*. Reprint, Chicago: University of Chicago Press.

Mead, Margaret. (1928) 1961. *Coming of Age in Samoa*. New York: William Morrow.

———. 1937. *Cooperation and Competition among Primitive Peoples*. New York: McGraw-Hill.

———. (1942) 1965. *And Keep Your Powder Dry: An Anthropologist Looks at America*. New York: Morrow Quill.

Mehta, Uday Singh. 1999. *Liberalism and Empire: A Study in Nineteenth-Century British Liberal Thought*. Chicago: University of Chicago Press.

Meier, August, and Elliott Rudwick. 1976. *From Plantation to Ghetto*. 3rd ed. New York: Hill and Wang.

Meiners, Erica R. 2007. *Right to Be Hostile: Schools, Prisons, and the Making of Public Enemies*. New York: Routledge.

Meister, Robert. 2011. "Debt and Taxes: Can the Financial Industry Save Public Higher Education?" *Representations* 116:128–47.

Melamed, Jodi. 2011. *Represent and Destroy: Rationalizing Violence in the New Racial Capitalism*. Minneapolis: University of Minnesota Press.

Melville, Herman. (1851) 1971. *Moby-Dick; or, The Whale*. Edited by Harrison Hayford, Hershel Parker, and G. Thomas Tanselle. Evanston, IL: Northwestern University Press; Chicago: Newberry Library.

Mendoza, Mary. 2019. "Caging Out, Caging In: Building a Carceral State at the U.S.-Mexico Divide." *Pacific Historical Review* 88 (1): 86–109.

Mendoza, Victor Román. 2015. *Metroimperial Intimacies: Fantasy, Racial-Sexual Governance, and the Philippines in U.S. Imperialism, 1899–1913*. Durham, NC: Duke University Press.

Mensch, Elizabeth. 1982. "The History of Mainstream Legal Thought." In *The Politics of Law: A Progressive Critique*, edited by David Kairys, 23–53. New York: Basic Books.

Meranze, Michael. 1996. *Laboratories of Virtue: Punishment, Revolution, and Authority in Philadelphia, 1760–1835*. Chapel Hill: University of North Carolina Press.

Mercer, Kobena. 1994. *Welcome to the Jungle: New Positions in Black Cultural Studies*. New York: Routledge.

Merchant, Carolyn. 1980. *The Death of Nature: Women, Ecology, and the Scientific Revolution*. San Francisco: HarperCollins.

———. 1996. "Reinventing Eden: Western Culture as a Recovery Narrative." In *Uncommon Ground: Rethinking the Human Place in Nature*, edited by William Cronon, 132–59. New York: Norton.

Merish, Lori. 2000. *Sentimental Materialism: Gender, Commodity Culture, and Nineteenth-Century American Literature*. Durham, NC: Duke University Press.

Meriwether, James H. 2002. *Proudly We Can Be Africans: Black Americans and Africa, 1935–61*. Chapel Hill: University of North Carolina Press.

Merleau-Ponty, Maurice. (1945) 2002. *The Phenomenology of Perception*. Reprint, London: Routledge.

Metz, Tamara. 2010. *Untying the Knot: Marriage, the State, and the Case for Their Divorce*. Princeton, NJ: Princeton University Press.

Meyer, John M. 2001. *Political Nature: Environmentalism and the Interpretation of Western Thought*. Cambridge: MIT Press.

Meyer, Richard. 2002. *Outlaw Representation: Censorship and Homosexuality in Twentieth-Century American Art*. New York: Oxford University Press.

Meyerowitz, Joanne. 2004. *How Sex Changed: A History of Transsexuality*.

Michaels, Walter Benn. 1987. "Corporate Fiction." In *The Gold Standard and the Logic of Naturalism: American Literature at the Turn of the Century*, 181–213. Berkeley: University of California Press.

———. 1990. "The Vanishing American." *American Literary History* 2 (2): 220–41.

———. 2016. "A Universe of Exploitation." *Nation*, December 16, 2016.

Mignolo, Walter. 2005. *The Idea of Latin America*. Malden, MA: Blackwell.

Migrant Rights International. n.d. Accessed 2012. www .migrantwatch.org.

Migration Policy Institute. n.d. "About MPI." Accessed 2012. www.migrationpolicy.org.

Miles, Robert, and Rudy Torres. 2007. "Does 'Race' Matter? Transatlantic Perspectives on Racism after 'Race Relations.'" In *Race and Racialization: Essential Readings*, edited by Tania Das Gupta, Carl E. James, Roger C. A. Maaka, Grace-Edward Galabuzi, and Chris Andersen, 65–73. Toronto: Canadian Scholars' Press.

Milian, Claudia, ed. 2017. "Special Issue: Theorizing LatinX." *Cultural Dynamics* 29 (3).

Mill, John Stuart. (1859) 1999. *On Liberty*. London: Longman, Roberts, & Green. Reprint, New York: Bartleby.com.

———. (1869) 1976. *The Subjection of Women. Three Essays*. New York: Oxford University Press.

Miller, Perry. 1960. *Errand into the Wilderness*. Cambridge, MA: Harvard University Press.

Miller, Toby. 1993. *The Well-Tempered Self: Citizenship, Culture, and the Postmodern Subject*. Baltimore: Johns Hopkins University Press.

———. 2001. "Introducing . . . Cultural Citizenship." *Social Text* 69 (19:4): 1–5.

———. 2012. *Blow Up the Humanities.* Philadelphia: Temple University Press.

Miller, Toby, Nitin Govil, John McMurria, and Richard Maxwell. 2001. *Global Hollywood.* London: British Film Institute.

Millet, Damien, and Eric Toussaint. 2004. *Who Owes Who? 50 Questions about World Debt.* London: Zed Books.

———. 2010. *Debt, the IMF, and the World Bank: Sixty Questions, Sixty Answers.* New York: Monthly Review Press.

Mills, Charles W. 1997. *The Racial Contract.* Ithaca, NY: Cornell University Press.

Milner, Yeshimabeit, Lucas Brown, Max Clermont, and Nicole Morris. 2018a. "About Data for Black Lives." Data for Black Lives. http://d4bl.org.

———. 2018b. Data for Black Lives. http://d4bl.org.

Mindt, Mark L. 2005. *Koda the Warrior.* Harvey, ND: Pony Gulch.

Mintz, Sidney. 1985. *Sweetness and Power: The Place of Sugar in Modern History.* New York: Viking.

Mirabeau, Victor de Riqueti, Marquis de. (1756–58) 1970. *L'ami des hommes: ou, Traité de la population.* 2 vols. Aalen, Germany: Scientia.

Mirzoeff, Nicholas. 1999. *Introduction to Visual Culture.* London: Routledge.

Mises, Ludwig von. 1949. *Human Action.* New Haven: Yale University Press.

Mishel, Lawrence R., John Bivens, Elise Gould, and Heidi Shierholz. 2012. *The State of Working America.* 12th ed. Ithaca, NY: ILR.

Mishra, Vijay. 1996. "The Diasporic Imaginary: Theorizing the Indian Diaspora." *Textual Practice* 10 (3): 421–47.

Mitchell, David T., and Sharon Snyder, eds. 1997. *The Body and Physical Difference: Discourses of Disability.* Ann Arbor: University of Michigan Press.

———. 2001. *Narrative Prosthesis: Disability and the Dependencies of Discourse.* Ann Arbor: University of Michigan Press.

———. 2015. *The Biopolitics of Disability: Neoliberalism, Ablenationalism, and Peripheral Embodiment.* Ann Arbor: University of Michigan Press.

Mitchell, Don. 2003. *The Right to the City: Social Justice and the Fight for Public Space.* New York: Guilford.

Mitchell, Lee Clark. 1996. *Westerns: Making the Man in Fiction and Film.* Chicago: University of Chicago Press.

Mitchell, Timothy. 2000. "The Stage of Modernity." In *Questions of Modernity*, edited by Timothy Mitchell, 1–34. Minneapolis: University of Minnesota Press.

———. 2002. *Rule of Experts: Egypt, Techno-Politics, Modernity.* Berkeley: University of California Press.

———. 2005. "Economists and the Economy in the Twentieth Century." In *The Politics of Method in the Human Sciences: Positivism and Its Epistemological Others*, edited by George Steinmetz, 126–41. Durham, NC: Duke University Press.

———. 2013. *Carbon Democracy: Political Power in the Age of Oil.* Verso.

Mitchell, W. J. T. 1994. *Picture Theory: Essays on Verbal and Visual Representation.* Chicago: University of Chicago Press.

———. 2011. *Cloning Terror: The War of Images, 9/11 to the Present.* Chicago: University of Chicago Press.

Miyoshi, M. 1993. "A Borderless World? From Colonialism to Transnationalism and the Decline of the Nation State." *Critical Inquiry* 19 (4): 726–51.

Mizen, Phillip. 2002. "Putting the Politics Back into Youth Studies: Keynesianism, Monetarism, and the Changing State of Youth." *Journal of Youth Studies* 5 (1): 5–20.

Mnookin, Jennifer. 1998. "The Image of Truth: Photographic Evidence and the Power of Analogy." *Yale Journal of Law and the Humanities* 10 (1): 1–74.

Moallem, Minoo. 2005. *Between Warrior Brother and Veiled Sister: Islamic Fundamentalism and the Cultural Politics of Patriarchy in Iran.* Berkeley: University of California Press.

Moffitt, Benjamin. 2017. *The Global Rise of Populism: Performance, Political Style, and Representation.* Palo Alto, CA. Stanford University Press.

Mogul, Joey L., Andrea J. Ritchie, and Kay Whitlock. 2011. *Queer (In)Justice: The Criminalization of LGBT People in the United States.* Boston: Beacon.

Mohanty, Chandra Talpade. 2003. *Feminism without Borders: Decolonizing Theory, Practicing Solidarity.* Durham, NC: Duke University Press.

Mohanty, Chandra Talpade, Anna Russo, and Lourdes Torres. 1991. *Third World Women and the Politics of Feminism.* Bloomington: Indiana University Press.

Mohler, R. Albert, Jr. 2015. *We Cannot Be Silent: Speaking Truth to a Culture Redefining Sex, Marriage, and the Very Meaning of Right and Wrong.* Nashville, TN: Thomas Nelson Press.

Momaday, N. Scott. 1968. *House Made of Dawn.* New York: Harper & Row.

Money, John, and Anke Ehrhardt. 1972. *Man and Woman, Boy and Girl: The Differentiation and Dimorphism of Gender Identity from Conception to Maturity.* Baltimore: Johns Hopkins University Press.

Montagu, Ashley. 1942. *Man's Most Dangerous Myth: The Fallacy of Race.* New York: Columbia University Press.

Montesquieu, Charles de Secondat, Baron de. 1748. *De l'esprit des lois.* Amsterdam: Chez Chatelain.

Montgomery, David. 1987. *The Fall of the House of Labor.* Cambridge: Cambridge University Press.

Moore, Jason W., ed. 2015. *Capitalism in the Web of Life: Ecology and the Accumulation of Capital*. London: Verso.

———. 2016. *Anthropocene or Capitalocene: Nature, History and the Crisis of Capitalism*. Oakland, CA: PM.

Moraga, Cherríe. 1983. *Loving in the War Years: Lo que nunca pasó por sus labios*. Boston: South End.

Moraga, Cherríe, and Gloria Anzaldúa. 1981. *This Bridge Called My Back: Writings by Radical Women of Color*. Watertown, MA: Persephone.

———. 1983. *This Bridge Called My Back: Writings by Radical Women of Color*. 2nd ed. New York: Kitchen Table / Women of Color.

Morais, Herbert M. 1934. *Deism in Eighteenth-Century America*. New York: Columbia University Press.

Moreton, Bethany. 2009. *To Serve God and Wal-Mart: The Making of Christian Free Enterprise*. Cambridge, MA: Harvard University Press.

Morgan, Edmund S. 1975. *American Slavery, American Freedom: The Ordeal of Colonial Virginia*. New York: Norton.

Morgan, Jennifer L. 2004. *Laboring Women: Reproduction and Gender in New World Slavery*. Philadelphia: University of Pennsylvania Press.

Morgan, Jo-Ann. 2007. *"Uncle Tom's Cabin" as Visual Culture*. Columbia: University of Missouri Press.

Morgan, William. 2004. *Questionable Charity: Gender, Humanitarianism, and Complicity in U.S. Literary Realism*. Hanover, NH: University Press of New England.

Morgensen, Scott Lauria. 2011a. "The Biopolitics of Settler Colonialism: Right Here, Right Now." *Settler Colonial Studies* 1 (1): 52–76.

———. 2011b. *Spaces between Us: Queer Settler Colonialism and Indigenous Decolonization*. Minneapolis: University of Minnesota Press.

Morone, James A. 2003. *Hellfire Nation: The Politics of Sin in American History*. New Haven: Yale University Press.

Morpeau, Louis. 1925. *Anthologie d'un siècle de poésie haïtienne*. Paris: Editions Bossard.

Morrison, Ewan. 2011. "Are Books Dead, and Can Authors Survive?" *Guardian*, August 22, 2011.

Morrison, Toni. 1987. *Beloved*. New York: Knopf.

———. 1992. *Playing in the Dark: Whiteness and the Literary Imagination*. Cambridge, MA: Harvard University Press.

———. 1993. *Playing in the Dark: Whiteness in the Literary Imagination*. New York: Random House.

Mortimer-Sandilands, Catriona, and Bruce Erickson. 2010. *Queer Ecologies: Sex, Nature, Desire*. Bloomington: Indiana University Press.

Moses, Wilson J. 1998. *Afrotopia: The Roots of Popular African American History*. Cambridge: Cambridge University Press.

Moten, Fred. 2003. *In the Break: The Aesthetics of the Black Radical Tradition*. Minneapolis: University of Minnesota Press.

Mouffe, Chantal. 1992. "Democratic Citizenship and the Political Community." In *Dimensions of Radical Democracy: Pluralism, Citizenship and Community*, edited by Chantal Mouffe, 225–39. London: Verso.

———. 1995. "Citizenship." In *The Encyclopedia of Democracy*, edited by Seymour Martin Lipset, 217–21. Vol. 1. Washington, DC: Congressional Quarterly.

———. 2018. *For a Left Populism*. London. Verso Books.

Mounk, Yascha. 2018. *The People vs. Democracy: Why Our Freedom Is in Danger and How to Save It*. Harvard University Press.

Movement. 2016. Haymarket Books.

Movement for Black Lives. 2016. "Invest-Divest." https://policy.m4bl.org.

Moynihan, Daniel Patrick. 1965. *The Negro Family: The Case for National Action*. Washington, DC: US Department of Labor.

———. 1979. "Further Thoughts on Words and Foreign Policy." *Policy Review* (Spring 1979): 53, 58–59.

Mudde, Cas, and Cristobal Rovira Kaltwasser. 2018. *Populism: A Very Short Introduction*. Oxford University Press.

Mulvey, Laura. 1975. "Visual Pleasure and Narrative Cinema." *Screen* 16 (3): 6–18.

Mumford, Kevin. 1997. *Interzones: Black/White Sex Districts in Chicago and New York in the Early Twentieth Century*. New York: Columbia University Press.

Mumford, Lewis. 1931. *Brown Decades: A Study of the Arts in America, 1865–1895*. New York: Harcourt, Brace.

Muñoz, José Esteban. 1999. *Disidentifications: Queers of Color and the Performance of Politics*. Minneapolis: University of Minnesota Press.

———. 2000. "Feeling Brown: Ethnicity and Affect in Ricardo Bracho's *The Sweetest Hangover (and Other STDs)*." *Theater Journal* 52 (1): 67–79.

———. 2006a. "Feeling Brown, Feeling Down: Latina Affect, the Performativity of Race, and the Depressive Position." *Signs* 31 (3): 675–88.

———. 2006b. "The Vulnerability Artist: Nao Bustamante and the Sad Beauty of Reparation." *Women & Performance: A Journal of Feminist Theory* 16 (2): 191–200.

———. 2009. *Cruising Utopia: The Then and There of Queer Futurity*. New York: New York University Press.

Murphie, Andrew. 2008. "Clone Your Technics—Research-Creation, Radical Empiricism and the Constraints of Models." *Inflexions: A Journal for Research-Creation*, no. 1. www.inflexions.org.

Murphree, Daniel. 2004. "Race and Religion on the Periphery:

Disappointment and Missionization in the Spanish Flori-
das, 1566–1763." In *Race, Nation, and Religion in the Americas*, edited by Henry Goldschmidt and Elizabeth McAlister,
35–59. New York: Oxford University Press.

Murray, Charles. 2008. *Real Education: Four Simple Truths for
Bringing America's Schools Back to Reality*. Crown Forum.

Murray, Pauli, and Mary O. Eastwood. 1965. "Jane Crow and
the Law: Sex Discrimination and Title VII." *George Washington Law Review* 34 (2): 232–56.

Musser, Amber Jamilla. 2014. *Sensational Flesh: Race, Power,
and Masochism*. New York: New York University Press.

Myrdal, Gunnar. 1944. *An American Dilemma: The Negro Problem and Modern Democracy*. New York: Harper.

Nakamura, Lisa. 2002. *Cybertypes: Race, Ethnicity, and Identity
on the Internet*. New York: Routledge.

———. 2008. *Digitizing Race: Visual Cultures in the Internet*. Minneapolis: University of Minnesota.

Nakamura, Lisa, and Peter A. Chow-White, eds. 2012. *Race
after the Internet*. New York: Routledge.

Nance, Susan. 2009. *How the Arabian Nights Inspired the American Dream, 1790–1935*. Chapel Hill: University of North
Carolina Press.

Nanda, Mira. 2003. *Prophets Facing Backward: Postmodern Critiques of Science and Hindu Nationalism in India*. New Brunswick, NJ: Rutgers University Press.

Nandy, Ashis. 1990. "Dialogue and the Diaspora: Conversation with Nikos Papastergiadis." *Third Text* 11:99–108.

Nasaw, David. 1993. *Going Out: The Rise and Fall of Public
Amusements*. New York: HarperCollins.

Nash, Gary B. 1986. *Race, Class, and Politics: Essays on Colonial
and Revolutionary Society*. Urbana: University of Illinois
Press.

Nash, George. 1976. *The Conservative Intellectual Movement in
America since 1945*. New York: Basic Books.

Nash, Roderick. 1982. *Wilderness and the American Mind*. 3rd
ed. New Haven: Yale University Press.

National Academy of Science. 1979. *Carbon Dioxide and Climate*. Washington, DC: National Academic of Science.

National Endowment for the Humanities. "NEH Launches
Initiative to Develop 10 Regional Humanities Centers
throughout the Nation." Press release, May 10, 1999. www
.neh.gov.

Nava, Gregory, dir. 1983. *El Norte*. American Playhouse / PBS.

Negt, Oskar, and Alexander Kluge. 1993. *Public Sphere and
Experience: Toward an Analysis of the Bourgeois and Proletar-
ian Public Sphere*. Translated by Peter Labanyi, Jamie Owen
Daniel, and Assenka Oksiloff. Minneapolis: University of
Minnesota Press.

Nel, Philip, and Lissa Paul. 2011. *Keywords for Children's Literature*. New York: New York University Press.

Nelson, Alondra. 2002. "Introduction: Future Texts." *Social
Text* 71 (20.2): 1–15.

Nelson, Benjamin. 1973. "Civilizational Complexes and Inter-
civilizational Encounters." *Sociological Analysis* 34:79–105.

Nelson, Cary, ed. 1997. *Will Work for Food: Academic Labor in
Crisis*. Minneapolis: University of Minnesota Press.

Nelson, Dana. 1992. *The Word in Black and White: Reading
"Race" in American Literature, 1638–1867*. Oxford: Oxford
University Press.

———. 1998. *National Manhood: Capitalist Citizenship and the
Imagined Fraternity of White Men*. Durham, NC: Duke University Press.

Nelson, Jennifer. 2003. *Women of Color and the Reproductive
Rights Movement*. New York: New York University Press.

Nelson, Lowry. 1949. "The American Rural Heritage." *American Quarterly* 1 (3): 225–34.

Nesbitt, Nick. 1999. "Négritude." In *Africana: The Encyclopedia
of the African and African American Experience*, edited by
Kwame Anthony Appiah and Henry Louis Gates Jr. New
York: Basic Books.

Nevins, Joseph. 2002. *Operation Gatekeeper: The Rise of the Illegal Alien and the Making of the U.S.-Mexico Boundary*. New
York: Routledge.

Newfield, Christopher. 1998. "Corporate Culture Wars." In *Corporate Futures: The Diffusion of the Culturally Sensitive Corporate
Form*, edited by George E. Marcus, 23–62. Chicago: University
of Chicago Press.

———. 2003. *Ivy and Industry: Business and the Making of the
American University, 1880–1980*. Durham, NC: Duke University Press.

———. 2008. *Unmaking the Public University: The Forty-Year Assault on the Middle Class*. Cambridge, MA: Harvard University Press.

———. 2016. *The Great Mistake: How We Wrecked Public Universities and How We Can Fix Them*. Baltimore: Johns Hopkins
University Press.

Newman, Louise. 1999. *White Women's Rights: The Racial
Origins of Feminism in the United States*. New York: Oxford
University Press.

New Social History Project. 1989–92. *Who Built America?* 2 vols.
New York: Pantheon.

Newton, Esther. 1972. *Mother Camp: Female Impersonators in
America*. Chicago: University of Chicago Press.

New York Times. 1981. "Excerpts from State Department Memo
on Human Rights." November 5, 1981.

Ngai, Mae. 2004. *Impossible Subjects: Illegal Aliens and the*

Making of Modern America. Princeton, NJ: Princeton University Press.

Ngai, Sianne. 2005. *Ugly Feelings*. Cambridge, MA: Harvard University Press.

Ngũgĩ wa Thiong'o. 1998. *Penpoints, Gunpoints, and Dreams: Towards a Critical Theory of the Arts and the State in Africa*. Oxford: Oxford University Press.

Nguyen, Mimi T. 2012. *The Gift of Freedom: War, Debt, and Other Refugee Passages*. Durham, NC: Duke University Press.

Nichols, Roberts. 2018. "Theft is Property! The Recursive Logic of Dispossession." *Political Theory* 46 (1): 3–28.

Nickerson, Michelle. 2012. *Mothers of Conservatism: Women and the Postwar Right*. Princeton, NJ: Princeton University Press.

Nieto-Phillips, John M. 2004. *The Language of Blood: The Making of Spanish-American Identity in New Mexico, 1880s–1930s*. Albuquerque: University of New Mexico Press.

Niewert, David. 1999. *In God's Country: The Patriot Movement and the Pacific Northwest*. Pullman: Washington State University Press.

Nixon, Rob. n.d. "The Great Acceleration and the Great Divergence: Vulnerability in the Anthropocene." *Profession*. Accessed May 30, 2013. http://profession.commons.mla.org.

Noble, David F. 1977. *America by Design: Science, Technology, and the Rise of Corporate Capitalism*. New York: Knopf.

———. 1995. *Progress without People: New Technology, Unemployment, and the Message of Resistance*. Toronto: Between the Lines.

Noble, David W. 2002. *Death of a Nation*. Minneapolis: University of Minnesota Press.

Noble, Safiya Umoja. 2018. *Algorithms of Oppression: How Search Engines Reinforce Racism*. New York: New York University Press.

Noiriel, Gerárd. 1991. *La tyrannie du national*. Paris: Calmann Levy.

NoiseCat, Julian Brave, and Anne Spice. n.d. "A History and Future of Resistance." Last modified September 8, 2016. www.jacobinmag.com.

Noland, Carrie. 2009. *Agency and Embodiment: Performing Gestures/Producing Culture*. Cambridge, MA: Harvard University Press.

Noland, Carrie, and Sally Ann Ness, eds. 2008. *Migrations of Gesture*. Minneapolis: University of Minnesota Press.

Norgren, Jill. 2004. *The Cherokee Cases: Two Landmark Federal Decisions in the Fight for Sovereignty*. Norman: University of Oklahoma Press.

Noriega, Chon, and Chela Sandoval, eds. 2011. *The Chicano Studies Reader: An Anthology of Aztlán, 1970–2010*. Los Angeles: UCLA Chicano Studies Research Center Press.

Norman, Donald A. 1998. *The Invisible Computer: Why Good Products Can Fail, the Personal Computer Is So Complex, and Information Appliances Are the Solution*. Cambridge: MIT Press.

Normand, Roger, and Sarah Zaidi. 2007. *Human Rights at the UN: The Political History of Universal Justice*. Bloomington: Indiana University Press.

Norquist, Grover. 2001. Interview. *Morning Edition*. National Public Radio, May 25, 2001.

North, Michael. 1994. *The Dialect of Modernism: Race, Language, and Twentieth-Century Literature*. New York: Oxford University Press.

Norton, Mary Beth. 1996. *Founding Mothers and Fathers: Gendered Power and the Formation of American Society*. New York: Knopf.

Novick, Peter. 1988. *That Noble Dream: The "Objectivity Question" and the American Historical Profession*. Cambridge: Cambridge University Press.

Nowviskie, Bethany, ed. 2014. *#Alt-Academy 01: Alternative Academic Careers for Humanities Scholars*. New York: MediaCommons.

Nunberg, Geoffrey. 2004. "The -Ism Schism: How Much Wallop Can a Simple Word Pack?" *New York Times*, July 11, 2004.

Nussbaum, Martha C. 1995. *Poetic Justice: The Literary Imagination and Public Life*. Boston: Beacon.

Nwankwo, Ifeoma Kiddoe. 2005. *Black Cosmopolitanism: Racial Consciousness and Transnational Identity in the Nineteenth-Century Americas*. Philadelphia: University of Pennsylvania Press.

Oakes, James. 2003. "The Peculiar Fate of the Bourgeois Critique of Slavery." In *Slavery and the American South*, edited by Winthrop Jordan, 29–48. Jackson: University Press of Mississippi.

O'Brien, Jean M. 2003. "Why Here? Scholarly Locations for American Indian Studies." *American Quarterly* 55 (4): 689–96.

———. 2010. *Firsting and Lasting: Writing Indians out of Existence in New England*. Minneapolis: University of Minnesota Press.

O'Brien, Ruth. 2001. *Crippled Justice: The History of Modern Disability Policy in the Workplace*. Chicago: University of Chicago Press.

O'Connor, Alice. 2002. *Poverty Knowledge: Social Science, Social Policy, and the Poor in Twentieth Century U.S. History*. Princeton, NJ: Princeton University Press.

Office of Diversity and Inclusion, World Bank. 2013. http://web.worldbank.org.

O'Gorman, Edmundo. 1961. *The Invention of America: An Inquiry into the Historical Nature of the New World and the Meaning of its History*. Bloomington: Indiana University Press.

Ogunnaike, Oludamini. 2016. "From Heathen to Sub-human: A Genealogy of the Influence of the Decline of Religion on the Rise of Modern Racism." *Open Theology* 2:785–803.

Okihiro, Gary Y. 1994. *Margins and Mainstreams: Asians in American History and Culture*. Seattle: University of Washington Press.

Oliver, Melvin, and Thomas Shapiro. 1995. *Black Wealth, White Wealth: A New Perspective on Racial Inequality*. New York: Routledge.

Olson, Joel. 2004. *The Abolition of White Democracy*. Minneapolis: University of Minnesota Press.

Omi, Michael, and Howard Winant. (1986) 1994. *Racial Formation in the United States: From the 1960s to the 1980s*. New York: Routledge.

O'Neill. Cathy. 2016. *Weapons of Math Destruction: How Big Data Increases Inequality and Threatens Democracy*. New York: Penguin.

Ong, Aihwa. 1996. "Cultural Citizenship as Subject Making: Immigrants Negotiate Racial and Cultural Boundaries in the United States." *Current Anthropology* 37 (5): 737–62.

———. 2006. *Neoliberalism as Exception: Mutations in Citizenship and Sovereignty*. Durham, NC: Duke University Press.

Ongiri, Amy Abugo. 2010. *Spectacular Blackness: The Cultural Politics of the Black Power Movement and the Search for a Black Aesthetic*. Charlottesville: University of Virginia Press.

Onwuachi-Willig, Angela. 2005. "The Return of the Ring: Welfare Reform's Marriage Cure as the Revival of Postbellum Control." *California Law Review* 93 (6): 1647–96.

Orderson, J. W. (1842) 2002. *Creoleana: Or, Social and Domestic Scenes and Incidents in Barbados in Days of Yore*. Edited by John Gilmore. Oxford: Macmillan.

Ordover, Nancy. 2003. *American Eugenics: Race, Queer Anatomy, and the Science of Nationalism*. Minneapolis: University of Minnesota Press.

Ortiz, Fernando. 1946. *El engaño de las razas*. Havana: Editorial Páginas.

Ortiz, Paul. 2005. *Emancipation Betrayed: The Hidden History of Black Organizing and White Violence in Florida from Reconstruction to the Bloody Election of 1920*. Berkeley: University of California Press.

Orwell, George. 1945. "You and the Atom Bomb." *Tribune* (London), October 19, 1945.

Osborne, Peter. 1995. *The Politics of Time: Modernity and Avant-Garde*. New York: Verso.

Oshinsky, David M. 2008. *Worse Than Slavery: Parchman Farm and the Ordeal of Jim Crow Justice*. New York: Simon & Schuster.

Ospina, William. 2000. *Mestizo America: The Country of the Future*. New York: Villegas Editores.

Ostiguy, Pierre. 2017. "Populism: A Socio-cultural Approach." In *The Oxford Handbook of Populism*. New York: Oxford University Press.

O'Sullivan, John L. 1839. "The Great Nation of Futurity." *United States Democratic Review* 6 (23): 426–30.

———. 1845. "Annexation." *Democratic Review*, July–August 1845.

Osumare, Halifu. 2007. *The Africanist Aesthetic in Global Hip-Hop*. New York: Palgrave Macmillan.

Otiono, Nduku. 2011. "Tracking Skilled Diasporas: Globalization, Brain Drain, and the Postcolonial Condition of Nigeria." *Transfers* 1 (3): 5–23.

Oxford English Dictionary Online. 2018. www.oed.com.

Padden, Carol A., and Tom L. Humphries. 1990. *Deaf in America: Voices from a Culture*. Cambridge, MA: Harvard University Press.

———. 2006. *Inside Deaf Culture*. Cambridge, MA: Harvard University Press.

Paine, Thomas. (1776) 1953. *Common Sense and Other Political Writings*. Indianapolis: Bobbs-Merrill.

———. (1791) 1999. *Rights of Man*. Mineola, NY: Dover.

Painter, Nell Irvin. 2010. *The History of White People*. New York: Norton.

Panizza, Francisco, ed. 2005. *Populism and the Mirror of Democracy*. London: Verso.

Paranjape, Makarand. 1998. "Theorising Postcolonial Difference: Culture, Nation, Civilization." *SPAN: Journal of the South Pacific Association for Commonwealth Literature and Language Studies* 47:1–17.

Paredes, Américo. 1958. *With His Pistol in His Hand: A Border Ballad and Its Hero*. Austin: University of Texas Press.

———. 1990. *George Washington Gómez: A Mexicotexan Novel*. Houston: Arte Público.

Parédez, Deborah. 2009. *Selenidad: Selena, Latinos, and the Performance of Memory*. Durham, NC: Duke University Press.

Parenti, Christian. 1999. *Lockdown America: Police and Prisons in the Age of Crisis*. London: Verso.

Park, Robert Ezra. 1936. "Succession, an Ecological Concept." *American Sociological Review* 1:2, 171–79.

———. 1939. "Symbiosis and Socialization: A Frame of Reference for the Study of Society." *American Journal of Sociology* 45:1–25.

———. 1950. *Race and Culture: The Collected Papers of Robert*

Ezra Park. Edited by Everett C. Hughes, Charles S. Johnson, Jitsuichi Masuoka, Robert Redfield, and Louis Wirth. Glencoe, IL: Free Press.

———. 1952. *Human Communities: The City and Human Ecology.* Glencoe, IL: Free Press.

Parker, Andrew, Mary Russo, Doris Sommer, and Patricia Yaeger, eds. 1992. *Nationalisms and Sexualities*. New York: Routledge.

Parker, Geoffrey. 2014. *Global Crisis: War, Climate Change, and Catastrophe in the Seventeenth Century*. New Haven: Yale University Press.

Parker, Theodore. (1863) 1973. *Sermons on War*. Edited by Frances P. Cobbe. New York: Garland.

Parlapiano, Alice. 2011. "(Not) Spreading the Wealth." *Washington Post*, June 18, 2011. www.washingtonpost.com.

Parreñas, Rhacel Salazar. 2001. *Servants of Globalization: Women, Migration, and Domestic Work*. Stanford, CA: Stanford University Press.

Parrington, Vernon Lewis, Jr., ed. 1953. "Vernon Parrington's View: Economics and Criticism." *Pacific Northwest Quarterly* 44 (3): 97–105.

Parsons, Lucy. 2004. *Freedom, Equality and Solidarity: Writings and Speeches, 1878–1937*. Edited by Gale Ahrens. Chicago: Charles H. Kerr.

Passmore, Kevin. 2006. *Fascism: A Very Short Introduction*. New York: Oxford University Press.

Patel, Raj, and Jason Moore. 2018. *A History of the World in Seven Cheap Things: A Guide to Capitalism, Nature, and the Future of the Planet*. Berkeley: University of California Press.

Pateman, Carole. 1988. *The Sexual Contract*. Stanford, CA: Stanford University Press.

Patterson, Orlando. 1982. *Slavery and Social Death: A Comparative Study*. Cambridge, MA: Harvard University Press.

Patterson, Sarah. 2015. "Toward Meaning-Making in the Digital Age: Black Women, Black Data and Colored Conventions." *Common-Place* 16 (1).

Patton, Cindy. 1985. *Sex and Germs: The Politics of AIDS*. Boston: South End.

———. 1996. *Fatal Advice: How Safe-Sex Education Went Wrong*. Durham, NC: Duke University Press.

Paulicelli, Eugenia, and Hazel Clark. 2009. *The Fabric of Cultures: Fashion, Identity, and Globalization*. New York: Routledge.

Paxton, Robert. 2005. *Anatomy of Fascism*. New York: Vintage.

———. 2010. "The Scholarly Flaws of Liberal Fascism." History News Network. https://historynewsnetwork.org.

———. 2017. "American Duce: Is Donald Trump a Fascist or a Plutocrat?" *Harper's Magazine*, May 2017.

Payne, Daniel G. 1996. *Voices in the Wilderness: American Nature Writing and Environmental Politics*. Hanover, NH: University Press of New England.

Payne, Stanley. 1996. *A History of Fascism 1914–1945*. Laramie: University of Wisconsin Press.

Pease, Donald E. 1993. "New Perspectives on U.S. Culture and Imperialism." In *Cultures of United States Imperialism*, edited by Amy Kaplan and Donald E. Pease, 22–37. Durham, NC: Duke University Press.

———. 2009a. *The New American Exceptionalism*. Minneapolis: University of Minnesota Press.

———. 2009b. "Re-thinking American Studies after US Exceptionalism." *American Literary History* 21 (1): 19–27.

Peck, Jamie, and Adam Tickell. 1995. "Searching for a New Institutional Fix: The After-Fordist Crisis and the Global-Local Disorder." In *Post-Fordism: A Reader*, edited by Ash Amin, 280–315. Oxford, UK: Blackwell.

Peck, R., dir. 2017. *The Young Karl Marx*. Agat Films & Cie.

Pedersen, Susan, and Caroline Elkins, eds. 2005. *Settler Colonialism in the Twentieth Century*. New York: Routledge.

Peirce, Charles Sanders. 1991. "On the Nature of Signs." In *Peirce on Signs: Writings on Semiotic by Charles Sanders Peirce*, edited by James Hoopes, 141–43. Chapel Hill: University of North Carolina Press.

Peiss, Kathy. 1986. *Cheap Amusements: Working Women and Leisure in Turn-of-the-Century New York*. Philadelphia: Temple University Press.

Peled, Micha, dir. 2005. *China Blue*. Teddy Bear Films.

Pellegrini, Ann. 2009. "Feeling Secular." *Women & Performance* 19 (2): 205–18.

Pelletier, Kevin. 2015. *Apocalyptic Sentimentalism: Love and Fear in U.S. Antebellum Literature*. Athens: University of Georgia Press.

Perdue, Theda. 1979. *Slavery and the Evolution of Cherokee Society, 1540–1866*. Knoxville: University of Tennessee Press.

Pérez, Hiram. 2015. *A Taste for Brown Bodies: Gay Modernity and Cosmopolitan Desire*. New York: New York University Press.

Pérez, Laura Elisa. 2007. *Chicana Art: The Politics of Spiritual and Aesthetic Altarities*. Durham, NC: Duke University Press.

Perlstein, Rick. 2001. *Before the Storm: Barry Goldwater and the Unmaking of American Conservatism*. New York: Hill and Wang.

———. 2008. *Nixonland: The Rise of a President and the Fracturing of America*. New York: Scribner.

———. 2014. *The Invisible Bridge: The Fall of Nixon and the Rise of Ronald Reagan*. New York: Simon & Schuster.

Perry, Pamela. 2002. *Shades of White: White Kids and Racial Identities in High School*. Durham, NC: Duke University Press.

Perry, Pamela, and Alexis Shotwell. 2009. "Relational Understanding and White Antiracist Praxis." *Sociological Theory* 27 (1): 33–50.

Petchesky, Rosalind Pollack. 1981. "Antiabortion, Antifeminism, and the Rise of the New Right." *Feminists Studies* 7:206–46.

Pew Research Center. n.d. "U.S. Muslims Concerned about Their Place in Society, but Continue to Believe in American Dream." www.pewforum.org.

Pexa, Christopher J. 2016. "More Than Talking Animals: Charles Alexander Eastman's Animal Peoples and Their Kinship Critiques of United States Colonialism." *PMLA* 131 (3): 652–67.

Philip, Cynthia Owen, ed. 1973. *Imprisoned in America: Prison Communications, 1776 to Attica*. New York: Harper & Row.

Phillips, Kevin. 2002. *Wealth and Democracy: A Political History of the American Rich*. New York: Broadway Books.

Phillips-Fein, Kim. 2009. *Invisible Hands: The Making of the Conservative Movement from the New Deal to Reagan*. New York: W. W. Norton.

Pick, Daniel. 2012. *The Pursuit of the Nazi Mind: Hitler, Hess, and the Analysts*. New York: Oxford University Press.

Piketty, Thomas. 2014. *Capital in the Twenty-First Century*. Translated by Arthur Goldhammer Cambridge, MA: Harvard University Press.

———. 2016. "Thomas Piketty on the Rise of Bernie Sanders: The US Enters a New Political Era." *Guardian*, February 16, 2016. www.theguardian.com.

Piore, Michael, and Charles F. Sabel. 1984. *The Second Industrial Divide: Possibilities for Prosperity*. New York: Basic Books.

Pitts-Taylor, Victoria. 2016. *The Brain's Body: Neuroscience and Corporeal Politics*. Durham, NC: Duke University Press.

Plummer, Brenda Gayle. 1996. *Rising Wind: Black Americans and Foreign Affairs, 1935–1960*. Chapel Hill: University of North Carolina Press.

Pocock, J. G. A. (1975) 2009. *Machiavellian Moment: Florentine Political Thought and the Atlantic Republican Tradition*. Princeton, NJ: Princeton University Press.

Polanyi, Karl. (1944) 2001. *The Great Transformation*. New York: Farrar and Rinehart. Reprint, Boston: Beacon.

Polikoff, Nancy D. 2008. *Beyond (Straight and Gay) Marriage: Valuing All Families under the Law*. Boston: Beacon.

Pollin, Robert. 2003. *Contours of Descent: U.S. Economic Fractures and the Landscape of Global Austerity*. London: Verso.

Poovey, Mary. 1986. "'Scenes of an Indelicate Character': The Medical 'Treatment' of Victorian Women." *Representations* 14:137–68.

———. 1998. *A History of the Modern Fact: Problems of Knowledge in the Sciences of Wealth and Society*. Chicago: University of Chicago Press.

———. 2008. *Genres of the Credit Economy: Mediating Value in Eighteenth- and Nineteenth-Century Britain*. Chicago: University of Chicago Press.

Porter, James I. 1997. Foreword to *The Body and Physical Difference: Discourses of Disability in the Humanities*, edited by David T. Mitchell and Sharon Snyder, xiii–xiv. Ann Arbor: University of Michigan Press.

Posner, Miriam, and Lauren F. Klein. 2017. "Data as Media." *Feminist Media Histories* 3 (3): 1–8.

Post, Margaret, Elaine Ward, Nicholas Longo, and John Saltmarsh. 2016. *Publicly Engaged Scholars: Next-Generation Engagement and the Future of Higher Education*. Sterling, VA: Stylus.

Poster, Mark. 1997. "CyberDemocracy: Internet and the Public Sphere." In *Internet Culture*, edited by David Foster. New York: Routledge.

Postman, Neil. 1993. *Technopoly: The Surrender of Culture to Technology*. New York: Vintage.

Povinelli, Elizabeth A. 2006. *The Empire of Love: Toward a Theory of Intimacy, Genealogy, and Carnality*. Durham, NC: Duke University Press.

———. 2011. *Economies of Abandonment: Social Belonging and Endurance in Late Liberalism*. Durham, NC: Duke University Press.

Povinelli, Elizabeth A., and George Chauncey. 1999. "Thinking Sexuality Transnationally: An Introduction." *GLQ* 5 (4): 439–50.

Powell, John A. 1990. "New Property Disaggregated: A Model to Address Employment Discrimination." *University of San Francisco Law Review* 24:363–83.

Prakash, Gyan. 1999. *Another Reason: Science and the Imagination of Modern India*. Princeton, NJ: Princeton University Press.

Prashad, Vijay. 2000. *Karma of Brown Folk*. Minneapolis: University of Minnesota Press.

———. 2001. *Everybody Was Kung Fu Fighting: Afro-Asian Connections and the Myth of Cultural Purity*. Boston: Beacon.

———. 2007. "Orientalism." In *Keywords for American Cultural Studies*, edited by Bruce Burgett and Glenn Hendler, 174–77. New York: New York University Press.

Pratt, Lloyd. 2010. *Archives of American Time: Literature and Modernity in the Nineteenth Century*. Philadelphia: University of Pennsylvania Press.

Preciado, Paul B. 2013. *Testo Junkie: Sex, Drugs, and Biopolitics in the Pharmacopornographic Era*. Translated by Bruce Benderson. New York: Feminist Press at City University of New York.

Prescott, William. 1843. *History of the Conquest of Mexico*. New York: Harper.

Price, Melanye. 2018. "Ayanna Pressley and the Might of the Black Political Left." *New York Times*, September 6, 2018. www.nytimes.com.

Price, Richard. 1953. "Letter to Thomas Jefferson, July 2, 1785." In *The Papers of Thomas Jefferson*, edited by Julian Boyd. Vol. 8. Princeton, NJ: Princeton University Press.

Prince, Mary. (1831) 2000. *The History of Mary Prince*. Edited by Sara Salih. New York: Penguin.

"Principles of Environmental Justice." 1991. First National People of Color Environmental Leadership Summit. Accessed July 15, 2019. www.ejnet.org.

Prosser, Jay. 1998. *Second Skins: The Body Narratives of Transsexuality*. New York: Columbia University Press.

Prucha, Francis Paul. 1981. "The Image of the Indian in Pre-Civil War America." In *Indian Policy in the United States: Historical Essays*, 49–63. Lincoln: University of Nebraska Press.

Puar, Jasbir K. 2005. "On Torture: Abu Ghraib." *Radical History Review* 93:13–38.

———. 2007. *Terrorist Assemblages: Homonationalism in Queer Times*. Durham, NC: Duke University Press.

———. 2017. *The Right to Maim: Debility, Capacity, Disability*. Durham, NC: Duke University Press.

Pulido, Laura. 1996. *Environmentalism and Economic Justice*. Tucson: University of Arizona Press.

Purdy, Jedediah. 2015. *After Nature: A Politics for the Anthropocene*. Harvard: Harvard University Press.

Purvis, Dara. 2016. "Boycotts." First Amendment Encyclopedia. Middle Tennessee State University. https://mtsu.edu.

Putnam, Robert D. 1993. "The Prosperous Community." *American Prospect* 13:35–42.

———. 2000. *Bowling Alone: The Collapse and Revival of American Community*. New York: Simon & Schuster.

Quadagno, Jill. 1994. *The Color of Welfare: How Racism Undermined the War on Poverty*. Oxford: Oxford University Press.

Quart, Alissa. 2018. *Squeezed: Why Our Families Can't Afford America*. New York: Ecco.

Quayson, Ato. 2007. *Aesthetic Nervousness: Disability and the Crisis of Representation*. New York: Columbia University Press.

Queers for Economic Justice. 2010. "A Military Job Is Not Economic Justice." http://q4ej.org.

Quetelet, Adolphe. 1835. *Sur l'homme et le développement de ses facultés, ou Essai de physique sociale*. Paris: Bachiliers.

Quiroga, José. 2000. *Tropics of Desire: Interventions from Queer Latino America*. New York: New York University Press.

Rabaka, Reiland. 2010. *Forms of Fanonism: Fanon's Critical Theory and the Dialectics of Decolonization*. Lanham, MD: Lexington Books.

Rabinowitz, Paula. 1991. *Labor and Desire: Women's Revolutionary Fiction in Depression America*. Chapel Hill: University of North Carolina Press.

Raboteau, Albert. 1978. *Slave Religion: The "Invisible Institution" in the Antebellum South*. New York: Oxford University Press.

Radano, Ronald, and Philip V. Bohlman. 2000. *Music and the Racial Imagination*. Chicago: University of Chicago Press.

Radway, Jan. 2002. "What's in a Name?" In *The Futures of American Studies*, edited by Donald Pease and Robyn Wiegman, 45–75. Durham, NC: Duke University Press.

Rafael, Vicente. 1988. *Contracting Colonialism: Translation and Christian Conversion in Tagalog Society under Early Spanish Rule*. Ithaca, NY: Cornell University Press.

Raheja, Michelle H. 2011. *Reservation Reelism: Redfacing, Visual Sovereignty, and Representations of Native Americans in Film*. Lincoln: University of Nebraska Press.

Rainsford, Marcus. 1805. *An Historical Account of the Black Empire of Hayti: Comprehending a View of the Principal Transactions in the Revolution of Saint Domingo; with Its Ancient and Modern State*. London: Albion.

Rajshekar, V. T. 2009. *Dalit: The Black Untouchables of India*. Atlanta: Clarity.

Rana, Junaid. 2011. *Terrifying Muslims: Race and Labor in the South Asian Diaspora*. Durham, NC: Duke University Press.

Rancière, Jacques. 1998. *Disagreement: Politics and Philosophy*. Minneapolis: University of Minnesota Press.

———. 2010. *Dissensus: On Politics and Aesthetics*. London: Continuum.

Ransby, Barbara. 2003. *Ella Baker and the Black Freedom Movement: A Radical Democratic Vision*. Chapel Hill: University of North Carolina Press.

Ransom, John Crowe. 1965. "Forms and Citizens." In *The World's Body*, 29–54. Baton Rouge: Louisiana State University Press.

Raphael, Ray. 2001. *A People's History of the American Revolution*. New York: New Press.

Ratcliffe, Krista. 2006. *Rhetorical Listening: Identification, Gender, Whiteness*. Carbondale: Southern Illinois University Press.

Ratto, Matt. 2011. "Critical Making: Conceptual and Material Studies in Technology and Social Life." *Information Society* 27 (4): 252–60.

Ravenstein, Ernest George. 1885. "The Laws of Migration." *Journal of the Statistical Society of London* 48 (2): 167–235.

Ravinet, Laurette Aimée Mozard Nicodami de. 1844. *Mémoires d'une créole de Port-au-Prince (Ile Saint-Domingue)*. Paris: Librairie-Papeterie.

Rawson, Katie, and Trevor Munoz. 2019. "Against Cleaning." In *Debates in the Digital Humanities 2019*, edited by Matthew K. Gold and Lauren Klein. Minneapolis: University of Minnesota Press.

Ray, Sarah Jaquette. 2013. *The Ecological Other: Environmental Exclusion in American Culture*. Tucson: University of Arizona Press.

Raz, Joseph. 1977. "The Rule of Law and Its Virtue." *Law Quarterly Review* 93:195–211.

Razack, Sherene. 2012. "'We Didn't Kill 'Em, We Didn't Cut Their Head Off': Abu Ghraib Revisited." In *Racial Formation in the Twenty-First Century*, edited by Daniel Martinez HoSang, Oneka LaBennett, and Laura Pulido, 217–45. Berkeley: University of California Press.

Readings, Bill. 1997. *The University in Ruins*. Boston: Harvard University Press.

Reagan, Ronald. 1983. "Remarks at the Annual Convention of the National Association of Evangelicals in Orlando, Florida." Ronald Reagan Presidential Library and Museum. www.reaganlibrary.gov.

———. 1987. "Remarks on East-West Relations at the Brandenburg Gate in West Berlin." Ronald Reagan Presidential Library. www.reagan.utexas.edu.

———. 1985. "Second Inaugural Address of Ronald Reagan." Avalon Project: Documents in Law, History, & Diplomacy, Yale Law School. http://avalon.law.yale.edu.

Recollet, Karyn. 2016. "Getting Indigenous Futurities through the Remix." *Dance Research Journal* 48 (1): 91-105.

Reddy, Chandan. 2011. *Freedom with Violence: Race, Sexuality, and the US State*. Durham, NC: Duke University Press.

Reece, E. 2016. *Utopia Drive: A Road Trip through America's Most Radical Idea*. New York: Farrar, Strauss and Giroux.

Reed, T. V. 1999. "Theory and Method in American/Cultural Studies: A Bibliographic Essay." American Studies at the University of Virginia. http://xroads.virginia.edu.

———. 2005. *The Art of Protest: Culture and Activism from the Civil Rights Movement to the Streets of Seattle*. Minneapolis: University of Minnesota Press.

Reich, Robert B. 1991. "Secession of the Successful." *New York Times*, January 20, 1991. www.nytimes.com.

Reich, Wilhelm. (1933) 1980. *The Mass Psychology of Fascism*. New York: Farrar, Straus and Giroux.

Reid-Ross, Alexander. 2017. *Against the Fascist Creep*. Oakland, CA: AK.

Reinhardt, Carmen, and Kenneth Rogoff. 2009. *This Time Is Different: Eight Centuries of Financial Folly*. Princeton, NJ: Princeton University Press.

Renan, Ernest. (1882) 1990. "What Is a Nation?" In *Nation and Narration*, edited by Homi K. Bhabha, 8–22. London: Routledge.

Renda, Mary A. 2001. *Taking Haiti: Military Occupation and the Culture of U.S. Imperialism, 1915-1940*. Chapel Hill: University of North Carolina Press.

Repo, Jemima. 2016. *The Biopolitics of Gender*. New York: Oxford University Press.

Resnick, Stephen A., and Richard D. Wolff. 1987. *Knowledge and Class: A Marxian Critique of Political Economy*. Chicago: University of Chicago Press.

Reverby, Susan. 2009. *Examining Tuskegee: The Infamous Syphilis Study and Its Legacy*. Chapel Hill: University of North Carolina Press.

Reynolds, David S. 1989. *Beneath the American Renaissance: The Subversive Imagination in the Age of Emerson and Melville*. Cambridge, MA: Harvard University Press.

Rhoads, Robert. 2003. "How Civic Engagement Is Reframing Liberal Education." *Peer Review* 5 (3). American Association of Colleges and Universities.

Rhodes, Lorna A. 2004. *Total Confinement: Madness and Reason in the Maximum Security Prison*. Berkeley: University of California Press.

Ricardo, David. 1817. *On the Principles of Political Economy and Taxation*. London: Murray. www.econlib.org.

Rich, Adrienne. (1980) 1983. "Compulsory Heterosexuality and Lesbian Existence." In *Powers of Desire: The Politics of Sexuality*, edited by Ann Snitow, Christine Stansell, and Sharon Thompson, 177–205. New York: Monthly Review Press.

———. 1986. "Sources: IV." In *Your Native Land, Your Life*. New York: Norton.

Richie, Beth E. 2012. *Arrested Justice: Black Women, Violence, and America's Prison Nation*. New York: New York University Press.

Richie, Beth E., Dana-Ain Davis, and LaTosha Traylor. 2012. "Feminist Politics, Racialized Imagery, and Social Control." *Souls: A Critical Journal of Black Politics, Culture and Society* 14 (1–2): 54–66.

Rickard, Jolene. 1995. "Sovereignty: A Line in the Sand." In *Strong Hearts: Native American Visions and Voices*, edited by Peggy Roalf, 51–60. New York: Aperture.

Ridge, John Rollin. (1854) 1977. *Life and Adventures of Joaquin Murieta: Celebrated California Bandit*. Norman: University of Oklahoma Press.

Riefenstahl, Leni, dir. 1935. *Triumph of the Will*. Leni

Riefenstahl-Produktion / Reichspropagandaleitung der NSDAP.

Rifkin, Jeremy. 2000. *The Age of Access: The New Culture of Hypercapitalism, Where All of Life Is a Paid-For Experience.* New York: Jeremy P. Tarcher / Putnam.

Rifkin, Mark. 2011. *When Did Indians Become Straight? Kinship, the History of Sexuality, and Native Sovereignty.* New York: Oxford University Press.

Riofrancos, Thea. 2017. "Democracy without the People: Left Populism vs. Insipid Pluralism." *N+1 Magazine*, Spring 2017.

Rivera, Raquel Z. 2003. *New York Ricans from the Hip Hop Zone.* New York: Palgrave Macmillan.

Rivera-Servera, Ramon H. 2012. *Performing Queer Latinidad: Dance, Sexuality, Politics.* Ann Arbor: University of Michigan Press.

Rivlin, Gary. 2010. *Broke, USA: From Pawnshops to Poverty, Inc.—How the Working Poor Became Big Business.* New York: HarperBusiness.

Roach, Joseph. 1996. *Cities of the Dead: Circum-Atlantic Performance.* New York: Columbia University Press.

Roanhorse, Rebecca, Elizabeth LaPensee, Johnnie Jae, and Darcie Little Badger. 2017. "Decolonizing Science Fiction and Imagining Futures: An Indigenous Futurisms Roundtable." Strange Horizons. http://strangehorizons.com.

Robbins, Bruce. 1993. "Introduction: The Public as Phantom." In *The Phantom Public Sphere*, edited by Bruce Robbins, vii–xxvi. Minneapolis: University of Minnesota Press.

Roberts, Brian. 2017. *Race, Reform, and Identity in American Popular Music, 1812–1925.* Chicago: University of Chicago Press.

Roberts, Dorothy E. 1993. "Racism and Patriarchy in the Meaning of Motherhood." *American University Journal of Gender and Law* 1:1–38.

———. 1998. *Killing the Black Body: Race, Reproduction, and the Meaning of Liberty.* New York: Vintage.

———. 2009. "Race, Gender, and Genetic Technologies: A New Reproductive Dystopia." *Signs* 34 (4): 783–804.

———. 2011. *Fatal Invention: How Science, Politics, and Big Business Re-create Race in the Twenty-First Century.* New York: New Press.

Robespierre, Maximilien. 2007. *Slavoj Žižek Presents Robespierre: Virtue and Terror.* Edited by Slavoj Žižek. New York: Verso.

Robin, Corey. 2004. *Fear: The History of a Political Idea.* New York: Oxford University Press.

———. 2011. *The Reactionary Mind: Conservatism from Edmund Burke to Sarah Palin.* Oxford: Oxford University Press.

Robinson, Cedric J. (1983) 2000. *Black Marxism: The Making of the Black Radical Tradition.* Chapel Hill: University of North Carolina Press.

———. 1984. *Black Marxism: The Making of the Black Radical Tradition.* London: Zed Books.

Robinson, Danielle. 2015. *Modern Moves: Dancing Race during the Ragtime and Jazz Eras.* New York: Oxford University Press.

Robinson, Forrest G. 1997. "Clio Bereft of Calliope: Literature and the New Western History." In *The New Western History: The Territory Ahead*, edited by Forrest G. Robinson, 61–98. Tucson: University of Arizona Press.

Rodgers, Tara. 2010. *Pink Noises: Women on Electronic Music and Sound.* Durham, NC: Duke University Press.

Rodríguez, Clara E. 2000. *Changing Race: Latinos, the Census, and the History of Ethnicity in the United States.* New York: New York University Press.

Rodríguez, Dylan. 2006. *Forced Passages: Imprisoned Radical Intellectuals and the U.S. Prison Regime.* Minneapolis: University of Minnesota Press.

———. 2012. "Racial/Colonial Genocide and the 'Neoliberal Academy': In Excess of a Problematic." *American Quarterly* 64 (4): 809–13.

Rodríguez, Juana María. 2003. *Queer Latinidad: Identity Practices, Discursive Spaces.* New York: New York University Press.

———. 2014. *Sexual Futures, Queer Gestures, and Other Latina Longings.* New York: New York University Press.

Rodríguez, Richard T. 2009. *Next of Kin: The Family in Chicano/a Cultural Politics.* Durham, NC: Duke University Press.

Rodríguez-Silva, Ileana M. 2005. "*Libertos* and *Libertas* in the Construction of the Free Worker in Postemancipation Puerto Rico." In *Gender and Slave Emancipation in the Atlantic World*, edited by Pamela Scully and Diana Paton, 199–222. Durham, NC: Duke University Press.

Roediger, David R. 1991. *The Wages of Whiteness: Race and the Making of the American Working Class.* London: Verso.

———. 1994. *Toward the Abolition of Whiteness: Essays on Race, Politics, and Working-Class History.* London: Verso.

———. 1999. *The Wages of Whiteness: Race and the Making of the American Working Class.* Rev. ed. London: Verso.

———. 2007. *The Wages of Whiteness: Race and the Making of the American Working Class.* Rev. ed. Haymarket Series. New York: Verso.

Roelvink, G., G. St. Martin, and J. K. Gibson-Graham, eds. 2015. *Making Other Worlds Possible: Performing Diverse Economies.* Minneapolis: University of Minnesota Press.

Rogers, Simon. 2010. "Data Are or Data Is?" *Guardian*, July 8, 2010. www.theguardian.com.

Rogin, Michael. 1987. *Ronald Reagan, the Movie, and Other Episodes in Political Demonology*. Berkeley: University of California Press.

———. 1996. *Black Face, White Noise: Jewish Immigrants in the Hollywood Melting Pot*. Berkeley: University of California Press.

Rohy, Valerie. 2009. *Anachronism and Its Others: Sexuality, Race, Temporality*. Albany: State University of New York Press.

Román, Ediberto. 2013. *Those Damned Immigrants: America's Hysteria over Undocumented Immigration*. New York: New York University Press.

Román, Miriam Jiménez, and Juan Flores, eds. 2010. *The Afro-Latin@ Reader: History and Culture in the United States*. Durham, NC: Duke University Press.

Romero, Lora. 1997. *Home Fronts: Domesticity and Its Critics in the Antebellum United States*. Durham, NC: Duke University Press.

Romero, Mary. 1992. *Maid in the U.S.A.* New York: Routledge.

Roosevelt, Theodore. (1889) 2016. *The Winning of the West Complete*. Scotts Valley, CA: Create Space Independent Publishing Platform.

———. 1894. "True Americanism." *Forum*, April 1894.

———. 1904. "Fourth Annual Message to Congress, December 6, 1904." In *A Compilation of the Messages and Papers of the Presidents: 1789–1908*, edited by James D. Richardson, 802–38. Vol. 10. Washington, DC: Bureau of National Literature and Art.

———. 1909. *Report of the Country Life Commission*. Washington, DC: Government Printing Office.

Root, Regina A. 2010. *Couture and Consensus: Fashion and Politics in Postcolonial Argentina*. Minneapolis: University of Minnesota Press.

Rosa, Andrew Juan. 1996. "El que no tiene dingo, tiene mandingo: The Inadequacy of the 'Mestizo' as a Theoretical Construct in the Field of Latin American Studies—the Problem and Solution." *Journal of Black Studies* 27 (2): 278–91.

Rosaldo, Michelle Z. 1984. "Toward an Anthropology of Self and Feeling." In *Culture Theory: Essays on Mind, Self and Emotion*, edited by Richard A. Shweder and Robert A. LeVine, 137–57. New York: Cambridge University Press.

Rosaldo, Renato. 1999. "Cultural Citizenship, Inequality, and Multiculturalism." In *Race, Identity, and Citizenship: A Reader*, edited by Rodolfo D. Torres, Louis F. Miron, and Jonathan Xavier Inda, 253–61. Oxford, UK: Blackwell.

Rosales, Francisco A. 1997. *Chicano! The History of the Mexican American Civil Rights Movement*. 2nd rev. ed. Houston: Arte Público.

Rosas, Gilberto. 2006. "The Thickening Borderlands: Diffused Exceptionality and 'Immigrant' Social Struggles during the 'War on Terror.'" *Cultural Dynamics* 18 (3): 335–49.

Rose, Mark. 1995. *Authors and Owners: The Invention of Copyright*. Cambridge, MA: Harvard University Press.

———. 2014. *The Mind at Work: Valuing the Intelligence of the American Worker*. New York: Penguin Books.

Rose, Nikolas. 1999. *The Powers of Freedom*. Cambridge: Cambridge University Press.

———. 2006. *The Politics of Life Itself: Biomedicine, Biopower, and Subjectivity in the Twenty-First Century*. Princeton, NJ: Princeton University Press.

Rose, Nikolas, and Peter Miller. 2008. *Governing the Present: Administering Economic, Social, and Personal Life*. Malden, MA: Polity.

Rose, Tricia. 1994. *Black Noise: Rap Music and Black Culture in Contemporary America*. Hanover, NH: Wesleyan University Press.

Rosenberg, Daniel. 2013. "Data before the Fact." In *"Raw Data" Is an Oxymoron*, 15–40. Cambridge: MIT Press.

Rosenberg, Samuel. 2003. *American Economic Development since 1945*. New York: Palgrave Macmillan.

Rosenthal, C. E. 2018. *Accounting for Slavery: Masters and Management*. Cambridge, MA: Harvard University Press.

Ross, Andrew. 1990. "Hacking Away at the Counterculture." *Postmodern Culture* 1 (1). http://pmc.iath.virginia.edu.

———. 1997. *No Sweat: Fashion, Free Trade, and the Rights of Garment Workers*. New York: Verso.

———. 2003. *No-Collar: The Humane Workplace and Its Hidden Costs*. New York: Basic Books.

———. 2004. *No Collar: The Humane Workplace and Its Hidden Costs*. Philadelphia: Temple University Press.

———. 2009. *Nice Work If You Can Get It: Life and Labor in Precarious Times*. New York: New York University Press.

———. 2014. *Creditocracy and the Case for Debt Refusal*. New York: OR Books.

Rossi, Alice S., ed. 1973. *The Feminist Papers: From Adams to de Beauvoir*. New York: Columbia University Press.

Rothenberg, Winifred Barr. 1992. *From Market-Places to a Market Economy: The Transformation of Rural Massachusetts, 1750–1850*. Chicago: University of Chicago Press.

Rothman, David. 1971. *The Discovery of the Asylum: Social Order and Disorder in the New Republic*. Boston: Little, Brown.

Rottenberg, Catherine. 2017. "Neoliberal Feminism and the Future of Human Capital." *Signs* 42 (2): 329–48.

Round, Phillip H. 2010. *Removable Type: Histories of the Book in Indian Country, 1663–1880*. Chapel Hill: University of North Carolina Press.

Rousseau, Jean-Jacques. (1754) 1984. *A Discourse on Inequality*. Translated by Maurice Cranston. New York: Penguin.

———. (1762) 1968. *The Social Contract*. Translated by Maurice Cranston. London: Penguin.

Rowe, John Carlos, ed. 2000. *Post-nationalist American Studies*. Berkeley: University of California Press.

Roy, William G. 1997. *Socializing Capital: The Rise of the Large Industrial Corporation in America*. Princeton, NJ: Princeton University Press.

Ruben, Matthew. 2002. "Suburbanization and Urban Poverty under Neoliberalism." In *The New Poverty Studies: The Ethnography of Power, Politics, and Impoverished People in the United States*, edited by Judith G. Goode and Jeff Maskovsky, 434–69. New York: New York University Press.

Rubin, Gayle. 1975. "The Traffic in Women: Notes on the 'Political Economy' of Sex." In *Toward an Anthropology of Women*, edited by Rayna R. Reiter, 157–210. New York: Monthly Review Press.

———. 1984. "Thinking Sex: Notes for a Radical Theory of the Politics of Sexuality." In *Pleasure and Danger: Exploring Female Sexuality*, edited by Carole S. Vance, 267–319. Boston: Routledge and Kegan Paul.

———. 2002. "Studying Sexual Subcultures: Excavating the Ethnography of Gay Communities in Urban North America." In *Out in Theory: The Emergence of Lesbian and Gay Anthropology*, edited by Ellen Lewin and William L. Leap, 17–67. Urbana: University of Illinois Press.

Ruccio, David F. 2003. "Globalization and Imperialism." *Rethinking Marxism* 15:75–94.

Ruccio, David F., and J. K. Gibson-Graham. 2001. "'After' Development: Reimagining Economy and Class." In *Re/presenting Class: Essays in Postmodern Political Economy*, edited by J. K. Gibson-Graham, Stephen Resnick, and Richard Wolff, 158–81. Durham, NC: Duke University Press.

Rugemer, Edward Bartlett. 2008. *The Problem of Emancipation: The Caribbean Roots of the American Civil War*. Baton Rouge: Louisiana State University Press.

Russ, Joanna. 1975. *The Female Man*. New York: Bantam.

———. 1995. "Speculations: The Subjunctivity of Science Fiction." In *To Write like a Woman: Essays in Feminism and Science Fiction*, 15–25. Bloomington: Indiana University Press.

Ryan, Mary P. 1975. *Womanhood in American from Colonial Times to the Present*. New York: New Viewpoints.

———. 1981. *Cradle of the Middle Class: The Family in Oneida County, New York, 1790–1865*. New York: Cambridge University Press.

Ryan, Susan M. 2003. *The Grammar of Good Intentions: Race and the Antebellum Culture of Benevolence*. Ithaca, NY: Cornell University Press.

Rybczynski, Witold. 1988. *Home: A Short History of an Idea*. London: Longman.

Sabol, William J., and Heather Couture. 2008. *Prisoners at Midyear 2007*. NCJ221944. Washington, DC: US Department of Justice, Bureau of Justice Statistics.

Safran, William. 1991. "Diasporas in Modern Societies: Myths of Homeland and Return." *Diaspora* 1 (1): 83–99.

Said, Edward W. 1978. *Orientalism*. New York: Vintage.

———. 1981. *Covering Islam: How the Media and the Experts Determine How We See the Rest of the World*. New York: Vintage.

———. 1993. *Culture and Imperialism*. New York: Random House.

Saint-Simon, Henri de. (1813) 1965. *Mémoire sur la science de l'homme: La physiologie sociale*. Edited by G. Gurwitch. Paris: Presses Universitaires de France.

Saito, Leland. 2009. *The Politics of Exclusion: The Failure of Race-Neutral Policies in Urban America*. Stanford, CA: Stanford University Press.

Sakai, Naoki. 2000. "'You Asians': On the Historical Role of the West and Asia Binary." *South Atlantic Quarterly* 99 (4): 789–817.

Sakai, Naoki, and Meaghan Morris. 2005. "The West." In *New Keywords: A Revised Vocabulary of Culture and Society*, edited by Tony Bennett, Lawrence Grossberg, and Meaghan Morris. London: Blackwell.

Saks, Eva. 1988. "Representing Miscegenation Law." *Raritan* 8:39–69.

Salazar, James B. 2010. *Bodies of Reform: The Rhetoric of Character in Gilded Age America*. New York: New York University Press.

Saldaña-Portillo, María Josefina. 2001. "Who's the Indian in Aztlán? Re-writing Mestizaje, Indianism, and Chicanismo from the Lacandón." In *Latin American Subaltern Studies Reader*, edited by Ileana Rodríguez, 402–23. Durham, NC: Duke University Press.

———. 2003. *The Revolutionary Imagination in the Americas and the Age of Development*. Durham, NC: Duke University Press.

———. 2016. *Indian Given: Racial Geographies across Mexico and the United States*. Durham, NC: Duke University Press.

Saldívar, José David. 1993. "Américo Paredes and Decolonization." In *Cultures of United States Imperialism*, edited by Amy Kaplan and Donald Pease, 292–311. Durham, NC: Duke University Press.

———. 1997. *Border Matters: Remapping American Cultural Studies*. Berkeley: University of California Press.

Saldivar, Ramon. 2006. *The Borderlands of Culture: Américo*

Paredes and the Transnational Imaginary. Durham, NC: Duke University Press.

Saldívar-Hull, Sonia. 2000. *Feminism on the Border: Chicana Gender Politics and Literature*. Berkeley: University of California Press.

Salles, Walter, dir. 2004. *The Motorcycle Diaries*. FilmFour.

Salter, Mark. 2006. "The Global Visa Regime and the Political Technologies of the International Self: Borders, Bodies, Biopolitics." *Alternatives* 31:167–89.

Saltmarsh, John, and Matthew Hartley. 2016. "The Inheritance of Next-Generation Engagement Scholars." In *Publicly Engaged Scholars: Next Generation Engagement and the Future of Higher Education*, edited by Margaret Post, Elaine Ward, Nicholas Longo, and John Saltmarsh. Sterling, VA: Stylus.

Samuels, Ellen. 2002. "Critical Divides: Judith Butler's Body Theory and the Question of Disability." *NWSA Journal* 14 (3): 58–76.

Samuels, Robert. 2013. *Why Public Higher Education Should Be Free: How to Decrease Cost and Increase Quality at American Universities*, New Brunswick, NJ: Rutgers University Press.

Samuels, Shirley, ed. 1992. *The Culture of Sentiment: Race, Gender, and Sentimentality in Nineteenth-Century America*. New York: Oxford University Press.

———. 1996. *Romances of the Republic: Women, the Family, and Violence in the Literature of the Early American Nation*. New York: Oxford University Press.

Samuelson, Paul A., and William D. Nordhaus. 2004. *Economics*. 18th ed. New York: McGraw-Hill / Irwin.

Sanchez, George J. 2012. "Crossing Figueroa: The Tangled Web of Diversity and Democracy." In *Collaborative Futures: Critical Reflections on Publicly Active Graduate Education*, edited by Amanda Gilvin, Georgia M. Roberts, and Craig Martin. Syracuse: Syracuse University Press.

Sánchez, María Carla. 2008. *Reforming the World: Social Activism and the Problem of Fiction in Nineteenth-Century America*. Iowa City: University of Iowa Press.

Sanchez, Rebecca. 2015. *Deafening Modernism: Embodied Language and Visual Poetics in American Literature*. New York: New York University Press.

Sánchez-Eppler, Karen. 1993. *Touching Liberty: Abolition, Feminism, and the Politics of the Body*. Berkeley: University of California Press.

Sandahl, Carrie, and Philip Auslander, eds. 2005. *Bodies in Commotion: Disability and Performance*. Ann Arbor: University of Michigan Press.

Sanders, Ashley. 2014. "Going Alt-Ac: How to Begin: What Is Alt-Ac? What Is an Alt-Ac Job? And How Do You Find One?" Inside Higher Ed. Accessed August 20, 2018. www.insidehighered.com.

Sanders, Bernie. 2012. "What If There Were 83 Women Senators?" Bernie Sanders's Senate website. www.sanders.senate.gov.

Sandoval, Tomás F. Summers, Jr. 2008. "Disobedient Bodies: Racialization, Resistance, and the Mass (Re)Articulation of the Mexican Immigrant Body." *American Behavioral Scientist* 52 (4): 580–97.

Sandvig, Christian. 2012. "Connection at Eqiiaapaayp Mountain: Indigenous Internet Infrastructure." In *Race after the Internet*, edited by Lisa Nakamura, Peter Chow-White, and Alondra Nelson, 168–200. New York: Routledge.

Sanger, Margaret. 1914. *Family Limitation*. New York: printed by the author.

Sangtin Writers Collective and Richa Nagar. 2006. *Playing with Fire: Feminist Thought and Activism through Seven Lives in India*. Minneapolis: University of Minnesota Press.

Sansay, Leonora. (1808) 2007. *Secret History or the Horrors of Santo Domingo and Laura*. Edited by Michael Drexler. Ontario, Canada: Broadview Editions.

Santiago, Silviano. (1971) 1973. *Latin American Literature: The Space in Between*. Translated by Stephen Moscov. Buffalo: Council on International Studies, State University of New York at Buffalo.

Sarachild, Kathie. 1978. "Consciousness Raising: A Radical Weapon." In *Feminist Revolution*, edited by Redstockings of the Women's Liberation Movement, 144–50. New York: Random House.

Sarat, Austin. 1982. "Going to Court: Access, Autonomy, and the Contradictions of Liberal Legality." In *The Politics of Law: A Progressive Critique*, edited by David Kairys, 97–114. New York: Basic Books.

Sargent, Daniel. 2014. "Oasis in the Desert? America's Human Rights Rediscovery." In *The Breakthrough: Human Rights in the 1970s*, edited by Jan Eckel and Samuel Moyn, 125–45. Philadelphia: University of Pennsylvania Press.

Sarmiento, Domingo Faustino. (1845) 2004. *Facundo: Civilization and Barbarism*. Translated by Kathleen Ross. Berkeley: University of California Press.

Sassen, Saskia. 1991. *The Global City*. Princeton, NJ: Princeton University Press.

———. 1992. "Why Migration?" *Report on the Americas* 26 (1): 14–19.

———. 1998. *Globalization and Its Discontents: Essays on the New Mobility of People and Money*. New York: New Press.

———. 2009. "Incompleteness and the Possibility of Making:

Towards Denationalized Citizenship?" *Cultural Dynamics* 21:227–54.

Savarese, D. J. 2017. "Passive Plants." *Iowa Review* 47 (1). https://iowareview.org.

Savran, David. 2009. *Highbrow/Lowdown: Theater, Jazz, and the Making of the New Middle Class*. Ann Arbor: University of Michigan Press.

Sawyer, Suzana. 2004. *Crude Chronicles: Indigenous Politics, Multinational Oil, and Neoliberalism in Ecuador*. Durham, NC: Duke University Press.

Saxton, Alexander. 1990. *The Rise and Fall of the White Republic*. New York: Verso.

Sayers, Jentery, ed. 2011. "Tinker-Centric Pedagogy in Literature and Language Classrooms." In *Collaborative Approaches to the Digital in English Studies*, edited by Laura McGrath, 279–300. Logan: Utah State University Press.

———, ed. 2018. *The Routledge Companion to Media Studies and Digital Humanities*. New York: Routledge.

Sayles, John, dir. 1996. *Lone Star*. Columbia Pictures Corporation / Rio Dulce.

Sayre, Gordon. 2010. "Renegades from Barbary: The Transnational Turn in Captivity Studies." *American Literary History* 22 (2): 347–59.

Scarry, Elaine. 1985. *The Body in Pain: The Making and Unmaking of the World*. New York: Oxford University Press.

———. 2001. *On Beauty and Being Just*. Princeton, NJ: Princeton University Press.

Schafer, R. Murray. 1977. *The Soundscape: Our Sonic Environment and the Tuning of the World*. New York: Knopf.

Schiebinger, Londa. 1989. *The Mind Has No Sex? Women in the Origins of Modern Science*. Cambridge, MA: Harvard University Press.

———. 1993. *Nature's Body: Gender in the Making of Modern Science*. Boston: Beacon.

Schiller, Friedrich. (1794) 1954. *On the Aesthetic Education of Man in a Series of Letters*. Translated by Reginald Snell. New Haven: Yale University Press.

———. (1794) 1982. *On the Aesthetic Education of Man in a Series of Letters*. Edited and translated by Elizabeth M. Wilkinson and L. A. Willoughby. Oxford, UK: Clarendon; New York: Oxford University Press.

Schilling, Vincent. 2018. "Now There`s 573! 6 VA Tribes Get Federal Recognition as President Signs Bill." *Indian Country Today*, January 30, 2018. https://newsmaven.io.

Schivelbusch, Wolfgang. (1977) 1986. *The Railway Journey: The Industrialization of Time and Space in the 19th Century*. Berkeley: University of California Press.

Schlesinger, Arthur M., Jr. 1945. *The Age of Jackson*. Boston: Little, Brown.

———. 1998. *The Disuniting of America: Reflections on a Multicultural Society*. Rev. ed. New York: Norton.

Schlund-Vials, Cathy, Linda Vo, and K. Scott Wong. Forthcoming. *Keywords for Asian American Studies*. New York: New York University Press.

Schmalzer, Sigrid, Daniel Chard, and Alyssa Bothelo, eds. 2018. *Science for the People: Documents from America's Movement of Radical Scientists*. Amherst: University of Massachusetts Press.

Schmandt-Besserat, Denise, and Michael Erard. 2008. "Writing Systems." In *Encyclopedia of Archaeology*, edited by Deborah M. Pearsall, 2222–34. Vol. 3. Oxford, UK: Academic Press. Gale Virtual Reference Library. https://doi.org/10.1016/B978-012373962-9.00325-3.

Schmidt, Leigh Eric. 2000. *Hearing Things: Religion, Illusion, and the American Enlightenment*. Cambridge: Cambridge University Press.

Schmidt Camacho, Alicia. 2008. *Migrant Imaginaries: Latino Cultural Politics and the Mexico-U.S. Borderlands*. New York: New York University Press.

———. 2010. "Hailing the Twelve Million: U.S. Immigration Policy, Deportation, and the Imaginary of Lawful Violence." *Social Text* 105 (28.4): 1–24.

Schmitt, Carl. (1923) 1985. *The Crisis of Parliamentary Democracy*. Translated by Ellen Kennedy. Cambridge: MIT Press.

———. 1986. *Four Chapters on the Concept of Sovereignty*. Translated by George Schwab. Cambridge: MIT Press.

Schneider, Rebecca. 2011. *Performing Remains: Art and War in Times of Theatrical Reenactment*. New York: Routledge.

Schoolman, Martha. 2014. *Abolitionist Geographies*. Minneapolis: University of Minnesota Press.

Schrader, Paul, dir. 1978. *Blue Collar*. Universal Pictures.

Schuller, Kyla. 2018. *The Biopolitics of Feeling: Race, Sex, and Science in the Nineteenth Century*. Durham, NC: Duke University Press.

Schwartz, Nelson D. 2013. "Corporate Profits Soar as Worker Income Limps." *New York Times*, March 3, 2013. www.nytimes.com.

Schwarz, Roberto. (1970) 1992. "Culture and Politics in Brazil, 1964–1969." In *Misplaced Ideas: Essays on Brazilian Culture*. London: Verso.

Schweik, Susan. 2009. *The Ugly Laws: Disability in Public*. New York: New York University Press.

Scott, David. 1995. "Colonial Governmentality." *Social Text* 43:191–220.

———. 2005. *Conscripts of Modernity: The Tragedy of Colonial Enlightenment*. Durham, NC: Duke University Press.

Scott, Joan. (1988) 2018. *Gender and the Politics of History*. New York: Columbia University Press.

Scott, Pamela. 2002. "'This Vast Empire': The Iconography of the Mall, 1791–1848." In *The Mall in Washington, 1791–1991*, edited by Richard Longstreth, 37–60. Washington, DC: National Gallery of Art; New Haven: Yale University Press.

Seacole, Mary. 2005. *Wonderful Adventures of Mrs. Seacole in Many Lands*. Edited by Sarah Salih. London: Penguin Classics.

Sears, John F. 1989. *Sacred Places: American Tourist Attractions in the Nineteenth Century*. Amherst: University of Massachusetts Press.

Sedgwick, Eve Kosofsky. 1990. *Epistemology of the Closet*. Berkeley: University of California Press.

———. 1993. "Queer and Now." In *Tendencies*, 1–20. Durham, NC: Duke University Press.

———. 2003. *Touching Feeling*. Durham, NC: Duke University Press.

Sedgwick, Eve Kosofsky, and Adam Frank, eds. 1995. *Shame and Its Sisters: A Silvan Tompkins Reader*. Durham, NC: Duke University Press.

Segura, Denise, and Patricia Zavella, eds. 2007. *Women and Migration in the U.S.-Mexico Borderlands*. Durham, NC: Duke University Press.

Sekula, Allan. 1986. "The Body and the Archive." *October* 39:3–64.

Sellers, Charles. 1991. *The Market Revolution: Jacksonian America, 1815–1846*. New York: Oxford University Press.

Sen, Amartya. 1999. *Development as Freedom*. New York: Random House.

Senghor, Léopold Sedar. 1964. *Négritude et humanisme*. Paris: Editions du Seuil.

Senna, Danzy. 1999. *Caucasia: A Novel*. New York: Riverhead.

———. 2010. *Where Did You Sleep Last Night? A Personal History*. New York: Picador.

Sernett, Milton C. 1997. *Bound for the Promised Land: African American Religion and the Great Migration*. Durham, NC: Duke University Press.

Sewall, Samuel. (1697) 1997. *Phaemonena quaedam Apocalyptica ad aspectum Novi Orbis configurata; or, Some Few Lines towards a Description of the New Heaven*. Edited by Rainer Slominski. Lincoln: University of Nebraska–Lincoln Electronic Texts in American Studies. http://digitalcommons.unl.edu.

Shabecoff, Philip. 1983. "Haste of Global Warming Trend Exposed." *New York Times*, October 21, 1983.

Shah, Nayan. 2001. *Contagious Divides: Epidemics and Race in San Francisco's Chinatown*. Berkeley: University of California Press.

———. 2012. *Stranger Intimacy: Contesting Race, Sexuality, and the Law in the North American West*. Berkeley: University of California Press.

Shaheen, Jack G. 2001. *Reel Bad Arabs: How Hollywood Vilifies a People*. New York: Olive Branch.

Shain, Yossi. 1994–95. "Ethnic Diaspora and U.S. Foreign Policy." *Political Science Quarterly* 109 (5): 811–42.

Shanley, Kathryn W. 1997. "The Indians America Loves to Love and Read: American Indian Identity and Cultural Appropriation." *American Indian Quarterly* 21 (4): 675–702.

Sharma, Meara. 2014. "Blackness as the Second Person: Interview with Claudia Rankine." *Guernica*, November 17, 2014. www.guernicamag.com.

Sharpe, Jenny. 1995. "Is the United States Postcolonial? Transnationalism, Immigration, and Race." *Diaspora* 4 (2): 181–99.

Sheehi, Stephen. 2011. *Islamophobia: The Ideological Campaign against Muslims*. Atlanta: Clarity.

Shekhovstovm, Anton. 2017. *Russia and the Western Far Right: Tango Noir*. New York: Routledge.

Shell, Marc, ed. 2002. *American Babel: Literatures of the United States from Abnaki to Zuni*. Cambridge, MA: Harvard University Press.

Shiekh, Irum. 2011. *Muslims' Stories of Detention and Deportation in America after 9/11*. New York: Palgrave Macmillan.

Shigematsu, Setsu, and Keith Camacho, eds. 2010. *Militarized Currents: Toward a Decolonized Future in Asia and the Pacific*. Minneapolis: University of Minnesota Press.

Shinozuka, Jeannie. 2013. "Deadly Perils: Japanese Beetles and the Pestilential Immigrant, 1920–1930." *American Quarterly* 65 (4): 521–42.

Shohat, Ella. 1992. "Notes on the 'Post-colonial.'" *Social Text* 31–32: 99–113.

Shukin, Nicole. 2009. *Animal Capital: Rendering Life in Biopolitical Times*. Minneapolis: University of Minnesota Press.

Sidbury, James. 1997. *Ploughshares into Swords: Race, Rebellion, and Identity in Gabriel's Virginia, 1730–1810*. Cambridge: Cambridge University Press.

Siebers, Tobin. 2004. "Disability as Masquerade." *Literature and Medicine* 23 (1): 1–22.

Silko, Leslie Marmon. 1991. *Almanac of the Dead: A Novel*. New York: Simon & Schuster.

Silvers, Anita. 1998. *Disability, Difference, Discrimination*. New York: Rowman & Littlefield.

Simmel, Georg. 1957. "Fashion." *American Journal of Sociology* 62 (6): 541–58.

Simon, Jonathan. 2007. *Governing through Crime: How the War on Crime Transformed American Democracy and Created a Culture of Fear*. New York: Oxford University Press.

Simpson, Audra. 2014. *Mohawk Interruptus: Political Life across the Borders of Settler States*. Durham, NC: Duke University Press.

Sinclair, Upton. (1906) 1988. *The Jungle*. Introduction by James Barrett. Urbana: University of Illinois Press.

Singer, Peter W. 2003. *Corporate Warriors: The Rise of the Privatized Military Industry*. Ithaca, NY: Cornell University Press.

Singh, Nikhil Pal. 2004. *Black Is a Country: Race and the Unfinished Struggle for Democracy*. Cambridge, MA: Harvard University Press.

———. 2012. "Racial Formation in the Age of Permanent War." In *Racial Formation in the Twenty-First Century*, edited by Daniel Martinez HoSang, Oneka LaBennett, and Laura Pulido, 276–301. Berkeley: University of California Press.

———. 2017. *Race and America's Long War*. Cambridge MA: Harvard University Press.

Sinha, Manisha. 2016. *The Slave's Cause: A History of Abolition*. New Haven: Yale University Press.

Sinha, Mrinalinhi. 1995. *Colonial Masculinity: The "Manly Englishman" and the "Effeminate Bengali" in the Late Nineteenth Century*. Manchester: Manchester University Press.

Sjoberg, Laura, and Sandra E. Via. 2010. *Gender, War, and Militarism: Feminist Perspectives*. Santa Barbara, CA: Praeger.

Skawennati. 2014. Time Traveller™. www.timetravellertm.com.

Skelton, Tracey, and Gill Valentine, eds. 1998. *Cool Places: Geographies of Youth Cultures*. London: Routledge.

Skinner, Quentin. 1978. *Foundations of Modern Political Thought*. 2 vols. Cambridge: Cambridge University Press.

Sklair, Leslie. 1991. *Sociology of the Global System*. Hertfordshire, UK: Harvester Wheatsheaf.

Slotkin, Richard. 1973. *Regeneration through Violence: The Mythology of the American Frontier, 1600–1860*. Middletown, CT: Wesleyan University Press.

———. 1985. *The Fatal Environment: The Myth of the Frontier in the Age of Industrialization, 1800–1890*. Middletown, CT: Wesleyan University Press.

———. 1992. *Gunfighter Nation: The Myth of the Frontier in Twentieth-Century America*. New York: Atheneum.

Smallwood, Stephanie. 2004. "Commodified Freedom: Interrogating the Limits of Anti-slavery Ideology in the Early Republic." *Journal of the Early Republic* 24:289–98.

Smiley, Jane. 1991. *A Thousand Acres*. New York: Knopf.

Smith, Adam. (1759) 1966. *The Theory of Moral Sentiments*. New York: Augustus M. Kelley.

———. (1776) 1937. *An Inquiry into the Nature and Causes of the Wealth of Nations*. Edited by Edwin Canaan. New York: Modern Library.

Smith, Adam C. 2003. "No Telling If Voter Rolls Are Ready for 2004." *St. Petersburg Times*, December 21, 2003. www.sptimes.com.

Smith, Andrea. 2005. *Conquest: Sexual Violence and American Indian Genocide*. Boston: South End.

———. 2010. "Indigeneity, Settler Colonialism, White Supremacy." *Global Dialogue* 12 (2). http://worlddialogue.org.

Smith, Barbara. 1982. "Toward a Black Feminist Criticism." In *All the Women Are White, All the Blacks Are Men, but Some of Us Are Brave: Black Women's Studies*, edited by Gloria T. Hull, Patricia Bell Scott, and Barbara Smith, 157–75. New York: Feminist.

Smith, Caleb. 2009. *The Prison and the American Imagination*. New Haven: Yale University Press.

Smith, David L. 1991. "Huck, Jim and American Racial Discourse." In *Satire or Evasion? Black Perspectives on "Huckleberry Finn,"* edited by James S. Leonard, Thomas A. Tenney, and Thadious M. Davis, 103–20. Durham, NC: Duke University Press.

Smith, Henry Nash. 1950. *Virgin Land: The American West as Symbol and Myth*. Cambridge, MA: Harvard University Press.

———. 1967. *Popular Culture and Industrialism, 1865–1890*. Garden City, NY: Anchor Books.

Smith, Jon, and Deborah N. Cohn. 2004. *Look Away! The U.S. South in New World Studies*. Durham, NC: Duke University Press.

Smith, Mark M. 1997. *Mastered by the Clock: Time, Slavery, and Freedom in the American South*. Chapel Hill: University of North Carolina Press.

———. 2000. "Listening to the Heard Worlds of Antebellum America." *Journal of the Historical Society* 1:63–97.

Smith, Martha Nell. 1998. "Dickinson's Manuscripts." In *The Emily Dickinson Handbook*, edited by Gudrun Grabher, Roland Hagenbüchle, and Cristanne Miller, 113–37. Amherst: University of Massachusetts Press.

———. 2007. "The Human Touch, Software of the Highest Order: Revisiting Editing as Interpretation." *Textual Cultures: Texts, Contexts, Interpretation* 2 (1): 1–15.

Smith, Neil. 1983. *Uneven Development: Nature, Capital, and the Production of Space*. Athens: University of Georgia Press.

———. 2004. *The Endgame of Globalization*. New York: Routledge.

Smith, Paul Chaat, and Robert Warrior. 1996. *Like a Hurricane: The Indian Movement from Alcatraz to Wounded Knee*. New York: New Press.

Smith, Rogers M. 1997. *Civic Ideals: Conflicting Visions of Citizenship in U.S. History*. New Haven: Yale University Press.

Smith, Shawn Michelle. 1999. *American Archives: Gender, Race, and Class in Visual Culture*. Princeton, NJ: Princeton University Press.

Smith, Valerie. 1998. *Not Just Race, Not Just Gender: Black Feminist Readings*. New York: Routledge.

Smith, Wilfred Cantwell. 1964. *The Meaning and End of Religion*. New York: New American Library.

Smith-Rosenberg, Carroll. 2010. *This Violent Empire: The Birth of an American National Identity*. Chapel Hill: University of North Carolina Press.

Snorton, C. Riley. 2017. *Black on Both Sides: A Racial History of Trans Identity*. Minneapolis: University of Minnesota Press.

Snow, C. P. 1959. *The Two Cultures and the Scientific Revolution*. Cambridge: Cambridge University Press.

Snyder, Sharon L., and David T. Mitchell. 2001. "Re-engaging the Body: Disability Studies and the Resistance to Embodiment." *Public Culture* 13 (3): 367–89.

———. 2006. *Cultural Locations of Disability*. Chicago: University of Chicago Press.

Snyder, Timothy. 2010. *Bloodlands: Europe between Hitler and Stalin*. New York: Basic Books.

Soderbergh, Steven, dir. 2000a. *Erin Brockovich*. Universal City, CA: Universal Pictures.

———, dir. 2000b. *Traffic*. Bedford Falls Productions.

Soja, Edward. 1989. *Postmodern Geographies: The Reassertion of Space in Postmodern Geographies*. London: Verso.

Sokal, Alan. 1996a. "A Physicist Experiments with Cultural Studies." *Lingua Franca* 6 (4): 62–64.

———. 1996b. "Transgressing the Boundaries: Toward a Transformative Hermeneutics of Quantum Gravity." *Social Text* 46–47 (14:1–2): 217–52.

Solanas, Valerie. (1968) 2004. *The SCUM Manifesto*. Introduction by Avital Ronell. New York: Verso.

Sollors, Werner. 1986. *Beyond Ethnicity: Consent and Descent in American Culture*. New York: Oxford University Press.

———, ed. 1998. *Multilingual America: Transnationalism, Ethnicity, and the Languages of American Literature*. New York: New York University Press.

Somerville, Siobhan B. 2000. *Queering the Color Line: Race and the Invention of Homosexuality in American Culture*. Durham, NC: Duke University Press.

Sone, Monica. (1953) 1979. *Nisei Daughter*. Seattle: University of Washington Press.

Sonnenschein, William. 1999. *The Diversity Toolkit: How You Can Build and Benefit from a Diverse Workforce*. New York: McGraw-Hill.

Sontag, Susan. 2003. *Regarding the Pain of Others*. New York: Farrar, Straus and Giroux.

Soto, Sandra K. 2010. *Reading Chican@ like a Queer: The Demastery of Desire*. Austin: University of Texas Press.

Spade, Dean. 2006. "Mutilating Gender." In *Transgender Studies Reader*, edited by Susan Stryker and Stephen Whittle, 315–22. London: Routledge.

———. 2007. "Documenting Gender." *Hastings Law Journal* 59:731.

———. 2011. *Normal Life: Administrative Violence, Critical Trans Politics, and the Limits of Law*. Cambridge, MA: South End.

———. 2013. "Intersectional Resistance and Law Reform." *Signs: Journal of Women in Culture and Society* 38 (4): 1031–55.

———. 2015. *Normal Life: Administrative Violence, Critical Trans Politics, and the Limits of Law*. Rev. ed. Durham, NC: Duke University Press.

Spade, Dean, and Craig Willse. 2000. "Confronting the Limits of Gay Hate Crimes Activism: A Radical Critique." *UCLA Chicano-Latino Law Review* 21:38–52.

Spanierman, Lisa B., Nathan R. Todd, and Carolyn J. Anderson. 2009. "Psychosocial Costs of Racism to Whites: Understanding Patterns among University Students." *Journal of Counseling Psychology* 56 (2): 239–52.

Spence, Mark David. 1999. *Dispossessing the Wilderness: Indian Removal and the Making of the National Parks*. New York: Oxford University Press.

Spencer, Herbert. 1874–75. *Principles of Sociology*. Vol. 1. London: Williams and Norgate.

Spillers, Hortense. 1987. "Mama's Baby, Papa's Maybe: An American Grammar Book." *Diacritics* 17:65–81.

———. 2003. *Black, White, and in Color: Essays on American Literature and Culture*. Chicago: University of Chicago Press.

Spiro, Peter J. 2008. *Beyond Citizenship: American Identity after Globalization*. New York: Oxford University Press.

Spivak, Gayatri Chakravorty. 1988. "Can the Subaltern Speak?" In *Marxism and the Interpretation of Culture*, edited by Cary Nelson and Lawrence Grossberg, 271–313. Urbana: University of Illinois Press.

———. 1990. *The Post-colonial Critic: Interviews, Strategies, Dialogues*. Edited by Sarah Harasym. New York: Routledge.

———. 1993. "Scattered Speculations on the Question of Cultural Studies." In *Outside in the Teaching Machine*, 255–84. New York: Routledge.

———. 1999. *A Critique of Postcolonial Reason: Toward a History of the Vanishing Present*. Cambridge, MA: Harvard University Press.

Spivak, Gayatri Chakravorty, and Judith Butler. 2007. *Who Sings the Nation-State? Language, Politics, Belonging*. London: Seagull Books.

Squier, Susan Merrill. 2004. *Liminal Lives: Imagining the Human at the Frontiers of Biomedicine*. Durham, NC: Duke University Press.

Stacey, Judith. 1990. *Brave New Families: Stories of Domestic Upheaval in Late-Twentieth-Century America*. New York: Basic Books.

Stack, Carol B. 1996. *Call to Home: African-Americans Reclaim the Rural South*. New York: Basic Books.

Stadler, Gustavus. 2010. "Introduction: Breaking Sound Barriers." *Social Text* 102 (28.1): 1–12.

Staiger, Janet, Ann Cvetkovich, and Ann Reynolds, eds. 2010. *Political Emotions*. New York: Routledge.

Stallybrass, Peter. 2001. "Books and Scrolls: Navigating the Bible." In *Material Texts: Books and Readers in Early Modern England*, edited by Jennifer Andersen and Elizabeth Sauer. Philadelphia: University of Pennsylvania Press.

Stallybrass, Peter, and Allon White. 1986. *The Politics and Poetics of Transgression*. Ithaca, NY: Cornell University Press.

Stange, Maren. 1989. *Symbols of Ideal Life: Social Documentary Photography in America, 1890–1950*. New York: Cambridge University Press.

Stanley, Amy Dru. 1996. "Home Life and the Morality of the Market." In *The Market Revolution in America: Social, Political, and Religious Expressions, 1800–1880*, edited by Melvyn Stokes and Stephen Conway, 74–96. Charlottesville: University of Virginia Press.

———. 1998. *From Bondage to Contract: Wage Labor, Marriage, and the Market in the Age of Slave Emancipation*. New York: Cambridge University Press.

Stanley, Jason. 2018. *How Fascism Works: The Politics of Us and Them*. New York, NY. Random House.

Stanley, Sara G. (1860) 1997. "What, to the Toiling Millions There, Is This Boasted Liberty?" In *Lift Every Voice: African American Oratory, 1787–1900*, edited by Philip Foner and Robert James Branham, 284–87. Tuscaloosa: University of Alabama Press.

Stannard, David. 1992. *American Holocaust: The Conquest of the New World*. Oxford: Oxford University Press.

Stansell, Christine. 1986. *City of Women: Sex and Class in New York, 1789–1860*. New York: Knopf.

Stanton, Elizabeth Cady. 1868a. "Marriages and Mistresses." *Revolution*, October 15, 1868.

———. 1868b. "Miss Becker on the Difference in Sex." *Revolution*, September 24, 1868.

Stark, Rodney, and Roger Finke. 1992. *The Churching of America, 1776–1990: Winners and Losers in Our Religious Economy*. New Brunswick, NJ: Rutgers University Press.

———. 2000. *Acts of Faith: Explaining the Human Side of Religion*. Berkeley: University of California Press.

Starobinski, Jean. 1988. *1789: The Emblems of Reason*. Cambridge: MIT Press.

"Statement on North Carolina HB 2." 2016. Council of the American Studies Association. May 9, 2016.

Stauffer, John. 2004. *The Black Hearts of Men: Radical Abolition and the Transformation of Race*. Cambridge, MA: Harvard University Press.

Stecopoulos, Harilaos. 2008. *Reconstructing the World: Southern Fictions and U.S. Imperialisms, 1898–1976*. Ithaca, NY: Cornell University Press.

Stegner, Wallace. 1992. *Where the Bluebird Sings to the Lemonade Springs: Living and Writing in the West*. New York: Random House.

Steigmann-Gall, Richard. 2016. "What the American Left Doesn't Understand about Fascism." Huffington Post. www.huffpost.com.

Stein, Gertrude. (1925) 1995. *The Making of Americans: Being a History of a Family's Progress*. Normal, IL: Dalkey Archive.

Steinberg, Stephen. 1995. *Turning Back: The Retreat from Racial Justice in American Thought and Policy*. Boston: Beacon.

Stephen, Lynn. 2007. *Transborder Lives: Indigenous Oaxacans in Mexico, California, and Oregon*. Durham, NC: Duke University Press.

Sterling, Dorothy, ed. 1976. *The Trouble They Seen: The Story of Reconstruction in the Words of African Americans*. Garden City, NY: Doubleday.

Stern, Alexandra Minna. 2019. *Proud Boys and the White Ethnostate: How the Alt-Right Is Warping the American Imagination*. Boston: Beacon.

———. 1999a. "Buildings, Boundaries and Blood: Medicalization and Nation-Building on the U.S.-Mexico Border, 1910–1930." *Hispanic American Historical Review* 79 (1): 41–82.

———. 1999b. "Secrets under the Skin: New Historical Perspectives on Disease, Deviation, and Citizenship." *Comparative Studies in Society and History* 41 (3): 589–96.

Sterne, Jonathan. 2003. *The Audible Past: Cultural Origins of Sound Reproduction*. Durham, NC: Duke University Press.

Sternhell, Zeev. 1995. *The Birth of Fascist Ideology: From Cultural Rebellion to Political Revolution*. Princeton, NJ: Princeton University Press.

Stevens, George, dir. 1953. *Shane*. Paramount.

Stevens, Jacqueline. 1999. *Reproducing the State*. Princeton, NJ: Princeton University Press.

———. 2004. "The Politics of LGBTQ Scholarship." *GLQ* 10 (2): 220–26.

Stewart, Kathleen. 1996. *A Space at the Side of the Road: Cultural Poetics in an "Other" America*. Princeton, NJ: Princeton University Press.

———. 2007. *Ordinary Affects*. Durham, NC: Duke University Press.

Stiglitz, Joseph E. 2002. *Globalization and Its Discontents*. New York: Norton.

———. 2013. *The Price of Inequality: How Today's Divided Society Endangers Our Future*. New York: Norton.

Stiglitz, Joseph E., and Carl E. Walsh. 2002. *Economics*. 3rd ed. New York: Norton.

Stoeker, Randy. 2016. *Liberating Service Learning and the Rest of Higher Education Civic Engagement*. Philadelphia: Temple University Press.

Stoever-Ackerman, Jennifer. 2010. "Splicing the Sonic Color-Line: Tony Schwartz Remixes Postwar Nueva York." *Social Text* 102 (28.1): 59–85.

Stokoe, William C., Dorothy C. Casterline, and Carl G. Croneberg. 1965. *A Dictionary of American Sign Languages on Linguistic Principles*. Washington, DC: Gallaudet College Press.

Stolberg, Sheryl Gay. 2009. "A Pregnant Pause." *New York Times*, November 29, 2009. www.nytimes.com.

Stoler, Ann Laura. 1995. *Race and the Education of Desire: Foucault's History of Sexuality and the Colonial Order of Things*. Durham, NC: Duke University Press.

———, ed. 2006. *Haunted by Empire: Geographies of Intimacy in North American History*. Durham, NC: Duke University Press.

———. 2010. *Carnal Knowledge and Imperial Power: Race and the Intimate in Colonial Rule*. Berkeley: University of California Press.

Stone, Allucquère Rosanne. 1996. *The War of Desire and Technology at the Close of the Mechanical Age*. Cambridge: MIT Press.

Stone, Deborah A. 1984. *The Disabled State*. Philadelphia: Temple University Press.

Stone, Sandy. 1991. "The 'Empire' Strikes Back: A Posttranssexual Manifesto." In *Body Guards: The Cultural Politics of Gender Ambiguity*, edited by Kristina Straub and Julia Epstein, 280–304. New York: Routledge.

Stowe, Harriet Beecher. (1852) 1981. *Uncle Tom's Cabin, or, Life among the Lowly*. New York: Penguin.

Strachey, William. (1610) 1964. "A True Reportory of the Wreck and Redemption of Sir Thomas Gates, Knight." *A Voyage to Virginia in 1609: Two Narratives*, edited by Louis B. Wright, 1–102. Charlottesville: University of Virginia Press.

Streeby, Shelley. 2002. *American Sensations: Class, Empire, and the Production of Popular Culture*. Berkeley: University of California Press.

———. 2013. *Radical Sensations: World Movements, Violence, and Visual Culture*. Durham, NC: Duke University Press.

———. 2018. *Imagining the Future of Climate Change: World Making through Science Fiction and Activism*. Oakland: University of California Press.

Strike Debt. 2014. *Debt Resistors Operations Manual*. Oakland, CA: PM.

Stryker, Susan. 2008. *Transgender History*. Berkeley, CA: Seal.

Stuckey, Sterling. 1987. *Slave Culture: Nationalism and the Foundations of Black America*. New York: Oxford University Press.

Sturken, Marita, and Lisa Cartwright. 2009. *Practices of Looking: An Introduction to Visual Culture*. New York: Oxford University Press.

Sturm, Circe. 2003. *Blood Politics: Race, Culture, and Identity in the Cherokee Nation of Oklahoma*. Berkeley: University of California Press.

Suarez, Michael, and H. R. Woodhuysen, eds. 2010. *Oxford Companion to the Book*. Oxford: Oxford University Press.

Suárez-Orozco, Marcelo, Carola Suárez-Orozco, and Carolyn Sattin-Bajaj. 2010. "Making Migration Work." *Peabody Journal of Education*, October 2010.

Sudarkasa, Niara. 1988. "Interpreting the African Heritage in AfroAmerican Family Organization." In *Black Families*, edited by Harriett P. McAdoo, 37–53. Beverly Hills, CA: Sage.

Sudbury, Julia. 1998. *"Other Kinds of Dreams": Black Women's Organisations and the Politics of Transformation*. London: Routledge.

Suisman, David, and Susan Strasser, eds. 2009. *Sound in the Age of Mechanical Reproduction*. Philadelphia: University of Pennsylvania Press.

Sullivan, Shannon. 2014. *Good White People: The Problem with Middle-Class White Anti-racism*. Albany: State University of New York Press.

Sunshine, Spencer. 2014. "The Right Hand of Occupy Wall Street: From Libertarians to Nazis, the Fact and Fiction of Right Wing Involvement." Political Research Associates. www.politicalresearch.org.

Susman, Warren I. 1984. *Culture as History: The Transformation of American Society in the Twentieth Century*. New York: Pantheon.

Sutherland, William. 1717. *Britain's Glory; or, Ship-Building Unvail'd, Being a General Director, for Building and Compleating the Said Machines*. London, Tho. Norris.

"Swadeshi Movements and Gandhi." 2004. *Journal of Human Values* 10 (1): 41–51. https://doi.org/10.1177/0971685804010000105.

Swatos, William H., Jr., and Daniel V. A. Olson, eds. 2000. *The Secularization Debate*. Lanham, MD: Rowman & Littlefield.

Sweet, John. 2003. *Bodies Politic: Renegotiating Race in the American North, 1730–1830*. Baltimore: Johns Hopkins University Press.

Swinth, Kirsten. 2005. "Review: Strangers, Neighbors, Aliens in a New America: Migration Stories for the Twenty-First Century." *American Quarterly* 57 (2): 507–21.

Sylvia Rivera Law Project. 2009. "SRLP Opposes the Matthew Shepard and James Byrd, Jr. Hate Crimes Prevention Act." http://srlp.org.

Sylvia Rivera Law Project, FIERCE, Queers for Economic Justice, Peter Cicchino Youth Project, and the Audre Lorde Project. 2009. "SRLP Announces Non-support of the Gender Employment Non-discrimination Act." http://srlp.org.

Szatmary, David. 1980. *Shays' Rebellion: The Making of an Agrarian Insurrection*. Amherst: University of Massachusetts Press.

Sze, Julie. 2017. "Gender and Environmental Justice." In *Routledge Handbook of Gender and Environment*, edited by Sherilyn MacGregor, 159–68. London: Routledge.

Szeman, Imre. 2007. "System Failure: Oil, Futurity, and the Anticipation of Disaster." *SAQ* 106 (4): 805–23.

Szwed, John. 1998. *Space Is the Place: The Lives and Times of Sun Ra*. New York: Da Capo.

Tagg, John. 1988. *The Burden of Representation: Essays on Photographies and Histories*. Minneapolis: University of Minnesota Press.

Tahmahkera, Dustin. 2011. "'An Indian in a White Man's Camp': Johnny Cash's Indian Country Music." In *Sound Clash: Listening to American Studies*, edited by Kara Keeling and Josh Kun, 147–74. Baltimore: Johns Hopkins University Press.

Takaki, Ronald. (1979) 1990. *Iron Cages: Race and Culture in Nineteenth-Century America*. New York: Oxford University Press.

———. 1987. *From Different Shores: Perspectives on Race and Ethnicity in America*. Edited by Ronald Takaki. New York: Oxford University Press.

———. 1989. *Strangers from a Different Shore: A History of Asian Americans*. Boston: Little, Brown.

———. 1993. *A Different Mirror: A History of Multicultural America*. Boston: Little, Brown.

Tarter, Jim. 2002. "Some Live More Downstream Than Others: Cancer, Gender, and Environmental Justice." In *The Environmental Justice Reader: Politics, Poetics, and Pedagogy*, edited by Joni Adamson, Mei Mei Evans, and Rachel Stein, 213–28. Tucson: University of Arizona Press.

Tate, Claudia. 1992. *Domestic Allegories of Political Desire: The Black Heroine's Text at the Turn of the Century*. New York: Oxford University Press.

Tatonetti, Lisa. 2014. *The Queerness of Native American Literature*. Minneapolis: University of Minnesota Press.

Tatum, Stephen. 1997. "The Problem of the 'Popular' in the New Western History." In *The New Western History: The Territory Ahead*, edited by Forrest G. Robinson, 153–90. Tucson: University of Arizona Press.

———. 2007. "Spectrality and the Postregional Interface." In *Postwestern Horizons: Literature, Theory, Space*, edited by Susan Kollin, 3–30. Lincoln: University of Nebraska Press.

Taub, Nadine, and Elizabeth M. Schneider. 1982. "Women's Subordination and the Role of Law." In *The Politics of Law: A Progressive Critique*, edited by David Kairys, 328–55. New York: Basic Books.

Taylor, Charles. 1992. *Multiculturalism and "The Politics of Recognition."* Princeton, NJ: Princeton University Press.

———. 2002. *Varieties of Religion Today*. Cambridge, MA: Harvard University Press.

———. 2004. *Modern Social Imaginaries*. Durham, NC: Duke University Press.

Taylor, Diana. 2003. *The Archive and the Repertoire: Performing Cultural Memory in the Americas*. Durham, NC: Duke University Press.

Taylor, Dorceta E. 2014. *Toxic Communities: Environmental Racism, Industrial Pollution, and Residential Mobility*. New York: New York University Press.

Taylor, Frederick Winslow. (1911) 2010. *The Principles of Scientific Management*. New York: Cosimo.

Taylor, Peter J. 1999. *Modernities: A Geohistorical Interpretation*. Minneapolis: University of Minnesota Press.

Teaiwa, Teresia K. 1998. "Yaqona/Yagona: Roots and Routes of a Displaced Native." Edited by Stephen Muecke and Meaghan Morris. *UTS Review* 4 (2): 92–106.

———. 2005. "Native Thoughts: A Pacific Studies Take on Cultural Studies and Diaspora." In *Indigenous Diasporas and Dislocations*, edited by Graham Harvey and Charles D. Thompson, 15–35. London: Ashgate.

Teare, Chris. 2015. "STEM Study Begins with the Liberal Arts." *Forbes*, August 15, 2015. www.forbes.com.

Terry, Jennifer. 1999. *An American Obsession: Science, Medicine, and Homosexuality in Modern Society*. Chicago: University of Chicago Press.

Teune, Henry. 2008. "Citizenship Deterritorialized: Global Citizenships." In *The Future of Citizenship*, edited by Jose V. Ciprut. Cambridge: MIT Press.

Thomas, Deborah A., and Kamari Maxine Clarke. 2006. "Introduction: Globalization and the Transformations of Race." In *Globalization and Race: Transformations in the Cultural Production of Blackness*, edited by Kamari Maxine Clarke and Deborah A. Thomas, 1–34. Durham, NC: Duke University Press.

Thomas, Paul. 2001. "Modalities of Consent." In *Beyond Nationalism?*, edited by Fred Dallmayr and José Maria Rosales, 3–18. Lanham, MD: Lexington Books.

Thomas, William I., and Florian Znanieki. 1918–20. *The Polish Peasant in Europe and America*. 5 vols. Boston: Gorham.

Thompson, E. P. 1961a. "The Long Revolution (Part I)." *New Left Review* 9:24–33.

———. 1961b. "The Long Revolution (Part II)." *New Left Review* 10:34–39.

———. 1963. *The Making of the English Working Class*. New York: Vintage.

———. 1967. "Time, Work-Discipline, and Industrial Capitalism." *Past and Present* 38:56–97.

Thompson, Emily. 2004. *The Soundscape of Modernity: Architectural Acoustics and the Culture of Listening in America, 1900–1933*. Cambridge: MIT Press.

Thompson, J. Philip. 2017. "The Future of Urban Populism: Will Cities Turn the Political Tides?" *New Labor Forum*, January 5, 2017. http://journals.sagepub.com.

Thoreau, Henry David. (1849) 1966. "On Civil Disobedience." In *Walden and Civil Disobedience*, edited by Owen Thomas, 276–300. New York: Norton.

———. (1849) 1985. "A Week on the Concord River and Merrimack." In *A Week, Walden, Maine Woods, Cape Cod*, 1–320. New York: Library of America.

———. (1854) 1966. *Walden; or, Life in the Woods: Walden and Civil Disobedience*, edited by Owen Thomas, 2–275. New York: Norton.

———. (1855) 1958. "Letter to Thomas Cholmondeley, November 8, 1855." In *The Correspondence of Henry David Thoreau*, edited by W. Harding and C. Bode, 398. New York: New York University Press.

Thrift, Nigel. 2008. *Non-representational Theory: Space, Politics, Affect*. New York: Routledge.

Thuma, Emily L. 2019. *All Our Trials: Prisons, Policing, and the Feminist Fight to End Violence*. Champaign: University of Illinois Press.

Tinker, Hugh. 1974. *A New System of Slavery: The Export of Indian Labour Overseas, 1830–1920*. Oxford: Oxford University Press.

Tocqueville, Alexis de. (1835) 2004. *Democracy in America*. Translated by Arthur Goldhammer. New York: Library of America.

Todd, Janet. 1986. *Sensibility: An Introduction*. New York: Methuen.

Tölölyan, Khachig. 1996. "Rethinking Diaspora(s): Stateless Power in the Transnational Moment." *Diaspora* 5 (1): 3–36.

Tomlinson, Barbara. 2019. *Undermining Intersectionality: The Perils of Powerblind Feminism*. Philadelphia: Temple University Press.

Tompkins, Jane. 1985. *Sensational Designs: The Cultural Work of American Fiction, 1790–1860*. New York: Oxford University Press.

Tompkins, Kyla Wazana. 2012. *Racial Indigestion: Eating Bodies in the Nineteenth Century*. New York: New York University Press.

Tongson, Karen. 2011. *Relocations: Queer Suburban Imaginaries*. New York: New York University Press.

Toomer, Jean. (1923) 1969. *Cane*. New York: Liveright.

Torpey, John. 2000. *The Invention of the Passport*. Cambridge: Cambridge University Press.

Tougaw, Jason. 2018. *The Elusive Brain: Literary Experiments in the Age of Neuroscience*. New Haven: Yale University Press.

Townsend, Robert, dir. 1987. *Hollywood Shuffle*. Samuel Goldwyn.

Toynbee, Arnold J. 1934–61. *The Study of History*. 12 vols. Oxford: Oxford University Press.

Trachtenberg, Alan. 1979. *Brooklyn Bridge: Fact and Symbol*. Chicago: University of Chicago Press.

———. 1982. *The Incorporation of America: Culture and Society in the Gilded Age*. New York: Farrar, Straus and Giroux.

Treichler, Paula A. 1999. *How to Have Theory in an Epidemic: Cultural Chronicles of AIDS*. Durham, NC: Duke University Press.

Trent, James W., Jr. 1994. *Inventing the Feeble Mind: A History of Mental Retardation in the United States*. Berkeley: University of California Press.

Tribe, Keith. 1978. *Land, Labour and Economic Discourse*. London: Routledge and Kegan Paul.

Trouillot, Michel-Rolph. 1995. *Silencing the Past: Power and the Production of History*. Boston: Beacon.

Truax, Barry. 1984. *Acoustic Communication*. Norwood, NJ: Ablex.

Truettner, William, and Roger B. Stein, eds. 1999. *Picturing Old New England: Image and Memory*. Washington, DC: National Museum of American Art, Smithsonian Institution; New Haven: Yale University Press.

Trump, Donald (@realDonaldTrump). 2018. "The greatest economy in the HISTORY of America." Twitter, June 4, 2018. https://twitter.com/realDonaldTrump/status/1003738744061603843.

Tsien, Tsuen-Hsuin. 2004. *Written on Bamboo and Silk: The Beginnings of Chinese Books and Inscriptions*. Chicago: University of Chicago Press.

Tsing, Anna. 2011. *Friction: An Ethnography of Global Connection*. Princeton, NJ: Princeton University Press.

Tu, Thuy Linh Nguyen. 2011. *The Beautiful Generation: Asian Americans and the Cultural Economy of Fashion*. Durham, NC: Duke University Press.

Tuan, Yi-fu. 1977. *Space and Place: The Perspective of Experience*. Minneapolis: University of Minnesota Press.

Tuck, Eve, and Reuben Gaztambide-Fernandez. 2013. "Curriculum Replacement and Settler Futurity." *Journal of Curriculum Theorizing* 29 (1): 72–89.

Tuck, Eve, and K. Wayne Yang. 2012. "Decolonization Is Not a Metaphor." *Decolonization: Indigeneity, Education, and Society* 1 (1): 1–40.

Tucker, Kenneth H., Jr. 2010. *Workers of the World Enjoy! Aesthetic Politics from Revolutionary Syndicalism to the Global Justice Movement*. Philadelphia: Temple University Press.

Turner, Bryan S. 1993. *Citizenship and Social Theory*. London: Sage.

———. 2006. *Vulnerability and Human Rights*. University Park: Penn State University Press.

Turner, Frederick Jackson. (1893) 1920. *The Frontier in American History*. New York: Holt.

Turner, Victor. 1969. *The Ritual Process: Structure and Anti-structure*. Chicago: Aldine.

Tuveson, Ernest Lee. 1968. *Redeemer Nation: The Idea of America's Millennial Role*. Chicago: University of Chicago Press.

Twain, Mark. 1874. "A True Story, Repeated Word for Word as I Heard It." *Atlantic Monthly*, November 1874.

———. (1885) 1985. *Adventures of Huckleberry Finn*. Berkeley: University of California Press.

Tyler, Royall. 1797. *The Algerine Captive; or, the Life and Adventures of Doctor Updike Underhill: Six Years a Prisoner among the Algerines*. Walpole, NH: David Carlisle.

Tylor, Edward Burnett. 1871. *Primitive Culture: Researches into the Development of Mythology, Philosophy, Religion, Art, and Custom*. London: J. Murray.

Tyrell, Ian. 1991. "American Exceptionalism in an Age of International History." *American Historical Review* 96:1031–55.

Uchitelle, Louis. 2007. *The Disposable American: Layoffs and Their Consequences*. 60571st ed. New York: Vintage.

United Nations. 2005. "Who Are Indigenous Peoples?" Fact sheet produced by the UN Permanent Forum on the Rights of Indigenous Peoples. www.un.org.

———. 2007. "Declaration on the Rights of Indigenous Peoples." Adopted by General Assembly Resolution 61/295. http://daccess-dds-ny.un.org.

———. 2009. *State of the World's Indigenous Peoples*. Department of Economic and Social Affairs, Division of Social Policy and Development, Secretariat of the Permanent Forum on Indigenous Issues. New York: United Nations.

Urton, Gary. 2003. *Signs of the Inka Khipu: Binary Coding in the Andean Knotted-String Records*. Austin: University of Texas Press.

US Bureau of Labor Statistics. 2011. "2010 Union Members Summary." www.bls.gov.

U.S. News and World Report. (1966) 2004. "Success Story of One Minority Group in the United States." December 26, 1966. Reprinted in *Asian American Studies: A Reader*, edited by Jean Yu-Wen Shen Wu and Min Song, 158–63. New Brunswick, NJ: Rutgers University Press.

US Senate, Committee on Energy and Natural Resources. 1988. "Greenhouse Effect and Global Climate Change, Part 2." 100th Congress, 1st Session, June 23, 1988.

Vaid, Urvashi. 1996. *Virtual Equality: The Mainstreaming of Gay and Lesbian Liberation*. New York: Anchor Books.

Vaidhyanathan, Siva. 2001. *Copyrights and Copywrongs: The Rise of Intellectual Property and How It Threatens Creativity*. New York: New York University Press.

———. 2011. *The Googlization of Everything (and Why We Should Worry)*. Berkeley: University of California Press.

Vaillant, Derek W. 2002. "Sounds of Whiteness: Local Radio, Racial Formation, and Public Culture in Chicago, 1921–1935." *American Quarterly* 54 (1): 25–66.

Valdez, Louis, and Stan Steiner, ed. (1969) 1972. "El Plan Espiritual de Aztlán." In *Aztlán: An Anthology of Mexican American Literature*, 1–5. New York: Vintage.

Valdez, Luis. 1972. "La Plebe." In *Aztlán: An Anthology of Mexican American Literature*, edited by Luis Valdez and Stan Steiner, xiii–xxxiv. New York: Vintage.

Valdman, Albert. 1984. "The Linguistic Situation of Haiti." In

Haiti-Today and Tomorrow, edited by Charles R. Foster and Albert Valdman. Lanham, MD: University Press of America.

———. 2005. "Haitian Creole at the Dawn of Independence." *Yale French Studies: Nineteenth-Century French Studies* 107:146–61.

Valentine, David. 2007. *Imagining Transgender: An Ethnography of a Category*. Durham, NC: Duke University Press.

Valenzuela, Angela. 1999. *Subtractive Schooling: U.S.-Mexican Youth and the Politics of Caring*. Albany: State University of New York Press.

Valverde, Mariana. 2007. "Genealogies of European States: Foucauldian Reflections." *Economy and Society* 36:159–78.

van Wyck, Peter C. 1997. *Primitives in the Wilderness: Deep Ecology and the Missing Human Subject*. Albany: State University of New York Press.

Vargas, Deborah R. 2012. *Dissonant Divas in Chicana Music: The Limits of La Onda*. Minneapolis: University of Minnesota Press.

Vasak, Karel. 1977. "A 30-Year Struggle." *UNESCO Courier*, November 1977.

Vasconcelos, José. (1925) 1997. *The Cosmic Race*. Translated by Didier T. Jaén. Baltimore: Johns Hopkins University Press.

Vazquez, Alexandra T. 2013. *Listening in Detail: Performances of Cuban Music*. Durham, NC: Duke University Press.

Veblen, Thorstein. (1899) 1994. *The Theory of the Leisure Class*. New York: Dover.

Vento, Arnoldo Carlos. 2002. *Mestizo: The History, Culture, and Politics of the Mexican and the Chicano, the Emerging Mestizo-Americans*. New York: University Press of America.

Venturelli, Shalini. 2001. *From the Information Economy to the Creative Economy: Moving Culture to the Center of International Public Policy*. Washington, DC: Center for Arts and Culture.

Vera, Hernán, and Andrew Gordon. 2003. *Screen Saviors: Hollywood Fictions of Whiteness*. New York: Rowman & Littlefield.

Vermont Arts Council. n.d. "Cultural Heritage Toolkit." Accessed February 16, 2012. www.vermontartscouncil.org.

Vials, Christopher. 2014. *Haunted by Hitler: Liberals, the Left, and the Fight against Fascism in the United States*. Amherst: University of Massachusetts Press.

Vidal, Gore. 2004. "State of the Union, 2004." *Nation*, September 13, 2004.

Viego, Antonio. 2007. *Dead Subjects: Toward a Politics of Loss in Latino Studies*. Duke University Press.

Villa, Pablo. 2003. *Ethnography at the Border*. Minneapolis: University of Minnesota Press.

Villa, Raul. 2000. *Barriologos*. Austin: University of Texas Press.

Virno, Paolo. 2010. "The Soviets of the Multitude: On Collectivity and Collective Work." Interview by Alexei Penzin. *Mediations* 25. www.mediationsjournal.org.

Vizenor, Gerald, and A. Robert Lee. 1999. *Postindian Conversations*. Lincoln: University of Nebraska Press.

Vo, Linda Trinh. 2004. *Mobilizing an Asian American Community*. Philadelphia: Temple University Press.

Von Eschen, Penny. 1997. *Race against Empire: Black Americans and Anticolonialism, 1937–1957*. Ithaca, NY: Cornell University Press.

———. 2004. *Satchmo Blows Up the World: Jazz Ambassadors Play the Cold War*. Cambridge, MA: Harvard University Press.

Von Mises, Ludwig. (1944) 1996. *Bureaucracy*. Grove City, PA: Libertarian Press.

Von Nardroff, Ellen. 1962. "The American Frontier as a Safety Valve: The Life, Death, Reincarnation, and Justification of a Theory." *Agricultural History* 36 (3): 123–42.

Voyles, Traci Brynne. 2015. *Wastelanding: Legacies of Uranium Mining in Navajo Country*. Minneapolis: University of Minnesota Press.

Wacquant, Loïc. 2002. "From Slavery to Mass Incarceration: Rethinking the 'Race Question' in the U.S." *New Left Review* 13:41–60.

———. 2009. *Punishing the Poor: The Neoliberal Government of Social Insecurity*. Durham, NC: Duke University Press.

Wade, Nicholas. 2015. *A Troublesome Inheritance: Genes, Race and Human History*. New York: Penguin.

Wajcman, Judy. 1991. *Feminism Confronts Technology*. Cambridge, UK: Polity.

Walcott, Rinaldo, ed. 2000. *Rude: Contemporary Black Canadian Cultural Criticism*. Toronto: Insomniac.

Wald, Priscilla. 1995. *Constituting Americans: Cultural Anxiety and Narrative Form*. Durham, NC: Duke University Press.

Waldstreicher, David. 2010. *Slavery's Constitution: From Revolution to Ratification*. New York: Hill and Wang.

Waligora-Davis, Nicole. 2011. *Sanctuary: African Americans and Empire*. New York: Oxford University Press.

Walker, Alice. 1982. *The Color Purple: A Novel*. New York: Harcourt, Brace, Jovanovich.

Walker, David. (1829) 1995. *David Walker's Appeal, in Four Articles, Together with a Preamble, to the Coloured Citizens of the World, but in Particular, and Very Expressly, to Those of the United States of America*. New York: Hill and Wang.

Walker, Rebecca. 2002. *Black, White, and Jewish: Autobiography of a Shifting Self*. New York: River Trade.

Wallace-Sanders, Kimberly. 2008. *Mammy: A Century of Race, Gender, and Southern Memory*. Ann Arbor: University of Michigan Press.

Wallerstein, Immanuel. 1976. *The Modern World-System*. New York: Academic.

———. 2001. *Unthinking Social Science: The Limits of Nineteenth-Century Paradigms*. 2nd ed. Philadelphia: Temple University Press.

———. 2004. *World-Systems Theory: An Introduction*. Durham, NC: Duke University Press.

Wallis, Brian. 1995. "Black Bodies, White Science: Louis Agassiz's Slave Daguerreotypes." *American Art* 9 (2): 38–61.

Walzer, Michael, ed. 1995. *Toward a Global Civil Society*. New York: Berghahn Books.

Ward, Candace. 2017. *Crossing the Line: Early Creole Novels and Anglophone Caribbean Culture in the Age of Emancipation*. Charlottesville: University of Virginia Press.

Ward, Jesmyn. 2011. *Salvage the Bones*. New York: Bloomsbury.

———. 2017. *Sing, Unburied, Sing*. New York: Scribner.

Wardrip-Fruin, Noah, and Nick Monfort. 2003. *The New Media Reader*. Cambridge: MIT Press.

Wark, McKenzie. 2004. *A Hacker Manifesto*. Cambridge, MA: Harvard University Press.

Warner, Michael. 1990. *The Letters of the Republic: Publication and the Public Sphere in Eighteenth-Century America*. Cambridge, MA: Harvard University Press.

———. 1999. *The Trouble with Normal: Sex, Politics, and the Ethics of Queer Life*. New York: Free Press.

———. 2002. "Publics and Counter-publics." *Public Culture* 14 (1): 49–90.

Warner, Susan. (1850) 1993. *The Wide Wide World*. New York: Feminist.

Warner, W. Lloyd, and Leo Srole. 1945. *The Social Systems of American Ethnic Groups*. Chicago: University of Chicago.

Warner-Lewis, Maureen. 1998. "Trinidad Yoruba: Its Theoretical Implications for Creolisation Processes." *Caribbean Quarterly* 44:50–61.

Warren, Kenneth W. 1993. "Appeals for (Mis)recognition: Theorizing the Diaspora." In *Cultures of United States Imperialism*, edited by Amy Kaplan and Donald E. Pease, 392–406. Durham, NC: Duke University Press.

Warrior, Robert Allen. 2003. "A Room of One's Own at the ASA: An Indigenous Provocation." *American Quarterly* 55 (4): 681–87.

Washington, Mary Helen. 1998. "Disturbing the Peace: What Happens to American Studies If You Put African American Studies at Its Center: Presidential Address to the American Studies Association, October 29, 1997." *American Quarterly* 50 (1): 1–23.

Washington Post. 1981. "For the Record." June 4, 1981.

Watkins, Evan. 1998. *Everyday Exchanges: Marketwork and Capitalist Common Sense*. Stanford, CA: Stanford University Press.

Wayne, Michael. 2003. "Post-Fordism, Monopoly Capitalism, and Hollywood's Media Industrial Complex." *International Journal of Cultural Studies* 6 (1): 82–103.

Webb, Walter Prescott. (1931) 1981. *The Great Plains*. Lincoln: University of Nebraska Press.

Weber, Max. (1905) 1958. *The Protestant Ethic and the Spirit of Capitalism*. Translated by Talcott Parsons. New York: Scribner's.

———. 1968. *Economy and Society: An Outline of Interpretive Sociology*. New York: Bedminster.

———. 1983. *Max Weber on Capitalism, Bureaucracy, and Religion: A Selection of Texts*, edited by Stanislav Andreski. London: Allen and Unwin.

Weheliye, Alexander G. 2014. *Habeas Viscus: Racializing Assemblages, Biopolitics, and Black Feminist Theories of the Human*. Durham, NC: Duke University Press.

Weinbaum, Alys Eve. 2004. *Wayward Reproductions: Genealogies of Race and Nation in Transatlantic Modern Thought*. Durham, NC: Duke University Press.

Weiser, Mark. 1991. "The Computer for the 21st Century." *Scientific American*, September 1991.

Weitz, Eric. 1997. *Creating German Communism 1890–1990: From Popular Protest to Socialist State*. Princeton, NJ: Princeton University Press.

Welke, Barbara Young. 2010. *Law and the Borders of Belonging in the Long Nineteenth Century United States*. New York: Cambridge University Press.

Wendell, Susan. 1989. "Toward a Feminist Theory of Disability." *Hypatia* 4 (2): 104–24.

West, Cornel. 1994. *Race Matters*. New York: Vintage Books.

Westad, Odd Arne. 2007. *The Global Cold War: Third World Interventions and the Making of Our Times*. Cambridge: Cambridge University Press.

Westheider, James E. 1997. *Fighting on Two Fronts: African Americans and the Vietnam War*. New York: New York University Press.

Wettstein, Howard. 2002. Introduction to *Diasporas and Exiles: Varieties of Jewish Identity*, edited by Howard Wettstein, 1–17. Berkeley: University of California Press.

Wexler, Laura. 2000. *Tender Violence: Domestic Visions in an Age of U.S. Imperialism*. Chapel Hill: University of North Carolina Press.

Wheatley, Phillis. (1773) 1999. *Poems on Various Subjects, Religious and Moral*. Charlottesville: University of Virginia Press.

———. (1775) 2001. "To His Excellency General Washington."

In *Phillis Wheatley: Complete Writings*, 88–99. New York: Penguin.

Whelchel, Toshio. 1999. *From Pearl Harbor to Saigon: Japanese American Soldiers and the Vietnam War*. London: Verso.

White, G. Edward. 1986. "From Legal Realism to Critical Legal Studies: A Truncated Intellectual History." *Southwestern Law Journal* 4:819–43.

White, Hayden. 1978. *Tropics of Discourse: Essays in Cultural Criticism*. Baltimore: Johns Hopkins University Press.

———. 1982. "The Politics of Historical Interpretation: Discipline and De-sublimation." *Critical Inquiry* 9:113–37.

Whitlock, Katherine. 2001. *In a Time of Broken Bones: A Call to Dialogue on Hate Violence and the Limitations of Hate Crime Laws*. Philadelphia: American Friends Service Committee.

Whitlock, Kay, and Michael Bronski. 2015. *Considering Hate: Violence, Goodness, and Justice in American Culture and Politics*. Boston: Beacon.

Whitman, James Q. 2003. *Harsh Justice: Criminal Punishment and the Widening Divide between America and Europe*. Oxford: Oxford University Press.

———. 2017. *Hitler's American Model: The United States and the Making of Nazi Race Law*. Princeton, NJ: Princeton University Press.

Whitman, Walt. (1855) 1965. *Leaves of Grass*. Edited by Harold W. Blodgett and Sculley Bradley. New York: New York University Press.

———. (1855) 1999. "Whitman's Preface to *Leaves of Grass*." In *Selected Poems, 1855–1892: A New Edition*, edited by Gary Schmidgall, 3–14. New York: St. Martin's.

———. 1932. *Franklin Evans; or the Inebriate*. In *The Uncollected Poetry and Prose of Walt Whitman*, edited by Emory Holloway, 103–221. New York: Peter Smith.

Whyte, Kyle Powys. 2014. "Indigenous Women, Climate Change Impacts, and Collective Action." *Hypatia: A Journal of Feminist Philosophy* 29 (3): 599–616. https://doi.org/10.1111/hypa.12089.

———. 2016. "Is It Colonial Déjà Vu? Indigenous Peoples and Climate Justice." In *Humanities for the Environment: Integrating Knowledges, Forging New Constellations of Practice*, edited by Joni Adamson, Michael Davis, and Hsinya Huang, 88–104. London: Earthscan.

———. 2017. "Indigenous Climate Change Studies: Indigenizing Futures, Decolonizing the Anthropocene." *English Language Notes* 55 (1–2): 153–62.

———. 2018. "Indigenous Science (Fiction) for the Anthropocene: Ancestral Dystopias and Fantasies of Climate Change Crises." *Environment and Planning E: Nature and Space* 1 (1–2): 224–42.

Widmer, Edward L. 1999. *Young America: The Flowering of Democracy in New York City*. New York: Oxford University Press.

Wiegman, Robyn. 1997. *American Anatomies*. Durham, NC: Duke University Press.

Wiencek, Henry. 2012. "The Dark Side of Thomas Jefferson." *Smithsonian Magazine*, October 2012. www.smithsonianmag.com.

Wildcat, Daniel. 2009. *Red Alert! Saving the Planet with Indigenous Knowledge*. Golden, CO: Fulcrum.

Wilder, Craig Steven. 2013. *Ebony and Ivy: Race, Slavery, and the Troubled History of America's Universities*. New York: Bloomsbury.

Wilentz, Sean. 1984a. "Against Exceptionalism: Class Consciousness and the American Labor Movement." *International labor and Working Class History* 26:1–24.

———. 1984b. *Chants Democratic: New York City and the Rise of the American Working Class, 1788–1850*. New York: Oxford University Press.

Wilkins, David E., and Heidi Kiiwetinepinesiik Stark. 2011. *American Indian Politics and the American Political System*. 3rd ed. Lanham, MD: Rowman & Littlefield.

Willey, Angela. 2016. *Undoing Monogamy: The Politics of Science and the Possibilities of Biology*. Durham, NC: Duke University Press.

Williams, Eric. (1944) 1994. *Capitalism and Slavery*. Chapel Hill: University of North Carolina Press.

Williams, Jeffrey J. 2006. "Debt Education: Bad for the Young, Bad for America." *Dissent Magazine*, Summer 2006. www.dissentmagazine.org.

———. 2008. "Student Debt and the Spirit of Indenture." *Dissent*, Fall 2008.

———. 2016. "Innovation for What? The Politics of Inequality in Higher Education." *Dissent Magazine*, Winter 2016. www.dissentmagazine.org.

Williams, Linda. 2002. *Playing the Race Card: Melodramas of Black and White from Uncle Tom to O. J. Simpson*. Princeton, NJ: Princeton University Press.

Williams, Randall. 2010. *The Divided World: Human Rights and Its Violence*. Minneapolis: University of Minnesota Press.

Williams, Raymond. 1958. *Culture and Society, 1780–1950*. New York: Columbia University Press.

———. 1973. *The Country and the City*. New York: Oxford University Press.

———. (1974) 2000. *Television: Technology and Cultural Form*. London: Routledge.

———. (1976) 1983. *Keywords: A Vocabulary of Culture and Society*. London: Fontana; New York: Oxford University Press.

——. (1977) 1997. *Marxism and Literature*. Oxford: Oxford University Press.

——. 1980. "Ideas of Nature." In *Problems in Materialism and Culture*, 67–85. London: Verso.

——. 1982. *The Sociology of Culture*. New York: Schocken Books.

Williams, Robert A., Jr. 2005. *Like a Loaded Weapon: The Rehnquist Court, Indian Rights, and the Legal History of Racism in America*. Minneapolis: University of Minnesota Press.

Williams, Sherley Anne. 1986. *Dessa Rose*. New York: William Morrow.

Williams, William Appleman. 1992. "The Frontier Thesis and American Foreign Policy." In *A William Appleman Williams Reader*, edited by Henry W. Berger, 89–104. Chicago: Ivan R. Dee.

Willis, Paul. 1977. *Learning to Labor: How Working-Class Kids Get Working-Class Jobs*. New York: Columbia University Press.

Wilson, Bryan. 1998. "Secularization: The Inherited Model." In *Religion in American History: A Reader*, edited by Jon Butler and Harry S. Stout, 335–44. New York: Oxford University Press.

Wilson, Elizabeth A. (1985) 2003. *Adorned in Dreams: Fashion and Modernity*. New Brunswick, NJ: Rutgers University Press.

——. 2004. *Psychosomatic: Feminism and the Neurological Body*. Durham, NC: Duke University Press.

——. 2015. *Gut Feminism*. Durham, NC: Duke University Press.

Wilson, George. 1855. *What Is Technology? An Inaugural Lecture Delivered in the University of Edinburgh*. Edinburgh: Sutherland and Knox.

Wilson, Harriet. (1859) 1983. *Our Nig; or, Sketches from the Life of a Free Black*. New York: Vintage.

Wilson, James Q., and George L. Kelling. 1982. "Broken Windows: The Police and Neighborhood Safety." *Atlantic Monthly* 249:29–38.

Wilson, Rob. 2000. *Reimagining the American Pacific: From "South Pacific" to Bamboo Ridge and Beyond*. Durham, NC: Duke University Press.

Wilson, Woodrow. 1917. "Address to a Joint Session of Congress Requesting a Declaration of War against Germany, April 2, 1917." American Presidency Project. Accessed April 27, 2014. www.presidency.ucsb.edu.

Winant, Howard. 1994. *Racial Conditions: Politics, Theory, Comparisons*. Minneapolis: University of Minnesota Press.

——. 2001. *The World Is a Ghetto: Race and Democracy since World War II*. New York: Basic Books.

Winthrop, John. (1630) 1838. "A Modell of Christian Charity." In *Collections of the Massachusetts Historical Society*, 3rd ser., vol. 7, 31–48. Boston: Charles C. Little and James Brown.

Wirtén, Eva Hemmungs. 2008. *Terms of Use: Negotiating the Jungle of the Intellectual Commons*. Toronto: University of Toronto Press.

Witschi, Nicolas S., ed. 2011. *A Companion to the Literature and Culture of the American West*. New York: Blackwell.

Wolf, Eric. 1982. *Europe and the People without History*. Berkeley: University of California Press.

Wolfe, Patrick. 2006. "Settler Colonialism and the Elimination of the Native." *Journal of Genocide Research* 8 (4): 387–410.

Wolff, Richard. 2012. *Democracy at Work: A Cure for Capitalism*. New York: Haymarket.

Wolff, R., and S. Resnick. 2012. *Contending Economic Theories: Neoclassical, Keynesian, and Marxian*. Cambridge: MIT Press.

Wolin, Richard. 2006. *The Seduction of Unreason: The Intellectual Romance with Fascism from Nietzsche to Post-modernism*. Princeton, NJ: Princeton University Press.

Wollstonecraft, Mary. (1790, 1792) 2009. *"A Vindication of the Rights of Woman" and "A Vindication of the Rights of Men."* Oxford: Oxford University Press.

Womack, Craig S. 1999. *Red on Red: Native American Literary Separatism*. Minneapolis: University of Minnesota Press.

Womack, Ytasha L. 2013. *The World of Black Sci-Fi and Culture*. Chicago: Lawrence Hill Books.

Women Who Rock. 2012. *Women Who Rock: Making Scenes, Building Communities*. Seattle: University of Washington Libraries. http://womenwhorockcommunity.org.

"Women Working, 1800–1930" (digital archive). n.d. Harvard University Library Open Collections Program. http://ocp.hul.harvard.edu.

Wood, Gordon S. 1992. *The Radicalism of the American Revolution*. New York: Knopf.

Woodmansee, Martha, and Peter Jaszi, eds. 1994. *The Construction of Authorship: Textual Appropriation in Law and Literature*. Durham, NC: Duke University Press.

Woodward, C. Vann. 1955. *The Strange Career of Jim Crow*. New York: Oxford University Press.

Woolf, Virginia. (1924) 1989. "Mr. Bennett and Mrs. Brown." In *The Essays of Virginia Woolf*. Vol. 3, *1919–1924*, edited by Andrew McNeillie, 384–89. San Diego, CA: Harcourt Brace.

Woolsey, Theodore Dwight. 1878. *Political Science; or, the State Theoretically and Practically Considered*. Vol. 1. New York: Scribner, Armstrong.

Wray, Matt. 2006. *Not Quite White: White Trash and the Boundaries of Whiteness*. Durham, NC: Duke University Press.

Wright, Erik Olin. 1985. *Classes*. London: Verso.

Wright, Melissa W. 1999. "The Dialectics of Still Life: Murder, Women and the Maquiladoras." *Public Culture* 11:453–74.

Wright, Michelle M. 2004. *Becoming Black: Creating Identity in the African Diaspora*. Durham, NC: Duke University Press.

———. 2015. *The Physics of Blackness: Beyond the Middle Passage Epistemology*. Minnesota: University of Minnesota Press.

Wright, Richard. (1956) 1995. *The Color Curtain: A Report on the Bandung Conference*. Jackson, MS: Banner Books.

Wyler, William, dir. 1959. *Ben-Hur*. Metro-Goldwyn-Mayer.

Wynter, Sylvia. 2003. "Unsettling the Coloniality of Being/Power/Truth/Freedom: Towards the Human, after Man, Its Overrepresentation—an Argument." *CR: The New Centennial Review* 3 (3): 257–337.

Yancy, George. 2012. *Look, a White! Philosophical Essays on Whiteness*. Philadelphia: Temple University Press.

Yeh, Chiou-ling. 2008. *Making an American Festival: Chinese New Year in San Francisco's Chinatown*. Berkeley: University of California Press.

Yellin, Jean Fagan. 1992. *Women and Sisters: Antislavery Feminists in American Culture*. New Haven: Yale University Press.

Yelvington, Kevin. 2001. "The Anthropology of Afro-Latin America and the Caribbean: Diasporic Dimensions." *Annual Review of Anthropology* 30:227–60.

Yoneyama, Lisa. 2005. "Liberation under Siege: U.S. Military Occupation and Japanese Women's Enfranchisement." *American Quarterly* 57 (3): 885–910.

Young, Alex Trimble. 2013. "Settler Sovereignty and the Rhizomatic West, or, The Significance of the Frontier in Postwestern Studies." *Western American Literature* 48 (1–2): 115–40.

———. 2018. "Settler." *Western American Literature* 53:1, 75–80.

Young, Alfred F. 1976. *The American Revolution: Explorations in the History of American Radicalism*. DeKalb: Northern Illinois University Press.

———. 1993. *Beyond the American Revolution: Explorations in the History of American Radicalism*. DeKalb: Northern Illinois University Press.

Young, Ezra. Forthcoming. "Demarginalizing Trans Rights." In *A Companion to On Intersectionality: Essential Writings*. New York: New Press.

Young, Harvey. 2010. *Embodying Black Experience: Stillness, Critical Memory, and the Black Body*. Ann Arbor: University of Michigan Press.

Young, Iris Marion. 1990. *Justice and the Politics of Difference*. Princeton, NJ: Princeton University Press.

———. 2000. *Inclusion and Democracy*. New York: Oxford University Press.

Young, Jock. 1971. *The Drugtakers: The Social Meaning of Drug Use*. London: Paladin.

Yu, Henry. 2001. *Thinking Orientals: Migration, Contact, and Exoticism in Modern America*. New York: Oxford University Press.

Yúdice, George. 2003. *The Expediency of Culture: Uses of Culture in the Global Era*. Durham, NC: Duke University Press.

———. 2018. "The Challenges of the New Media Scene for Public Policies." In *The Routledge Handbook of Global Cultural Policy*, edited by Victoria Durrer, Toby Miller, and Dave O'Brien, 382–96. London: Routledge.

Yusoff, Kathryn. 2018. *A Billion Black Anthropocenes or None*. Minneapolis: University of Minneapolis Press.

Yuval-Davis, Nira. 1997. *Gender and Nation*. London: Sage.

Yuval-Davis, Nira, and Floya Anthias, eds. 1989. *Women–Nation–State*. London: Macmillan.

Zagarri, Rosemarie. 2007. *Revolutionary Backlash: Women and Politics in the Early American Republic*. Philadelphia: University of Pennsylvania Press.

Zakaria, Fareed. 2008. *The Post-American World*. New York: Norton.

Zalasiewicz, Jan, Mark Williams, and Colin N. Waters. 2016. "Anthropocene." In *Keywords for Environmental Studies*, edited by Joni Adamson, William A. Gleason, and David N. Pellow, 14–16. New York: New York University Press.

Zavella, Patricia. 2011. *I'm Neither Here nor There*. Durham, NC: Duke University Press.

Zeskind, Leonard. 2009. *Blood and Politics: The History of the White Nationalist Movement from Margins to Mainstream*. New York: Farrar, Straus and Giroux.

Zimmermann, Eberhard August Wilhelm von. 1787. *A Political Survey of the Present State of Europe*. London: C. Dilly.

Zinn, Howard. 1965. *The New Abolitionists*. Boston: Beacon.

———. 1980. *A People's History of the United States*. New York: Harper & Row.

Žižek, Slavoj. 1999. *The Ticklish Subject: The Absent Centre of Political Ontology*. London: Verso.

———. 2010. "How to Begin from the Beginning." In *The Idea of Communism*, edited by Costas Douzinas and Slavoj Žižek, 209–26. London: Verso.

Zukin, Sharon. 2010. *Naked City: The Death and Life of Authentic Urban Places*. New York: Oxford University Press.

Zunshine, Lisa. 2006. *Why We Read Fiction: Theory of Mind and the Novel*. Columbus: Ohio State University Press.

About the Contributors

Note: A complete list of contributors is available at keywords.nyupress.org.

Vermonja R Alston is Associate Professor in the Department of Humanities at York University in Toronto. Among her recent publications are "Environment" in *Keywords for Environmental Studies* and "Water: Rivers and Forests of Survival" in the *Journal of Commonwealth and Postcolonial Studies*.

Lee Bebout is a Professor of English and Affiliate Faculty with the School of Transborder Studies, the School of Social Transformation, and the Program in American Studies at the University of Arizona. His articles have appeared in *Aztlán*, *MELUS*, *Latino Studies*, and other scholarly journals. He is the author of *Mythohistorical Interventions: The Chicano Movement and Its Legacies* and *Whiteness on the Border: Mapping the US Racial Imagination in Brown and White*.

Lauren Berlant is George M. Pullman Distinguished Service Professor of English at the University of Chicago. Her recent books include *The Hundreds* (with Kathleen Stewart) and *Cruel Optimism*.

Amaranth Borsuk is Associate Professor and Associate Director of the MFA in Creative Writing and Poetics in the School of Interdisciplinary Arts and Sciences at the University of Washington Bothell. She is the author of *The Book* and five volumes of poetry.

Marc Bousquet has retired from a position as Associate Professor of Film and Media at Emory University. He is the author of *How the University Works: Higher Education and the Low-Wage Nation*.

Laura Briggs is Professor of Women, Gender, Sexuality Studies at the University of Massachusetts Amherst. She is the author of *Taking Children: A History of American Terror* and *How All Politics Became Reproductive Politics: From Welfare Reform to Foreclosure to Trump*.

June Wayee Chau is a PhD Candidate in Cultural Studies at the University of California, Davis and is currently working on a project that uses a critical environmental justice lens to explore issues of migrant water access, transnational air pollution, and agribusiness extractions in California's Imperial Valley.

Kandice Chuh is Professor of English, American Studies, and Critical Social Psychology at the City University of New York, Graduate Center. She is the author of *The Difference Aesthetics Makes: On the Humanities "After Man"* and *Imagine Otherwise: On Asian Americanist Critique*.

Ann Cvetkovich is Director of the Pauline Jewett Institute of Women's and Gender Studies at Carleton University. She is the author of *Depression: A Public Feeling* and *An*

Archive of Feelings: Trauma, Sexuality, and Lesbian Public Cultures.

Marlene L. Daut is Professor of African Diaspora Studies at the University of Virginia. She is the author of *Tropics of Haiti: Race and the Literary History of the Haitian Revolution in the Atlantic World, 1789–1865* and *Baron de Vastey and the Origins of Black Atlantic Humanism.* She is currently working on a collaborative project, *An Anthology of Haitian Revolutionary Fictions.*

Ashley Dawson is Professor of English at the City University of New York. He is the author of *People's Power, Extreme Cities: The Peril and Promise of Urban Life in the Age of Climate Change,* and *Extinction: A Radical History.*

Angela D. Dillard is Richard A. Meisler Collegiate Professor of Afroamerican and African Studies in the Residential College at the University of Michigan. She is the author of *Guess Who's Coming to Dinner Now? Multicultural Conservatism in America* and *Faith in the City: Preaching Radical Social Change in Detroit.*

Lisa Duggan is Professor of Social and Cultural Analysis at New York University. She is the author of *Mean Girl: Ayn Rand and the Culture of Greed* and *Twilight of Equality? Neoliberalism, Cultural Politics and the Attack on Democracy.*

Brian T. Edwards is Professor of English and Dean of the School of Liberal Arts at Tulane University. He is the author of *Morocco Bound: Disorienting America's Maghreb* and *After the American Century: The Ends of U.S. Culture in the Middle East* and co-editor of *Globalizing American Studies.*

Robert Fanuzzi is Associate Professor of English and American Studies at St. John's University. He is the author

of *Abolition's Public Sphere*, "Frederick Douglass's Everlasting Now," and "Lydia Maria Child's Abolition Democracy, and Ours." He is the recipient of an American Studies Community Partnership Grant and Humanities New York Action Grant (2016) supporting publicly engaged African American studies programs.

Cynthia G. Franklin is Professor of English at the University of Hawai'i and author of *Academic Lives: Memoir, Cultural Theory and the University Today.* She is co-editor of *Biography,* where she recently produced a special issue on "Life in Occupied Palestine." She is a member of the Organizing Collective of the US Campaign for the Academic and Cultural Boycott of Israel.

Kevin K. Gaines is the Julian Bond Professor of Civil Rights and Social Justice in the Corcoran Department of History and the Carter G. Woodson Institute for African American and African Studies at the University of Virginia. He is the author of *Uplifting the Race: Black Leadership, Politics, and Culture during the Twentieth Century* and *American Africans in Ghana: Black Expatriates and the Civil Rights Era.*

Alyshia Gálvez is a Cultural and Medical Anthropologist and a Professor of Latin American and Latino Studies and Anthropology at Lehman College and the Graduate Center of the City University of New York. She is the author of *Eating NAFTA: Trade, Food Policies and the Destruction of Mexico* and two prior books on Mexican migration.

Kirsten Silva Gruesz is Professor of Literature at the University of California, Santa Cruz. She is the author of *Ambassadors of Culture: The Transamerican Origins of Latino Writing.*

Sandra M. Gustafson is Professor of English and Concurrent Professor of American Studies at the University of Notre Dame. She is the author of *Eloquence Is Power: Oratory and Performance in Early America* and *Imagining Deliberative Democracy in the Early American Republic*. Gustafson also edited the first volume of the *Norton Anthology of American Literature*.

Jack Halberstam is Professor of English and Gender Studies at Columbia University. His recent publications include *Female Masculinity*, *Trans*: A Quick and Quirky Account of Gender Variance*, and *Wild Things: The Disorder of Desire*. The journal *Places* awarded Halberstam its Arcus/Places Prize in 2018 for innovative public scholarship on the relationship between gender, sexuality, and the built environment.

Christina B. Hanhardt is Associate Professor of American Studies at the University of Maryland, College Park. She is the author of *Safe Space: Gay Neighborhood History and the Politics of Violence*.

Scott Herring is James H. Rudy Professor of English at Indiana University. He is the author of *The Hoarders: Material Deviance in Modern American Culture* and *Another Country: Queer Anti-Urbanism*.

Rebecca Hill is Professor of American Studies at Kennesaw State University. She is the author of *Men, Mobs and Law: Anti-Lynching and Labor Defense in U.S. Radical History* and editor, with Elizabeth Duclos-Orsello and Joseph Entin, of *Teaching American Studies: State of the Classroom as State of the Field*.

Daniel Martinez HoSang is Associate Professor of Ethnicity, Race, and Migration and American Studies at Yale University. He is co-author (with Joseph Lowndes) of *Producers, Parasites and Patriots: Race and the New Right-Wing Politics of Precarity*.

Matthew Frye Jacobson is William Robertson Coe Professor of American Studies and History at Yale University. He is the author of *Odetta's One Grain of Sand* and *The Historian's Eye: Photography, History, and the American Present*.

E. Patrick Johnson is Carlos Montezuma Professor of Performance Studies and African American Studies at Northwestern University. He is the author of *Sweet Tea: Black Gay Men of the South* and *Honeypot: Black Southern Women Who Love Women*.

Walter Johnson is Winthrop Professor of History at Harvard University. He is the author of *The Broken Heart of America: St. Louis and the Violent History of the United States*.

J. Kēhaulani Kauanui is Professor of American Studies and Affiliate Faculty in Anthropology at Wesleyan University. She is the author of *Hawaiian Blood: Colonialism and the Politics of Sovereignty and Indigeneity* and *Paradoxes of Hawaiian Sovereignty: Land, Sex, and the Colonial Politics of State Nationalism* and the editor of *Speaking of Indigenous Politics: Conversations with Activists, Scholars, and Tribal Leaders*. She is one of the six cofounders of the Native American and Indigenous Studies Association (NAISA), established in 2008.

David Kazanjian is Professor of English and Comparative Literature at the University of Pennsylvania. He is the author of *The Brink of Freedom: Improvising Life in the Nineteenth-Century Atlantic World*.

Lauren F. Klein is Associate Professor of English and Quantitative Theory and Methods at Emory University. She is the author of *An Archive of Taste: Race and Eating in the Early United States* and co-author (with Catherine D'Ignazio) of *Data Feminism*.

Erica Kohl-Arenas is Associate Professor of American Studies and Faculty Director of Imagining America: Artists and Scholars in Public Life at the University of California, Davis. She is the author of *The Self Help Myth: How Philanthropy Fails to Alleviate Poverty*.

Josh Kun is Chair in Cross-Cultural Communication and Professor of Communication, Journalism, and American Studies and Ethnicity at the University of Southern California Annenberg School of Communication. He is the author of *Audiotopia: Music, Race, and America* and *The Tide Was Always High: The Music of Latin America in Los Angeles*.

Oneka LaBennett is Associate Professor of American Studies and Ethnicity at the University of Southern California. She is the author of *She's Mad Real: Popular Culture and West Indian Girls in Brooklyn* and "'Beyoncé and Her Husband': Representing Infidelity and Kinship in a Black Marriage." She is currently working on a book that centers on Guyana's global gendered racializations.

George Lipsitz is Professor of Black Studies and Sociology at the University of California, Santa Barbara. He is the author of *The Possessive Investment in Whiteness* and *How Racism Takes Place*.

Eric Lott is Distinguished Professor of English and American Studies at the Graduate Center, City University of New York. He is the author of *Black Mirror: The Cultural Contradictions of American Racism* and *Love and Theft: Blackface Minstrelsy and the American Working Class*.

Lisa Lowe is Samuel Knight Professor of American Studies at Yale University. She is the author of *Immigrant Acts: On Asian American Cultural Politics* and *The Intimacies of Four Continents*.

Joseph Lowndes is Professor of Political Science at the University of Oregon. He is the author of *From the New Deal to the New Right: Race and the Southern Origins of Modern Conservatism* and co-author (with Daniel Martinez HoSang) of *Producers, Parasites, Patriots: Race and the New Right-Wing Politics of Precarity*.

Sunaina Maira is Professor of Asian American Studies at the University of California, Davis. She is the author of *The 9/11 Generation: Youth, Rights, and Solidarity in the War on Terror* and *Boycott! The Academy and Justice for Palestine*.

Erin Manning is Professor of Fine Arts at Concordia University. She is the author of *For a Pragmatics of the Useless* and *The Minor Gesture*.

Kembrew McLeod is Professor of Communication Studies at the University of Iowa. He is the author of *The Downtown Pop Underground* and *Blondie's Parallel Lines*.

Tara McPherson is Professor and Chair of Cinema and Media Studies at the University of Southern California. She is the author of *Feminist in a Software Lab: Difference and Design* and founding Principal Investigator on the publishing platform *Scalar*.

Robert McRuer is Professor of English at George Washington University. He is the author of *Crip Times: Disability, Globalization, and Resistance* and *Crip Theory: Cultural Signs of Queerness and Disability*.

Leerom Medovoi is Professor of English and Social, Cultural, and Critical Theory at the University of Arizona.

He is the author of *Rebels: Youth and the Cold War Origins of Identity*.

Jodi Melamed is Associate Professor of English at Marquette University. She is co-editor of a special issue of *Social Text* on "Economies of Dispossession: Indigeneity, Race, and Capitalism" and the author of *Represent and Destroy: Rationalizing Violence in the New Racial Capitalism*.

Timothy Mitchell is Professor of Middle Eastern, South Asian, and African Studies at Columbia University. He is the author of *Rule of Experts: Egypt, Technopolitics, Modernity* and *Carbon Democracy: Political Power in the Age of Oil*.

Lisa Nakamura is Gwendolyn Calvert Baker Collegiate Professor of American Studies and Director of the Digital Studies Institute at the University of Michigan, Ann Arbor. She is the author of four books on race, gender, and digital culture.

Christopher Newfield is Distinguished Professor of Literature and American Studies at the University of California, Santa Barbara. He is the author of *The Great Mistake: How We Wrecked Public Universities and How We Can Fix Them* and *Unmaking the Public University*.

Tavia Nyong'o is Professor of American Studies at Yale University. He is the author of *The Amalgamation Waltz: Race, Performance, and the Ruses of Memory* and *Afro-Fabulations: The Queer Drama of Black Life*.

Crystal Parikh is Professor of Social and Cultural Analysis and English and Director of the Asian/Pacific/American Institute at New York University. She is the author of *Writing Human Rights: The Political Imaginaries of Writers*

of Color and *An Ethics of Betrayal: The Politics of Otherness in Emergent U.S. Literature and Culture*.

Miriam Posner is Assistant Professor of Information Studies and Digital Humanities at the University of California, Los Angeles. She is working on a book on global supply chain software.

Junaid Rana is Associate Professor of Asian American Studies at the University of Illinois at Urbana-Champaign. He is the author of *Terrifying Muslims: Race and Labor in the South Asian Diaspora* and co-editor of *With Stones in Our Hands: Writings on Racism, Muslims, and Empire*.

Juana María Rodríguez is Professor of Ethnic Studies at the University of California, Berkeley. She is the author of *Sexual Futures, Queer Gestures, and Other Latina Longings* and *Queer Latinidad: Identity Practices, Discursive Spaces*.

Valerie Rohy is Professor of English at the University of Vermont. She is the author of *Chances Are: Contingency, Queer Theory, and American Literature* and *Lost Causes: Narrative, Etiology, and Queer Theory*.

Andrew Ross is Professor of Social and Cultural Analysis at New York University. He is the author of *Stone Men: The Palestinians Who Built Israel*, *Creditocracy and the Case for Debt Refusal*, and *Nice Work If You Can Get It: Life and Labor in Precarious Times*.

David F. Ruccio is Professor Emeritus of Economics at the University of Notre Dame. He is the author of *Development and Globalization: A Marxian Class Analysis* and (with J. Amariglio) *Postmodern Moments in Modern Economics*.

George J. Sanchez is Professor of American Studies and Ethnicity and History at the University of Southern California. He is the author of *Becoming Mexican American: Ethnicity, Culture and Identity in Chicano Los Angeles, 1900–1945* and "'What's Good for Boyle Heights Is Good for the Jews': Creating Multiracialism on the Eastside during the 1950s."

Jentery Sayers is Associate Professor of English and Cultural, Social, and Political Thought at the University of Victoria. He is the editor of *Making Things and Drawing Boundaries: Experiments in the Digital Humanities.*

Kyla Schuller is Associate Professor of Women's, Gender, and Sexuality Studies at Rutgers University, New Brunswick. She is the author of *The Biopolitics of Feeling: Race, Sex, and Science in the Nineteenth Century* and co-editor of "The Origins of Biopolitics in the Americas," a special issue of *American Quarterly.*

Stephanie Smallwood is Associate Professor in the Department of History and the Comparative History of Ideas at the University of Washington Seattle. She is the author of *Saltwater Slavery: A Middle Passage from Africa to American Diaspora.*

Caleb Smith is Professor of English and American Studies at Yale University. He is the author of *The Prison and the American Imagination* and the editor of Austin Reed's *The Life and the Adventures of a Haunted Convict.*

Siobhan B. Somerville is Associate Professor of English and Gender and Women's Studies at the University of Illinois at Urbana-Champaign. She is the author of *Queering the Color Line: Race and the Invention of Homosexuality in American Culture* and editor of the *Cambridge Companion to Queer Studies.*

Dean Spade is Associate Professor at the School of Law at Seattle University. He is the author of *Normal Life: Administrative Violence, Critical Trans Politics and the Limits of Law.* His writing and video projects are available at deanspade.net.

Julie Sze is Professor of American Studies at the University of California, Davis. She is the author of three books, most recently, *Environmental Justice in a Moment of Danger.*

John Kuo Wei Tchen is the Inaugural Clement A. Price Chair of Public History and Humanities at Rutgers University–Newark and Director of the Clement Price Institute on Ethnicity, Culture, and the Modern Experience. He is Founding Director of the Asian/Pacific/American Studies Institute at New York University and cofounded the Museum of Chinese in America in 1979–80. He is the author of *Yellow Peril: An Archive of Anti-Asian Fear.*

Rebecca Wanzo is Associate Professor of Women, Gender, and Sexuality Studies at Washington University in St. Louis. She is the author of *The Suffering Will Not Be Televised: African American Women and Sentimental Political Storytelling* and *The Content of Our Caricature: African American Comic Art and Political Belonging.*

Alys Eve Weinbaum is Professor of English at the University of Washington Seattle. She is the author of *The Afterlife of Reproductive Slavery: Biocapitalism and Black Feminism's Philosophy of History* and *Wayward Reproductions: Genealogies of Race and Nation in Transatlantic Modern Thought.*

Henry Yu is Associate Professor of History at the University of British Columbia. He is the author of *Thinking*

Orientals: Migration, Contact, and Exoticism in Modern America and co-editor of *Within and Without the Nation: Canadian History as Transnational History*.

George Yúdice is Professor of Modern Languages and Literatures at the University of Miami. He is the author of *The Expediency of Culture: The Uses of Culture in the Global Era* and "For a New Institutional Paradigm."